Don Green

Merriam-Webster's
Pocket
Geographical
Dictionary

W9-BNH-260

Merriam-Webster, Incorporated
Springfield, Massachusetts

A GENUINE MERRIAM-WEBSTER

The name *Webster* alone is no guarantee of excellence. It is used by a number of publishers and may serve mainly to mislead an unwary buyer.

Merriam-Webster™ is the name you should look for when you consider the purchase of dictionaries or other fine reference books. It carries the reputation of a company that has been publishing since 1831 and is your assurance of quality and authority.

Copyright © 1999 by Merriam-Webster, Incorporated

Philippines Copyright © 1999 by Merriam-Webster, Incorporated

ISBN: 0-87779-506-1

Made in the United States of America
45678910NFWP040302

Preface

Merriam-Webster's Pocket Geographical Dictionary gives basic information about the countries of the world and their most important regions, cities, and physical features. The information includes spelling, end-of-line division, and pronunciation of the name, nature of the feature, its location, and for more important entries statistical data. Cities in the United States having 19,000 or more inhabitants at the 1990 census and incorporated places in Canada having 21,500 or more inhabitants in the 1991 census have been included.

This dictionary shares many details of presentation with other members of the Merriam-Webster family, such as *Merriam-Webster's Collegiate Dictionary, Tenth Edition,* from which the material in this book is drawn. However, the nature of the material presented here requires special treatment of entries, and users of this dictionary need to be familiar with the following features.

Main entries follow one another in alphabetical order. Centered periods within the entries show points at which a hyphen may be put when the word is broken at the end of a line.

Variant spellings and **alternative names** that are in common use appear at the main entry usually following the word *or.* If use of the variant spelling or alternative name is limited in some way, an additional italic label is included to indicate the fact, as *or formerly* for spellings or names that are no longer in common use and *or F* for spellings or names that are most common in contexts where French spellings and names are used. Variant spellings can also be shown after derivatives.

Derivatives are shown following a dash at the end of many entries. Such derivatives usually end in *-an* or *-ian* and may function as adjectives or nouns or both. Derived adjectives mean "of or relating to (the place named in the entry)." Derived nouns mean "a native or inhabitant of (the place named in the entry)."

Run-in entries are place-names related to the main entry that appear in boldface within an entry.

Cross-reference entries are entries that direct the user from a variant spelling, alternative name, or a related place-name that appears as a run-in to the main entry where they appear. Cross-reference entries appear only for forms that fall more than a page away from the main entry at which they appear.

Pronunciation information is either given explicitly or implicitly for nearly every entry in the dictionary. Pronunciation respellings are placed within reversed slant lines following the boldface words to which they apply. Where the pronunciation is not indicated at a particular entry, the pronunciation is to be inferred from an earlier indicated pronunciation. Pronunciations are not shown for words that are listed elsewhere in the dictionary. Hence, at the entry for

Booker T. Washington National Monument, no pronunciation is given for *Washington,* as the pronunciation of that word appears at the entry for *Washington.* Neither are pronunciations shown for common English words that appear within place-names. Hence at the entry for *Alibates Flint Quarries National Monument,* a pronunciation is shown only for *Alibates,* as the other words in that name are common English words whose pronunciations are readily available in any good dictionary.

A full list of pronunciation symbols used is shown on the page following this Preface.

Hyphens that are a fixed part of hyphenated compounds as *Cap-de-la-Madeleine* are converted to a special double hyphen when the compound appears in lightface type and that hyphen comes at the end of a line in this dictionary. This indicates that the hyphen is to be retained when the word is not shown at the end of a line. Fixed hyphens in boldface words are shown as short boldface dashes, which are a bit larger than ordinary hyphens. These short dashes in boldface words are retained at the end of a line in this dictionary.

Guide words are shown in boldface type at the top left- and right-hand corners of each two-page spread. The guidewords are the first and last main entry on each spread.

Abbreviations used in this dictionary are listed in the section Abbreviations in This Work that follows this Preface. The letters N, E, S, and W when not followed by a period indicate direction and are not part of a place-name; thus N Vietnam indicates northern Vietnam and not North Vietnam. The symbol ✳ denotes a capital.

Areas, altitudes, and lengths are given first in conventional units with metric equivalents in parentheses.

The Pinyin transliteration of place-names for the People's Republic of China is the first spelling shown; the Wade-Giles transliteration is second. Where no variant is given, the two spellings are identical.

Abbreviations in This Work

ab   about
AD   anno Domini
adj   adjective
Ala   Alabama
Alta   Alberta
anc   ancient
Ar   Arabic
Ariz   Arizona
Ark   Arkansas
BC   before Christ, British Columbia
bet   between
bib   biblical
Brit   British
Calif   California
cen   central
Colo   Colorado
Conn   Connecticut
Dan   Danish
DC   District of Columbia
Del   Delaware
E   east, eastern
ENE   east-northeast
ESE   east-southeast
esp   especially
F   French
Fla   Florida
Flem   Flemish
ft   feet
G   German
Ga   Georgia
Gk   Greek
Heb   Hebrew
Ill   Illinois
Ind   Indiana
IrGael   Irish Gaelic
Is   Island
It   Italian
Kans   Kansas
km   kilometer
Ky   Kentucky
L   Latin
La   Louisiana
LL   Late Latin

m   meters
Man   Manitoba
Mass   Massa-chusetts
Md   Maryland
mi   miles
Mich   Michigan
Minn   Minnesota
Mo   Missouri
Mont   Montana
Mt   Mount
n   noun
N   north, northern
NB   New Brunswick
NC   North Carolina
ND, N Dak   North Dakota
NE   northeast, northeastern
Nebr   Nebraska
Nev   Nevada
Nfld   Newfound-land
NGk   New Greek
NH   New Hampshire
NJ   New Jersey
N Mex   New Mexico
NNE   north-northeast
NNW   north-northwest
Norw   Norwegian
NS   Nova Scotia
NW   northwest, northwestern
NY   New York
Okla   Oklahoma
Ont   Ontario
Oreg   Oregon
orig   originally
Pa   Pennsylvania
pop   population

PEI   Prince Edward Island
Que   Quebec
RI   Rhode Island
Russ   Russ
S   south, southern
Sask   Saskatchewan
SC   South Carolina
ScGael   Scottish Gaelic
SD, S Dak   South Dakota
SE   southeast, southeastern
Serb   Serbian
Sp   Spanish
sq km   square kilometers
sq mi   square miles
SSE   south-southeast
SSW   south-southwest
St   Saint
SW   southwest, southwestern
Tenn   Tennessee
Tex   Texas
US   United States
USSR   Union of Soviet Socialist Republics
usu   usually
VA   Virginia
Vt   Vermont
W   west, western
Wash   Washington
Wis   Wisconsin
WNW   west-northwest
WSW   west-southwest
W Va   West Virginia
Zech   Zecharia

Pronunciation Symbols

ə   banana, collide, abut; raised \ᵊ\ in \ᵊl\, \ᵊn\ as in battle, cotton, in \lᵊ, mᵊ, rᵊ\ as in French table, prisme, titre

'ə, ˌə   humbug, abut

ər   operation, further

a   map, patch

ā   day, fate

ä   bother, cot, father

à   father as pronounced by those who do not rhyme it with bother

aù   now, out

b   baby, rib

ch   chin, catch

d   did, adder

e   set, red

ē   beat, nosebleed, easy

f   fifty, cuff

g   go, big

h   hat, ahead

hw   whale

i   tip, banish

ī   site, buy

j   job, edge

k   kin, cook

k̇   German ich, Buch

l   lily, cool

m   murmur, dim

n   nine, own; raised \ⁿ\ indicates that a preceding vowel or diphthong is pronounced through both nose and mouth, as in French bon \bōⁿ\

ŋ   sing, singer, finger, ink

ō   bone, hollow

ȯ   saw, cork

œ   French bœuf, German Hölle

œ̄   French feu, German Höhle

ȯi   toy, sawing

p   pepper, lip

r   rarity

s   source, less

sh   shy, mission

t   tie, attack

th   thin, ether

th   then, either

ü   boot, few \'fyü\

ù   put, pure \'pyùr\

ue   German füllen

ūe   French rue, German fühlen

v   vivid, give

w   we, away

y   yard, cue \'kyü\; raised \ʸ\ indicates that preceding \l\, \n\, or \w\ is modified by the placing of the tongue tip against the lower front teeth, as in French digne \dēnʸ\

z   zone, raise

zh   vision, pleasure

\   slant line used in pairs to mark the beginning and end of a transcription

ˈ   mark at the beginning of a syllable that has primary (strongest) stress: \'penmən,ship\

ˌ   mark at the beginning of a syllable that has secondary (next-strongest) stress: \'penmən,ship\

-    mark of syllable division

()   indicate that what is shown between is present in some utterances but not in others: factory \'fak-t(ə-)rē\

÷   indicates that many regard as unacceptable the pronunciation immediately following: cupola \'kyü-pə-,lə, ÷ -,lō\

sic   indicates that the preceding pronunciation is correct despite the spelling: Kiribati \'kir-ə-bas—sic\

A

Aa·chen \ˈä-kən, -kən\ *or* F **Aix-la-Cha·pelle** \ˌāks-ˌlä-shä-ˈpel, ˌeks-\ city W Germany near Belgian & Dutch borders *pop* 241,861

Aai·ún, El \el-ˈī-ˈün\ *or* F **La·youne** *or* **La'·youn** \lä-ˈyün\ town NW Africa ✱ of Western Sahara

Aalborg — see ÅLBORG

Aalst \ˈälst\ *or* **Alost** \ä-ˈlóst\ commune *cen* Belgium WNW of Brussels *pop* 76,382

Aa·rau \ˈär-ˌaú\ commune N Switzerland ✱ of Aargau canton *pop* 15,836

Aa·re \ˈär-ə\ *or* **Aar** \ˈär\ river 183 *mi* (294 *km*), *cen* & N Switzerland flowing E & NE into the Rhine

Aar·gau \ˈär-ˌgaú\ *or* F **Ar·go·vie** \ˌär-gō-ˈvē\ canton N Switzerland ✱ Aarau *area* 542 *sq mi* (1409 *sq km*), *pop* 489,567

Aarhus — see ÅRHUS

Ab·a·co \ˈa-bə-ˌkō\ two islands of Bahamas (**Great Abaco & Little Abaco**) N of New Providence Is. *area* 776 *sq mi* (2018 *sq km*)

Aba·dan \ˌä-bə-ˈdän, ˌa-bə-ˈdan\ 1 island W Iran in delta of Shatt al Arab 2 town & port on Abadan Is.

Aba·kan \ˌə-bə-ˈkän\ town S Russia in Asia ✱ of Khakassia *pop* 158,000

Abay *or* **Ab·bai** \ä-ˈbī\ the upper course of the Blue Nile

Ab·be·ville \ˈáb-ˌvēl, ˈa-bi-ˌvil\ commune N France on the Somme NW of Amiens *pop* 24,588

Ab·er·dare \ˌa-bər-ˈdar, -ˈder\ town S Wales in Mid Glamorgan *pop* 36,621

Ab·er·deen 1 \ˈa-bər-ˌdēn\ city NE S.Dak. *pop* 24,927 2 \ˌa-bər-ˈdēn\ *or* **Ab·er·deen·shire** \-ˌshir, -shər\ former county NE Scotland ✱ Aberdeen 3 city & port NE Scotland ✱ of Grampian *pop* 211,080 — **Ab·er·do·ni·an** \ˌa-bər-ˈdō-nē-ən\ *adj or n*

Ab·er·yst·wyth \ˌa-bə-ˈris-ˌtwith, -ˈrəs-\ borough W Wales in Dyfed on Cardigan Bay *pop* 8666

Ab·i·djan \ˌä-bē-ˈjän, ˌa-bi-\ city & port ✱ of Ivory Coast *pop* 1,934,342

Abila — see MUSA (Jebel)

Ab·i·lene \ˈa-bə-ˌlēn\ city NW *cen* Tex. *pop* 106,654

Ab·i·ti·bi \ˌa-bə-ˈti-bē\ 1 lake Canada on E boundary of Ont. *area* 356 *sq mi* (926 *sq km*) 2 river 230 *mi* (368 *km*) Canada flowing N into Moose River

Ab·khaz Republic \ab-ˈkaz, əb-ˈkäs\ autonomous republic NW Republic of Georgia on Black Sea ✱ Sukhumi *area* 3320 *sq mi* (8599

sq km), pop 533,800 — **Ab·khas** \\-'käs\ *n* — **Ab·kha·sian** *or* **Ab·kha·zian** \\-'kä-zh(ē-)ən, -'kä-zē-ən\ *adj or n*

Abo·mey \\ə-bō-'mā, ə-'bō-mē\ city S Benin *pop* 54,418

Abruz·zi \\ä-'brüt-sē, ə-\ region *cen* Italy bordering on the Adriatic & including highest of the Apennines ✴ L'Aquila *pop* 1,249,388; with Molise (to S), formerly comprised **Abruzzi e Mo·li·se** \\ä-'mō-li-,zä\ region

Ab·sa·ro·ka Range \\ab-'sär-ə-kə, -'sór-kē, -'zór-\ mountain range S Mont. & NW Wyo. E of Yellowstone National Park — see FRANCS PEAK

Ab·se·con Inlet \\ab-'sē-kən\ inlet SE N.J. bet. barrier islands N of Atlantic City

Abu Dha·bi \\ä-bü-'dä-bē, -'thä-\ **1** sheikhdom, member of United Arab Emirates **2** town, its ✴ & ✴ of United Arab Emirates *pop* 347,000

Abu·ja \\ä-'bü-jä\ city *cen* Nigeria, its ✴ since 1991

Abu Qir \\ä-bü-'kir, ,ä-\ **1** bay N Egypt bet. Alexandria & Rosetta mouth of the Nile **2** village on this bay

Abu Sim·bel \\ä-,bü-'sim-bəl\ locality S Egypt on left bank of the Nile SW of Aswân; site of two rock temples which were moved 1964–66 to higher ground when area was flooded after completion of Aswân High Dam

Aby·dos \\ə-'bī-dəs\ **1** ancient town Asia Minor on the Hellespont **2** ancient town S Egypt on left bank of the Nile S of Thebes

Abyla — see MUSA (Jebel)

Abys·sin·ia \\a-bə-'si-nē-ə, -nyə\ — see ETHIOPIA — **Ab·ys·sin·ian** \\-nē-ən, -nyən\ *adj or n*

Aca·dia \\ə-'kā-dē-ə\ *or F* **Aca·die** \\ä-kä-'dē\ NOVA SCOTIA — an early name — **Aca·di·an** \\-dē-ən\ *adj or n*

Acadia National Park section of coast of Maine including chiefly mountainous areas on Mount Desert Is. & Isle au Haut

Aca·pul·co \\ä-kä-'pül-(,)kō, ,a-\ *or* **Acapulco de Juá·rez** \\dä-'hwär-,es, thä-\ city & port S Mexico in Guerrero on the Pacific *pop* 592,187

Ac·ar·na·nia \\a-kər-'nā-nē-ə, -'nā-nyə\ region W Greece on Ionian Sea — **Ac·ar·na·nian** \\a-kər-'nā-nē-ən, -'nā-nyən\ *adj or n*

Ac·cad \\'a-,kad, 'ä-,käd\ — see AKKAD — **Ac·ca·di·an** \\ə-'kā-dē-ən, -'kä-\ *adj or n*

Ac·cra \\'ä-krə, 'a-; ə-'krä\ city & port ✴ of Ghana on Gulf of Guinea *pop* 867,459

Ac·cring·ton \\'a-kriŋ-tən\ town NW England in SE Lancashire N of Manchester

Achaea \\ə-'kē-ə\ *or* **Acha·ia** \\ə-'kī-ə, -'kā-\ region S Greece in Peloponnese bordering on Gulfs of Corinth & Patras — **Achae·an** \\ə-'kē-ə\ *or* **Acha·ian** \\ə-'kī-ən, -'kā-\ *adj or n*

Ach·e·lo·us \\a-kə-'lō-əs\ *or NGk* **Akhe·lō·os** \\ä-ke-'lō-ōs\ river 137 *mi* (220 *km*) W Greece flowing S to Ionian Sea

Ach·ill \\'a-kəl\ island 15 *mi* (24 *km*) long NW Ireland in County Mayo

Achray, Loch \\ə-'krā\ lake *cen* Scotland in SW Tayside

Acon·ca·gua \\ä-kōn-'kä-gwä\ mountain 22,834 *ft* (6960 *m*) W Argentina WNW of Mendoza near Chilean border; highest in Andes & western hemisphere

Açores — see AZORES

Acragas — see AGRIGENTO

Acre \'ä-krē, -(,)krä\ state W Brazil bordering on Peru & Bolivia ✳ Rio Branco *area* 59,343 *sq mi* (153,698 *sq km*), *pop* 417,437

Acre \'ä-kər, 'ä-kər, 'ä-krə\ *or* Heb **'Ak·ko** *or Old Testament* **Ac·cho** \'ä-kō, 'ä-\ *or New Testament* **Ptol·e·ma·ïs** \,tä-lə-'mā-əs\ city & port NW Israel N of Mt. Carmel *pop* 37,400

Ac·te \'ak-tē\ *or Gk* **Ak·ti** \äk-'tē\ peninsula NE Greece, the most easterly of the three peninsulas of Chalcidice — see ATHOS

Ac·ti·um \'ak-shē-əm, 'ak-tē-\ promontory & ancient town W Greece in NW Acarnania

Adak \'ä-,dak\ island SW Alaska in Andreanof group

Adalia — see ANTALYA

Ad·ams, Mount \'a-dəmz\ **1** mountain 5798 *ft* (1767 *m*) N N.H. in White Mountains N of Mt. Washington **2** mountain 12,307 *ft* (3751 *m*) SW Wash. in Cascade Range SSE of Mt. Rainier

Ad·am's Bridge \'a-dəmz\ chain of shoals 30 *mi* (48 *km*) long bet. Sri Lanka & SE India

Adam's Peak *or Sinhalese* **Sa·ma·na·la** \'sə-mə-nə-lə\ mountain 7360 *ft* (2243 *m*) S *cen* Sri Lanka

Ada·na \,ä-dä-'nä, ə-'dä-nə\ *or formerly* **Sey·han** \sä-'hän\ city S Turkey on Seyhan River *pop* 916,150

Ada·pa·za·ri \,ä-də-,pä-zə-'ri\ city NW Turkey E of Istanbul *pop* 171,225

Ad Dam·mām \,äd-däm-'mäm\ *or* **Dam·mam** \də-'mam\ town & port Saudi Arabia on Persian Gulf

Ad·dis Aba·ba \'ä-dis-'ä-bä-,bä, ,ä-dəs-'a-bə-bə\ city *cen* Ethiopia, its ✳ *pop* 1,408,068

Ad·di·son \'a-də-sən\ village NE Ill. W of Chicago *pop* 32,058

Ad·e·laide \'a-dᵊl-,ād\ city Australia ✳ of S. Australia *metropolitan area pop* 917,000

Aden \'ä-dᵊn, 'ā-\ **1** former Brit. protectorate S Arabia comprising coast area bet. Yemen on W & Oman on E; became part of People's Democratic Republic of Yemen 1967 *area* 112,000 *sq mi* (291,200 *sq km*) **2** former Brit. colony on coast of & surrounded by Aden protectorate comprising Aden & Little Aden peninsulas, a small area of hinterland, & Perim Is.; became part of People's Democratic Republic of Yemen 1967 *area* 75 *sq mi* (195 *sq km*) **3** city & port S Yemen; formerly ✳ of People's Democratic Republic of Yemen & before that ✳ of Aden colony & protectorate *pop* 240,370

Aden, Gulf of arm of Indian Ocean bet. Aden & Somalia

Adi·ge \'ä-dē-,jä\ river 255 *mi* (410 *km*) N Italy flowing SE into the Adriatic

Ad·i·ron·dack Mountains \,a-də-'rän-,dak\ mountains NE N.Y.

Adjar·i·an Autonomous Republic \ə-'jär-ē-ən\ *or* **Adzhar** \'ä-jär, ə-'jär\ *or* **Adzhar·ia** *or* **Ajar·ia** \ə-'jär-ē-ə\ autonomous republic SW Republic of Georgia on Black Sea ✳ Batumi *area* 1158 *sq mi* (2999 *sq km*), *pop* 381,500

Ad·mi·ral·ty Inlet \'ad-m(ə-)rəl-tē\ branch of Puget Sound NW Washington

Admiralty Island island 90 *mi* (145 *km*) long SE Alaska in N Alexander Archipelago

Admiralty Islands islands W Pacific N of New Guinea in Bismarck Archipelago *area* 800 *sq mi* (2080 *sq km*), *pop* 30,160

Adour \a-'dùr\ river 208 *mi* (335 *km*) SW France flowing from the Pyrenees NW & W into Bay of Biscay

Adri·an \'ā-drē-ən\ city SE Mich. SW of Detroit *pop* 22,097

Adrianople — see EDIRNE

Adri·at·ic Sea \ˌā-drē-'a-tik, ˌa-\ arm of the Mediterranean bet. Italy & Balkan Peninsula

Ad·vent Bay \'ad-ˌvent, -vənt\ inlet of Arctic Ocean West Spitsbergen on W coast

Ad·wa \'äd-(ˌ)wä\ town N Ethiopia S of Asmara *pop* 17,476

Ady·gea or **Ady·ge·ya** \ˌä-də-'gā-ə\ republic S Russia in Europe ✳ Maykop *area* 2934 *sq mi* (7599 *sq km*), *pop* 437,400

Adzhar or **Adzharia** — see ADJARIAN AUTONOMOUS REPUBLIC — **Adzhar** *n* — **Adzhar·i·an** \ə-'jär-ē-ən\ *adj or n*

Aegates — see EGADI

Ae·ge·an Islands \i-'jē-ən\ islands Aegean Sea including the Cyclades & the Northern & Southern Sporades

Aegean Sea arm of the Mediterranean bet. Asia Minor & Greece — **Aegean** *adj*

Ae·gi·na \i-'jī-nə\ or *Gk* **Aí·yi·na** \'e-yē-ˌnä\ island & ancient state SE Greece in Saronic Gulf — **Ae·gi·ne·tan** \ˌē-jə-'nē-tᵊn\ *adj or n*

Ae·gos·pot·a·mi \ˌē-gə-'spä-tə-ˌmī\ or **Ae·gos·pot·a·mos** \-məs\ river & town of ancient Thrace in the Chersonese

Aemilia — see EMILIA-ROMAGNA

Ae·o·lis \'ē-ə-ləs\ or **Ae·o·lia** \ē-'ō-lē-ə, -'ōl-yə\ ancient country of NW Asia Minor

Ae·to·lia \ē-'tō-lē-ə, -'tōl-yə\ region W *cen* Greece N of Gulf of Patras & E of Acarnania — **Ae·to·lian** \-lē-ən, -yən\ *adj or n*

Afars and the Issas, French Territory of the — see DJIBOUTI

Af·ghan·i·stan \af-'ga-nə-ˌstan, -'gä-nə-ˌstän\ country W Asia E of Iran; a republic ✳ Kabul *area* 250,775 *sq mi* (649,507 *sq km*), *pop* 18,052,000 — **Af·ghan** \'af-ˌgan *also* -gən\ *adj or n*

Afog·nak \ə-'fog-ˌnak, -'fäg-\ island S Alaska N of Kodiak Is.

Af·ri·ca \'a-fri-kə *also* ä-\ continent of the eastern hemisphere S of the Mediterranean & adjoining Asia on NE *area* 11,677,239 *sq mi* (30,244,049 *sq km*) — **Af·ri·can** \-fri-kən\ *adj or n*

Afyon \ä-'fyōn\ or **Afyon·ka·ra·hi·sar** \ä-'fyōn-ˌkär-ə-hi-'sär\ city W *cen* Turkey *pop* 98,618

Aga·dir \ˌä-gə-'dir, -ˌ\ city & port SW Morocco *pop* 110,479

Aga·na \ä-'gä-nyä\ town ✳ of Guam on W coast *pop* 1139

Agar·ta·la \ˌə-gər-tə-'lä\ city E India ✳ of Tripura *pop* 157,636

Ag·ate Fossil Beds National Monument \'a-gət\ reservation W Nebr.

Ag·a·wam \'a-gə-ˌwäm\ town SW Mass. *pop* 27,323

Age·nais \ˌä-zhə-'nā\ or **Age·nois** \ˌä-zhe-'nwä\ ancient region SW France S of Périgord ✳ Agen

Aghrim — see AUGHRIM

Agin·court \'a-jin-ˌkōrt, 'ä-zhən-ˌkùr\ or *Fr* **Azin·court** \ˌà-zaⁿ-'kūr\ village N France WNW of Arras

Ag·no \'äg-(ˌ)nō\ river 128 *mi* (206 *km*) Philippines in NW Luzon

Agou·ra Hills \ə-'gür-ə\ city SW Calif. W of Los Angeles *pop* 20,390

Agra \'ä-grə, 'ə-\ **1** region N India roughly equivalent to present Uttar Pradesh excluding Oudh region **2** city N India in W Uttar Pradesh SSE of Delhi *pop* 891,790

Agri Dagi — see ARARAT

Agri·gen·to \ˌä-grē-ˈjen-(ˌ)tō, ˌa-\ *or formerly* **Gir·gen·ti** \jər-ˈjen-tē\ *or anc* **Ag·ri·gen·tum** \ˌa-grə-ˈjen-təm\ *or* **Ac·ra·gas** \ˈä-krä-ˌgäs\ commune Italy in SW Sicily near south coast *pop* 54,603

Agua·di·lla \ˌä-gwä-ˈthē-yä\ city NW Puerto Rico *pop* 59,335

Aguas·ca·lien·tes \ˌä-gwä-skäl-ˈyen-ˌtäs\ **1** state *cen* Mexico *area* 2158 *sq mi* (5589 *sq km*), *pop* 719,659 **2** city, its * *pop* 506,384

Agul·has, Cape \ə-ˈgə-ləs\ headland Republic of S. Africa in S Western Cape province; southernmost point of Africa, at 34°50′S, 20°E

Ahag·gar Mountains \ə-ˈhä-gər, ˌä-hə-ˈgär\ *or* **Hog·gar Mountains** \ˈhä-gər, hə-ˈgär\ mountains S Algeria in W *cen* Sahara; highest Tahat 9842 *ft* (3000 *m*)

Ah·mad·abad \ˈä-mə-də-ˌbäd, -ˌbad\ city W India N of Bombay in Gujarat *pop* 2,954,526

Ah·vaz \ä-ˈväz\ *or* **Ah·waz** \ä-ˈwäz\ city SW Iran on the Karun *pop* 579,826

Ai·ken \ˈä-kən\ city W S.C. SW of Columbia *pop* 19,872

Ail·sa Craig \ˈāl-zə-ˌkräg\ small rocky island Scotland S of Arran at mouth of Firth of Clyde

Ain \ˈaⁿ\ river 120 *mi* (195 *km*) E France rising in Jura Mountains & flowing SSW into the Rhône

Aintab — see GAZIANTEP

Air·drie \ˈar-drē, ˈer-\ burgh S *cen* Scotland in Strathclyde E of Glasgow *pop* 45,643

Aire \ˈar, ˈer\ river 70 *mi* (113 *km*) N England in W Yorkshire flowing to the Ouse; its valley is **Aire·dale** \-ˌdāl\

Aisne \ˈān\ river *ab* 165 *mi* (265 *km*) N France flowing NW & W from Argonne Forest into the Oise near Compiègne

Aix-en-Pro·vence \ˌāks-ˌäⁿ-prō-ˈväⁿs, ˌeks-\ *or* **Aix** \ˈäks, ˈeks\ city SE France N of Marseille *pop* 126,854

Aix-la-Chapelle — see AACHEN

Aix-les-Bains \ˌäks-lā-ˈbaⁿ, ˌeks-\ commune E France N of Chambéry *pop* 24,826

Ajac·cio \ä-ˈyä-(ˌ)chō, ä-zhäk-ˈsyō\ city & port France in Corsica *pop* 59,318

Ajan·ta \ə-ˈjən-tə\ village W *cen* India in N *cen* Maharashtra in Ajanta Range NNE of Aurangabad; caves

Ajaria — see ADJARIAN AUTONOMOUS REPUBLIC

Ajax \ˈā-ˌjaks\ town Canada in SE Ont. *pop* 57,350

'Aj·man \äj-ˈmán\ sheikhdom, member of United Arab Emirates

Aj·mer \əj-ˈmir, -ˈmer\ city NW India in Rajasthan SW of Delhi *pop* 402,700

Akhelóos — see ACHELOUS

Ak·hi·sar \ˌäk-hi-ˈsär, ˌä-ki-\ *or anc* **Thy·a·ti·ra** \ˌthī-ə-ˈtī-rə\ city W Turkey in Asia NE of Izmir *pop* 151,957

Aki·ta \ä-ˈkē-tä, ˈä-kē-ˌtä\ city & port Japan in N Honshu on Sea of Japan *pop* 302,359

Ak·kad *or* **Ac·cad** \ˈa-ˌkad, ˈä-ˌkäd\ **1** the N division of ancient Babylonia **2** *or* **Aga·de** \ə-ˈgä-də\ ancient city, its * — **Ak·ka·di·an** \ə-ˈkä-dē-ən\ *adj or n*

Akkerman — see BELGOROD-DNESTROVSKI

'Akko — see ACRE

Akmola — see AQMOLA

Ak·ron \'a-krən\ city NE Ohio SE of Cleveland *pop* 223,019

Ak·sum *also* **Ax·um** \'äk-,süm\ town N Ethiopia ✻ of an ancient kingdom (the Axumite Empire)

Akti — see ACTE

Akyab — see SITTWE

Al·a·bama \,a-lə-'ba-mə\ **1** river 315 *mi* (507 *km*) S Ala. flowing SW into Tensaw & Mobile rivers — see TALLAPOOSA **2** state SE U.S. ✻ Montgomery *area* 51,705 *sq mi* (133,916 *sq km*), *pop* 4,040,587 — **Al·a·bam·i·an** \-'ba-mē-ən\ *or* **Al·a·bam·an** \-'ba-mən\ *adj or n*

Ala·go·as \,ä-lə-'gō-əs\ state NE Brazil ✻ Maceió *area* 11,238 *sq mi* (29,184 *sq km*), *pop* 2,512,515

Alai \'ä-,lī\ mountain range SW Kyrgyzstan; highest peak 19,554 *ft* (5960 *m*)

Al·'A·mä·rah \,al-ha-'mä-rə\ city SE Iraq on the Tigris

Al·a·me·da \,a-lə-'mē-də\ city & port W Calif. on island in San Francisco Bay near Oakland *pop* 76,459

Alamein, El — see EL ALAMEIN

Al·a·mo·gor·do \,a-lə-mə-'gór-(,)dō\ city S N.Mex. *pop* 27,596

Aland \'ō-,län(d)\ *or* **Ahv·e·nan·maa** \'ä-ve-nän-,mä\ **1** archipelago SW Finland in Baltic Sea ✻ Mariehamn **2** island, chief of this group

Ala·nia \ə-'lä-nyə, -nē-ə\ *or* **North Os·se·tia** \ä-'sē-sh(ē-)ə\ autonomous republic SE Russia in Europe on the N slopes of Caucasus Mountains ✻ Vladikavkaz *area* 3089 *sq mi* (8001 *sq km*), *pop* 695,000

Al·'Aqabah — see AQABA

Ala·se·hir \,a-lə-shə-'hir, ,ä-\ *or anc* **Philadelphia** city W Turkey 75 *mi* (121 *km*) E of Izmir *pop* 36,535

Alas·ka \ə-'las-kə\ state (territory 1912–59) of the U.S. NW N. America ✻ Juneau *area* 591,004 *sq mi* (1,530,700 *sq km*), *pop* 550,043 — **Alas·kan** \-kən\ *adj or n*

Alaska, Gulf of inlet of the Pacific off S Alaska between Alaska Peninsula on W & Alexander Archipelago on E

Alaska Peninsula peninsula SW Alaska SW of Cook Inlet

Alaska Range mountain range S Alaska extending from Alaska Peninsula to Yukon boundary — see MCKINLEY (Mount)

Ala Tau \'ä-lə-'taủ\ several ranges of the Tian Shan mountain system E Kazakhstan & Kyrgyzstan around & NE of Issyk Kul

Ala·va \'ä-lə-və\ province N Spain S of Vizcaya; in Basque Country ✻ Vitoria *area* 1176 *sq mi* (3046 *sq km*), *pop* 272,447

Al·a·va, Cape \'a-lə-və\ cape NW Wash. S of Cape Flattery; westernmost point of conterminous U.S., at 124°44'W

Al·'Ayzarīyah — see BETHANY 2

Al·ba·ce·te \,äl-bä-'sä-tä\ **1** province SE Spain N of Murcia province *area* 5737 *sq mi* (14,859 *sq km*), *pop* 342,677 **2** commune, its ✻ *pop* 130,023

Al·ba Lon·ga \,al-bə-'lóŋ-gə\ ancient city *cen* Italy SE of Rome

Al·ban Hills \'ól-bən, 'al-\ *or anc* **Al·ba·nus Mons** \äl-'bä-nəs-'món(t)s\ mountain group Italy SE of Rome

Al·ba·nia \al-'bā-nē-ə, -nyə\ *also* ól-\ **1** ancient country Europe in E Caucasus region on W side of Caspian Sea **2** country S Europe in Balkan Peninsula on the Adriatic; a republic ✻ Tiranë *area* 11,100

sq mi (28,749 sq km), pop 3,357,000 — **Al·ba·nian** \-nē-ən, -nyən\ *adj or n*

Al·ba·no, Lake \al-'bä-(,)nō, äl-\ *or anc* **Al·ba·nus La·cus** \äl-'bā-nəs-'lā-kəs\ lake Italy SE of Rome

Al·ba·ny \'òl-bə-nē\ **1** city SW Ga. *pop* 78,122 **2** city ✷ of N.Y., on Hudson River *pop* 101,082 **3** city NW Oreg. S of Salem *pop* 29,462 **4** \'al-\ river 610 *mi* (982 *km*) Canada in N Ont. flowing E into James Bay — **Al·ba·ni·an** \òl-'bā-nē-ən\ *adj or n*

Al Basrah — see BASRA

Al·be·marle Sound \'al-bə-,märl\ inlet of Atlantic Ocean NE N.C.

Al·bert, Lake \al-'bərt\ lake 100 *mi* (161 *km*) long E Africa bet. Uganda & Democratic Republic of the Congo in course of the Victoria Nile

Al·ber·ta \al-'bərt-ə\ province W Canada ✷ Edmonton *area* 246,422 *sq mi* (638,232 *sq km*), *pop* 2,545,553 — **Al·ber·tan** \-'bər-t³n\ *adj or n*

Albert Nile — see NILE

Albertville — see KALEMIE

Al·bi \al-'bē\ commune S France NE of Toulouse *pop* 48,707

Al Biqa — see BEKAA

Al·borg *or* **Aal·borg** \'òl-,bòrg\ city & port Denmark in NE Jutland *pop* 155,664

Al·bu·quer·que \'al-bə-,kər-kē\ city *cen* N.Mex. *pop* 384,736 — **Al·bu·quer·que·an** \-kē-ən\ *n*

Al·ca·mo \'äl-kä-,mò\ commune Italy in NW Sicily *pop* 43,231

Al·ca·traz \'al-kə-,traz\ island Calif. in San Francisco Bay

Al·coy \äl-'kòi\ commune E Spain N of Alicante *pop* 65,514

Al·da·bra \äl-'dä-brə\ island (atoll) NW Indian Ocean N of Madagascar, chief of Aldabra group belonging to Seychelles

Al·dan \äl-'dän\ river 1393 *mi* (2241 *km*) E Russia in Asia, in Sakha Republic flowing into the Lena

Al·der·ney \'òl-dər-nē\ island in English Channel, northernmost of the Channel Islands ✷ St. Anne *area* 3 *sq mi* (7.8 *sq km*), *pop* 2086

Al·der·shot \'òl-dər-,shät\ borough S England in NE Hampshire *pop* 32,654

Aleksandrovsk — see ZAPOROZH 'YE

Aleksandrovsk–Grushevski — see SHAKHTY

Alen·çon \a-,län²-'sō²\ city NW France N of Le Mans *pop* 32,917

Alep·po \ə-'le-(,)pō\ *or anc* **Be·roea** \bə-'rē-ə\ city N Syria *pop* 1,445,000 — **Alep·pine** \ə-'le-pən, -,pīn, -,pēn\ *adj or n*

Ales·san·dria \ä-le-'sän-drē-ä\ commune NW Italy *pop* 90,475

Aleu·tian Islands \ə-'lü-shən\ islands SW Alaska extending in an arc 1700 *mi* (2735 *km*) SW & W from Alaska Peninsula — see ANDREANOF ISLANDS, FOX ISLANDS, NEAR ISLANDS, RAT ISLANDS

Aleutian Range mountain range SW Alaska, the SW extension of Alaska Range, running along NW shore of Cook Inlet to SW tip of Alaska Peninsula with mountains of the Aleutian chain forming its SW extension — see SHISHALDIN

Al·ex·an·der Archipelago \,a-lig-'zan-dər, ,e-\ archipelago of *ab* 1100 islands SE Alaska — see ADMIRALTY ISLAND, BARANOF, CHICHAGOF, KUPREANOF, PRINCE OF WALES ISLAND, REVILLAGIGEDO ISLAND

Alexander I Island island Antarctica W of base of Antarctic Peninsula

Alexandretta — see ISKENDERUN

Al·ex·an·dria \a-lig-'zan-drē-ə, ,e-\ **1** city *cen* La. *pop* 49,188 **2** city N Va. on the Potomac S of Washington, D.C. *pop* 111,183 **3** city & port N Egypt bet. Lake Mareotis & the Mediterranean *pop* 3,170,000 — **Al·ex·an·dri·an** \-drē-ən\ *adj or n*

Al Fayyūm — see EL FAIYÛM

Al·föld \'ȯl-,fə(r)ld, -,fœld\ the central plain of Hungary

Al Fu·jay·rah \,äl-fù-'jī-rə\ *or* **Fu·jai·rah** \-'jī-rə\ sheikhdom, member of United Arab Emirates *area* 450 *sq mi* (1166 *sq km*)

Al·gar·ve \äl-'gär-və, al-\ medieval Moorish kingdom now a province of Portugal on S coast

Al·ge·ci·ras \,al-jə-'sir-əs, ,äl-thē-'thē-räs\ city & port SW Spain W of Gibraltar on Bay of Algeciras *pop* 101,256

Al·ge·ria \al-'jir-ē-ə\ country NW Africa bordering on the Mediterranean ✳ Algiers *area* 918,497 *sq mi* (2,390,315 *sq km*), *pop* 22,971,000 — **Al·ge·ri·an** \-ē-ən\ *adj or n*

Al·giers \al-'jirz\ **1** former Barbary state N Africa now Algeria **2** city & port ✳ of Algeria on **Bay of Algiers** (inlet of Mediterranean) *pop* 1,365,400 — **Al·ge·rine** \,al-jə-'rēn\ *adj or n*

Al·goa Bay \al-'gō-ə\ inlet of Indian Ocean S Republic of S. Africa on SE coast of Eastern Cape province

Al Hamad — see HAMAD, AL

Al·ham·bra \al-'ham-brə, *for 2 also* ə-'lam-brə\ **1** city SW Calif. E of Los Angeles *pop* 82,106 **2** hill in Granada, Spain; site of remains of the palace of the Moorish kings

Al-Ha·sa \äl-'hä-sə\ *or* **Hasa** region NE Saudi Arabia in E Nejd bordering on Persian Gulf

Al Hijāz — see HEJAZ

Al Hu·day·dah \äl-hȯ-'dā-də, -dī-\ *or* **Ho·dei·da** \hō-'dā-də\ city & port W Yemen *pop* 155,110

Al Hu·fuf \,äl-hȯ-'füf\ *or* **Ho·fuf** \hō-'füf\ city NE Saudi Arabia in E Nejd

Al·i·ba·tes Flint Quarries National Monument \,a-lə-'bä-tēz\ archaeological site N Tex. NE of Amarillo

Ali·can·te \,a-lə-'kan-tē, ,ä-lē-'kän-tā\ **1** province E Spain on the Mediterranean S of Valencia province *area* 2264 *sq mi* (5864 *sq km*), *pop* 1,292,563 **2** city & port, its ✳ *pop* 265,473

Al·ice \'a-ləs\ city S Tex. W of Corpus Christi *pop* 19,788

Ali·garh \,ə-lē-'gər, ,ä-lē-,gär\ city N India in NW Uttar Pradesh N of Agra *pop* (including old town of **Ko·il** \'kō-əl\) 480,520

Al Ittihad — see MADINAT ASH SHA'B

Al Jazirah — see GEZIRA

Al Jizah — see GIZA

Al Khums \äl-'kȯms, al-'kùmz\ town & port Libya ESE of Tripoli; nearby are ruins of ancient Leptis Magna

Alk·maar \'alk-,mär\ commune NW Netherlands *pop* 91,817

Al Ku·frah \äl-'kü-frə\ *or* **Ku·fra** \'kü-frə\ group of five oases SE Libya

Al Kut city SE *cen* Iraq on the Tigris SE of Baghdad

Al·lah·abad \'ä-lä-hä-,bäd, 'a-lə-hə-,bad\ city N India in S Uttar Pradesh on the Ganges W of Varanasi *pop* 806,486

Al·le·ghe·ny \,a-lə-'gā-nē *also* -'ge-\ river 325 *mi* (523 *km*) W Pa. & SW N.Y. uniting with the Monongahela at Pittsburgh to form the Ohio — **Al·le·ghe·ni·an** \-'gā-nē-ən, -'ge-\ *adj*

Al·le·ghe·ny Mountains mountains of Appalachian system E U.S. in Pa., Md., Va., & W.Va.

Al·len Park \'a-lən\ city SE Mich. WSW of Detroit *pop* 31,092

Allenstein — see OLSZTYN

Al·len·town \'a-lən-ˌtaun\ city E Pa. on the Lehigh *pop* 105,090

Al·lep·pey \ə-'le-pē\ city & port S India in Kerala *pop* 174,606

Al·li·ance \ə-'lī-ən(t)s\ city NE Ohio NE of Canton *pop* 23,376

Al·lier \al-'yā\ river *ab* 250 *mi* (402 *km*) S *cen* France flowing to the Loire

Al·ma \'al-mə\ **1** river 50 *mi* (80 *km*) in SW Crimea **2** city Canada in E Que. on the Saguenay *pop* 25,910

Al·ma-Ata \ˌal-'mä-ə-ˌtä; ˌal-mə-'ä-tə, -ə-'tä\ *or* **Al·maty** \ˌal-'mä-tē\ *or formerly* **Ver·nyi** \'vern-yē\ city SE Kazakhstan, formerly its ✳ *pop* 1,156,200

Al·ma·dén \ˌäl-mä-'dän, -'thän\ town S *cen* Spain in Sierra Morena *pop* 8012

Al Mansurah — see EL MANSÛRA

Al·me·lo \'äl-mə-ˌlō\ commune E Netherlands *pop* 63,383

Al·me·ría \ˌal-mä-'rē-ä\ **1** province S Spain SE of Granada province *area* 3388 *sq mi* (8775 *sq km*), *pop* 455,496 **2** city & port, its ✳ *pop* 155,120

Al Minya — see EL MINYA

Al Mu·kal·la \ˌäl-mù-'kà-ˌlä\ *or* **Mu·kal·la** \mù-'ka-lə\ town & port Yemen on Gulf of Aden; chief town of the Hadhramaut

Al Mukhā — see MOCHA

Alor \'a-ˌlòr, 'ä-\ island Indonesia in Lesser Sunda Is. N of Timor; with **Pan·tar** \'pan-ˌtär\, forms **Alor Islands** group

Alor Se·tar \sə-'tär\ city Malaysia in NW Peninsular Malaysia ✳ of Kedah *pop* 66,179

Alost — see AALST

Al·phe·us \al-'fē-əs\ *or NGk* **Al·fiós** \äl-'fyòs\ river *ab* 75 *mi* (121 *km*) S Greece in W Peloponnese flowing NW into Ionian Sea

Alps \'alps\ mountain system S *cen* Europe extending from Mediterranean coast at border bet. France & Italy to the W Balkan Peninsula — see MONT BLANC — **Al·pine** \'al-ˌpīn\ *adj*

Al·sace \al-'sas, -'säs; ál-'zás\ *or G* **El·sass** \'el-ˌzäs\ *or anc* **Al·sa·tia** \al-'sā-sh(ē-)ə\ region & former province NE France bet. Rhine River & Vosges Mountains — **Al·sa·tian** \al-'sā-shən\ *adj or n*

Alsace-Lor·raine \-lə-'rän, -lò-\ region NE France including Alsace & part of Lorraine

Al·sek \'al-ˌsek\ river 260 *mi* (418 *km*) NW Canada & SE Alaska flowing S into the Pacific

Al·ta California \'al-tə\ former Spanish & Mexican province (1772–1848) comprising the present state of Calif. — a name used to differentiate it from Baja California

Al·tai \al-'tī\ mountain system *cen* Asia bet. Mongolia (republic) & Xinjiang Uygur region of W China & bet. Kazakhstan & Russia in Asia — **Al·ta·ic** \al-'tā-ik\ *adj*

Al·ta·ma·ha \'òl-tə-mə-ˌhò\ river 137 *mi* (220 *km*) SE Ga. formed by junction of the Ocmulgee & the Oconee & flowing SE into **Al·tamaha Sound** (estuary)

Al·ta·mi·ra \ˌal-tä-'mē-rä\ caverns N Spain WSW of Santander

Al·ta·monte Springs \'al-tə-ˌmänt\ city *cen* Fla. *pop* 34,879

Al·tay or **Al·tai** \al-ˈtī\ territory SW Russia in Asia ✳ Barnaul *area* 101,042 *sq mi* (261,699 *sq km*), *pop* 2,666,000

Alt·dorf \ˈalt-ˌdȯrf, ˈält-\ or **Al·torf** \ˈal-ˌtȯrf, ˈäl-\ town *cen* Switzerland ✳ of Uri canton *pop* 8249

Al·ten·burg \ˈäl-tᵊn-ˌbu̇rg\ city E *cen* Germany E of Weimar *pop* 48,926

Al·to Adi·ge \ˈäl-tō-ˈä-dē-ˌjä\ or **Upper Adige** or **South Tirol** district N Italy in S Tirol in N Trentino-Alto Adige region

Al·ton \ˈȯl-tᵊn\ city SW Ill. on the Mississippi *pop* 32,905

Al·too·na \al-ˈtü-nə\ city S *cen* Pa. *pop* 51,881

Alto Paraná — see PARANÁ

Al·trinc·ham \ˈȯl-triŋ-əm\ borough NW England in Greater Manchester SSW of Manchester *pop* 39,641

Al·tun or **Al·tyn** \äl-ˈtün\ mountain range W China in S Xinjiang Uygur; highest peak *ab* 25,000 *ft* (7620 *m*)

Al·tus \ˈal-təs\ city SW Okla. *pop* 21,910

Al·vin \ˈal-vən\ city SE Tex. S of Houston *pop* 19,220

Ama·do·ra \ˌä-mə-ˈdȯr-ə, -ˈdȯr\ city W Portugal *pop* 95,518

Ama·ga·sa·ki \ˌä-mä-gä-ˈsä-kē\ city Japan in W *cen* Honshu on Osaka Bay *pop* 497,333

Amal·fi \ä-ˈmäl-fē\ commune & port S Italy in Campania on Gulf of Salerno — **Amal·fi·an** \-fē-ən\ *adj* or n

Ama·mi \ä-ˈmä-mē\ island group W Pacific in *cen* Ryukyus *area* 498 *sq mi* (1295 *sq km*)

Ama·pá \ˌä-mə-ˈpä\ state N Brazil NW of Amazon delta ✳ Macapá *area* 54,965 *sq mi* (142,359 *sq km*), *pop* 289,050

Am·a·ril·lo \ˌa-mə-ˈri-(ˌ)lō, -lə\ city NW Tex. *pop* 157,615 — **Am·a·ril·lo·an** \-ˈri-lō-ən\ n

Am·a·zon \ˈa-mə-ˌzän, -zən\ river *ab* 3900 *mi* (6276 *km*) N S. America flowing from Peruvian Andes into the Atlantic in N Brazil — see UCAYALI, SOLIMÕES — **Am·a·zo·nian** \ˌa-mə-ˈzō-nē-ən, -nyən\ *adj*

Ama·zo·nas \ˌä-mə-ˈzō-nəs\ state NW Brazil ✳ Manaus *area* 604,032 *sq mi* (1,564,443 *sq km*), *pop* 2,088,682

Ama·zo·nia \ˌa-mə-ˈzō-nē-ə\ region N S. America, the basin of the Amazon

Am·ba·to \äm-ˈbä-(ˌ)tō\ city *cen* Ecuador S of Quito *pop* 124,166

Am·bon \äm-ˈbȯn, ˈam-ˌbän\ or **Am·boi·na** \am-ˈbȯi-nə\ 1 island E Indonesia in the Moluccas S of Ceram *area* 314 *sq mi* (816 *sq km*) 2 city & port on Ambon Is. *pop* 276,955 — **Am·boi·nese** \ˌam-ˌbȯi-ˈnēz, -ˈnēs, and -bȯi-\ or **Am·bo·nese** \ˌam-bə-ˈnēz, ˈnēs\ *adj* or n

Am·bra·cian Gulf \am-ˈbrā-shən\ or **Gulf of Ar·ta** \ˈär-tə\ or Gk **Am·vra·ki·kós Kól·pos** \ˌäm-ˈvrä-kē-ˌkȯs-ˈkȯl-ˌpȯs\ inlet of Ionian Sea 25 *mi* (40 *km*) long W Greece in S Epirus

Am·brose \ˈam-ˌbrōz\ dredged channel SE N.Y. at entrance to N.Y. harbor S of Sandy Hook; 40 *ft* (12 *m*) deep, 2000 *ft* (606 *m*) at widest point

Am·chit·ka \am-ˈchit-kə\ island SW Alaska at E end of Rat group

Amer·i·ca \ə-ˈmer-ə-kə\ 1 either continent (N. America or S. America) of the western hemisphere 2 or the **Amer·i·cas** \-kəz\ the lands of the western hemisphere including N., Central, & S. America & the W. Indies 3 UNITED STATES OF AMERICA — **Amer·i·can** \ə-ˈmer-ə-kən, -ˈmar-, -i-kən\ *adj* or n

American Samoa *or* **Eastern Samoa** island group of E Samoa SW *cen* Pacific ✱ Pago Pago (on Tutuila Is.) *area* 76 *sq mi* (198 *sq km*), *pop* 49,600

American Samoa National Park reservation American Samoa comprising three sections

Amers·foort \'ä-mərz-ˌfōrt, -mərs-, -ˌfòrt\ commune *cen* Netherlands NE of Utrecht *pop* 104,390

Ames \'āmz\ city *cen* Iowa N of Des Moines *pop* 47,198

Am·ga \əm-'gä\ river 800 *mi* (1280 *km*) E *cen* Russia in Asia, flowing NE to the Aldan

Am·hara \am-'har-ə, äm-'här-ə\ former kingdom (now a province) NW Ethiopia ✱ Gondar

Am·herst \'a-(ˌ)mərst, *chiefly by outsiders* 'am-ˌhərst\ town W *cen* Mass. N of Springfield *pop* 35,228

Amiens \äm-'yaⁿ\ city N France on the Somme *pop* 136,234

Amin·di·vi \ˌə-mən-'dē-vē\ island group India in the N Laccadives

Am·i·rante \'a-mə-ˌrant\ islands W Indian Ocean SW of Seychelles; a dependency of Seychelles

Am·man \ä-'män, a-, -'man\ *or anc* **Philadelphia** *or bib* **Rab·bah Am·mon** \ˌra-bə-'a-mən\ *or* **Rab·bath Am·mon** \ˌra-bəth\ city ✱ of Jordan, NE of Dead Sea *pop* 1,213,300

Am·mon \'a-mən\ ancient country NW Arabia E of Gilead ✱ Rabbah

Ammonium — see SIWA

Amne Machin — see A'NYÊMAQÊN

Amo — see BLACK

Amor·gós \ä-(ˌ)mór-'gós\ island Greece in the Aegean in SE Cyclades SE of Naxos *area* 47 *sq mi* (122 *sq km*)

Amoy — see XIAMEN

Am·ra·va·ti \ˌəm-'rä-və-tē, äm-\ *or formerly* **Am·rao·ti** \-'raú-tē\ city *cen* India in NE Maharashtra, chief city of Berar region *pop* 421,576

Am·rit·sar \ˌəm-'rit-sər\ city N India in NW Punjab *pop* 709,456

Am·ster·dam \'am(p)-stər-ˌdam, *for 2 also* 'äm(p)-stər-ˌdäm\ **1** city E N.Y. on the Mohawk *pop* 20,714 **2** city & port, official ✱ of Netherlands *pop* 713,407 — **Am·ster·dam·mer** \-ˌda-mər, -ˌdä-\ *n*

Amu Dar'·ya \ä-mü-'där-yə\ *or anc* **Ox·us** \'äk-səs\ river over 1500 *mi* (2400 *km*), *cen* & W Asia flowing from Pamir plateau into Aral Sea

Amund·sen Gulf \'ä-mən-sən, 'a-\ arm of Beaufort Sea N Canada

Amundsen Sea arm of the S Pacific W Antarctica off Marie Byrd Land

Amur \ä-'múr\ *or* **Chin Hei·long** *or* **Hei–lung** \'hā-'lúŋ\ river *ab* 1780 *mi* (2865 *km*) E Asia formed by junction of the Shilka & the Argun, flowing into the Pacific at N end of Tatar Strait, & forming part of boundary bet. China & Russia

Ana·dyr \ˌä-nə-'dir, ˌa-\ river 694 *mi* (1117 *km*) E Russia in Asia flowing S & E to Gulf of Anadyr

Anadyr, Gulf of *or* **Gulf of Ana·dir** \ˌä-nə-'dir, ˌa-\ inlet of N Bering Sea E Russia in Asia S of Chukchi Peninsula

An·a·heim \'a-nə-ˌhīm\ city SW Calif. E of Long Beach *pop* 266,406

Aná·huac \ä-'nä-ˌwäk\ the central plateau of Mexico

An·a·to·lia \ˌa-nə-ˈtō-lē-ə, -ˈtōl-yə\ the part of Turkey comprising the peninsula of Asia Minor — **An·a·to·lian** \-ˈtō-lē-ən, -ˈtōl-yən\ *adj or n*

An·cas·ter \ˈaŋ-ˌkas-tər, ˈan-\ town Canada in SE Ont. W of Hamilton *pop* 21,988

An·ch'ing — see ANQING

An·chor·age \ˈaŋ-k(ə-)rij\ city S *cen* Alaska at head of Cook Inlet *pop* 226,338

An·co·hu·ma \ˌäŋ-kō-ˈü-mä, -ˈhü-\ mountain peak 20,958 *ft* (6388 *m*) W Bolivia; highest in the Illampu massif

An·co·na \äŋ-ˈkō-nə, an-\ city & port *cen* Italy ✳ of Marche on the Adriatic *pop* 101,179

An·da·lu·sia \ˌan-də-ˈlü-zh(ē-)ə\ *or Sp* **An·da·lu·cía** \ˌän-dä-(ˌ)lü-ˈsē-ä\ region S Spain including Sierra Nevada & valley of the Guadalquivir — **An·da·lu·sian** \ˌan-də-ˈlü-zhən\ *adj or n*

An·da·man and Nic·o·bar \ˈan-də-mən...ni-kə-ˌbar, -ˌman-\ union territory India comprising Andaman & Nicobar groups ✳ Port Blair *area* 3202 *sq mi* (8293 *sq km*), *pop* 280,661

Andaman Islands islands India in Bay of Bengal S of Myanmar & N of Nicobar Islands *area* 2461 *sq mi* (6374 *sq km*) — **An·da·man·ese** \ˌan-də-mə-ˈnēz, -ˈnēs\ *adj or n*

Andaman Sea sea SE Asia, the E section of Bay of Bengal

An·der·lecht \ˈän-dər-ˌlekt\ commune *cen* Belgium, *pop* 87,884

An·der·matt \ˈän-dər-ˌmät\ commune *cen* Switzerland S of Altdorf

An·der·son \ˈan-dər-sən\ **1** city *cen* Ind. *pop* 59,459 **2** city NW S.C. *pop* 26,184 **3** river 430 *mi* (692 *km*) Canada in Northwest Territories flowing W & N into Beaufort Sea

An·des \ˈan-(ˌ)dēz\ mountain system of S. America extending along W coast from Panama to Tierra del Fuego — see ACONCAGUA — **An·de·an** \ˈan-dē-ən, an-ˈdē-\ *adj* — **An·dine** \ˈan-ˌdēn, -ˌdīn\ *adj*

An·dhra Pra·desh \ˌän-drə-prə-ˈdāsh, -ˈdesh\ state SE India N of Tamil Nadu state bordering on Bay of Bengal ✳ Hyderabad *area* 106,272 *sq mi* (275,244 *sq km*), *pop* 66,508,008

An·di·zhan *or* **An·di·jon** \ˌan-di-ˈzhan, ˌän-di-ˈzhän\ city Uzbekistan ESE of Tashkent *pop* 298,300

An·dor·ra \an-ˈdȯr-ə, -ˈdär-ə\ country SW Europe in E Pyrenees bet. France & Spain; a republic ✳ Andorra la Vella *area* 180 *sq mi* (482 *sq km*), *pop* 57,100 — **An·dor·ran** \-ən\ *adj or n*

An·do·ver \ˈan-ˌdō-vər, -də-\ town NE Mass. *pop* 29,151

An·dre·a·nof Islands \ˌan-drē-ˈä-ˌnȯf, ˌän-drē-ˈä-nəf\ islands SW Alaska in *cen* Aleutian chain — see ADAK, ATKA

An·dria \ˈän-drē-ə\ commune SE Italy in Puglia *pop* 89,762

Andropov — see RYBINSK

An·dros 1 \ˈan-drəs\ island, largest of Bahamas *area* 1600 *sq mi* (4160 *sq km*) **2** \ˈan-drəs, -ˌdräs; ˈän-thrȯs\ island 25 *mi* (40 *km*) long Greece in N Cyclades

An·dros·cog·gin \ˌan-drə-ˈskä-gən\ river 157 *mi* (253 *km*) NE N.H. & SW Maine flowing into the Kennebec

Ane·to, Pi·co de \ˈpē-(ˌ)kō-ˌdā-ä-ˈnā-(ˌ)tō\ *or F* **Pic de Né·thou** \ˌpēk-də-(ˌ)nā-ˈtü\ mountain 11,168 *ft* (3404 *m*) NE Spain; highest in the Pyrenees

An·ga·ra \ˌəŋ-gə-ˈrä, ˌäŋ-gə-ˈrä\ river 1100 *mi* (1770 *km*) Russia, flowing from Lake Baikal into the Yenisey — see TUNGUSKA

An·garsk \ən-'gärsk\ city S Russia in Asia on the Angara NW of Irkutsk *pop* 269,000

An·gel Falls \'än-jəl\ waterfall 3212 *ft* (979 *m*) SE Venezuela on Auyán-tepuí mountain in a headstream of the Caroní

An·gers \äⁿ-zhā\ city W France ENE of Nantes *pop* 146,163

Ang·kor \'aŋ-,kôr\ ruins of ancient city NW Cambodia N of Tonle Sap; ✳ of the Khmers

An·gle·sey *or* **An·gle·sea** \'aŋ-gəl-sē\ **1** *or anc* **Mo·na** \'mō-nə\ island NW Wales **2** former county comprising Anglesey Is. & Holyhead Is. ✳ Llangefni

Anglia 1 — see ENGLAND **2** — see EAST ANGLIA — **An·gli·an** \'aŋ-glē-ən\ *adj or n*

Anglo–Egyptian Sudan — see SUDAN

An·go·la \aŋ-'gō-lə, an-\ *or formerly* **Portuguese West Africa** country SW Africa S of mouth of the Congo; until 1975 a dependency of Portugal ✳ Luanda *area* 481,351 *sq mi* (1,251,513 *sq km*), *pop* 10,609,000 — **An·go·lan** \-lən\ *adj or n*

An·gou·lême \äⁿ-gü-'läm, -'lem\ city W France *pop* 46,194

An·gou·mois \äⁿ-gü-'mwä\ region & former duchy & province W France S of Poitou ✳ Angoulême

An·guil·la \aŋ-'gwi-lə, an-\ island Brit. West Indies NW of St. Kitts *area* 35 *sq mi* (91 *sq km*) — **An·guil·lan** \-'gwi-lən\ *adj or n*

An·gus \'aŋ-gəs\ *or earlier* **For·far** \'fôr-far\ *or* **For·far·shire** \-,shir, -shər\ former county E Scotland ✳ Forfar

An·halt \'än-,hält\ former state *cen* Germany ✳ Dessau

An·hui *or* **An·hwei** \'än-'hwä, -'wä\ province E China W of Jiangsu ✳ Hefei *area* 54,015 *sq mi* (140,439 *sq km*), *pop* 56,180,813

An·i·ak·chak Crater \,a-nē-'ak-,chak\ active volcano SW Alaska on Alaska Peninsula in **Aniakchak National Monument**; crater 6 *mi* (10 *km*) in diameter

A–ni–ma–ch'ing — see A'NYÊMAQÊN

An·jou \'an-jü, äⁿ-'zhü\ **1** region & former province NW France in Loire valley ✳ Angers **2** town Canada in S Que. *pop* 37,210 — **An·ge·vin** \'an-jə-vən\ *adj or n*

An·ka·ra \'aŋ-kə-rə, 'äŋ-\ *or formerly* **An·go·ra** \aŋ-'gôr-ə, an-, -'gòr-\ *or anc* **An·cy·ra** \an-'sī-rə\ city ✳ of Turkey in N *cen* Anatolia *pop* 2,559,471

Ann, Cape \'an\ peninsula NE Mass.

An·na·ba \ä-'nä-bə\ *or formerly* **Bône** \'bōn\ commune & port NE Algeria NE of Constantine *pop* 305,526

An Na·fūd \,än-nä-'füd\ *or* **Na·fud** \na-'füd\ desert N Saudi Arabia in N Nejd

An Na·jaf \än-'nä-,jäf\ city S *cen* Iraq W of the Euphrates *pop* 242,603

An·nam \a-'nam, ə-; 'a-,nam\ region & former kingdom E Indochina in *cen* Vietnam ✳ Hue *area ab* 57,000 *sq mi* (148,200 *sq km*) — **An·nam·ese** \,a-nə-'mēz, -'mēs\ *adj or n* — **An·nam·ite** \'a-nə-,mīt\ *adj or n*

An·nap·o·lis \ə-'na-pə-lis\ city & port ✳ of Md. *pop* 33,187

Annapolis Basin inlet of Bay of Fundy Canada in W N.S.

An·na·pur·na \,a-nə-'pur-nə, -'pər-\ massif N Nepal in the Himalayas; highest peak 26,504 *ft* (8078 *m*)

Ann Ar·bor \(,)an-'är-bər\ city SE Mich. W of Detroit *pop* 109,592

An·ne·cy \än-'sē\ city E France ENE of Lyon *pop* 51,143

An Nhon \ˈän-ˈnōn\ *or formerly* **Binh Dinh** \ˈbin-ˈdin\ city *cen* Vietnam in S Annam

An·nis·ton \ˈa-nə-stən\ city NE Ala. *pop* 26,623

An·qing *or* **An–ch'ing** \ˈän-ˈchin\ *or* **An·king** \ˈän-ˈkin\ *or formerly* **Hwai·ning** \ˈhwī-ˈnin\ city E China in Anhui on the Chang *pop* 250,718

An·shan \ˈän-ˈshän\ city NE China in E *cen* Liaoning SSW of Shenyang *pop* 1,203,986

An·ta·kya \ˌän-tä-ˈkyä\ *or* **An·ta·ki·yah** \-ˈkē-yə\ *or anc* **An·ti·och** \ˈan-tē-ˌäk\ city S Turkey on the Orontes *pop* 123,871

An·tal·ya \än-ˈtäl-ˈyä\ *or formerly* **Ada·lia** \ə-ˈdä-lē-ə\ city & port SW Turkey on Gulf of Antalya *pop* 378,208

An·ta·nan·a·ri·vo \ˌän-tä-ˌnä-nä-ˈrē-(ˌ)vō\ *or Malagasy* **Ta·nan·a·ri·vo** \tä-ˌnä-nä-ˈrē-(ˌ)vō\ *or formerly* **Ta·nan·a·rive** \tə-ˈna-nə-ˌrēv\ city ✳ of Madagascar *pop* 802,390

Ant·arc·tic \ant-ˈärk-tik, -ˈär-tik\ region including Antarctica, Antarctic Peninsula, and the Antarctic Ocean

Ant·arc·ti·ca \-ˈärk-ti-kə, -ˈär-tik\ body of land around the S. Pole; a plateau covered by a great ice cap & mountain peaks *area ab* 5,500,000 *sq mi* (14,300,000 *sq km*), divided into **West Antarctica** (including Antarctic Peninsula) & **East Antarctica** by Transantarctic Mountains

Antarctic Archipelago — see PALMER ARCHIPELAGO

Antarctic Ocean ocean surrounding Antarctica including the southern regions of the S. Atlantic, S. Pacific, & Indian oceans esp. S of *ab* 60°S

Antarctic Peninsula *or formerly* **Palmer Peninsula** peninsula *ab* 700 *mi* (1126 *km*) long W Antarctica and S end of S. America

An·tibes \äⁿ-ˈtēb\ city & port SE France SW of Nice *pop* 70,688

Antibes, Cap d' — see CAP D'ANTIBES

An·ti·cos·ti Island \ˌan-tə-ˈkä-stē\ island E Canada in E Que. at mouth of the St. Lawrence *area* 3043 *sq mi* (7912 *sq km*)

An·tie·tam Creek \an-ˈtē-təm\ creek S Pa. & N Md. flowing S into the Potomac N of Harpers Ferry, W.Va.

An·ti·gua \an-ˈtē-gə, -gwə\ **1** island Brit. West Indies in the Leewards *area* 108 *sq mi* (281 *sq km*); with Barbuda an independent nation (**Antigua and Barbuda**) since 1981 (*pop* 83,000) — see WEST INDIES ASSOCIATED STATES **2** *or* Antigua Guatemala city S *cen* Guatemala; former ✳ of Guatemala *pop* 20,715 — **An·ti·guan** \an-ˈtē-gən, -gwən\ *adj or n*

An·ti–Leb·a·non \an-tī-ˈle-bə-nən, -ˌnän\ mountain range SW Asia E of Bekaa Valley on Syria-Lebanon border — see HERMON (Mount)

An·til·les \an-ˈti-lēz\ the W. Indies excluding Bahamas — see GREATER ANTILLES, LESSER ANTILLES — **An·til·le·an** \an-ˈti-lē-ən\ *adj*

An·ti·och \ˈan-tē-ˌäk\ **1** city W Calif. NE of Oakland *pop* 62,195 **2** — see ANTAKYA **3** ancient city Asia Minor in Pisidia, at certain periods within boundaries of Phrygia; ruins in W *cen* Turkey — **An·ti·o·chene** \ˈan-tī-ə-ˌkēn, ˌan-tē-(ˌ)ä-ˈkēn\ *adj or n* — **An·ti·och·i·an** \ˌan-tē-ˈō-kē-ən, -ˈä-\ *adj or n*

An·ti·sa·na \ˌan-tē-ˈsä-nä\ volcano 18,714 *ft* (5704 *m*) N *cen* Ecuador

An·to·fa·gas·ta \ˌän-tō-fä-ˈgäs-tä\ city & port N Chile N of Santiago *pop* 218,754

An·trim \'an-trəm\ **1** traditional county NE Northern Ireland **2** district E Northern Ireland, established 1974 *area* 217 *sq mi* (564 *sq km*), *pop* 44,322

An·tsi·ra·na·na \ˌän-tsē-'rä-nə-nə\ *or formerly* **Di·é·go–Sua·rez** \dē-'ā-gō-'swä-res\ city & port Madagascar near N tip of island *pop* 54,418

Antung — see DANDONG

Ant·werp \'ant-ˌwərp, 'an-ˌtwərp\ *or F* **An·vers** \äⁿ-'ver(s)\ *or Flem* **Ant·wer·pen** \'änt-ˌver-pə(n)\ **1** province N Belgium *area* 1104 *sq mi* (2870 *sq km*), *pop* 1,605,167 **2** city & port, its * on the Schelde *pop* 467,518

Anu·ra·dha·pu·ra \ə-ˌnúr-ə-də-ˌpúr-ə\ town N *cen* Sri Lanka; an ancient * of Ceylon *pop* 37,000

An·yang \'än-'yäŋ\ **1** city E China in N Henan *pop* 480,668 **2** city NW S. Korea *pop* 361,577

A'·nyê·ma·qên \ä-'nyā-ˌmä-'chen\ *or* **Am·ne Ma·chin** \'äm-nē-mä-'chin\ *or* **A–ni–ma–ch'ing** \'ä-nē-'mä-'chiŋ\ range of the Kunlun Mountains W China in E *cen* Qinghai; highest peak *ab* 20,500 *ft* (6250 *m*)

An·zio \'änt-sē-ˌō, 'an-zē-ˌō\ city & port Italy SSE of Rome *pop* 33,523

Ao·mo·ri \ä-'ō-mō-rē\ city & port N Japan in NE Honshu on Mutsu Bay *pop* 287,354

Aorangi — see COOK (Mount)

Aos·ta \ä-'ò-stä\ **1** commune NW Italy in Piedmont at junction of Great & Little Saint Bernard passes *pop* 36,339 **2** — see VALLE D'AOSTA

Ap·a·lach·i·co·la \ˌa-pə-ˌla-chi-'kō-lə\ river 90 *mi* (145 *km*) NW Fla. flowing from Lake Seminole S into **Apalachicola Bay** (inlet of Gulf of Mexico)

Apa·po·ris \ˌä-pä-'pōr-(ˌ)ēs, -'pór-\ river *ab* 550 *mi* (885 *km*) S Colombia flowing SE into the Japurá on Colombia-Brazil boundary

Apel·doorn \'ä-pəl-ˌdōrn, -ˌdórn\ commune E *cen* Netherlands N of Arnhem *pop* 148,745

Ap·en·nines \'a-pə-ˌnīnz\ mountain chain Italy extending the length of the peninsula — see CORNO (Monte) — **Ap·en·nine** \-ˌnīn\ *adj*

Apia \ä-'pē-ä\ town & port Samoa * of Western Samoa on Upolu Is.

Apo, Mount \'ä-(ˌ)pō\ volcano 9692 *ft* (2954 *m*) S Philippines in SE Mindanao; highest peak in the Philippines

Ap·pa·la·chia \ˌa-pə-'lā-chə, -'la-chə, -'lā-shə\ region E U.S. comprising Appalachian Mountains from S *cen* N.Y. to *cen* Ala.

Ap·pa·la·chian Mountains \ˌa-pə-ˌlā-ch(ē-)ən, -ˌsh(ē-)ən, -'la-ch(ē-)ən\ mountain system E N. America extending from SE Que., Nfld., & N.B. SW to N Ala.; highest peak Mt. Mitchell 6684 *ft* (2037 *m*)

Ap·pen·zell \'ä-pən-ˌzel, 'ä-pən(t)-ˌsel\ former canton NE Switzerland, now divided into two cantons (formerly half cantons): **Appenzell Inner Rhodes** \'rōdz\ *or G* **Appenzell Inner Rho·den** \'i-nə(r)-'rō-dᵊn\ (* Appenzell *area* 67 *sq mi or* 174 *sq km, pop* 13,656) & **Appenzell Outer Rhodes** *or G* **Appenzell Aus·ser Rhoden** \'aú-sə(r)\ (* Herisau *area* 94 *sq mi or* 243 *sq km, pop* 51,167)

Ap·pi·an Way \'a-pē-ən\ ancient paved highway extending from Rome to the Adriatic

Ap·ple·ton \'a-pəl-tən\ city E Wis. *pop* 65,695

Apple Valley 1 town SE Calif. N of San Bernardino *pop* 46,079 2 city SE Minn. *pop* 34,598

Apra Harbor \'ä-prä\ seaport Guam on W coast

Ap·she·ron \,əp-shi-'rón\ peninsula E Azerbaijan projecting into the Caspian Sea

Apu·lia — see PUGLIA — **Apu·lian** \ə-'pyül-yən, -'pyü-lē-ən\ *adj or n*

Apu·re \ä-'pü-rä\ river 509 *mi* (819 *km*) W Venezuela flowing E into the Orinoco

Apu·rí·mac \,ä-pü-'rē-,mäk\ river 428 *mi* (689 *km*) S & *cen* Peru flowing N to unite with the Urubamba forming the Ucayali

Aqa·ba \'ä-kä-bə\ or **Al-'A·qa·bah** \,äl-\ *or anc* **Elath** \'ē-,lath\ town & port SW Jordan on border of Israel at head of NE arm **(Gulf of Aqaba)** of Red Sea

Aq·mo·la or **Ak·mo·la** \ak-'mó-lə\ town N *cen* Kazakhstan, its ✻ since 1997

Aquid·neck Island \ə-'kwid-,nek\ or **Rhode Island** island SE R.I. in Narragansett Bay; site of city of Newport

Aq·ui·taine \'a-kwə-,tān\ old region of SW France comprising area later known as Guienne ✻ Toulouse

Aq·ui·ta·nia \,a-kwə-'tā-nyə, -nē-ə\ a Roman division of SW Gaul under Caesar consisting of country bet. Pyrenees & Garonne River & under Augustus expanded to Loire & Allier rivers — **Aq·ui·ta·nian** \-nyən, -nē-ən\ *adj or n*

'Ara·bah, Wadi \'wä-dē-'är-à-bə\ or **Wadi al-'Arabah** or **Wadi el-'Arabah** \-,äl-, -,el-\ valley extending S from Dead Sea to Gulf of Aqaba

Arabian Desert desert E Egypt bet. the Nile & the Red Sea

Arabian Peninsula or **Ara·bia** \ə-'rā-bē-ə\ peninsula SW Asia *ab* 1200 *mi* (1930 *km*) long & 1300 *mi* (2090 *km*) wide including Saudi Arabia, Yemen, & Persian Gulf States; in early times divided into **Arabia Pe·trae·a** \pə-'trē-ə\, "Rocky Arabia", the NW part; **Arabia De·ser·ta** \di-'zər-tə\, "Desert Arabia", the N part; & **Arabia Fe·lix** \'fē-liks\, "Fertile Arabia", the main part but by some geographers restricted to Yemen — **Ar·ab** \'ar-əb, 'er-\ *adj or n* — **Ara·bi·an** \-bē-ən\ *adj*

Arabian Sea sea, NW section of the Indian Ocean bet. India & Arabian Peninsula

Ara·by \'ar-ə-bē\ ARABIA

Ara·ca·ju \,är-ə-kə-'zhü\ city & port NE Brazil ✻ of Sergipe *pop* 293,285

Arad \ä-'räd\ city W Romania on the Mures *pop* 191,428

Ara·fu·ra Sea \,ä-rä-'fü-rä\ sea bet. N Australia & W New Guinea

Ar·a·gon \'ar-ə-,gän, -gən\ \ä-rä-'gón\ region NE Spain bordering on France; once an independent kingdom ✻ Saragossa — **Ar·a·go·nese** \,ar-ə-gə-'nēz, -'nēs\ *adj or n*

Ara·gua·ia or **Ara·gua·ya** \,är-à-'gwī-ə\ river *ab* 1365 *mi* (2195 *km*), *cen* Brazil flowing N into the Tocantins

Arāk \ä-'räk, ə-'rak\ city W Iran SW of Tehran *pop* 265,349

Ara·kan \,ar-ə-'kän, -'kan\ coast region SW Myanmar on Bay of Bengal; chief town Sittwe

Araks \ə-'räks\ *or* **Aras** \ə-'räs\ *or anc* **Arax·es** \ə-'rak-(ˌ)sēz\ river 635 *mi* (1022 *km*) W Asia rising in mountains of Turkish Armenia & flowing E to join the Kura in E Azerbaijan

Ar·al Sea \'ar-əl\ *or formerly* **Lake Aral** brackish lake bet. Kazakhstan & Kyrgyzstan *area formerly more than* 25,500 *sq mi* (66,000 *sq km*)

Ar·am \'ar-əm, 'er-\ ancient Syria — its Hebrew name

Ar·an Islands \'ar-ən\ islands W Ireland off coast of Galway; largest island Inishmore

Aran·sas Bay \ə-'ran(t)-səs\ inlet of Gulf of Mexico S Tex. NE of Corpus Christi Bay bet. mainland & St. Joseph Is.

Aransas Pass channel S Tex. bet. Mustang & St. Joseph islands leading to Corpus Christi & Aransas bays

Ar·a·rat \'ar-ə-ˌrat\ *or* **Ag·ri Da·gi** \ä-grē-dä-'gē\ mountain 16,946 *ft* (5165 *m*) E Turkey near border of Iran

Ara·val·li Range \ä-'rä-və-(ˌ)lē\ mountain range NW India E of Thar Desert; highest peak Mt. Abu 5650 *ft* (1722 *m*)

Ar·bil *or* **Ir·bil** *or* **Er·bil** \ər-'bēl\ city N Iraq E of Mosul *pop* 460,758

Ar·bon \är-'bōn\ commune NE Switzerland *pop* 11,333

Ar·buck·le Mountains \'är-ˌbək-ᵊl\ hilly region S *cen* Okla.

Ar·ca·dia \är-'kā-dē-ə\ **1** city SW Calif. ENE of Los Angeles *pop* 48,290 **2** mountainous region S Greece in *cen* Peloponnese — **Ar·ca·di·an** \-dē-ən\ *adj or n*

Archangel, Gulf of — see DVINA GULF

Arch·es National Park \'är-chəz\ reservation E Utah including wind-eroded natural arch formations

Ar·cos de la Fron·te·ra \'är-kōs-ˌthä-lä-frōn-'tä-rä\ commune SW Spain NE of Cádiz *pop* 26,946

Ar·cot \är-'kät\ city SE India in N Tamil Nadu WSW of Madras; once ✻ of the nawabs of Carnatic *pop* 45,193

Arc·tic \'ärk-tik, 'är-tik\ the Arctic Ocean and lands in it and adjacent to it

Arctic Archipelago archipelago N & E Northwest Territories, Canada in Arctic Ocean

Arctic Ocean ocean N of the Arctic Circle

Arctic Red river 310 *mi* (499 *km*) Canada in W Northwest Territories, flowing N into the Mackenzie

Ar·cueil \är-'kœi, -'kü-ē\ commune N France S of Paris *pop* 20,303

Ar·da·bil *or* **Ar·de·bil** \är-də-'bēl\ city NW Iran in E Azerbaijan region *pop* 281,973

Ar·den \'är-dᵊn\ district *cen* England in SW Warwickshire W of Stratford-upon-Avon; site of former **Forest of Arden**

Ar·dennes \är-'den\ wooded plateau region in NE France, W Luxembourg, & SE Belgium E of the Meuse

Ard·more \'ärd-ˌmȯr, -ˌmȯr\ city S Okla. *pop* 23,079

Ards \'ärdz\ district E Northern Ireland, established 1974 *area* 143 *sq mi* (372 *sq km*), *pop* 64,026

Are·ci·bo \ä-rä-'sē-(ˌ)bō\ city & port N Puerto Rico *pop* 93,385

Are·na, Point \ə-'rē-nə\ promontory N Calif. in the Pacific *ab* midway bet. Cape Mendocino & San Francisco Bay

Are·qui·pa \ä-rā-'kē-pä\ city S Peru at foot of El Misti *pop* 621,700

Arez·zo \ä-'ret-(ˌ)sō, ä-\ commune *cen* Italy in Tuscany *pop* 91,527

Ar·gen·tan \är-zhən-'täⁿ\ commune NW France in Normandy NNW of Alençon *pop* 16,063

Ar·gen·teuil \är-zhən-'təi, -'tü-ē\ commune N France on the Seine NNW of Paris *pop* 94,162

Ar·gen·ti·na \är-jən-'tē-nə\ *or* **the Ar·gen·tine** \'är-jən-,tīn, -,tēn\ country S S. America bet. the Andes & the Atlantic S of the Pilcomayo; a federal republic ✻ Buenos Aires *area* 1,072,156 *sq mi* (2,776,884 *sq km*), *pop* 33,070,000 — **Argentine** *adj or n* — **Argen·tin·ean** *or* **Ar·gen·tin·i·an** \,är-jən-'ti-nē-ən\ *adj or n*

Ar·gi·nu·sae \,är-jə-'nü-(,)sē, -'nyü\ group of small islands in the Aegean SE of Lesbos

Ar·go·lis \'är-gə-ləs\ district & ancient country S Greece in E Peloponnese comprising a plain around Argos & area between Gulf of Argolis & Saronic Gulf — **Ar·gol·ic** \är-'gä-lik\ *adj*

Argolis, Gulf of inlet of the Aegean S Greece on E coast of Peloponnese

Ar·gonne \är-'gón, -'gän\ wooded plateau NE France S of the Ardennes near Belgian border bet. the Meuse & the Aisne

Ar·gos \'är-,gös, -gəs\ town Greece in E Peloponnese on Argive plain at head of Gulf of Argolis; once a Greek city-state — **Argive** \'ä-,jīv, -,gīv\ *adj or n*

Argovie — *see* AARGAU

Ar·guel·lo, Point \är-'gwe-(,)lō\ cape SW Calif. WNW of Santa Barbara

Ar·gun \'är-'gün\ river 450 *mi* (724 *km*) NE Asia forming boundary bet. Inner Mongolia (China) & Russia & uniting with the Shilka to form the Amur

Ar·gyll \är-'gīl, -'gil\ *or* **Ar·gyll·shire** \-,shir, -shər\ former county W Scotland ✻ Lochgilphead

Ar·hus *or* **Aar·hus** \'ór-,hüs\ city & port Denmark in E Jutland on the Kattegat *pop* 259,493

Aria \'är-ē-ə, ə-'rī-ə\ **1** an E province of ancient Persian Empire; district now in NW Afghanistan & E Iran **2** — *see* HERAT

Ari·ca \ə-'rē-kə\ city & port N Chile *pop* 177,330 — *see* TACNA

Ar·i·ma·thea \,ar-ə-mə-'thē-ə\ town in ancient Palestine; location not certainly identified

Ariminum — *see* RIMINI

Ari·pua·nã \,är-ē-pwə-'näⁿ\ river 400 *mi* (644 *km*) W *cen* Brazil rising in Mato Grosso state & flowing N into the Madeira

Arius — *see* HARI

Ar·i·zo·na \,ar-ə-'zō-nə\ state SW U.S. ✻ Phoenix *area* 113,909 *sq mi* (296,163 *sq km*), *pop* 3,665,228 — **Ar·i·zo·nan** \-nən\ *or* **Ari·zo·nian** \-nē-ən, -nyən\ *adj or n*

Ar·kan·sas \'är-kən-,só; *1 is also* är-'kan-zəs\ **1** river 1450 *mi* (2334 *km*) SW *cen* U.S. rising in *cen* Colo. & flowing E & SE through S Kans., NE Okla., & Ark. into the Mississippi **2** state S *cen* U.S. ✻ Little Rock *area* 53,187 *sq mi* (137,754 *sq km*), *pop* 2,350,725 — **Ar·kan·san** \är-'kan-zən\ *adj or n*

Ar·khan·gel'sk \är-'kän-,gelsk, ər-'kän-gilsk\ *or* **Arch·an·gel** \'är-,kān-jəl\ city & port Russia in Europe on the Northern Dvina *pop* 414,000

Arl·berg \'är(-ə)l-,bərg, -,berk\ Alpine valley, pass, & tunnel W Austria in the Tirol

Ar·les \'är(-ə)l\ **1** medieval kingdom E & SE France; also called Kingdom of Burgundy **2** *or anc* **Ar·e·las** \'ar-ə-,las\ *or* **Ar·e·la·te** \,ar-ə-'lā-tē\ city SE France on the Rhône *pop* 52,593 — **Ar·le·sian** \är-'lē-zhən\ *n*

Ar·ling·ton \'är-liŋ-tən\ **1** town E Mass. NW of Boston *pop* 44,630 **2** city N Tex. E of Fort Worth *pop* 261,721 **3** unincorporated population center N Va. *pop* 170,936

Arlington Heights village NE Ill. NW of Chicago *pop* 75,460

Ar·lon \är-'lōⁿ\ commune SE Belgium ✳ of Luxembourg province *pop* 23,422

Ar·magh \är-'mä, 'är-\ **1** traditional county SE Northern Ireland **2** district S Northern Ireland, established 1974 *area* 260 *sq mi* (676 *sq km*), *pop* 51,331 **3** town *cen* Armagh district, Northern Ireland *pop* 49,100

Ar·ma·gnac \,är-mán-'yák\ district SW France in old province of Gascony; chief town Auch

Ar·me·nia \är-'mē-nē-ə, -nyə\ **1** *or bib* **Min·ni** \'mi-,nī\ former kingdom W Asia in mountainous region SE of Black Sea & SW of Caspian Sea; area now divided bet. Armenia, Turkey, & Iran **2** independent country SE Europe; a constituent republic (**Ar·me·ni·an Republic** \-nē-ən\) of the U.S.S.R. 1936–91 ✳ Yerevan *area* 11,506 *sq mi* (29,800 *sq km*), *pop* 3,426,000 — see LESSER ARMENIA — **Armenian** *adj or n*

Ar·men·tières \,är-mäⁿ-'tyer, -,är-mən-'tirz\ commune N France W of Lille *pop* 26,240

Ar·mor·i·ca \är-'mòr-ə-kə, -'mär-\ **1** *or* **Ar·e·mor·i·ca** \,ar-ə-\ ancient region NW France bet. the Seine & the Loire **2** BRITTANY — **Ar·mor·i·can** \-i-kən\ *or* **Ar·mor·ic** \-ik\ *adj or n*

Arn·hem \'ärn-,hem, 'är-nəm\ commune E Netherlands ✳ of Gelderland *pop* 132,928

Arn·hem Land \'är-nəm\ region N Australia on N coast of Northern Territory

Ar·no \'är-(,)nō\ *or anc* **Ar·nus** \-nəs\ river 150 *mi* (241 *km*) *cen* Italy flowing W from the Apennines through Florence into Ligurian Sea

Aroos·took \ə-'rüs-tək, -'rús-\ river 140 *mi* (225 *km*) N Maine flowing NE across N.B. border & into St. John River

Ar·ran \'ar-ən\ island SW Scotland in Firth of Clyde *area* 165 *sq mi* (429 *sq km*)

Ar·ras \à-'rás, 'ar-əs\ city N France SSW of Lille *pop* 42,715

Arsanias — see MURAT

Arta, Gulf of — see AMBRACIAN GULF

Ar·tois \är-'twä\ former province N France bet. Flanders & Picardy ✳ Arras

Aru·ba \ə-'rü-bə\ internally self-governing Dutch island off NW Venezuela; chief town Oranjestad *area* 69 *sq mi* (179 *sq km*), *pop* 69,000

Aru Islands *or formerly* **Aroe Islands** \'är-(,)ü\ islands E Indonesia S of W New Guinea *area* 3305 *sq mi* (8593 *sq km*), *pop* 29,604

Arun·a·chal Pra·desh \'är-ə-,nä-chəl-prə-'dāsh, -'desh\ *or formerly* **North East Frontier Agency** state NE India N of Assam ✳ Itanagar *area* 32,269 *sq mi* (83,577 *sq km*), *pop* 864,558

Aru·wi·mi \,ä-rü-'wē-mē\ river 620 *mi* (998 *km*) N Democratic Republic of the Congo flowing SW & W into Congo River

Ar·va·da \är-'va-də\ city N *cen* Colo. NW of Denver *pop* 89,235

Ar·wad \är-'wad, -'wäd\ *or bib* **Ar·vad** \'är-,vad\ island Syria off coast of S Latakia

Asa·hi·ka·wa \,ä-sə-hē-'kä-wə, ä-,sä-'hē-kä-\ *or* **Asa·hi·ga·wa** \-'gä-wə, -gä-wə\ city Japan in *cen* Hokkaido *pop* 361,736

Asa·ma \ä-'sä-mä\ *or* **Asa·ma·ya·ma** \ä-,sä-mä-'yä-mä\ volcano 8300 *ft* (2530 *m*) Japan in *cen* Honshu

Asan·sol \,ə-sənsól\ city NE India in W. Bengal *pop* 261,836

As·cen·sion \ə-'sen(t)-shən\ island in S Atlantic belonging to Brit. colony of St. Helena *area* 34 *sq mi* (88 *sq km*), *pop* 1400

As·co·li Pi·ce·no \'äs-kō-(,)lē-pē-'chā-(,)nō\ *or anc* **As·cu·lum Pi·ce·num** \'as-kyə-ləm-(,)pī-'sē-nəm\ commune *cen* Italy in Marche NE of Rome *pop* 52,371

Ascoli Sa·tria·no \,sä-trē-'ä-(,)nō\ *or anc* **As·cu·lum Ap·u·lum** \,as-kyə-ləm-'a-pyə-ləm\ *or* **Aus·cu·lum Apulum** \'ós-\ commune SE Italy in Puglia S of Foggia

As·cot \'as-kət\ village S England in Berkshire SW of London

As·cut·ney, Mount \-'skət-nē\ mountain 3320 *ft* (1012 *m*) SE Vt.

Ashan·ti \ə-'shan-tē, -'shän-\ region *cen* Ghana; formerly a native kingdom & later a Brit. colony ✴ Kumasi *area* 9417 *sq mi* (24,390 *sq km*), *pop* 2,090,100

Ash·bur·ton \'ash-,bər-tᵊn\ river *ab* 400 *mi* (644 *km*) in NW Western Australia flowing NW into Indian Ocean

Ash·dod \'ash-,däd\ city & port Israel W of Jerusalem *pop* 76,600

Ashe·ville \'ash-,vil, -'vil\ city W N.C. *pop* 61,607

Ashkh·a·bad \'ash-kə-,bad, -,bäd\ *or* **Ash·ga·bat** \'äsh-gə-,bät\ *or formerly* **Pol·to·ratsk** \,päl-tə-'rätsk\ city ✴ of Turkmenistan *pop* 412,200

Ash·land \'ash-lənd\ **1** city NE Ky. on the Ohio *pop* 23,622 **2** city N *cen* Ohio *pop* 20,079

Ash·ley \'ash-lē\ river 40 *mi* (64 *km*) S S.C. flowing SE into Charleston harbor

Ash·qe·lon \'ash-kə-,län\ ancient city & port SW Palestine, site in Israel WSW of Jerusalem

Ash Sha·ri·qah \,àsh-'shä-rē-kə\ *or* **Shar·jah** \'shär-jə\ sheikhdom, member of United Arab Emirates

Ash·ta·bu·la \,ash-tə-'byü-lə\ city NE Ohio on Lake Erie *pop* 21,633

Asia \'ā-zhə, -shə\ continent of the eastern hemisphere N of equator forming a single landmass with Europe (the conventional dividing line bet. Asia & Europe being the Ural Mountains & main range of the Caucasus Mountains); has numerous large offshore islands including Cyprus, Sri Lanka, Malay Archipelago, Taiwan, the Japanese chain, & Sakhalin *area* 17,139,445 *sq mi* (44,391,162 *sq km*) — **Asian** \-zhən, -shən\ *adj or n*

Asia Minor peninsula forming W extremity of Asia bet. Black Sea on N, Mediterranean Sea on S, & Aegean Sea on W — see ANATOLIA

Asir \a-'sir\ province S Saudi Arabia on Red Sea SE of Hejaz ✴ As Sabya *area* 40,130 *sq mi* (103,937 *sq km*)

As·ma·ra \az-'mär-ə, -'mar-ə\ city ✴ of Eritrea *pop* 342,706

As·nières \än-'yer\ commune N France NW of Paris

Aso \'ä-(,)sō\ *or* **Aso·san** \'ä-sō-,sän\ volcanic mountain Japan in *cen* Kyushu; has five volcanic cones grouped around crater 15 *mi* (24 *km*) long with walls 2000 *ft* (610 *m*) high

Aso·lo \'ä-zō-,lō\ commune NE Italy NW of Treviso

Asphaltites, Lacus — see DEAD SEA

As·sam \a-'sam, a-; 'a-,sam\ state NE India on edge of Himalayas ✻ Dispur *area* 30,318 *sq mi* (78,827 *sq km*), *pop* 22,414,322 — **As·sam·ese** \,a-sə-'mēz, -ēs\ *adj or n*

As·sen \'ä-s³n\ commune NE Netherlands ✻ of Drenthe *pop* 50,880

As·sin·i·boine \ə-'si-nə-,bóin\ river 665 *mi* (1070 *km*) Canada rising in SE Sask. & flowing S & E across S Man. into Red River

Assiniboine, Mount mountain 11,870 *ft* (3618 *m*) Canada in SW Alta. on B.C. border

As·si·si \ə-'si-sē, -'sē-, -zē\ commune *cen* Italy ESE of Perugia *pop* 24,669

As·syr·ia \ə-'sir-ē-ə\ *or bib* **As·sur** \ä-'sùr, 'ä-\ *or* **Ashur** \'ä-,shùr\ ancient empire W Asia extending along middle Tigris & over foothills to the E; early ✻ Calah, later ✻ Nineveh — **As·syr·i·an** \-ē-ən\ *adj or n*

Astacus — see IZMIT

Asti \'äs-tē\ commune NW Italy W of Alessandria *pop* 74,649

As·tra·khan \'as-trə-,kan, -kən\ city Russia in Europe, on the Volga at head of its delta *pop* 512,000

As·tu·ri·as \ə-'stùr-ē-əs, a-, -'styùr-\ **1** region & old kingdom NW Spain on Bay of Biscay **2** province NW Spain *area* 4079 *sq mi* (10,565 *sq km*), *pop* 1,093,937 — **As·tu·ri·an** \-ē-ən\ *adj or n*

Asun·ción \ä-sün-'syōn\ city ✻ of Paraguay on Paraguay River at confluence with the Pilcomayo *pop* 502,426

As·wân \a-'swän, ä-\ *or anc* **Sy·e·ne** \sī-'ē-nē\ city S Egypt on right bank of the Nile near site of dam built 1898–1902 & of **Aswân High Dam** (completed 1970 to form **Lake Nas·ser** \'nä-sər, 'na-\) *pop* 191,461

As·yût \äs-'yüt\ city *cen* Egypt on left bank of the Nile *pop* 273,191

Ata·ca·ma \,ä-tä-'kä-mä\ — see PUNA DE ATACAMA

Atacama Desert desert N Chile bet. Copiapó & Peru border

Atas·ca·de·ro \ə-,tas-kə-'der-(,)ō\ city W Calif. *pop* 23,138

At·ba·ra \'at-bə-rə, 'ät-\ river *ab* 500 *mi* (805 *km*) NE Africa rising in N Ethiopia & flowing through E Sudan into the Nile

Atchaf·a·laya \(ə-),cha-fə-'lī-ə\ river 225 *mi* (362 *km*) S La. flowing S into **Atchafalaya Bay** (inlet of Gulf of Mexico)

Ath·a·bas·ca *or* **Ath·a·bas·ka** \,a-thə-'bas-kə, ,ä-\ river 765 *mi* (1231 *km*) Canada in Alta. flowing NE & N into Lake Athabasca

Athabasca, Lake lake Canada on Alta.-Sask. boundary *area* 3058 *sq mi* (7951 *sq km*)

Ath·ens \'a-thənz\ **1** city NE Ga. *pop* 45,734 **2** city SE Ohio *pop* 21,265 **3** *or Gk* **Athí·nai** \ä-'thē-(,)ne\ *or anc* **Athe·nae** \ə-'thē-(,)nē\ city ✻ of Greece near Saronic Gulf *pop* 748,110 — **Athe·nian** \ə-'thē-nē-ən, -nyən\ *adj or n*

Athos \'a-,thōs, 'ä\ mountain NE Greece at E end of Acte Peninsula; site of a number of monasteries comprising **Mount Athos** (autonomous area)

Ati·tlán \ä-tē-'tlän\ lake 12 *mi* (19 *km*) long SW Guatemala at 4700 *ft* (1432 *m*) altitude occupying a crater 1000 *ft* (305 *m*) deep N of **Atitlán Volcano**

At·ka \'at-kə, 'ät-\ island SW Alaska in Andreanof group

At·lan·ta \ət-'lan-tə, at-\ city NW *cen* Ga., its ✳ *pop* 394,017 — **At·lan·tan** \-'lan-t³n\ *adj or n*

At·lan·tic City \ət-'lan-tik, at-\ city SE N.J. on Atlantic coast *pop* 37,986

Atlantic Ocean ocean separating N. & S. America from Europe & Africa *area* 31,814,640 *sq mi* (82,399,918 *sq km*); often divided into **North Atlantic Ocean** & **South Atlantic Ocean** — **Atlantic** *adj*

Atlantic Provinces the Canadian provinces of Nfld., N.B., N.S., & P.E.I. — see MARITIME PROVINCES

At·las Mountains \'at-ləs\ mountains NW Africa extending from SW Morocco to NE Tunisia; its highest peaks are in the **Grand,** or **High, Atlas** in SW *cen* Morocco — see TOUBKAL (Jebel)

Atrek \ä-'trek\ *or* **Atrak** \-'trak\ river 300 *mi* (483 *km*) NE Iran flowing into the Caspian Sea on Turkmenistan border

Atropatene — see AZERBAIJAN

At·ta·wa·pis·kat \ˌa-tə-wə-'pis-kət\ river 465 *mi* (748 *km*) Canada in N Ont. flowing N into James Bay

At·ti·ca \'a-ti-kə\ region E Greece, chief city Athens; a state of ancient Greece — **At·tic** \'a-tik\ *adj or n*

At·tle·boro \'a-t³l-ˌbər-ō\ city SE Mass. *pop* 38,383

At·tu \'a-(ˌ)tü\ island SW Alaska, most westerly of the Aleutians in Near group — see WRANGELL (Cape)

At·wa·ter \'at-ˌwȯ-tər, -, wä-\ city *cen* Calif. *pop* 22,282

Aube \'ōb\ river 154 *mi* (248 *km*) N *cen* France flowing into the Seine

Au·ber·vil·liers \ˌō-bər-ˌvēl-'yā\ commune N France *pop* 72,859

Au·burn \'ȯ-bərn\ **1** city E Ala. *pop* 33,830 **2** city SW Maine *pop* 24,309 **3** city *cen* N.Y. *pop* 31,258 **4** city W Wash. *pop* 33,102

Auck·land \'ȯ-klənd\ city & port N New Zealand on North Is. *pop* 315,668 — **Auck·land·er** \-klən-dər\ *n*

Audenarde — see OUDENAARDE

Au·ghrim *or* **Aghrim** \'ȯ-grəm\ town W Ireland in E Galway

Au·gra·bies Falls \ȯ-'grä-bēz\ waterfall 480 *ft* (146 *m*) Republic of S. Africa in Orange River in Northern Cape province

Augs·burg \'ȯgz-ˌbərg, 'au̇gz-ˌbu̇rk\ city S Germany in Bavaria on the Lech *pop* 256,877

Au·gus·ta \ȯ-'gəs-tə, ə-\ **1** city E Ga. on Savannah River *pop* 44,639 **2** city ✳ of Maine on the Kennebec *pop* 21,325

Au·lis \'ȯ-ləs\ harbor E Greece in Boeotia on Evripos Strait

Au·nis \ō-'nēs\ former province W France on Gironde Estuary & Bay of Biscay ✳ La Rochelle

Au·rang·a·bad \au̇-'rəŋ-gə-ˌbäd, -'rəŋ-ə-, -ˌbad\ city W India in *cen* Maharashtra ENE of Bombay *pop* 573,272

Au·rès \ȯ-'res\ massif *ab* 7600 *ft* (2316 *m*) NE Algeria in Saharan Atlas

Au·ri·gnac \ˌō-rēn-'yak\ village SW France SW of Toulouse

Au·ril·lac \ˌō-rē-'yak\ city S France *pop* 32,654

Au·ro·ra \ə-'rȯr-ə, ȯ-, -'rȯr-\ **1** city N *cen* Colo. E of Denver *pop* 222,103 **2** city NE Ill. *pop* 99,581 **3** town Canada in SE Ont. *pop* 29,454

Au·sa·ble \ȯ-'sā-bəl\ river 20 *mi* (32 *km*) NE N.Y. flowing E into Lake Champlain through **Ausable Chasm** gorge

Auschwitz — see OŚWIĘCIM

Austerlitz — see SLAVKOV

Aus·tin \'òs-tən, 'äs-\ **1** city S Minn. *pop* 21,907 **2** city ✳ of Tex. on the Colorado *pop* 465,622

Aus·tral Islands \'òs-trəl, 'äs-\ islands S Pacific S of Tahiti belonging to France *pop* 6509

Aus·tral·asia \ˌòs-trə-'lā-zhə, ˌäs-, -'lā-shə\ Australia, Tasmania, New Zealand, & Melanesia — **Aus·tral·asian** \-zhən, -shən\ *adj or n*

Aus·tra·lia \ò-'strāl-yə, ä-, ə-\ **1** continent of the eastern hemisphere SE of Asia & S of the equator *area* 2,948,366 *sq mi* (7,665,751 *sq km*) **2** *or* **Commonwealth of Australia** dominion of the Commonwealth of Nations including the continent of Australia & island of Tasmania ✳ Canberra *area* 2,967,909 *sq mi* (7,716,563 *sq km*), *pop* 17,562,000 — **Aus·tra·lian** \-yən\ *adj or n*

Australian Alps mountain range SE Australia in E Victoria & SE New S. Wales forming S end of Great Dividing Range

Australian Capital Territory *or formerly* **Federal Capital Territory** district SE Australia including two areas, one around Canberra & the other on Jervis Bay, surrounded by New S. Wales *area* 939 *sq mi* (2441 *sq km*), *pop* 229,000

Aus·tra·sia *or* **Os·tra·sia** \ò-'strā-zhə, ä-, -shə\ the E dominions of the Merovingian Franks extending from the Meuse to Böhmerwald — **Aus·tra·sian** \-zhən, -shən\ *adj or n*

Aus·tria \'òs-trē-ə, 'äs-\ *or G* **Ös·ter·reich** \'ē-stə(r)-ˌrīk\ country *cen* Europe in & N of E Alps with the Danube crossing it in N; a republic ✳ Vienna *area* 32,375 *sq mi* (84,175 *sq km*), *pop* 7,812,100 — **Aus·tri·an** \-ən\ *adj or n*

Austria–Hun·ga·ry \-'həŋ-gə-rē\ dual monarchy 1867–1918 *cen* Europe including Bohemia, Moravia, Bukovina, Transylvania, Galicia, and what is now Austria, Hungary, Slovenia, Croatia, & NE Italy — **Aus·tro–Hun·gar·i·an** \ˌòs-(ˌ)trō-ˌhəŋ-'gar-ē-ən, ˌäs-, -'ger-\ *adj or n*

Aus·tro·ne·sia \ˌòs-trə-'nē-zhə, ˌäs-, -'nē-shə\ **1** the islands of the S Pacific **2** area extending from Madagascar through the Malay Peninsula & Archipelago to Hawaii & Easter Is.

Au·teuil \ō-'tȯi, -'tə(r)\ district in W Paris, France

Au·vergne \ō-'vernʸ, -'vərn\ region & former province S *cen* France ✳ Clermont (now Clermont-Ferrand)

Auvergne Mountains mountains S *cen* France; highest in the Massif Central — see SANCY (Puy de)

Aux Cayes — see CAYES

Aux Sources, Mont \ˌmōⁿ-ˌtō-'sùrs\ mountain 10,822 *ft* (3298 *m*) N Lesotho in Drakensberg Mountains on South Africa border

Au·yán–te·puí \aù-ˌyän-tā-'pwē\ *or* **Devil Mountain** plateau *ab* 20 *mi* (32 *km*) long SE Venezuela E of the Caroní — see ANGEL FALLS

Au·yuit·tuq National Park \aú-'yü-ə-tək\ reservation NE Canada in E Baffin Is.

Av·a·lon \'a-və-ˌlän\ peninsula Canada in SE Newfoundland

Avalon, Isle of — see ISLE OF AVALON

Ave·bury \'āv-b(ə-)rē, *US also* -ˌber-ē\ village S England in Wiltshire E of Bristol; has megalithic remains

Avel·la·ne·da \ä-vä-zhä-'nä-thä\ city E Argentina, E suburb of Buenos Aires, on Río de la Plata *pop* 346,620

Avenches \ä-'väsh\ *or anc* **Aven·ti·cum** \ə-'ven-ti-kəm\ town W Switzerland in Vaud canton ✳ of ancient Helvetia

Av·en·tine \'a-vən-,tīn, -,tēn\ hill in Rome, Italy, one of seven (including also the Caelian, Capitoline, Esquiline, Palatine, Quirinal, & Viminal) on which the ancient city was built

Aver·nus, Lake \ə-'vər-nəs\ *or It* **Lago d'Aver·no** \'lä-gō-dä-'ver-(,)nō\ lake S Italy in crater of extinct volcano W of Naples

Avi·gnon \ȧ-(,)vēn-'yō\ city SE France *pop* 89,440

Ávi·la \'ä-vi-lä, -vē-,lä\ **1** province *cen* Spain area 3107 *sq mi* (8047 *sq km*), *pop* 174,378 **2** city, its ✳, WNW of Madrid *pop* 45,977

Avlona — see VLORË

Avon \'ā-vən, 'a-, *US also* 'ā-,vän\ **1** river 96 *mi* (154 *km*) *cen* England rising in Northamptonshire & flowing WSW past Stratford-upon-Avon into Severn River at Tewkesbury **2** river 65 *mi* (105 *km*) S England rising near Devizes in Wiltshire & flowing S into English Channel **3** river 75 *mi* (121 *km*) SW England rising in Gloucestershire & flowing S & W through city of Bristol into Bristol Channel at Avonmouth **4** \'a-vən\ — see SWAN **5** \'ā-vən, 'a-, *US also* 'ā-,vän\ county SW England ✳ Bristol area 535 *sq mi* (1386 *sq km*), *pop* 919,800

Avranches \äv-'räsh\ town NW France in SW Normandy

Awa·ji \ä-'wä-jē\ island Japan S of Honshu & NE of Shikoku

Awash \'ä-,wäsh\ river 500 *mi* (805 *km*) E Ethiopia flowing NE

Ax·el Hei·berg \'ak-səl-'hī-,bərg\ island N Canada in the Sverdrup Islands W of Ellesmere Is. area 15,779 *sq mi* (41,025 *sq km*)

Axum — see AKSUM — **Ax·um·ite** \'ak-sə-mīt\ adj or n

Aya·cu·cho \,ī-ä-'kü-(,)chō\ town S Peru SE of Lima *pop* 101,600

Ay·dın \ī-'din\ city SW Turkey SE of Izmir *pop* 107,011

Ayers Rock \'arz, 'erz\ outcrop *cen* Australia in SW Northern Territory; 1143 *ft* (348 *m*) high

Ayles·bury \'ālz-b(ə-)rē, *US also* -,ber-ē\ borough SE *cen* England ✳ of Buckinghamshire *pop* 41,288

Ayl·mer \'āl-mər\ town Canada in SW Que. *pop* 32,244

Ayr \'ar, 'er\ **1** *or* **Ayr·shire** \-,shir, -shər\ former county SW Scotland **2** burgh & port SW Scotland in Strathclyde *pop* 49,481

Ayut·tha·ya \ä-yü-'tī-ə\ *or in full* **Phra Na·khon Si Ayutthaya** \prä-nä-'kȯn-sē-\ city S Thailand N of Bangkok *pop* 60,561

Azer·bai·jan \,a-zər-,bī-'jän, ,ä-\ independent country SE Europe bordering on Caspian Sea; a constituent republic of the U.S.S.R. 1936–91 ✳ Baku area 33,200 *sq mi* (86,320 *sq km*), *pop* 7,029,000

Azerbaijan *or anc* **At·ro·pa·te·ne** \a-trō-pə-'tē-nē\ *or* **Me·dia Atropatene** \'mē-dē-ə\ region NW Iran; chief city Tabriz

Azincourt — see AGINCOURT

Azores \'ā-,zȯrz, -,zȯrz, ,ə-\ *or Pg* **Aço·res** \ə-'sȯr-ēsh\ islands N Atlantic belonging to Portugal & lying *ab* 800 *mi* (1287 *km*) off coast of Portugal; chief town Ponta Delgada area 905 *sq mi* (2344 *sq km*), *pop* 236,500 — **Azor·e·an** *or* **Azor·i·an** \ā-'zȯr-ē-ən, -'zȯr-, ə-\ adj or n

Azov, Sea of \'a-,zȯf, 'ā-, ə-'zȯf\ gulf of the Black Sea E of Crimea connected with the Black Sea by the Kerch Strait area 14,517 *sq mi* (37,599 *sq km*)

Az·tec Ruins National Monument \'az-,tek\ reservation NW N.Mex. NE of Farmington; site of a prehistoric pueblo

Azu·sa \ə-'zü-sə\ city SW Calif. ENE of Los Angeles *pop* 41,333

Az Zaqāzīg — see ZAGAZIG

B

Baal·bek \'bā-əl-,bek, 'bäl-,bek\ town E Lebanon N of Damascus on site of ancient city of **He·li·op·o·lis** \,hē-lē-'äp-(ə-)ləs\

Ba·bar Islands \'bä-,bär\ islands Indonesia ENE of Timor

Bab el Man·deb \'bäb-el-'män-dəb\ strait between SW Arabia & Africa connecting Red Sea & Gulf of Aden

Ba·bel·thu·ap \,bä-bəl-'tü-,äp\ island W Pacific, chief island in Palau *area* 143 *sq mi* (372 *sq km*)

Babruysk — see BOBRUYSK

Ba·bu·yan \,bä-bü-'yän\ chief island of the Babuyan group

Babuyan Islands *or* **Ba·bu·ya·nes** \,bä-bü-'yä-nās\ islands of N Philippines N of Luzon *area* 225 *sq mi* (585 *sq km*)

Bab·y·lon \'ba-bə-lən, -,län\ ancient city ✳ of Babylonia; its site *ab* 55 *mi* (89 *km*) S of Baghdad near the Euphrates

Bab·y·lo·nia \,ba-bə-'lō-nyə, -nē-ə\ ancient country in valley of the lower Euphrates & the Tigris ✳ Babylon — **Bab·y·lo·ni·an** \-nē-ən\ *adj or n*

Ba·cau \bə-'kaù\ city E *cen* Romania *pop* 193,269

Back \'bak\ river 605 *mi* (974 *km*) Canada in Northwest Territories flowing ENE into Arctic Ocean

Ba·co·lod \bä-'kō-,lòd\ city Philippines on Negros Is. *pop* 364,000

Bactra — see BALKH

Bac·tria \'bak-trē-ə\ ancient country SW Asia between Hindu Kush & Oxus River ✳ Bactra — see BALKH — **Bac·tri·an** \'bak-trē-ən\ *adj or n*

Ba·da·joz \,bä-thä-'hòs, ,bä-də-'hòz\ **1** province SW Spain in valley of the Guadiana *area* 8362 *sq mi* (21,658 *sq km*), *pop* 650,388 **2** city, its ✳ *pop* 122,225

Ba·da·lo·na \,bä-thä-'lō-nä, ,bä-dəl-'ō-nə\ city & port NE Spain on the Mediterranean NE of Barcelona *pop* 218,725

Bad Ems — see EMS

Ba·den \'bä-dᵊn\ **1** region SW Germany bordering on Switzerland & France; formerly a grand duchy (1805–1918), a state of the Weimar Republic (1918–33), an administrative division of the Third Reich (1933–49), & a state of the Bonn Republic (1949–51) ✳ Karlsruhe — see BADEN-WÜRTTEMBERG **2** BADEN-BADEN

Ba·den-Ba·den \,bä-dᵊn-'bä-dᵊn\ *or* **Baden** city & spa SW Germany in Baden-Württemberg SSW of Karlsruhe *pop* 52,524

Ba·den–Würt·tem·berg \,bä-dᵊn-'wər-təm-,bərg, -'wür-; -'vᵊr-təm-,berk\ state SW Germany W of Bavaria; formed 1951 from former Baden, Württemberg-Baden, & Württemberg-Hohenzollern states ✳ Stuttgart *area* 13,803 *sq mi* (35,750 *sq km*), *pop* 9,822,000

Bad Godesberg — see GODESBERG

Bad Hom·burg \bät-'hòm-,bùrk, -'häm-,bərg\ city SW *cen* Germany N of Frankfurt am Main *pop* 51,663

Bad·lands National Park \'bad-,landz\ reservation SW S.Dak. E of Black Hills comprising an area of badlands topography

Bad Mergentheim — see MERGENTHEIM

Baer·um \'bar-əm\ city SE Norway, a suburb of Oslo *pop* 89,221

Baf·fin Bay \'ba-fən\ inlet of the Atlantic bet. W Greenland & E Baffin Is.

Baffin Island island NE Canada N of Hudson Strait; largest in Arctic Archipelago *area* 183,810 *sq mi* (477,906 *sq km*)

Ba·fing \bə-'faŋ, bȧ-'fēⁿ\ river 350 *mi* (560 *km*) W Africa in W Mali & Guinea; the upper course of the Senegal

Bagh·dad \'bag-,dad, ,bäg-'däd\ city ✳ of Iraq on the middle Tigris *pop* 3,841,268 — **Bagh·dadi** \bag-'da-dē\ *n*

Ba·guio \bä-gē-'ō\ city, summer ✳ of the Philippines, in NW *cen* Luzon *pop* 183,000

Ba·ha·mas \bə-'hä-məz, *by outsiders also* -'hä-\ islands in the Atlantic SE of Fla.; an independent member of the Commonwealth of Nations since 1973 ✳ Nassau *area* 4404 *sq mi* (11,450 *sq km*), *pop* 268,000 — see TURKS AND CAICOS — **Ba·ha·mi·an** \bə-'hä-mē-ən, -'hä-\ *adj or n*

Ba·ha·wal·pur \bə-'hä-wəl-,pùr\ region Pakistan in SW Punjab; until 1947 a princely state of India

Ba·hia \bə-'hē-ə, bä-'ē-ə\ **1** *or formerly* **Ba·ía** \bä-'ē-ə\ state E Brazil ✳ Salvador *area* 216,612 *sq mi* (561,025 *sq km*), *pop* 11,801,810 **2** — see SALVADOR — **Ba·hi·an** \-ən\ *adj or n*

Ba·hía Blan·ca \bä-,ē-ə-'blaŋ-kə, bä-,ē-ə-'bläŋ-kä\ city & port E Argentina SW of Buenos Aires *pop* 271,467

Bahnasa, El — see OXYRHYNCHUS

Bah·rain *also* **Bah·rein** \bä-'rān\ **1** islands in Persian Gulf off coast of Arabia; an independent sultanate ✳ Manama (on Bahrain Is.) *area* 255 *sq mi* (661 *sq km*), *pop* 485,600 **2** island, largest of the group, 27 *mi* (43 *km*) long — **Bah·raini** *or* **Bah·reini** \-'rā-nē\ *adj or n*

Bahr al–Gha·zal \,bär-ȧl-gȧ-'zäl\ river 445 *mi* (716 *km*) SW Sudan flowing E to unite with the Bahr el Jebel forming the White Nile

Ba·ia–Ma·re \,bä-yä-'mä-rä\ city NW Romania *pop* 150,456

Baie–Co·meau \,bā-'kō-(,)mō, ,bā-kə-'mō\ town Canada in SE Que. *pop* 26,012

Bai·kal, Lake *or* **Lake Bay·kal** \bī-'käl, -'kal\ lake Russia in Asia; 5715 *ft* (1742 *m*) deep, *ab* 395 *mi* (636 *km*) long

Baile Atha Cliath — see DUBLIN

Ba·ja California \'bä-(,)hä\ peninsula 760 *mi* (1216 *km*) long NW Mexico bet. the Pacific & Gulf of California; divided into the states of **Baja California** (to the N ✳ Mexicali *area* 27,071 *sq mi or* 70,114 *sq km, pop* 1,660,855) & **Baja California Sur** \'sùr\ (to the S ✳ La Paz *area* 28,447 *sq mi or* 73,678 *sq km, pop* 317,764)

Bakan — see SHIMONOSEKI

Ba·ker Island \'bā-kər\ atoll *cen* Pacific near the equator at 176°31'W; belongs to U.S.

Baker, Mount mountain 10,778 *ft* (3266 *m*) NW Wash. in Cascade Range

Baker Lake — see DUBAWNT

Ba·kers·field \'bā-kərz-ˌfēld\ city S *cen* Calif. on the Kern *pop* 174,820

Bākh·ta·rān \ˌbäk-tə-'rän\ *or formerly* **Ker·man·shah** \ker-ˌmän-'shä\ city W Iran *pop* 560,514

Ba·ku \bä-'kü\ city, ✳ of Azerbaijan *pop* 1,150,000

Bakwanga — see MBUJI-MAYI

Ba·la·kla·va \ˌba-lə-'klä-və, -'kla-; ˌba-lə-'klä-və\ village in Crimea SE of Sevastopol

Bal·a·ton, Lake \'ba-lə-ˌtän, 'bò-lò-ˌtōn\ *or G* **Plat·ten·see** \'plä-t⁽ə⁾n-ˌzā\ lake W Hungary; largest in *cen* Europe *area* 232 *sq mi* (601 *sq km*)

Bal·boa Heights \(ˌ)bal-'bō-ə\ town Panama at Pacific entrance to Panama Canal adjacent to Panama (city); former administrative center of Canal Zone

Bald·win \'bòl-dwən\ borough SW Pa. S of Pittsburgh *pop* 21,923

Baldwin Park city SW Calif. E of Los Angeles *pop* 69,330

Bâle — see BASEL

Bal·e·ar·es \ˌba-lē-'ar-ēz, ˌbä-lē-'är-ās\ **1** BALEARIC ISLANDS **2** province E Spain comprising the Balearic Islands ✳ Palma *area* 1936 *sq mi* (5034 *sq km*), *pop* 709,138

Bal·e·ar·ic Islands \ˌba-lē-'ar-ik\ islands E Spain in the W Mediterranean — see BALEARES, IBIZA, MAJORCA, MINORCA

Ba·li \'bä-lē, 'ba-\ island Indonesia off E Java *area* 2147 *sq mi* (5582 *sq km*), *pop* 2,777,811 — **Ba·li·nese** \ˌbä-li-'nēz, ˌba-, -'nēs\ *adj or n*

Ba·lı·ke·sir \ˌbä-li-ke-'sir\ city NW Turkey in Asia *pop* 170,589

Ba·lik·pa·pan \ˌbä-lik-'pä-ˌpän\ city & port Indonesia on SE Borneo on inlet of Makassar Strait *pop* 309,492

Bal·kan Mountains \'bòl-kən\ mountain range *cen* Bulgaria extending from Yugoslavia border to Black Sea; highest point Botev Peak 7793 *ft* (2375 *m*)

Balkan Peninsula peninsula SE Europe bet. Adriatic & Ionian seas on W & Aegean & Black seas on E — **Balkan** *adj* — **Bal·kan·ic** \bòl-'ka-nik\ *adj*

Bal·kans \'bòl-kənz\ *also* **Balkan States** the countries occupying the Balkan Peninsula; Slovenia, Croatia, Bosnia and Herzegovina, Macedonia, Yugoslavia, Romania, Bulgaria, Albania, Greece, & Turkey in Europe

Bal·kar·ia \bòl-'kar-ē-ə, bal-, -'ker-\ mountain region S Russia in Europe, in S Kabardino-Balkaria Republic

Balkh \'bälk\ **1** district N Afghanistan corresponding closely to ancient Bactria **2** *or anc* **Bac·tra** \'bak-trə\ town N Afghanistan ✳ of ancient Bactria

Bal·khash, Lake \bal-'kash, bäl-'käsh\ lake 376 *mi* (605 *km*) long SE Kazakhstan *area ab* 7100 *sq mi* (18,390 *km*)

Bal·la·rat \'ba-lə-ˌrat\ city SE Australia in *cen* Victoria *pop* 34,501

Bal·ly·me·na \ˌba-lē-'mē-nə\ district NE Northern Ireland, established 1974 *area* 246 *sq mi* (640 *sq km*), *pop* 56,032

Bal·ly·mon·ey \ˌba-lē-'mə-nē\ district N Northern Ireland, established 1974 *area* 162 *sq mi* (421 *sq km*), *pop* 23,984

Bal·sas \'bòl-səs, 'bäl-säs\ river 426 *mi* (682 *km*) *cen* Mexico flowing from Tlaxcala to the Pacific on border bet. Michoacán & Guerrero

Baltic Sea 28

Bal·tic Sea \'bȯl-tik\ arm of the Atlantic N Europe enclosed by Denmark & Scandinavia *area ab* 160,000 *sq mi* (256,000 *sq km*) — **Baltic** *adj*

Bal·ti·more \'bȯl-tə-,mȯr, -,mȯr, -,mȯr; 'bȯlt-mər; *by residents usu* 'bȯl-tē-,mȯr *or* 'bȯl-mər\ city & port N *cen* Md. on the Patapsco estuary near Chesapeake Bay *pop* 736,014 — **Bal·ti·mor·e·an** \,bȯl-tə-'mȯr-ē-ən, -'mȯr-\ *n*

Bal·ti·stan \,bȯl-tə-'stan, ,bəl-, -'stän\ region Ladakh district N Kashmir; under Pakistani control

Ba·lu·chi·stan \bə-,lü-chə-'stan, -'stän; bə-'lü-chə-,\ **1** arid region S Asia bordering on Arabian Sea in SW Pakistan & SE Iran S & SW of Afghanistan **2** province SW Pakistan ✳ Quetta *pop* 4,305,000 — **Ba·lu·chi** \bə-'lü-chē\ *n*

Ba·ma·ko \'bä-mä-,kō\ city ✳ of Mali on Niger River *pop* 745,787

Bam·ba·ri \'bäm-bä-rē\ town S *cen* Central African Republic *pop* 52,100

Bam·berg \'bam-,bərg, 'bäm-,berk\ city S *cen* Germany in N Bavaria NNW of Nuremberg *pop* 70,689

Ba·na·ba \bä-'nä-bä\ *or* **Ocean Island** island W Pacific ESE of Nauru; belongs to Kiribati *area over* 2 *sq mi* (5 *sq km*), *pop* 284

Ba·na·hao, Mount \bä-'nä-,haů\ extinct volcano 7141 *ft* (2142 *m*) Philippines on S Luzon SE of Manila

Ba·na·na River \bə-'na-nə\ lagoon E Fla. bet. Canaveral Peninsula & Merritt Is.

Banaras — see VARANASI

Ba·nat \bə-'nät, 'bä-,nät\ region SE *cen* Europe in Danube basin bet. the Tisza & the Mures & the Transylvanian Alps; once entirely in Hungary, divided 1919 bet. Yugoslavia & Romania

Ban·bridge \ban-'brij\ district SE Northern Ireland, established 1974 *area* 171 *sq mi* (445 *sq km*), *pop* 33,102

Ban·da Islands \'ban-də, 'bän-\ islands Indonesia in Moluccas S of Ceram *area* 16 *sq mi* (42 *sq km*)

Banda Sea sea E Malay Archipelago SE of Sulawesi, S of the Moluccas, W of Aru Islands, & NE of Timor

Ban·da Ori·en·tal \'bän-də-,ȯr-ē-,en-'täl, -,ȯr-\ URUGUAY — a former name, used with reference to its position on E shore of Río de la Plata

Bandar — see MACHILIPATNAM

Bandar 'Abbas *or* **Bandar–e–Abbas** \,bən-dər(-ē)-ə-'bäs\ city S Iran on Strait of Hormuz *pop* 201,642

Bandar–e Khomeyni *or* **Bandar Khomeyni** \,bən-dər(-ē)-,kō-mā-'nē, -kō-'mä-nē\ town & port SW Iran at head of Persian Gulf ENE of Abadan *pop* 49,355

Bandar Lampung — see TANJUNGKARANG

Ban·dar Se·ri Be·ga·wan \,bən-dər-,ser-ē-bə-'gä-wän\ *or formerly* **Brunei** town, ✳ of Brunei *pop* 21,484

Ban·de·lier National Monument \,ban-də-'lir\ reservation N *cen* N.Mex. W of Santa Fe containing cliff-dweller ruins

Ban·dung *or* D **Ban·doeng** \'bän-,důŋ\ city Indonesia in W Java SE of Jakarta *pop* 2,057,442

Banff \'bam(p)f\ *or* **Banff·shire** \-,shir, -shər\ former county NE Scotland ✳ Banff

Banff National Park reservation W Canada in SW Alta. on E slope of Rocky Mountains

Ban·ga·lore \'baŋ-gə-,lōr, -,lȯr\ city S India W of Madras ✻ of Karnataka *pop* 3,302,296

Bang·ka *or* **Ban·ka** \'baŋ-kə\ island Indonesia off SE Sumatra; chief town Pangkalpinang *area* 4609 *sq mi* (11,983 *sq km*), *pop* 251,639

Bang·kok \'baŋ-,käk, baŋ-'\ *or Thai* **Krung Thep** \'krùŋ-'tep\ city & port ✻ of Thailand on the Chao Phraya *ab* 25 *mi* (40 *km*) above its mouth *pop* 5,620,591

Ban·gla·desh \,bäŋ-glə-'desh, ,baŋ-, ,bəŋ-, -'däsh\ country S Asia E of India on Bay of Bengal; a republic in the Commonwealth of Nations since 1971 ✻ Dhaka *area* 55,126 *sq mi* (143,328 *sq km*), *pop* 115,075,000 — see EAST PAKISTAN — **Ban·gla·deshi** \-'de-shē, -'dä-\ *adj or n*

Ban·gor \'baŋ-,gȯr & 'baŋ-,gȯr (*these usual for 1*), 'baŋ-gər\ **1** city E *cen* Maine on the Penobscot *pop* 33,181 **2** town SE Northern Ireland in North Down district *pop* 46,585 **3** borough & city NW Wales in Gwynedd *pop* 12,174

Ban·gui \bäŋ-'gē\ city ✻ of Central African Republic, on the Ubangi *pop* 300,723

Bang·we·u·lu, Lake \,bäŋ-gwā-'ü-(,)lü\ lake *ab* 50 *mi* (80 *km*) long N Zambia in swamp region; its area fluctuates seasonally; drains into the Luapula, a headstream of Congo River

Ban·jar·ma·sin \'bän-jär-,mä-sin\ city Indonesia in S Borneo *pop* 481,371

Ban·jul \bän-'jül\ *or formerly* **Bath·urst** \'ba-(,)thərst\ city & port ✻ of Gambia on island of St. Mary in Gambia River *pop* 44,188

Banks Island \'baŋks\ island N Canada at W end of Canadian Arctic Archipelago *area ab* 27,000 *sq mi* (69,900 *sq km*)

Banks Islands islands SW Pacific N of Vanuatu *pop* 5521

Ban·nock·burn \'ba-nək-,bərn, ,ba-nək-'\ town *cen* Scotland in Central region SSE of Stirling

Ban·tam \'ban-təm\ village Indonesia in NW corner of Java; once ✻ of Sultanate of Bantam

Ban·try Bay \'ban-trē\ bay SW Ireland in SW County Cork

Bao·ding *or* **Pao·ting** \'baù-'diŋ\ *or formerly* **Tsing·yuan** \'chiŋ-yü-'en\ city NE China SW of Beijing *pop* 483,155

Bao·ji *or* **Pao·chi** \'baù-'jē\ city N *cen* China in SW Shaanxi on the Wei W of Xi'an *pop* 337,765

Bao·tou *or* **Pao·t'ou** \'baù-'tō\ city N China in SW Inner Mongolia on the Huang *pop* 983,508

Ba·paume \bä-'pōm, ba-\ town N France S of Arras *pop* 3683

Bar·ra·cal·do \,bä-rä-'käl-dō\ commune N Spain W of Bilbao *pop* 104,883

Ba·ra·coa \,bä-rä-'kō-ä\ city & port E Cuba on N coast near E tip of island *pop* 76,873

Ba·ra·na·gar \bə-'rä-nə-gər\ city E India in W. Bengal N of Calcutta *pop* 223,770

Ba·ra·nof \'bar-ə-,nóf, bə-'rä-nəf\ island SE Alaska in Alexander Archipelago S of Chichagof Is. *area ab* 1600 *sq mi* (4160 *sq km*)

Bar·a·tar·ia Bay \,bar-ə-'tar-ē-ə, -'ter-\ lagoon SE La. on coast NW of delta of Mississippi River

Bar·ba·dos \bär-'bā-(,)dōs, -dəs, -(,)dōz\ island Brit. West Indies in Lesser Antilles E of the Windward group; a dominion of the Commonwealth of Nations since 1966 ✳ Bridgetown *area* 166 *sq mi* (432 *sq km*), *pop* 260,000 — **Bar·ba·di·an** \-'bä-dē-ən\ *adj or n*

Bar·ba·ry \'bär-b(ə-)rē\ region N Africa on **Barbary Coast** extending from Egyptian border to the Atlantic & including the former **Barbary States** (Morocco, Algiers, Tunis, & Tripoli) — a chiefly former name

Bar·bers Point \'bär-bərz\ *or* **Ka·la·e·loa Point** \kä-,lä-(,)ā-'lō-ä\ cape Hawaii at SW corner of Oahu W of Pearl Harbor

Bar·ber·ton \'bär-bər-tən\ city NE Ohio SW of Akron *pop* 27,623

Bar·bi·zon \,bär-bē-'zōⁿ, 'bär-bə-,zän\ village N France SSE of Paris

Bar·bu·da \bär-'bü-də\ island Brit. West Indies in the Leewards *area* 62 *sq mi* (161 *sq km*) — see ANTIGUA 1

Bar·ce·lo·na \,bär-sə-'lō-nə\ **1** province NE Spain in Catalonia on the Mediterranean *area* 2986 *sq mi* (7734 *sq km*), *pop* 4,654,407 **2** city & port, its ✳ *pop* 1,623,542 **3** city NE Venezuela near coast *pop* 109,061 — **Bar·ce·lo·nan** \-'lō-nən\ *n* — **Bar·ce·lo·nese** \-lō-'nēz, -'nēs, -'lō-\ *adj or n*

Bar·di·yah *or* **Bar·dia** \'bär-dē-ə, bär-'dē-ə\ town & port Libya in NE Cyrenaica

Ba·reil·ly *or* **Ba·re·li** \bə-'rā-lē\ **1** city N India in NW *cen* Uttar Pradesh ESE of Delhi *pop* 590,661 **2** — see ROHILKHAND

Bar·ents Sea \'bar-ən(t)s, 'bär-\ sea comprising the part of the Arctic Ocean bet. Spitsbergen & Novaya Zemlya

Ba·ri \'bär-ē\ *or anc* **Bar·i·um** \'bar-ē-əm, 'ber-\ commune & port SE Italy ✳ of Puglia on the Adriatic *pop* 341,273

Ba·ri·lo·che \,bä-rē-'lō-chā\ *or* **San Car·los de Bariloche** \sän-'kär-lōs-thā-\ town SW Argentina on Lake Nahuel Huapí *pop* 15,995

Ba·ri·nas \bä-'rē-näs\ town W *cen* Venezuela *pop* 152,853

Bar·i·sāl \'bar-ə-,säl\ city S Bangladesh in Ganges delta *pop* 180,014

Bar·ka \'bär-kə\ town Libya in NW Cyrenaica

Bar·king and Dag·en·ham \,bär-kiŋ-ən(d)-'da-gᵊn-ᵊm\ borough of E Greater London, England *pop* 139,900

Bar·let·ta \bär-'le-tə\ commune & port SE Italy in Puglia on the Adriatic *pop* 88,074

Bar·na·ul \,bär-nə-'ül\ city Russia in Asia on the Ob ✳ of Altay territory *pop* 606,000

Bar·ne·gat Bay \'bär-ni-,gat, -gət\ inlet of the Atlantic E N.J.

Barnes \'bärnz\ former municipal borough SE England, now part of Richmond

Bar·net \'bär-nət\ borough of N Greater London, England *pop* 283,000

Barns·ley \'bärnz-lē\ town N England in S. Yorkshire *pop* 217,300

Barn·sta·ble \'bärn-stə-bəl\ town SE Mass. *pop* 40,949

Ba·ro·da \bə-'rō-də\ **1** former state W India near head of Gulf of Khambhat ✳ Baroda *area* 8176 *sq mi* (21,258 *sq km*) **2** — see VADODARA

Ba·rot·se·land \bä-'rōt-sā-,land\ region W Zambia; formerly a protectorate

Bar·qui·si·me·to \,bär-kē-sə-'mä-(,)tō\ city NW Venezuela *pop* 602,622

Bar·ran·quil·la \ˌbär-än-ˈkē-yä\ city & port N Colombia on the Magdalena *pop* 1,018,800

Barren Grounds treeless plains N Canada W of Hudson Bay

Bar·rie \ˈbar-ē\ city Canada in SE Ont. *pop* 62,728

Bar·row, Point \ˈbar-(ˌ)ō\ most northerly point of Alaska & of the U.S., at *ab* 71°25′N 156°30′W

Bar·row–in–Fur·ness \ˌbar-ō-in-ˈfər-nəs\ port NW England in S Cumbria *pop* 71,900

Bar·stow \ˈbär-ˌstō\ city S Calif. NNE of San Bernardino *pop* 21,472

Bar·tles·ville \ˈbär-t°lz-ˌvil\ city NE Okla. *pop* 34,256

Bart·lett \ˈbärt-lət\ **1** village NE Ill. W of Chicago *pop* 19,373 **2** city SW Tenn. *pop* 26,989

Ba·rú \bä-ˈrü\ *or formerly* **Chi·ri·quí** \ˌchē-rē-ˈkē\ volcano 11,400 ft (3475 m) Panama near Costa Rican border

Ba·sel \ˈbä-zəl\ *or F* **Bâle** *or older* **Basle** \ˈbäl\ **1** former canton NW Switzerland, now divided into two half cantons: **Ba·sel–Land** \ˈbä-zəl-ˌlänt\ (✷ Liestal *area* 165 *sq mi or* 429 *sq km, pop* 234,910) & **Ba·sel–Stadt** \-ˌshtät\ (✷ Basel *area* 14 *sq mi or* 36 *sq km, pop* 197,403) **2** city NW Switzerland ✷ of Basel–Stadt *pop* 171,465

Ba·shan \ˈbā-shən\ region in ancient Palestine E & NE of Sea of Galilee

Ba·shi Channel \ˈbä-shē\ strait between Philippines & Taiwan

Bash·kor·to·stan \bäsh-ˈkȯr-tə-ˌstän, -ˌstan\ *or* **Bash·kir Republic** \ˌbash-ˈkir, ˌbäsh-\ autonomous republic E Russia in European S Ural Mountains ✷ Ufa *area* 55,443 *sq mi* (143,597 *sq km), pop* 4,008,000

Ba·si·lan \bä-ˈsē-ˌlän\ **1** island Philippines SW of Mindanao *area* 495 *sq mi* (1287 *sq km*) **2** city comprising Basilan Is. and several small nearby islands

Bas·il·don \ˈba-zəl-dən\ town SE England in Essex *pop* 157,500

Ba·si·li·ca·ta \bä-ˌzē-lē-ˈkä-tä\ *or formerly* **Lu·ca·nia** \lü-ˈkä-nyə, -ˈkä-\ region S Italy on Gulf of Taranto ✷ Potenza *pop* 591,897

Basin Ranges — SEE GREAT BASIN

Basque Country \ˈbask, ˈbäsk\ autonomous region N Spain on Bay of Biscay including provinces of Alava, Guipúzcoa, & Vizcaya — **Basque** *adj or n*

Bas·ra \ˈbäs-rə, ˈbəs-, ˈbas-, ˈbäz-, ˈbəz-, ˈbaz-\ *or* **Al–Bas·rah** \al-\ city & port S Iraq on Shatt-al-Arab *pop* 310,950

Bass Strait \ˈbas\ strait separating Tasmania & continent of Australia

Bas·sein \bə-ˈsān\ city S Myanmar W of Yangon *pop* 126,045

Basse·terre \bas-ˈter, bäs-\ town & port Brit. West Indies ✷ of St. Kitts Is. & of St. Kitts-Nevis state *pop* 14,725

Basse–Terre \bas-ˈter, bäs-\ **1** island French West Indies constituting the W part of Guadeloupe *area* 364 *sq mi* (946 *sq km*) **2** town & port ✷ of Guadeloupe *pop* 14,107

Bas·tia \ˈbas-tē-ə, ˈbäs-\ city & port France on NE coast of Corsica *pop* 38,728

Bas·togne \ba-ˈstōn, -ˈstó-nyə\ town SE Belgium in the Ardennes *pop* 12,187

Basutoland — SEE LESOTHO

Ba·ta \ˈbä-tä\ city ✷ of Mbini, Equatorial Guinea *pop* 30,474

Ba·taan \bə-'tan, -'tän\ peninsula Philippines in W Luzon on W side of Manila Bay

Ba·ta·via \bə-'tā-vē-ə\ — see JAKARTA — **Ba·ta·vi·an** \-vē-ən\ *adj or n*

Batavian Republic the Netherlands under the French (1795–1806)

Bath \'bath, 'báth\ city SW England in Avon *pop* 79,900

Bathurst — see BANJUL

Bathurst Island island N Canada in Parry group

Bat·on Rouge \,ba-tᵊn-'rüzh\ city ✳ of La. on Mississippi River *pop* 219,531

Bat·ter·sea \'ba-tər-sē\ former metropolitan borough SW London, England, on S bank of the Thames, now part of Wandsworth

Bat·tle Creek \,ba-tᵊl-'krēk\ city S Mich. *pop* 53,540

Ba·tu·mi \bä-'tü-mē\ city & port SW Republic of Georgia on Black Sea ✳ of Adjarian Republic *pop* 137,500

Baut·zen \'baút-sən\ city E Germany on the Spree ENE of Dresden *pop* 47,131

Ba·var·ia \bə-'ver-ē-ə, -'var-\ *or G* **Bay·ern** \'bī-ərn\ state SE Germany bordering on Austria & the Czech Republic ✳ Munich *area* 27,239 *sq mi* (70,549 *sq km*), *pop* 11,448,800 — **Ba·var·i·an** \bə-'vər-ē-ən\ *adj or n*

Ba·ya·món \,bī-ä-'mōn\ city NE *cen* Puerto Rico *pop* 220,262

Bay City city E Mich. near head of Saginaw Bay *pop* 38,936

Ba·yeux \bī-'yü, bä-; bä-'yə(r); bá-'yœ\ town NW France WNW of Caen *pop* 15,106

Baykal, Lake — see BAIKAL (Lake)

Bay·onne \bā-'ōn\ city & port NE N.J. *pop* 61,444

Ba·yonne \bā-'ōn, bä-'yón\ city SW France on the Adour near Bay of Biscay *pop* 41,846

Bay·reuth \bī-'róit, 'bī-,\ city Germany in Bavaria NE of Nuremberg *pop* 72,777

Bay·town \'bā-,taún\ city SE Tex. on Galveston Bay *pop* 63,850

Beachy Head \'bē-chē\ headland SE England on coast of E. Sussex

Bear \'bar, 'ber\ river 350 *mi* (563 *km*) N Utah, SW Wyo., & SE Idaho flowing to Great Salt Lake

Beard·more \'bird-,mōr, -,mór\ glacier Antarctica descending to Ross Ice Shelf at *ab* 170°E

Bear Mountain mountain 1305 *ft* (398 *m*) SE N.Y. on the Hudson

Bé·arn \bā-'arn\ region & former province SW France in Pyrenees SW of Gascony ✳ Pau

Be·as *or* **Bi·as** \'bē-,äs\ river *ab* 300 *mi* (483 *km*) N India in the Punjab

Beau·fort Sea \'bō-fərt\ sea comprising the part of the Arctic Ocean NE of Alaska & NW of Canada

Beau·mar·is \bō-'mar-əs\ borough NW Wales in Gwynedd on E Anglesey Is. on **Beaumaris Bay** *pop* 2088

Beau·mont \'bō-,mänt, bō-'\ city & port SE Tex. on the Neches *pop* 114,323

Beaune \'bōn\ commune E France SSW of Dijon *pop* 22,171

Beau·port \bō-'pòr, 'bō-(,)pòrt\ city Canada in S Que. *pop* 69,158

Beau·so·leil \,bō-sə-'lā\ commune SE France N of Monaco

Beau·vais \bō-'vā\ commune N France NNW of Paris *pop* 56,278

Bea·ver \'bē-vər\ **1** river 280 *mi* (451 *km*) NW Okla. forming upper course of the N. Canadian **2** river 305 *mi* (491 *km*) Canada in Alta. & Sask. flowing E into the Churchill

Bea·ver·creek \'bē-vər-,krēk\ city SW Ohio E of Dayton *pop* 33,626

Bea·ver·head Mountains \'bē-vər-,hed\ mountains on Idaho-Mont. boundary; SE part of Bitterroot Range of the Rockies — see GARFIELD MOUNTAIN

Bea·ver·ton \'bē-vər-tən\ city NW Oreg. W of Portland *pop* 53,310

Bé·char \bā-'shär\ *or formerly* **Co·lomb–Béchar** \kə-,lōⁿ-\ commune NW Algeria SSE of Oran *pop* 107,311

Bech·u·a·na·land \bech-'wä-nə-,land, ,be-chə-\ **1** region S Africa N of Orange River & including Kalahari Desert & Okanvango Swamps **2** — see BOTSWANA **3** *or* **British Bechuanaland** former Brit. colony in the region S of the Molopo; became part of Union of South Africa 1895 — **Bech·u·a·na** \bech-'wä-nə, ,be-chə-\ *adj or n*

Beck·en·ham \'be-kə-nəm, 'bek-nəm\ former urban district SE England in Kent, now part of Bromley

Bed·ford \'bed-fərd\ **1** city N Tex. *pop* 43,762 **2** borough SE *cen* England ✳ of Bedfordshire *pop* 74,245

Bed·ford·shire \'bed-fərd-,shir, -shər\ *or* **Bed·ford** \'bed-fərd\ county SE *cen* England *area* 494 *sq mi* (1279 *sq km*), *pop* 514,200

Bedloe's Island — see LIBERTY ISLAND

Bę·dzin \'ben-jēn\ commune S Poland in Silesia *pop* 75,800

Beer·she·ba \bir-'shē-bə, ber-, bər-\ town S Israel in N Negeb, in biblical times marking extreme S limit of Palestine *pop* 128,400

Behistun — see BISITUN

Bei·jing \'bā-'jiŋ\ *or* **Pe·king** \'pē-'kiŋ, 'pā-\ *or formerly* **Pei·ping** \'pā-'piŋ, 'bā-\ municipality NE China, its ✳ *pop* 10,819,407

Bei·ra \'bā-rə\ town & port SE Mozambique; chief port for *cen* Mozambique & landlocked Zimbabwe & Malawi *pop* 298,847

Bei·rut \bā-'rüt\ *or anc* **Be·ry·tus** \bə-'rī-təs\ city & port ✳ of Lebanon — **Bei·ruti** \bā-'rü-tē\ *n*

Be·jaïa \bā-'zhī-ə\ *or formerly* **Bou·gie** \bü-'zhē\ city & port NE Algeria *pop* 89,500

Be·kaa \bi-'kä\ *or* **Al Bi·qa'** \,àl-be-'kä\ *or anc* **Coe·le–Syr·ia** \,sē-lē-'sir-ē-ə\ valley Lebanon bet. Lebanon & Anti-Lebanon mountain ranges

Be·la·rus \bē-lə-'rüs, bye-lə-\ independent country N *cen* Europe; a constituent republic (**Belorussia** *or* **Byelorussia**) of the U.S.S.R. 1919–91 ✳ Minsk *area* 80,154 *sq mi* (207,599 *sq km*), *pop* 10,353,000 — **Be·la·ru·san** \-'rü-sən\ *adj or n* — **Be·la·ru·si·an** \-'rü-sē-ən, 'rə-shən\ *or* **Be·la·rus·sian** \-'rə-shən\ *adj or n*

Belau — see PALAU

Be·la·wan \bā-'lä-,wän\ town & port Indonesia in NE Sumatra

Be·la·ya \'bye-lə-yə\ river Russia in Europe rising in the S Urals & flowing N, W & NW to the Kama

Be·lém \be-'lem\ *or* **Pa·rá** \pà-'rä\ city N Brazil ✳ of Pará state on Pará River *pop* 1,200,000

Bel·fast \'bel-,fast, bel-\ **1** district E Northern Ireland, established 1974 *area* 54 *sq mi* (140 *sq km*), *pop* 283,746 **2** city & port ✳ of Northern Ireland at head of **Belfast Lough** (inlet) *pop* 295,100

Bel·fort \bel-'fòr, bā-'fòr\ commune E France commanding **Belfort Gap** (wide pass bet. Vosges & Jura mountains) *pop* 51,913

Belgian Congo — see CONGO 2

Belgian East Africa — see RUANDA-URUNDI

Bel·gium \'bel-jəm\ *or* F **Bel·gique** \bel-'zhēk\ *or* Flem **Bel·gië** \'bel-kē-ə\ country W Europe bordering on North Sea; a constitutional monarchy ✳ Brussels *area* 11,781 *sq mi* (30,513 *sq km*), *pop* 9,978,681 — **Bel·gian** \-jən\ *adj or n*

Bel·go·rod–Dnes·trov·ski *or* **Belgorod–Dnes·trov·skiy** \'bel-gə-,räd-(,)ne-'stròf-skē, -'stròv-, 'byel-gə-rət-dne-\ *or formerly* Turk & Russ **Ak·ker·man** \'ä-kər-,män\ city SW Ukraine on the Dniester estuary *pop* 29,000

Bel·grade \'bel-,gräd, -,gräd, -,grad, bel-'\ *or* **Beo·grad** \bā-'ò-,gräd \ city ✳ of Yugoslavia & of Serbia *pop* 1,553,854

Bel·gra·via \bel-'grā-vē-ə\ district of W *cen* London, England, in Kensington and Chelsea borough S of Hyde Park

Be·li·tung \bā-'lē-tən\ *or* **Bil·li·ton** \-,tän\ island Indonesia bet. Sumatra & Borneo *area* 1866 *sq mi* (4852 *sq km*), *pop* 102,375

Be·lize \bə-'lēz\ *or formerly* **British Honduras** country Central America bordering on the Caribbean; an independent member of the Commonwealth of Nations ✳ Belmopan *area* 8867 *sq mi* (22,966 *sq km*), *pop* 184,340 — **Be·liz·ean** \-'lē-zē-ən\ *adj or n*

Belize City seaport Belize; formerly ✳ of British Honduras *pop* 45,158

Bell \'bel\ city SW Calif. SE of Los Angeles *pop* 34,365

Bel·la Coo·la \be-lə-'kü-lə\ river *ab* 60 *mi* (96 *km*) Canada in B.C. flowing W to Burke Channel E of Queen Charlotte Sound

Bel·leau \be-'lō, 'be-,\ village N France NW of Château-Thierry & N of **Belleau Wood** (*F* Bois de Bel·leau \bwä-də-be-'lō\)

Belle Fourche \bel-'füsh\ river NE Wyo. & W S.Dak. flowing NE & E into Cheyenne River

Belle Isle, Strait of \bel-'īl\ channel bet. N tip of Newfoundland (island) & SE Labrador

Belle·ville \'bel-,vil\ **1** city SW Ill. *pop* 42,785 **2** town NE N.J. N of Newark *pop* 34,213 **3** city Canada in SE Ont. *pop* 37,243

Belle·vue \'bel-,vyü\ **1** city E Nebr. S of Omaha *pop* 30,982 **2** city W Wash. E of Seattle *pop* 86,874

Bell·flow·er \'bel-,flaù(-ə)r\ city SW Calif. E of Los Angeles *pop* 61,815

Bell Gardens city SW Calif. E of Los Angeles *pop* 42,355

Bel·ling·ham \'be-liŋ-,ham\ city & port NW Wash. on **Bellingham Bay** (inlet at N end of Puget Sound) *pop* 52,179

Bel·lings·hau·sen Sea \'be-liŋz-,haù-zən\[ʰ] sea comprising a large bay of the S Pacific W of base of Antarctic Peninsula

Bel·lin·zo·na \,be-lən-'zō-nə\ commune S Switzerland E of Locarno ✳ of Ticino *pop* 17,142

Bell·wood \'bel-,wúd\ village NE Ill. W of Chicago *pop* 20,241

Bel·mont \'bel-,mänt\ **1** city W Calif. SE of San Francisco *pop* 24,127 **2** town E Mass. W of Boston *pop* 24,720

Bel·mo·pan \,bel-mō-'pän\ city ✳ of Belize *pop* 3687

Be·lo Ho·ri·zon·te \'bā-lō-,ör-ē-'zōn-tē\ city E Brazil ✳ of Minas Gerais *pop* 2,300,000

Be·loit \bə-'lòit\ city S Wis. on Ill. border *pop* 35,573

Be·lo·rus·sia \be-lō-'rə-shə, ,bye-lō-\ *or* **Bye·lo·rus·sia** \bē-,e-lō-, ,bye-lō-\ constituent republic of the U.S.S.R. bordering on Poland, Lithuania, & Latvia; became independent 1991 — see BELARUS — **Be·lo·rus·sian** \-shən\ *adj or n*

Beloye More — see WHITE SEA

Bel·sen \'bel-zən, -sən\ *or* **Ber·gen–Belsen** \,ber-gən-, ,bər-\ locality N Germany on Lüneburg Heath NW of Celle; site of Nazi concentration camp during World War II

Be·lu·kha \bə-'lü-kə\ mountain 15,157 *ft* (4620 *m*) Russia in Asia; highest in Altai mountain range

Benares — see VARANASI

Ben·brook \'ben-,brúk\ village N Tex. SW of Fort Worth *pop* 19,564

Bend \'bend\ city *cen* Oreg. on the Deschutes *pop* 20,469

Ben·di·go \'ben-di-,gō\ city SE Australia in *cen* Victoria NNW of Melbourne *pop* 30,133

Be·ne·lux \'be-nə-l,əks\ economic union comprising Belgium, the Netherlands, & Luxembourg; formed 1947

Be·ne·ven·to \,bā-nā-'ven-(,)tō\ commune S Italy in Campania NE of Naples *pop* 62,683

Ben·gal \ben-'gól, beŋ-, -'gäl\ region E India (subcontinent) including delta of the Ganges & the Brahmaputra; formerly a presidency & (1937–47) a province of Brit. India; divided 1947 bet. Pakistan & India (republic) — see EAST BENGAL, EAST PAKISTAN, WEST BENGAL — **Ben·gal·ese** \,beŋ-gə-'lēz, ,ben-, -'lēs\ *adj or n*

Bengal, Bay of arm of the Indian Ocean between India & Sri Lanka on the W & Myanmar & Malay Peninsula on the E

Beng·bu *or* **Pang–pu** *or* **Peng–pu** *all* 'bəŋ-'bü\ city E China in N Anhui *pop* 449,245

Ben·gha·zi \ben-'gä-zē, beŋ-, -'ga-\ *or anc* **Ber·e·ni·ce** \,ber-ə-'nī-sē\ city & port NE Libya, a former * of Libya *pop* 446,250

Ben·guela \ben-'gwä-lä\ city & port W Angola *pop* 40,996

Be·ni \'bā-nē\ river *ab* 1000 *mi* (1609 *km*) *cen* & N Bolivia flowing N to unite with Mamoré River forming Madeira River

Be·ni·cia \bə-'nē-shə\ city *cen* Calif. NNE of Oakland *pop* 24,437

Be·nin \bə-'nēn, -'nin; 'be-nin\ **1** river *ab* 100 *mi* (161 *km*) S Nigeria W of the Niger flowing into Bight of Benin **2** former kingdom W Africa on lower Niger River; incorporated in Nigeria after 1897 **3** *or formerly* **Da·ho·mey** \də-'hō-mē\ country W Africa on Gulf of Guinea; a republic, formerly a territory of French West Africa * Porto-Novo *area* 43,483 *sq mi* (112,621 *sq km*), *pop* 5,074,000 **4** *or* **Benin City** city SW Nigeria in W delta of Niger River *pop* 202,800 — **Be·ni·nese** \bə-,ni-'nēz, -,nē-; ,be-ni-'nēz, -'nēs\ *adj or n*

Benin, Bight of the N section of Gulf of Guinea W Africa SW of Nigeria

Be·ni Su·ef \,be-nē-sü-'āf\ city N *cen* Egypt on W bank of the Nile *pop* 174,000

Ben Lomond — see LOMOND (Ben)

Ben Nev·is \ben-'ne-vəs\ mountain 4406 *ft* (1343 *m*) W Scotland in Grampian Hills; highest in Great Britain

Be·no·ni \be-'nō-nē\ city NE Republic of South Africa in Gauteng on the Witwatersrand E of Johannesburg *pop* 151,294

Be·nue \'bān-(ˌ)wä\ river 870 *mi* (1400 *km*) W Africa flowing W into Niger River

Ben Ve·nue \ˌben-və-'nü, -'nyü\ mountain 2393 *ft* (729 *m*) *cen* Scotland S of Loch Katrine

Ben·xi \'bən-'shē\ *or* **Pen–hsi** \'bən-'shē\ *or* **Pen–ch'i** \-'chē\ city NE China in E *cen* Liaoning *pop* 768,778

Be·rar \bā-'rär, bə-\ region *N cen* India; in Central Provinces & Berar 1903–47, in Madhya Pradesh 1947–56, in Bombay 1956–60, in Maharashtra since 1960; chief city Amravati

Ber·be·ra \'bər-b(ə-)rə\ town & port N Somalia *pop* 12,219

Be·rea \bə-'rē-ə\ **1** city NE Ohio SW of Cleveland *pop* 19,051 **2** — see VÉROIA

Be·re·zi·na \bə-'rā-zᵊn-ə, -'re-\ river 365 *mi* (587 *km*) Belarus flowing SE into the Dnieper

Bergama — see PERGAMUM

Ber·ga·mo \'ber-gä-ˌmō, 'bər-\ commune N Italy in Lombardy NE of Milan *pop* 115,655

Ber·gen **1** \'bər-gən, 'ber-\ city & port SW Norway *pop* 211,826 **2** — see MONS

Ber·gen·field \'bər-gən-ˌfēld\ borough NE N.J. *pop* 24,458

Be·ring Sea \'bir-iŋ, 'ber-\ arm of the N Pacific bet. Alaska & NE Siberia & bet. the Aleutians & Bering Strait *area* 885,000 *sq mi* (2,292,150 *sq km*)

Bering Strait strait at narrowest point 53 *mi* (85 *km*) wide separating Asia (Russia) from N. America (Alaska)

Berke·ley \'bər-klē\ city W Calif. on San Francisco Bay N of Oakland *pop* 102,724

Berk·shire \'bərk-ˌshir, -shər\ **1** hills W Mass. W of Connecticut River — see GREYLOCK (Mount) **2** *Brit usu* 'bärk-\ county S England in Thames River basin ✳ Reading *area* 502 *sq mi* (1300 *sq km*), *pop* 716,500

Ber·lin \(ˌ)bər-'lin, *G* ber-'lēn\ city, official ✳ of (reunified) Germany on Spree River, before 1945 ✳ of Germany & of Prussia, divided under postwar occupation bet. E. & W. Germany, E. Berlin being made ✳ of E. Germany (1949) & W. Berlin a state (not formally incorporated) of W. Germany — **Ber·lin·er** \(ˌ)bər-'li-nər\ *n*

Ber·me·jo \ber-'mā-(ˌ)hō\ river 650 *mi* (1046 *km*) N Argentina rising on Bolivian frontier & flowing SE into Paraguay River

Ber·mond·sey \'bər-mən(d)-zē\ former metropolitan borough E *cen* London, England, now part of Southwark

Ber·mu·da \(ˌ)bər-'myü-də\ islands W Atlantic ESE of Cape Hatteras; a self-governing Brit. colony ✳ Hamilton *area* 20 *sq mi* (52 *sq km*), *pop* 61,700 — **Ber·mu·di·an** \-dē-ən\ *or* **Ber·mu·dan** \-dᵊn\ *adj or n*

Bermuda Triangle triangular area N. Atlantic Ocean bet. Bermuda, Fla., & Puerto Rico; site of numerous reported disappearances of planes & ships

Bern \'bərn, 'bern\ **1** canton NW & W *cen* Switzerland *area* 2327 *sq mi* (6027 *sq km*), *pop* 942,721 **2** city, its ✳ & ✳ of Switzerland on the Aare *pop* 135,825 — **Ber·nese** \(ˌ)bər-'nēz, -'nēs\ *adj or n*

Bern·burg \'bərn-ˌbərg, 'bern-ˌbürk\ city *cen* Germany W of Dessau *pop* 39,006

Ber·ner Al·pen \,ber-nər-'äl-pən\ *or* **Ber·nese Ober·land** \(,)bər-'nēz-'ō-bər-,länt, -'nēs-\ *or* **Bernese Alps** *or* **Oberland** section of the Alps S Switzerland in Bern & Valais cantons bet. Lake of Thun & Brienz on the N & the valley of the upper Rhône on the S

Ber·ni·cia \(,)bər-'ni-sh(ē-)ə\ Anglian kingdom of 6th century A.D. located bet. Tyne & Forth rivers ✲ Bamborough

Ber·ni·na \(,)bər-'nē-nə\ the S extension of Rhaetian Alps on border bet. Italy & Switzerland; highest peak **Piz Bernina** \,pēts-\ (highest in the Rhaetian Alps) 13,200 *ft* (4023 *m*)

Beroea 1 — see ALEPPO **2** — see VÉROIA

Ber·ry \be-'rē\ former province *cen* France ✲ Bourges

Ber·thoud Pass \'bər-thəd\ mountain pass 11,315 *ft* (3449 *m*) N Colo. in Front range WNW of Denver

Ber·wick \'ber-ik\ *or* **Ber·wick·shire** \-,shir, -shər\ former county SE Scotland ✲ Duns

Ber·wyn \'bər-wən\ city NE Ill. W of Chicago *pop* 45,426

Berytus — see BEIRUT

Be·san·çon \bə-'zan(t)-sən, bə-zän-'sōⁿ\ city E France E of Dijon *pop* 119,194

Bes·kids \'bes-,kidz, be-'skēdz\ mountain ranges *cen* Europe in W Carpathians; include **West Beskids** (in Poland, Slovakia, & the Czech Republic) & **East Beskids** (in Poland & NE Slovakia)

Bes·sa·ra·bia \,be-sə-'rā-bē-ə\ region SE Europe bet. the Dniester & Prut rivers; now mostly in Moldova — **Bes·sa·ra·bi·an** \-bē-ən\ *adj or n*

Bes·se·mer \'be-sə-mər\ city N *cen* Ala. *pop* 33,497

Beth·a·ny \'be-thə-nē\ **1** city cen. Okla. *pop* 20,075 **2** *or now* **Al-'Ay·zar·i·yah** \,äl-,ī-zä-'rē-yə\ biblical village Palestine E of Jerusalem on Mount of Olives *pop* 3560

Beth·el \'be-thəl, be-'thel\ ruined town Palestine in W Jordan N of Jerusalem

Beth·el Park \'be-thəl\ borough SW Pa. *pop* 33,823

Be·thes·da \bə-'thez-də\ population center Md., a N suburb of Washington, D.C. *pop* 62,936

Beth·le·hem \'beth-li-,hem, -lē-həm, -lē-əm\ **1** city E Pa. on the Lehigh *pop* 71,428 **2** city Palestine in Judea SW of Jerusalem *pop* 34,180

Beth·nal Green \'beth-nəl\ former metropolitan borough E London, England, now part of Tower Hamlets

Beth·sa·i·da \beth-'sā-ə-də\ ruined town Palestine on NE side of Sea of Galilee E of the Jordan; its site in SE Syria

Be·tio \'bā-chē-,ō, -shē-\ islet & village W Pacific in N Kiribati at S end of Tarawa

Bet·ten·dorf \'be-tⁿn-,dórf\ city E Iowa E of Davenport *pop* 28,132

Beuthen — see BYTOM

Bev·er·ley \'be-vər-lē\ town N England in Humberside *pop* 109,500

Bev·er·ly \'be-vər-lē\ city NE Mass. *pop* 38,195

Beverly Hills city SW Calif. within city of Los Angeles *pop* 31,971

Bex·ley \'bek-slē\ borough of E Greater London, England *pop* 211,200

Bey·o·glu \bā-ō-'glü\ *or formerly* **Pera** \'per-ə\ section of Istanbul, Turkey, comprising area N of the Golden Horn

Bé·ziers \bāz-'yā\ city S France SW of Montpellier *pop* 72,362

Bezwada — see VIJAYAWADA

Bha·gal·pur \'bä-gəl-ˌpúr\ city E India on the Ganges in E Bihar *pop* 254,993

Bhak·ra Dam \'bə-krə, 'bä-\ hydroelectric & irrigation dam 740 *ft* (226 *m*) N India in Punjab NW of Bilaspur in gorge of the Sutlej

Bha·mo \bə-'mó, -'mō\ city N Myanmar on the upper Irrawaddy *pop* 13,767

Bhat·pa·ra \bät-'pär-ə\ city E India in W. Bengal *pop* 315,976

Bhav·na·gar *or* **Bhau·na·gar** \baú-'nə-gər\ city & port W India in S Gujarat on Gulf of Khambhat *pop* 402,338

Bho·pal \bō-'päl\ **1** former state N *cen* India in & N of Vindhya Mountains ✷ Bhopal; now part of Madhya Pradesh **2** city N *cen* India NW of Nagpur ✷ of Madhya Pradesh *pop* 1,062,771

Bhu·ba·nes·war *or* **Bhu·ba·nesh·war** \ˌbú-və-'näsh-wər\ city E India S of Cuttack ✷ of Orissa *pop* 411,542

Bhu·tan \bü-'tan, -'tan\ country Asia in Himalayas on NE border of India; a protectorate of India ✷ Thimphu *area* 18,000 *sq mi* (46,800 *sq km*), *pop* 1,546,000 — **Bhu·ta·nese** \ˌbü-tᵊn-'ēz, -'ēs\ *adj or n*

Bi·a·fra \bē-'ä-frə, bē-, -'a-\ name adopted by the SE part of Nigeria during its secession 1967–70 — **Bi·a·fran** \-frən\ *adj or n*

Biafra, Bight of *or* **Bight of Bon·ny** \'bä-nē\ the E section of Gulf of Guinea, W Africa

Bi·ak \bē-'yäk\ island off W New Guinea; largest of the Schoutens

Bia·ly·stok \bē-'ä-li-ˌstók, byä-'wi-stók\ city NE Poland *pop* 268,085

Biar·ritz \byä-'rēts\ commune SW France on Bay of Biscay *pop* 28,887

Bias — see BEAS

Bid·de·ford \'bi-də-fərd\ city SW Maine SW of Portland *pop* 20,710

Biel \'bēl\ *or F* **Bienne** \bē-'en\ commune NW Switzerland in Bern canton *pop* 52,670

Bie·le·feld \'bē-lə-ˌfelt\ city W *cen* Germany E of Münster *pop* 322,132

Biel·sko–Bia·la \bē-ˌel-skō-bē-'ä-lə, ˌbyel-skó-'byä-wä\ city S Poland *pop* 179,879

Big Bend **1** area W Tex. in large bend of the Rio Grande; partly included in **Big Bend National Park** **2** section of Columbia River E *cen* Wash.

Big Black river 330 *mi* (531 *km*) W *cen* Miss. flowing to Mississippi River

Big Diomede — see DIOMEDE ISLANDS

Big·horn \'big-ˌhórn\ river 336 *mi* (541 *km*) N Wyo. & SE Mont. flowing N into Yellowstone River — see WIND

Bighorn Mountains mountains N Wyo. extending S from Mont. border E of Bighorn River — see CLOUD PEAK

Big Sandy river 22 *mi* (35 *km*) bet. W.Va. & Ky. flowing N into Ohio River

Big Sioux \'sü\ river 420 *mi* (676 *km*) S.Dak. & Iowa flowing S to Missouri River & forming Iowa-S.Dak. boundary

Big Spring city W Tex. NE of Odessa *pop* 23,093

Big Stone lake *ab* 30 *mi* (48 *km*) long bet. W Minn. & NE S.Dak. — see MINNESOTA 1

Big Sur \'sər\ region W Calif. centering on Big Sur River & extending *ab* 80 *mi* (129 *km*) along coast SE of Point Sur

Big Thicket wilderness area E Tex. NE of Houston *area ab* 450 *sq mi* (1170 *sq km*)

Bi·har \bi-'här\ **1** state NE India bordering on Nepal; winter ✳ Patna, summer ✳ Ranchi *area* 67,184 *sq mi* (174,006 *sq km*), *pop* 86,374,465 **2** city *cen* Bihar state SE of Patna *pop* 200,976 — **Bi·ha·ri** \-'hä-rē\ *adj or n*

Bi·ka·ner \,bi-kə-'nir, 'be-kə-,ner\ city NW India in N Rajasthan in Thar Desert *pop* 416,289

Bi·ki·ni \bi-'kē-nē\ island (atoll) W Pacific in Marshall Islands — **Bi·ki·ni·an** \-nē-ən\ *n*

Bi·las·pur \bə-'läs-,púr\ city E *cen* India in SE Madhya Pradesh SE of Jabalpur *pop* 233,570

Bil·bao \bil-'bä-,ō, -'baú, -'bä-(,)ō\ city N Spain ✳ of Vizcaya *pop* 369,839

Bil·ler·i·ca \(,)bil-'ri-kə\ town NE Mass. *pop* 37,609

Bil·lings \'bi-liŋz\ city S *cen* Mont. *pop* 81,151

Billiton — see BELITUNG

Bi·loxi \bə-'lək-sē, -'läk-\ city & port SE Miss. *pop* 46,319

Bim·i·ni \'bi-mə-nē\ two islands of Bahamas NW of Andros

Bing·en \'biŋ-ən\ city W Germany *pop* 24,272

Bing·ham·ton \'biŋ-əm-tən\ city S *cen* N.Y. *pop* 53,008

Binh Dinh — see AN NHON

Bío-Bío \,bē-ō-'bē-(,)ō\ river 238 *mi* (383 *km*) S *cen* Chile flowing into the Pacific at Concepción

Bi·o·ko \bē-'ō-(,)kō\ *or formerly* **Fer·nan·do Póo** \fer-'nän-(,)dō-'pō\ *or* 1973–79 **Ma·cí·as Ngue·ma Bi·yo·go** \mä-'sē-äs-əŋ-'gwä-mə-bē-'yō-(,)gō\ island Equatorial Guinea in Bight of Biafra *area* 779 *sq mi* (2018 *sq km*)

Bir·ken·head \'bər-kən-,hed, ,bər-kən-'\ borough NW England in Merseyside on the Mersey estuary opposite Liverpool *pop* 123,907

Bir·ming·ham \'bər-miŋ-,ham, *Brit usu* -miŋ-əm\ **1** city N cen Ala. *pop* 265,968 **2** city SE Mich. N of Detroit *pop* 19,997 **3** city & borough W *cen* England in West Midlands *pop* 934,900

Bi·ro·bi·dzhan \,bir-ō-bi-'jän, -'jan\ city Russia in Asia ✳ of Jewish Autonomous Oblast *pop* 86,300

Biscay *or* **Biscaya** — see VIZCAYA — **Bis·cay·an** \bis-'kī-ən, -'kā-\ *adj or n*

Bis·cay, Bay of \'bis-,kā, -kē\ inlet of the Atlantic bet. W coast of France & N coast of Spain

Bis·cayne Bay \bis-'kān, 'bis-,\ inlet of the Atlantic SE Fla.; S part forms **Biscayne National Park**

Bish·kek \bish-'kek\ *or* 1926–91 **Frun·ze** \'frün-zi\ city on Chu River ✳ of Kyrgyzstan *pop* 641,400

Bi·sho \'bē-(,)shō\ town S Republic of South Africa; formerly ✳ of Ciskei

Bi·si·tun \,bē-sə-'tün\ *or* **Be·his·tun** \,bā-his-\ *or* **Bi·su·tun** \,bē-sə-\ ruined town W Iran E of Kermanshah

Bis·kra \'bis-krə, -,(,)krä\ city NE Algeria at an oasis on S edge of Atlas Mountains *pop* 128,747

Bis·marck \'biz-,märk\ city ✳ of N.Dak. on Missouri River *pop* 49,256

Bismarck Archipelago archipelago W Pacific N of E end of New Guinea *area* 19,173 *sq mi* (49,658 *sq km*)

Bismarck Range mountain range North-East New Guinea NW of Owen Stanley Range; highest Mt. Wilhelm

Bismarck Sea sea comprising the part of the W Pacific enclosed by the islands of the Bismarck Archipelago

Bis·sau \bi-'saú\ city & port ✳ of Guinea-Bissau *pop* 125,000

Bi·thyn·ia \bə-'thi-nē-ə\ ancient country NW Asia Minor bordering on the Sea of Marmara & Black Sea — **Bi·thyn·i·an** \-nē-ən\ *adj or n*

Bi·to·la \'bi-tō-lä\ *or* **Bi·tolj** \'bē-,tōl(-yə), -,tói\ *or* **Mon·a·stir** \,mä-nə-'stir\ city S Macedonia *pop* 122,173

Bitter Lakes two lakes (Great Bitter Lake & Little Bitter Lake) in NE Egypt N of Suez; connected & traversed by the Suez Canal

Bit·ter·root Range \'bi-tə(r)-,rüt, -,rút\ range of the Rocky Mountains on Idaho-Mont. boundary — see BEAVERHEAD MOUNTAINS, GARFIELD MOUNTAIN

Bi·wa \'bē-(,)wä\ lake 40 *mi* (64 *km*) long Japan on W *cen* Honshu

Biysk \'bēsk\ city Russia in Asia, in E Altay territory *pop* 235,000

Bi·zerte \bə-'zər-tē, bi-'zert\ *or* **Bi·zer·ta** \bə-'zert-ə\ city & port N Tunisia on Lake Bizerte (a deep lagoon) *pop* 62,856

Black *or in China* **Amo** \'ä-'mō\ *or in Vietnam* **Da** \'dä\ river 500 *mi* (805 *km*) SE Asia rising in *cen* Yunnan, China & flowing SE to Red River in N Vietnam

Black·burn \'blak-(,)bərn\ borough NW England in Lancashire *pop* 132,800

Blackburn, Mount mountain 16,390 *ft* (4996 *m*) S Alaska; highest in the Wrangell Mountains

Black Canyon **1** canyon of Colorado River bet. Ariz. & Nev. S of Hoover Dam **2** canyon of the Gunnison SW *cen* Colo. partly in **Black Canyon of the Gunnison National Monument**

Black Forest *or G* **Schwarz·wald** \'shvärts-,vält\ forested mountain region SW Germany along the upper Rhine bet. the Neckar River & Swiss border

Black Hills mountains W S.Dak. & NE Wyo. — see HARNEY PEAK

Black Mountains mountains W N.C., a range of the Blue Ridge Mountains — see MITCHELL (Mount)

Black·pool \'blak-,pül\ borough NW England in Lancashire on Irish Sea *pop* 144,500

Blacks·burg \'blaks-,bərg\ city W Va. W of Roanoke *pop* 34,590

Black Sea *or anc* **Pon·tus Eux·i·nus** \'pän-təs-,yük-'sī-nəs\ *or* **Pontus** sea bet. Europe & Asia connected with Aegean Sea through the Bosporus, Sea of Marmara, & Dardanelles *area more than* 160,000 *sq mi* (414,400 *sq km*)

Black Volta — see VOLTA

Black Warrior river 178 *mi* (286 *km*) *cen* Ala. flowing into the Tombigbee

Bla·go·vesh·chensk \,blə-gə-'vyäsh-chən(t)sk\ city Russia in Asia on the Amur *pop* 214,000

Blaine \'blān\ city E Minn. N of St. Paul *pop* 38,975

Blain·ville \'blān-,vil, blēⁿ-'vēl\ town Canada in S Que. *pop* 22,679

Blanc, Cape \'blaŋk, bläⁿ\ **1** cape N Tunisia: northernmost point of Africa, at 37°14′N **2** promontory NW Africa on the Atlantic in Mauritania at SW tip of Río de Oro

Blanc, Mont — see MONT BLANC

Blan·ca Peak \'blaŋ-kə, 'blän-\ mountain 14,345 *ft* (4372 *m*) S Colo.; highest in Sangre de Cristo Mountains

Blan·co, Cape \'blaŋ-(,)kō\ cape SW Oreg.

Blan·tyre \'blan-,tīr\ city S Malawi *pop* 333,120

Blar·ney \'blär-nē\ town SW Ireland in *cen* County Cork *pop* 1952

Blen·heim \'ble-nəm\ *or* **Blind·heim** \'blint-,hīm\ village S Germany in Bavaria NNW of Augsburg *pop* 1619

Bli·da \'blē-də\ city N Algeria SW of Algiers *pop* 170,182

Block Island \'bläk\ island R.I. in the Atlantic at E entrance to Long Island Sound

Bloem·fon·tein \'blüm-fən-,tān, -,fän-\ city *cen* Republic of South Africa, judicial ✳ of the Republic *pop* 149,836

Blois \'blwä\ city N *cen* France SW of Orléans *pop* 51,549

Bloom·field \'blüm-,fēld\ 1 town N *cen* Conn. NW of Hartford *pop* 18,608 2 town NE N.J. *pop* 45,061

Bloo·ming·ton \'blü-miŋ-tən\ 1 city *cen* Ill. *pop* 51,972 2 city SW *cen* Ind. *pop* 60,633 3 village SE Minn. *pop* 86,335

Blooms·bury \'blümz-b(ə-)rē, *US also* -,ber-ē\ district of N *cen* London, England, in borough of Camden

Blue Grotto sea cave Italy on N shore of Capri

Blue Island city NE Ill. S of Chicago *pop* 21,203

Blue Mountains 1 mountains NE Oreg. & SE Wash.; highest Rock Creek Butte 9105 *ft* (2775 *m*) 2 mountains SE Australia in Great Dividing Range in E New S. Wales; highest 4460 *ft* (1359 *m*) 3 mountains E Jamaica; highest Blue Mountain Peak 7402 *ft* (2256 *m*)

Blue Nile river 850 *mi* (1368 *km*) Ethiopia & Sudan flowing from Lake Tana NNW into the Nile at Khartoum — see ABBAI

Blue Ridge the E range of the Appalachians E U.S. extending from South Mountain, S Pa. into N Ga. — see MITCHELL (Mount)

Blue Springs city W Mo. SE of Independence *pop* 40,153

Bluff \'bləf\ town S New Zealand; port for Invercargill *pop* 2720

Blythe·ville \'blī-vəl, 'blīth-,vil\ city NE Ark. *pop* 22,906

Bo·bo–Diou·las·so \'bō-(,)bō-dyü-'lä-(,)sō\ town W Burkina Faso *pop* 300,000

Bo·bruysk *or* **Ba·bruysk** \bə-'brü-isk\ city *cen* Belarus on the Berezina *pop* 223,000

Bo·ca Ra·ton \,bō-kə-rə-'tōn\ city SE Fla. N of Fort Lauderdale *pop* 61,492

Bo·chum \'bō-kəm\ city W Germany in Ruhr valley *pop* 398,578

Bodensee — see CONSTANCE (Lake)

Bodh Ga·ya \'bōd-'gī-ä\ *or* **Bud·dha Gaya** \'bü-də\ *or* **Buddh Gaya** \'büd\ village NE India in *cen* Bihar *pop* 21,686

Bod·min \'bäd-min\ borough SW England, a ✳ of Cornwall and Isles of Scilly *pop* 12,148

Boe·o·tia \bē-'ō-sh(ē-)ə\ *or NGk* **Voi·o·tía** \,vē-ō-'tē-ä\ district E *cen* Greece NW of Attica — **Boe·o·tian** \bē-'ō-shən\ *adj or n*

Boetoeng — see BUTON

Bo·go·tá \,bō-gō-'tä, -'tó, 'bō-gə-,\ city ✳ of Colombia on plateau in the Andes *pop* 4,921,300

Bo Hai *or* **Po Hai** \'bō-'hi\ *or* **Gulf of Chih·li** \'chē-'lē, 'jir-\ arm of Yellow Sea NE China bounded on NE by Liaodong Peninsula & on SE by Shandong Peninsula

Bo·he·mia \bō-'hē-mē-ə\ or **Če·chy** \'che-kē, -kē\ region W Czech Republic; once a kingdom, later a province ✳ Prague — **Bo·he·mi·an** \-mē-ən\ adj or n

Bohemian Forest or G **Böh·mer Wald** \'bǣ-mər-,vält\ forested mountain region Czech Republic & Germany along boundary bet. E Bavaria & SW Bohemia

Bo·hol \bō-'hōl\ island S cen Philippines, one of the Visayan Islands, N of Mindanao area 1492 sq mi (3879 sq km)

Bois de Belleau — see BELLEAU

Bois de Bou·logne \,bwä-də-bü-'lōn, -'lō-nyə, -'lȯin\ park France W of Paris

Boi·se \'bȯi-sē, -zē\ city ✳ of Idaho on Boise River (60 mi or 96 km long) pop 125,738

Bo·ja·dor, Cape \'bä-jə-,dȯr\ headland NW Africa in the Atlantic on W coast of Western Sahara

Bokhara — see BUKHARA

Boks·burg \'bäks-,bərg\ city NE Republic of South Africa in Gauteng E of Johannesburg pop 110,832

Bo·lan Pass \bō-'län\ mountain pass 5900 ft (1798 m) Pakistan in N Baluchistan

Bolbitine — see ROSETTA

Bo·ling·brook \'bō-liŋ-,bru̇k\ city NE Ill. SW of Chicago pop 40,843

Bo·lí·var, Cer·ro \'ser-(,)ō-bō-'lē-,vär\ or formerly **La Pa·ri·da** \,lä-pä-'rē-dä\ iron mountain 2018 ft (615 m) E Venezuela S of Ciudad Bolívar

Bo·lí·var, Pi·co \'pē-(,)kō-bō-'lē-,vär\ mountain 16,427 ft (5007 m) W Venezuela in Cordillera de Mérida; highest in Venezuela

Bo·liv·ia \bə-'li-vē-ə\ country W cen S. America; a republic; administrative ✳ La Paz, constitutional ✳ Sucre area ab 424,200 sq mi (1,102,920 sq km), pop 7,715,000 — **Bo·liv·i·an** \-vē-ən\ adj or n

Bo·lo·gna \bə-'lō-nyä\ or cen **Bo·no·nia** \bə-'nō-nē-ə\ commune N Italy ✳ of Emilia-Romagna at foot of the Apennines pop 404,322 — **Bo·lo·gnan** \bə-'lō-nyən\ or **Bo·lo·gnese** \bō-lə-'nēz, -'nēs, -'nyēz, -'nyēs\ adj or n

Bol·se·na, Lake \bōl-'sā-nə\ lake cen Italy in NW Lazio

Bol·ton \'bōl-t°n\ borough NW England in NW Greater Manchester pop 253,300

Bol·za·no \bōlt-'sä-(,)nō, bōl-'zä-\ **1** former province N Italy in S Tirol, now part of Trentino-Alto Adige region **2** commune in Trentino-Alto Adige region pop 98,233

Bo·ma \'bō-mə\ city & port W Republic of the Congo on Congo River pop 246,207

Bom·bay \bäm-'bā\ **1** former state W India ✳ Bombay; divided 1960 into Gujarat & Maharashtra states; once a presidency & (1937–47) a province of Brit. India **2** or **Mum·bai** \'məm-,bī\ city & port W India ✳ of Maharashtra & of former Bombay state area pop 9,925,891

Bombay Island island W India on which city of Bombay is situated area 24 sq mi (62 sq km)

Bo·mu \'bō-(,)mü\ or **Mbo·mou** \əm-'bō-(,)mü\ river 500 mi (805 km) W cen Africa forming boundary bet. Democratic Republic of the Congo & Central African Republic & uniting with the Uele to form the Ubangi

Bon, Cape \'bōⁿ\ *or* *Ar* **Ra's at Tib** \,räs-át-'tēb\ headland NE Tunisia on **Cape Bon Peninsula**

Bo·na, Mount \'bō-nə\ mountain *ab* 16,500 *ft* (5030 *m*) S Alaska at W end of Wrangell Mountains

Bon·aire \bə-'nar, -'ner\ island Netherlands Antilles E of Curaçao *area* 111 *sq mi* (287 *sq km*), *pop* 11,058

Bon·di \'bän-,dī\ town SE Australia, SE suburb of Sydney, S of entrance to Port Jackson on **Bondi Beach**

Bône — *see* ANNABA

Bo·nin Islands \'bō-nən\ *or* **Oga·sa·wa·ra Islands** \(,)ō-gä-sä-'wär-ä\ islands W Pacific *ab* 600 *mi* (966 *km*) SSE of Tokyo; belong to Japan; administered by U.S. 1945–68 *area* 40 *sq mi* (104 *sq km*), *pop* 1507

Bonn \'bän, 'bon\ city W Germany on the Rhine SSE of Cologne; seat of German parliament and ✱ of Federal Republic of Germany (sometimes called **Bonn Republic**) before reunification *pop* 296,244

Bon·ne·ville Salt Flats \'bä-nə-,vil\ broad level area of Great Salt Lake Desert E of Wendover, Utah

Bonny, Bight of — *see* BIAFRA, BIGHT OF

Book·er T. Wash·ing·ton National Monument \'bu̇-kər-,tē-'wȯ-shiŋ-tən, -'wä-\ historic site W *cen* Va. SE of Roanoke

Boo·thia, Gulf of \'bü-thē-ə\ gulf N Canada bet. Baffin Is. & Melville Peninsula on E & Boothia Peninsula on W

Boothia Peninsula peninsula N Canada W of Baffin Is.; its N tip (at *ab* 72°N, 94°W) is the northernmost point on N. American mainland

Boo·tle \'bü-t²l\ borough NW England in W Merseyside *pop* 62,463

Bo·phu·tha·tswa·na \,bō-(,)pü-tät-'swä-nä\ former group of noncontiguous black enclaves in the Republic of South Africa ✱ Mmabatho; granted independence 1977; abolished 1994

Bo·ra-Bo·ra \,bŏr-ə-'bŏr-ə, ,bŏr-ə-'bŏr-ə\ island S Pacific in Leeward group of the Society Islands NW of Tahiti *area ab* 15 *sq mi* (38 *sq km*)

Bo·rah Peak \'bŏr-ə, 'bŏr-\ mountain 12,662 *ft* (3859 *m*) E *cen* Idaho in Lost River Range; highest point in state

Bo·rås \bü-'ro̅s\ city SW Sweden E of Göteborg *pop* 102,840

Bor·deaux \bŏr-'dō\ city & port SW France on the Garonne *pop* 213,274 — **Bor·de·lais** \bŏr-d²l-'ā\ *n*

Bor·ders \'bŏr-dərz\ region S Scotland, established 1975 ✱ Newtown St. Boswells *area* 1814 *sq mi* (4698 *sq km*), *pop* 105,300

Bor·di·ghe·ra \,bŏr-di-'ger-ə\ commune & port NW Italy in Liguria *pop* 11,559

Borgne, Lake \'bŏrn\ inlet of the Mississippi Sound E of New Orleans, La.

Bor·neo \'bŏr-nē-,ō\ island Malay Archipelago SW of Philippines *area* 290,320 *sq mi* (751,929 *sq km*) — *see* BRUNEI, KALIMANTAN, SABAH, SARAWAK — **Bor·ne·an** \-nē-ən\ *adj or n*

Born·holm \'bŏrn-,hōm, -,hŏm\ island Denmark in Baltic Sea ✱ Rönne *area* 227 *sq mi* (588 *sq km*), *pop* 45,991

Bos·nia \'bäz-nē-ə, 'bŏz-\ region S Europe in the Balkans; with Herzegovina forms independent state of **Bosnia and Her·ze·go·vi·na** \,hert-sə-gō-'vē-nə, ,hərt-, -'gō-və-nə\; a federated republic of

Yugoslavia 1946–92 ✳ Sarajevo *area* 19,904 *sq mi* (51,750 *sq km*), *pop* 4,422,000 — **Bos·ni·an** \-nē-ən\ *adj or n*

Bos·po·rus \'bäs-p(ə-)rəs\ *or* **Bos·pho·rus** \-f(ə-)rəs\ strait *ab* 18 *mi* (29 *km*) long bet. Turkey in Europe & Turkey in Asia connecting Sea of Marmara & Black Sea — **Bos·po·ran** \-pə-rən\ *adj*

Bos·sier City \'bō-zhər\ city NW La. *pop* 52,721

Bos·ton \'bòs-tən\ **1** city & port ✳ of Mass. on Massachusetts Bay *pop* 535,721 **2** borough & port E England in SE Lincolnshire in Parts of Holland *pop* 52,600 — **Bos·to·nian** \bò-'stō-nē-ən, -nyən\ *adj or n*

Boston Mountains mountains NW Ark. & E Okla. in Ozark Plateau

Bo·ta·fo·go Bay \,bō-tä-'fō-(,)gō\ inlet of Guanabara Bay in Rio de Janeiro, Brazil

Bot·a·ny Bay \'bä-tⁿn-ē\ inlet of the S Pacific SE Australia in New South Wales on S border of city of Sydney

Both·nia, Gulf of \'bäth-nē-ə\ arm of Baltic Sea bet. Sweden & Finland

Bo·tswa·na \bät-'swä-nə\ country S Africa N of the Molopo; an independent republic since 1966, formerly Brit. protectorate of **Bechuanaland** ✳ Gaborone *area ab* 220,000 *sq mi* (569,800 *sq km*), *pop* 1,406,000

Bot·trop \'bä-,träp\ city W Germany NNW of Essen *pop* 118,758

Bou·cher·ville \'bü-shər-,vil, ,bü-shā-'vēl\ town Canada in S Que. NE of Montreal *pop* 33,796

Bou·gain·ville \'bü-gən-,vil, 'bō-, 'bù-\ island S Pacific, largest of the Solomons; chief town Kieta *area* 3880 *sq mi* (10,088 *sq km*)

Bougie — see BEJAÏA

Bouil·lon \'bü-'yōⁿ\ town SE Belgium in the Ardennes *pop* 5468

Boul·der \'bōl-dər\ city N cen Colo. *pop* 83,312

Boulder Dam — see HOOVER DAM

Bou·logne \bü-'lòn, -'lò-nyə, -'lòin\ *or* **Bou·logne-sur-Mer** \-,sùr-'mer\ city & port N France on English Channel *pop* 44,244

Boulogne-Bil·lan·court \-,bē-,yäⁿ-'kür\ commune N France SW of Paris on the Seine *pop* 103,527

Bound·ary Peak \'baùn-d(ə-)rē\ mountain 13,140 *ft* (4005 *m*) SW Nev. in White Mountains; highest in state

Boun·ti·ful \'baùn-ti-fəl\ city N Utah N of Salt Lake City *pop* 36,659

Bour·bon·nais \,bùr-bò-'nā\ former province *cen* France W of Burgundy

Bourges \'bürzh\ commune *cen* France SSE of Orléans *pop* 78,773

Bourgogne — see BURGUNDY

Bourne·mouth \'bòrn-məth, 'bòrn-, 'bùrn-\ town S England in Dorset on English Channel *pop* 154,400

Bou·vet \'bü-(,)vā\ island S Atlantic SSW of Cape of Good Hope at *ab* 54°S. 5°E; belongs to Norway

Bow \'bō\ river 315 *mi* (507 *km*) Canada in SW Alta. rising in Banff National Park

Bow·ie \'bü-ē\ town Md. NE of Washington, D.C. *pop* 37,589

Bowl·ing Green \'bō-liŋ-'grēn\ **1** city S Ky. *pop* 40,641 **2** city NW Ohio S of Toledo *pop* 28,176

Boyne \'bòin\ river 70 *mi* (113 *km*) E Ireland in Leinster flowing to Irish Sea S of Drogheda

Boyn·ton Beach \'boin-tᵊn\ city SE Fla. *pop* 46,194

Bo·yo·ma Falls \bòi-'ō-mä\ *or formerly* **Stanley Falls** series of seven cataracts NE Democratic Republic of the Congo in the Lualaba near head of Congo River with total fall of *ab* 200 *ft* (61 *m*) in 60 *mi* (96 *km*)

Boz·caa·da \,bôz-jä-'dä\ *or anc* **Ten·e·dos** \'te-nə-,däs\ island Turkey in NE Aegean Sea S of the Dardanelles

Boze·man \'bōz-mən\ city SW Mont. *pop* 22,660

Bra·bant \brə-'bant; brə-'bant, -'bänt\ 1 old duchy of W Europe including region now forming N. Brabant province of Netherlands & of Brabant & Antwerp provinces of Belgium 2 province *cen* Belgium ✳ Brussels *pop* 1,302,577

Bra·den·ton \'brä-dᵊn-tən\ city & port W Fla. N of Sarasota *pop* 43,779

Brad·ford \'brad-fərd\ city N England in W. Yorkshire *pop* 280,691

Bra·ga \'brä-gə\ commune NW Portugal NNE of Porto *pop* 63,033

Bra·gan·ça \brə-'gȧn-sə\ commune NE Portugal near Spanish border *pop* 14,181

Brah·ma·pu·tra \,brä-mə-'pü-trə\ river *ab* 1800 *mi* (2900 *km*) S Asia flowing from the Himalayas in Tibet to the Ganges delta in E India (subcontinent) — see JAMUNA, TSANGPO

Bra·i·la \brə-'ē-lä\ city E Romania on the Danube *pop* 242,595

Brain·tree \'brān-(,)trē\ town E Mass. S of Boston *pop* 33,836

Brak·pan \'brak-,pan\ city NE Republic of South Africa in Gauteng on the Witwatersrand S of Johannesburg *pop* 85,044

Bramp·ton \'bramp-tən\ city Canada in SE Ont. W of Toronto *pop* 234,445

Bran·co, Rio \,rē-ō-'braŋ-kü\ river 350 *mi* (563 *km*) N Brazil flowing S into Negro River

Bran·den·burg \'bran-dən-,bərg, 'brän-dən-,bûrk\ 1 region & former province NE *cen* Germany 2 city E Germany *pop* 88,760

Bran·don \'bran-dən\ city Canada in SW Man. *pop* 38,567

Bran·dy·wine \'bran-dē-,wīn\ creek *ab* 20 *mi* (32 *km*) SE Pa. & N Del. flowing SE to Wilmington, Del.

Bran·ford \'bran-fərd\ town S Conn. E of New Haven *pop* 27,603

Brant·ford \'brant-fərd\ city Canada in SE Ont. *pop* 81,997

Bras d'Or Lake \brä-'dòr\ tidal lake *ab* 50 *mi* (80 *km*) long Canada in N.S. on Cape Breton I.

Bra·sí·lia \brə-'zil-yə\ city ✳ of Brazil in Federal District *metropolitan area pop* 1,803,478

Bra·sov \brä-'shòv\ *or formerly* **Sta·lin** \'stä-lən, 'sta-, -,lēn\ *or* **Ora·sul Stalin** \ó-,rä-shü̇, -shûl\ city *cen* Romania in foothills of Transylvanian Alps *pop* 352,640

Bra·ti·sla·va \,brȧ-tə-'slä-və, ,brä-\ *or G* **Press·burg** \'pres-,bərg, -,bûrk\ *or Hung* **Po·zsony** \'pō-,zhō-nyə\ city SW Slovakia, its ✳, on the Danube *pop* 441,453

Bratsk \'brätsk\ city Russia in Asia, NNE of Irkutsk near site of **Bratsk Dam** (in the Angara) *pop* 259,000

Braunschweig — see BRUNSWICK

Bravo, Río — see RIO GRANDE

Bray \'brā\ town & port E Ireland *pop* 25,101

Bra·zil *or Pg* **Bra·sil** \brə-'zil\ country E S. America; a federal republic ✳ Brasília *area ab* 3,280,000 *sq mi* (8,495,200 *sq km*), *pop* 150,051,784 — **Bra·zil·ian** \brə-'zil-yən\ *adj or n*

Braz·os \\'braz-əs\\ river *ab* 840 *mi* (1350 *km*), *cen* Tex. flowing SE into Gulf of Mexico

Braz·za·ville \\'brä-zə-ˌvil, 'brä-zə-ˌvēl\\ city & port ✻ of Republic of the Congo on W bank of Pool Malebo in Congo River *pop* 937,579

Brea \\'brā-ə\\ city SW Calif. SE of Los Angeles *pop* 32,873

Brec·on \\'bre-kən\\ *or* **Breck·nock** \\'brek-ˌnäk, -nək\\ **1** *or* **Brec·on·shire** *or* **Breck·nock·shire** \\-ˌshir, -shər\\ former county SE Wales ✻ Brecon **2** borough SE Wales in Powys *pop* 7422

Brecon Beacons two mountain peaks SE Wales in S Powys

Bre·da \\brā-ˈdä\\ commune S Netherlands in N. Brabant province *pop* 162,951

Bre·genz \\'brā-ˌgents\\ commune W Austria on Lake Constance ✻ of Vorarlberg *pop* 27,236

Bre·men \\'bre-mən, 'brā-\\ **1** former duchy N Germany bet. the lower Weser & the lower Elbe **2** state NW Germany *area* 156 *sq mi* (404 *sq km*), *pop* 681,700 **3** city & port, its ✻, on the Weser *pop* 552,746

Bre·mer·ha·ven \\'bre-mər-ˌhä-vᵊn, ˌbrā-mər-ˈhä-fᵊn\\ city & port NW Germany in Bremen state at mouth of the Weser; includes former site of Wesermünde *pop* 130,938

Brem·er·ton \\'bre-mər-tən, -tᵊn\\ city & port W Wash. on Puget Sound *pop* 38,142

Bren·ner Pass \\'bre-nər\\ mountain pass *ab* 4495 *ft* (1370 *m*) in the Alps bet. Austria & Italy

Brent \\'brent\\ *or formerly* **Brentford and Chis·wick** \\'brent-fərd-ᵊn-'chi-zik\\ borough of W Greater London, England *pop* 226,100

Bren·ta \\'bren-tä\\ river 100 *mi* (161 *km*) N Italy flowing SE into the Adriatic S of Chioggia

Bre·scia \\'bre-shä, 'brā-\\ *or anc* **Brix·ia** \\'brik-sē-ə\\ commune N Italy in E Lombardy ENE of Milan *pop* 200,722

Breslau — see WROCŁAW

Brest \\'brest\\ **1** *or formerly* **Brest Li·tovsk** \\li-'tofsk\\ city SW Belarus on Bug River *pop* 277,000 **2** commune & port NW France in Brittany *pop* 153,099

Bre·ton, Cape \\kāp-'bre-tᵊn, kə-'bre-, -'bri-\\ headland Canada, easternmost point of Cape Breton Is. & of N.S., at 59°48′W

Bridge·port \\'brij-ˌpōrt, -ˌpȯrt\\ city SW Conn. on Long Island Sound *pop* 141,686

Bridge·town \\'brij-ˌtaún\\ city & port Brit. West Indies ✻ of Barbados *pop* 6070

Bridge·wa·ter \\'brij-ˌwȯ-tər, -ˌwä-\\ city SE Mass. S of Brockton *pop* 21,249

Brie \\brē\\ district & medieval county NE France E of Paris; chief town Meaux

Bri·enne \\brē-'en\\ **1** former county NE France in Champagne NNE of Troyes **2** town, its ✻

Bri·enz \\brē-'ents\\ town Switzerland in SE Bern canton at NE end of **Lake of Brienz** (9 *mi* or 14 *km* long, in course of the Aare)

Brigh·ton \\'brī-tᵊn\\ borough S England in E. Sussex on English Channel *pop* 133,400

Brin·di·si \\'brin-də-(ˌ)zē, 'brēn-\\ *or anc* **Brun·di·si·um** \\ˌbrən-'di-zē-əm, -zhē-\\ city & port SE Italy in Puglia *pop* 91,778

Bris·bane \'briz-bən, -,bān\ city & port E Australia ✻ of Queensland on **Brisbane River** (215 *mi or* 344 *km*) near its mouth *pop* 751,115

Bris·tol \'bris-t^əl\ **1** city W *cen* Conn. WSW of Hartford *pop* 60,640 **2** town E R.I. SE of Providence *pop* 21,625 **3** city NE Tenn. *pop* 23,421 **4** city & port SW England in Avon on Avon River near Severn estuary *pop* 370,300 — **Bris·to·li·an** \bri-'stōl-ē-ən, -'stōl-yən\ *n*

Bristol Bay arm of Bering Sea SW Alaska W of Alaska Peninsula

Bristol Channel channel bet. S Wales & SW England

Brit·ain \'bri-t^ən\ **1** *or L* **Bri·tan·nia** \brə-'ta-nyə, -nē-ə\ the island of Great Britain **2** UNITED KINGDOM **3** COMMONWEALTH OF NATIONS — **Brit·ish** \-tish\ *adj or n*

British America 1 *or* **British North America** CANADA **2** all Brit. possessions in & adjacent to N. & S. America

British Bechuanaland — see BECHUANALAND

British Cameroons former Brit. trust territory W equatorial Africa comprising two areas in the Cameroons bet. Nigeria & Cameroon ✻ Buea; divided 1961 bet. Nigeria (N section) & Cameroon (S section)

British Columbia province W Canada on Pacific coast ✻ Victoria *area* 344,663 *sq mi* (892,677 *sq km*), *pop* 3,282,061 — **British Co·lum·bi·an** \kə-'ləm-bē-ən\ *n or adj*

British Commonwealth COMMONWEALTH OF NATIONS — a former name

British East Africa 1 KENYA — a former name **2** the former Brit. dependencies in E Africa: Kenya, Uganda, Zanzibar, & Tanganyika

British Empire Great Britain & the Brit. dominions & dependencies — a former usage

British Guiana — see GUYANA

British Honduras — see BELIZE

British India the part of India formerly under direct Brit. administration — see INDIAN STATES

British Indian Ocean Territory Brit. colony in Indian Ocean comprising Chagos Archipelago & formerly Aldabra, Farquhar, & Desroches islands (returned to Seychelles 1976) *area* 23 *sq mi* (60 *sq km*)

British Isles island group W Europe comprising Great Britain, Ireland, & adjacent islands

British Malaya former dependencies of Great Britain on Malay Peninsula & in Malay Archipelago including Malaya (federation), Singapore, N. Borneo, Sarawak, & Brunei

British Solomon Islands former Brit. protectorate comprising the Solomons (except Bougainville, Buka, & adjacent small islands) & the Santa Cruz Islands ✻ Honiara (on Guadalcanal)

British Somaliland former Brit. protectorate E Africa bordering on Gulf of Aden ✻ Hargeisa; since 1960 part of Somalia

British Virgin Islands the E islands of the Virgin Islands group; a Brit. possession ✻ Road Town (on Tortola Is.) *area* 59 *sq mi* (153 *sq km*), *pop* 14,786

British West Indies islands of the West Indies including Jamaica, Bahamas, Caymans, Brit. Virgin Islands, Brit. Leeward & Windward Islands, Trinidad, & Tobago

Brit·ta·ny \'bri-tᵊn-ē\ *or* F **Bre·tagne** \brə-'tànʸ\ region & former province NW France SW of Normandy — **Bret·on** \'bre-tᵊn\ *adj or n*

Br·no \'bər-(,)nō\ *or* G **Brünn** \'brœn, 'brùn\ city E Czech Republic, chief city of Moravia *pop* 387,986

Broad \'bród\ **1** river 220 *mi* (354 *km*) N.C. & S.C. — see SALUDA **2** river 70 *mi* (113 *km*) S S.C. flowing into the Atlantic

Broads \'brödz\ low-lying district E England in Norfolk (the **Norfolk Broads**) & Suffolk (the **Suffolk Broads**)

Brock·en \'brä-kən\ mountain 3747 *ft* (1142 *m*) cen Germany near former E. Germany–W. Germany border; highest in Harz Mountains

Brock·ton \'bräk-tən\ city SE Mass. *pop* 92,788

Brock·ville \'bräk-,vil\ city Canada in SE Ont. *pop* 21,582

Bro·ken Ar·row \'brō-kən-'ar-ō\ city NE Okla. SE of Tulsa *pop* 58,043

Broken Hill 1 city SE Australia in W New South Wales *pop* 23,739 **2** — see KABWE

Bromberg — see BYDGOSZCZ

Brom·ley \'bräm-lē\ borough of SE Greater London, England *pop* 281,700

Bronx \'bränks\ *or* **The Bronx** borough of New York City on the mainland NE of Manhattan Is. *pop* 1,203,789

Brook·field \'brük-,fēld\ city SE Wis. W of Milwaukee *pop* 35,184

Brook·line \'brük-,lin\ town E Mass. W of Boston *pop* 54,718

Brook·lyn \'brük-lən\ borough of New York City at SW end of Long Is. *pop* 2,300,664 — **Brook·lyn·ite** \-klə-,nīt\ *n*

Brooklyn Center village SE Minn. NW of Minneapolis *pop* 28,887

Brooklyn Park village E Minn. NW of Minneapolis *pop* 56,381

Brook Park \'brük\ city NE Ohio *pop* 22,865

Brooks Range \'brüks\ mountain range N Alaska extending from Kotzebue Sound to Canadian border; highest peak over 9000 *ft* (2740 *m*)

Broom·field \'brüm-,fēld, 'brúm-\ city N cen Colo. NNW of Denver *pop* 24,638

Bros·sard \brö-'sär(d)\ town Canada in S Que. *pop* 64,793

Browns·ville \'braunz-,vil, -vəl\ city & port S Tex. *pop* 98,962

Bruce \'brüs\ peninsula SE Ontario, Canada, projecting bet. Lake Huron & Georgian Bay

Brug·ge \'brü-gə, 'brœ-kə\ *or* F **Bruges** \'brüzh, 'brœzh\ commune NW Belgium ✳ of W. Flanders *pop* 116,700

Bru·nei \brù-'nī, 'brü,nī\ **1** independent sultanate & former Brit. protectorate NW Borneo ✳ Bandar Seri Begawan *area* 2226 *sq mi* (5788 *sq km*), *pop* 260,863 **2** — see BANDAR SERI BEGAWAN — **Bru·nei·an** \brù-'nī-ən\ *adj or n*

Bruns·wick \'brənz-(,)wik\ **1** town SW Maine *pop* 20,906 **2** city NE Ohio SSW of Cleveland *pop* 28,230 **3** *or* G **Braun·schweig** \'braun-,shvīk\ former state cen Germany ✳ Brunswick **4** *or* G **Braunschweig** city N cen Germany W of Berlin *pop* 259,127

Brus·sels \'brə-səlz\ *or* F **Bru·xelles** \brü(k)-'sel\ *or* Flem **Brussel** \'brœ-səl\ city ✳ of Belgium & of Brabant *pop* 136,424 — **Bru·xel·lois** \brœ-sel-'wà *also* brük-\ *adj or n*

Bruttium — see CALABRIA

Bry·an \'brī-ən\ city E cen Tex. *pop* 55,002

49 **Bulgaria**

Bry·ansk \brē-'änsk\ city Russia in Europe SW of Moscow *pop* 461,000

Bryce Canyon National Park \'brīs\ reservation S Utah NE of Zion National Park

Bu·bas·tis \byü-'bas-təs\ ancient city N Egypt near modern Zagazig

Bu·ca·ra·man·ga \,bü-kä-rä-'mäŋ-gä\ city N Colombia NNE of Bogotá *pop* 349,400

Bu·cha·rest \'bü-kə-,rest, 'byü-\ *or Romanian* **Bu·cu·reş·ti** \,bü-kə-'resht\, -'resh-tē\ city ✷ of Romania *pop* 2,036,894

Bu·chen·wald \'bü-kən-,wôld, -,vält\ village *cen* Germany NW of Weimar; site of Nazi concentration camp

Buck·ing·ham·shire \'bə-kiŋ-əm-,shir, -shər, *US also* -kiŋ-,ham-\ *or* **Buckingham** *or* **Bucks** \'bəks\ county SE *cen* England ✷ Aylesbury *area* 753 *sq mi* (1950 *sq km*), *pop* 651,700

Buck Island Reef National Monument \'bək\ reservation St. Croix, Virgin Islands; contains marine gardens

Bu·da·pest \'bü-də-,pest *also* 'bü-, 'byü-, -,pesht\ city ✷ of Hungary on the Danube *pop* 2,008,546

Buddha Gaya, Buddh Gaya — see BODH GAYA

Budweis — see CESKE BUDEJOVICE

Bue·na Park \'bwā-nə\ city Calif. W of Anaheim *pop* 68,784

Bue·na·ven·tu·ra \,bwā-nä-ven-'tü-rä\ city & port W Colombia on the Pacific *pop* 115,770

Bue·nos Ai·res \,bwā-nəs-'ar-ēz, *Sp* ,bwā-nōs-'ī-räs\ city & port ✷ of Argentina on Río de la Plata *pop* 2,960,976

Buenos Aires, Lake lake 80 *mi* (129 *km*) long S Argentina & S Chile

Buf·fa·lo \'bə-fə-,lō\ city & port N.Y. on Lake Erie & the Niagara *pop* 328,123 — **Buf·fa·lo·ni·an** \,bə-fə-'lō-nē-ən\ *n*

Buffalo Grove city NE Ill. *pop* 36,427

Bug \'büg\ **1** river over 450 *mi* (720 *km*) *cen* Poland rising in W Ukraine, & flowing into the Vistula **2** river over 500 *mi* (805 *km*) SW Ukraine flowing SE to the Dnieper estuary

Bu·gan·da \bü-'gän-dä, byü-\ region & former native kingdom E Africa in SE Uganda ✷ Kampala

Bu·jum·bu·ra \,bü-jəm-'bur-ä\ *or formerly* **Usum·bu·ra** \,ü-səm-\ city ✷ of Burundi on Lake Tanganyika *pop* 236,334

Bu·ka \'bü-kä\ island N Pacific in the Solomons N of Bougainville *pop* 33,770

Bu·ka·vu \bü-'kä-(,)vü\ *or formerly* **Cos·ter·mans·ville** \'käs-tər-mənz-,vil\ city E Democratic Republic of the Congo at S end of Lake Kivu *pop* 209,566

Bu·kha·ra \bü-'kär-ə, -'kar-, -'kär-\ *or* **Bo·kha·ra** \bō-\ **1** former emirate W Asia around city of Bukhara **2** city W Uzbekistan E of the Amu Darya *pop* 249,600 — **Bu·kha·ran** *or* **Bo·kha·ran** \-ən\ *adj or n*

Bu·ko·vi·na *or* **Bu·co·vi·na** \,bü-kō-'vē-nə\ region E *cen* Europe in foothills of E Carpathians; now in NE Romania & W Ukraine

Bu·la·wa·yo \,bü-lä-'wä-yō\ city SW Zimbabwe, chief town of Matabeleland *pop* 495,317

Bul·gar·ia \,bəl-'gar-ē-ə, bůl-, -'ger-\ country SE Europe on Black Sea; a republic ✷ Sofia *area* 42,823 *sq mi* (110,912 *sq km*), *pop* 8,466,000 — **Bul·gar·i·an** \'bəl-,gär, 'bůl-\ *n* — **Bul·gar·i·an** \bəl-'gar-ē-ən, bůl-, -'ger-\ *adj or n*

Bull·head City \'bul-,hed\ city W Ariz., across Colorado River from Nev. *pop* 21,951

Bull Run \'bul-'rən\ stream 20 *mi* (32 *km*) N Va. W of Washington, D.C., flowing into Occquan Creek (small tributary of the Potomac)

Bun·del·khand \'bun-dᵊl-,kənd\ region N *cen* India containing headwaters of the Yamuna; now chiefly in N Madhya Pradesh

Bundesrepublik Deutschland — see GERMANY

Bun·ker Hill \'bəŋ-kər\ height in Charlestown section of Boston, Mass.

Bur·bank \'bər-,baŋk\ **1** city SW Calif. *pop* 93,643 **2** city NE Ill. *pop* 27,600

Bur·gas \bur-'gäs\ city & port SE Bulgaria on an inlet of Black Sea *pop* 204,915

Bur·gen·land \'bər-gən-,land, 'bur-gən-,länt\ province E Austria SE of Vienna on Hungarian border ✳ Eisenstadt

Bur·gos \'bur-,gōs\ **1** province N Spain *area* 5509 *sq mi* (14,268 *sq km*), *pop* 352,722 **2** city, its ✳ & once ✳ of Old Castile *pop* 160,278

Bur·gun·dy \'bər-gən-dē\ *or F* **Bour·gogne** \bur-'gónⁿ\ **1** region & with varying limits former kingdom, duchy, & province E France S of Champagne **2** former county France E of Burgundy province; later called **Franche–Com·té** \,frän⁼sh-kōⁿ-'tā\ — **Bur·gun·di·an** \(,)bər-'gən-dē-ən\ *adj or n*

Bur·ki·na Fa·so \bur-'kē-nə-'fä-sō, bər-\ *or formerly* **Upper Vol·ta** \'vōl-tə, 'vol-, 'väl-\ republic W Africa; until 1958 a French territory ✳ Ouagadougou *area* 105,869 *sq mi* (274,201 *sq km*), *pop* 9,780,000

Bur·lin·game \'bər-liŋ-,gām\ city W Calif. *pop* 26,801

Bur·ling·ton \'bər-liŋ-tən\ **1** city SE Iowa *pop* 27,208 **2** town NE Mass. *pop* 23,302 **3** city N *cen* N.C. *pop* 39,498 **4** city NW Vt. *pop* 39,127 **5** city Canada in SE Ont. N of Hamilton *pop* 129,575

Burma — see MYANMAR — **Bur·mese** \,bər-'mēz, -'mēs\ *adj or n*

Bur·na·by \'bər-nə-bē\ municipality Canada in SW B.C. *pop* 158,858

Burn·ley \'bərn-lē\ borough NW England in SE Lancashire *pop* 89,000

Burns·ville \'bərnz-,vil\ village SE Minn. S of Minneapolis *pop* 51,288

Bur·rard Inlet \bə-'rärd\ inlet of Strait of Georgia W Canada in B.C.; city of Vancouver is situated on it

Bur·sa \bur-'sä, 'bər-sə\ *or formerly* **Bru·sa** \brü-'sä, 'brü-sə\ city NW Turkey in Asia near Sea of Marmara *pop* 834,576

Bur·ton \'bər-tᵊn\ city SE *cen* Mich. SE of Flint *pop* 27,617

Bu·run·di \bu̇-'rün-dē, -'rün-\ *or formerly* **Urun·di** \u̇-'rün-\ country E *cen* Africa; a republic ✳ Bujumbura *area ab* 10,700 *sq mi* (27,700 *sq km*), *pop* 5,665,000 — see RUANDA-URUNDI — **Bu·run·di·an** \-dē-ən\ *adj or n*

Bury \'ber-ē\ borough NW England in Greater Manchester NNW of Manchester *pop* 172,200

Bur·yat·ia \bur-'yä-tē-ə\ *or* **Bur·yat Republic** \bur-'yät, ,bur-ē-'ät\ autonomous republic S Russia in Asia adjacent to Mongolia & E of Lake Baikal ✳ Ulan-Ude *area* 135,637 *sq mi* (351,300 *sq km*), *pop* 1,059,000 — **Buryat** *n*

Bury Saint Ed·munds \,ber-ē-sānt-'ed-mən(d)z, -sənt-\ borough SE England in Suffolk *pop* 28,914

Bu·shehr \bü-'sher\ city & port SW Iran *pop* 120,787

Bu·ta·ri·ta·ri \bü-,tä-rē-'tä-rē\ atoll W Pacific at N end of Kiribati *area* 4 *sq mi* (10 *sq km*)

Bute \'byüt\ **1** island SW Scotland W of Firth of Clyde **2** *or* **Bute·shire** \-,shir, -,shər\ former county SW Scotland comprising several islands in the Firth of Clyde ✶ Rothesay (on Bute)

Bu·ton \'bü-,tón\ *or* **Bu·tung** *or D* **Boe·toeng** \'bü-,tüη\ island Indonesia off SE Sulawesi *area ab* 2000 *sq mi* (5200 *sq km*), *pop* 253,262

Butte \'byüt\ city SW Mont. in plateau of Rockies *pop* 33,336

Bu·zau \bə-'zō, -'zaú\ city E Romania *pop* 145,423

Buz·zards Bay \'bə-zərdz\ inlet of the Atlantic SE Mass. W of Cape Cod

Byd·goszcz \'bid-,gósh(ch)\ *or G* **Brom·berg** \'bräm-,berg, 'bróm-,berk\ city NW cen Poland NE of Poznan *pop* 380,385

Byelorussia — see BELORUSSIA — **Bye·lo·rus·sian** \bē-,e-lō-'rə-shən, ,bye-lō-\ *adj or n*

By·tom \'bē-,tóm, 'bi-\ *or G* **Beu·then** \'bói-t⁸n\ city SW Poland in Silesia *pop* 229,851

Byzantium — see ISTANBUL — **Byz·an·tine** \'bi-z⁸n-,tēn, 'bī-, -,tīn; bə-'zan-,, bī-\ *adj or n*

C

Ca·ba·na·tuan \,kä-bä-nä-'twän\ city Philippines in S *cen* Luzon *pop* 173,000

Ca·bi·mas \kä-'bē-mäs\ city NW Venezuela on NE coast of Lake Maracaibo *pop* 165,755

Ca·bin·da \kä-'bin-dä\ territory W equatorial Africa on the Atlantic bet. Republic of the Congo & Democratic Republic of the Congo; belongs to Angola ✶ Cabinda *area* 3000 *sq mi* (7800 *sq km*), *pop* 58,547

Cab·ot Strait \'ka-bət\ strait *ab* 70 *mi* (113 *km*) wide E Canada bet. SW Newfoundland & Cape Breton Is. connecting Gulf of Saint Lawrence with the Atlantic

Ca·bril·lo National Monument \kə-'brē-(,)yō\ historic site SW Calif. on San Diego Bay

Ca·ca·hua·mil·pa \,kä-kē-wä-'mēl-pä\ caverns S Mexico in Guerrero NNE of Taxco

Cá·ce·res \'kä-sə-,räs\ **1** province W Spain in N Extremadura *area* 7701 *sq mi* (19,946 *sq km*), *pop* 411,464 **2** city, its ✶ *pop* 74,589

Cache la Pou·dre \,kash-lə-'pü-dər\ river 125 *mi* (201 *km*) N Colo. flowing into the S. Platte

Cad·do Lake \'ka-(,)dō\ lake 20 *mi* (32 *km*) long NW La. & NE Tex. draining to Red River

Cá·diz \kə-'diz; 'kä-dəz, 'kä-, 'ka-; *Sp* 'kä-(,)thēs\ **1** province SW Spain in Andalusia *area* 2851 *sq mi* (7384 *sq km*), *pop*

1,078,404 **2** *or anc* **Ga·dir** \'gā-dər\ *or* **Ga·des** \'gā-(,)dēz\ city & port, its ✻, on Bay of Cádiz NW of Gibraltar *pop* 154,347

Cádiz, Gulf of arm of the Atlantic SW Spain

Cae·li·an \'sē-lē-ən\ hill in Rome, Italy, one of seven on which the ancient city was built — see AVENTINE

Caen \'kän\ city NW France in Normandy *pop* 115,624

Caerdydd — see CARDIFF

Caer·nar·von *or* **Caer·nar·fon** \kär-'när-vən, kə(r)-\ **1** *or* **Caer·nar·von·shire** \-,shir, -shər\ former county NW Wales **2** borough NW Wales ✻ of Gwynedd *pop* 9506

Cae·sa·rea \,sē-zə-'rē-ə; ,se-sə-, ,se-zə-\ **1** ancient seaport Palestine S of Haifa **2** *or* **Caesarea Mazaca** — see KAYSERI

Caesarea Phi·lip·pi \'fi-lə-,pī, fə-'li-,pī\ ancient city N Palestine SW of Mt. Hermon; site at modern village of Baniyas \,ba-nē-'yas\ in SW Syria

Caesena — see CESENA

Ca·ga·yan \,kä-gä-'yän\ *or* **Rio Gran·de de Cagayan** \,rē-ō-'grän-dā-dä-\ river 220 *mi* (354 *km*) Philippines in NE Luzon flowing N

Ca·glia·ri \'käl-yə-(,)rē\ commune & port Italy ✻ of Sardinia *pop* 219,095

Ca·guas \'kä-,gwäs\ town E *cen* Puerto Rico *pop* 92,429

Ca·ho·kia Mounds \kə-'hō-kē-ə\ group of prehistoric Indian mounds Ill. ENE of E. St. Louis

Ca·hors \kä-'ór\ city SW France N of Toulouse *pop* 20,787

Caicos — see TURKS AND CAICOS

Cairn·gorm \'karn-,górm, 'kern-\ mountain 4084 *ft* (1245 *m*) in Cairngorm Mountains on boundary bet. Highlands and Grampian regions

Cairngorm Mountains mountain range of the Grampians NE *cen* Scotland; highest point Ben Macdhui 4296 *ft* (1309 *m*)

Cairns \'karnz, 'kernz\ city & port NE Australia in NE Queensland *pop* 54,862

Cai·ro \'kī-(,)rō\ city N Egypt, its ✻ *pop* 6,663,000 — **Cai·rene** \kī-'rēn\ *adj or n*

Caith·ness \'käth-nis, ,käth-'nes\ *or* **Caith·ness–shire** \-nish-,shir, -shər; -'nesh-\ former county N Scotland ✻ Wick

Ca·ja·mar·ca \,kä-hə-'mär-kä\ city N Peru *pop* 92,600

Ca·jon Pass \kə-'hōn\ pass 4301 *ft* (1303 *m*) S Calif. NW of San Bernardino bet. San Bernardino Mountains & San Gabriel Mountains

Cal·a·bar \'ka-lə-,bär\ city & port SE Nigeria *pop* 153,900

Ca·la·bria \kə-'lä-brē-ə, -'lä-\ **1** district of ancient Italy comprising area forming heel of the Italian Peninsula; now the S part of Puglia **2** *or* It **Le Ca·la·brie** \lā-kä-'lä-brē-,ā\ *or anc* **Brut·ti·um** \'brú-tē-əm, 'brə-\ region S Italy occupying toe of the Italian Peninsula ✻ Catanzaro *area* 5822 *sq mi* (15,079 *sq km*), *pop* 2,152,539 — **Ca·la·bri·an** \kə-'lä-brē-ən, -'lä-\ *adj or n*

Ca·lah \'kā-lə\ ancient city ✻ of Assyria on the Tigris 20 *mi* (32 *km*) SE of modern Mosul, Iraq; site now called **Nim·rud** \nim-'rüd\

Ca·lais \ka-'lā, kä-'le\ city & port N France on Strait of Dover *pop* 75,836

Calais, Pas de — see DOVER (Strait of)

Ca·la·mian \,kä-lä-mē-'än\ islands W Philippines NE of Palawan Is.

53 **Cambodia**

Cal·ca·sieu \'kal-kə-ˌshü\ river 200 *mi* (322 *km*) SW La. flowing
through **Calcasieu Lake** (*ab* 15 *mi* or 24 *km* long) & **Calcasieu
Pass** (channel 5 *mi* or 8 *km* long) into Gulf of Mexico

Cal·cut·ta \kal-'kə-tə\ city & port E India on the Hugli ✱ of W.
Bengal *metropolitan area pop* 11,021,915 — **Cal·cut·tan** \-'kə-tᵊn\
n

Cal·e·don \'ka-lə-dən\ town Canada in SE Ont. *pop* 34,965

Cal·e·do·nia \ˌka-lə-'dō-nyə, -nē-ə\ **1** town E Wisconsin *pop*
20,999 **2** — see SCOTLAND — **Cal·e·do·nian** \-nyən, -nē-ən\ *adj
or n*

Caledonian Canal ship canal N Scotland connecting Loch Linnhe
& Moray Firth & uniting Lochs Ness, Oich, Lochy, & Eil

Cal·ga·ry \'kal-gə-rē\ city Canada in SW Alta. *pop* 710,677 — **Cal·
gar·i·an** \kal-'gar-ē-ən, -'ger-\ *n*

Ca·li \'kä-lē\ city W Colombia on the Cauca *pop* 1,624,400

Cal·i·cut \'ka-li-(ˌ)kət\ or **Ko·zhi·kode** \'kō-zhə-ˌkōd\ city & port
SW India on Malabar Coast in Kerala *pop* 456,618

Cal·i·for·nia \ˌka-lə-'fȯr-nyə\ state SW U.S. ✱ Sacramento *area*
158,706 *sq mi* (411,048 *sq km*), *pop* 29,760,020 — **Cal·i·for·nian**
\-nyən\ *adj or n* — **Cal·i·for·nio** \-nyō\ *n*

California, Gulf of arm of the Pacific NW Mexico bet. Baja California & states of Sonora & Sinaloa

Cal·lao \kä-'yä-(ˌ)ō, -'yaù\ city & port W Peru on Callao Bay W of
Lima *pop* 588,600

Ca·loo·sa·hatch·ee \kə-ˌlü-sə-'ha-chē\ river 75 *mi* (121 *km*) S Fla.
flowing W into Gulf of Mexico

Calpe — see GIBRALTAR (Rock of)

Cal·ta·nis·set·ta \ˌkäl-tä-nē-'se-tä\ commune Italy in *cen* Sicily *pop*
60,162

Cal·u·met \'kal-yə-ˌmet, -mət\ industrial region NW Ind. & NE Ill.
SE of & adjacent to Chicago; includes chiefly cities of E. Chicago,
Gary, & Hammond, Ind., & Calumet City & Lansing, Ill.

Calumet City city NE Ill. S of Chicago *pop* 37,840

Cal·va·dos Reef \ˌkal-və-'dōs\ or *F* **Ro·chers du Calvados** \rō-
ˌshä-dē-\ long reef of rocks NW France in English Channel at
mouth of the Orne

Cal·va·ry \'kal-v(ə-)rē\ or *Heb* **Gol·go·tha** \'gäl-gə-thə, gäl-'gä-thə\
place outside ancient Jerusalem where Jesus was crucified

Cal·y·don \'ka-lə-ˌdän, -dᵊn\ ancient city *cen* Greece in S Aetolia
near Gulf of Patras — **Cal·y·do·nian** \ˌka-lə-'dō-nyən, -nē-ən\ *adj*

Cam \'kam\ river 40 *mi* (64 *km*) E *cen* England in Cambridgeshire
flowing into the Ouse

Ca·ma·güey \ˌkä-mä-'gwä\ city E *cen* Cuba *pop* 283,008

Ca·margue \kä-'märg\ or **La Camargue** \ˌlä-\ marshy island S
France in delta of the Rhône

Cam·a·ril·lo \ˌka-mə-'rē-(ˌ)ō\ city SW Calif. W of Los Angeles *pop*
52,303

Cambay — see KHAMBHAT

Cambay, Gulf of — see KHAMBHAT (GULF OF)

Cam·ber·well \'kam-bər-ˌwel, -wəl\ **1** city SE Australia in S Victoria E of Melbourne *pop* 83,799 **2** former metropolitan borough S
London, England, now part of Southwark

Cam·bo·dia \kam-'bō-dē-ə\ or **Kam·pu·chea** \ˌkam-pù-'chē-ə\ or
1970–75 **Khmer Republic** \kə-'mer\ country SE Asia bordering

on Gulf of Thailand ✳ Phnom Penh *area ab* 70,000 *sq mi* (181,300 *sq km*), *pop* 9,287,000 — **Cam·bo·di·an** \-ən\ *adj or n*

Cam·brai *or formerly* **Cam·bray** \kam-'brā, käⁿ-'bre\ city N France on the Schelde *pop* 34,210

Cam·bria \'kam-brē-ə\ — see WALES

Cam·bri·an \'kam-brē-ən\ mountains *cen* Wales

Cam·bridge \'kām-brij\ **1** city E Mass. W of Boston *pop* 95,802 **2** city Canada in SE Ont. *pop* 92,772; includes former cities of Galt & Preston **3** *or ML* **Can·ta·brig·ia** \,kan-tə-'bri-j(ē-)ə\ city & borough E England ✳ *of* Cambridgeshire *pop* 92,772 — **Can·ta·brig·i·an** \-ən\ *adj or n*

Cam·bridge·shire \'kām-brij-,shir, -shər\ *or* **Cambridge** *or formerly* **Cambridgeshire and Isle of Ely** \'ē-lē\ county E England ✳ Cambridge *area* 1364 *sq mi* (3533 *sq km*), *pop* 640,700

Cam·den \'kam-dən\ **1** city & port SW N.J. on Delaware River opposite Philadelphia, Pa. *pop* 87,492 **2** borough of N Greater London, England *pop* 170,500

Cam·er·oon \,ka-mə-'rün\ **1** massif *ab* 13,350 *ft* (4069 *m*) Cameroon (republic) NW of Buea **2** *or* **Cam·er·oun** \-'rün\ country W equatorial Africa in Cameroons region; a republic, formerly a trust territory under France ✳ Yaoundé *area ab* 183,590 *sq mi* (475,500 *sq km*), *pop* 13,103,000 — **Cam·er·oo·nian** \-'rü-nē-ən, -nyən\ *adj or n*

Cam·er·oons \,ka-mə-'rünz\ region W Africa bordering on NE Gulf of Guinea formerly comprising Brit. & French Cameroons but now divided bet. Nigeria & Cameroon — **Cam·er·oo·nian** \-'rü-nē-ən, -nyən\ *adj or n*

Ca·mi·guin \,kä-mē-'gēn\ **1** island N Philippines NE of Luzon; site of Camiguin Volcano 2602 *ft* (793 *m*) **2** island S Philippines off N coast of Mindanao — see HIBOKHIBOK

Ca·mo·tes Sea \kä-'mō-,täs\ sea S *cen* Philippines W of Leyte

Cam·pa·gna di Ro·ma \käm-'pä-nyä-dē-'rō-mä, -'pa-\ *or* **Roman Campagna** region *cen* Italy around Rome

Cam·pa·nia \käm-'pä-nyä, kam-'pä-nyə\ region S Italy bordering on Tyrrhenian Sea ✳ Naples *area* 5250 *sq mi* (13,598 *sq km*), *pop* 5,808,705 — **Cam·pa·nian** \-nyən, -nē-ən\ *adj or n*

Camp·bell \'kam-bel, 'ka-məl\ city W Calif. SW of San José *pop* 36,048

Cam·pe·che \kam-'pē-chē, käm-'pā-chā\ **1** state SE Mexico in W Yucatán Peninsula *area* 21,666 *sq mi* (56,115 *sq km*), *pop* 535,185 **2** city & port, its ✳, on Bay of Campeche *pop* 172,208

Campeche, Bay of the SW section of Gulf of Mexico

Cam·pi·na Gran·de \,käm-,pē-nə-'grän-dē\ city E Brazil in E Paraíba *pop* 326,153

Cam·pi·nas \käm-'pē-nəs\ city SE Brazil in E São Paulo state *pop* 846,084

Cam·po·bel·lo \,kam-pə-'be-(,)lō\ island Canada in SW N.B.

Cam·po·for·mi·do \,kam-(,)pō-'fȯr-mə-,dō\ *or formerly* **Cam·po For·mio** \-mē-,ō\ village NE Italy SW of Udine

Cam·po Gran·de \,käm-(,)pü-'grän-dē\ city SW Brazil ✳ of Mato Grosso do Sul *pop* 525,612

Cam·pos \'käm-pəs\ city SE Brazil in Rio de Janeiro state on the Paraíba *pop* 349,036

Cam Ranh Bay \\'käm-'rän\\ inlet of S. China Sea SE Vietnam *ab* 180 *mi* (290 *km*) NE of Ho Chi Minh City

Ca·na \\'kä-nə\\ village in Galilee NE of Nazareth; now in Israel

Ca·naan \\'kā-nən\\ ancient region corresponding vaguely to later Palestine — **Ca·naan·ite** \\'kā-nə-,nīt\\ *adj or n*

Can·a·da \\'ka-nə-də\\ country N N. America including Newfoundland & Arctic islands N of mainland; a dominion of the Commonwealth of Nations ✳ Ottawa *area* 3,851,809 *sq mi* (10,014,703 *sq km*), *pop* 27,296,859 — **Ca·na·di·an** \\kə-'nā-dē-ən\\ *adj or n*

Canadian *or, above its junction with the N. Canadian,* **South Canadian** river 906 *mi* (1458 *km*) S *cen* U.S. flowing E from NE N. Mex. to Arkansas River in E Okla.

Canadian Shield *or* **Lau·ren·tian Plateau** \\lȯ-'ren(t)-shən\\ plateau region E Canada & NE U.S. extending from Mackenzie River basin E to Davis Strait & S to S Que., NE Minn., N Wis., NW Mich., & NE N.Y. including the Adirondacks

Canal Zone *or* **Panama Canal Zone** strip of territory Panama; ceased to exist as a formal political entity Oct. 1, 1979, but remains under U.S. control through 1999 for administration of the Panama Canal — **Zon·ian** \\'zō-nē-ən, -nyən\\ *adj or n*

Can·an·dai·gua \\,ka-nən-'dā-gwə\\ lake 15 *mi* (24 *km*) long W *cen* N.Y.; one of the Finger Lakes

Ca·nary Islands \\kə-'ner-ē\\ islands in the Atlantic off NW Africa belonging to Spain *area* 2796 *sq mi* (7242 *sq km*), *pop* 1,493,784 — see LAS PALMAS, SANTA CRUZ DE TENERIFE — **Ca·nar·i·an** \\kə-'ner-ē-ən\\ *adj or n*

Ca·nav·er·al, Cape \\kə-'nav-rəl, -'na-və-\\ *or 1963–1973 officially* **Cape Ken·ne·dy** \\'ke-nə-dē\\ cape on E shore of Canaveral Peninsula; site of Air Force Missile Test Center & John F. Kennedy Space Center

Canaveral Peninsula peninsula E Fla. enclosing Indian River (lagoon)

Can·ber·ra \\'kan-b(ə-)rə, -,ber-ə\\ city ✳ of Australia in Australian Capital Territory SW of Sydney

Can·cún \\,kan-'kün, kän-\\ resort SE Mexico on island off NE coast of Yucatán Peninsula

Can·dia \\'kan-dē-ə, kän-\\ **1** CRETE **2** — see IRÁKLION

Candia, Sea of — see CRETE (Sea of)

Ca·nea \\kə-'nē-ə\\ *or anc* **Cy·do·nia** \\sī-'dō-nē-ə, -nyə\\ city & port Greece on N coast of W Crete *pop* 50,077

Can·i·a·pis·kau \\,ka-nē-ə-'pis-(,)kō\\ river 575 *mi* (925 *km*) Canada in N Que. flowing N to unite with the Larch forming the Koksoak

Can·nae \\'ka-(,)nē\\ ancient town SE Italy in Puglia WSW of modern Barletta

Can·na·nore \\'ka-nə-,nōr, -,nȯr\\ **1** *or* **Ka·na·nur** \\,kə-nə-'nùr\\ city SW India in Kerala NNW of Calicut *pop* 65,233 **2** — see LACCADIVE ISLANDS

Cannes \\'kan, 'kän\\ commune & port SE France SW of Nice *pop* 69,363

Ca·no·pus \\kə-'nō-pəs\\ ancient city N Egypt E of Alexandria at modern Abu Qir — **Ca·no·pic** \\-'nō-pik, -'nä-\\ *adj*

Can·so, Cape \\'kan(t)-(,)sō\\ cape Canada on NE N.S. mainland

Canso, Strait of narrow channel Canada separating Cape Breton Is. from N.S. mainland

Can·ta·bria \kän-'tä-brē-ä\ *or formerly* **San·tan·der** \sän-'tän-der\ province N Spain in N Old Castile bordering on Bay of Biscay ✱ Santander *area* 2042 *sq mi* (5289 *sq km*), *pop* 527,326

Can·ta·bri·an Mountains \kan-'tä-brē-ən\ mountains N & NW Spain running E–W near coast of Bay of Biscay — *see* CERREDO

Cantabrigia — *see* CAMBRIDGE

Can·ter·bury \'kan-tə(r)-,ber-ē, -b(ə-)rē\ **1** city SE Australia in E New South Wales, SW suburb of Sydney *pop* 129,232 **2** city & county borough SE England in Kent *pop* 34,404 — **Can·ter·bu·ri·an** \,kan-tə(r)-'byùr-ē-ən\ *adj*

Can·ti·gny \käⁿ-,tē-'nyē\ village N France S of Amiens

Can·ton \'kan-tⁿn\ **1** city NE Ohio SSE of Akron *pop* 84,161 **2** — *see* GUANGZHOU — **Can·ton·ese** \,kan-tⁿn-'ēz, -'ēs\ *adj or n*

Canyon de Chelly National Monument \də-'shā\ reservation NE Ariz. containing cliff-dweller ruins

Can·yon·lands National Park \'kan-yən-,lan(d)z\ reservation SE Utah surrounding junction of Colorado & Green rivers

Cap d'An·tibes \,kàp-däⁿ-'tēb\ cape SE France SW of Antibes

Cap de la Hague \,kàp-də-là-'àg\ cape NW France at tip of Cotentin Peninsula

Cap–de–la–Ma·de·leine \,kàp-də-là-,màd-'len\ city Canada in S Que. on St. Lawrence River ENE of Trois-Rivières *pop* 33,716

Cape Breton — *see* BRETON (Cape)

Cape Bret·on Highlands National Park \kāp-'bre-tⁿn, kə-'bre-, -'bri-\ reservation Canada in NE N.S. near N end of Cape Breton Is.

Cape Breton Island island Canada in NE N.S. *area* 3970 *sq mi* (10,322 *sq km*)

Cape Cod — *see* COD (Cape)

Cape Cod Bay the S end of Massachusetts Bay W of Cape Cod

Cape Cor·al \'kòr-əl, 'kär-\ city SW Fla. *pop* 74,991

Cape Fear \'fir\ **1** river 202 *mi* (325 *km*) *cen* & SE N.C. flowing SE into the Atlantic **2** — *see* FEAR (Cape)

Cape Gi·rar·deau \jə-'rär-(,)dō, -jə-'rä-də\ city SE Mo. on Mississippi River *pop* 34,438

Cape Horn — *see* HORN (Cape)

Cape Kru·sen·stern National Monument \'krü-zən-,stərn\ reservation NW Alaska on Chukchi Sea

Cape of Good Hope 1 — *see* GOOD HOPE (Cape of) **2** *or* **Cape Province** *or* **Kaap·land** \'käp-,länt\ *or earlier* **Cape Colony** former province S Republic of South Africa ✱ Cape Town *area* 278,465 *sq mi* (724,009 *sq km*)

Ca·per·na·um \kə-'pər-nā-əm, -nē-\ city of ancient Palestine on NW shore of Sea of Galilee

Cape Sable — *see* SABLE (Cape)

Cape Sa·ble Island \'sā-bəl\ island 7 *mi* (11 *km*) long Canada off S coast of N.S.

Cape Town \'kāp-,taún\ city & port, legislative ✱ of Republic of South Africa & formerly ✱ of Cape of Good Hope, on Table Bay *pop* 776,617 — **Cape·to·ni·an** \kāp-'tō-nē-ən\ *n*

Cape Verde — *see* VERDE (Cape)

Cape Verde \'vərd\ country E Atlantic comprising the Cape Verde Islands; until 1975 belonged to Portugal ✱ Praia *area* 1557 *sq mi* (4048 *sq km*), *pop* 350,000 — **Cape Verd·ean** \'vər-dē-ən\ *adj or n*

Cape Verde Islands islands in the Atlantic off W Africa

Cape York Peninsula \'york\ peninsula NE Australia in N Queensland having at its N tip **Cape York** (on Torres Strait)

Cap Hai·tien \kap-'hā-shən\ *or F* **Cap–Ha·i·tien** \kȧ-pȧ-ē-'syaⁿ, -ē-'tyaⁿ\ city & port N Haiti *pop* 92,122

Cap·i·to·line \'ka-pə-tᵊl-,īn, *Brit often* kə-'pi-tᵊl-\ hill in Rome, Italy, one of seven on which the ancient city was built — *see* AVENTINE

Cap·i·tol Reef National Park \'ka-pə-tᵊl\ reservation S *cen* Utah containing archaeological remains, petrified forests, & unusual erosion forms

Capodistria — *see* KOPER

Caporetto — *see* KOBARID

Cap·pa·do·cia \,ka-pə-'dō-sh(ē-)ə\ ancient district E Asia Minor chiefly in valley of the upper Kizil Irmak in modern Turkey ✳ Caesarea Mazaca — **Cap·pa·do·cian** \-sh(ē-)ən\ *adj or n*

Ca·pri \kä-'prē, kə-; 'kä-(,)prē, 'ka-\ *or anc* **Ca·pre·ae** \ka-prē-,ē\ island Italy S Bay of Naples *area* 4 *sq mi* (10 *sq km*) — **Ca·pri·ote** \'kä-prē-,ōt, 'kä-, -prē-ət\ *n*

Capsa — *see* GAFSA

Cap·ua \'ka-pyü-wə, 'kä-pü-ä\ commune S Italy on the Volturno N of Naples NW of site of ancient city of Capua *pop* 17,967

Cap·u·lin, Mount \kȧ-pyǘ-lən, -pü-\ cinder cone 8368 *ft* (2550 *m*) NE N. Mex.; main feature of **Capulin Volcano National Monument**

Cap Vert — *see* VERT (Cape)

Ca·ra·cas \kä-'rä-käs, -'ra-\ city ✳ of Venezuela near Caribbean coast *metropolitan area pop* 1,824,892

Car·bon·dale \'kär-bən-,dāl\ city SW Ill. *pop* 27,033

Car·cas·sonne \,kär-kä-'sȯn, -'sȯn\ city S France *pop* 44,991

Car·che·mish \'kär-kə-,mish, kär-'kē-mish\ ruined city S Turkey on the Euphrates at Syrian border N of modern Jarabulus, Syria

Cár·de·nas \'kär-thā-,näs\ city & port N Cuba E of Matanzas *pop* 75,651

Car·diff \'kär-dif\ *or W* **Caer·dydd** \kīr-'dēth\ borough & port ✳ of Wales & of S. Glamorgan *pop* 272,600

Car·di·gan \'kär-di-gən\ *or* **Car·di·gan·shire** \-,shir, -shər\ former county W Wales ✳ Aberystwyth

Cardigan Bay inlet of St. George's Channel on W coast of Wales

Ca·ren·tan \,kä-rä[n]-'tä[n]\ town NW France at base of Cotentin Peninsula

Car·ia \'kar-ē-ə, 'ker-\ ancient region SW Asia Minor bordering on Aegean Sea ✳ Halicarnassus — **Car·i·an** \-ē-ən\ *adj or n*

Ca·rib·be·an Sea \,kar-ə-'bē-ən, kə-'ri-bē-\ arm of the Atlantic bounded on N & E by West Indies, on S by S. America, & on W by Central America — **Caribbean** *adj*

Car·ib·bees \'kar-ə-,bēz\ LESSER ANTILLES

Car·i·boo \'kar-ə-,bü\ mountains W Canada in E *cen* B.C. W of the Rocky Mountains; highest point *ab* 11,750 *ft* (3581 *m*)

Ca·rin·thia \kə-'rin(t)-thē-ə\ region *cen* Europe in E Alps; once a duchy, Austrian crown land 1849–1918, divided bet. Austria & Yugoslavia 1918 — **Ca·rin·thi·an** \-thē-ən\ *adj or n*

Car·lisle \kär-'līl, kər-, 'kär-,\ city & borough NW England ✳ of Cumbria *pop* 99,800

Car·low \'kär-ˌlō\ **1** county SE Ireland in Leinster *area* 346 *sq mi* (900 *sq km*), *pop* 40,942 **2** town, its ✳ *pop* 11,275

Carls·bad \'kär(-ə)lz-ˌbad\ **1** caverns SE N. Mex. in **Carlsbad Caverns National Park 2** city SW Calif. NNW of San Diego *pop* 63,126 **3** city SE N. Mex. on the Pecos *pop* 24,952

Carmana, Carmania — see KERMAN

Car·mar·then \kär-'mär-thən, kə(r)-\ **1** *or* **Car·mar·then·shire** \-ˌshir, -shər\ former county S Wales ✳ Carmarthen **2** borough & port S Wales ✳ of Dyfed *pop* 54,800

Car·mel 1 \kär-'mel\ city W Calif. S of Monterey Bay *pop* 4239 **2** \'kär-məl\ city *cen* Ind. N of Indianapolis *pop* 25,380

Car·mel, Mount \'kär-məl\ mountain ridge NW Israel; highest point 1791 *ft* (546 *m*)

Car·men de Pat·a·go·nes \'kär-men-thä-ˌpä-tä-'gō-nās\ town Argentina on the Negro River opposite Viedma *pop* 13,981

Car·nat·ic \kär-'na-tik\ region SE India bet. Eastern Ghats & Coromandel coast now in Andhra Pradesh & Karnataka

Carnic Alps \'kär-nik\ mountain range E Alps bet. Austria & Italy

Car·nio·la \ˌkär-nē-'ō-lə, kär-'nyō-\ region S & W Slovenia NE of Istrian Peninsula — **Car·nio·lan** \-lən\ *adj*

Car·o·li·na \ˌkar-ə-'lī-nə\ English colony 1663–1729 on E coast of N. America divided 1729 into N.C. & S.C. (the **Car·o·li·nas** \-nəz\) — **Car·o·lin·ian** \ˌkar-ə-'li-nē-ən, -nyən\ *n*

Ca·ro·li·na \ˌkä-rō-'lē-nä\ city NE *cen* Puerto Rico *pop* 177,806

Car·o·line Islands \'kar-ə-ˌlīn, -lin\ islands W Pacific Ocean comprising Palau & the Federated States of Micronesia; formerly part of Trust Territory of the Pacific Islands

Car·ol Stream \'kar-əl\ village NE Ill. W of Chicago *pop* 31,716

Ca·ro·ní \ˌkä-rō-'nē\ river E Venezuela flowing N into the Orinoco

Car·pa·thi·an Mountains \kär-'pā-thē-ən\ mountain system E *cen* Europe along boundary bet. Slovakia & Poland & extending through Ukraine & E Romania — see GERLACHOVKA, TATRY, TRANSYLVANIAN ALPS

Carpathian Ruthenia, Carpatho–Ukraine — see ZAKARPATS'KA

Car·pen·tar·ia, Gulf of \ˌkär-pən-'ter-ē-ə, -'tar-\ inlet of Arafura Sea on N coast of Australia

Car·pen·ters·ville \'kär-pən-tərz-ˌvil\ village NE Ill. NW of Chicago *pop* 23,049

Car·qui·nez Strait \kär-'kē-nəs\ strait 8 *mi* (13 *km*) long Calif. joining San Pablo & Suisun bays

Car·ran·tuo·hill \ˌkar-ən-'tü-əl\ mountain 3414 *ft* (1041 *m*) SW Ireland in County Kerry; highest in Macgillicuddy's Reeks & in Ireland

Car·ra·ra \kä-'rär-ä\ commune N Italy ESE of La Spezia *pop* 68,528

Car·rhae \'kar-(ˌ)ē\ ancient city N Mesopotamia SSE of modern Urfa

Car·rick·fer·gus \ˌkar-ik-'fər-gəs\ district E Northern Ireland, established 1974 *area* 34 *sq mi* (88 *sq km*), *pop* 32,439

Car·rick on Shan·non \'kar-ik-ˌon-'sha-nən, -ˌän-\ town N *cen* Ireland ✳ of County Leitrim *pop* 1621

Car·roll·ton \'kar-əl-tən\ city N Tex. *pop* 82,169

Car·shal·ton \kär-'shȯl-tən, kər-\ former urban district S England in Surrey, now part of Sutton

Carso — see KARST
Car·son \'kär-s°n\ **1** river W Nev. flowing NE into **Carson Lake 2** city SW Calif. SE of Los Angeles *pop* 83,995
Carson City city * of Nev. E of Lake Tahoe *pop* 40,443
Carson Sink intermittent lake W Nev. S of Humboldt Lake
Carstensz, Mount — see PUNCAK JAYA
Car·ta·ge·na \,kär-tä-'gā-nä, -'hā-, -'jē-\ **1** city & port NW Colombia *pop* 688,300 **2** city & port SE Spain on the Mediterranean *pop* 166,736
Car·ta·go \kär-'tä-(,)gō\ city *cen* Costa Rica *pop* 21,753
Car·ter·et \,kär-tə-'ret\ borough NE N.J. S of Elizabeth *pop* 19,025
Car·thage \'kär-thij\ *or anc* **Car·tha·go** \kär-'tä-(,)gō, -'thä-\ ancient city & state N Africa on coast NE of modern Tunis — **Car·tha·gin·ian** \,kär-thə-'ji-nyən, -nē-ən\ *adj or n*
Cary \'kar-ē, 'ker-ē\ city E *cen* N.C. *pop* 43,858
Ca·sa·blan·ca \,ka-sə-'blaŋ-kə, ,kä-sə-'bläŋ-, -zə-\ *or Ar* **Dar el Bei·da** \,där-,el-bā-'dä\ city & port W Morocco on the Atlantic *pop* 3,102,000
Casa Gran·de Ruins National Monument \,ka-sə-'gran-dē\ reservation S Ariz. SE of Phoenix; prehistoric ruins
Cas·cade Range \(,)kas-'kād\ mountain range W U.S., N continuation of the Sierra Nevada extending N from Lassen Peak across Oreg. & Wash. — see COAST MOUNTAINS, COAST RANGES, RAINIER (Mount)
Cas·co Bay \'kas-(,)kō\ inlet of the Atlantic S Maine
Ca·ser·ta \kä-'zer-tä, -'zʌr-\ commune S Italy *pop* 68,811
Cash·el \'ka-shəl\ town S Ireland in *cen* Tipperary at base of **Rock of Cashel** (hill with ruins of cathedral & castle) *pop* 2473
Cashmere — see KASHMIR
Ca·si·qui·a·re *or* **Cas·si·qui·a·re** \,kä-sē-'kyä-rā\ river S Venezuela connecting the upper course of Negro River with Orinoco River
Cas·per \'kas-pər\ city *cen* Wyo. on N. Platte River *pop* 46,742
Cas·pi·an Gates \'kas-pē-ən\ pass on W shore of Caspian Sea near Derbent
Caspian Sea sea (salt lake) bet. Europe & Asia; *ab* 90 *ft* (27 *m*) below sea level *area* 143,550 *sq mi* (371,795 *sq km*)
Cas·si·no \kä-'sē-(,)nō\ commune *cen* Italy ESE of Frosinone; site of Monte Cassino monastery *pop* 32,803
Cas·tel Gan·dol·fo \(,)kä-,stel-gän-'dōl-(,)fō\ commune *cen* Italy on Lake Albano SE of Rome *pop* 6784
Cas·tel·lón \,käs-tēl-'yōn\ province E Spain *area* 2579 *sq mi* (6680 *sq km*), *pop* 446,744
Cas·tel·lón de la Pla·na \,käs-tel-'yōn-thä-lä-'plä-nä\ city & port, * of Castellón province, Spain, on the Mediterranean NE of Valencia *pop* 133,180
Castellorizo *or* **Castelrosso** — see KASTELLORIZON
Cas·tile \ka-'stēl\ *or Sp* **Cas·til·la** \kä-'stēl-yä, -'stē-yä\ region & ancient kingdom *cen* & N Spain divided by the Sierra de Guadarrama into regions & old provinces of **Old Castile** *or Sp* **Castilla la Vie·ja** \lä-'vyä-hä\ (to the N, * Burgos) & **New Castile** *or Sp* **Castilla la Nue·va** \lä-'nwä-vä\ (to the S, * Toledo) — **Cas·til·ian** \ka-'stil-yən\ *adj or n*
Cas·til·lo de San Mar·cos National Monument \kä-'stē-yō-də-san-'mär-(,)kōs\ historic site NE Fla.; contains a Spanish fort

Cas·tle·bar \\ka-səl-'bär\ town NW Ireland ✳ of Mayo *pop* 6071

Castle Clin·ton National Monument \'klin-tᵊn\ historic site Manhattan Is. SE N.Y.; contains a fort

Cast·le·reagh \'ka-səl-(,)rā\ district E Northern Ireland, established 1974 *area* 33 *sq mi* (85 *sq km*), *pop* 60,649

Castres \'kästrᵊ\ city S France E of Toulouse *pop* 46,292

Cas·tries \'kas-,trēz, -,trēs\ city & port ✳ of St. Lucia *pop* 11,147

Ca·strop-Raux·el \,käs-,tróp-'raùk-səl\ city W Germany SSW of Münster *pop* 79,065

Ça·tal·ca \chä-tᵊl-'jä\ city Turkey in Europe W of Istanbul

Cat·a·li·na \,ka-tᵊl-'ē-nə\ *or* **San·ta Catalina** \'san-tə\ island SW Calif. in Channel Islands *area* 70 *sq mi* (182 *sq km*)

Cat·a·lo·nia \,ka-tᵊl-'ō-nyə, -nē-ə\ *or Sp* **Ca·ta·lu·ña** \,kä-tä-'lü-nyä\ autonomous region NE Spain bordering on France & the Mediterranean; chief city Barcelona *area* 12,328 *sq mi* (31,930 *sq km*), *pop* 6,059,494 — **Cat·a·lan** \'ka-tə-lən, -,lan\ *n* — **Cat·a·lo·nian** \-'ō-nyən, -nē-ən\ *adj or n*

Ca·ta·mar·ca \,kä-tä-'mär-kä\ city NW Argentina *pop* 110,489

Ca·ta·nia \kə-'tä-nyə, -'tä-\ *or anc* **Cat·a·na** \'ka-tə-nə\ commune Italy in E Sicily on E coast on Gulf of Catania *pop* 330,037

Ca·tan·za·ro \,kä-,tänd-'zär-(,)ō, -,tänt-'sär-\ city S Italy ✳ of Calabria *pop* 93,464

Ca·taw·ba \kə-'tó-bə\ river 250 *mi* (402 *km*) flowing S from W N.C. into S.C. — see WATEREE

Cathay \ka-'thā\ CHINA — an old name

Ca·the·dral City \kə-'thē-drəl\ city SW Calif. *pop* 30,085

Catherine, Mount — see KATHERINA (Gebel)

Ca·toc·tin Mountain \kə-'täk-tən\ mountain ridge NW Md. & N Va. in Blue Ridge Mountains

Cats·kill Mountains \'kat-,skil\ mountains SE N.Y. in the Appalachian system W of Hudson River — see SLIDE MOUNTAIN

Cattaro — see KOTOR

Cau·ca \'kaù-kä\ river 838 *mi* (1348 *km*) W Colombia flowing N into the Magdalena

Cau·ca·sia \kó-'kä-zhə, -shə\ *or* **Cau·ca·sus** \'kó-kə-səs\ region SE Europe bet. the Black & Caspian seas; divided by Caucasus Mountains into **Cis·cau·ca·sia** \,sis-\ (to the N) & **Trans·cau·ca·sia** \,tran(t)s-\ (to the S) — **Cau·ca·sian** \kó-'kä-zhən, kä-, *also* -'kazhən\ *adj or n*

Caucasus Indicus — see HINDU KUSH

Caucasus Mountains mountain system SE Europe in Russia, Georgia, Azerbaijan, and Armenia

Cau·dine Forks \'kó-,dīn, -,dēn\ two mountain passes S Italy in the Apennines bet. Benevento & Capua

Caul·field \'kól-,fēld\ city SE Australia in S Victoria SE of Melbourne; part of Greater Melbourne *pop* 67,776

Causses \'kōs\ limestone region S *cen* France on S border of Massif Central

Cau·ve·ry \'kó-və-rē\ *or* **Kā·ve·ri** \'kä-və-rē\ river 475 *mi* (764 *km*) S India flowing E & entering Bay of Bengal in a wide delta

Cauvery Falls *or* **Kā·ve·ri Falls** \'kä-və-rē\ waterfall India in the Cauvery on Karnataka-Tamil Nadu boundary

Cav·an \'ka-vən\ **1** county NE Ireland (republic) in Ulster *area* 730 *sq mi* (1898 *sq km*), *pop* 52,756 **2** town, its ✳ *pop* 3332

Ca·vi·te \kä-'vē-tē\ city Philippines in Luzon on **Cavite Peninsula** in Manila Bay SW of Manila *pop* 92,000

Ca·xi·as \kə-'shē-əs\ **1** town NE Brazil in Maranhão WNW of Teresina *pop* 145,709 **2** — see DUQUE DE CAXIAS **3** *or* **Caxias do Sul** \də-'sül\ city S Brazil in Rio Grande do Sul *pop* 290,968

Cay·enne \kī-'en, kā-\ city & port ✻ of French Guiana on island in Cayenne River near the coast *pop* 37,097

Cayes \'kī\ *or* **Aux Cayes** \ō-'kī\ city & port SW Haiti *pop* 105,383

Ca·yey \kä-'yä\ city SE *cen* Puerto Rico *pop* 46,553

Cay·man Islands \(,)kä-'man, *attributively* 'kā-mən\ islands W. Indies NW of Jamaica; a Brit. colony ✻ George Town (on **Grand Cayman**, chief island) *area* 100 *sq mi* (259 *sq km*), *pop* 23,881 — **Cay·man·i·an** \kā-'ma-nē-ən\ *adj or n*

Ca·yu·ga \kā-'yü-gə, kī-, kē-, kə-\ lake 40 *mi* (64 *km*) long W *cen* N.Y.; one of the Finger Lakes

Ce·a·rá \sä-ə-'rä\ state NE Brazil bordering on the Atlantic ✻ Fortaleza *area* 57,147 *sq mi* (148,011 *sq km*), *pop* 6,353,346

Ce·bu \sā-'bü\ **1** island E *cen* Philippines, one of the Visayans *area* 1707 *sq mi* (4438 *sq km*) **2** city on E Cebu Is. *pop* 610,000

Čechy — see BOHEMIA

Ce·dar \'sē-dər\ river 329 *mi* (529 *km*) SE Minn. & E Iowa flowing SE into the Iowa

Cedar Breaks National Monument \'bräks\ reservation SW Utah NE of Zion National Park containing unusual erosion forms

Cedar Falls city NE Iowa NW of Waterloo *pop* 34,298

Cedar Hill town NE Tex. SW of Dallas *pop* 19,976

Cedar Rapids city E Iowa on the Cedar *pop* 108,751

Ce·le·bes \'se-lə-ˌbēz, sə-'lē-bēz\ — see SULAWESI

Celebes Sea arm of W Pacific enclosed on N by Mindanao & the Sulu Archipelago, on S by Sulawesi, & on W by Borneo — **Cel·e·be·sian** \ˌse-lə-'bē-zhən\ *adj*

Ce·les·tial Empire \sə-'les-chəl, -'lesh-, -'les-tē-əl\ the former Chinese Empire

Cel·le \'(t)se-lə\ city N Germany NE of Hannover *pop* 72,609

Celt·ic Sea \'kel-tik, 'sel-\ inlet of the Atlantic in British Isles SE of Ireland, SW of Wales, & W of Cornwall

Ce·nis, Mont \môⁿ-sə-'nē\ **1** mountain pass 6831 *ft* (2082 *m*) bet. France & Italy over Mont Cenis massif in Graian Alps **2** *or* **Fré·jus** \frā-'zhüs, -'zhēs\ railroad tunnel 8.5 *mi* (13.6 *km*) long piercing the Fréjus massif SW of Mont Cenis

Cen·ter·ville \'sen-tər-ˌvil, -vəl\ city SW Ohio *pop* 21,082

Central region *cen* Scotland, established 1975 ✻ Stirling *area* 1017 *sq mi* (2635 *sq km*), *pop* 272,900

Central African Republic *or 1976–79* **Central African Empire** *or earlier* **Ubangi–Shari** republic N *cen* Africa ✻ Bangui *area* 240,376 *sq mi* (624,978 *sq km*), *pop* 2,998,000

Central America 1 the narrow S portion of N. America connecting with S. America & extending from the Isthmus of Tehuantepec to the Isthmus of Panama **2** the republics of Guatemala, El Salvador, Honduras, Nicaragua, & Costa Rica & often also Panama & Belize

Central Europe the countries of *cen* Europe — usu. considered as including the countries extending from Baltic Sea on the N to Alps on the S and from Russia, Lithuania, Belarus, & Ukraine on the E to North Sea & France on the W

Central India former group of 89 Indian states N *cen* India ✳ Indore; area now chiefly in W & N Madhya Pradesh

Central Karroo — see KARROO

Central Provinces and Be·rar \bä-'rär, bə-\ former province of India reorganized 1950 & renamed Madhya Pradesh

Central Valley valley *cen* Calif. comprising the valleys of the Sacramento & San Joaquin rivers

Ceos — see KEA

Ceph·a·lo·nia \se-fə-'lō-nyə, -nē-ə\ *or NGk* **Ke·fal·li·nía** \ke-fä-lä-'nē-ä\ island W Greece in the Ionians *area* 288 *sq mi* (746 *sq km*)

Ce·ram *or* **Se·ram** \'sā-,räm\ island E Indonesia in *cen* Moluccas *area* 6621 *sq mi* (17,215 *sq km*), *pop* 96,797

Ce·res \'sir-(,)ēz\ city *cen* Calif. SE of Modesto *pop* 26,314

Cernauti — see CHERNIVTSI

Cer·re·do \se-'rā-(,)thō\ *or* **Tor·re de Cerredo** \'tōr-ā-thā-\ mountain 8787 *ft* (2678 *m*) N Spain SW of Santander; highest in the Cantabrians

Cer·ri·tos \sə-'rē-təs\ city SW Calif. NE of Long Beach *pop* 53,240

Cerro Bolívar — see CERRO BOLÍVAR (Cerro)

Cer·ro de Pas·co \'ser-ō-thä-'päs-(,)kō\ **1** mountain 15,100 *ft* (4602 *m*) *cen* Peru NE of Lima **2** city near the mountain *pop* 170,500

Cerro de Pun·ta \thä-'pün-tä\ mountain *ab* 4390 *ft* (1338 *m*), *cen* Puerto Rico in Cordillera Central; highest on the island

Cerro Gor·do \'gór-(,)dō\ mountain pass E Mexico bet. Veracruz & Jalapa

Cervin, Mont — see MATTERHORN

Ce·se·na \chā-'zā-nä\ *or anc* **Cae·se·na** \sə-'zē-nə\ commune N Italy in Emilia-Romagna SE of Forlì *pop* 89,606

Ces·ke Bu·de·jo·vi·ce \'ches-ke-'bü-de-,yó-vēt-se\ *or G* **Bud·weis** \'bút-,vīs\ city Czech Republic in S Bohemia *pop* 97,283

Ce·ti·nje \'(t)se-tē-,nyä\ town S Yugoslavia SE of Kotor near coast; formerly ✳ of Montenegro *pop* 20,258

Cette — see SÈTE

Ceu·ta \'thä-ü-,tä, 'syü-tä\ city & port N Morocco opposite Gibraltar; a Spanish presidio *pop* 73,483

Cé·vennes \sā-'ven\ mountain range S France W of the Rhône at E edge of Massif Central — see MÉZENC

Cey·lon \si-'län, sā-\ **1** *or Ar* **Ser·en·dib** \'ser-ən-,dib, -,dip\ *or L & Gk* **Ta·prob·a·ne** \tə-'präb-ə-(,)nē\ island 270 *mi* (434 *km*) long & 140 *mi* (225 *km*) wide in Indian Ocean off S India **2** — see SRI LANKA — **Cey·lon·ese** \sā-lə-'nēz, ,sē-, ,se-, -'nēs\ *adj or n*

Chaco — see GRAN CHACO

Chad *or F* **Tchad** \'chad\ country N *cen* Africa ✳ N'Djamena; a republic; until 1959 a territory of French Equatorial Africa *area* 495,752 *sq mi* (1,288,955 *sq km*), *pop* 5,200,000 — **Chad·ian** \'cha-dē-ən\ *adj or n*

Chad, Lake shallow lake N *cen* Africa at junction of boundaries of Chad, Niger, & Nigeria

Chae·ro·nea \,ker-ə-'nē-ə, ,kir-\ ancient city E *cen* Greece in W Boeotia SE of Mt. Parnassus

Cha·gos Archipelago \'chä-gəs\ archipelago *cen* Indian Ocean S of Maldives; comprises Brit. Indian Ocean Territory — see DIEGO GARCIA

Cha·gres \'chä-grəs, 'cha-\ river Panama flowing through Gatun Lake to the Caribbean

Cha·gua·ra·mas \chä-gwä-'rä-mäs\ district NW Trinidad W of Port of Spain on **Chaguaramas Bay** (inlet of Gulf of Paria)

Cha·har \'chä-'här\ former province NE China in E Inner Mongolia ✻ Kalgan

Chalcedon — see KADIKOY

Chal·cid·i·ce \kal-'si-də-(‚)sē\ *or Gk* **Khal·ki·di·kí** \‚käl-kē-thē-'kē\ peninsula NE Greece in E Macedonia projecting SE into N Aegean Sea; terminates in three peninsulas, the most notable of which is Acte — see ACTE

Chalcis — see KHALKÍS — **Chal·cid·i·an** \kal-'si-dē-ən\ *adj or n*

Chal·dea \kal-'dē-ə\ ancient region SW Asia on Euphrates River & Persian Gulf — **Chal·da·ic** \kal-'dā-ik, kòl-, käl-\ *adj or n* — **Chal·de·an** \kal-'dē-ən, kòl-, käl-\ *adj or n* — **Chal·dee** \'kal-‚dē, 'kòl-, 'käl-\

Cha·leur Bay \shə-'lùr, -'lər\ inlet of Gulf of St. Lawrence SE Canada bet. N N.B. & Gaspé Peninsula, Que.

Cha·lon \shà-'lō⁽ⁿ⁾\ *or* **Chalon-sur-Saône** \-‚sùer-'sòn\ city E *cen* France N of Mâcon *pop* 56,259

Châ·lons \shä-'lō⁽ⁿ⁾\ *or* **Châlons-sur-Marne** \-‚sùer-'märn\ commune NE France on the Marne *pop* 51,533

Cham·bal \'chəm-bəl\ river 650 *mi* (1046 *km*) *cen* India flowing from Vindhya Mountains E into the Yamuna

Cham·bé·ry \shä⁽ⁿ⁾-bā-'rē\ city E France E of Lyon *pop* 55,603

Cham·bord \shä⁽ⁿ⁾-'bór\ village N *cen* France NE of Blois *pop* 214

Cha·mi·zal \‚shä-mə-'zäl, ‚chä-mi-'säl\ tract of land 437 *acres* (177 *hectares*) on N bank of the Rio Grande formerly in El Paso, Tex.; ceded to Mexico 1963 — see CORDOVA ISLAND

Cha·mo·nix \‚shà-mō-'nē\ **1** valley SE France NW of Mont Blanc **2** *or* **Chamonix–Mont-Blanc** \-(‚)mō⁽ⁿ⁾-'blä⁽ⁿ⁾\ town SE France in Chamonix valley *pop* 5907

Cham·pagne \sham-'pān\ region & former province NE France W of Lorraine & N of Burgundy ✻ Troyes

Cham·paign \sham-'pān\ city E *cen* Ill. *pop* 63,502

Cham·pi·gny–sur–Marne \shä⁽ⁿ⁾-(‚)pē-nyē-‚sùer-'märn\ commune N France, SSE suburb of Paris *pop* 80,189

Cham·plain, Lake \sham-'plān\ lake 125 *mi* (201 *km*) long bet. N.Y. & Vt. extending N into Que. *area* 430 *sq mi* (1114 *sq km*)

Chan–chiang — see ZHENJIANG

Chan·der·na·gore \‚chən-dər-nə-'gòr, -'gòr\ *or* **Chan·dan·na·gar** \‚chən-də-'nə-gər\ *or* **Chan·dar·na·gar** \-dər-'nə-gər\ *or* **Chan·der·na·gor** \-nə-'gòr\ city E India in W. Bengal N of Calcutta; before 1950 part of French India *pop* 421,256

Chan·di·garh \'chən-dē-gər\ city N India N of Delhi; a union territory administered by the national government; ✻ of Punjabi Suba & of Haryana; founded 1953, *pop* 510,565

Chan·dler \'chan(d)-lər\ city SW *cen* Ariz. *pop* 90,533

Chan·dra·pur \'chən-drə-'pùr\ *or formerly* **Chan·da** \'chən-də\ town *cen* India in E Maharashtra *pop* 225,841; ✻ of anc. Gond dynasty

Chang \'chäŋ\ *or* **Yang·tze** \'yaŋ-'sē, 'yaŋ(k)t-'sē; 'yäŋ-'tsə\ river 3434 *mi* (5525 *km*) *cen* China flowing from Kunlun Mountains in SW Qinghai E into E. China Sea

Changan — see XI'AN

Ch'ang-chia-k'ou — see ZHANGJIAKOU

Chang-chou — see ZHANGZHOU

Chang·chun \'chäŋ-'chùn\ city NE China ✳ of Jilin *pop* 1,679,270

Chang·de *or* **Ch'ang-te** \'chäŋ-'də\ city SE *cen* China in N Hunan on the Yuan *pop* 301,276

Chang·sha \'chäŋ-'shä\ city SE *cen* China ✳ of Hunan on the Xiang *pop* 1,113,212

Chang·zhou *or* **Ch'ang-chou** \'chäŋ-'jō\ *or formerly* **Wu·tsin** \'wüd-'zin\ city E China in S Jiangsu *pop* 531,470

Channel Islands 1 *or* **Santa Barbara Islands** Calif. in the Pacific off SW coast — see CATALINA, SAN CLEMENTE ISLAND, SANTA CRUZ, SANTA ROSA ISLAND 2 islands in English Channel, a possession of Brit. Crown *area* 75 *sq mi* (195 *sq km*), *pop* 135,694 — see ALDERNEY, GUERNSEY, JERSEY, SARK

Channel Islands National Park reserve SW Calif. in Channel Islands including areas on Anacapa Islands (E of Santa Cruz Is.) & Santa Barbara Is. (W of Santa Catalina Is.)

Chan·til·ly \,shäⁿ-tē-'yē, shan-'ti-lē\ town N France NNE of Paris *pop* 11,525

Chao-'an \'chaù-'än\ *or* **Chao·zhou** *or* **Ch'ao-chou** *or* **Chao-chow** \'chaù-'jō\ city E China in NE Guangdong on Han River *pop* 101,000

Chao Phra·ya \chaù-'prī-ə, prä-'yä\ *or* **Me Nam** \mä-'näm\ river 227 *mi* (365 *km*) W *cen* Thailand formed by confluence of Nan & Ping rivers & flowing S into Gulf of Thailand

Cha·pa·la, Lake \chä-'pä-lä lake 50 *mi* (80 *km*) long W *cen* Mexico in Jalisco & Michoacán SE of Guadalajara

Chap·el Hill \'cha-pəl\ town N N.C. SW of Durham *pop* 38,719

Cha·rente \shä-'räⁿt\ river *ab* 225 *mi* (362 *km*) W France flowing W into Bay of Biscay

Cha·ri *or* **Sha·ri** \'shär-ē\ river *ab* 590 *mi* (949 *km*) N *cen* Africa in Chad flowing NW into Lake Chad

Char·i·ton \'shar-ə-tⁿn\ river 280 *mi* (451 *km*) S Iowa & N Mo. flowing S into the Missouri

Charle·roi \'shär-lə-,ròi, -lər-,wä\ city SW Belgium in Hainaut *pop* 206,800

Charles \'chär(-ə)lz\ river 47 *mi* (76 *km*) Mass. flowing into Boston harbor

Charles, Cape cape E Va. N of entrance to Chesapeake Bay

Charles·bourg \shärl-'bùr, 'chär(-ə)lz-,bərg\ city Canada in SE Que. NE of Quebec city *pop* 70,788

Charles·ton \'chär(-ə)l-stən\ 1 city E *cen* Ill. *pop* 20,398 2 city & port SE S.C. *pop* 80,414 3 city ✳ W. Va. on the Kanawha *pop* 57,287 — **Charles·to·nian** \,chär(-ə)l-'stō-nē-ən, -nyən\ *n*

Charleston Peak mountain 11,919 *ft* (3633 *m*) SE Nev. WNW of Las Vegas

Charles·town \'chär(-ə)lz-,taùn\ section of Boston, Mass., on Boston harbor between mouths of Charles & Mystic rivers

Char·lotte \'shär-lət\ city S N.C. near S.C. border *pop* 395,934

Charlotte Ama·lie \ə-'mäl-yə, 'a-mə-lē\ *or formerly* **Saint Thom·as** city & port ✳ of Virgin Islands of the U.S., on St. Thomas Is. *pop* 12,331

Charlotte Harbor inlet of Gulf of Mexico SW Fla.

Char·lottes·ville \'shär-ləts-,vil, -vəl\ city *cen* Va. *pop* 40,341

Char·lotte·town \'shär-lət-,taún\ city & port Canada ✳ of P.E.I. on Northumberland Strait *pop* 15,396

Chartres \'shärt, 'shärtrᵊ\ city N *cen* France SW of Paris *pop* 41,850

Châ·teau·guay \'sha-tə-,gā\ town Canada in S Que. SW of Montreal *pop* 39,833

Châ·teau·roux \,shá-tō-'rü\ commune *cen* France S of Orléans *pop* 35,691

Châ·teau–Thier·ry \,shà-,tō-,tye-'rē\ town N France on the Marne SW of Reims *pop* 15,830

Chat·ham \'cha-təm\ **1** — see SAN CRISTÓBAL **2** city Canada in SE Ont. E of Lake Saint Clair *pop* 43,557 **3** borough SE England in Kent *pop* 43,557

Chatham Islands islands S Pacific belonging to New Zealand & comprising two islands (Chatham & Pitt) *area* 372 *sq mi* (967 *sq km*)

Chatham Strait strait SE Alaska bet. Admiralty Is. & Kuiu Is. on E & Baranof Is. & Chichagof Is. on W

Chat·ta·hoo·chee \,cha-tə-'hü-chē\ river 436 *mi* (702 *km*) SE U.S. rising in N Ga., flowing SW & S along Ala.-Ga. boundary into Lake Seminole

Chat·ta·noo·ga \,cha-tə-'nü-gə, ,cha-tᵊn-'ü-\ city SE Tenn. on Tennessee River *pop* 152,466

Chau·tau·qua \shə-'tȯ-kwə\ lake 18 *mi* (29 *km*) long SW N.Y.

Che·bok·sa·ry \,che-,bäk-'sär-ē\ city Russia in Europe ✳ of Chuvash Republic WNW of Kazan *pop* 442,000

Che·cheno–In·gush Republic \,chə-,che-nō-in-'güsh\ former autonomous republic U.S.S.R. on N slopes of Caucasus Mountains; split into republics of Chechnya and Ingushetia within Russia 1992

Chech·nya *or* **Chech·e·nya** *or* **Chech·e·nia** \chech-'nyä, 'chech-nyə\ *or* **Che·chen Republic** \chi-'chen\ republic SE Russia in Europe on N slopes of Caucasus Mountains

Che·du·ba \chə-'dü-bə\ island W Myanmar *area* 202 *sq mi* (523 *sq km*), *pop* 2635

Chefoo — see YANTAI

Che·ju \'chā-,jü\ *or formerly* **Quel·part** \'kwel-,pärt\ island S. Korea in N E. China Sea *area* 706 *sq mi* (1829 *sq km*)

Chekiang — see ZHEJIANG

Che·lan, Lake \shə-'lan\ lake *ab* 55 *mi* (88 *km*) long N *cen* Wash.

Chelms·ford 1 \'chemz-fərd *also* 'chelmz-\ town NE Mass. S of Lowell *pop* 32,383 **2** \'chelmz-, 'chemz-\ borough SE England ✳ of Essex *pop* 150,000

Chel·sea \'chel-sē\ **1** city E Mass. NE of Boston *pop* 28,710 **2** former metropolitan borough SW London, England, on N bank of Thames River, now part of Kensington and Chelsea

Chel·ten·ham \'chelt-nəm, -nᵊn-əm, -nᵊn-,ham\ borough SW *cen* England in Gloucestershire *pop* 85,900

Che·lya·binsk \chel-'yä-bən(t)sk\ city W Russia in Asia S of Sverdlovsk *pop* 1,143,000

Che·lyu·skin, Cape \chel-'yü-skən\ headland Russia in Asia on Taymyr Peninsula; northernmost point of Asian mainland, at 77°35′N, 105°E

Chem·nitz \'kem-ˌnits, -nəts\ or 1953–90 **Karl–Marx–Stadt** \(ˌ)kärl-'märk-ˌshtät, -ˌstät\ city E Germany SE of Leipzig pop 287,511

Chemulpo — see INCHON

Che·nab \chə-'näb\ river ab 600 mi (965 km) NW India (subcontinent) in Kashmir & the Punjab flowing SW to unite with the Sutlej forming the Panjnad

Chen–chiang — see ZHENJIANG

Cheng–chou — see ZHENGZHOU

Cheng·de or **Ch'eng–te** \'chəŋ-'də\ or **Je·hol** \jə-'hōl, 'rō-'hō\ city NE China in NE Hebei NE of Beijing pop 246,799

Cheng·du or **Ch'eng–tu** \'chəŋ-'dü\ city SW cen China ✳ of Szechwan on Min River pop 1,713,255

Chenstokhov — see CZESTOCHOWA

Cher \'sher\ river 217 mi (349 km), cen France flowing into the Loire

Cher·bourg \'sher-ˌbür(g), sher-'bür\ city & port NW France on Cotentin Peninsula on English Channel pop 28,773

Che·rem·kho·vo \chə-'rem-kə-vō, ˌcher-əm-'kȯ-və\ city Russia in Asia NW of Irkutsk pop 73,600

Cher·kessk \chir-'kyesk\ city S Russia in Europe in N Caucasus region SE of Stavropol ✳ of Karachay-Cherkessia pop 119,000

Cher·ni·gov \chir-'nē-gəf\ city N Ukraine pop 306,000

Cher·niv·tsi \chir-'nift-sē\ or **Cher·nov·tsy** \chir-'nȯft-sē\ or Romanian **Cer·na·uti** \ˌcher-nə-'üts, -'üt-sē\ city W Ukraine on the Prut near Romania border pop 259,000

Cher·no·byl \chər-'nō-bəl, (ˌ)cher-\ site N Ukraine of town abandoned after 1986 nuclear accident

Cher·o·kee Outlet \ˌcher-ə-(ˌ)kē\ strip of land N Okla. along S border of Kans. E of 100° W opened to settlement 1893; 50 mi (80 km) wide, ab 220 mi (354 km) long

Cher·so·nese \'kər-sə-ˌnēz, -ˌnēs\ or anc **Cher·so·ne·sus** \ˌkər-sə-'nē-səs\ any of several peninsulas: as (1) Jutland (the **Cim·bri·an Chersonese** \'sim-brē-ən\ or **Cim·bric Chersonese** \-brik\); (2) the Malay Peninsula (the **Golden Chersonese**); (3) the Crimea (the **Tau·ric Chersonese** \'tȯr-ik\); (4) the Gallipoli Peninsula (the **Thra·cian Chersonese** \'thrā-shən\)

Cher·well \'chär-wəl\ river 30 mi (48 km) cen England in Northamptonshire & Oxfordshire flowing S into the Thames at Oxford

Ches·a·peake \'che-sə-ˌpēk, 'ches-ˌpēk\ city SE Va. S of Norfolk pop 151,976

Chesapeake Bay inlet of the Atlantic 193 mi (311 km) long in Va. & Md.

Chesh·ire \'che-shər, -ˌshir\ **1** town S Conn. SW of Meriden pop 25,684 **2** or **Ches·ter** \'ches-tər\ county NW England ✳ Chester area 929 sq mi (2406 sq km), pop 937,300

Ches·ter \'ches-tər\ **1** city SE Pa. pop 41,856 **2** city NW England ✳ of Cheshire on Dee River pop 58,436

Ches·ter·field \'ches-tər-ˌfēld\ **1** city E Mo. W of St. Louis *pop* 37,991 **2** borough N *cen* England in Derbyshire S of Sheffield *pop* 99,700

Chesterfield Inlet inlet N Canada on NW coast of Hudson Bay

Che·tu·mal \ˌchā-tü-ˈmäl\ city SE Mexico ✻ of Quintana Roo

Chev·i·ot \'che-vē-ət, 'che-\ peak 2676 *ft* (816 *m*) highest in the Cheviot Hills

Cheviot Hills hills extending NE to SW along English-Scottish border

Chey·enne \shī-'an, -'en\ **1** river 527 *mi* (850 *km*) S. Dak. flowing NE into Missouri River **2** city ✻ of Wyo. *pop* 50,008

Chia–i \'jyä-'ē\ city W *cen* Taiwan *pop* 258,664

Chia–mu–ssu — see JIAMUSI

Chiang Mai \'jyäŋ-'mī\ city NW Thailand on the Ping *pop* 161,541

Chia·pas \chē-'ä-päs\ state SE Mexico bordering on the Pacific ✻ Tuxtla Gutiérrez *area* 28,528 *sq mi* (73,888 *sq km*), *pop* 3,210,496

Chi·ba \'chē-bä\ city E Japan in Honshu on Tokyo Bay E of Tokyo *pop* 829,467

Chi·ca·go \shə-'kä-(ˌ)gō, -'kȯ-, -gə\ **1** river Chicago, Ill., having two branches (N. Branch & S. Branch) & orig. flowing E into Lake Michigan but now flowing S through S. Branch & Chicago Sanitary & Ship Canal into Des Plaines River **2** city & port NE Ill. on Lake Michigan *pop* 2,783,726 — **Chi·ca·go·an** \-'kä-gō-ən, -'kȯ-\ *n*

Chicago Heights city NE Ill. S of Chicago *pop* 33,072

Chich·a·gof \'chi-chə-ˌgȯf, -ˌgäf\ island SE Alaska in Alexander Archipelago N of Baranof Is. *area* 2100 *sq mi* (5460 *sq km*)

Chi·chén It·zá \chē-ˌchen-ēt-'sä, -'ēt-sə\ village SE Mexico in Yucatán ESE of Mérida at site of ruins of important Mayan city

Chich·es·ter \'chi-chəs-tər\ city & borough S England ENE of Portsmouth ✻ of W. Sussex *pop* 24,189

Ch'i–ch'i–ha–erh — see QIQIHAR

Chick·a·hom·i·ny \ˌchi-kə-'hä-mə-nē\ river 90 *mi* (145 *km*) E Va. flowing SE into James River

Chi·cla·yo \chē-'klī-(ˌ)ō\ city NW Peru near coast *pop* 419,600

Chi·co \'chē-(ˌ)kō\ city W Calif. N of Sacramento *pop* 40,079

Chic·o·pee \'chi-kə-(ˌ)pē\ city SW Mass. *pop* 56,632

Chi·cou·ti·mi \shə-'kü-tə-mē\ **1** river 100 *mi* (161 *km*) Canada in S Que. flowing N into the Saguenay **2** city Canada in S *cen* Que. on the Saguenay *pop* 62,670

Chihli — see HEBEI

Chihli, Gulf of — see BO HAI

Chi·hua·hua \chē-'wä-(ˌ)wä, chə-, -wə\ **1** state N Mexico bordering on the U.S. *area* 95,400 *sq mi* (247,086 *sq km*), *pop* 2,441,873 **2** city, its ✻ *metropolitan area pop* 530,487

Chi·le \'chi-lē, 'chē-(ˌ)lā\ country S S. America bet. the Andes & the Pacific; a republic ✻ Santiago *area* 292,257 *sq mi* (756,946 *sq km*), *pop* 11,275,440 — **Chil·e·an** \'chi-lē-ən, chə-'lā-ən\ *adj or n*

Chil·koot \'chil-ˌküt\ pass 3502 *ft* (1067 *m*) bet. SE Alaska & SW Yukon Territory, Canada, in N Coast Mountains

Chil·li·cothe \ˌchi-lə-'kä-thē, -'kȯ-\ city S Ohio *pop* 21,923

Chil·li·wack \'chi-lə-ˌwak\ municipality Canada in S B.C. *pop* 49,531

Chi·loé \chē-lō-ˈā\ island S cen Chile area 4700 sq mi (12,220 sq km), pop 65,161

Chil·pan·cin·go \ˌchēl-pän-ˈsēŋ-(ˌ)gō\ city S Mexico ✻ of Guerrero pop 136,243

Chil·tern Hills \ˈchil-tərn\ hills S cen England in Oxfordshire, Buckinghamshire, Hertfordshire, & Bedfordshire

Chi·lung \jē-ˈlúŋ\ or **Keelung** \ˈkē-ˈlúŋ\ city & port N Taiwan pop 347,828

Chim·bo·ra·zo \ˌchēm-bō-ˈrä-(ˌ)zō\ mountain 20,561 ft (6267 m) in cen Ecuador

Chimkent — see SHYMKENT

China, People's Republic of \ˈchī-nə\ country E Asia; a republic, ✻ Beijing; area 3,691,502 sq mi (9,597,905 sq km), pop 1,179,467,000 — **Chi·nese** \chī-ˈnēz, -ˈnēs\ adj or n

China, Republic of — see TAIWAN

Chinan — see JINAN

China Sea the E. & S. China seas

Chin–chou, Chinchow — see JINZHOU

Chin·co·teague Bay \ˌshiŋ-kə-ˈtēg\ bay Md. & Va. on Atlantic coast

Chin·dwin \ˈchin-ˈdwin\ river NW Myanmar flowing S into the Ir-rawaddy

Chinese Turkestan region W China in W & cen Xinjiang Uygur

Ch'ing Hai — see QINGHAI

Chin Hills \ˈchin\ hills W Myanmar; highest Mt. Victoria 10,016 ft (3053 m)

Ch'in–huang–tao, Chin·wang·tao — see QINHUANGDAO

Chinkiang — see ZHENJIANG

Chinnampo — see NAMPO

Chinnereth, Sea of — see GALILEE (Sea of)

Chi·no \ˈchē-(ˌ)nō\ city SW Calif. E of Los Angeles pop 59,682

Chiog·gia \kē-ˈò-jä\ commune & port NE Italy on island in Lagoon of Venice pop 52,582

Chi·os \ˈkī-ˌäs\ or NGk **Khí·os** \ˈkē-ˌós\ **1** island E Greece in the Aegean off W coast of Turkey area 325 sq mi (842 sq km) pop 52,691 **2** city & port Greece on E shore of Chios Is. — **Chi·an** \ˈkī-ən\ adj or n

Chip·pe·wa \ˈchip-ə-ˌwò, -ˌwä, -ˌwā, -wə\ river 183 mi (294 km) NW Wis. flowing S into Mississippi River

Chir·i·ca·hua National Monument \ˌchir-ə-ˈkä-wə, locally also ˈchir-ə-ˌkaú\ reservation SE Ariz. containing curious natural rock formations

Chiriquí — see BARÚ

Chis·holm Trail \ˈchi-zəm\ pioneer cattle trail bet. San Antonio (Tex.) & Abilene (in E cen Kans.), used esp. 1866–85

Chi·și·nău \ˌkē-shē-ˈnaú\ or **Ki·shi·nev** \ˌki-shi-ˈnyóf; ˈki-shə-ˌnef, -ˌnev\ city cen Moldova, its ✻ pop 665,000

Chis·le·hurst and Sid·cup \ˈchi-zəl-ˌhorst-ən(d)-ˈsid-kəp\ former urban district SE England in Kent, now partly in Bexley, partly in Bromley

Chi·ta \chi-ˈtä, ˈchē-\ city Russia in Asia E of Lake Baikal pop 377,000

Chi·tral \chi-ˈträl\ river 300 mi (483 km) N Pakistan & Afghanistan flowing SW into Kabul River

Chit·ta·gong \'chi-tə-ˌgäŋ, -ˌgòŋ\ city & port SE Bangladesh on Bay of Bengal *pop* 1,566,070

Chi·tun·gwi·za \ˌchē-tüŋ-'gwē-zä\ city NE *cen* Zimbabwe, SSE of Harare *pop* 274,035

Chiu·si \'kyü-sē\ *or anc* **Clu·si·um** \'klü-zhē-əm, -zē-\ town *cen* Italy in Tuscany SE of Siena

Chkalov — see ORENBURG

Choaspes — see KARKHEH

Choi·seul \shwä-'zə(r)l, -'zē\ island W Pacific in the Solomons SE of Bougainville Is.; nearly surrounded by barrier reef

Choi·sy \shwä-'zē\ *or* **Choi·sy–le–Roi** \shwä-ˌzē-lər-'wä\ commune N France on the Seine SSE of Paris *pop* 38,629

Cho·lon \shə-'lōn, chə-'lən\ former city S Vietnam, now part of Ho Chi Minh City

Cho·lu·la \chō-'lü-lä\ town SE *cen* Mexico in Puebla state

Cho·mo Lha·ri \ˌchō-mō-'lär-ē\ mountain 23,997 *ft* (7314 *m*) in the Himalayas bet. Tibet & NW Bhutan; sacred to Buddhists

Chomolungma — see EVEREST (Mount)

Ch'ong·ju \'chȯŋ-ˌjü\ city W *cen* S. Korea N of Taejon *pop* 350,256

Chong·qing *or* **Ch'ung–ch'ing** \'chùŋ-'chin\ *or* **Chung·king** \'chùŋ-'kiŋ\ city SE Sichuan on the Chang; ✳ of China 1937–43 *pop* 2,266,772

Chon·ju \'jən-ˌjü\ city SW S. Korea SW of Taejon *pop* 426,473

Cho Oyu \'chō-ō-'yü\ mountain 26,750 *ft* (8153 *m*) Nepal & Tibet in the Himalayas; 6th highest in the world

Cho·ras·mia \kə-'raz-mē-ə\ province of ancient Persia on Oxus River extending W to Caspian Sea; equivalent to Khwarazm — see KHIVA

Cho·rzow \'kȯ-ˌzhüf, 'kȯ-, -ˌzhüv\ city SW Poland in Silesia *pop* 132,674

Chosen — see KOREA

Cho·ta Nag·pur \'chō-tə-'näg-ˌpùr\ plateau region E India N of Mahanadi basin in N Orissa & S Bihar

Chou–shan — see ZHOUSHAN

Cho·wan \chə-'wän\ river 50 *mi* (80 *km*) NE N.C. flowing into Albemarle Sound

Christ·church \'krīs(t)-ˌchərch\ city New Zealand on E coast of South Is. *pop* 292,858 — see LYTTELTON

Christiania — see OSLO

Chris·tian·sted \'kris-chən-ˌsted, 'krish-\ town Virgin Islands of the U.S. on N coast of St. Croix Is. *pop* 2555

Christ·mas Island \'kris-məs\ **1** island E Indian ocean 225 *mi* (360 *km*) S of W end of Java; administered by Australia *area* 52 *sq mi* (135 *sq km*), *pop* 1200 **2** — see KIRITIMATI

Chu \'chü\ **1** — see ZHU **2** river *over* 1000 *mi* (1609 *km*) SE Kazakhstan flowing E into Issyk Kul

Ch'üan–chou, Chuanchow — see QUANZHOU

Chubb Crater — see NEW QUEBEC CRATER

Chu·but \chü-'büt, -'vüt\ river 500 *mi* (805 *km*) S Argentina flowing E across Patagonia into the Atlantic

Chu–chou, Chuchow — see ZHUZHOU

Chudskoe — see PEIPUS

Chu·gach Mountains \\'chü-,gach *also* -,gash\\ mountains S Alaska extending along coast from Cook Inlet to St. Elias Range; highest 13,176 *ft* (4016 *m*)

Chuk·chi Peninsula \\'chək-chē, 'chúk-\\ peninsula NE Russia in Asia, bet. Bering & Chukchi seas

Chukchi Sea sea of the Arctic Ocean N of Bering Strait

Chu·la Vis·ta \\,chü-lə-'vis-tə\\ city SW Calif. S of San Diego *pop* 135,163

Chu·lym *or* **Chu·lim** \\chə-'lim\\ river Russia in Asia flowing W into the Ob

Ch'ung–ch'ing, Chungking — see CHONGQING

Chur \\'kùr\\ *or* F **Coire** \\'kwär\\ commune E Switzerland ✳ of Graubünden canton *pop* 31,078

Chur·chill \\'chər-,chil\\ **1** river *ab* 1000 *mi* (1609 *km*) Canada flowing E across N Sask. & N Man. into Hudson Bay **2** *or formerly* **Hamilton** river 208 *mi* (335 *km*) Canada in Nfld. in S cen Labrador flowing E to Lake Melville

Churchill Falls *or formerly* **Grand Falls** waterfall 245 *ft* (75 *m*) high Canada in W Labrador in Churchill River

Chuuk \\'chük\\ *or* **Truk** \\'trək, 'trúk\\ islands cen Carolines, part of Federated States of Micronesia

Chu·vash Republic \\chü-'väsh\\ autonomous republic E cen Russia in Europe S of the Volga ✳ Cheboksary area 7066 *sq mi* (18,301 *sq km*), *pop* 1,393,000

Chu·zen·ji \\chü-'zen-jē\\ lake Japan in cen Honshu W of Nikko

Cí·bo·la \\'sē-bə-lə, 'si-\\ historical region in present N N. Mex. including seven pueblos (the **Seven Cities of Cíbola**) believed by early Spanish explorers to contain vast treasures

Cic·ero \\'si-sə-,rō\\ town NE Ill. W of Chicago *pop* 67,436

Cien·fue·gos \\syen-'fwä-(,)gōs\\ city & port W cen Cuba on S coast on Cienfuegos Bay *pop* 123,600

Cie·szyn \\'che-shin\\ *or* G **Te·schen** \\'te-shən\\ region cen Europe in Silesia; once an Austrian duchy; divided 1920 bet. Poland & Czechoslovakia (now the Czech Republic)

Ci·la·cap *or* **Tji·la·tjap** \\chē-'lä-chäp\\ city & port Indonesia in S Java ESE of Bandung

Ci·li·cia \\sə-'li-sh(ē-)ə\\ ancient country SE Asia Minor extending along Mediterranean coast S of Taurus Mountains — see LITTLE ARMENIA — **Ci·li·cian** \\-'li-shən\\ *adj or n*

Cilician Gates mountain pass S Turkey in Taurus Mountains

Cim·ar·ron \\'si-mə-,rän, -,rōn, -,rən\\ river flowing E from NE N. Mex. through SW Kans. into Arkansas River in NE Okla.

Cimbrian Chersonese, Cimbric Chersonese — see CHERSONESE

Cim·me·ri·an Bosporus \\sə-'mir-ē-ən\\ KERCH STRAIT

Cin·cin·nati \\,sin(t)-sə-'na-tē, -'na-tə\\ city SW Ohio on Ohio River *pop* 364,040 — **Cin·cin·nat·i·an** \\-'na-tē-ən\\ *n*

Cinque Ports \\'siŋk\\ group of seaport towns SE England on coast of Kent & Sussex, orig. five (Dover, Sandwich, Romney, Hastings, & Hythe) to which were later added Winchelsea, Rye, & other minor places, granted special privileges (abolished in 19th century) in return for services in coast defense

Cintra — see SINTRA

Circars — see NORTHERN CIRCARS

Cir·cas·sia \(ˌ)sər-'ka-sh(ē-)ə\ region S Russia in Europe on Black Sea N of W end of Caucasus Mountains — **Cir·cas·sian** \-ən\ *adj or n*

Ci·re·bon \ˈchē-re-ˈbȯn\ city Indonesia in W Java on N coast E of Jakarta *pop* 245,307

Cirenaica — see CYRENAICA

Cis·al·pine Gaul \(ˌ)sis-ˈal-ˌpīn\ the part of Gaul lying S & E of the Alps

Ciscaucasia — see CAUCASIA

Cis·kei \ˈsis-ˌkī\ former black enclave in the Republic of South Africa ✻ Bisho; granted independence 1981; abolished 1994 — **Cis·kei·an** \(ˌ)sis-ˈkī-ən\ *adj or n*

Ci·thae·ron \sə-ˈthē-ˌrän\ *or NGk* **Ki·thai·rón** \ˌkē-the-ˈrȯn\ *or formerly* **El·a·tea** \ˌe-lə-ˈtē-ə\ mountain 4623 *ft* (1409 *m*) Greece on NW border of ancient Attica

Ci·tlal·te·petl \sēt-ˌläl-ˈtä-ˌpe-tᵊl\ *or* **Ori·za·ba** \ˌȯr-ə-ˈzä-bə, ˌō-rē-ˈsä-vä\ inactive volcano 18,700 *ft* (5700 *m*) SE Mexico on Puebla-Veracruz boundary; highest mountain in Mexico & 3d highest in N. America

Cit·rus Heights \ˈsi-trəs\ urban center N *cen* Calif. NE of Sacramento *pop* 107,439

Città del Vaticano — see VATICAN CITY

Ciu·dad Bo·lí·var \syü-ˈthäth-bō-ˈlē-ˌvär, ˌsē-ü-ˈdad-\ city & port E *cen* Venezuela on the Orinoco *pop* 225,846

Ciudad Gua·ya·na \gwä-ˈyä-nä\ city E Venezuela near junction of the Caroní & the Orinoco *pop* 536,506

Ciudad Juá·rez *or* **Juárez** \ˈhwär-es, -wär-\ city Mexico in Chihuahua on Rio Grande opposite El Paso, Tex. *pop* 789,522

Ciudad Re·al \rā-ˈäl\ **1** province S *cen* Spain *area* 7625 *sq mi* (17,749 *sq km*), *pop* 475,435 **2** commune, its ✻, S of Toledo *pop* 56,315

Ciudad Trujillo — see SANTO DOMINGO

Ciudad Vic·to·ria \vik-ˈtȯr-ē-ə, -ˈtȯr-\ city E *cen* Mexico ✻ of Tamaulipas *pop* 94,304

Ci·vi·ta·vec·chia \ˌchē-ˌvē-tä-ˈve-(ˌ)kyä\ commune & port *cen* Italy in Lazio on Tyrrhenian Sea WNW of Rome *pop* 50,856

Clack·man·nan \klak-ˈma-nən\ *or* **Clack·man·nan·shire** \-ˌshir, -shər\ **1** former county *cen* Scotland bordering on the Forth **2** town, its ✻

Clac·ton \ˈklak-tən\ *or* **Clacton–on–Sea** town SE England in Essex on North Sea *pop* 43,571

Clare \ˈklär, ˈkler\ county N Ireland in Munster ✻ Ennis *area* 1231 *sq mi* (3201 *sq km*), *pop* 90,918

Clare·mont \-ˌmänt\ city SW Calif. E of Los Angeles *pop* 32,503

Clark Fork \ˈklärk\ river 300 *mi* (483 *km*) W Mont. & N Idaho flowing NW into Pend Oreille Lake

Clarks·dale \ˈklärks-ˌdāl\ city NW Miss. *pop* 19,717

Clarks·ville \ˈklärks-ˌvil, -vəl\ **1** town S Ind. *pop* 19,833 **2** city N Tenn. NW of Nashville *pop* 75,494

Clear·field \ˈklir-ˌfēld\ city N Utah S of Ogden *pop* 21,435

Clear·wa·ter \ˈklir-ˌwȯ-tər, -ˌwä-\ city W Fla. NW of St. Petersburg on Gulf of Mexico *pop* 98,784

Clearwater Mountains mountains N *cen* Idaho; highest *ab* 8000 *ft* (2438 *m*)

Cle·burne \'klē-bərn\ city NE *cen* Tex. *pop* 22,205

Clee Hills \'klē\ hills W England in S Shropshire

Cler·mont–Fer·rand \kler-ˌmōⁿ-fe-'räⁿ\ city S *cen* France in Allier valley on edge of Auvergne Mountains *pop* 140,167

Cleve·land \'klēv-lənd\ **1** city & port NE Ohio on Lake Erie *pop* 505,616 **2** city SE Tenn. ENE of Chattanooga *pop* 30,354 **3** county N England N of N. Yorkshire ✱ Middlesbrough *area* 233 *sq mi* (603 *sq km*), *pop* 541,100; includes the **Cleveland Hills** — **Cleve·land·er** \-lən-dər\ *n*

Cleveland, Mount mountain 10,455 *ft* (3185 *m*) N Mont., highest in Glacier National Park

Cleveland Heights city NE Ohio E of Cleveland *pop* 54,052

Cli·chy \klē-'shē\ commune N France NW of Paris *pop* 48,204

Cliff·side Park \'klif-(ˌ)sīd\ borough NE N.J. *pop* 20,393

Clif·ton \'klif-tən\ city NE N.J. N of Newark *pop* 71,742

Clinch \'klinch\ river *ab* 300 *mi* (480 *km*) SW Va. & E Tenn. flowing SW into Tennessee River

Cling·mans Dome \'kliŋ-mənz\ mountain 6643 *ft* (2025 *m*) on N.C.-Tenn. boundary; highest in Great Smoky Mountains

Clin·ton \'klin-tᵊn\ **1** city E Iowa on Mississippi River *pop* 29,201 **2** town SW *cen* Miss. *pop* 21,847

Clon·mel \klän-'mel\ town S Ireland ✱ of County Tipperary *pop* 11,759

Cloud Peak \'klaùd\ mountain 13,165 *ft* (4013 *m*) N Wyo.; highest in Bighorn Mountains

Clo·vis \'klō-vəs\ **1** city *cen* Calif. NE of Fresno *pop* 50,323 **2** city E N. Mex. *pop* 30,954

Cluj–Na·po·ca \'klüzh-'nä-pō-kə\ city NW *cen* Romania in Transylvania *pop* 317,914

Clu·ny \'klü-nē, klü-'\ town E *cen* France NNW of Lyon *pop* 4724

Clusium — see CHIUSI

Clu·tha \'klü-thə\ river 210 *mi* (338 *km*) New Zealand in SE South Is. flowing SE into the Pacific

Clwyd \'klü-id\ county NE Wales ✱ Mold *area* 937 *sq mi* (2436 *sq km*), *pop* 401,900

Clyde \'klīd\ river 106 *mi* (171 *km*) SW Scotland flowing NW into **Firth of Clyde** (estuary)

Clyde·bank \'klīd-ˌbaŋk\ burgh W *cen* Scotland in Strathclyde on Clyde River *pop* 46,920

Clydes·dale \'klīdz-ˌdāl\ valley of the upper Clyde River in Scotland

Cni·dus \'nī-dəs\ ancient town SW Asia Minor in Caria

Cnossus — see KNOSSOS

Coa·chel·la Valley \kō-'che-lə\ valley SE Calif. bet. Salton Sea & San Bernardino Mountains

Coa·hui·la \ˌkō-ä-'wē-lä, kwä-'wē-\ state N Mexico bordering on the U.S. ✱ Saltillo *area* 58,522 *sq mi* (151,572 *sq km*), *pop* 1,972,340

Coast Mountains mountains Canada in W B.C.; N continuation of Cascade Range

Coast Ranges mountain ranges W N. America extending along Pacific coast W of Sierra Nevada & Cascade Range & N through Vancouver Is., B.C., to Kenai Peninsula & Kodiak Is., Alaska — see LOGAN (Mount)

Coat·bridge \'kōt-(ˌ)brij\ burgh S *cen* Scotland in Strathclyde *pop* 50,866

Coats Land \'kōts\ section of Antarctica SE of Weddell Sea

Cobh \'kōv\ *or formerly* **Queens·town** \'kwēnz-ˌtaún\ town & port SW Ireland on island in Cork harbor *pop* 6369

Coblenz — see KOBLENZ

Co·burg 1 \'kō-ˌbərg\ city SE Australia in S Victoria, N suburb of Melbourne *pop* 50,625 **2** \-ˌbórg, -ˌbúrk\ city *cen* Germany in N Bavaria NW of Bayreuth *pop* 44,693

Co·cha·bam·ba \ˌkō-chä-'bäm-bä\ city W *cen* Bolivia *pop* 404,102

Co·chin \kō-'chin\ region SW India in Kerala on Malabar Coast — see TRAVANCORE

Co·chin China \'kō-ˌchin\ region S Vietnam bordering on S. China Sea & Gulf of Thailand *area* 29,974 *sq mi* (77,932 *sq km*)

Cochinos, Bahía de — see PIGS (Bay of)

Co·co \'kō-(ˌ)kō\ *or formerly* **Se·go·via** \sä-'gō-vyä, sə-, -vē-ä\ river *over* 450 *mi* (724 *km*) N Nicaragua flowing NE into the Caribbean & forming part of Honduras-Nicaragua boundary

Co·co·ni·no Plateau \ˌkō-kə-'nē-(ˌ)nō, -'nē-nə\ plateau NW Ariz. S of Grand Canyon

Co·co·nut Creek \'kō-kə-(ˌ)nət\ city SE Fla. NNW of Fort Lauderdale *pop* 27,485

Co·cos Islands \'kō-kəs\ *or* **Kee·ling Islands** \'kē-liŋ\ islands E Indian Ocean belonging to Australia *area* 5.5 *sq mi* (14 *sq km*), *pop* 600

Cod, Cape \'käd\ peninsula 65 *mi* (105 *km*) long SE Mass. — **Cape Cod·der** \'kä-dər\ *n*

Coele–Syria — see BEKAA

Coeur d'Alene \ˌkór-dᵊl-'ān\ city N Idaho *pop* 24,563

Coeur d'Alene Lake lake *ab* 37 *mi* (59 *km*) long N Idaho E of Spokane, Wash.; drained by Spokane River

Co·glians, Mon·te \ˌmōn-tā-kōl-'yän(t)s\ mountain 9217 *ft* (2809 *m*) on Austria-Italy border; highest in the Carnic Alps

Coim·ba·tore \ˌkóim-bə-'tōr, -'tór\ city S India in W Tamil Nadu on S slope of Nilgiri Hills *pop* 816,321

Co·im·bra \kō-'im-brə, kü-\ city W *cen* Portugal *pop* 145,724

Coire — see CHUR

Col·ches·ter \'kōl-ˌches-tər, -chəs-\ borough SE England in Essex *pop* 141,100

Col·chis \'käl-kəs\ ancient country bordering on Black Sea S of Caucasus Mountains; area now constitutes W part of Republic of Georgia — **Col·chi·an** \'käl-kē-ən\ *adj or n*

Cole·raine \kōl-'rān, 'kōl-\ district N Northern Ireland, established 1974 *area* 187 *sq mi* (484 *sq km*), *pop* 51,062

Co·li·ma \kō-'lē-mä\ **1** volcano SW Mexico in S Jalisco **2** state SW Mexico bordering on the Pacific *area* 2106 *sq mi* (5454 *sq km*), *pop* 428,510 **3** city, its ✻, SSW of Guadalajara *pop* 106,967

Col·lege Park \'kä-lij\ **1** city NW Ga. S of Atlanta *pop* 20,457 **2** city SW Md. NE of Washington, D.C. *pop* 21,927

College Station city E *cen* Tex. SE of Bryan *pop* 52,456

Col·lins·ville \'kä-lənz-ˌvil\ city SW Ill. NE of E. St. Louis *pop* 22,446

Col·mar *or G* **Kol·mar** \'kōl-ˌmär, kōl-\ commune NE France at E edge of Vosges Mountains *pop* 64,889

Co·logne \kə-'lōn\ *or G* **Köln** \'kœln\ city W Germany in N. Rhine-Westphalia on the Rhine *pop* 956,690

Colomb–Béchar — see BÉCHAR

Co·lombes \kȯ-'lōⁿb, -'lōm\ commune N France, NW suburb of Paris *pop* 79,058

Co·lom·bia \kə-'ləm-bē-ə *also* -'lōm-\ country NW S. America bordering on Caribbean Sea & Pacific Ocean ✻ Bogotá *area* 439,735 *sq mi* (1,138,914 *sq km*), *pop* 26,525,670 — **Co·lom·bi·an** \-bē-ən\ *adj or n*

Co·lom·bo \kə-'ləm-(,)bō\ city & port ✻ of Sri Lanka *pop* 615,000

Co·lón \kō-'lōn\ city & port N Panama on the Caribbean at entrance to Panama Canal *pop* 54,469

Colón, Archipiélago de — see GALÁPAGOS ISLANDS

Col·o·phon \'kä-lə-fən, -,fän\ ancient city W Asia Minor in Lydia

Col·o·ra·do \,kä-lə-'ra-(,)dō, -'rä-\ **1** river 1450 *mi* (2334 *km*) SW U.S. & NW Mexico rising in N Colo. & flowing SW into Gulf of California **2** river 600 *mi* (950 *km*) S Tex. flowing SE into Gulf of Mexico **3** state W U.S. ✻ Denver *area* 104,247 *sq mi* (271,042 *sq km*), *pop* 3,294,394 **4** river 530 *mi* (853 *km*) *cen* Argentina flowing SE to the Atlantic — **Col·o·ra·dan** \-'ra-dᵊn, -'rä-\ *adj or n* — **Col·o·ra·do·an** \-'ra-də-ən, -'rä-\ *adj or n*

Colorado Desert desert SE Calif. W of Colorado River

Colorado National Monument reservation W Colo. W of Grand Junction containing many unusual erosion formations

Colorado Plateau plateau SW U.S. W of Rocky Mountains in Colorado River basin in N Ariz., S & E Utah, W Colo., & NW N. Mex

Colorado Springs city *cen* Colo. E of Pikes Peak *pop* 281,140

Co·los·sae \kə-'lä-(,)sē\ ancient city SW *cen* Asia Minor in SW Phrygia — **Co·los·sian** \kə-'lä-shən\ *adj or n*

Col·ton \'kōl-tᵊn\ city SW Calif. S of San Bernardino *pop* 40,213

Co·lum·bia \kə-'ləm-bē-ə\ **1** river 1214 *mi* (1953 *km*) SW Canada & NW U.S. rising in SE B.C. & flowing S & W into the Pacific **2** city *cen* Mo. *pop* 69,101 **3** city ✻ of S.C. *pop* 98,052 **4** city *cen* Tenn. *pop* 28,583 — **Co·lum·bi·an** \-bē-ən\ *adj or n*

Columbia, Cape cape N Canada on Ellesmere Is.; northernmost point of Canada, at 83°07′N

Columbia, District of — see DISTRICT OF COLUMBIA

Columbia Plateau plateau E Wash., E Oreg., & SW Idaho in Columbia River basin

Co·lum·bus \kə-'ləm-bəs\ **1** city W Ga. on the Chattahoochee *pop* 178,681 **2** city S *cen* Ind. *pop* 31,802 **3** city E Miss. *pop* 23,799 **4** city E Nebr. *pop* 19,480 **5** city *cen* Ohio, its ✻ *pop* 632,910

Col·ville \'kōl-,vil, 'käl-\ river 375 *mi* (603 *km*) N Alaska flowing NE into Beaufort Sea

Col·wyn Bay \'käl-wən\ borough N Wales in Clwyd *pop* 26,278

Co·mil·la *or* **Ku·mil·la** \kủ-'mi-lə\ city E Bangladesh SE of Dhaka *pop* 164,509

Commander — see KOMANDORSKIE ISLANDS

Common Market — see EUROPEAN ECONOMIC COMMUNITY

Commonwealth of Independent States association of the former constituent republics of the U.S.S.R. except for Lithuania, Latvia, & Estonia; formed 1991

Commonwealth of Nations or **Commonwealth** political organization consisting of nations loyal to the British monarch

Com·mu·nism Peak \'käm-yə-ˌni-zəm\ or Russ **Pik Kom·mu·niz·ma** \'pēk-kə-mü-'nēs-mə\ mountain 24,590 ft (7495 m) NE Tajikistan in Pamirs; highest in Tajikistan & the former U.S.S.R.

Co·mo \'kō-(ˌ)mō\ commune N Italy in Lombardy at SW end of **Lake Como** (37 mi or 59 km long) pop 85,955

Co·mo·do·ro Ri·va·da·via \ˌkō-mō-'thōr-(ˌ)ō-ˌrē-vä-'thä-vē-ä\ city & port S Argentina pop 96,865

Com·o·rin, Cape \'kä-mə-rən; kə-'mōr-ən, -'mòr-, -'mär-\ cape S India in Tamil Nadu; southernmost point of India, at 8°5′N

Com·o·ros \'kä-mə-ˌrōz\ group of islands comprising a country off SE Africa bet. Mozambique & Madagascar; formerly a French possession; a republic (except for Mayotte Is., which remains French) since 1975 ✴ Moroni area 719 sq mi (1862 sq km), pop 519,527

Com·piègne \kōⁿ-'pyenʸ\ town N France on the Oise pop 44,703

Compostela — see SANTIAGO 3

Comp·ton \'käm(p)-tən\ city SW Calif. SSE of Los Angeles pop 90,454

Com·stock Lode \'käm-ˌstäk\ gold & silver lode at Virginia City, Nev.

Con·a·kry \'kä-nə-krē\ city & port ✴ of Guinea on the Atlantic pop 581,000

Co·nan·i·cut Island \kə-'na-ni-kət\ island R.I. in Narragansett Bay W of Aquidneck Is.

Con·cep·ción \ˌkōn-sep-'syón\ city S cen Chile pop 267,891

Con·chos \'kōn-(ˌ)chōs\ river 300 mi (483 km) N Mexico flowing NE into Rio Grande

Con·cord 1 \'kän-ˌkòrd, 'kän-\ city W Calif. NE of Oakland pop 111,348 **2** \'kän-kərd\ town E Mass. NW of Boston pop 17,076 **3** \'kän-kərd\ city ✴ of N.H. on the Merrimack pop 36,006 **4** \'kän-ˌkòrd, 'kän-\ city S cen N.C. pop 27,347

Co·ney Island \'kō-nē\ resort section of New York City in S Brooklyn; formerly an island

Con·ga·ree \'kän-gə-(ˌ)rē\ river 60 mi (96 km) cen S.C. flowing SE to unite with the Wateree forming the Santee

Congaree Swamp National Monument reservation cen S.C. S of Columbia

Con·go \'kän-(ˌ)gō\ **1** or **Zaire** river more than 2700 mi (4344 km) cen Africa flowing N, W & SW into the Atlantic — see LUALABA **2** or **Democratic Republic of the Congo** or 1971–97 **Za·ire** \zä-'ir\ or 1908–60 **Belgian Congo** or 1885–1908 **Congo Free State** country cen Africa comprising most of Congo River basin E of lower Congo River ✴ Kinshasa area 905,356 sq mi (2,344,872 sq km), pop 43,775,000 **3** or **Republic of the Congo** or formerly **Middle Congo** country W cen Africa W of the lower Congo ✴ Brazzaville area 132,047 sq mi (342,002 sq km), pop 2,775,000 — see FRENCH EQUATORIAL AFRICA — **Con·go·lese** \ˌkän-gə-'lēz, -'lēs\ adj or n

Con·nacht \'kä-ˌnòt\ or formerly **Con·naught** \'kä-ˌnòt\ province W Ireland area 6611 sq mi (17,189 sq km) pop 422,909

Con·nect·i·cut \kə-'ne-ti-kət\ **1** river 407 mi (655 km) NE U.S. rising in N N.H. & flowing S into Long Island Sound **2** state NE U.S. ✴ Hartford area 5018 sq mi (12,997 sq km), pop 3,287,116

Con·ne·ma·ra \,kä-nə-'mär-ə\ district Ireland in W Galway

Con·roe \'kän-(,)rō\ city E Tex. *pop* 27,610

Con·stance \'kän(t)-stən(t)s\ *or G* **Kon·stanz** \'kón-,stänts\ commune S Germany on Lake Constance *pop* 76,162

Constance, Lake *or G* **Bo·den·see** \-bō-d°n-,zā\ lake 46 *mi* (74 *km*) long W Europe on border bet. Germany, Austria, & Switzerland

Con·stan·ţa \kən-'stän(t)-sə\ city & port SE Romania on Black Sea *pop* 315,917

Con·stan·tine \'kän(t)-stən-,tēn\ city NE Algeria *pop* 440,842

Constantinople — see ISTANBUL — **Con·stan·ti·no·pol·i·tan** \,kän-,stan-t°n-ō-'pä-lə-t°n\ *adj*

Continental Divide *or* **Great Divide** the watershed of N. America comprising the line of highest points of land separating the waters flowing W from those flowing N or E coinciding with various ranges of the Rockies, and extending SSE from NW Canada to NW S. America

Con·way \'kän-,wā\ city *cen* Ark. N of Little Rock *pop* 26,481

Cooch Be·har \,küch-bə-'här\ former state NE India W of Assam; since 1947 attached to West Bengal

Cook, Mount \'kuk\ *or formerly* **Ao·rangi** \aù-'räṅ-ē\ mountain 12,349 *ft* (3764 *m*) New Zealand in W *cen* South Is.; highest peak in Southern Alps & New Zealand

Cooke·ville \'kuk-,vil, -vəl\ city N *cen* Tenn. *pop* 21,744

Cook Inlet inlet of the Pacific S Alaska W of Kenai Peninsula

Cook Islands islands S Pacific SW of Society Islands; self-governing territory of New Zealand ✻ Avarua (on Rarotonga Is.) *area* 92 *sq mi* (238 *sq km*), *pop* 17,614

Cooks·town \'kuks-,taún\ district *cen* Northern Ireland, established 1974 *area* 241 *sq mi* (627 *sq km*), *pop* 30,808

Cook Strait strait New Zealand bet. North Is. & South Is.

Coon Rapids \'kün\ city E Minn. N of St. Paul *pop* 52,978

Coo·per City \'kü-pər\ city SE Fla. WNW of Hollywood *pop* 20,791

Coorg *or* **Kurg** \'kùrg\ former state S India ✻ Mercara; merged with Mysore state (now Karnataka) 1956

Coo·sa \'kü-sə\ river 286 *mi* (460 *km*) NW Ga. & N Ala. flowing SW to join Tallapoosa River forming Alabama River

Coos Bay \'küs\ inlet of the Pacific SW Oreg.

Co·pán \kō-'pän\ ruins of Mayan city W Honduras

Co·pen·ha·gen \,kō-pən-'hā-gən, -'hä-; 'kō-pən-,\ *or Dan* **Kö·ben·havn** \,kœ-bən-'haún\ city & port ✻ of Denmark on E Sjælland Is. & N Amager Is. *pop* 467,850 — **Co·pen·ha·gen·er** \,kō-pən-'hā-gə-nər, -'hä-; 'kō-pən-,\ *n*

Co·pia·pó \,kō-pyä-'pō\ city N *cen* Chile *pop* 79,268

Cop·per·as Cove \'kä-p(ə-)rəs\ city *cen* Tex. *pop* 24,079

Cop·per·mine \'kä-pər-,mīn\ river 525 *mi* (845 *km*) N Canada in Northwest Territories flowing NW into Arctic Ocean

Coquilhatville — see MBANDAKA

Cor·al Ga·bles \'kór-əl-'gā-bəlz, 'kär-\ city SE Fla. SW of Miami *pop* 40,091

Coral Sea arm of the SW Pacific bounded on W by Queensland, Australia, on N by the Solomons, & on E by Vanuatu & New Caledonia

Coral Springs city SE Fla. *pop* 79,443

Cor·co·va·do \\,kȯr-kō-'vä-(,)dü\ mountain 2310 *ft* (704 *m*) SE Brazil on S side of city of Rio de Janeiro

Cor·dil·le·ra Cen·tral \\,kȯr-dᵊl-'yer-ə-,sen-'träl, ,kȯr-də-'ler-, ,kȯr-dē-'yer-\ **1** range of the Andes in Colombia **2** range of the Andes in Peru E of the Marañón **3** chief range of the Dominican Republic **4** range Philippines in N Luzon — see PULOG (Mount) **5** range S *cen* Puerto Rico — see CERRO DE PUNTA

Cordillera de Mé·ri·da \thä-'mā-rē-,thä\ *or* **Sier·ra Ne·va·da de Mérida** \'syer-ä-ne-'vä-thä-,thä\ mountain range W Venezuela — see BOLÍVAR (Pico)

Cór·do·ba \'kȯr-thō-bə, 'kȯr-thō-,vä\ **1** province S Spain *area* 5297 *sq mi* (13,179 *sq km*) *pop* 754,452 **2** *or* **Cor·do·va** \'kȯr-thō,vä\ city, its ✻, on the Guadalquivir *pop* 300,229 **3** city N *cen* Argentina *pop* 1,179,067 — **Cor·do·ban** \-bən\ *adj or n* — **Cor·do·van** \'kȯr-də-vən\ *adj*

Cor·do·va Island \'kȯr-də-və, 'kȯr-thō-,vä\ tract on the Rio Grande 385 *acres* (156 *hectares*) adjoining Chamizal, formerly belonging to Mexico; 193 *acres* (78 *hectares*) ceded to U.S. in 1963

Cor·fu \kȯr-'fü; 'kȯr-(,)fü, -(,)fyü\ *or NGk* **Kér·ky·ra** \'ker-kē-,rä\ *or anc* **Cor·cy·ra** \kȯr-'sī-rə\ **1** island NW Greece, one of the Ionian Islands *area* 229 *sq mi* (593 *sq km*) *pop* 105,043 **2** city & port on E Corfu *pop* 36,875 — **Cor·fi·ote** \'kȯr-fē-,ōt, -ət\ *n*

Cor·inth \'kȯr-ən(t)th, 'kär-\ *or NGk* **Kó·rin·thos** \'kȯr-ēn-,thȯs\ *or Lat* **Co·rin·thia** \kə-'rin(t)-thē-ə\ region of ancient Greece occupying most of Isthmus of Corinth & part of NE Peloponnese — **Co·rin·thi·an** \kə-'rin(t)-thē-ən\ *adj or n*

Corinth, Gulf of inlet of Ionian Sea *cen* Greece W of **Isthmus of Corinth** (neck of land 20 *mi* or 32 *km* long connecting Peloponnese with rest of Greece)

Cork \'kȯrk\ **1** county SW Ireland in Munster *area* 2880 *sq mi* (7459 *sq km*), *pop* 283,116 **2** city & port, its ✻, at head of Cork harbor *pop* 127,024

Corn \'kȯrn\ two small islands Nicaragua in the Caribbean

Cor·ner Brook \'kȯr-nər-,brük\ city Canada on W Nfld. on Gulf of Saint Lawrence *pop* 22,410

Corneto — see TARQUINIA

Cor·no, Mon·te \mȯn-tā-'kȯr-(,)nō\ mountain 9560 *ft* (2897 *m*) *cen* Italy NE of Rome; highest in the Apennines

Corn·wall \'kȯrn-,wȯl, -wəl\ **1** city Canada in SE Ont. *pop* 47,137 **2** *or since 1974* **Cornwall and Isles of Scil·ly** \'si-lē\ county SW England ✻ Bodmin & ✻ Truro *area* 1418 *sq mi* (3673 *sq km*), *pop* 469,300 — **Cor·nish** \'kȯr-nish\ *adj* — **Cor·nish·man** \-mən\ *n*

Co·ro \'kȯr-(,)ō, 'kȯr-\ city NW Venezuela near coast *pop* 124,616

Cor·o·man·del \,kȯr-ə-'man-dᵊl, ,kär-\ coast region SE India on Bay of Bengal S of the Krishna

Co·ro·na \kə-'rō-nə\ city SW Calif. E of Los Angeles *pop* 76,095

Co·ro·na·do \,kȯr-ə-'nä-(,)dō, ,kär-\ city SW Calif. on San Diego Bay opposite San Diego *pop* 26,540

Cor·pus Chris·ti \,kȯr-pəs-'kris-tē\ city & port S Tex. on **Corpus Christi Bay** (inlet of Gulf of Mexico) at mouth of the Nueces *pop* 257,453

Cor·reg·i·dor \kə-'re-gə-,dȯr\ island N Philippines at entrance to Manila Bay *area ab* 2 *sq mi* (5 *sq km*)

Cor·rien·tes \ˌkȯr-ē-ˈen-ˌtās\ city NE Argentina *pop* 267,742

Cor·si·ca \ˈkȯr-si-kə\ *or F* **Corse** \ˈkȯrs\ island France in the Mediterranean N of Sardinia *area* 3360 *sq mi* (8702 *sq km*), *pop* 250,634 — **Cor·si·can** \ˌkȯr-si-kən\ *adj or n*

Cor·si·ca·na \ˌkȯr-sə-ˈka-nə\ city NE Tex. *pop* 22,911

Cor·ti·na *or* **Cortina d'Am·pez·zo** \ˌkȯr-ˈtē-nä-ˌdäm-ˈpet-(ˌ)sō\ resort village N Italy in the Dolomites N of Belluno

Cort·land \ˈkȯrt-lənd\ city S *cen* N.Y. *pop* 19,801

Cor·to·na \kȯr-ˈtō-nä\ commune *cen* Italy NW of Perugia *pop* 22,352

Coruña, La; Corunna — see LA CORUÑA

Cor·val·lis \kȯr-ˈva-ləs\ city W Oreg. SW of Salem *pop* 44,757

Cos — see KOS

Co·sen·za \kō-ˈzen(t)-sä\ commune S Italy in Calabria *pop* 87,140

Cos·ta Bra·va \ˌkōs-tä-ˈbrä-vä, ˌkȯs-\ coast region NE Spain in Catalonia on the Mediterranean extending NE from Barcelona

Costa del Sol \-del-ˈsōl, -thel-, -ˈsōl\ coast region S Spain on the Mediterranean extending E from Gibraltar

Costa Me·sa \ˈmā-sə\ city SW Calif. SE of Long Beach on Pacific coast *pop* 96,357

Costa Ri·ca \ˈrē-kə\ country Central America bet. Nicaragua & Panama; a republic ✳ San José *area* 19,652 *sq mi* (50,899 *sq km*), *pop* 3,199,000 — **Cos·ta Ri·can** \-kən\ *adj or n*

Costermansville — see BUKAVU

Côte d'A·zur \ˌkōt-də-ˈzür, -dä-ˈzŭ̇r\ coast region SE France on the Mediterranean; part of the Riviera

Côte d'Ivoire — see IVORY COAST

Côte d'Or \kōt-ˈdȯr\ range of hills E France SW of Dijon

Co·ten·tin Peninsula \kō-ˌtäⁿ-ˈtaⁿ\ peninsula NW France projecting into English Channel W of mouth of the Seine

Côte–Saint–Luc \ˌkōt-saⁿ-ˈlük, -sänt-, -sənt-\ city Canada in S Que. W of Montreal *pop* 28,700

Co·to·nou \ˌkō-tō-ˈnü\ city & port S Benin, former ✳ of Dahomey *pop* 449,000

Co·to·paxi \ˌkō-tō-ˈpak-sē\ volcano 19,347 *ft* (5897 *m*) N *cen* Ecuador

Cots·wold \ˈkät-ˌswōld, -swəld\ hills SW *cen* England in Gloucestershire; highest point Cleeve Cloud 1031 *ft* (314 *m*)

Cot·tage Grove \ˈkä-tij\ city E Minn. *pop* 22,935

Cott·bus *or* **Kott·bus** \ˈkät-bəs, -ˌbu̇s\ city E Germany on Spree River SE of Berlin *pop* 123,321

Cot·ti·an Alps \ˈkä-tē-ən\ range of W Alps France & Italy — see VISO

Coun·cil Bluffs \ˌkau̇n(t)-səl-ˈbləfs\ city SW Iowa on Missouri River *pop* 54,315

Cou·ran·tyne \ˈkȯr-ən-ˌtīn, ˈkȯr-\ *or D* **Co·ran·tijn** \-ˌtīn\ river *ab* 475 *mi* (764 *km*) N S. America flowing N into the Atlantic & forming boundary bet. Guyana & Suriname

Cour·be·voie \ˌkür-bə-ˈvwä\ commune N France on the Seine NW of Paris *pop* 65,649

Cour·land \ˈku̇r-lənd, ˈkür-ˌlänt\ region W Latvia bordering on the Baltic & Gulf of Riga

Courland Lagoon *or Ger* **Kur·isch·es Haff** \'kûr-i-shəs-'häf\ *or Russ* **Kur·skiy Za·liv** \'kûr-skē-'zä-lif\ inlet of the Baltic on border bet. Lithuania & Russia *area* 625 *sq mi* (1625 *sq km*)

Cour·ma·yeur \,kûr-mə-'yər\ resort village NW Italy in Valle d'Aosta SE of Mont Blanc

Courtrai — see KORTRIJK

Cov·en·try 1 \'kə-vən-trē\ town W R.I. *pop* 31,083 **2** \'kä-, 'kə-\ city *cen* England in W. Midlands *pop* 292,500

Co·vi·na \kō-'vē-nä\ city SW Calif. E of Los Angeles *pop* 43,207

Cov·ing·ton \'kə-viŋ-tən\ city N Ky. *pop* 43,264

Cowes \'kauz\ town S England on Isle of Wight *pop* 19,663

Cow·litz \'kau-ləts\ river 130 *mi* (209 *km*) SW Wash. flowing into Columbia River

Co·zu·mel \,kō-sü-'mel, ,kä-zə-\ island SE Mexico off Quintana Roo

Cracow — see KRAKÓW

Craig·av·on \krā-'ga-vən\ district *cen* Northern Ireland, established 1974 *area* 147 *sq mi* (381 *sq km*), *pop* 74,494

Cra·io·va \krä-'yō-vä\ city S Romania *pop* 300,030

Cran·ston \'kran(t)-stən\ city E R.I. S of Providence *pop* 76,060

Cra·ter Lake \'krā-tər\ lake 1932 *ft* (589 *m*) deep SW Oreg. in Cascade Range at altitude of 6164 *ft* (1879 *m*); main feature of **Crater Lake National Park**

Craters of the Moon National Monument reservation SE *cen* Idaho including lava flows & other volcanic formations

Cré·cy \krā-'sē, 'kre-sē\ *or* **Cré·cy–en–Pon·thieu** \krā-'sē-,äⁿ-pōⁿ-'tyə(r), -'tyœ\ commune N France NW of Amiens

Cre·mo·na \krā-'mō-nä\ commune N Italy in Lombardy on the Po ESE of Milan *pop* 73,404 — **Cre·mo·nese** \,kre-mə-'nēz, -'nēs\ *adj*

Crete \'krēt\ *or Gk* **Krí·ti** \'krē-tē\ island Greece in the E Mediterranean ✳ Iráklion *area* 3189 *sq mi* (8260 *sq km*), *pop* 536,980 — **Cre·tan** \'krē-t^ən\ *adj or n*

Crete, Sea of *or formerly* **Sea of Can·dia** \'kan-dē-ə\ the S section of Aegean Sea bet. Crete & the Cyclades

Crewe \'krü\ borough NW England in Cheshire *pop* 47,759

Cri·mea \krī-'mē-ə, krə-\ *or Russ* **Krim** \'krim\ peninsula SE Europe, extending into Black Sea SW of Sea of Azov — **Cri·me·an** \krī-'mē-ən, krə-\ *adj*

Cris·to·bal \kri-'stō-bəl\ *or Sp* **Cris·tó·bal** \krē-'stō-väl\ town N Panama adjoining Colón at Caribbean entrance to Panama Canal

Cro·a·tia \krō-'ā-sh(ē-)ə\ independent country SE Europe; a constituent republic of Yugoslavia 1946–91 comprising Croatia, Slavonia, & most of Istria & the Dalmatian coast ✳ Zagreb *area* 21,829 *sq mi* (56,537 *sq km*), *pop* 4,821,000 — **Cro·at** \'krō-,at *also* 'krō(-ə)t\ *n* — **Cro·a·tian** \krō-'ā-shən\ *adj or n*

Crocodile — see LIMPOPO

Cros·by \'krôz-bē\ *or* **Great Crosby** borough NW England in Merseyside on Irish Sea NNW of Liverpool *pop* 53,660

Cross \'krôs\ river 300 *mi* (483 *km*) W Africa in W Cameroon & SE Nigeria flowing W & S into Gulf of Guinea

Cro·ton \'krō-t^ən\ river 60 *mi* (95 *km*) SE N.Y. flowing into the Hudson

Cro·to·ne \krō-'tō-nä\ *or anc* **Cro·to·na** \-nə\ *or* **Cro·ton** \'krō-
ˌtän, 'krō-t°n\ commune S Italy in Calabria on Gulf of Taranto *pop*
55,633

Croy·don \'kròi-d°n\ borough of S Greater London, England *pop*
299,600

Cro·zet Islands \krō-'zā\ islands S Indian Ocean WNW of Kerguelen; a French dependency

Crys·tal \'kris-t°l\ city SE Minn. N of Minneapolis *pop* 23,788

Crystal Lake city N Ill. *pop* 24,512

Cte·si·phon \'te-sə-ˌfän, 'tē-\ ancient city *cen* Iraq on the Tigris opposite Seleucia * of Parthia & of later Sassanid empire

Cuan·za *or* **Kwan·za** \'kwän-zä\ river 600 *mi* (965 *km*) SW Africa
in *cen* Angola flowing NW into the Atlantic

Cu·ba \'kyü-bə, 'kü-\ **1** island in the W. Indies N of Caribbean
Sea *area* 41,620 *sq mi* (107,800 *sq km*) **2** country largely coextensive with island; a republic — * Havana *area* 42,804 *sq mi* (110,862
sq km), *pop* 10,892,000 — **Cu·ban** \'kyü-bən\ *adj or n*

Cubango — see OKAVANGO

Cú·cu·ta \'kü-kü-tä\ city N Colombia near Venezuela border *pop*
450,300

Cud·a·hy \'kə-də-(ˌ)hē\ city SW Calif. NW of Downey *pop* 22,817

Cuen·ca \'kweŋ-kä\ **1** city S Ecuador *pop* 194,981 **2** province E
cen Spain *area* 6587 *sq mi* (17,060 *sq km*), *pop* 205,198 **3** commune, its *, ESE of Madrid *pop* 42,615

Cuer·na·va·ca \ˌkwer-nä-'vä-kä, -'va-\ city S *cen* Mexico S of
Mexico City * of Morelos *pop* 281,752

Cu·lia·cán \ˌkül-yä-'kän\ **1** river 175 *mi* (282 *km*) NW Mexico
flowing SW into the Pacific at mouth of Gulf of California **2** city
NW Mexico on the Culiacán * of Sinaloa *pop* 602,114

Cul·lo·den Moor \kə-'lä-d°n, -'lō-\ moorland N Scotland in N
Highland region E of Inverness

Cul·ver City \'kəl-vər\ city SW Calif. *pop* 38,793

Cu·mae \'kyü-(ˌ)mē\ ancient town S Italy on Tyrrhenian coast W of
modern Naples — **Cu·mae·an** \kyü-'mē-ən\ *adj*

Cu·ma·ná \ˌkü-mä-'nä\ city & port NE Venezuela on the Caribbean
NE of Barcelona *pop* 212,492

Cum·ber·land \'kəm-bər-lənd\ **1** river 687 *mi* (1106 *km*) S Ky. &
N Tenn. flowing W into Ohio River **2** city NW Md. on the Potomac
pop 23,706 **3** town NE R.I. *pop* 29,038 **4** former county NW England * Carlisle — see CUMBRIA **5** settlement Canada in SE Ont.
on Ottawa River NE of Ottawa *pop* 40,697

Cumberland Caverns caverns *cen* Tenn. SE of McMinnville

Cumberland Falls falls SE Ky. in upper course of Cumberland
River

Cumberland Gap mountain pass 1640 *ft* (500 *m*) NE Tenn.
through a ridge of the Cumberlands SE of Middlesboro, Ky.

Cumberland Plateau mountain region E U.S., part of the S Appalachian Mountains W of Tennessee River extending from S W.Va.
to NE Ala.

Cumbre, La — see USPALLATA

Cum·bria \'kəm-brē-ə\ **1** — see STRATHCLYDE **2** county NW England including former counties of Cumberland & Westmorland *
Carlisle *area* 2724 *sq mi* (7055 *sq km*), *pop* 486,900 — **Cum·bri·
an** \'kəm-brē-ən\ *adj or n*

Cumbrian Mountains mountains NW England chiefly in Cumbria & Lancashire — see SCAFELL PIKE

Cu·naxa \kyü-'nak-sə\ town in ancient Babylonia NW of Babylon

Cu·ne·ne or **Ku·ne·ne** \kü-'nā-nə\ river 700 mi (1126 km) SW Africa in SW Angola flowing S & W into the Atlantic

Cu·par \'kü-pər\ burgh E Scotland ✳ of Fife pop 6642

Cu·per·ti·no \,kü-pər-'tē-(,)nō\ city W Calif. W of San José pop 40,263

Cu·ra·cao \,kür-ə-'saü, ,kyür-, -'sō, -'sä-,ō\ island Netherlands Antilles in the S Caribbean; chief town Willemstad area 182 sq mi (471 sq km), pop 143,816

Cu·ri·ti·ba \,kür-ə-'tē-bə\ city S Brazil ✳ of Paraná pop 1,966,426

Cush or **Kush** \'kəsh, 'küsh\ ancient country NE Africa in Nile valley S of Egypt — **Cush·ite** \'kə-,shīt, 'kü-\ adj or n — **Cush·it·ic** \,kə-'shit-ik, kü-\ adj or n

Cut·tack \'kə-tək\ city E India in Orissa pop 440,295

Cux·ha·ven \'kúks-,hä-fən\ city & port NW Germany on North Sea at mouth of the Elbe pop 56,328

Cuy·a·ho·ga \,kī-(ə-)'hō-gə, kə-'hō-, -'hä-, -'hò\ river 100 mi (161 km) NE Ohio flowing into Lake Erie at Cleveland

Cuyahoga Falls city NE Ohio N of Akron pop 48,950

Cu·yu·ni \kü-'yü-nē\ river 350 mi (563 km) N S. America rising in E Venezuela & flowing E into the Essequibo in N Guyana

Cuz·co or **Cus·co** \'küs-(,)kō\ city S Peru pop 316,804

Cwm·bran \küm-'brän\ urban town SE Wales ✳ of Gwent

Cyc·la·des \'si-klə-,dēz\ or NGk **Ki·klá·dhes** \kē-'klä-(,)thes\ islands Greece in the S Aegean area 993 sq mi (2572 sq km), pop 95,083 — **Cy·clad·ic** \si-'kla-dik, sī-\ adj

Cydonia — see CANEA — **Cy·do·nian** \sī-'dō-nē-ən, -nyən\ adj or n

Cymru — see WALES — **Cym·ric** \'kəm-rik, 'kim-\ adj — **Cym·ry** \-rē\ n

Cy·press \'sī-prəs\ city SW Calif. SE of Los Angeles pop 42,655

Cy·prus \'sī-prəs\ **1** island E Mediterranean S of Turkey **2** country coextensive with the island; a republic of the Commonwealth of Nations ✳ Nicosia area 3572 sq mi (9287 sq km), pop 764,000 — **Cyp·ri·ot** \'si-prē-ət, -,ät\ or **Cyp·ri·ote** \-,ōt, -ət\ adj or n

Cy·re·na·ica \,sir-ə-'nā-ə-kə, ,sī-rə-\ or It **Ci·re·na·ica** \same or ,chē-rā-'nä-ē-(,)kä\ **1** or **Cy·re·na·ica** \sī-'rē-(,)nē\ ancient coastal region N Africa dominated by city of Cyrene **2** region E Libya, formerly a province — **Cy·re·na·ic** \,sir-ə-'nā-ik, ,sī-rə-\ adj or n — **Cy·re·na·ican** \-'nä-ə-kən\ adj or n

Cy·re·ne \sī-'rē-(,)nē\ ancient city N Africa on the Mediterranean in NE Libya — **Cy·re·ni·an** \-'nē-ən\ adj or n

Cyz·i·cus \'si-zi-kəs\ **1** — see KAPIDAGI **2** ancient city in Mysia on isthmus leading to Kapidagi Peninsula

Czech·o·slo·va·kia \,che-kə-slō-'vä-kē-ə, -slə-, -'va-\ country 1918–92 cen Europe; a republic ✳ Prague area 49,371 sq mi (127,871 sq km), pop 15,567,666; divided Jan. 1, 1993 into separate countries of Czech Republic & Slovakia — **Czech** \'chek\ adj or n — **Czech·o·slo·vak** \-'slō-,väk, -,vak\ adj or n — **Czech·o·slo·va·ki·an** \-slō-'vä-kē-ən, -slə-, -'va-\ adj or n

Czech Republic country *cen* Europe; a constituent republic of Czechoslovakia 1918–92 ✳ Prague *area* 30,450 *sq mi* (78,866 *sq km*), *pop* 10,332,000

Cze·sto·cho·wa \chen(t)-stə-'kō-və\ *or Russ* **Chen·sto·khov** \chen(t)-stə-'kóf, -'kóv\ city S Poland on the Warta *pop* 258,700

D

Da — see BLACK

Da·bro·wa Gor·ni·cza \dón-'bró-vä-gùr-'nē-chä\ city S Poland *pop* 139,200

Dacca — see DHAKA

Da·chau \'dä-,kaú, -,kaù\ city S Germany in S Bavaria *pop* 35,892; site of Nazi concentration camp

Da·cia \'dā-sh(ē-)ə\ ancient country & Roman province SE Europe roughly equivalent to Romania & Bessarabia — **Da·cian** \-shən\ *adj or n*

Da·dra and Na·gar Ha·ve·li \də-'drä . . . ,nə-gər-ə-'ve-lē\ union territory India bordering on Gujarat and Maharashtra *area* 189 *sq mi* (491 *sq km*), *pop* 138,477

Dag·en·ham \'da-gə-nəm, 'dag-nəm\ former municipal borough SE England in Essex, now part of Barking and Dagenham

Da·ge·stan *or* **Da·ghe·stan** \,da-gə-'stan, ,dä-gə-'stän\ autonomous republic SE Russia in Europe, on W shore of the Caspian ✳ Makhachkala *area* 19,421 *sq mi* (50,300 *sq km*), *pop* 1,890,000

Dahomey — see BENIN — **Da·ho·man** \də-'hō-mən\ *adj or n* — **Da·ho·me·an** \-mē-ən\ *or* **Da·ho·mey·an** \-mē-ən\ *adj or n*

Da·kar \'da-,kär, dä-'kär\ city & port ✳ of Senegal *pop* 1,729,823

Dakh·la \'dä-klə\ *or formerly* **Vil·la Cis·ne·ros** \,vē-yə-sis-'ner-ōs\ town & port NW Africa in Western Sahara ✳ of Río de Oro

Da·ko·ta \də-'kō-tə\ **1** — see JAMES 1 **2** territory (1861–89) NW U.S. divided 1889 into states of N.D. & S.D. (the **Da·ko·tas** \-təz\) — **Da·ko·tan** \-'kō-tən\ *adj or n*

Dal·e·car·lia \,da-lə-'kär-lē-ə\ region W *cen* Sweden — **Dal·e·car·li·an** \-lē-ən\ *adj*

Da·lian *or* **Ta·lien** \'dä-'lyen\ *or* **Lu·da** *or* **Lu–ta** \'lü-'dä\ *or* **Dairen** \'dī-'ren\ city NE China in S Liaoning on Liaodong Peninsula *pop* 1,723,302

Dal·las \'da-ləs, -lis\ city NE Tex. on Trinity River *pop* 1,006,877 — **Dal·las·ite** \'da-lə-,sīt\ *n*

Dal·ma·tia \dal-'mä-sh(ē-)ə\ region W Balkan Peninsula on the Adriatic — **Dal·ma·tian** \-shən\ *adj or n*

Dal·ton \'dól-tᵊn\ city NW Ga. *pop* 21,761

Da·ly City \'dā-lē\ city W Calif. S of San Francisco *pop* 92,311

Da·man \də-'män, -'man\ *or* **Da·mão** \də-'maúⁿ\ district W India on Gulf of Khambhat; a constituent part of the union territory of **Daman and Diu** (*area* 36 *sq mi or* 93 *sq km, pop* 101,586) — see GOA, PORTUGUESE INDIA

Da·man·hûr \da-mən-'hûr\ city N Egypt E of Alexandria *pop* 216,000

Da·mas·cus \də-'mas-kəs\ city SW Syria, its ✳ *pop* 1,451,000 — **Dam·a·scene** \'da-mə-,sēn, ,da-mə-'\ *adj or n*

Dam·a·vand \'da-mə-,vand\ *or* **Dem·a·vend** \'de-mə-,vend\ mountain 18,934 *ft* (5771 *m*) N Iran; highest in Elburz Mountains

Dam·i·et·ta \,da-mē-'e-tə\ city & port N Egypt *pop* 93,488

Dammam — see AD DAMMAM

Da·mo·dar \'dä-mə-,där\ river 368 *mi* (592 *km*) NE India in *cen* Bihar & W. Bengal flowing ESE into the Hugli

Dan \'dan\ **1** river 180 *mi* (290 *km*) S Va. & N N.C. flowing E into Roanoke River **2** ancient village at N extremity of Palestine

Da Nang \(,)dä-'näŋ, -'naŋ\ *or formerly* **Tou·rane** \tü-'rän\ city & port cen Vietnam in Annam *pop* 369,734

Da·na Point \dā-nə\ coastal city S Calif. *bet* Los Angeles and San Diego *pop* 31,896

Dan·bury \'dan-,ber-ē, -b(ə-)rē\ city SW Conn. *pop* 65,585

Dan·dong \'dän-'dúŋ\ *or* **An·tung** \'än-'dúŋ\ *or* **Tan·tung** \'dän-'dúŋ\ city & port NE China in SE Liaoning at mouth of the Yalu *pop* 523,699

Danger Islands — see PUKAPUKA

Danish West Indies the W islands of the Virgin Islands group that were until 1917 a Danish possession & now constitute the Virgin Islands of the U.S.

Danmark — see DENMARK

Dan·ube \'dan-(,)yüb\ *or G* **Do·nau** \'dō-,naú\ *or anc* **Da·nu·bi·us** \də-'nü-bē-əs, da-, -'nyü-\ *or* **Is·ter** \'is-tər\ river 1771 *mi* (2850 *km*) cen & SE Europe flowing SE from S Germany into Black Sea — **Da·nu·bi·an** \də-'nyü-bē-ən\ *adj*

Dan·vers \'dan-vərz\ town NE Mass. N of Lynn *pop* 24,174

Dan·ville \'dan-,vil\ **1** city W Calif. E of Oakland *pop* 31,306 **2** city E Ill. *pop* 33,828 **3** city S Va. on Dan River *pop* 53,056

Dan·zig \'dan(t)-sig, 'dän(t)-\ **1** — see GDANSK **2** territory surrounding & including Gdansk that (1920–39) constituted a free city under the League of Nations

Danzig, Gulf of — see GDANSK, GULF OF

Dar·da·nelles \,där-d²n-'elz\ *or* **Hel·les·pont** \'he-lə-,spänt\ *or anc* **Hel·les·pon·tus** \,he-lə-'spän-təs\ strait NW Turkey connecting Sea of Marmara with the Aegean

Dar el Beida — see CASABLANCA

Dar es Sa·laam \,där-,e(s)-sə-'läm\ city & port ✳ of Tanzania & of Tanganyika on Indian Ocean *pop* 1,360,850

Dar·fur \där-'fúr\ region W Sudan; chief city El Fasher

Dar·i·én \,dar-ē-'en, ,der-, ,där-\ Spanish colonial settlement Central America W of Gulf of Darien

Darien, Gulf of inlet of the Caribbean bet. E Panama & NW Colombia

Darien, Isthmus of — see PANAMA (Isthmus of)

Dar·jee·ling *or* **Dar·ji·ling** \där-'jē-liŋ\ city NE India in W. Bengal on Sikkim border

Dar·ling \'där-liŋ\ river *ab* 1700 *mi* (2735 *km*) SE Australia in Queensland & New South Wales flowing SW into Murray River

Darling Range mountain range SW Western Australia extending *ab* 250 *mi* (400 *km*) N–S along coast; highest point Mt. Cooke 1910 *ft* (582 *m*)

Dar·ling·ton \'där-liŋ-tən\ town N England in Durham *pop* 96,700

Darm·stadt \'därm-,stat, -,shtät, -,stät\ city *cen* Germany in Hesse SSW of Frankfurt am Main *pop* 140,040

Dar·nah \'där-nə, 'dar-\ *or* **Der·na** \'der-\ city & port NE Libya

Dart·moor \'därt-,múr, -,mōr, -,mòr\ tableland SW England in S Devon *area* 365 *sq mi* (945 *sq km*)

Dart·mouth \'därt-məth\ **1** town SE Mass. W of New Bedford *pop* 27,244 **2** city Canada in S N.S. on Halifax harbor opposite Halifax *pop* 67,798 **3** town & port SW England in S Devon on Dart River *pop* 6298

Dar·win \'där-wən\ city & port N Australia ✳ of Northern Territory on Port Darwin (inlet of Timor Sea) *pop* 70,071

Da·tong \'dä-'túŋ\ *or* **Ta·tung** \'dä-'túŋ\ city NE China in N Shanxi *pop* 798,319

Dau·gav·pils \'daú-gəf-,pilz\ *or Russ* **Dvinsk** \də-'vin(t)sk\ city E Latvia on Dvina River *pop* 129,000

Dau·phi·né \,dō-fē-'nā\ region & former province SE France N of Provence ✳ Grenoble

Da·vao \'dä-,vaú, dä-'vaú\ city Philippines on Davao Gulf *pop* 850,000

Davao Gulf gulf of the Pacific, Philippines in SE Mindanao

Dav·en·port \'da-vən-,pōrt, -,pòrt\ city E Iowa on Mississippi River *pop* 95,333

Da·vid \'dä-'vēth\ town W Panama *pop* 65,635

Da·vie \'dä-vē\ city S Fla. *pop* 47,217

Da·vis \'dä-vəs\ city W Calif. W of Sacramento *pop* 46,209

Davis Mountains mountains W Tex. N of the Big Bend of the Rio Grande

Davis Strait strait connecting Baffin Bay with the Atlantic

Daw·son \'dò-sᵊn\ city N Canada in Yukon *pop* 972

Dax \'däks\ commune SW France in the Landes on the Adour NE of Biarritz *pop* 20,119

Day·ton \'dā-tᵊn\ city SW Ohio on Miami River *pop* 182,044

Day·to·na Beach \dā-'tō-nə, də-\ city NE Fla. *pop* 61,921

Da Yunhe — see GRAND CANAL

Dead Sea *or bib* **Salt Sea** \'sòlt\ *or L* **La·cus As·phal·ti·tes** \'lā-kəs-,as-,fòl-'tī-tēz\ salt lake *ab* 50 *mi* (80 *km*) long on boundary bet. Israel & Jordan *area* 370 *sq mi* (962 *sq km*), surface 1312 *ft* (400 *m*) below sea level

Dean, Forest of \'dēn\ forested district SW England in W Glouces-ter bet. Severn & Wye rivers; an ancient royal forest

Dear·born \'dir-,bòrn, -,bərn\ city SE Mich. *pop* 89,286

Dearborn Heights city SE Mich. W of Detroit *pop* 60,838

Death Valley \'deth\ arid valley E Calif. & S Nev. containing low-est point in the U.S. at 282 *ft* (86 *m*) below sea level; most of area included in **Death Valley National Monument**

Deau·ville \'dō-,vil, dō-'vēl\ town NW France on Bay of the Seine SSW of Le Havre *pop* 4380

De·bre·cen \'de-bret-,sen\ city E Hungary *pop* 222,300

De·cap·o·lis \di-'ka-pə-lis\ confederation of 10 ancient cities N Pal-estine in region chiefly SE of Sea of Galilee

De·ca·tur \di-'kā-tər\ **1** city N Ala. *pop* 48,761 **2** city *cen* Ill. *pop* 83,885

Dec·can \'de-kən, -,kan\ plateau region S *cen* India lying bet. Eastern Ghats & Western Ghats

Ded·ham \'de-dəm\ town E Mass. SW of Boston *pop* 23,782

Dee \'dē\ **1** river 87 *mi* (140 *km*) NE Scotland flowing E into North Sea **2** river 50 *mi* (80 *km*) S Scotland flowing S into Solway Firth **3** river 70 *mi* (113 *km*) N Wales & W England flowing E & N into Irish Sea

Deep South region SE U.S. — usu. considered as including Ala., Ga., La., Miss., N.C., S.C., and all or part of the adjacent states of Fla., Va., Tenn., Ark., & Tex.

Deer·field Beach \'dir-,fēld\ city SE Fla. N of Fort Lauderdale *pop* 46,325

Deer Park \'dir\ city SE Tex. *pop* 27,652

De·hi·wa·la–Mount La·vin·ia \,dä-hē-'wä-lə . . . lə-'vi-nē-ə\ town W Sri Lanka on coast S of Colombo *pop* 193,000

Deh·ra Dun \,der-ə-'dün\ city N India in NW Uttar Pradesh *pop* 270,028

De Kalb \di-'kalb\ city N Ill. *pop* 34,925

Del·a·goa Bay \,de-lə-'gō-ə\ inlet of Indian Ocean S Mozambique

Del·a·no \də-'lā-(,)nō\ city S Calif. NNW of Bakersfield *pop* 22,762

Del·a·ware \'de-lə-,war, -,wer, -wər\ **1** river 296 *mi* (476 *km*) E U.S. flowing S from S N.Y. into Delaware Bay **2** state E U.S. ✳ Dover *area* 2057 *sq mi* (5348 *sq km*), *pop* 666,168 **3** city *cen* Ohio NNW of Columbus *pop* 20,030 — **Del·a·war·ean** \,de-lə-'war-ē-ən, -'wer-\ *adj*

Delaware Bay inlet of the Atlantic bet. SW N.J. & E Del.

Del City \'del\ city *cen* Okla. E of Oklahoma City *pop* 23,928

De·lé·mont \də-lā-'mōⁿ\ commune NW Switzerland ✳ of Jura canton *pop* 11,467

Delft \'delft\ commune SW Netherlands *pop* 90,066

Del·ga·do, Cape \del-'gä-(,)dō\ cape NE Mozambique

Del·hi \'de-lē\ **1** union territory N India W of Uttar Pradesh ✳ Delhi *area* 573 *sq mi* (1484 *sq km*), *pop* 9,420,644 **2** city, its ✳ *pop* 7,206,704 — see NEW DELHI

Dells of the Wisconsin *or* **Wisconsin Dells** \'delz\ gorge of Wisconsin River in S *cen* Wis.

Del·mar·va Peninsula \del-'mär-və\ peninsula E U.S. bet. Chesapeake & Delaware bays comprising Del. & parts of Md. & Va. — see EASTERN SHORE

Del·men·horst \'del-mən-,hörst\ city NW Germany in Lower Saxony WSW of Bremen *pop* 75,967

De·los \'dē-,läs\ *or Gk* **Dhí·los** \'thē-,lòs\ island Greece in *cen* Cyclades *area* 2 *sq mi* (5.2 *sq km*) — **De·lian** \'dē-lē-ən, 'dēl-yən\ *adj or n*

Del·phi \'del-,fī\ ancient town *cen* Greece in Phocis on S slope of Mt. Parnassus near present village of **Dhel·foí** \thel-'fē\ — **Del·phi·an** \'del-fē-ən\ *adj* — **Del·phic** \'del-fik\ *adj*

Del·ray Beach \del-'rā\ city SE Fla. S of Palm Beach *pop* 47,181

Del Rio \del-'rē-(,)ō\ city S Tex. on Rio Grande *pop* 30,705

Del·ta \'del-tə\ municipality Canada in SW B.C. *pop* 88,978

Delta, The region NW Miss. bet. Mississippi & Yazoo rivers

Demavend — see DAMAVEND

Dem·e·ra·ra \,de-mə-'rär-ə, -'rar-\ river 200 *mi* (322 *km*) Guyana flowing N into the Atlantic

Denali, Denali National Park — see MCKINLEY (Mount)

Den·bigh \'den-bē\ *or* Den·bigh·shire \-,shir, -shər\ former county N Wales ✳ Ruthin

Den·der·mon·de \,den-dər-'män-də\ *or* F **Ter·monde** \ter-'mōⁿd\ commune NW *cen* Belgium *pop* 42,499

Den Hel·der \dən-'hel-dər\ commune W Netherlands in N. Holland on an outlet from Wadden Zee to North Sea *pop* 61,149

Den·i·son \'de-nə-sən\ city NE Tex. on Red River *pop* 21,505

De·niz·li \,de-naz-'lē\ city SW Turkey SE of Izmir *pop* 204,118

Den·mark \'den-,märk\ *or* Dan **Dan·mark** \'dän-,märk\ country N Europe occupying most of Jutland Peninsula & adjacent islands in Baltic & North seas; a kingdom ✳ Copenhagen *area* 16,629 *sq mi* (43,069 *sq km*), *pop* 5,129,778 — **Dane** \'dān\ *n* — **Dan·ish** \'dā-nish\ *adj or n*

Denmark Strait strait 130 *mi* (209 *km*) wide bet. SE Greenland & Iceland connecting Arctic Ocean with the Atlantic

Dent Blanche \däⁿ-'bläⁿsh\ mountain 14,295 *ft* (4357 *m*) S Switzerland in Pennine Alps

Dent du Mi·di \däⁿ-dē-mē-'dē\ mountain 10,686 *ft* (3257 *m*) SW Switzerland in W Alps

Den·ton \'den-t⁰n\ city N Tex. NW of Dallas *pop* 66,270

D'En·tre·cas·teaux Islands \,dän-trə-'kas-(,)tō\ islands SW Pacific N of E tip of New Guinea belonging to Papua New Guinea *area* 1200 *sq mi* (3120 *sq km*), *pop* 38,894

Den·ver \'den-vər\ city NE *cen* Colo., its ✳ *pop* 467,610 — **Den·ver·ite** \-və-,rīt\ *n*

Dept·ford \'det-fərd\ former metropolitan borough SE London, England, now part of Lewisham

Der·be \'dər-(,)bē\ ancient town S Asia Minor in S Lycaonia on border of Cilicia; exact site unknown

Der·bent *or* Der·bend \dər-'bent\ city S Russia in Europe in Dagestan on Caspian Sea *pop* 81,500

Der·by \'där-bē, *chiefly U.S.* 'dər-\ city N *cen* England in Derbyshire *pop* 214,000

Der·by·shire \'där-bē-,shir, -shər; *US also* -bē-\ *or* **Derby** county N *cen* England ✳ Matlock *area* 1052 *sq mi* (2725 *sq km*), *pop* 914,600

Derna — see DARNAH

Der·ry \'der-ē\ **1** city SE N.H. SE of Manchester *pop* 29,603 **2** *or* Lon·don·der·ry \,lən-dən-'der-ē; 'lən-dən-,der-ē, -d(ə-)rē\ district NW Northern Ireland, established 1974 *area* 148 *sq mi* (383 *sq km*), *pop* 94,918 **3** *or* **Londonderry** county borough & port, NW Derry district *pop* 62,697

Der·went \'dər-wənt\ river more than 105 *mi* (170 *km*) Australia in Tasmania flowing SE into Tasman Sea

Derwent Water lake NW England in Lake District in Cumbria

Desaguadero — see SALADO

Des·chutes \dā-'shüt\ river 250 *mi* (402 *km*) *cen* & N Oreg. E of Cascade Range flowing N into Columbia River

Des·er·et \,de-zə-'ret\ provisional state of the U.S. S of 42d parallel & W of the Rockies organized 1849 by Mormons

Des Moines \di-ˈmȯin\ **1** river 327 *mi* (526 *km*) Iowa flowing SE into Mississippi River **2** city ✻ of Iowa on Des Moines River *pop* 193,187

Des·na \dyi-ˈsnä\ river 550 *mi* (885 *km*) SW Russia in Europe & N Ukraine flowing S into the Dnieper

De So·to \di-ˈsō-(ˌ)tō\ city NE Tex. S of Dallas *pop* 30,544

Des Plaines \des-ˈplānz\ **1** river 150 *mi* (241 *km*) NE Ill. flowing S to unite with Kankakee River forming Illinois River **2** city NE Ill. NW of Chicago *pop* 53,223

Des·roches \dā-ˈrȯsh\ island NW Indian Ocean NNE of Madagascar belonging to Seychelles

Des·sau \ˈde-ˌsau̇\ city *cen* Germany NE of Halle *pop* 95,097

De·troit \di-ˈtrȯit, *locally also* ˈdē-,\ **1** river 31 *mi* (50 *km*) Ont. & SE Mich. connecting Lake Erie & Lake Saint Clair **2** city SE Mich. on Detroit River *pop* 1,027,974 — **De·troit·er** \di-ˈtrȯi-tər\ *n*

Detskoe Selo — see PUSHKIN

Deur·ne \ˈdər-nə, ˈdərn\ commune N Belgium, E suburb of Antwerp

Deutsche Demokratische Republik — see GERMANY

Deutschland — see GERMANY

De·ven·ter \ˈdā-vən-tər\ commune E Netherlands *pop* 68,004

Devil Mountain — see AUYÁN-TEPUÍ

Dev·il's Island \ˈde-vᵊlz\ *or F* Île du Dia·ble \ˌēl-dǖē-ˈdyäbl\ island French Guiana in the Safety Islands group; former penal colony

Devils Post·pile \ˈpōst-ˌpīl\ lava formation E *cen* Calif. SE of Yosemite National Park; feature of **Devils Postpile National Monument**

Devils Tower *or* **Ma·to Tepee** \ˈmä-(ˌ)tō\ columnar rock formation NE Wyo. rising 865 *ft* (264 *m*) in **Devils Tower National Monument**

Dev·on \ˈde-vən\ *or* **Dev·on·shire** \ˈde-vən-ˌshir, -shər\ county SW England ✻ Exeter *area* 2686 *sq mi* (6957 *sq km*), *pop* 998,200

Devon Island island Northwest Territories, Canada in E Parry Islands N of Baffin Is. *area* 20,861 *sq mi* (54,239 *sq km*)

Dews·bury \ˈdüz-ˌber-ē, ˈdyüz-, -b(ə-)rē\ town N England in W. Yorkshire S of Leeds *pop* 48,339

Dez \ˈdez\ river 250 *mi* (402 *km*) W Iran flowing S to the Karun

Dezh·nev, Cape \ˈdezh-nyif\ *or Russ* **Mys Dezh·ne·va** \ˈmis-ˌdezh-ˈnyȯ-və, ˌdesh-\ cape NE Russia in Asia at E end of Chukchi Peninsula

Dhah·ran \dä-ˈrän, thäh-ˈran\ town SE Saudi Arabia on Persian Gulf near Bahrain Islands *pop* 12,500

Dha·ka \ˈdä-kə\ *or* **Dac·ca** \ˈda-kə, ˈdä-\ city ✻ of Bangladesh *pop* 3,637,892

Dhau·la·gi·ri, Mount \ˌdau̇-lə-ˈgir-ē\ mountain 26,810 *ft* (8172 *m*) W *cen* Nepal in the Himalayas

Di·a·blo, Mount \dē-ˈä-(ˌ)blō, dī-ˈa-\ mountain 3849 *ft* (1173 *m*) *cen* Calif. at N end of **Diablo Range**

Di·a·man·ti·na \ˌdī-ə-ˌman-ˈtē-nə\ intermittent river maximum length 560 *mi* (901 *km*) E *cen* Australia in SW Queensland flowing SW into the Warburton **2** \ˌdē-ə-\ city E Brazil in *cen* Minas Gerais *pop* 26,075

Di·a·mond \ˈdī-(ə-)mənd\ *or* **Kum·gang** \ˈkùm-ˌgän\ mountains SE N. Korea; highest 5374 *ft* (1638 *m*)

Diamond Bar city S Calif. E of Los Angeles *pop* 53,672
Diamond Head promontory Hawaii on Oahu Is. in SE Honolulu
Die·go Gar·cia \dē-ˌā-gō-ˌgär-'sē-ə\ island in Indian Ocean, chief island of Chagos Archipelago
Diégo–Suarez — see ANTSIRANANA
Dien Bien Phu \dyen-ˌbyen-'fü\ village NW Vietnam
Dieppe \'dyep\ city & port N France N of Rouen *pop* 25,607
Di·jon \dē-'zhōⁿ\ city E France *pop* 151,636
Diks·mui·de or **Dix·mui·de** \dik-'smī-də\ or **Dix·mude** \dēk-'smüd\ town W Belgium in W. Flanders N of Ieper *pop* 15,273
Di·li or **Dil·li** \'di-lē\ city & port N Timor, formerly ✱ of Portuguese Timor
Di·mi·trov·grad \də-'mē-trəf-ˌgrad, -ˌgrát\ city S Bulgaria on the Maritsa ESE of Plovdiv *pop* 56,882
Dimitrovo — see PERNIK
Di·nar·ic Alps \də-'nar-ik\ range of E Alps W Slovenia, W Croatia, Bosnia and Herzegovina, & Montenegro; highest point 8274 *ft* (2522 *m*)
Din·gle Bay \'diŋ-gəl\ inlet of the Atlantic SW Ireland
Ding·wall \'diŋ-ˌwȯl\ burgh N Scotland NW of Inverness *pop* 4815
Di·no·saur National Monument \'dī-nə-ˌsȯr\ reservation NW Colo. & NE Utah at junction of Green & Yampa rivers; rich fossil deposits
Di·o·mede Islands \'dī-ə-ˌmēd\ islands in Bering Strait comprising **Big Diomede** (Russia) & **Little Diomede** (U.S.)
Diospolis — see THEBES
Di·re Da·wa \ˌdē-rā-'daů-ä\ city E Ethiopia *pop* 121,887
Disko — see QEQERTARSUAQ
Dis·mal Swamp \'diz-məl\ or **Great Dismal Swamp** swamp SE Va. & NE N.C. between Chesapeake Bay & Albemarle Sound *ab* 37 *mi* (60 *km*) long, 10 *mi* (16 *km*) wide
District of Co·lum·bia \kə-'ləm-bē-ə\ federal district E U.S. coextensive with city of Washington *area* 69 *sq mi* (179 *sq km*), *pop* 609,909
Dis·tri·to Fe·de·ral \dē-'strē-tō-ˌfā-thā-'räl\ **1** district E Argentina largely comprising ✱ city of Buenos Aires *area* 77 *sq mi* (199 *sq km*), *pop* 2,960,976 **2** — see FEDERAL DISTRICT 1 **3** or **Federal District** district *cen* Mexico including ✱ city of Mexico City *area* 579 *sq mi* (1500 *sq km*), *pop* 8,235,744 **4** or **Federal District** district N Venezuela including ✱ city of Caracas *area* 745 *sq mi* (1937 *sq km*), *pop* 2,103,661
Diu \'dē-(ˌ)ü\ district W India at S end of Kathiawar Peninsula; a constituent part of the union territory of Daman and Diu — see GOA, PORTUGUESE INDIA
Di·yar·ba·kir \di-ˌyär-bä-'kir\ or **Di·ar·bekr** \-'be-kər\ city SE Turkey on the Tigris *pop* 381,144
Djakarta — see JAKARTA
Djawa — see JAVA
Djerba — see JERBA
Dji·bou·ti \jə-'bü-tē\ **1** or formerly **French Territory of the Afars and the Is·sas** \'ä-ˌfär(z) . . . ē-'sä(z)\ or earlier **French Somaliland** country E Africa on Gulf of Aden; a republic *area* 8880 *sq mi* (23,088 *sq km*), *pop* 510,000 **2** city, its ✱ *pop* 300,000

Dnie·per \'nē-pər\ river 1420 *mi* (2285 *km*) Ukraine, E Belarus, & W Russia in Europe rising in S Valdai Hills & flowing S into Black Sea

Dnies·ter \'nēs-tər\ river 877 *mi* (1411 *km*) W Ukraine & E Moldova rising on N slope of Carpathian Mountains near Polish border & flowing SE into Black Sea

Dni·pro·dzer·zhyns'k or **Dne·pro·dzer·zhinsk** \də-,nye-prə-dzir-'zhēnsk\ city E *cen* Ukraine on the Dnieper W of Dnipropetrovs'k *pop* 284,000

Dni·pro·pe·trovs'k or **Dne·pro·pe·trovsk** \də-,nye-prə-pə-'trófsk\ or *formerly* **Eka·te·ri·no·slav** \i-,kä-ti-'rē-nə-,släf, -,släv\ city E Ukraine *pop* 1,189,000

Do·be·rai \'dō-bə-,rī\ or *formerly* **Vo·gel·kop** \'vō-gəl-,käp\ peninsula Indonesia in NW W. Irian

Do·bru·ja or **Do·bru·dja** \'dō-brü-jä, -jə\ region S Europe in Romania & Bulgaria on Black Sea S of the Danube

Do·de·ca·nese \dō-'de-kə-,nēz, -,nēs; ,dō-di-kə-\ islands Greece in the SE Aegean comprising the Southern Sporades S of Ikaria & Samos; belonged to Italy 1923–47 — *area* 486 *sq mi* (1264 *sq km*) *pop* 162,439 — see RHODES — **Do·de·ca·ne·sian** \(,)dō-,de-kə-'nē-zhən, ,dō-di-kə-, -shən\ *adj or n*

Dodge City \'däj\ city S Kans. on Arkansas River *pop* 21,129

Do·do·ma \dō-'dō-(,)mä\ town NE *cen* Tanzania, since 1974 designated as the future national ✳

Dog·ger Bank \'dó-gər, 'dä-\ submerged sandbank *ab* 150 *mi* (241 *km*) long in North Sea E of N England

Do·ha \'dō-(,)hä\ city & port ✳ of Qatar on Persian Gulf *pop* 217,294

Dol·gel·lau \dòl-'ge-(,)(h)lī, -'geth-,lī\ town W Wales in Gwynedd, formerly ✳ of Merionethshire

Dol·lard–des–Or·meaux \dò-,lär-,dā-,zór-'mō\ town Canada in S Que. NW of Montreal *pop* 46,922

Do·lo·mites \'dō-lə-,mīts, 'dä-\ range of E Alps NE Italy bet. Adige & Piave rivers — see MARMOLADA

Dol·ton \'dōl-tᵊn\ village NE Ill. S of Chicago *pop* 23,930

Dôme, Puy de \'pwē-də-'dōm\ mountain 4806 *ft* (1465 *m*) S *cen* France in Auvergne Mountains

Dom·i·ni·ca \,dä-mə-'nē-kə, ÷də-'mi-nə-kə\ island Brit. West Indies in the Lesser Antilles; a republic of the Commonwealth of Nations since 1978 ✳ Roseau *area* 289 *sq mi* (749 *sq km*), *pop* 74,000

Do·min·i·can Republic \də-'mi-ni-kən\ or *formerly* **San·to Do·min·go** \,san-tə-də-'miŋ-(,)gō, ,san-tō-tə-thō-\ or **San Domingo** \,san-də-, ,sän-dō-\ country W. Indies on E Hispaniola; a republic ✳ Santo Domingo *area* 18,657 *sq mi* (48,322 *sq km*), *pop* 7,634,000 — **Dominican** *adj or n*

Don \'dän\ river 1224 *mi* (1969 *km*) Russia in Europe flowing SE & then SW into Sea of Azov

Donau — see DANUBE

Don·cas·ter \'däŋ-kəs-tər\ borough N England in S. Yorkshire *pop* 81,610

Don·e·gal \,dä-ni-'gòl, ,də-\ county NW Ireland (republic) in Ulster ✳ Lifford *area* 1865 *sq mi* (4849 *sq km*), *pop* 128,117

Donegal Bay inlet of the Atlantic NW Ireland

Do·nets \də-'nets, -'nyets\ river *over* 630 *mi* (1014 *km*) SE Ukraine & SW Russia in Europe flowing SE into Don River

Donets Basin *or* **Don·bass** *or* **Don·bas** \dən-'bas\ region E Ukraine SW of the Donets

Do·netsk \də-'nyetsk\ *or formerly* **Sta·li·no** \'stä-lyi-,nō, 'sta-\ *or* **Sta·lin** \'stä-lyin, 'sta-, -,lēn\ city E Ukraine in Donets Basin *pop* 1,121,000

Don·ner Pass \'dä-nər\ mountain pass *ab* 7090 *ft* (2160 *m*) E Calif. in Sierra Nevada

Don·ny·brook \'dä-nē-,brúk\ city E Ireland in Leinster, SE suburb of Dublin

Doornik — see TOURNAI

Door Peninsula \'dōr, 'dór\ peninsula E Wis. bet. Green Bay & Lake Michigan

Dor·ches·ter \'dór-chəs-tər, -,ches-\ borough S England ✴ of Dorset *pop* 14,049

Dor·dogne \dór-'dōn, -'dó-nyə\ river 293 *mi* (471 *km*) SW France flowing SW & W to unite with the Garonne forming the Gironde Estuary

Dor·drecht \'dór-,drekt, -,drekt\ commune SW Netherlands in S. Holland on the Meuse *pop* 112,687

Dore, Monts \mō'-,dór, -'dór\ mountain group S *cen* France in Auvergne Mountains — see SANCY (Puy de)

Do·ris \'dōr-əs, 'dór-, 'där-\ 1 ancient country *cen* Greece bet. Mounts Oeta & Parnassus 2 ancient district SW Asia Minor on coast of Caria — **Do·ri·an** \-ē-ən\ *adj or n* — **Dor·ic** \-ik\ *adj*

Dor·noch \'dór-nək, -,nək\ royal burgh N Scotland in Highland region N of Inverness

Dorpat — see TARTU

Dor·set \'dór-sət\ *or* **Dor·set·shire** \-,shir, -shər\ county S England ✴ Dorchester *area* 1062 *sq mi* (2750 *sq km*), *pop* 645,200

Dort·mund \'dórt-,múnt, -mənd\ city W Germany in the Ruhr *pop* 601,007

Do·than \'dō-thən\ city SE Ala. *pop* 53,589

Dou·ai \dü-'ā\ city N France S of Lille *pop* 44,195

Dou·a·la \dü-'ä-lä\ city & port SW Cameroon on Bight of Biafra *pop* 810,000

Doug·las \'də-gləs\ borough ✴ of Isle of Man *pop* 22,214

Dou·ro \'dōr-(,)ü, 'dór-\ *or Sp* **Due·ro** \'dwā-rō\ river 556 *mi* (895 *km*) N Spain & N Portugal flowing W into the Atlantic

Do·ver \'dō-vər\ 1 city *cen* Del., its ✴ *pop* 27,630 2 city SE N.H. *pop* 25,042 3 borough SE England in Kent on Strait of Dover *pop* 32,843

Dover, Strait of *or F* **Pas de Ca·lais** \,päd-kà-'lā\ channel bet. SE England & N France, easternmost section of English Channel; 20 *mi* (32 *km*) wide at narrowest point

Down \'daún\ 1 district SE Northern Ireland, established 1974 *area* 250 *sq mi* (650 *sq km*), *pop* 57,511 2 traditional county SE Northern Ireland

Dow·ners Grove \daú-nərz\ village NE Ill. *pop* 46,858

Dow·ney \'daú-nē\ city SW Calif. SE of Los Angeles *pop* 91,444

Down·pat·rick \daún-'pa-trik\ town SE Northern Ireland in Down district *pop* 8245

Downs \'daúnz\ **1** two ranges of hills SE England — see NORTH DOWNS, SOUTH DOWNS **2** roadstead in English Channel along E coast of Kent protected by the Goodwin Sands

Down Under Australia or New Zealand

Dra·chen·fels \'drä-kən-ˌfels\ hill 1053 *ft* (321 *m*) W Germany in the Siebengebirge on the Rhine S of Bonn

Dra·cut \'drā-kət\ town NE Mass. N of Lowell *pop* 25,594

Dra·kens·berg \'drä-kənz-ˌbərg\ *or* **Kwath·lam·ba** \kwät-'läm-bə\ mountains E Republic of S. Africa & in Lesotho; highest Thabana Ntlenyana 11,425 *ft* (3482 *m*)

Drake Passage \'drāk\ strait S of S. America bet. Cape Horn & S. Shetlands

Dram·men \'drä-mən\ city & port SE Norway *pop* 51,978

Dran·cy \dräⁿ-'sē\ commune N France, NE of Paris *pop* 60,928

Dra·va *or* **Dra·ve** \'drä-və\ river 447 *mi* (719 *km*) S Austria, NE Slovenia, & N tip of Croatia flowing SE into the Danube

Dren·the \'dren-tə\ province NE Netherlands ✳ Assen *area* 1037 *sq mi* (2686 *sq km*), *pop* 448,256

Dres·den \'drez-dən\ city E Germany in Saxony *pop* 485,132

Dri·na \'drē-nə\ river 285 *mi* (459 *km*) flowing N along the border bet. Bosnia & Serbia into the Sava

Dro·ghe·da \'dròi-ə-də, 'drò-i-də\ town & port E Ireland in County Louth on the Boyne *pop* 23,845

Drug — see DURG

Drum·mond·ville \'drə-mən(d)-ˌvil\ town Canada in S Que. NE of Montreal *pop* 35,462

Dry Tor·tu·gas \tòr-'tü-gəz\ island group S Fla. W of Key West; site of **Dry Tortugas National Monument**

Duar·te \'dwär-tē, dü-'är-\ city SW Calif. *pop* 20,688

Du·bawnt \dü-'bònt\ river 580 *mi* (933 *km*) N Canada flowing NE through Dubawnt Lake to **Ba·ker Lake** \'bā-kər\ (W expansion of Chesterfield Inlet)

Dubawnt Lake lake N Canada in SE Northwest Territories E of Great Slave Lake

Du·bayy *or* **Du·bai** \(ˌ)dü-'bī\ **1** sheikhdom, member of United Arab Emirates 1500 *sq mi* (3885 *sq km*) **2** city, its ✳ *pop* 265,702

Dub·lin \'də-blən\ *or for 2 and 3 IrGael* **Bai·le Atha Cli·ath** \blä-'klē-ə\ **1** city W Calif. NE of Oakland *pop* 23,229 **2** county E Ireland in Leinster *area* 356 *sq mi* (926 *sq km*), *pop* 546,915 **3** city & county borough & port ✳ of Ireland (republic) & of County Dublin at mouth of the Liffey on **Dublin Bay** (inlet of Irish Sea) *pop* 477,675 — **Dub·lin·er** \'də-blə-nər\ *n*

Du·brov·nik \'dü-ˌbròv-nik, dü-'bròv-nik\ city & port S Croatia *pop* 55,638

Du·buque \də-'byük\ city E Iowa on Mississippi River *pop* 57,546

Dud·ley \'dəd-lē\ borough W *cen* England in W. Midlands NNW of Birmingham *pop* 300,400

Duis·burg \'dü-əs-ˌberg, 'düz-, 'dyüz-\, *G* \'dēs-ˌbúrk\ *or formerly* **Duis·burg-Ham·born** \-ˌhäm-'bòrn\ city W Germany at junction of Rhine & Ruhr rivers *pop* 537,441

Du·luth \də-'lüth\ city & port NE Minn. at W end of Lake Superior *pop* 85,493 — **Du·luth·ian** \-'lü-thē-ən\ *adj or n*

Dul·wich \'də-lij, -lich\ a SE district of London, England

Dum·bar·ton \dəm-'bär-tᵊn\ **1** burgh W *cen* Scotland in Strath-clyde *pop* 79,750 **2** *or* **Dum·bar·ton·shire** \-,shir, -shər\ DUNBAR-TON

Dum·fries \dəm-'frēs, -'frēz\ **1** *or* **Dum·fries·shire** \-'frēsh-,shir, -shər\ former county S Scotland ✳ Dumfries **2** burgh S Scotland ✳ of Dumfries and Galloway *pop* 32,084

Dumfries and Gal·lo·way \'ga-lə-,wā\ region S Scotland, estab-lished 1975 ✳ Dumfries *area* 2481 *sq mi* (6425 *sq km*), *pop* 147,900

Dun·bar·ton \dən-'bär-tᵊn\ *or* **Dun·bar·ton·shire** \-,shir, -shər\ former county W *cen* Scotland ✳ Dumbarton

Dun·can \'dəŋ-kən\ city S Okla. *pop* 21,732

Dun·can·ville \'dəŋ-kən-,vil, -vəl\ city NE Tex. *pop* 35,748

Dun·dalk \,dən-'do(l)k\ town & port NE Ireland (republic) on **Dun-dalk Bay** (inlet of Irish sea) ✳ of County Louth *pop* 26,669

Dun·das \'dən-dəs\ town Canada in SE Ont. *pop* 21,868

Dun·dee \,dən-'dē\ city & port E Scotland ✳ of Tayside on Firth of Tay *pop* 172,860

Dun·e·din \,də-'nē-dᵊn\ **1** city W Fla. N of Clearwater *pop* 34,012 **2** — see EDINBURGH **3** city New Zealand on SE coast of South Is. at head of Otago Harbor *pop* 116,577

Dun·ferm·line \,dən-'fərm-lən\ royal burgh E Scotland in Fife *pop* 129,910

Dun·gan·non \,dən-'ga-nən\ district S Northern Ireland, established 1974 *area* 301 *sq mi* (783 *sq km*), *pop* 45,322

Dun·kerque *or* **Dun·kirk** \'dən-,kərk, ,dən-'\ city & port N France on Strait of Dover *pop* 71,071

Dun Laoghai·re \,dən-'ler-ə\ *or formerly* **Kings·town** \'kinz-,taûn\ borough & port E Ireland in Leinster on Dublin Bay *pop* 54,715

Dun·net Head \'də-nət\ headland N Scotland on N coast W of John o'Groat's; northernmost point of mainland, at 58°50′N

Duns \'dənz\ burgh SE Scotland in Borders region *pop* 2249

Du·que de Ca·xi·as \dü-kē-dē-kə-'shē-əs\ city S Brazil in Rio de Janeiro state N of city of Rio de Janeiro *pop* 664,643

Du·ran·go \dü-'raŋ-(,)gō, dyù-; dü-'räŋ-gō\ **1** state NW *cen* Mexico *area* 46,196 *sq mi* (119,648 *sq km*), *pop* 1,349,378 **2** city, its ✳ *pop* 414,015

Dur·ban \'dər-bən\ city & port E Republic of South Africa in E KwaZulu-Natal on Natal Bay *pop* 736,852

Durg \'dùrg\ *or formerly* **Drug** \'drüg\ city E *cen* India in SE Madhya Pradesh E of Nagpur *pop* 150,513

Dur·ham \'dər-əm, 'də-rəm, 'dùr-əm\ **1** city NE *cen* N.C. NW of Raleigh *pop* 136,611 **2** county N England bordering on North Sea *area* 974 *sq mi* (2523 *sq km*), *pop* 589,800 **3** city, its ✳, S of New-castle *pop* 26,422

Dur·res \'dùr-əs\ *or* It **Du·raz·zo** \dü-'rät-(,)sō\ *or anc* **Ep·i·dam-nus** \,e-pə-'dam-nəs\ *or* **Dyr·ra·chi·um** \də-'rä-kē-əm\ city & port Albania on Adriatic Sea W of Tiranë *pop* 85,500

Du·shan·be \dü-'sham-bə, dyü-, -'shäm-, 'dyü-,; ,dyü-shäm-'bä\ *or formerly* **Sta·lin·a·bad** \,stä-lyi-nə-'bäd, ,sta-li-nə-'bad\ city ✳ of Tajikistan *pop* 595,000

Düs·sel·dorf \'dü-səl-,dórf, 'dyü-, 'dœ-\ city W Germany on the Rhine N of Cologne ✳ of N. Rhine-Westphalia *pop* 577,561

Dutch Borneo — see KALIMANTAN

Dutch Guiana — see SURINAME

Dutch New Guinea — see IRIAN JAYA

Dvi·na, Northern \dvē-'nä, 'dvē-nə\ river 466 *mi* (750 *km*) N Russia in Europe flowing NW into White Sea

Dvina, Western river 634 *mi* (1020 *km*) Latvia, W Belarus, & W Russia in Europe rising in Valdai Hills & flowing W into Gulf of Riga

Dvina Gulf *or* **Dvina Bay** *or formerly* **Gulf of Arch·an·gel** \'är-ˌkän-jəl\ arm of White Sea N Russia in Europe

Dvinsk — see DAUGAVPILS

Dyf·ed \'də-ved, -vəd\ county SW Wales ✳ Carmarthen *area* 2227 *sq mi* (5768 *sq km*), *pop* 341,600

Dzaudzhikau — see VLADIKAVKAZ

Dzer·zhinsk \dzər-'zhēn(t)sk\ city *cen* Russia in Europe on Oka River W of Nizhniy Novgorod *pop* 287,000

Dzungaria *or* **Dzungarian Basin** — see JUNGGAR

E

Ea·gan \'ē-gən\ city SE Minn. *pop* 47,409

Ea·gle Lake \'ē-gəl\ lake 13 *mi* (21 *km*) long N Calif. ENE of Lassen Peak

Eagle Pass city SW Tex. on Rio Grande *pop* 20,651

Ea·ling \'ē-liŋ\ borough of W Greater London, England *pop* 263,600

East An·glia \'aŋ-glē-ə\ region E England including Norfolk & Suffolk; one of kingdoms in Anglo-Saxon heptarchy *pop* 1,366,300 —
East An·gli·an \-ən\ *adj or n*

East Antarctica — see ANTARCTICA

East Bengal the part of Bengal now in Bangladesh

East Beskids — see BESKIDS

East·bourne \'ēs(t)-ˌbȯrn, -ˌbȯrn\ town S England in E. Sussex on English Channel *pop* 83,200

East Chicago city NW Ind. SE of Chicago, Ill. *pop* 33,892

East China Sea sea W Pacific bet. China (on W), S. Korea (on N), Japan & Ryukyu Islands (on E), & Taiwan (on S)

East Cleveland city NE Ohio NE of Cleveland *pop* 33,096

East Detroit city SE Mich. NE of Detroit *pop* 35,283

Eas·ter Island \'ē-stər\ *or* **Ra·pa Nui** \ˌrä-pə-'nü-ē\ *or Sp* **Is·la de Pas·cua** \ˌēs-lä-thā-'päs-kwä\ island Chile in SE Pacific 2000 *mi* (3200 *km*) W of coast *area* 46 *sq mi* (119 *sq km*) — **Easter Islander** *n*

Eastern Cape *or* **Oos Kaap** \ˌōs-'käp\ province SE Republic of South Africa *area* 65,483 *sq mi* (169,600 *sq km*), *pop* 6,504,000

Eastern Ghats \'gäts, 'gȯts, 'gəts\ chain of mountains SE India extending SW & S from near delta of the Mahanadi in Orissa to W Tamil Nadu; highest point Mt. Dodabetta (in Nilgiri Hills) 8640 *ft* (2633 *m*) — see WESTERN GHATS

Eastern Rumelia region S Bulgaria including Rhodope Mountains & the Maritsa valley

Eastern Samoa — see AMERICAN SAMOA

Eastern Shore region E Md. & E Va. E of Chesapeake Bay; sometimes considered as including Del. — see DELMARVA PENINSULA

Eastern Thrace — see THRACE

Eastern Transvaal — see MPUMALANGA

East Flanders province NW *cen* Belgium ✳ Ghent *area* 1151 *sq mi* (2981 *sq km*), *pop* 1,335,793

East Frisian — see FRISIAN ISLANDS

East Germany the German Democratic Republic — see GERMANY

East Ham \'ēst-'ham\ former county borough SE England in Essex, now part of Newham

East Hartford town *cen* Conn. *pop* 50,452

East Ha·ven \'ēst-,hā-vən\ town S Conn. SE of New Haven *pop* 26,144

East Indies 1 *or* **East India** southeastern Asia including India, Indochina, Malaya, & Malay Archipelago — a chiefly former name **2** the Malay Archipelago — **East Indian** *adj or n*

East·lake \'ēst-,lāk\ city NE Ohio NE of Cleveland *pop* 21,161

East Lansing city S Mich. *pop* 50,677

East London city & port S Republic of South Africa in SE Eastern Cape on Indian Ocean *pop* 119,727

East Los Angeles urban center SW Calif. *pop* 126,379

East Lo·thi·an \'lō-thē-ən\ *or* **Had·ding·ton** \'ha-diŋ-tən\ *or* **Hadding·ton·shire** \-,shir, -shər\ former county SE Scotland ✳ Haddington — see LOTHIAN

East·main \'ēst-,mān\ river *ab* 500 *mi* (804 *km*) Canada in W Que.

East Malaysia the parts of Malaysia on the island of Borneo, comprising Sabah and Sarawak

East Moline city NW Ill. on Mississippi River *pop* 20,147

Eas·ton \'ēs-tən\ **1** city SE Mass. SW of Brockton *pop* 19,807 **2** city E Pa. NE of Allentown *pop* 26,276

East Orange city NE N.J. NW of Newark *pop* 73,552

East Pakistan the former E division of Pakistan comprising the E portion of Bengal — see BANGLADESH

East Palo Alto city W Calif. *pop* 23,451

East Peoria city N *cen* Ill. *pop* 21,378

East Point \'ēst-,point\ city NW *cen* Ga. SW of Atlanta *pop* 34,402

East Providence city E R.I. *pop* 50,380

East Prussia region N Europe bordering on the Baltic E of Pomerania; formerly a province of Prussia, for a time (1919–39) separated from rest of Prussia by Polish Corridor; divided 1945 bet. Poland & U.S.S.R. (Russia & Lithuania)

East Punjab — see PUNJAB

East Ridge \'ēst-,rij\ town SE Tenn. SE of Chattanooga *pop* 21,101

East Riding — see YORK

East River strait SE N.Y. connecting Upper New York Bay with Long Island Sound & separating Manhattan Is. from Long Is.

East Saint Louis city SW Ill. *pop* 40,944

East Siberian Sea sea, arm of Arctic Ocean N of E Russia in Asia extending from New Siberian Islands to Wrangel Is.

East Strouds·burg \'straudz-,bərg\ borough E Pa. *pop* 8781

East Suffolk — see SUFFOLK

East Sus·sex \'sə-siks, *US also* -,seks\ county SE England ✳ Lewes *area* 718 *sq mi* (1860 *sq km*), *pop* 670,600

East York borough Canada in SE Ont. near Toronto *pop* 102,696

Eau Claire \ō-'klar, -'kler\ city W Wis. *pop* 56,856

Eb·bw Vale \'e-bü-'väl\ town SE Wales in W Gwent *pop* 24,422

Eboracum — see YORK

Ebro \'ā-(,)brō\ river 565 *mi* (909 *km*) NE Spain flowing from Cantabrian Mountains ESE into the Mediterranean

Ecbatana — see HAMADAN

Ec·ua·dor \'e-kwə-,dór, ,e-kwä-'thór\ country W S. America bordering on the Pacific; a republic ✳ Quito *area* 109,483 *sq mi* (283,561 *sq km*), *pop* 10,985,000 — **Ec·ua·dor·an** \,e-kwə-'dór-ən, -'dór-\ *adj or n* — **Ec·ua·dor·ean** or **Ec·ua·dor·ian** \-ē-ən\ *adj or n*

Edam \'ē-dəm, -,dam, D ā-'däm\ commune NW Netherlands on the IJsselmeer NNE of Amsterdam *pop* 23,853

Ede 1 \'ā-də\ commune E Netherlands W of Arnhem *pop* 96,044 **2** \'ā-,dā\ city SW Nigeria NE of Ibadan *pop* 271,000

Eden Prairie \'ē-d³n\ village SE *cen* Minn., a suburb of Minneapolis *pop* 39,311

Edes·sa \i-'de-sə\ **1** city N Greece in W Macedonia; ancient ✳ of Macedonian kings *pop* 17,624 **2** — see URFA

Edi·na \i-'dī-nə\ village SE Minn. SW of Minneapolis *pop* 46,070

Ed·in·boro \'e-d³n-,bər-ə, -,bə-rə\ borough NW corner of Pa. *pop* 7736

Ed·in·burg \'e-d³n-,bərg\ city S Tex. NW of Brownsville *pop* 29,885

Ed·in·burgh \'e-d³n-,bər-ə, -,bə-rə, -b(ə-)rə\ **1** or *ScGael* **Dun·e·din** \,də-'nē-d³n\ city ✳ of Scotland & of Lothian region on Firth of Forth *pop* 434,520 **2** or **Ed·in·burgh·shire** \-,shir, -shər\ — see MIDLOTHIAN

Edir·ne \ā-'dir-nə\ or *formerly* **Adri·a·no·ple** \,ā-drē-ə-'nō-pəl\ city Turkey in Europe on the Maritsa *pop* 102,345

Ed·is·to \'e-də-,stō\ river 150 *mi* (241 *km*) S S.C. flowing SE into the Atlantic

Edith Ca·vell, Mount \'ē-dəth-'ka-vəl, -kə-'vel\ mountain 11,033 *ft* (3363 *m*) Canada in SW Alta. in Jasper National Park

Ed·mond \'ed-mənd\ city *cen* Okla. N of Oklahoma City *pop* 52,315

Ed·monds \'ed-mən(d)z\ city W Wash. N of Seattle *pop* 30,744

Ed·mon·ton \'ed-mən-tən\ **1** city Canada ✳ of Alta. on the N. Saskatchewan *pop* 616,741 **2** former municipal borough SE England in Middlesex, now part of Enfield — **Ed·mon·to·ni·an** \,ed-mən-'tō-nē-ən, -nyən\ n

Edo — see TOKYO

Edom \'ē-dəm\ or **Id·u·maea** or **Id·u·mea** \,i-dyü-'mē-ə\ ancient country SW Asia S of Judea & the Dead Sea — **Edom·ite** \'ē-də-,mīt\ n

Ed·ward, Lake \'ed-wərd\ lake E Africa SW of Lake Albert on boundary bet. NE Democratic Republic of the Congo & SW Uganda *area* 830 *sq mi* (2158 *sq km*)

Ed·wards \'ed-wərdz\ plateau 2000–5000 *ft* (610–1524 *m*) SW Tex.

Efa·te \ā-'fä-,tā\ or *F* **Va·té** \vä-'tā\ island SW Pacific in *cen* Vanuatu; chief town Port-Vila (✳ of Vanuatu) *area* 353 *sq mi* (914 *sq km*), *pop* 30,422

Ef·fi·gy Mounds National Monument \'e-fə-jē\ site NE Iowa on Mississippi River NW of Dubuque including prehistoric mounds

Ega·di Islands \\'e-gə-dē\\ *or anc* **Ae·ga·tes Islands** \\ē-'gä-tēz\\ islands Italy off W coast of Sicily *area* 15 *sq mi* (6 *sq km*), *pop* 4335

Eger \\'ā-gər\\ *or Czech* **Ohře** \\'ȯr-zhə\\ river 193 *mi* (311 *km*) E Germany & NW Czech Republic flowing NE into the Elbe

Eg·mont, Mount \\'eg-ˌmänt\\ *or* **Ta·ra·na·ki** \\ˌtä-rä-'nä-kē\\ mountain 8260 *ft* (2518 *m*) New Zealand in W *cen* North Is.

Egypt \\'ē-jipt\\ *or Ar* **Miṣr** \\'misrʰ\\ country NE Africa bordering on Mediterranean & Red seas ✳ Cairo *area* 386,900 *sq mi* (1,002,071 *sq km*), *pop* 57,673,000 — see UNITED ARAB REPUBLIC — **Egyp·tian** \\i-'jip-shən\\ *adj or n*

Ei·fel \\'ī-fəl\\ plateau region W Germany NW of the Moselle & NE of Luxembourg

Ei·ger \\'ī-gər\\ mountain 13,025 *ft* (3970 *m*) W *cen* Switzerland NE of the Jungfrau

Eind·ho·ven \\'īnt-ˌhō-və(n), 'änt-\\ commune S Netherlands in N. Brabant *pop* 193,966

Eire — see IRELAND

Ei·se·nach \\'ī-zⁿn-ˌäk, -ˌäk\\ city *cen* Germany in Thuringia W of Erfurt *pop* 44,266

Ekaterinodar — see KRASNODAR

Ekaterinoslav — see DNIPROPETROVS'K

El Aiún — see AAIÚN, EL

El Al·a·mein \\ˌel-ˌa-lə-'mān\\ village NW Egypt on the Mediterranean N of NE corner of Qattara Depression

Elam \\'ē-ləm\\ *or* **Su·si·ana** \\ˌsü-zē-'a-nə, -'ä-, -'ā-\\ ancient kingdom SW Asia at head of Persian Gulf E of Babylonia ✳ Susa — **Elam·ite** \\'ē-lə-ˌmīt\\ *adj or n*

Elat \\'ē-ˌlat, ā-'lät\\ town & port S Israel at head of Gulf of Aqaba *pop* 29,900

Elatea — see CITHAERON

Elath \\'ē-ˌlath\\ — see AQABA

Ela·zig \\e-lə-'zə, -'zē(g)\\ city E *cen* Turkey in valley of the upper Murat *pop* 204,603

El·ba \\'el-bə\\ island Italy in the Mediterranean bet. Corsica & mainland; chief town Portoferraio *area* 86 *sq mi* (224 *sq km*)

El Bahnasa — see OXYRHYNCHUS

El·be \\'el-bə, 'elb\\ *or Czech* **La·be** \\'lä-be\\ river 720 *mi* (1159 *km*) N Czech Republic & NE Germany flowing NW into North Sea

El·bert, Mount \\'el-bərt\\ mountain 14,433 *ft* (4399 *m*) *cen* Colo. in Sawatch Range; highest in Colo. & Rocky Mountains

El·blag \\'el-ˌblȯŋk\\ *or G* **El·bing** \\'el-biŋ\\ city & port N Poland near the Frisches Haff *pop* 125,154

El'·brus *or* **El·brus** \\'el-'brüz, -'brüs\\ mountain 18,510 *ft* (5642 *m*) S Russia in Europe; highest in the Caucasus & in Europe

El·burz Mountains \\el-'bürz\\ mountains N Iran parallel with S shore of Caspian Sea — see DAMAVAND

El Ca·jon \\ˌel-kə-'hōn\\ city SW Calif. E of San Diego *pop* 88,693

El Cen·tro \\el-'sen-(ˌ)trō\\ city S Calif. in Imperial Valley *pop* 31,384

El Cer·ri·to \\ˌel-sə-'rē-(ˌ)tō\\ city W Calif. on San Francisco Bay N of Berkeley *pop* 22,869

El·che \\'el-(ˌ)chä\\ city SE Spain SW of Alicante *pop* 188,062

El Do·ra·do \\ˌel-də-'rä-(ˌ)dō, -'rä-də\\ city S Ark. *pop* 23,146

Elec·tric Peak \i-'lek-trik, ē-\ mountain 10,992 *ft* (3350 *m*) S Mont. in Yellowstone National Park; highest in Gallatin Range

El·e·phan·ta \e-lə-'fan-tə\ *or* **Gha·ra·pu·ri** \gär-ə-'pür-ē\ island W India in Bombay harbor

El·e·phan·tine \e-lə-,fan-'tī-nē, -fən-, -'tē-\ island S Egypt in the Nile opposite Aswân *pop* 1814

Eleu·sis \i-'lü-səs\ ancient deme W Attica NW of Athens; ruins at modern town of **Elev·sís** \e-lef-'sēs\ in E Greece — **El·eu·sin·i·an** \,el-yù-'si-nē-ən\ *adj or n*

Eleu·thera \i-'lü-thə-rə\ island Bahamas E of New Providence Is. *area* 164 *sq mi* (426 *sq km*)

El Fai·yûm \el-fā-'yüm, -,(,)fī-\ *or* **Al Fay·yūm** \,al-\ city N Egypt SSW of Cairo *pop* 166,910

El Fa·sher \el-'fa-shər\ city W Sudan in Darfur

El Fer·rol \el-fe-'röl\ *or* **El Ferrol del Cau·dil·lo** \,thel-kaù-'thē-(,)yō, -'thēl-(,)yō\ city & port NW Spain on the Atlantic *pop* 83,045

El Gezira — see GEZIRA

El·gin \'el-jən\ city NE Ill. *pop* 77,010 **2** \'el-gən\ *or* **El·gin·shire** \-,shir, -shər\ — see MORAY **3** \'el-gən\ royal burgh NE Scotland in Moray district of Grampian region *pop* 18,905

El Giza — see GIZA

El·gon, Mount \'el-,gän\ extinct volcano 14,178 *ft* (4321 *m*) E Africa on boundary bet. Uganda & Kenya NE of Lake Victoria

Elikón — see HELICON

Elis \'ē-ləs\ *or NGk* **Ilía** \ē-'lē-ä\ region S Greece in NW Peloponnese S of Achaea bordering on Ionian Sea

Elisabethville — see LUBUMBASHI

Elisavetgrad — see KIROVOGRAD

Elisavetpol — see GANCA

Elis·ta \e-'lyē-stə, ē-'lis-tə\ town S Russia in Europe ✱ of Kalmykia *pop* 95,200

Eliz·a·beth \i-'li-zə-bəth\ **1** short river SE Va. flowing bet. cities of Norfolk & Portsmouth into Hampton Roads **2** city & port NE N.J. SW of Newark on Newark Bay *pop* 110,002

Elizabeth Islands islands SE Mass. bet. Buzzards Bay & Vineyard Sound

Elk Grove Village \'elk\ village NE Ill. NW of Chicago *pop* 33,429

Elk·hart \'el-,kärt\ city N Ind. E of S. Bend *pop* 43,627

Elk Island National Park reservation Canada in E *cen* Alta.

Ellás — see GREECE

Elles·mere Island \'elz-,mir\ island Canada in Northwest Territories W of NW Greenland — see COLUMBIA (Cape)

Ellice — see TUVALU

El·lis Island \'e-ləs\ island SE N.Y. in Upper New York Bay; served as immigrant station 1892–1954

El·lo·ra \e-'lōr-ə, -'lȯr-\ village W India in *cen* Maharashtra NW of Aurangabad; caves

Ells·worth Land \'elz-(,)wərth\ region W Antarctica on Bellingshausen Sea

El Maghreb al Aqsa — see MAGHREB

El Ma·hal·la El Ku·bra \,el-mə-'ha-lə-,el-'kü-brə\ city N Egypt in Nile delta NE of Tanta *pop* 400,000

El Man·sû·ra \el-man-'sûr-ə\ *or* **Al Man·su·rah** \,al-\ city N Egypt in Nile delta

Elm·hurst \'elm-ˌhərst\ city NE Ill. W of Chicago *pop* 42,029

El Min·ya \el-'min-yə\ *or* **Al Minya** \al-\ city *cen* Egypt on the Nile

El·mi·ra \el-'mī-rə\ city S N.Y. *pop* 33,724

El Misti — see MISTI

El Mon·te \el-'män-tē\ city SW Calif. E of Los Angeles *pop* 106,209

El Mor·ro National Monument \el-'mär-(ˌ)ō, -'mȯr-\ reservation W N.Mex. SE of Gallup; rock carvings, pueblo

Elm·wood Park \ˌelm-ˌwu̇d\ village NE Ill. *pop* 23,206

El Obeid \ˌel-ō-'bād\ city *cen* Sudan in Kordofan *pop* 66,270

El Paso \el-'pa-(ˌ)sō\ city Tex. at W tip on Rio Grande *pop* 515,342 — **El Paso·an** \-'pa-sō-ən\ *n*

El Sal·va·dor \el-'sal-və-ˌdȯr, ˌsal-və-'; ˌel-ˌsäl-vä-'thȯr\ country Central America bordering on the Pacific; a republic ✻ San Salvador *area* 8260 *sq mi* (21,393 *sq km*) *pop* 5,517,000 — **El Sal·va·dor·an** \-ˌsal-və-'dȯr-ən\ *n or adj*

Elsass — see ALSACE

Elsene — see IXELLES

Elu·ru \e-'lu̇r-(ˌ)ü\ *or formerly* **El·lore** \e-'lȯr, -'lȯr\ city SE India in E Andhra Pradesh *pop* 212,918

Ely \'ē-lē\ town E England in N *cen* Cambridgeshire

Ely, Isle of district & former administrative county (✻ Ely) E England in Cambridgeshire — see CAMBRIDGESHIRE

Elyr·ia \i-'lir-ē-ə\ city NE Ohio SW of Cleveland *pop* 56,746

Em·bar·ras *or* **Em·bar·rass** \'am-ˌbrò—*sic*\ river 185 *mi* (298 *km*) E Ill. flowing SE into the Wabash

Em·den \'em-dən\ city & port NW Germany at mouth of Ems River *pop* 51,103

Emesa — see HOMS

Emi·lia \ā-'mēl-yä\ **1** district N Italy comprising the W part of Emilia-Romagna region **2** — see EMILIA-ROMAGNA

Emilia–Ro·ma·gna \-rō-'mä-nyä\ *or formerly* **Emilia** *or anc* **Ae·mil·ia** \ē-'mil-yə\ region N Italy bounded by the Po, the Adriatic, & the Apennines ✻ Bologna *area* 8543 *sq mi* (22,126 *sq km*), *pop* 3,921,597

Em·me \'e-mə\ river *ab* 50 *mi* (80 *km*) *cen* Switzerland in E Bern canton

Em·men \'e-mən\ commune NE Netherlands *pop* 93,107

Em·po·ria \em-'pȯr-ē-ə, -'pȯr-\ city E *cen* Kans. *pop* 25,512

Empty Quarter RUBʿ AL KHALI

Ems \'emz, 'em(p)s\ **1** river 231 *mi* (372 *km*) NW Germany flowing N into North Sea **2** *or* **Bad Ems** \ˌbät-\ town W Germany SE of Koblenz *pop* 10,358

En·chant·ed Mesa \in-'chan-təd, en-\ sandstone butte W N.Mex. NE of Acoma

En·ci·ni·tas \ˌen(t)-sə-'nē-təs\ city S Calif. on coast N of San Diego *pop* 55,386

En·der·bury \'en-dər-ˌber-ē\ island (atoll) *cen* Pacific in the Phoenix Islands chain of Kiribati

En·di·cott Mountains \'en-di-kət, -də-ˌkät\ mountains N Alaska, the central range of Brooks Range

En·field \'en-ˌfēld\ **1** town N Conn. *pop* 45,532 **2** borough of N Greater London, England *pop* 248,900

En·ga·dine \\en-gə-'dēn, 'eŋ-gə-,\\ valley of upper Inn River 60 *mi* (96 *km*) long E Switzerland in Graubünden

En·gland \\'iŋ-glənd, 'iŋ-lənd\\ **1** *or LL* **An·glia** \\'aŋ-glē-ə\\ country S Great Britain; a division of the United Kingdom of Great Britain and Northern Ireland ✻ London *area* 50,333 *sq mi* (130,362 *sq km*), *pop* 46,161,000 **2** England & Wales **3** UNITED KINGDOM — **En·glish** \\'iŋ-glish\\ *adj or n* — **En·glish·man** \\-mən\\ *n* — **En·glish·wom·an** \\-,wü-mən\\ *n*

En·gle·wood \\'eŋ-gəl-,wud\\ **1** city N *cen* Colo. S of Denver *pop* 29,387 **2** city NE N.J. on the Hudson *pop* 24,850

English Channel *or F* **La Manche** \\lä-'mä°sh\\ strait bet. S England & N France connecting North Sea & Atlantic Ocean

Enid \\'ē-nəd\\ city N Okla. *pop* 45,309

Eni·we·tok \\,e-ni-'wē-,täk\\ island (atoll) W Pacific in the NW Marshalls

En·na \\'e-nä\\ commune Italy in *cen* Sicily *pop* 28,296

En·nis \\'e-nəs\\ town W Ireland ✻ of County Clare *pop* 13,746

En·nis·kil·len \\,e-nə-'ski-lən\\ *or* **In·nis·kil·ling** \\,i-nə-'ski-liŋ\\ town SW Northern Ireland in *cen* Fermanagh district

Enns \\'enz, 'en(t)s\\ river 160 *mi* (257 *km*) *cen* Austria flowing E & N from Styria into the Danube

En·sche·de \\'en(t)-skə-,dā, -skə-\\ commune E Netherlands in Overijssel near German frontier *pop* 147,199

En·se·na·da \\,en(t)-sə-'nä-də, ,en-sā-'nä-thä\\ city & port NW Mexico in Baja California on the Pacific SE of Tijuana *pop* 260,905

En·teb·be \\en-'te-bə, -bē\\ town S Uganda on N shore of Lake Victoria; former ✻ of Uganda *pop* 41,638

En·ter·prise \\'en-tə(r)-,prīz\\ city SE Ala. *pop* 20,123

Eph·e·sus \\'e-fə-səs\\ ancient city W Asia Minor in Ionia near Aegean coast; its site SSE of Izmir — **Ephe·sian** \\i-'fē-zhən\\ *adj or n*

Ephra·im \\'ē-frē-əm\\ **1** *or* **Mount Ephraim** \\...\\ hilly region *cen* Palestine in N Jordan E of Jordan River **2** — see ISRAEL — **Ephra·im·ite** \\-frē-ə-,mīt\\ *n*

Epidamnus — see DURRES

Ep·i·dau·rus \\,e-pə-'dȯr-əs\\ ancient town S Greece in Argolis on Saronic Gulf

Épi·nal \\,ā-pi-'näl\\ commune NE France on the Moselle *pop* 39,480

Epi·rus \\i-'pī-rəs\\ *or Gk* **Epei·ros** \\'ē-pē-,rȯs\\ region NW Greece bordering on Ionian Sea — **Epi·rote** \\i-'pī-,rōt, -rət\\ *n*

Ep·ping Forest \\'e-piŋ\\ forested region SE England in Essex NE of London & S of town of Epping

Equa·to·ri·al Guinea \\,ē-kwə-'tȯr-ē-əl, ,e-\\ country W Africa on Bight of Biafra comprising former Spanish Guinea; an independent republic since 1968 ✻ Malabo *area* 10,825 *sq mi* (28,037 *sq km*), *pop* 376,000— see SPANISH GUINEA

Erbil — see ARBIL

Er·ci·yas \\,er-jē-'yäs\\ mountain 12,848 *ft* (3916 *m*) *cen* Turkey; highest in Asia Minor

Er·e·bus, Mount \\'er-ə-bəs\\ volcano 12,450 *ft* (3795 *m*) E Antarctica on Ross Is. in SW Ross Sea

Ere·gli \\,er-ā-'lē, -'glē\\ **1** city S Turkey SSE of Ankara *pop* 74,332 **2** town & port NW Turkey in Asia on Black Sea *pop* 63,776

Er·furt \'er-fərt, -,fu̇rt\ city *cen* Germany WSW of Leipzig *pop* 204,912

Erie \'ir-ē\ city & port NW Pa. on Lake Erie *pop* 108,718

Erie, Lake lake E *cen* N. America on boundary bet. the U.S. & Canada; one of the Great Lakes *area* 9910 *sq mi* (25,667 *sq km*)

Erie Canal canal 363 *mi* (584 *km*) long N.Y. from Hudson River at Albany to Lake Erie at Buffalo; built 1817–25; superseded by **New York State Barge Canal** (*ab* 525 *mi* or 840 *km* long)

Eriha — see JERICHO

Er·in \'er-ən\ IRELAND — a poetic name

Er·i·trea \,er-ə-'trē-ə, -'trā-\ country NE Africa bordering on Red Sea ✻ Asmara; incorporated (1962) into Ethiopia; voted (1993) in favor of independence *area* 45,405 *sq mi* (117,599 *sq km*), *pop* 3,317,611 — **Er·i·tre·an** \-ən\ *adj or n*

Er·lang·en \'er-,läŋ-ən\ city S Germany in Bavaria NNW of Nuremberg *pop* 102,433

Er·mou·po·lis or **Her·moú·po·lis** \er-'mü-pə-lis, -pō-,lēs\ or **Sí·ros** \'sī-,räs, 'sē-,rós\ town & port Greece on Síros; chief town of the Cyclades *pop* 12,987

Er Rif or **Er Riff** \er-'rif\ mountain range N Morocco on the Mediterranean

Erz·ge·bir·ge \'erts-gə-,bir-gə\ mountain range Germany & NW Czech Republic on boundary bet. Saxony & Bohemia; highest peak (in Czech Republic) 4080 *ft* (1244 *m*)

Er·zin·can \,er-zin-'jän\ city E *cen* Turkey on the Euphrates *pop* 90,799

Er·zu·rum \,er-zu̇-'rům\ city NE Turkey in mountains of W Turkish Armenia *pop* 242,391

Es·bjerg \'es-,byer(g)\ city & port SW Denmark in SW Jutland Peninsula on North Sea *pop* 81,843

Escaut — see SCHELDT

Es·con·di·do \,es-kən-'dē-(,)dō\ city SW Calif. N of San Diego *pop* 108,635

Es·dra·e·lon, Plain of \,ez-drə-'ē-lən\ plain N Israel NE of Mt. Carmel in valley of the upper Qishon

Es·fa·hān \,es-fə-'hän, -'han\ or **Is·fa·han** \is-\ or *formerly* **Is·pa·han** \,is-pə-\ city W *cen* Iran; former ✻ of Persia *pop* 986,753

Esher \'ē-shər\ town S England in N Surrey *pop* 61,446

Es·kils·tu·na \'es-kəl-,stü-nə\ city SE Sweden *pop* 89,584

Es·ki·se·hir \,es-ki-shə-'hir\ or **Es·ki-shehr** \-'sher\ city W *cen* Turkey on tributary of the Sakarya *pop* 413,082

España — see SPAIN

Española — see HISPANIOLA

Es·pí·ri·to San·to \ə-'spir-ə-,tü-'sän-(,)tü\ state E Brazil bordering on the Atlantic ✻ Vitória *area* 17,658 *sq mi* (45,734 *sq km*), *pop* 2,598,231

Es·pí·ri·tu San·to \ə-'spir-ə-,tü-'sän-(,)tü\ island SW Pacific in NW Vanuatu largest in the group *area* 1420 *sq mi* (3678 *sq km*), *pop* 22,663

Es·poo \'es-(,)pō\ town S Finland W of Helsinki *pop* 175,806

Es·qui·line \'es-kwə-,līn, -lən\ hill in Rome, Italy, one of seven on which the ancient city was built — see AVENTINE

Es·sa·oui·ra \,e-sə-'wir-ə\ or *formerly* **Mog·a·dor** \'mä-gə-,dòr\ city & port W Morocco on the Atlantic W of Marrakech *pop* 30,061

Es·sen \'e-s°n\ city W Germany in the Ruhr *pop* 626,989

Es·se·qui·bo \e-sə-'kē-(,)bō\ river 630 *mi* (1014 *km*) Guyana flowing N into the Atlantic through a wide estuary

Es·sex \'e-siks\ county SE England bordering on North Sea & N shore of Thames River; one of kingdoms in Anglo-Saxon heptarchy ✳ Chelmsford *area* 1470 *sq mi* (3807 *sq km*), *pop* 1,495,600

Ess·ling·en \'es-liŋ-ən\ city SW Germany on the Neckar *pop* 91,829

Es·te·rel \,es-tə-'rel\ forested mountain region SE France on coast bet. Fréjus & Cannes; highest point 2020 *ft* (616 *m*)

Es·tes Park \'es-tēz\ valley N Colo. in Front Range of the Rocky Mountains at E border of Rocky Mountain National Park

Es·to·nia \e-'stō-nē-ə, -nyə\ *or* **Es·tho·nia** \es-'thō-, es-'thō-\ country N Europe bordering on Baltic Sea; one of the Baltic Provinces of Russia 1721–1917, an independent republic 1918–40, a constituent republic (**Es·to·ni·an Republic** \-ən\) of the U.S.S.R 1940–91 ✳ Tallinn *area* 17,413 *sq mi* (45,100 *sq km*), *pop* 1,536,000 — **Esto·nian** *adj or n*

Es·to·ril \,ēsh-tə-'ril\ resort town Portugal on coast W of Lisbon *pop* 2524

Es·tre·ma·du·ra \,es-trə-mə-'dúr-ə\ region & old province W *cen* Portugal ✳ Lisbon

Ethi·o·pia \,ē-thē-'ō-pē-ə\ **1** ancient country NE Africa bordering on Red Sea and extending from S Egypt to N (present-day) Ethiopia **2** *or* **Ab·ys·sin·ia** \,a-bə-'sin-yə, -'si-nē-ə\ country E Africa; formerly an empire, since 1975 a republic ✳ Addis Ababa *area* 471,776 *sq mi* (1,226,618 *sq km*), *pop* 55,699,000 — **Ethi·o·pi·an** \-ən\ *adj or n*

Et·na, Mount \'et-nə\ volcano 10,902 *ft* (3323 *m*) Italy in NE Sicily

Eto·bi·coke \e-'tō-bi-,kō—*sic*\ city Canada in SE Ont. *pop* 309,993

Eton \'ē-t°n\ town SE *cen* England in Berkshire

Etru·ria \i-'trúr-ē-ə\ ancient country *cen* Italy coextensive with modern Tuscany & part of Umbria; home of the Etruscans — **Etrus·can** \i-'trəs-kən\ *adj or n*

Et·trick Forest \'e-trik\ region, formerly a forest & hunting ground, in SE Scotland in Borders region

Eu·boea \yú-'bē-ə\ *or* **Ev·voia** \'e-vē-ä\ island 90 *mi* (145 *km*) long E Greece in the Aegean NE of Attica & Boeotia *area* 1411 *sq mi* (3654 *sq km*) — **Eu·boe·an** \yú-'bē-ən\ *adj or n*

Eu·clid \'yü-kləd\ city NE Ohio NE of Cleveland *pop* 54,875

Eu·ga·ne·an Hills \yü-'gā-nē-ən, ,yü-gə-'nē-\ hills NE Italy in SW Veneto bet. Padua & the Adige

Eu·gene \yü-'jēn\ city N Oreg. on the Willamette *pop* 112,669

Eu·less \'yü-ləs\ city NE Tex. NE of Fort Worth *pop* 38,149

Eu·pen \'òi-pən, ,ȯ(r)-'pen, ˌē-'\ commune E Belgium E of Liège; formerly in Germany, transferred (with Malmédy) to Belgium 1919 *pop* 17,161

Eu·phra·tes \yú-'frā-(,)tēz\ river 1700 *mi* (2736 *km*) SW Asia flowing from E Turkey SW & SE to unite with the Tigris forming the Shatt al Arab — see KARA SU — **Eu·phra·te·an** \-'frā-tē-ən\ *adj*

Eur·asia \yú-'rā-zhə, -shə\ name given to Asia & Europe as one continent

Eure \'ər, 'œr\ river 140 *mi* (225 *km*) NW France flowing N into the Seine

Eu·re·ka \yú-'rē-kə\ city & port NW Calif. *pop* 27,025

Eu·rope \'yuṙ-əp\ **1** continent of the eastern hemisphere bet. Asia & the Atlantic *area* 3,997,929 *sq mi* (10,354,636 *sq km*), *pop* 498,000,000 **2** the European continent exclusive of the British Isles — **Eu·ro·pe·an** \,yuṙ-ə-'pē-ən\ *adj or n*

European Economic Community *or* **Common Market** economic organization subsumed within the European Union

European Union *or formerly* **European Communities** *or* **European Community** economic, scientific, and political organization consisting of Belgium, France, Italy, Luxembourg, Netherlands, Germany, Denmark, Greece, Ireland, United Kingdom, Spain, Portugal, Austria, Finland, & Sweden

Ev·ans, Mount \'e-vənz\ mountain 14,264 *ft* (4348 *m*) N *cen* Colo. in Front Range WSW of Denver

Ev·ans·ton \'e-vən(t)-stən\ city NE Ill. N of Chicago *pop* 73,233

Ev·ans·ville \'e-vənz-,vil\ city SW Ind. on Ohio River *pop* 126,272

Ev·er·est, Mount \'ev-rəst, 'e-və-\ *or Tibetan* **Cho·mo·lung·ma** \,chō-mō-'luṅ-mə\ mountain 29,028 *ft* (8848 *m*) S Asia on border bet. Nepal & Tibet in the Himalayas; highest in the world

Ev·er·ett \'ev-rət, 'e-və-\ **1** city E Mass. N of Boston *pop* 35,701 **2** city NW *cen* Wash. on Puget Sound N of Seattle *pop* 69,961

Ev·er·glades \'e-vər-,glādz\ swamp region S Fla. S of Lake Okeechobee; now partly drained; SW part forms **Everglades National Park**

Ev·er·green Park \'e-vər-,grēn\ village NE Ill. S of Chicago *pop* 20,874

Eve·sham \'ēv-shəm\ borough W *cen* England in Hereford and Worcester S of Birmingham in **Vale of Evesham** *pop* 15,271

Évian *or* **Évian–les–Bains** \ā-vyäⁿ-le-'baⁿ\ commune E France on Lake Geneva; health resort *pop* 7027

Evo·ra \'e-vu̇-rə\ city S *cen* Portugal *pop* 34,851

Évreux \āv-'rœ̄, -'rə(r)\ commune N France WNW of Paris *pop* 51,452

Ev·ri·pos \'ev-ri-,pós\ narrow strait E Greece bet. Euboea & mainland

Évros — see MARITSA

Ex·e·ter \'ek-sə-tər\ city SW England ✳ of Devon *pop* 101,100

Ex·moor \'eks-,mu̇r, -,mōr, -,mȯr\ moorland SW England in Somerset & Devon *area* 32 *sq mi* (83 *sq km*)

Ex·tre·ma·du·ra \,ek-strə-mə-'du̇r-ə, ,es-trā-mä-'thü-rä\ region & old province W Spain bordering on Portugal; area included in present Cáceres & Badajoz provinces

Ex·u·ma \ik-'sü-mə, ig-'zü-\ islands in *cen* Bahamas S of **Exuma Sound** (SE of New Providence Is.); chief island **Great Exuma**

Eyre, Lake \'ar, 'er\ intermittent lake *cen* Australia in NE S. Australia

Eyre Peninsula peninsula Australia in S S. Australia W of Spencer Gulf

Eyzies, Les — see LES EYZIES

F

Fa·en·za \fä-'en-zä, -'en(t)-sä\ commune N Italy *pop* 54,118

Faer·oe Islands *or* **Far·oe Islands** \'far-(,)ō, 'fer-\ islands Denmark in the NE Atlantic NW of the Shetlands ✹ Torshavn *area* 540 *sq mi* (1404 *sq km*), *pop* 47,653

Fa·ial \fə-'yäl, fī-'äl\ island *cen* Azores *area* 66 *sq mi* (171 *sq km*)

Fair·banks \'far-,baŋks, 'fer-\ city E *cen* Alaska *pop* 30,843

Fair·born \'far-,bȯrn, 'fer-\ city SW *cen* Ohio *pop* 31,300

Fair·fax \'far-,faks, 'fer-\ city NE Va. *pop* 19,622

Fair·field \'far-,fēld, 'fer-\ **1** city W Calif. NE of Berkeley *pop* 77,211 **2** city SW Conn. SW of Bridgeport *pop* 53,418 **3** city SW Ohio *pop* 39,729

Fair Lawn borough NE N.J. NE of Paterson *pop* 30,548

Fair·mont \'far-,mänt, 'fer-\ city N W.Va. *pop* 20,210

Fair·weath·er, Mount *or* **Fairweather Mountain** \'far-,we-thər, 'fer-\ mountain 15,300 *ft* (4663 *m*) on boundary bet. Alaska & B.C.

Fai·sa·la·bad \,fī-,sä-lə-'bäd, -,sa-lə-'bad\ *or formerly* **Lyall·pur** \lē-,äl-'pu̇r\ city NE Pakistan W of Lahore *pop* 1,092,000

Faiyûm, El — see EL FAIYÛM

Faiz·a·bad \'fī-zə-,bad, -,bäd\ **1** *or* **Fey·za·bad** \'fā-zä-,bäd\ city NE Afghanistan *pop* 70,871 **2** city N India in Uttar Pradesh *pop* 125,012

Fa·ka·ra·va \,fä-kä-'rä-vä\ island (atoll) S Pacific, principal island of the Tuamotu Archipelago *pop* 651

Fa·laise \fä-'lāz\ town NW France SSE of Caen *pop* 8387

Fal·kirk \'fȯl-(,)kərk\ royal burgh *cen* Scotland in Central region ENE of Glasgow *pop* 36,875

Falk·land Islands \'fȯ-klənd, 'fȯl-\ *or Sp* **Is·las Mal·vi·nas** \,ēs-läs-mäl-'vē-näs\ islands SW Atlantic E of S end of Argentina; a Brit. crown colony ✹ Stanley *area* 4700 *sq mi* (12,173 *sq km*), *pop* 2100

Falkland Islands Dependencies islands & territories in the S Atlantic & in Antarctica administered by the British from Falkland Islands, including S. Orkney, S. Sandwich, & S. Shetland Islands, S. Georgia Is., Antarctic Peninsula, & Palmer Archipelago

Fall River \'fȯl\ city & port SE Mass. *pop* 92,703

Fal·mouth \'fal-məth\ town SE Mass. on Cape Cod *pop* 27,960

False Bay \'fȯls\ inlet Republic of South Africa in SW Western Cape province E of Cape of Good Hope

Fal·ster \'fäl-stər, 'fȯl-\ island Denmark in Baltic Sea S of Sjælland *pop* 42,841

Fa·ma·gus·ta \,fä-mä-'güs-tä, ,fa-\ city & port E Cyprus on **Famagusta Bay** (inlet of the Mediterranean) *pop* 42,500

Fanning — see TABUAERAN

Far·al·lon Islands \'far-ə-,län\ islands in the Pacific W *cen* Calif. W of San Francisco

Far East the countries of E Asia & the Malay Archipelago — usu. considered as comprising the Asian countries bordering on the Pacific but sometimes as including also India, Sri Lanka, Bangladesh, Tibet, & Myanmar — **Far Eastern** *adj*

Fare·well, Cape \'far-,wel, 'fer-\ cape Greenland at S tip

Far·go \'fär-(,)gō\ city E N.Dak. on Red River *pop* 74,111

Farm·ers Branch \'fär-mərz\ city NE Tex. *pop* 24,250

Far·ming·ton \'fär-miŋ-tən\ **1** town N Conn. W of Hartford *pop* 20,608 **2** city NW N.Mex. *pop* 33,997

Farmington Hills city SE Mich. *pop* 74,652

Far·quhar Islands \'fär-kwər, -kər\ island group NW Indian Ocean NE of Madagascar belonging to Seychelles

Far·rukh·a·bad \fə-'rü-kə-,bad, -,bäd\ city N India in Uttar Pradesh on the Ganges WNW of Lucknow *pop* 160,927

Fársala — see PHARSALUS

Fashoda — see KODOK

Fá·ti·ma \'fa-tə-mə, 'fä-tē-\ village *cen* Portugal NNE of Lisbon

Fatshan — see FOSHAN

Fay·ette·ville \'fā-ət-,vil, -vəl; *2 is also* 'fed-vəl\ **1** city NW Ark. *pop* 42,099 **2** city SE *cen* N.C. on Cape Fear River *pop* 75,695

Fear, Cape \'fir\ cape SE N.C. at mouth of Cape Fear River

Feath·er \'fe-thər\ river 100 *mi* (161 *km*) N *cen* Calif. flowing S into Sacramento River

Federal Capital Territory — see AUSTRALIAN CAPITAL TERRITORY

Federal District 1 *or Pg* **Dis·tri·to Fe·de·ral** \dish-'trē-tü-,fe-di-'räl\ district E *cen* Brazil including ✳ city of Brasília *area* 2245 *sq mi* (5814 *sq km*), *pop* 1,596,174 **2** — see DISTRITO FEDERAL 3 **3** — see DISTRITO FEDERAL 4

Federated Malay States former Brit. protectorate (1895–1945) comprising the Malay states of Negeri Sembilan, Pahang, Perak, & Selangor ✳ Kuala Lumpur

Federated Shan States — see SHAN

Fen \'fən, 'fen\ river 300 *mi* (483 *km*) N China in *cen* Shanxi flowing SSE into the Huang

Fengtien 1 — see LIAONING **2** — see SHENYANG

Fer·ga·na \fər-'gä-nə\ valley W *cen* Asia in the Tian Shan in Kyrgyzstan, Tajikistan, & Uzbekistan SE of Tashkent

Fer·gu·son \'fər-gə-sən\ city E Mo. N of St. Louis *pop* 22,286

Fer·man·agh \fər-'ma-nə\ **1** district SW Northern Ireland, established 1974 *area* 724 *sq mi* (1875 *sq km*), *pop* 54,062 **2** traditional county N Northern Ireland

Fer·nan·do de No·ro·nha \fər-'nán-(,)dü-dē-nò-'rō-nyə\ island Brazil in the Atlantic NE of city of Natal *area* 10 *sq mi* (26 *sq km*)

Fernando Póo — see BIOKO

Fern·dale \'fərn-,dāl\ city SE Mich. N of Detroit *pop* 25,084

Fer·ra·ra \fe-'rär-ä\ commune N Italy in Emilia-Romagna NE of Bologna near the Po *pop* 137,336

Ferro — see HIERRO

Ferrol, El — see EL FERROL

Ferryville — see MENZEL-BOURGUIBA

Fertile Crescent semicircle of fertile land stretching from SE coast of Mediterranean around Syrian Desert N of Arabia to Persian Gulf

Fez \'fez\ *or* **Fès** \'fes\ city N *cen* Morocco *pop* 448,823

Fez·zan \fe-'zan\ region SW Libya, chiefly desert

Fich·tel·ge·bir·ge \'fik-t°l-gə-,bir-gə\ mountains Germany in NE Bavaria; highest Schneeberg 3453 *ft* (1052 *m*)

Fie·so·le \'fyä-zō-,lā\ *or anc* **Fae·su·lae** \'fē-zə-,lē\ commune *cen* Italy in Tuscany NE of Florence *pop* 15,056

Fife \'fīf\ *or* **Fife·shire** \-,shir, -shər\ region, formerly a county E Scotland bet. Firths of Tay & Forth ✻ Cupar *area* 509 *sq mi* (1319 *sq km*), *pop* 351,200

Fi·ji \'fē-(,)jē\ islands SW Pacific E of Vanuatu constituting (with Rotuma Is.) an independent dominion of the Commonwealth of Nations ✻ Suva (on Viti Levu) *area* 7055 *sq mi* (18,272 *sq km*), *pop* 715,735 — **Fi·ji·an** \'fē-(,)jē-ən, fi-\ *adj or n*

Filch·ner Ice Shelf \'filk-nər\ area of shelf ice Antarctica in Weddell Sea

Filipinas, República de — see PHILIPPINES

Finch·ley \'finch-lē\ former municipal borough SE England in Middlesex, now part of Barnet

Find·lay \'fin(d)-lē\ city NW Ohio *pop* 35,703

Fin·gal's Cave \'fiŋ-gəlz\ sea cave W Scotland on Staffa Is.

Fin·ger Lakes \'fiŋ-gər\ group of long narrow lakes W *cen* N.Y. comprising Cayuga, Seneca, Keuka, Canandaigua, Skaneateles, Owasco, & several smaller lakes

Fin·is·terre, Cape \,fi-nə-'ster, -'ster-ē\ cape NW Spain on coast of La Coruña province; westernmost point of Spanish mainland, at 9°18'W

Fin·land \'fin-lənd\ *or* **Finn Suo·mi** \'swȯ-mē\ country N Europe bordering on Gulf of Bothnia & Gulf of Finland; a republic ✻ Helsinki *area* 130,128 *sq mi* (337,032 *sq km*), *pop* 5,058,000 — **Fin·land·er** *n* — **Finn** \'fin\ *n* — **Fin·nish** \'fi-nish\ *adj or n*

Finland, Gulf of arm of Baltic Sea bet. Finland & Estonia

Fin·lay \'fin-lē\ river 250 *mi* (402 *km*) Canada in N *cen* B.C. flowing SE to unite with **Pars·nip** \'pär-snip\ River (145 *mi* or 232 *km*) forming Peace River

Fins·bury \'finz-,ber-ē, -b(ə-)rē\ former metropolitan borough E *cen* London, England, now part of Islington

Fin·ster·aar·horn \,fin(t)-stər-'är-,hȯrn\ mountain 14,019 *ft* (4273 *m*) S Switzerland; highest of the Berner Alpen

Fiord·land \'fē-'ȯrd-,land, 'fē-,; 'fyȯrd-\ mountain region S New Zealand in SW South Is.

Fitch·burg \'fich-,bərg\ city N *cen* Mass. *pop* 41,194

Fiume — see RIJEKA

Fiu·mi·ci·no \,fyü-mē-'chē-(,)nō\ town *cen* Italy on Tyrrhenian Sea SW of Rome & WNW of Ostia

Flag·staff \'flag-,staf\ city N *cen* Ariz. *pop* 45,857

Flam·bor·ough \'flam-,bər-ə, -,bə-rə, -b(ə-)rə\ town Canada in SE Ont. near Hamilton *pop* 29,616

Flamborough Head promontory NE England on Humberside coast

Flan·ders \'flan-dərz\ *or* F **Flan·dre** \fläⁿdr\ *or* Flem **Vlaan·de·ren** \'vlän-də-rə(n)\ **1** medieval county along coast of what is now Belgium and adjacent parts of France & Netherlands ✻ Lille **2** semiautonomous region W Belgium — see EAST FLANDERS, WEST FLANDERS — **Flem·ing** \'fle-miŋ\ *n* — **Flem·ish** \-mish\ *adj or n*

Flat·head \'flat-,hed\ river 245 *mi* (394 *km*) SE B.C. & NW Mont. flowing S through **Flathead Lake** (reservoir in Mont.) into Clark Fork

Flat·tery, Cape \'fla-tə-rē\ cape NW Wash. at entrance to Strait of Juan de Fuca

Flens·burg \'flenz-,bərg, 'flen(t)s-,bu̇rk\ city & port N Germany on inlet of the Baltic near Danish border *pop* 87,241

Fletsch·horn \'flech-ˌhȯrn\ mountain 13,107 *ft* (3995 *m*) S Switzerland in Pennine Alps S of Simplon Pass

Flevo·land \'fle-vō-ˌland\ province *cen* Netherlands ✻ Lelystad *area* 549 *sq mi* (1422 *sq km*), *pop* 243,441

Flin·ders \'flin-dərz\ river 520 *mi* (837 *km*) Australia in *cen* Queensland flowing NW into Gulf of Carpentaria

Flinders Ranges mountain ranges Australia in E S. Australia E of Lake Torrens

Flint \'flint\ **1** river 265 *mi* (426 *km*) W Ga. flowing S & SW into Lake Seminole **2** city SE *cen* Mich. NNW of Detroit *pop* 140,761 **3** or **Flint·shire** \-ˌshir, -shər\ former county NE Wales ✻ Mold

Flod·den \'flä-dᵊn\ hill N England in N Northumberland near Scottish border

Flor·ence \'flȯr-ən(t)s, 'flär-\ **1** city NW Ala. on Tennessee River *pop* 36,426 **2** city E S.C. *pop* 29,813 **3** or *It* **Fi·ren·ze** \fē-'rent-sä\ commune *cen* Italy on the Arno ✻ of Tuscany *pop* 402,316 — **Flor·en·tine** \'flȯr-ən-ˌtēn, 'flär-, -ˌtīn\ *n*

Flo·res \'flȯr-əs, 'flȯr-\ **1** island NW Azores *area* 58 *sq mi* (150 *sq km*) **2** island Indonesia in Lesser Sunda Islands

Flo·ri·a·nó·po·lis \ˌflȯr-ē-ə-'nō-pü-lis\ city S Brazil ✻ of Santa Catarina state on island off coast *pop* 254,944

Flor·i·da \'flȯr-ə-də, 'flär-\ state SE U.S. ✻ Tallahassee *area* 58,664 *sq mi* (151,940 *sq km*), *pop* 12,937,926 — **Flo·rid·i·an** \flə-'ri-dē-ən\ *adj or n* — **Flor·i·dan** \'flȯr-ə-dᵊn, 'flär-\ *adj or n*

Florida, Straits of channel bet. Florida Keys (on NW) & Cuba & Bahamas (on S & E) connecting Gulf of Mexico with the Atlantic

Flor·i·da Island \'flȯr-ə-də, 'flär-; flə-'rē-də\ island W Pacific in SE Solomons N of Guadalcanal

Florida Keys chain of islands S Florida extending SW from S tip of the peninsula

Flo·ris·sant \'flȯr-ə-sənt, 'flȯr-\ city E Mo. NNW of St. Louis *pop* 51,206

Florissant Fossil Beds National Monument reservation *cen* Colo.

Flush·ing \'flə-shiŋ\ **1** section of New York City on Long Is. in Queens **2** — see VLISSINGEN

Fly \'flī\ river 650 *mi* (1046 *km*) S New Guinea flowing SE into Gulf of Papua

Fog·gia \'fȯ-(ˌ)jä\ commune SE Italy in Puglia *pop* 155,042

Foggy Bottom section of Washington, D.C., near the Potomac where the State Department building is located

Foix \'fwä\ region & former province S France in the Pyrenees SE of Gascony

Folke·stone \'fōk-stən, *US also* -ˌstōn\ borough SE England in Kent on Strait of Dover *pop* 43,742

Fol·som \'fōl-səm\ city Calif. NE of Sacramento *pop* 29,802

Fond du Lac \ˌfän-dᵊl-ˌak, ˌfän-jə-ˌlak\ city E Wis. on Lake Winnebago *pop* 37,757

Fon·se·ca, Gulf of \fȯn-'sā-kä\ or **Fonseca Bay** inlet of the Pacific in Central America in El Salvador, Honduras, & Nicaragua

Fon·taine·bleau \ˌfän-tᵊn-ˌblō, ˌfȯⁿ-ten-'blō\ commune N France *pop* 18,037

Fon·tana \fän-'ta-nə\ city SW Calif. E of Los Angeles *pop* 87,535

Foochow — see FUZHOU

For·a·ker, Mount \'fȯr-i-kər, 'fär-\ mountain 17,400 ft (5304 m) S Alaska in Alaska Range SW of Mt. McKinley

For·far \'fȯr-fər\ **1** or **For·far·shire** \-,shir, -shər\ — see ANGUS **2** royal burgh E Scotland in Tayside pop 12,742

Fo·ril·lon National Park \,fȯr-ē(l)-'yōⁿ\ reservation E Canada in Gaspé Peninsula

For·lì \fȯr-'lē\ commune N Italy in Emilia-Romagna SE of Bologna pop 109,228

Formosa — see TAIWAN — **For·mo·san** \fȯr-'mō-sᵊn, fər-, -zᵊn\ adj or n

For·mo·sa Strait \fȯr-'mō-sə, fər-, -zə\ strait between Taiwan & China mainland connecting E. China & S. China seas

For·ta·le·za \,fȯr-tᵊl-'ā-zə\ city & port NE Brazil on the Atlantic ✳ of Ceará pop 1,700,000

Fort Col·lins \'kä-lənz\ city N Colo. pop 87,758

Fort–de–France \,fȯr-də-'fräⁿs\ city French West Indies ✳ of Martinique on W coast pop 93,598

Fort Dodge \'däj\ city NW cen Iowa pop 25,894

Fort Erie \'ir-ē\ town Canada in SE Ont. on Niagara River pop 26,006

Fort Fred·er·i·ca National Monument \,fre-də-'rē-kə, fre-'drē-\ reservation SE Ga. on W shore of St. Simons Is. containing site of fort built by Oglethorpe 1736

Fort George \'jȯrj\ river 480 mi (772 km) Canada in cen Que. flowing W into James Bay

Forth \'fȯrth, 'fōrth\ river 116 mi (187 km) S cen Scotland flowing E into **Firth of Forth** (estuary 48 mi or 77 km long, inlet of North Sea)

Fort Knox \'näks\ military reservation N cen Ky. SSW of Louisville; location of U.S. Gold Bullion Depository

Fort–Lamy — see N'DJAMENA

Fort Lau·der·dale \'lȯ-dər-,dāl\ city SE Fla. on the Atlantic pop 149,377

Fort Lee \'lē\ borough NE N.J. on the Hudson pop 31,997

Fort Ma·tan·zas National Monument \mə-'tan-zəs\ reservation SSE of St. Augustine, Fla., containing fort built ab 1736 by the Spanish

Fort Mc·Hen·ry National Monument \mə-'ken-rē\ site in Baltimore, Md., of a fort bombarded 1814 by the British

Fort Mc·Mur·ray \mək-'mər-ē\ city Canada in NE Alta. pop 34,706

Fort My·ers \'mī(-ə)rz\ city SW Fla. pop 45,206

Fort Nel·son \'nel-sən\ river 260 mi (418 km) Canada in NE B.C. flowing NW into the Liard

Fort Peck Lake \'pek\ reservoir ab 130 mi (209 km) long NE Mont. formed in Missouri River by **Fort Peck Dam**

Fort Pierce \'pirs\ city E Fla. on the Atlantic pop 36,830

Fort Pu·las·ki National Monument \pə-'las-kē, pyü-\ reservation E Ga. comprising island in mouth of Savannah River, site of a fort built 1829–47 to replace Revolutionary Fort Greene

Fort Smith \'smith\ city NW Ark. on Arkansas River pop 72,798

Fort Stan·wix National Monument \'stan-(,)wiks\ historic site E cen N.Y. in Rome

Fort Sum·ter National Monument \\'səm(p)-tər\ reservation S.C. at entrance to Charleston harbor containing site of Fort Sumter

Fort Union National Monument reservation NE N.Mex. ENE of Santa Fe containing site of military post 1851–91

Fort Wal·ton Beach \\'wȯl-tᵊn\ city NW Fla. E of Pensacola *pop* 21,471

Fort Wayne \\'wān\ city NE Ind. *pop* 173,072

Fort William — see THUNDER BAY

Fort Worth \\'wərth\ city N Tex. W of Dallas *pop* 447,619

Fo·shan \\'fō-'shän\ *or formerly* **Fat·shan** \\'făt-'shän\ city SE China in *cen* Guangdong SW of Guangzhou *pop* 303,160

Fos·sil Butte National Monument \\'fä-səl\ reservation SW Wyo. containing aquatic fossils

Fos·ter City \\'fȯs-tər, 'fäs-\ city W Calif. SSE of San Francisco *pop* 28,176

Foun·tain Valley \\'faȯn-tᵊn\ city SW Calif. SE of Los Angeles *pop* 53,691

Four Forest Cantons the cantons of Uri, Schwyz, Unterwalden, & Lucerne in *cen* Switzerland surrounding Lake of Lucerne

Fou·ta Djal·lon \\,fü-tə-jə-'lōn\ mountain region W Guinea; highest point *ab* 4970 *ft* (1515 *m*)

Fox \\'fäks\ **1** river 220 *mi* (354 *km*) SE Wis. & NE Ill. flowing S into Illinois River **2** river 175 *mi* (282 *km*) E Wis. flowing NE & N through Lake Winnebago into Green Bay

Foxe Basin \\'fäks\ inlet of the Atlantic N Canada in E Northwest Territories W of Baffin Is.; connected with Hudson Bay by **Foxe Channel**

Fox Islands islands SW Alaska in E Aleutians — see UMNAK, UN-ALASKA, UNIMAK

Foyle \\'fȯil\ river *ab* 20 *mi* (32 *km*) N Ireland flowing NE past city of Derry to **Lough Foyle** (inlet of the Atlantic 18 *mi or* 29 *km* long)

Fra·ming·ham \\'frā-miŋ-,ham\ town E Mass. WSW of Boston *pop* 64,989

France \\'fran(t)s, 'frãs\ country W Europe bet. English Channel & the Mediterranean; a republic * Paris *area* 212,918 *sq mi* (551,458 *sq km*), *pop* 54,257,300 — **French** \\'french\ *adj or n* — **French·man** \-mən\ *n* — **French·wom·an** \-,wu̇-mən\ *n*

Franche–Com·té \\,frãsh-kōⁿ-'tā\ region & former county & province E France E of the Saône * Besançon — see BURGUNDY

Fran·cis Case, Lake \\'fran(t)-səs-'kās\ reservoir *ab* 100 *mi* (161 *km*) long S S.Dak. formed in Missouri River by **Fort Ran·dall Dam** \\'ran-dᵊl\

Fran·co·nia \\fraŋ-'kō-nē-ə, -nyə\ former duchy in Austrasia, now included chiefly in Baden-Wurtemburg, Bavaria, & Hesse states, Germany — **Fran·co·ni·an** \-nē-ən, -nyən\ *adj or n*

Frank·fort \\'fraŋk-fərt\ city * of Ky., on Kentucky River E of Louisville *pop* 25,968

Frank·furt \\'fraŋk-fərt, 'fräŋk-,fu̇rt\ **1** *or in full* **Frankfurt am Main** \\(,)äm-'mīn\ city W Germany on Main River *pop* 654,679 **2** *or in full* **Frankfurt an der Oder** \\,än-dər-'ō-dər\ city E Germany on Oder River *pop* 85,357

Frank·lin \\'fraŋ-klən\ **1** town E *cen* Mass. *pop* 22,095 **2** town *cen* Tenn. S of Nashville *pop* 20,098 **3** city SE Wis., a SSW suburb of

Milwaukee *pop* 21,855 **4** former district Canada in N Northwest Territories including Arctic islands & Boothia & Melville peninsulas

Franklin D. Roo·se·velt Lake \'rō-zə-,velt, -vəlt *also* 'rü-\ reservoir 151 *mi* (243 *km*) long NE Wash. formed in Columbia River by Grand Coulee Dam

Franks Peak \'franks\ mountain 13,140 *ft* (4005 *m*) NW Wyo.; highest in Absaroka Range

Franz Jo·sef Land \,frants-'jō-zəf-,land, -səf-; ,fränts-'yō-zəf-,länt\ archipelago Russia in Arctic Ocean N of Novaya Zemlya

Fras·ca·ti \frä-'skä-tē\ commune *cen* Italy in Lazio SE of Rome *pop* 20,043

Fra·ser \'frā-zər, -zhər\ river 850 *mi* (1368 *km*) Canada in S *cen* B.C. flowing into Strait of Georgia

Frau·en·feld \'fraù-(ə)n-,felt\ commune NE Switzerland ✱ of Thurgau canton *pop* 19,538

Fred·er·ick \'fre-drik, 'fre-də-rik\ city N Md. *pop* 40,148

Fred·er·icks·burg \'fre-driks-,bərg, 'fre-də-riks-\ city NE Va. SW of Alexandria *pop* 19,027

Fred·er·ic·ton \'fre-drik-tən, 'fre-də-rik-\ city Canada ✱ of N.B. on St. John River *pop* 46,466

Fred·er·iks·berg \'fre-driks-,bərg, 'fre-də-riks-\ city Denmark on Sjælland Is., W suburb of Copenhagen *pop* 85,327

Free·port \'frē-,pōrt, -,pȯrt\ **1** city N Ill. W of Rockford *pop* 25,840 **2** village SE N.Y. on Long Is. *pop* 39,894 **3** city NW Bahamas on *cen* Grand Bahama Is. *pop* 26,574

Free State *or* **Vry·staat** \'frā-,stät, 'frī-\ *or formerly* **Or·ange Free State** \'ȯr-inj, 'är-, -ənj\ *or* **Oran·je Vrystaat** \ȯ-'rän-yə-\ province E *cen* Republic of South Africa bet. Orange & Vaal rivers *area* 49,992 *sq mi* (129,480 *sq km*), *pop* 2,767,000

Free·town \'frē-,taùn\ city & port ✱ of Sierra Leone on the Atlantic *pop* 178,600

Frei·burg \'frī-,bùrg, -,bərg, -,bùrk\ *or* **Freiburg im Breis·gau** \im-'brīs-,gaù\ city SW Germany at W foot of Black Forest *pop* 193,775

Fréjus — see CENIS (Mont) 2

Fré·jus, Mas·sif du \mä-,sēf-dü-frā-'zhēs\ mountain on border bet. France & Italy at SW end of Graian Alps

Fre·man·tle \'frē-,man-t⁽ᵊ⁾l\ city Australia in SW Western Australia at mouth of Swan River; port for Perth *pop* 23,834

Fre·mont \'frē-,mänt\ **1** city W Calif. SE of Oakland *pop* 173,339 **2** city E Nebr. *pop* 23,680

French Broad \'bȯd\ river 210 *mi* (338 *km*) flowing from W N.C. to E Tenn.

French Community former federation comprising France, its overseas departments & territories, & the former French territories in Africa that chose to maintain their ties with France

French Equatorial Africa *or earlier* **French Congo** former country W *cen* Africa N of Congo River comprising a federation of Chad, Gabon, Middle Congo, & Ubangi-Shari territories ✱ Brazzaville

French Guiana country N S. America; an overseas department of France ✱ Cayenne *area* 35,126 *sq mi* (90,976 *sq km*), *pop* 128,000

French Guinea — see GUINEA

French India former French possessions in India including Chandernagore (ceded to India 1950) & Pondicherry, Karikal, Yanaon, & Mahé (ceded to India 1954) ✳ Pondicherry

French Indochina — see INDOCHINA

French Morocco — see MOROCCO

French Polynesia *or formerly* **French Oceania** islands in S Pacific belonging to France & including Society, Marquesas, Tuamotu, Gambier, & Tubuai groups ✳ Papeete (on Tahiti) *pop* 212,000

French Somaliland — see DJIBOUTI

French Sudan — see MALI

French Territory of the Afars and the Issas — see DJIBOUTI

French Togo — see TOGOLAND

French Union former federation (1946–58) comprising metropolitan France & its overseas departments, territories, & associated states — see FRENCH COMMUNITY

French West Africa former federation of French dependencies W Africa consisting of Dahomey, French Guinea, French Sudan, Ivory Coast, Mauritania, Niger, Senegal, & Upper Volta

French West Indies islands of the W. Indies belonging to France & including Guadeloupe, Martinique, Désirade, Les Saintes, Marie Galante, St. Barthélemy, & part of St. Martin

Fres·no \'frez-(,)nō\ city S *cen* Calif. SE of San Francisco *pop* 354,202

Fria, Cape \'frē-ə\ cape NW Namibia on the Atlantic

Fri·bourg \frē-'bür\ **1** canton W *cen* Switzerland *area* 645 *sq mi* (1670 *sq km*), *pop* 203,878 **2** commune, its ✳, SW of Bern *pop* 33,913

Frid·ley \'frid-lē\ city SE Minn. N of St. Paul *pop* 28,335

Friends·wood \'fren(d)z-,wúd\ city SE Tex. SE of Houston *pop* 22,814

Fries·land \'frēs-,land, 'frēz-, -lənd; 'frēs-,länt\ **1** old region N Europe bordering on North Sea **2** province N Netherlands ✳ Leeuwarden *area* 1464 *sq mi* (3792 *sq km*), *pop* 603,998

Frio, Cape \'frē-(,)ô\ cape SE Brazil E of Rio de Janeiro

Fri·sches Haff \'fri-shəs-,häf\ lagoon N Poland & W Russia in Europe; inlet of Gulf of Gdansk

Fri·sian Islands \'fri-zhən, 'frē-\ islands NW Europe in North Sea including **West Frisian Islands** (off N Netherlands), **East Frisian Islands** (off NW Germany), & **North Frisian Islands** (off NW Germany & Denmark, including Helgoland & Sylt)

Fri·u·li \frē-'ü-lē\ district N Italy in Friuli-Venezia Giulia on Slovenia border — **Fri·u·li·an** \frē-'ü-lē-ən\ *adj or n*

Friuli–Ve·ne·zia Giu·lia \-ve-'net-sē-ə-'jül-yä\ region N Italy E of Veneto ✳ Trieste *area* 3028 *sq mi* (7842 *sq km*), *pop* 1,202,877

Fro·bi·sher Bay \'frō-bi-shər\ inlet of the Atlantic N Canada in E Northwest Territories on SE coast of Baffin Is.

Front Range \'frənt\ range of the Rockies extending from *cen* Colo. N into SE Wyo. — see GRAYS PEAK

Frost·belt \'fróst-,belt\ the N & NE states of the U.S.

Fro·ward, Cape \'frō-(w)ərd\ headland S Chile N of Strait of Magellan; southernmost point of mainland of S. America at *ab* 53°54′S

Frunze — see BISHKEK

Fu-chou — see FUZHOU

Fujairah *or* **Fujayrah, Al** — see AL FUJAYRAH

Fu·ji \'fü-jē\ or **Fu·ji·ya·ma** \,fü-jē-'yä-mä\ or **Fu·ji-san** \-'sän\ mountain 12,388 ft (3776 m) Japan in S cen Honshu; highest in Japan

Fu·jian \'fü-'jyen\ or **Fu·kien** \'fü-'kyen, -'jyen\ province SE China bordering on Formosa Strait ✳ Fuzhou area 47,529 sq mi (123,575 sq km), pop 30,048,224

Fu·ji·sa·wa \,fü-jē-'sä-wä\ city Japan on Honshu pop 358,757

Fu·ku·o·ka \,fü-kü-'ō-kä\ city & port Japan on N Kyushu on inlet of Tsushima Strait pop 1,261,658

Fu·ku·ya·ma \,fü-kə-'yä-mä\ city Japan on SW Honshu pop 365,615

Ful·da \'fül-də\ city cen Germany pop 57,180

Ful·ham \'fü-ləm\ former metropolitan borough SW London, England, now part of Hammersmith

Ful·ler·ton \'fü-lər-tən\ city SW Calif. NE of Long Beach pop 114,144

Fu·na·ba·shi \,fü-nä-'bä-shē\ city Japan on Honshu, a suburb of Tokyo pop 537,614

Fu·na·fu·ti \,fü-nä-'fü-tē\ island (atoll) S Pacific in cen Tuvalu Islands; contains ✳ of the group pop 1328

Fun·chal \fün-'shäl, ,fən-\ city & port Portugal ✳ of Madeira Islands pop 126,021

Fun·dy, Bay of \'fən-dē\ inlet of the Atlantic SE Canada bet. N.B. & N.S.

Fundy National Park reservation SE Canada in N.B. on upper Bay of Fundy

Fur·neaux \'fər-(,)nō\ islands Australia off NE Tasmania

Fur·ness \'fər-nəs\ district N England comprising peninsula in Irish Sea in SW Cumbria

Fürth \'fürt, 'fuert\ city S cen Germany NW of Nuremberg pop 105,297

Fu·shun \'fü-'shün\ city NE China in NE Liaoning E of Shenyang pop 1,202,388

Fu·tu·na \fü-'tü-nä\ 1 island SW Pacific in Futuna Islands 2 island SW Pacific in SE Vanuatu

Futuna Islands or **Hoorn Islands** \'hōrn, 'hȯrn\ islands SW Pacific NE of Fiji; formerly a French protectorate, since 1959 part of Wallis & Futuna Islands territory pop 4732

Fu·xin or **Fu·sin** \'fü-'shin\ city NE China in cen Liaoning

Fu·zhou \'fü-'jō\ or **Foo·chow** or **Fu–chou** \'fü-'jō, -'chaü\ or formerly **Min·how** \'min-'hō\ city & port SE China ✳ of Fujian on Min River pop 874,809

Fyn \'fin\ island Denmark in the Baltic bet. Sjælland & Jutland; chief city Odense area 1149 sq mi (2987 sq km), pop 458,111

G

Ga·bès \\'gä-,bes\ city & port SE Tunisia on **Gulf of Gabès** *or anc* **Syr·tis Minor** \\'sər-təs\ (arm of the Mediterranean) *pop* 83,610

Ga·bon \gȧ-'bōⁿ\ **1** *or* **Ga·boon** *or* **Ga·bun** \gə-'bün, ga-\ river NW Gabon flowing into the Atlantic through long wide estuary **2** country W Africa on the Atlantic; formerly a territory of French Equatorial Africa, since 1958 a republic ✻ Libreville *area* 102,317 *sq mi* (265,001 *sq km*), *pop* 1,280,000 — **Gab·o·nese** \,ga-bə-'nēz, -'nēs\ *adj or n*

Ga·bo·rone \,gä-bō-'rō-(,)nā, ,kä-\ *or formerly* **Ga·be·ro·nes** \-'rō-nəs\ town SE Botswana, its ✻ *pop* 133,468

Gad·a·ra \'ga-də-rə\ ancient town Palestine SE of Sea of Galilee — **Gad·a·rene** \'ga-də-,rēn, ,ga-də-'\ *adj or n*

Gades *or* **Gadir** — see CÁDIZ — **Gad·i·tan** \'ga-də-tən\ *adj or n*

Gads·den \'gadz-dən\ city NE Ala. on the Coosa *pop* 42,523

Gadsden Purchase tract of land S of Gila River in present Ariz. & N.Mex. purchased 1853 by the U.S. from Mexico *area* 29,640 *sq mi* (77,064 *sq km*)

Ga·e·ta \gä-'ā-tä\ city & port *cen* Italy in Lazio on **Gulf of Gaeta** (inlet of Tyrrhenian Sea N of Bay of Naples) *pop* 22,393

Gaf·sa \'gaf-sə\ *or anc* **Cap·sa** \'kap-sə\ oasis W *cen* Tunisia

Ga·han·na \gə-'ha-nə\ city *cen* Ohio NE of Columbus *pop* 27,791

Gaines·ville \'gānz-,vil, -vəl\ city N *cen* Fla. *pop* 84,770

Gaird·ner, Lake \'gard-nər, 'gerd-\ salt lake Australia in S. Australia W of Lake Torrens *area* 1840 *sq mi* (4784 *sq km*)

Gai·thers·burg \'gā-thərz-,bərg\ town W Md. NW of Washington, D.C. *pop* 39,542

Ga·lá·pa·gos Islands \gə-'lä-pə-gəs, -'lä-, -,gōs\ *or* **Ar·chi·pié·la·go de Co·lón** \,är-chē-'pyä-lä-gō-thä-kō-'lōn\ island group Ecuador in the Pacific W of mainland ✻ on San Cristóbal Is. *area* 3093 *sq mi* (8010 *sq km*), *pop* 9785 — see ISABELA

Ga·la·ta \'ga-lə-tə\ port & commercial section of Istanbul, Turkey

Ga·la·ți \gä-'läts, -'lät-sē\ city E Romania on the Danube *pop* 307,376

Ga·la·tia \gə-'lā-sh(ē-)ə\ ancient country & Roman province *cen* Asia Minor in region centered on modern Ankara, Turkey — **Ga·la·tian** \-shən\ *adj or n*

Gald·hø·pig·gen \'gäl-,hœ-,pē-gən\ mountain 8100 *ft* (2469 *m*) S *cen* Norway in Jotunheim Mountains

Gales·burg \'gā(ə)lz-,bərg\ city NW Ill. WNW of Peoria *pop* 33,530

Ga·li·cia \gə-'li-sh(ē-)ə\ **1** region E Europe including N slopes of the Carpathians & valleys of the upper Vistula, Dniester, Bug, & Seret rivers; former Austrian crown land; belonged to Poland bet. the two world wars; now divided bet. Poland & Ukraine **2** region & ancient kingdom NW Spain bordering on the Atlantic — **Ga·li·cian** \-'li-shən\ *adj or n*

Gal·i·lee \'ga-lə-,lē\ hill region N Israel N of Plain of Esdraelon — **Gal·i·le·an** \,ga-lə-'lē-ən\ *adj or n*

Galilee, Sea of *or mod* **Lake Ti·be·ri·as** \tī-'bir-ē-əs\ *or bib* **Lake of Gen·nes·a·ret** \gə-'ne-sə-,ret, -rət\ *or* **Sea of Tiberias** *or* **Sea of Chin·ne·reth** \'ki-nə-,reth\ *or Heb* **Yam Kin·ne·ret**

\'yäm-'ki-nə-,ret\ lake 13 *mi* (21 *km*) long & 7 *mi* (11 *km*) wide N Israel on Syrian border traversed by Jordan River; *ab* 700 *ft* (212 *m*) below sea level

Gal·la·tin \'ga-lə-t⁹n\ river 125 *mi* (201 *km*) SW Mont. — see THREE FORKS

Gallatin Range mountain range S Mont. — see ELECTRIC PEAK

Gal·li·nas, Point \gä-'yē-näs\ cape N Colombia; northernmost point of S. America, at 12°15′N

Gal·lip·o·li \gə-'li-pə-lē\ *or Turk* **Ge·li·bo·lu** \ge-'lē-bó-,lü\ peninsula Turkey in Europe bet. the Dardanelles & Saros Gulf — see CHERSONESE

Gal·lo·way \'ga-lə-,wā\ former district SW Scotland comprising area formerly in counties of Wigtown & Kirkcudbright — see DUMFRIES AND GALLOWAY — **Gal·we·gian** \gal-'wē-j(ē-)ən\ *adj or n*

Gal·lup \'ga-ləp\ city NW N.Mex. near Indian reservations *pop* 19,154

Galt \'gólt\ former city, Ont., Canada — see CAMBRIDGE

Gal·ves·ton \'gal-vəs-tən\ city SE Tex. on **Galveston Island** (30 *mi or* 48 *km* long) at entrance to **Galveston Bay** (inlet of Gulf of Mexico) *pop* 59,070 — **Gal·ves·to·nian** \,gal-və-'stō-nē-ən, -nyən\

Gal·way \'gól-,wā\ **1** county W Ireland in Connacht bordering on the Atlantic *area* 2293 *sq mi* (5962 *sq km*), *pop* 129,511 **2** municipal borough & port, its ✳, on **Galway Bay** (inlet) *pop* 50,842

Gam·bia \'gam-bē-ə, -,gäm-\ **1** river 700 *mi* (1126 *km*) W Africa flowing from Fouta Djallon in W Guinea W through Senegal into the Atlantic in Gambia **2** *or* **The Gambia** country W Africa; a republic in the Commonwealth of Nations ✳ Banjul *area* 4003 *sq mi* (10,368 *sq km*), *pop* 687,817 — **Gam·bi·an** \-bē-ən\ *adj or n*

Gam·bier Islands \'gam-,bir\ islands S Pacific SE of Tuamotu Archipelago belonging to France *pop* 620 — see MANGAREVA

Gan *or* **Kan** \'gän\ river over 500 *mi* (800 *km*) SE China in Jiangxi

Gana — see GHANA

Gan·ca \gän-'jä\ *or* **Gyan·dzha** \gyän-'jä\ *or 1935–90* **Ki·ro·va·bad** \kē-rə-və-'bät\ *or earlier* **Eli·sa·vet·pol** *or* **Ye·li·za·vet·pol** \yi-li-zə-'vyet-,pól\ city W Azerbaijan *pop* 282,200

Gand — see GHENT

Gan·dhi·na·gar \gən-də-,nə-gər\ town W India ✳ of Gujarat *pop* 121,746

Gan·ges \'gan-,jēz\ river 1550 *mi* (2494 *km*) N India flowing from the Himalayas SE & E to unite with the Brahmaputra & empty into Bay of Bengal through the vast **Ganges Delta** — see HUGLI

Gan·get·ic \gan-'je-tik\ *adj*

Gangetic Plain low-lying plains region India & Bangladesh formed by Ganges River & its tributaries

Gang·tok \'gaṅ-'täk, -,gəṅ-\ town NE India ✳ of Sikkim *pop* 24,971

Gan·nett Peak \'ga-nət\ mountain 13,804 *ft* (4208 *m*) cen Wyo.; highest in Wind River Range & in the state

Gan·su *or* **Kan·su** \'gän-'sü\ province N cen China ✳ Lanzhou *area* 137,104 *sq mi* (356,470 *sq km*), *pop* 22,371,141

Gar \'gär\ *or* **Ka·erh** \'kä-'ər\ town China in W Tibet

Gar·da, Lake \'gär-də\ lake *ab* 35 *mi* (56 *km*) long N Italy bet. Lombardy & Veneto draining through the Mincio into the Po

Gar·de·na \gär-'dē-nə\ city SW Calif. S of Los Angeles *pop* 49,847

Gar·den City \'gär-d°n\ **1** city W Kans. on Arkansas River *pop* 24,097 **2** city SE Mich. *pop* 31,846 **3** village SE N.Y. on Long Is. *pop* 21,686

Garden Grove city SW Calif. SW of Los Angeles *pop* 143,050

Gard·ner \'gärd-nər\ city N *cen* Mass. *pop* 20,125

Gar·field \'gär-,fēld\ city NE N.J. N of Newark *pop* 26,727

Garfield Heights city NE Ohio SSE of Cleveland *pop* 31,739

Garfield Mountain mountain 10,961 *ft* (3341 *m*) SW Mont. near Idaho border; highest in Beaverhead & Bitterroot ranges

Ga·ri·glia·no \,gär-ēl-'yä-(,)nō\ river 100 *mi* (161 *km*) *cen* Italy in Lazio flowing SE & SW into Gulf of Gaeta

Gar·land \'gär-lənd\ city NE Tex. NNE of Dallas *pop* 180,650

Gar·misch–Par·ten·kir·chen \'gär-mish-'pär-t°n,kir-kən\ city S Germany in Bavaria SW of Munich in foothills of the Alps *pop* 27,094

Ga·ronne \gə-'rän, gȧ-'rȯn\ river *ab* 355 *mi* (571 *km*) SW France flowing NW to unite with the Dordogne forming Gironde Estuary

Gar·ri·son Dam \'gar-ə-sən\ dam 210 *ft* (64 *m*) high in Missouri River W *cen* N. Dak. — see SAKAKAWEA (Lake)

Gary \'gar-ē, 'ger-\ city NW Ind. on Lake Michigan *pop* 116,646

Gas·co·nade \,gas-kə-'nād\ river 265 *mi* (426 *km*) S *cen* Mo. flowing NE into Missouri River

Gas·co·ny \'gas-kə-nē\ *or F* **Gas·cogne** \gȧ-'skȯnʸ\ region & former province SW France ✱ Auch

Ga·sher·brum \'gə-shər-,brüm, -,brům\ mountain 26,470 *ft* (8068 *m*) N Kashmir in Karakoram Range SE of K2

Gas·pé Peninsula \ga-'spā, 'ga-\ peninsula Canada in SE Que. bet. mouth of St. Lawrence River & Chaleur Bay — **Gas·pe·sian** \ga-'spē-zhən\ *adj*

Gas·ti·neau Channel \'gas-tə-,nō\ channel SE Alaska bet. Douglas Is. & mainland; Juneau is situated on it

Gas·to·nia \ga-'stō-nē-ə, -nyə\ city SW N.C. W of Charlotte *pop* 54,732

Gates·head \'gāts-,hed\ borough N England in Tyne and Wear county on the Tyne opposite Newcastle *pop* 196,500

Gates of the Arctic National Park wilderness area N *cen* Alaska in Brooks Range N of the Arctic Circle

Gath \'gath\ city of ancient Philistia ENE of Gaza

Gat·i·neau \,ga-t°n-'ō\ **1** river 240 *mi* (386 *km*) Canada in SW Que. flowing S into Ottawa River at Hull **2** town Canada in SW Que. *pop* 92,284

Ga·tun Lake \gä-'tün\ lake *cen* Panama formed by the **Gatun Dam** in the Chagres; formerly in Canal Zone

Gaul \'gȯl\ *or L* **Gal·lia** \'ga-lē-ə\ ancient country W Europe comprising chiefly the region occupied by modern France & Belgium & at one time including also the Po valley in N Italy — see CISALPINE GAUL, TRANSALPINE GAUL — **Gal·lic** \'ga-lik\ *adj* — **Gal·li·can** \-li-kən\ *adj* — **Gaul** \gȯl\ *n* — **Gaul·ish** \'gȯ-lish\ *adj or n*

Gau·teng \'gaú-,teŋ\ *or formerly* **Pretoria–Witwatersrand–Vereeniging** province *cen* NE Republic of South Africa *area* 7262 *sq mi* (18,810 *sq km*), *pop* 6,864,000

Ga·var·nie \gä-vȧr-'nē\ waterfall 1385 *ft* (422 *m*) SW France S of Lourdes in the **Cirque de Gavarnie** \sẽrk-də-\ (natural amphitheater at head of Gave de Pau) — see PAU

Gave de Pau — see PAU

Gav·ins Point Dam \'ga-vənz\ dam SE S.Dak. & NE Nebr. in Missouri River — see LEWIS AND CLARK LAKE

Gäv·le \'yev-lə\ city & port E Sweden on Gulf of Bothnia NNW of Stockholm *pop* 89,194

Ga·ya \gə-'yä\ city NE India in *cen* Bihar *pop* 291,220

Ga·za *or Ar* **Ghaz·ze** \'gä-zə, 'ga-\ city S Palestine near the Mediterranean; with surrounding coastal district (**Gaza Strip,** adjoining Sinai Peninsula), administered 1949–67 by Egypt, subsequently by Israel, self-rule accord signed 1994 *pop* 57,000 — **Ga·zan** \-zən\ *n*

Ga·zi·an·tep \gä-zē-,)än-'tep\ *or formerly* **Ain·tab** \īn-'täb\ city S Turkey N of Aleppo, Syria *pop* 603,434

Gdansk \gə-'dän(t)sk, -'dan(t)sk\ *or G* **Dan·zig** \'dan(t)-sig, 'dän(t)-sik\ city & port N Poland on Gulf of Gdansk *pop* 464,649

Gdansk, Gulf of *or* **Gulf of Danzig** inlet of S Baltic Sea in N Poland & W Russia

Gdyn·ia \gə-'di-nē-ə\ city & port N Poland on Gulf of Gdansk NNW of Gdansk *pop* 250,936

Gebel Katherina — see KATHERINA (Gebel)

Gebel Musa — see MUSA (Gebel)

Ge·diz \gə-'dēz\ *or* **Sa·ra·bat** \sär-ä-'bät\ river 217 *mi* (349 *km*) W Turkey in Asia flowing W into Gulf of Izmir

Gee·long \jə-'lòŋ\ city & port SE Australia in S Victoria on Port Phillip Bay SW of Melbourne *pop* 13,036

Geelvink Bay — see SARERA BAY

Gel·der·land \'gel-dər-,land, 'kel-dər-,länt\ province E Netherlands bordering on IJsselmeer ✳ Arnhem *area* 1981 *sq mi* (5131 *sq km*), *pop* 1,839,883

Gelibolu — see GALLIPOLI

Gel·sen·kir·chen \,gel-z°n-'kir-kən\ city W Germany in the Ruhr W of Dortmund *pop* 293,839

General San Martín — see SAN MARTÍN

Gen·e·see \,je-nə-'sē\ river 144 *mi* (232 *km*) W N.Y. flowing N into Lake Ontario

Ge·ne·va \jə-'nē-və\ *or F* **Ge·nève** \zhə-'nev\ *or G* **Genf** \'genf\ **1** canton SW Switzerland *area* 109 *sq mi* (282 *sq km*), *pop* 377,108 **2** city, its ✳, at SW tip of Lake Geneva on the Rhône *pop* 167,934 — **Gen·e·vese** \,je-nə-'vēz, -'vēs\ *adj or n*

Geneva, Lake *or* **Lake Le·man** \'lē-mən, 'le-; lə-'man; lā-'män\ lake 45 *mi* (72 *km*) long on border bet. SW Switzerland & E France; traversed by the Rhône

Gennesaret, Lake of — see GALILEE (Sea of)

Gen·oa \'je-nō-ə\ *or It* **Ge·no·va** \'je-nō-(,)vä\ *or anc* **Gen·ua** \'jen-yə-wə\ commune & port NW Italy ✳ of Liguria at foot of the Apennines & at head of **Gulf of Genoa** (arm of Ligurian Sea) *pop* 675,639 — **Gen·o·ese** \,je-nō-'ēz, -'ēs\ *adj or n* — **Gen·o·vese** \-nə-'vēz, -'vēs\ *adj or n*

Gen·tof·te \'gen-,tȯf-tə\ city Denmark on Sjælland Is., N suburb of Copenhagen *pop* 65,032

George \'jȯrj\ river 345 *mi* (555 *km*) Canada in NE Que. flowing N into Ungava Bay

George, Lake 1 lake 14 *mi* (22 *km*) long NE Fla. in course of St. Johns River WNW of Daytona Beach **2** lake 33 *mi* (53 *km*) long E N.Y. S of Lake Champlain

Georg·es Bank \'jòr-jəz\ submerged sandbank E of Mass.
George·town \'jòrj-,taún\ **1** section of Washington, D.C., in W part of the city **2** city & port ✻ of Guyana on the Atlantic *pop* 162,000
George Town \'jòrj-,taún\ **1** town ✻ of Cayman Islands on Grand Cayman Is. **2** *or* **Pe·nang** \pə-'naŋ, -'näŋ\ city & port Malaysia ✻ of Penang on Penang Is. *pop* 234,930
George Washington Birthplace National Monument historic site E Va.
George Washington Car·ver National Monument \'kär-vər\ historic site SW Mo. SE of Joplin
Geor·gia \'jòr-jə\ **1** state SE U.S. ✻ Atlanta *area* 58,910 *sq mi* (152,577 *sq km*), *pop* 6,478,216 **2** *or* **Republic of Georgia** independent country SE Europe bordering on Black Sea; an ancient & medieval kingdom & later (1936–91) a constituent republic of the U.S.S.R. ✻ Tbilisi *area* 26,911 *sq mi* (69,699 *sq km*), *pop* 5,493,000 — **Geor·gian** \'jòr-jən\ *adj or n*
Georgia, Strait of channel 150 *mi* (241 *km*) long NW Wash. & SW B.C. bet. S Vancouver Is. & mainland NW of Puget Sound
Georgian Bay inlet of Lake Huron, Canada, in SE Ont.
Georgian Bay Islands National Park reservation SE Canada including Flowerpot Is. SE of Manitoulin Is. & a group of small islands N of Midland, Ont.
Geor·gi·na \jòr-'jē-nə\ town Canada in SE Ont. *pop* 29,746
Ge·ra \'ger-ə\ city E Germany ESE of Erfurt *pop* 126,521
Ger·la·chov·ka \'ger-lə-,kóf-kə, -,kòv-\ *or* **Ger·la·chov·sky** \-skē\ mountain 8711 *ft* (2655 *m*) N Slovakia in Tatra Mountains; highest in Carpathians
German East Africa former country E Africa comprising Tanganyika & Ruanda-Urundi (now Rwanda & Burundi); a German protectorate 1885–1920
Ger·ma·nia \(,)jər-'mā-nē-ə, -nyə\ **1** region of ancient Europe E of the Rhine & N of the Danube **2** region of Roman Empire just W of the Rhine in what is now NE France & part of Belgium & the Netherlands
German Southwest Africa — see NAMIBIA
Ger·man·town \'jər-mən-,taún\ **1** city SW Tenn. *pop* 32,893 **2** a NW section of Philadelphia, Pa.
Ger·ma·ny \'jər-mə-nē\ *or* **G Deutsch·land** \'dòich-,länt\ country *cen* Europe bordering on North & Baltic seas, divided 1949–90 into two republics: **Federal Republic of Germany** *or* **Bun·des·re·pu·blik Deutschland** \,bùn-dəs-,rā-pü-'blēk\ to the W (✻ Bonn, *area ab* 96,000 *sq mi or* 249,600 *sq km*) & **German Democratic Republic** *or* **Deutsche De·mo·krat·ische Re·pu·blik** \'dòi-chə-,dä-mō-'krä-ti-shə-,rā-pü-'blēk\ to the E (✻ East Berlin *area ab* 42,000 *sq mi or* 108,780 *sq km*); ✻ Berlin 137,735 *sq mi* (356,734 *sq km*), *pop* 80,974,900 — **Ger·man** \'jər-mən\ *adj or n* — **Ger·man·ic** \,jər-'ma-nik\ *adj*
Ger·mis·ton \'jər-məs-tən\ city NE Republic of South Africa in Gauteng E of Johannesburg *pop* 221,972
Ge·ro·na \hā-'rō-nä, jə-\ **1** province NE Spain in NE Catalonia *area* 2273 *sq mi* (5887 *sq km*), *pop* 509,628 **2** *or* **Gi·ro·na** \hē-\ commune, its ✻ *pop* 68,656
Ge·zi·ra \jə-'zē-rə\ *or* **Gezira, El** \,el-\ *or* **Al Ja·zi·rah** \,al-jə-'zē-rə\ region E *cen* Sudan bet. the Blue Nile & the White Nile

Gha·da·mes or **Gha·da·mis** or **Ghu·da·mis** \gə-'da-məs, -'dä-\ oasis & town NW Libya in Tripolitania near Algerian border

Gha·gha·ra \'gä-gə-,rä\ river 570 mi (1207 km) S cen Asia flowing S from SW Tibet through Nepal into the Ganges in N India

Gha·na \'gä-nə, 'ga-\ **1** or **Ga·na** ancient empire W Africa in what is now W Mali; flourished 4th–13th centuries **2** or formerly **Gold Coast** country W Africa bordering on Gulf of Guinea; a republic within the Commonwealth of Nations; formerly (as Gold Coast) a Brit. territory comprising Gold Coast colony, Ashanti, Northern Territories, & Togoland trust territory * Accra area 92,100 sq mi (238,539 sq km), pop 15,636,000 — **Gha·na·ian** \gä-'nā-ən, ga-, -'nī-ən\ adj or n — **Gha·ni·an** \'gä-nē-ən, 'ga-, -nyən\ adj or n — **Gha·nese** \gä-'nēz, ga-, -'nēs\ adj

Gharapuri — see ELEPHANTA

Ghar·da·ïa \gär-'dī-ə\ commune N cen Algeria pop 89,415

Ghats — see EASTERN GHATS, WESTERN GHATS

Ghazal, Bahr el — see BAHR EL GHAZAL

Ghaz·ni \'gäz-nē\ city E cen Afghanistan; once * of a Muslim kingdom extending from the Tigris to the Ganges pop 35,900

Ghazze — see GAZA

Ghent \'gent\ or Flem **Gent** \'kent\ or F **Gand** \'gäⁿ\ city NW cen Belgium * of E. Flanders pop 230,246

Giant's Causeway formation of prismatic basaltic columns Northern Ireland on N coast of Moyle

Gib·e·on \'gi-bē-ən\ city of ancient Palestine NW of Jerusalem — **Gib·e·on·ite** \-ə-,nīt\ n

Gi·bral·tar \jə-'brȯl-tər\ town & port on Rock of Gibraltar; a Brit. colony area 2.5 sq mi (6.5 sq km), pop 29,760 — **Gi·bral·tar·i·an** \jə-,brȯl-'ter-ē-ən, ji-,brȯl-, -'tar-\ n

Gibraltar, Rock of or anc **Cal·pe** \'kal-(,)pē\ headland on S coast of Spain at E end of Strait of Gibraltar; highest point 1396 ft (426 m) — see PILLARS OF HERCULES

Gibraltar, Strait of passage bet. Spain & Africa connecting the Atlantic & Mediterranean ab 8 mi (12.8 km) wide at narrowest point

Gies·sen \'gē-sᵊn\ city W cen Germany N of Frankfurt am Main pop 73,763

Gi·fu \'gē-(,)fü\ city Japan in cen Honshu pop 410,318

Gi·jón \hē-'hōn\ city & port NW Spain in Asturias province on Bay of Biscay pop 259,067

Gi·la \'hē-lə\ river 630 mi (1014 km) N.Mex. & Ariz. flowing W into Colorado River

Gila Cliff Dwellings National Monument reservation SW N.Mex. including cliff-dweller ruins

Gil·bert \'gil-bərt\ town SW cen Ariz. SE of Mesa pop 29,188

Gilbert and El·lice \'e-lis\ island group W Pacific; until 1976 a Brit. colony; now divided into the independent countries of Kiribati and Tuvalu

Gilbert Islands islands Kiribati in cen Pacific — **Gil·bert·ese** \,gil-bər-'tēz, -'tēs\ n or adj

Gil·boa, Mount \gil-'bō-ə\ mountain 1631 ft (497 m) N Palestine W of Jordan River & S of Plain of Esdraelon

Gil·e·ad \'gi-lē-əd\ mountainous region of Palestine E of Jordan River; now in Jordan — **Gil·e·ad·ite** \-lē-ə-,dīt\ n

Gil·git \'gil-gət\ **1** region NW Kashmir; under Pakistani control **2** town NW Kashmir on Gilgit River (tributary of the Indus) *pop* 4671

Gil·ling·ham \'ji-liŋ-əm\ town SE England in Kent *pop* 93,300

Gil·roy \'gil-,roi\ city W Calif. SE of San Jose *pop* 31,487

Gin·za \'gin-zə, 'gēn-zä\ shopping street & entertainment district in downtown Tokyo, Japan

Gi·re·sun \gir-ə-'sün\ *or* **Ke·ra·sun** \,ker-ə-\ city & port NE Turkey on Black Sea W of Trabzon *pop* 67,536

Girgenti — see AGRIGENTO

Gi·ronde \jə-'ränd, zhə-; zhē-'rōⁿd\ estuary 45 *mi* (72 *km*) W France formed by junction of the Garonne & the Dordogne & flowing NW into Bay of Biscay

Gis·borne \'giz-bərn, -,bôrn\ borough & port New Zealand on E North Is. *pop* 31,400

Gi·za \'gē-zə\ *or* **El Giza** \el-\ *or* **Al Ji·zah** \äl-'jē-zə\ city N Egypt on W bank of the Nile near Cairo *pop* 2,096,000

Gju·he·zes, Cape \jü-'hə-,zəs\ *or formerly* **Cape Lin·guet·ta** \liŋ-'gwe-tä\ *or* **Cape Glos·sa** \'glä-sä, 'glô-\ cape SW Albania projecting into Strait of Otranto

Gla·cier Bay \'glä-shər *also* -zhər\ inlet SE Alaska at S end of St. Elias Range in **Glacier Bay National Park**

Glacier National Park 1 — see WATERTON-GLACIER INTERNATIONAL PEACE PARK **2** reservation W Canada in SE B.C. in Selkirk Mountains W of Yoho National Park

Glad·beck \'glät-,bek, 'glad-\ city W Germany in the Ruhr *pop* 80,127

Glades \'glädz\ EVERGLADES

Glad·sak·se \'gläth-,säk-sə\ city Denmark; a suburb of Copenhagen *pop* 61,198

Glad·stone \'glad-,stōn\ city N Mo. N of Kansas City *pop* 26,243

Gla·mor·gan \glə-'môr-gən\ *or* **Gla·mor·gan·shire** \-,shir, -shər\ former county SE Wales ✳ Cardiff — see MID GLAMORGAN, SOUTH GLAMORGAN, WEST GLAMORGAN

Gla·rus \'glär-əs\ *or F* **Gla·ris** \glä-'rēs\ **1** canton E *cen* Switzerland *area* 264 *sq mi* (684 *sq km*), *pop* 37,686 **2** commune, its ✳ *pop* 5623

Glas·gow \'glas-(,)gō, 'glaz-(,)gō\ city & port S *cen* Scotland on the Clyde ✳ of Strathclyde *pop* 681,470 — **Glas·we·gian** \glas-'wē-jən, glaz-\ *n or adj*

Glas·ton·bury 1 \'glas-tən-,ber-ē\ town *cen* Conn. SE of Hartford *pop* 27,901 **2** \'glas-tən-b(ə-)rē, 'gläs-\ town SW England in Somerset *pop* 6773

Glen Canyon Dam \'glen\ dam N Ariz. in Glen Canyon of Colorado River forming **Lake Pow·ell** \'paù(-ə)l\ (chiefly in SE Utah)

Glen·coe \glen-'kō\ valley W Scotland SE of Loch Leven

Glen Cove \'glen-'kōv\ city SE N.Y. on NW Long Is. *pop* 24,149

Glen·dale 1 \-,dāl\ city *cen* Ariz. NW of Phoenix *pop* 148,134 **2** city SW Calif. just N of Los Angeles *pop* 180,038

Glendale Heights city NE Ill. *pop* 27,973

Glen·do·ra \glen-'dôr-ə, -'dôr-\ city SW Calif. *pop* 47,828

Glen El·lyn \gle-'ne-lən\ village NE Ill. W of Chicago *pop* 24,944

Glen More \glen-'môr, -'môr\ valley *ab* 50 *mi* (80 *km*) long N Scotland running SW to NE & connecting Loche Linnhe & Moray Firth — see CALEDONIAN CANAL

Glen·view \'glen-ˌvyü\ village NE Ill. NNW of Chicago *pop* 37,093

Glit·ter·tind \'gli-tər-ˌtin\ mountain 8110 *ft* (2472 *m*) S *cen* Norway in Jotunheim Mountains; highest in Scandinavia

Gli·wi·ce \gli-'vēt-se\ *or G* **Glei·witz** \'glī-(ˌ)vits\ city SW Poland in Silesia W of Katowice *pop* 222,084

Glouces·ter \'gläs-tər, 'glós-\ **1** city NE Mass. on Cape Ann *pop* 28,716 **2** city Canada in SE Ont. near Ottawa *pop* 101,677 **3** town SW *cen* England W of Gloucestershire *pop* 91,800

Glouces·ter·shire \'gläs-tər-ˌshir, -shər, 'glós-\ *or* **Glouces·ter** \'gläs-tər, 'glós-\ county SW *cen* England *area* 1055 *sq mi* (2732 *sq km*), *pop* 520,600

Gnossus — see KNOSSOS

Goa *or Pg* **Gôa** \'gō-ə\ state W India on Malabar Coast; before 1962 belonged to Portugal; with Daman & Diu constituted a union territory 1962–1987; ✻ Panaji *area* 1404 *sq mi* (3636 *sq km*), *pop* 1,169,793 — see PORTUGUESE INDIA — **Go·an** \-ən\ *adj or n*

Goa·nese \ˌgō-ə-'nēz, -'nēs\ *adj or n*

Go·bi \'gō-(ˌ)bē\ desert E *cen* Asia in Mongolia & China *area ab* 500,000 *sq mi* (1,300,000 *sq km*)

Go·da·va·ri \gō-'dä-və-rē\ river 900 *mi* (1448 *km*) *cen* India flowing SE across the Deccan into Bay of Bengal

Go·des·berg \'gō-dəs-ˌbərg, -ˌberk\ *or* **Bad Godesberg** \ˌbät-\ former commune W Germany on the Rhine; became part of Bonn 1969

Godthåb — see NUUK

Godwin Austen — see K2

Go·ge·bic \gō-'gē-bik\ iron range N Wis. & NW Mich.

Goi·â·nia *or formerly* **Goy·a·nia** \ˌgói-'yä-nyə\ city SE *cen* Brazil ✻ of Goiás *pop* 920,838

Goi·ás *or formerly* **Goi·az** *or* **Goy·az** \gói-'äs\ state SE *cen* Brazil ✻ Goiânia *area* 131,339 *sq mi* (340,168 *sq km*), *pop* 4,024,547

Gök·çe·ada \ˌgœk-jä-ə-'dä\ *or formerly* **Im·roz** \im-'róz\ island Turkey in NE Aegean *area* 110 *sq mi* (286 *sq km*)

Go·lan Heights \'gō-ˌlän, -lən\ hilly region NE of Sea of Galilee; annexed by Israel 1981

Gol·con·da \gäl-'kän-də\ ruined city *cen* India in W Andhra Pradesh W of Hyderabad ✻ (1512–1687) of Golconda kingdom

Gold Coast **1** region W Africa on N shore of Gulf of Guinea bet. the Ivory Coast (on W) & the Slave Coast (on E) **2** — see GHA-NA **3** former Brit. colony in S Gold Coast region ✻ Accra; now part of Ghana

Golden Chersonese — see CHERSONESE

Golden Gate strait 2 *mi* (3.2 *km*) wide W Calif. connecting San Francisco Bay with Pacific Ocean

Golden Horn inlet of the Bosporus, Turkey; harbor of Istanbul

Golden Valley village E Minn. W of Minneapolis *pop* 20,971

Golds·boro \'gōl(d)z-ˌbər-ō\ city E *cen* N.C. *pop* 40,709

Golgotha — see CALVARY

Go·ma·ti \'gō-mə-tē\ *or formerly* **Gum·ti** \'gùm-tē\ river *ab* 500 *mi* (805 *km*) N India flowing SE into the Ganges

Go·mel \'gó-ˌmel, -'myel\ *or* **Ho·mel** \hó-\ *or* **Ho·myel'** \kō-'myel\ city SE Belarus *pop* 503,300

Go·mor·rah \gə-'mór-ə, -'mär-\ city of ancient Palestine in the plain of Jordan River

Go·nâve, Gulf of \gō-'näv\ arm of Caribbean Sea on W coast of Haiti

Gon·der \'gón-dər\ *or* **Gon·dar** \-dər, -,där\ city NW Ethiopia N of Lake Tana ✻ of Amhara & former ✻ of Ethiopia *pop* 98,352

Gond·wa·na·land \gän-'dwä-nə-,land\ *or* **Gond·wa·na** \-'dwä-nə\ hypothetical land area believed to have once connected the Indian subcontinent & the landmasses of the southern hemisphere

Gong·ga Shan \'goŋ-gə-'shän\ *or* **Min·ya Kon·ka** \,mi-nyə-'käŋ-kə\ mountain 24,790 *ft* (7556 *m*) W China in SW *cen* Szechwan; highest in China

Good Hope, Cape of \,gúd-'hōp\ cape S Republic of South Africa in SW Western Cape province W of False Bay, at 34°21′S — see CAPE OF GOOD HOPE 2

Good·win Sands \'gúd-win\ shoals SE England in Strait of Dover off E coast of Kent — see DOWNS

Goose Creek \'güs\ city SE S.C. *pop* 24,692

Go·rakh·pur \'gōr-ək-,púr, 'gór-\ city NE India in E Uttar Pradesh N of Varanasi *pop* 505,566

Go·ri·zia \gō-'rēt-syä\ commune NE Italy in Venetia *pop* 37,999

Gorki — see NIZHNIY NOVGOROD

Gör·litz \'gœr-,lits, -ləts\ city E Germany on Neisse River *pop* 70,448

Gor·lov·ka \'gór-ləf-kə\ *or* **Hor·liv·ka** \'hór-\ city E Ukraine in the Donets Basin N of Donetsk *pop* 337,000

Gor·no-Al·tay \'gór-nə-,äl-'tī\ *or formerly* **Oy·rot** \'ói-rət\ autonomous region S Russia in Asia in SE Altay Territory in Altay Mountains ✻ **Gorno-Al·taysk** \-'tīsk\ area 35,753 *sq mi* (92,600 *sq km*), *pop* 197,000

Gor·no-Ba·dakh·shan \'gór-(,)nō-bä-,däk-'shän\ autonomous region SE Tajikistan in the Pamirs ✻ Khorog area 24,595 *sq mi* (63,701 *sq km*), *pop* 167,100

Gor·zow Wiel·ko·pol·ski \'gó-zhúf-,vyel-kó-'pól-skē\ city W Poland *pop* 123,350

Go·shen \'gō-shən\ **1** city N Ind. *pop* 23,797 **2** district of ancient Egypt E of the Nile delta

Gos·port \'gäs-,pōrt, -,pórt\ town S England in Hampshire on Portsmouth harbor *pop* 72,800

Gö·te·borg \,yœ̄-tə-'bór-ē\ *or* **Goth·en·burg** \'gä-thən-,bərg\ city & port SW Sweden on the Kattegat *pop* 433,811

Go·tha \'gō-tə, 'gō-thä\ city *cen* Germany W of Erfurt *pop* 53,372

Goth·am \'gä-thəm\ NEW YORK CITY — an informal name — **Goth·am·ite** \-thə-,mīt\ *n*

Got·land \'gät-,land, -,länd\ island Sweden in the Baltic off SE coast; chief town Visby area 1225 *sq mi* (3173 *sq km*), *pop* 56,840

Göt·ting·en \'gœ-tiŋ-ən, 'ge-tiŋ-\ city *cen* Germany SSW of Brunswick *pop* 124,331

Gou·da \'gaú-də, 'gü-, 'kaú-\ commune SW Netherlands *pop* 67,146

Gow·er \'gaú-(-ə)r\ peninsula S Wales W of Swansea

Gra·ham Land \'grä-əm, 'gra(-ə)m\ the N section of the Antarctic Peninsula

Gra·hams·town \'grä-əmz-,taún, 'gra(-ə)mz-\ city S Republic of South Africa in Eastern Cape province ENE of Port Elizabeth *pop* 41,302

Gra·ian Alps \\'grā-ən, 'grī-\\ section of W Alps S of Mont Blanc on border bet. France & Italy — see GRAN PARADISO

Grain Coast \\'grān\\ region W Africa in Liberia on Gulf of Guinea

Gram·pi·an \\'gram-pē-ən\\ region NE *cen* Scotland, established 1975 ✳ Aberdeen *area* 3358 *sq mi* (8698 *sq km*), *pop* 528,100

Grampian Hills hills *cen* Scotland bet. the Lowlands & the Highlands — see BEN NEVIS

Gra·na·da \\grə-'nä-də, grä-'nä-thä\\ **1** city SW Nicaragua on NW shore of Lake Nicaragua *pop* 56,232 **2** medieval Moorish kingdom S Spain **3** province S Spain in Andalusia bordering on the Mediterranean *area* 4838 *sq mi* (12,530 *sq km*), *pop* 790,515 **4** city, ✳ of Granada province, Spain, in the Sierra Nevada *pop* 254,034

Gran·by \\'gran-bē\\ town Canada in S Que. *pop* 42,804

Gran Cha·co \\grän-'chä-(,)kō\\ *or* **Chaco** region S *cen* S. America drained by the Paraguay & its chief W tributaries the Pilcomayo & Bermejo; divided bet. Argentina, Bolivia, & Paraguay

Grand \\'grand\\ **1** river 260 *mi* (418 *km*) SW Mich. flowing N & W into Lake Michigan **2** river 300 *mi* (483 *km*) NW Mo. flowing SE into Missouri River **3** river 200 *mi* (322 *km*) N S.Dak. flowing SE into Missouri River **4** the Colorado River from its source to junction with Green River in SE Utah — a former name **5** — see NEOSHO

Grand Atlas — see ATLAS

Grand Bahama island Bahamas, NW island of group *area* 530 *sq mi* (1373 *sq km*)

Grand Banks shoals in W Atlantic SE of Newfoundland

Grand Canal *or* **Da Yun·he** \\'dä-'yün-'hä\\ canal *ab* 1000 *mi* (1609 *km*) long E China from Hengshui to Tianjin

Grand Canary *or* *Sp* **Gran Ca·na·ria** \\grän-kä-'när-yä\\ island Spain in the Canaries; chief city Las Palmas *area* 592 *sq mi* (1533 *sq km*)

Grand Canyon gorge of the Colorado NW Ariz. extending from mouth of the Little Colorado W to the Grand Wash Cliffs; over 1 *mi* (1.6 *km*) deep; area largely comprised in **Grand Canyon National Park** — see MARBLE CANYON

Grand Cayman — see CAYMAN

Grand Cou·lee \\'kü-lē\\ valley E Wash. extending SSW from S wall of canyon of Columbia River where it turns W in forming the Big Bend

Grand Coulee Dam dam NE *cen* Wash. in Columbia River — see FRANKLIN D. ROOSEVELT LAKE

Grande Prai·rie \\'grand-'prer-ē, -'prā-rē\\ city Canada in W Alta. *pop* 28,271

Grande, Rio 1 \\,rē-ō-'grand, -'gran-dē\\ river U.S. & Mexico — see RIO GRANDE **2** \\,rē-ō-'gran-dē\\ river 680 *mi* (1094 *km*) E Brazil in Minas Gerais flowing W to unite with Paranaíba River forming Paraná River

Grande–Terre \\grän-'ter\\ island French West Indies constituting the E portion of Guadeloupe *area* 220 *sq mi* (572 *sq km*)

Grand Falls — see CHURCHILL FALLS

Grand Forks city E N.Dak. on Red River *pop* 49,425

Grand Island city SE *cen* Nebr. near Platte River *pop* 39,386

Grand Junction city W Colo. on Colorado River *pop* 29,034

Grand Lac — see TONLE SAP

Grand Ma·nan Island \mə-'nan\ island 20 *mi* (32 *km*) long Canada in N.B. at entrance to Bay of Fundy

Grand Portage National Monument historic site NE Minn. on Lake Superior

Grand Prairie city NE *cen* Tex. W of Dallas *pop* 99,616

Grand Rapids city SW Mich. on Grand River *pop* 189,126

Grand Te·ton \'tē-,tän, 'tē-t°n\ mountain 13,770 *ft* (4197 *m*) W Wyo. in Grand Teton National Park; highest in Teton Range

Grand Teton National Park reservation NW Wyo. including Jackson Lake & main part of Teton Range

Grand Trav·erse Bay \'tra-vərs\ inlet of Lake Michigan in Mich. on NW coast of Lower Peninsula

Grand Turk — see TURKS AND CAICOS

Grand·view \'grand-,vyü\ city W Mo. *pop* 24,967

Grange·mouth \'grānj-məth, -,maúth\ burgh & port *cen* Scotland in Central region on Firth of Forth *pop* 21,666

Granicus — see KOCABAS

Gran·ite City \'gra-nət\ city SW Ill. on Mississippi River *pop* 32,862

Granite Peak mountain 12,799 *ft* (3901 *m*) S Mont. NE of Yellowstone National Park in Beartooth Range (spur of Absaroka Range); highest point in state

Gran Pa·ra·di·so \grän-,pär-ä-'dē-(,)zō\ mountain 13,323 *ft* (4061 *m*) NW Italy in NW Piedmont; highest in Graian Alps

Grape·vine \'grāp-,vīn\ city N Tex. NE of Fort Worth *pop* 29,202

Gras·mere \'gras-,mir\ lake 1 *mi* (1.6 *km*) long NW England in Cumbria in Lake District

Grasse \'gras, 'gräs\ commune SE France W of Nice *pop* 42,077

Grass·lands National Park \'gras-,landz, -ləndz\ reservation Canada in SW Sask.

Grau·bün·den \graú-'bún-dən, -'bɛn-\ *or F* **Gri·sons** \grē-'zōⁿ\ canton E Switzerland ✲ Chur *area* 2745 *sq mi* (7110 *sq km*), *pop* 177,096

Graudenz — see GRUDZIADZ

Gravenhage, 's — see HAGUE (The)

Graves·end \,grāvz-'end\ town SE England in Kent on Thames estuary *pop* 52,963

Grays Harbor \'grāz\ inlet of the Pacific W Wash.

Grays Peak mountain 14,270 *ft* (4349 *m*) *cen* Colo., highest in Front Range

Graz \'gräts\ city S Austria ✲ of Styria on the Mur *pop* 232,155

Great Abaco — see ABACO

Great Australian Bight wide bay on S coast of Australia; part of Indian Ocean

Great Barrier Reef coral reef 1250 *mi* (2012 *km*) long Australia in Coral Sea off NE coast of Queensland; in part comprises a marine park

Great Basin region W U.S. bet. Sierra Nevada & Wasatch Range including most of Nev. & parts of Calif., Idaho, Utah, Wyo. & Oreg. & having no drainage to ocean; contains many isolated mountain ranges (the **Basin Ranges**)

Great Basin National Park reservation E Nev. including Wheeler Peak & Lehman Caves

Great Bear Lake \'bar, 'ber\ lake Canada in W Northwest Territories *area* over 12,000 *sq mi* (31,200 *sq km*)

Great Brit·ain \'bri-tᵊn\ *or* **Britain 1** island W Europe comprising England, Scotland, & Wales *area* 88,150 *sq mi* (228,300 *sq km*), *pop* 53,917,000 **2** UNITED KINGDOM

Great Crosby — see CROSBY

Great Dismal — see DISMAL

Great Divide — see CONTINENTAL DIVIDE

Great Dividing Range mountain system E Australia extending from Cape York Peninsula to S Victoria &, interrupted by Bass Strait, into Tasmania — see KOSCIUSKO (Mount)

Greater Antilles group of islands in the West Indies including Cuba, Hispaniola, Jamaica, & Puerto Rico

Greater London — see LONDON 2

Greater Manchester metropolitan area NW England comprising Manchester and nearby boroughs *area* 514 *sq mi* (1331 *sq km*), *pop* 2,454,800

Greater Sunda Islands — see SUNDA ISLANDS

Greater Walachia — see MUNTENIA

Great Exuma — see EXUMA

Great Falls 1 waterfall 35 *ft* (11 *m*) in the Potomac N of Washington, D.C. **2** city W *cen* Mont. on Missouri River WSW of the **Great Falls of the Missouri** (waterfall, now in modified form) *pop* 55,097

Great Inagua — see INAGUA

Great Indian Desert — see THAR DESERT

Great Kabylia — see KABYLIA

Great Karroo — see KARROO

Great Lakes 1 chain of five lakes (Superior, Michigan, Huron, Erie, & Ontario) *cen* N. America in the U.S. & Canada draining through St. Lawrence River into the Atlantic **2** group of lakes E *cen* Africa including Lakes Turkana, Albert, Victoria, Tanganyika, & Malawi

Great Namaqualand — see NAMAQUALAND

Great Ouse — see OUSE

Great Plains elevated plains region W *cen* U.S. & W Canada E of Rocky Mountains & chiefly W of 100th meridian extending from NE B.C. & NW Alta. SE & S to include the Llano Estacado of N.Mex. & Tex.

Great Rift Valley depression SW Asia & E Africa extending with several breaks from valley of Jordan River S to *cen* Mozambique

Great Saint Ber·nard \,sänt-bər-'närd\ mountain pass 8090 *ft* (2468 *m*) through Pennine Alps bet. Switzerland & Italy

Great Salt Lake lake *ab* 80 *mi* (130 *km*) long N Utah having strongly saline waters & no outlet

Great Salt Lake Desert flat barren region NW Utah

Great Sand Dunes National Monument reservation S Colo. on W slope of Sangre de Cristo Mountains

Great Slave Lake \'slāv\ lake NW Canada in S Northwest Territories receiving Slave River on S & draining into Mackenzie River on W *area ab* 11,000 *sq mi* (28,490 *sq km*)

Great Smoky Mountains \'smō-kē\ mountains on N.C.-Tenn. boundary partly in **Great Smoky Mountains National Park** — see CLINGMANS DOME

Great Stour — see STOUR 3

Great Yarmouth — see YARMOUTH

Greece \'grēs\ *or NGk* **El·lás** \e-'läs\ *or anc Gk* **Hel·las** \'he-ləs\ country S Europe at S end of Balkan Peninsula; a republic ✻ Athens *area* 50,944 *sq mi* (131,945 *sq km*), *pop* 10,310,000 — **Greek** \'grēk\

Gree·ley \'grē-lē\ city N Colo. *pop* 60,536

Green \'grēn\ river 730 *mi* (1175 *km*) W U.S. flowing from Wind River Range in W Wyo. S into Colorado River in SE Utah

Green Bay 1 inlet of NW Lake Michigan 120 *mi* (193 *km*) long in NW Mich. & NE Wis. **2** city NE Wis. on Green Bay *pop* 96,466

Green·belt \'grēn-,belt\ city *cen* Md. *pop* 21,096

Green·field \'grēn-,fēld\ city SE Wis. near Milwaukee *pop* 33,403

Green·land \'grēn-lənd, -,land\ *or native* **Ka·laal·lit Nu·naat** \kä-'lät-,lēt-nü-'nät, -'lä-\ island in N Atlantic off NE N. America belonging to Denmark ✻ Nuuk *area* 839,999 *sq mi* (2,175,597 *sq km*), *pop* 55,171 — **Green·land·er** \-lən-dər, -,lan-\ n

Greenland Sea arm of Arctic Ocean bet. Greenland & Spitsbergen

Green Mountains mountains E N. America in Appalachian system extending from S Que. S through Vt. into W Mass. — see MANSFIELD (Mount)

Gree·nock \'grē-nək\ burgh & port SW Scotland in Strathclyde on Firth of Clyde *pop* 57,324

Greens·boro \'grēnz-,bər-ō\ city N *cen* N.C. *pop* 183,521

Green·ville \'grēn-,vil, -vəl\ **1** city W Miss. on Mississippi River *pop* 45,226 **2** city E N.C. *pop* 44,972 **3** city NW S.C. *pop* 58,282 **4** city N Tex. NE of Dallas on the Sabine *pop* 23,071

Green·wich 1 \'gre-nich, 'grēn-,wich, 'grin-,wich\ town SW Conn. on Long Island Sound *pop* 58,441 **2** \'gri-nij, 'gre-, -nich\ borough of E Greater London, England *pop* 200,800

Green·wich Village \'gre-nich\ section of New York City in Manhattan on lower W side

Green·wood \'grēn-,wüd\ **1** city *cen* Ind. *pop* 26,265 **2** city W S.C. *pop* 20,807

Gre·na·da \grə-'nā-də\ island Brit. West Indies in S Windward Islands; with S Grenadines, independent member of the Commonwealth of Nations since 1974 ✻ St. George's *area* 133 *sq mi* (346 *sq km*), *pop* 98,000 — **Gre·na·dan** \-'nā-dᵊn\ *adj or n* — **Gre·na·di·an** \-'nā-dē-ən\ *adj or n*

Gren·a·dines \,gre-nə-'dēnz, 'gre-nə-,\ islands Brit. West Indies in *cen* Windward Islands bet. Grenada & St. Vincent; divided administratively bet. Grenada & St. Vincent and the Grenadines

Gre·no·ble \grə-'nō-bəl, -'nóblᵊ\ city SE France on the Isère *pop* 153,973

Gresh·am \'gre-shəm\ city NW Oreg. E of Portland *pop* 68,235

Grey·lock, Mount \'grā-,läk\ mountain 3491 *ft* (1064 *m*) NW Mass.; highest in Berkshire Hills & in state

Grif·fin \'gri-fən\ city W *cen* Ga. *pop* 21,347

Grims·by \'grimz-bē\ borough E England in Humberside near mouth of the Humber *pop* 92,147

Grin·del·wald \'grin-dᵊl-,wòld, -,vält\ valley & village *cen* Switzerland in Bern canton in the Berner Alpen E of Interlaken

Gri·qua·land West \'gri-kwə-ˌland, 'grē-\ district NW Republic of South Africa in NE Northern Cape N of Orange River; chief town Kimberley

Gris–Nez, Cape \grē-'nā\ headland N France projecting into Strait of Dover

Grisons — see GRAUBÜNDEN

Grod·no \'gräd-(ˌ)nō, 'gród-nə\ or **Hrod·na** or **Hrod·no** \'kród-nə\ city W Belarus on the Neman *pop* 284,800

Gro·ning·en \'krō-niŋ-ən, 'krö-niŋ-ə(n)\ **1** province NE Netherlands *area* 934 *sq mi* (2419 *sq km*), *pop* 555,397 **2** city, its ✳ *pop* 169,387

Gros Morne National Park \grō-'mórn\ reservation Canada in Newfoundland (island)

Gross·glock·ner \'grōs-ˌglók-nər\ mountain 12,457 *ft* (3797 *m*) SW Austria, highest in the Hohe Tauern & in Austria

Gros Ventre \'grō-ˌvänt\ river 100 *mi* (161 *km*) W Wyo. flowing W into Snake River

Grot·on \'grä-tᵊn\ town SE Conn. at New London *pop* 45,144

Grove City \'grōv\ city *cen* Ohio *pop* 19,661

Groz·ny or **Groz·nyy** \'gróz-nē, 'gräz-\ city S Russia in Europe, N of Caucasus Mountains *pop* 388,000

Gru·dziadz \'grü-ˌjónts\ or *G* **Grau·denz** \'grau-ˌdents\ city N Poland on the Vistula NE of Bydgoszcz *pop* 100,861

Gua·da·la·ja·ra \ˌgwä-dᵊl-ə-'här-ə, ˌgwä-thä-lä-'hä-rä\ **1** city W *cen* Mexico ✳ of Jalisco *pop* 1,628,617 **2** province E *cen* Spain in NE New Castile *area* 4707 *sq mi* (12,191 *sq km*), *pop* 145,593 **3** commune, ✳ of Guadalajara province, Spain *pop* 62,943

Gua·dal·ca·nal \ˌgwä-dᵊl-kə-'nal, ˌgwä-ˌdä-kə-\ island W Pacific in the SE Solomons *pop* 23,922 — see HONIARA

Gua·dal·qui·vir \ˌgwä-dᵊl-ki-'vir, -'kwi-vər\ river 408 *mi* (656 *km*) S Spain flowing W & SW into Gulf of Cádiz

Gua·da·lupe \'gwä-dᵊl-ˌüp\ river SE Tex. flowing SE into San Antonio River

Gua·da·lupe Hi·dal·go \ˌgwä-dᵊl-ˌüp-hi-'dal-(ˌ)gō, ˌgwä-thä-'lü-pā-ē-'thäl-(ˌ)gō\ **1** former city *cen* Mexico N of Mexico City now part of city of Gustavo A. Madero **2** GUSTAVO A. MADERO (villa)

Guadalupe Mountains mountains S N.Mex. & W Tex., the S extension of Sacramento Mountains; highest point **Guadalupe Peak,** 8749 *ft* (2667 *m*) in **Guadalupe Mountains National Park** (in Tex.)

Gua·de·loupe \'gwä-dᵊl-ˌüp, ˌgwä-dᵊl-\ two islands, Basse-Terre (or Guadeloupe proper) & Grande-Terre, in French West Indies in *cen* Leeward Islands; an overseas department of France ✳ Basse-Terre (on Basse-Terre Is.) *area* 582 *sq mi* (1507 *sq km*), *pop* 418,000 — **Gua·de·lou·pe·an** \ˌgwä-dᵊl-'ü-pē-ən\ *n*

Gua·di·a·na \ˌgwä-thyä-nä\ river 515 *mi* (829 *km*) Spain & Portugal flowing W & S into Gulf of Cádiz

Guairá — see SETE QUEDAS

Guam \'gwäm\ island W Pacific in S Marianas belonging to U.S. ✳ Agana *area* 209 *sq mi* (541 *sq km*), *pop* 143,000 — **Gua·ma·ni·an** \gwä-'mä-nē-ən\ *adj* or *n*

Gua·na·ba·coa \ˌgwä-nä-bä-'kō-ä\ city W Cuba E of Havana *pop* 100,452

Gua·na·ba·ra Bay \,gwä-nä-'bär-ə\ inlet of Atlantic Ocean SE Brazil

Gua·na·jua·to \,gwä-nä-'hwä-(,)tō\ **1** state *cen* Mexico *area* 11,810 *sq mi* (30,588 *sq km*), *pop* 3,982,593 **2** city, its * *pop* 113,580

Guang·dong \'gwäŋ-'dùŋ\ *or* **Kwang·tung** \'gwäŋ-'dùŋ, 'kwäŋ-, -'tùŋ\ province SE China bordering on S. China Sea & Gulf of Tonkin * Guangzhou *area* 76,220 *sq mi* (197,410 *sq km*), *pop* (with Hainan) 62,829,236

Guang·xi Zhuang·zu \'gwäŋ-'shē-'jwäŋ-'dzü\ *or* **Kwang·si Chuang** \'gwäŋ-'sē-'chwäŋ\ region & former province S China W of Guangdong * Nanning *area* 85,096 *sq mi* (221,250 *sq km*), *pop* 42,245,765

Guang·zhou *or* **Kuang·chou** \'gwäŋ-'jō\ *or* **Can·ton** \'kan-,tän, kan-'\ city & port SE China * of Guangdong on Zhu River *pop* 2,914,281

Guan·tá·na·mo \gwän-'tä-nä-,mō\ city SE Cuba NW of **Guantánamo Bay** (inlet of the Caribbean; site of U.S. naval station) *pop* 200,381

Gua·po·ré \,gwä-pō-'rā\ **1** *or* **Ité·nez** \ē-'tā-nes\ river 1087 *mi* (1749 *km*) W Brazil & NE Bolivia flowing NW to the Mamoré **2** — see RONDÔNIA

Guar·da·fui, Cape \,g(w)är-də-'fwē, -'fü-ē\ cape NE Somalia at entrance to Gulf of Aden

Guá·ri·co \'gwär-i-,kō\ river W Venezuela flowing SW & S into the Apure

Gua·te·ma·la \,gwä-tə-'mä-lə, -tä-'mä-lä\ **1** country Central America S of Mexico bordering on the Pacific & the Caribbean; a republic *area* 42,042 *sq mi* (109,309 *sq km*), *pop* 9,713,000 **2** *or* **Guatemala City** city, its * *pop* 1,132,730 — **Gua·te·ma·lan** \-'mä-lən\ *adj or n*

Gua·via·re \gwä-'vyä-rā\ river 650 *mi* (1046 *km*) Colombia flowing E into the Orinoco

Gua·ya·ma \gwä-'yä-mä\ town SE Puerto Rico *pop* 21,692

Gua·ya·quil \gwī-ə-'kēl\ city & port W Ecuador on Guayas River 40 *mi* (64 *km*) from **Gulf of Guayaquil** (inlet of the Pacific) *pop* 1,508,444

Gua·yas \'gwī-äs\ river W Ecuador forming delta in Gulf of Guayaquil

Guay·mas \'gwī-mäs\ city & port NW Mexico in Sonora on Gulf of California *pop* 128,960

Guay·na·bo \gwī-'nä-(,)bō, -(,)vō\ city NE *cen* Puerto Rico *pop* 73,385

Guelph \'gwelf\ city Canada in SE Ont. *pop* 87,976

Guern·sey \'gərn-zē\ island English Channel in the Channel Islands * St. Peter Port *area* 24 *sq mi* (62 *sq km*), *pop* 55,421

Guer·re·ro \gä-'rä-rō\ state S Mexico bordering on the Pacific * Chilpancingo *area* 24,631 *sq mi* (63,794 *sq km*), *pop* 2,620,637

Gui \'gwē\ *or* **Kuei** \'gwä\ river 200 *mi* (322 *km*) SE China in E Guangxi Zhuangzu flowing S into the Xi

Gui·a·na \gē-'a-nə, -'ä-nə\ *or* **gī·'a-nə**\ region N S. America bordering on the Atlantic & bounded on W & S by Orinoco, Negro, & Amazon rivers; includes Guyana, French Guiana, Suriname, & adjoining parts of Brazil & Venezuela — **Gui·a·nan** \-nən\ *adj or n* — **Gui·a·nese** \ˌgī-ə-ˈnēz, ˌgē-ə-, -ˈnēs\ *adj or n*

Gui·enne *or* **Guy·enne** \gwē-ˈyen\ region & former province SW France bordering on Bay of Biscay ✴ Bordeaux — see AQUITAINE

Guil·ford \ˈgil-fərd\ city S Conn. on Long Island Sound *pop* 19,848

Gui·lin \ˈgwē-ˈlin\ *or* **Kuei·lin** *or* **Kwei·lin** \ˈgwā-ˈlin\ city S China in NE Guangxi Zhuangzu on the Gui *pop* 364,130

Guin·ea \ˈgi-nē\ *or F* **Gui·née** \gē-ˈnā\ 1 region W Africa bordering on the Atlantic from Gambia (on N) to Angola (on S) 2 *or formerly* **French Guinea** republic W Africa bordering on the Atlantic; formerly a territory of French West Africa ✴ Conakry *area* 94,925 *sq mi* (245,856 *sq km*), *pop* 7,300,000 — **Guin·ean** \ˈgi-nē-ən\ *adj or n*

Guinea, Gulf of arm of the Atlantic W *cen* Africa; includes Bights of Benin & Biafra

Guin·ea-Bis·sau \ˌgi-nē-bi-ˈsau̇\ *or formerly* **Portuguese Guinea** republic W Africa S of Senegal; until 1974 a Portuguese colony ✴ Bissau *area* 13,948 *sq mi* (36,265 *sq km*), *pop* 1,036,000

Gui·púz·coa \gē-ˈpüs-kō-ə, -ˈpüth-kō-ä\ province N Spain; in Basque Country ✴ San Sebastian *area* 771 *sq mi* (1997 *sq km*), *pop* 676,488

Gui·yang \ˈgwē-ˈyän\ *or* **Kuei–yang** *or* **Kwei·yang** \ˈgwā-ˈyän\ city S China ✴ of Guizhou *pop* 1,018,619

Gui·zhou \ˈgwē-ˈjō\ *or* **Kwei·chow** \ˈgwā-ˈjō, ˈkwā-\ province S China S of Szechwan ✴ Guiyang *area* 67,181 *sq mi* (174,671 *sq km*), *pop* 32,391,066

Gu·ja·rat *or* **Gu·je·rat** \ˌgü-jə-ˈrät, ˌgüj-ə-\ 1 region W India where Gujarati is spoken 2 state W India N & E of Gulf of Khambhat ✴ Gandhinagar *area* 72,236 *sq mi* (187,091 *sq km*), *pop* 41,309,582

Guj·ran·wala \ˌgüj-rən-ˈwä-lə, ˌgüj-\ city NE Pakistan N of Lahore *pop* 785,000

Gulf·port \ˈgəlf-ˌpȯrt, -ˌpȯrt\ city & port SE Miss. *pop* 40,775

Gulf Stream warm current in N Atlantic flowing from Gulf of Mexico NE along U.S. coast to Nantucket & thence eastward

Gulja — see YINING

Gumti — see GOMATI

Gun·ni·son \ˈgə-nə-sən\ river 150 *mi* (241 *km*) W *cen* Colo. flowing W & NW into Colorado River — see BLACK CANYON

Gun·tur \gün-ˈtu̇r\ city E India in *cen* Andhra Pradesh W of Machilipatnam *pop* 471,051

Gus·ta·vo A. Ma·de·ro, Vil·la \ˈvē-yä-gü-ˈstä-vō-ˌä-mä-ˈthä-rō\ city *cen* Mexico in Distrito Federal N of Mexico City *pop* 1,182,895

Guy·ana \gī-ˈa-nə\ *or formerly* **British Guiana** country N S. America on Atlantic coast; a republic within the Commonwealth of Nations since 1970 ✴ Georgetown *area* 83,000 *sq mi* (215,800 *sq km*), *pop* 755,000 — **Guy·a·nese** \ˌgī-ə-ˈnēz, -ˈnēs\ *adj or n*

Gwa·dar *or* **Gwa·dur** \ˈgwä-dər\ town & port SW Pakistan on Arabian Sea; until 1958 belonged to Sultan of Oman *pop* 17,000

Gwa·li·or \ˈgwä-lē-ˌȯr\ 1 former state N *cen* India ✴ Lashkar; part of Madhya Pradesh since 1956 2 city N *cen* India in NW Madhya Pradesh SSE of Agra *pop* 690,765

Gwent \ˈgwent\ county SE Wales ✴ Cwmbran *area* 531 *sq mi* (1381 *sq km*), *pop* 432,300

Gwyn·edd \'gwi-neth\ county NW Wales ✳ Caernarvon *area* 1494 *sq mi* (3869 *sq km*), *pop* 238,600
Gyandzha — see GANCA
Gyor \'jœr\ city NW Hungary WNW of Budapest *pop* 134,200

H

Haar·lem \'här-ləm\ city W Netherlands ✳ of N. Holland *pop* 149,788
Habana, La — see HAVANA
Ha·chi·o·ji \,hä-chē-'ō-jē\ city Japan on Honshu *pop* 466,373
Hack·en·sack \'ha-kᵊn-,sak\ city NE N.J. *pop* 37,049
Hack·ney \'hak-nē\ borough of N Greater London, England *pop* 164,200
Had·ding·ton \'ha-diŋ-tən\ **1** or **Had·ding·ton·shire** \-shir, -shər\ — see EAST LOTHIAN **2** royal burgh Scotland in Lothian *pop* 8117
Ha·dra·mawt or **Ha·dhra·maut** \,hä-drə-'maút\ region S Arabia bordering on Arabian Sea E of Aden, Yemen; chief town Al Mukal-la *area* 58,500 *sq mi* (152,100 *sq km*)
Hadrumetum — see SOUSSE
Hae·ju \'hī-(,)jü\ city SW N. Korea on inlet of Yellow Sea *pop* 195,000
Ha·erh–pin — see HARBIN
Ha·gen \'hä-gᵊn\ or **Hagen in West·fa·len** \in-,vest-'fä-lən\ city W Germany ENE of Düsseldorf *pop* 214,085
Ha·gers·town \'hā-gərz-,taún\ city N Md. *pop* 35,445
Hague, Cap de la — see CAP DE LA HAGUE
Hague, The \thə-'häg\ or *D* 's **Gra·ven·ha·ge** \'skrä-vᵊn-,hä-kə\ city SW Netherlands in S. Holland near coast of North Sea; de fac-to ✳ of the Netherlands *pop* 445,287
Haidarabad — see HYDERABAD
Hai·fa \'hī-fə\ city & port NW Israel at foot of Mt. Carmel *pop* 251,000
Hai·kou \'hī-'kō\ city & port SE China ✳ of Hainan *pop* 280,153
Hai·nan \'hī-'nän\ island SE China in S. China Sea; a province ✳ Haikou *area* 13,124 *sq mi* (33,991 *sq km*), *pop* 6,557,482
Hai·naut \ā-'nō, hā-\ **1** medieval county in Low Countries SE of Flanders in modern SW Belgium & N France **2** province SW Bel-gium ✳ Mons *area* 1463 *sq mi* (3789 *sq km*), *pop* 1,278,791
Hai·phong \'hī-'fŏŋ, -'fäŋ\ city & port N Vietnam in Tonkin in delta of Red River *pop* 449,747
Hai·ti \'hā-tē *also* hä-'ē-tē\ **1** — see HISPANIOLA **2** country W. In-dies on W Hispaniola; a republic ✳ Port-au-Prince *area* 10,714 *sq mi* (27,856 *sq km*), *pop* 6,902,000 — **Hai·tian** \'hā-shən *also* 'hä-tē-ən\ *adj or n*
Ha·ko·da·te \,hä-kō-'dä-tā\ city & port Japan in SW Hokkaido on Tsugaru Strait *pop* 307,251
Hal·ber·stadt \'häl-bər-,shtät, -,stät\ city *cen* Germany SE of Bruns-wick *pop* 47,713

Ha·le·a·ka·la Crater \hä-lā-ˌä-kä-ˈlä\ crater of dormant volcano 10,023 ft (3055 m) Hawaii on E Maui; more than 2500 ft (762 m) deep, 20 mi (32 km) in circumference; in **Haleakala National Park**

Hal·i·car·nas·sus \ˌha-lə-kär-ˈna-səs\ ancient city SW Asia Minor in SW Caria on Aegean Sea

Hal·i·fax \ˈha-lə-ˌfaks\ **1** city & port Canada ✳ of N.S. pop 114,455 **2** borough N England in W. Yorkshire pop 87,488 — **Hal·i·go·ni·an** \ˌha-lə-ˈgō-nē-ən\ n

Hal·lan·dale \ˈha-lən-ˌdāl\ city SE Fla. S of Fort Lauderdale pop 30,996

Hal·le \ˈhä-lə\ city E cen Germany on the Saale NW of Leipzig pop 232,396

Hall·statt \ˈhȯl-ˌstat, ˈhäl-ˌshtät, -ˌstät\ village W cen Austria on shore of **Hall·stät·ter Lake** \ˈhȯl-ˌste-tər; ˈhäl-ˌshte-, -ˌste-\

Hal·ma·he·ra \ˌhal-mə-ˈher-ə, ˌhäl-\ island E Indonesia in Moluccas; lies on the equator & is largest in group area 6928 sq mi (18,013 sq km), pop 54,000

Halm·stad \ˈhälm-ˌstä(d)\ city & port SW Sweden pop 81,084

Halq al–Wa·di \ˈhälk-äl-ˈwä-dē\ or **La Gou·lette** \lä-gü-ˈlet\ city N Tunisia on Bay of Tunis; port for Tunis pop 67,685

Hälsingborg — see HELSINGBORG

Hal·tom City \ˈhȯl-təm\ village N Tex. NE of Fort Worth pop 32,856

Hal·ton Hills \ˈhȯl-tᵊn\ town Canada in S Ont. pop 36,816

Halys — see KIZIL IRMAK

Ha·ma or **Ha·mah** \ˈhä-ˌmä\ or bib **Ha·math** \ˈhā-ˌmath\ city W Syria on the Orontes pop 229,000

Ha·mad, Al \ˌäl-hə-ˈmäd\ the SW portion of Syrian Desert

Ha·ma·dan \ˌha-mə-ˈdan, ˌhä-mə-ˈdän\ or anc **Ec·bat·a·na** \ek-ˈba-tᵊn-ə\ city W Iran WSW of Tehran pop 272,499

Ha·ma·ma·tsu \ˌhä-mä-ˈmät-(ˌ)sü\ city Japan in S Honshu SE of Nagoya near Pacific coast pop 534,624

Ham·burg \ˈham-ˌbərg; ˈhäm-ˌbu̇rg, -ˌbu̇rk\ city & port N Germany on the Elbe 68 mi (109 km) from its mouth; a state of the Federal Republic of Germany 1948–90 & of reunified Germany since then area 288 sq mi (749 sq km), pop 1,668,800 — **Ham·burg·er** \-ˌbər-gər, -ˌbu̇r-\ n

Ham·den \ˈham-dən\ town S Conn. N of New Haven pop 52,434

Ha·meln \ˈhä-məln\ or formerly **Ham·e·lin** \ˈha-mə-lən\ city N cen Germany in Lower Saxony SW of Hannover pop 58,906

Ham·hung \ˈhäm-ˌhu̇ŋ\ city E cen N. Korea near coast pop 701,000

Ham·il·ton \ˈha-məl-tən\ **1** city SW Ohio N of Cincinnati pop 61,368 **2** town & port ✳ of Bermuda pop 1100 **3** — see CHURCHILL **4** city & port Canada in SE Ont. on Lake Ontario pop 318,499 **5** city New Zealand on N cen North Is. pop 103,600

Hamilton, Mount mountain 4261 ft (1299 m) W Calif. E of San Jose

Hamilton Inlet inlet of the Atlantic 150 mi (241 km) long (with Lake Melville) Canada in SE Labrador

Hamm \ˈham, ˈhäm\ city W Germany on Lippe River pop 180,323

Ham·mer·fest \ˈha-mər-ˌfest, ˈhä-\ town & port N Norway on island in Arctic Ocean; northernmost town in Europe, at 70°38′N pop 6934

Ham·mer·smith and Ful·ham \'ha-mər-,smith-ənd-'fu̇-ləm\ borough of SW Greater London, England *pop* 136,500

Ham·mond \'ha-mənd\ city NW Ind. SE of Chicago *pop* 84,236

Hamp·shire \'hamp-,shir, -shər\ *or* **Hants** \'hants\ county S England on English Channel ❋ Winchester *area* 1509 *sq mi* (3908 *sq km*), *pop* 1,511,900

Hamp·stead \'hamp-stəd, -,sted\ former metropolitan borough NW London, England, now part of Camden

Hamp·ton \'hamp-tən\ city & port SE Va. E Newport News on Hampton Roads *pop* 133,793

Hampton Roads channel SE Va. through which James & Elizabeth rivers flow into Chesapeake Bay

Han \'hän\ 1 river E *cen* China in Shaanxi & Hubei flowing SE into the Chang 2 river *ab* 300 *mi* (483 *km*) N *cen* S. Korea flowing W & NW into Yellow Sea

HaNegev — see NEGEV

Han·ford \'han-fərd\ city S *cen* Calif. SE of Fresno *pop* 30,897

Hang·zhou \'häŋ-'jō\ *or* **Hang·chou** *or* **Hang·chow** \'haŋ-'chau̇, 'häŋ-'jō\ city E China ❋ of Zhejiang at head of **Hangzhou Bay** (inlet of E. China Sea) *pop* 1,099,660

Han·ko \'haŋ-,kō\ *or Sw* **Hangö** \'haŋ-,œ\ town & port SW Finland on Hanko (Hangö) Peninsula in the Baltic SE of Turku

Han·kow \'haŋ-,kau̇, -'kō; 'hän-'kō\ former city E *cen* China — see WUHAN

Han·ni·bal \'ha-nə-bəl\ city NE Mo. on Mississippi River *pop* 18,004

Han·no·ver *or* **Han·o·ver** \'ha-,nō-vər, -nə-vər, *G* hä-'nō-fər\ city N *cen* Germany WNW of Brunswick *pop* 517,476

Ha·noi \ha-'nȯi, hə-, hä-\ city ❋ of Vietnam in Tonkin on Red River; formerly ❋ of French Indochina & of N. Vietnam *metropolitan area pop* 1,089,760

Han·o·ver Park \'ha-,nō-vər, -nə-vər\ city NE Ill. *pop* 32,895

Han·yang \'hän-'yäŋ\ former city E *cen* China — see WUHAN

Haora — see HOWRAH

Ha·rap·pa \hə-'ra-pə\ locality W Pakistan in Indus valley NE of Multan; center of a prehistoric civilization

Ha·ra·re \hə-'rä-(,)rā\ *or formerly* **Salisbury** city ❋ of Zimbabwe *pop* 1,184,169

Har·bin \'här-bən, här-'bin\ *or* **Ha·erh·pin** \'hä-'ər-'bin\ *or formerly* **Pin·kiang** \'bin-'jyäŋ\ city NE China ❋ of Heilongjiang on Songhua River *pop* 2,443,398

Ha·rer \'här-ər\ city E Ethiopia E of Addis Ababa *pop* 76,890

Ha·ri \'här-ē\ *or* **Ha·ri Rud** \'rüd\ *or anc* **Ari·us** \'ar-ē-əs, 'er-; ə-'rī-əs\ river 700 *mi* (1126 *km*) NW Afghanistan, NE Iran, & S Turkmenistan flowing W & N into Kara Kum Desert

Har·in·gey \'har-iŋ-,gā\ borough of N Greater London, England *pop* 187,300

Har·lem \'här-ləm\ 1 river channel SE N.Y. NE of Manhattan Is.; with Spuyten Duyvil Creek, connects Hudson & East rivers 2 section of New York City in NE Manhattan bordering on Harlem & East rivers 3 HAARLEM — **Har·lem·ite** \-lə-,mīt\ *n*

Har·lin·gen 1 \'här-lən-jən\ city S Tex. NNW of Brownsville *pop* 48,735 2 \-liŋ-ən\ town & port N Netherlands in Friesland

Har·ney Lake \'här-nē\ intermittent salt lake SE Oreg. in **Harney Basin** (depression, area 2500 sq mi or 6500 sq km)

Harney Peak mountain 7242 ft (2207 m) SW S.Dak.; highest in Black Hills & in state

Harris — SEE LEWIS WITH HARRIS

Har·ris·burg \'har-əs-,bərg\ city ✳ of Pa. pop 52,376

Har·ri·son \'har-ə-sən\ village SE N.Y. on Long Island Sound pop 23,308

Har·ri·son·burg \'har-ə-sən-,bərg\ city N Va. pop 30,707

Har·ro·gate \'har-ə-gət, -,gāt\ borough N England in N. Yorkshire N of Leeds pop 66,475

Har·row \'har-(,)ō\ borough of NW Greater London, England pop 194,300

Hart·ford \'härt-fərd\ city N cen Conn., its ✳ pop 139,739 — **Hart·ford·ite** \-fər-,dīt\ n

Hart·le·pool \'härt-lē-,pül\ borough N England in Cleveland on North Sea pop 88,200

Har·vard, Mount \'här-vərd\ mountain 14,420 ft (4395 m) cen Colo. in Sawatch Mountains SE of Mt. Elbert

Har·vey \'här-vē\ city NE Ill. S of Chicago pop 29,771

Har·wich \'har-ij, -ich\ borough SE England in Essex on North Sea pop 15,076

Ha·ry·a·na \hə-rē-'ä-nə\ state NW India in E Punjab formed 1966 from southern part of former state of Punjab ✳ Chandigarh area 17,010 sq mi (44,226 sq km), pop 16,463,648

Harz \'härts\ mountains cen Germany bet. the Elbe & the Leine — SEE BROCKEN

Hasa or **Hasa, Al**— see AL-HASA

Has·selt \'hä-səlt\ commune NE Belgium ✳ of Limburg pop 66,611

Has·tings \'hās-tiŋz\ **1** city S Nebr. pop 22,837 **2** borough SE England in E. Sussex on Strait of Dover pop 78,100

Ha·tay \hä-'tī\ district S Turkey E of Gulf of Iskenderun

Hat·ter·as Island \'ha-tə-rəs\ island N.C. bet. Pamlico Sound & Atlantic Ocean; a long barrier island

Hatteras, Cape cape N.C. on SE Hatteras Is.

Hat·ties·burg \'ha-tēz-,bərg\ city SE Miss. pop 41,882

Hau·ra·ki Gulf \haü-'ra-kē, -'rä-\ inlet of the S Pacific N New Zealand on N coast of North Is.

Haute–Vol·ta \,ōt-vōl-'tä\ UPPER VOLTA — French name

Ha·vana \hə-'va-nə\ or Sp **La Ha·ba·na** \lä-ä-'vä-nä\ city & port ✳ of Cuba on Gulf of Mexico pop 2,096,054 — **Ha·van·an** \hə-'va-nən\ adj or n

Hav·ant \'ha-vənt\ town S England in Hampshire NE of Portsmouth pop 117,400

Hav·el \'hä-f'l\ river 212 mi (341 km) NE Germany flowing SW through Berlin into the Elbe

Have·lock \'hav-,läk, -lək\ city SE N.C. pop 20,268

Hav·er·ford·west \,ha-vər-fərd-'west, ,härt-fərd-\ borough & port SW Wales in Dyfed pop 9936

Ha·ver·hill \'hā-vrəl, 'hā-və-rəl\ city NE Mass. pop 51,418

Ha·ver·ing \'hāv-riŋ, 'hā-və-riŋ\ borough of NE Greater London, England pop 224,400

Ha·ví·rov \'hä-vē-,zhóf\ city E Czech Republic pop 86,267

Havre — see LE HAVRE

Ha·waii \hə-'wä-yē, -'wä-ē *also* -'vä- *or* -'wò-; *sometimes* -yə\ **1** *or* **Ha·wai·ian Islands** \-yən\ *or formerly* **Sand·wich Islands** \'sand-,wich\ group of islands *cen* Pacific belonging to U.S. **2** island SE Hawaii, largest of the group; chief city Hilo *area* 4021 *sq mi* (10,455 *sq km*) **3** state of the U.S. comprising Hawaiian Islands except Midway Islands; annexed 1898, a territory 1900–59 ✳ Honolulu *area* 6471 *sq mi* (16,760 *sq km*), *pop* 1,108,229 — **Hawaiian** *adj or n*

Hawaii Volcanoes National Park reservation Hawaii including Mauna Loa & Kilauea volcanoes on Hawaii (island)

Hawke Bay \'hòk\ inlet of the S Pacific N New Zealand on SE coast of North Is.

Haw·thorne \'hò-,thòrn\ **1** city SW Calif. SW of Los Angeles *pop* 71,349 **2** borough NE N.J. N of Paterson *pop* 17,084

Hay \'hā\ river 530 *mi* (853 *km*) Canada in N Alta. & SW Mackenzie district flowing NE into Great Slave Lake

Hayes \'hāz\ **1** river 300 *mi* (483 *km*) Canada in E Man. flowing NE into Hudson Bay **2** *or* **Hayes and Har·ling·ton** \'här-liŋ-tən\ former urban district SE England in Middlesex, now part of Hillingdon

Hay·ward \'hā-wərd\ city W Calif. SE of Oakland *pop* 111,498

Ha·zel Park \'hā-zəl\ city SE Mich. N of Detroit *pop* 20,051

Ha·zle·ton \'hā-zəl-tən\ city E Pa. S of Wilkes-Barre *pop* 24,730

Heard \'hərd\ island S Indian Ocean SE of Kerguelen, at 53°10'S 74°10'E; administered by Australia

He·bei \'hə-'bā\ *or* **Ho·peh** *or* **Ho·pei** \'hō-'bā\ *or formerly* **Chih·li** \'chē-'lē, 'jir-'lē\ province NE China ✳ Shijiazhuang *area* 77,079 *sq mi* (199,635 *sq km*), *pop* 61,082,439

Heb·ri·des \'he-brə-,dēz\ islands W Scotland in the Atlantic divided by Little Minch into **Inner Hebrides** (near the mainland) & **Outer Hebrides** (to NW) *area* 2900 *sq mi* (7540 *sq km*), *pop* 30,660 — see LEWIS WITH HARRIS, WESTERN ISLES — **Heb·ri·de·an** \,he-brə-'dē-ən\ *adj or n*

He·bron \'hē-brən\ *or anc* **Kir·jath-ar·ba** \,kər-yəth-'är-bə, ,kir-\ city *cen* Palestine SSW of Jerusalem in modern Jordan *pop* 79,087

Hec·ate Strait \'he-kət\ strait Canada in W B.C., inlet of the Pacific bet. Queen Charlotte Islands & the coast

Heer·len \'her-lən\ commune SE Netherlands in Limburg NE of Maastricht *pop* 95,001

He·fei *or* **Ho·fei** \'hə-'fā\ *or formerly* **Lu·chow** \'lü-'jō\ city E China ✳ of Anhui W of Nanjing *pop* 733,278

Hei·del·berg \'hī-d°l-,bərg, -,berk\ city SW Germany on the Neckar SE of Mannheim *pop* 139,392

Heil·bronn \'hīl-,brän, hīl-'brón\ city SW Germany on the Neckar N of Stuttgart *pop* 117,427

Heilong, Hei·lung — see AMUR

Hei·long·jiang *or* **Hei·lung·kiang** \'hā-'lùŋ-'jyän\ province NE China in N Manchuria bordering on the Amur ✳ Harbin *area* 178,996 *sq mi* (465,390 *sq km*), *pop* 35,214,873

He·jaz \he-'jaz, hi-\ *or* **Al Ḥi·jāz** \,äl-hi-'jaz\ region W Saudi Arabia on Red Sea; a viceroyalty ✳ Mecca *area* 134,600 *sq mi* (348,614 *sq km*), *pop* 1,400,000

Hek·la *or* **Hec·la** \'he-klä\ volcano 4747 *ft* (1447 *m*) SW Iceland

Hel·e·na \'he-lə-nə\ city W *cen* Mont., its ✳ *pop* 24,569

Hel·go·land \'hel-gō-,land, -,länt\ *or* **Hel·i·go·land** \'he-lə-gō-\ island NW Germany in North Sea, in N. Frisian Islands

Hel·i·con \'he-lə-,kän, -li-kən\ *or NGk* **Eli·kón** \,e-lē-'kón\ mountain 5735 *ft* (1748 *m*) E *cen* Greece in SW Boeotia near Gulf of Corinth

He·li·op·o·lis \,hē-lē-'ä-pə-lis\ **1** — see BAALBEK **2** ancient ruined city N Egypt S of modern Cairo **3** ancient ruined city NE of modern Cairo

Hellas — see GREECE — **Hel·lene** \'he-,lēn\ *n* — **Hel·len·ic** \he-'le-nik, hə-\ *adj or n* — **Hel·le·nis·tic** \,he-lə-'nis-tik\ *adj*

Hel·les, Cape \'he-(,)lēz\ headland Turkey in Europe at S tip of Gallipoli Peninsula

Hellespont, Hellespontus — see DARDANELLES

Hell Gate a narrow part of East River in New York City bet. Long Is. & Manhattan Is.

Hells Canyon \'helz\ canyon of Snake River on Idaho-Oreg. border

Hel·mand *or* **Hel·mund** \'hel-mənd\ river SW Afghanistan flowing SW & W into a morass on Iran border

Hel·mond \'hel-,mònt\ commune S Netherlands *pop* 70,574

Helm·stedt \'helm-,shtet, -,stet\ city Germany E of Brunswick near former E. Germany–W. Germany border *pop* 27,072

Hel·sing·borg *or* **Häl·sing·borg** \'hel-siŋ-,bòrg, -,bòr-ē\ city & port SW Sweden on Öresund opposite Helsingör, Denmark *pop* 108,359

Hel·sing·ör \,hel-siŋ-'œr\ city & port Denmark on N Sjælland Is. *pop* 56,754

Hel·sin·ki \'hel-,siŋ-kē, hel-'\ *or Sw* **Hel·sing·fors** \'hel-siŋ-,fòrs\ city & port ✻ of Finland on Gulf of Finland *pop* 490,629

Hel·vel·lyn \hel-'ve-lən\ mountain 3118 *ft* (950 *m*) NW England in Cumbria SW of Ullswater

Helvetia — see SWITZERLAND — **Hel·ve·tian** \hel-'vē-shən\ *adj or n*

Hem·et \'he-mət\ city SE Calif. SE of San Bernardino *pop* 36,094

Hemp·stead \'hem(p)-,sted, -stəd\ village SE N.Y. on Long Is. *pop* 49,453

He·nan \'hə-'nän\ *or* **Ho·nan** \'hō-'nän\ province E *cen* China ✻ Zhengzhou *area* 64,479 *sq mi* (167,645 *sq km*), *pop* 85,509,535

Hen·der·son \'hen-dər-sən\ **1** city NW Ky. *pop* 25,945 **2** city S Nev. *pop* 64,942

Hen·der·son·ville \'hen-dər-sən-,vil, -vəl\ city N Tenn. NE of Nashville *pop* 32,188

Hen·don \'hen-dən\ former urban district SE England in Middlesex, now part of Barnet

Heng·e·lo \'heŋ-ə-,lō\ commune E Netherlands in Overijssel *pop* 76,726

Heng·yang \'həŋ-'yäŋ\ city SE *cen* China in SE Hunan on the Xiang *pop* 487,148

Hen·ley \'hen-lē\ *or* **Henley on Thames** borough SE *cen* England in Oxfordshire W of London *pop* 31,744

Hen·lo·pen, Cape \hen-'lō-pən\ headland SE Del. at entrance to Delaware Bay

Hen·ry, Cape \'hen-rē\ headland SE Va. S of entrance to Chesapeake Bay

He·rat \he-'rät, hə-\ *or anc* **Aria** \'ar-ē-ə, 'er-; ə-'rī-ə\ city NW Afghanistan on the Hari *pop* 177,300

Her·cu·la·ne·um \,hər-kyə-'lā-nē-əm\ ancient city S Italy in Campania on Tyrrhenian Sea; destroyed A.D. 79 by eruption of Mt. Vesuvius

Her·e·ford \'her-ə-fərd, 'här-fərd\ **1** *or* **Her·e·ford·shire** \-,shir, -shər\ former county W England on Welsh border **2** town W England in Hereford and Worcester *pop* 49,800

Hereford and Worces·ter \'wùs-tər\ county W England ✱ Worcester *area* 1571 *sq mi* (4069 *sq km*), *pop* 667,800

Her·ford \'her-fört\ city W *cen* Germany in N. Rhine-Westphalia NE of Bielefeld *pop* 64,732

He·ri·sau \'her-ə-,zaù\ commune NE Switzerland ✱ of Appenzell Outer Rhodes half canton *pop* 15,560

Her·mon, Mount \'hər-mən\ mountain 9232 *ft* (2814 *m*) on border bet. Syria & Lebanon; highest in Anti-Lebanon Mountains

Her·mo·sil·lo \,er-mō-'sē-(,)yō\ city NW Mexico ✱ of Sonora on Sonora River *pop* 449,472

Hermoúpolis — see ERMOÚPOLIS

Her·ne \'her-nə\ city W Germany in the Ruhr *pop* 179,137

Her·ning \'her-niŋ, 'har-niŋ\ city Denmark in *cen* Jutland *pop* 56,376

Her·ten \'her-tᵊn\ city W Germany in N. Rhine-Westphalia N of Essen *pop* 69,374

Hert·ford \'här-fərd, 'härt-, *US also* 'hərt-\ borough SE England ✱ of Hertfordshire *pop* 21,412

Hert·ford·shire \'här-fərd-,shir, 'härt-, -shər, *US also* 'hərt-\ *or* **Hert·ford** \'här-fərd *also* 'härt-, *US also* 'hərt-\ county SE England *area* 654 *sq mi* (1699 *sq km*), *pop* 951,500

Hertogenbosch, 's — see 'S HERTOGENBOSCH

Her·ze·go·vi·na \,hert-sə-gō-'vē-nə, ,hərt-, -'gō-və-nə\ *or Serb* **Her·ce·go·vi·na** \,kert-sə-gō-vē-nə\ region S Europe S of Bosnia & NW of Montenegro; part of Bosnia and Herzegovina — **Her·ze·go·vi·nian** \,hert-sə-gō-'vē-nē-ən, ,hərt-, -nyən\ *adj*

Hes·pe·ria \he-'sper-ē-ə\ city SE Calif. N of San Bernardino *pop* 50,418

Hesse \'hes, 'he-sē\ *or G* **Hes·sen** \'he-sᵊn\ **1** region W *cen* Germany N of Baden-Württemberg divided into **Hesse–Darmstadt** (in the S) & **Hesse–Cas·sel** \'ka-sᵊl, -'kä-\ (in the N), the latter being united with Prussia in 1866 as part of the province of **Hesse–Nassau** along with the duchy of Nassau & the city of Frankfurt am Main **2** state of the Weimar Republic, equivalent to Hesse-Darmstadt **3** state of Germany & formerly of W. Germany including larger part of Hesse-Darmstadt & part of Hesse-Nassau ✱ Wiesbaden *area* 8151 *sq mi* (21,111 *sq km*), *pop* 5,763,300

Hes·ton and Isle·worth \'hes-tən-ənd-'ī-zəl-(,)wərth, 'he-sᵊn-\ former municipal borough SE England in Middlesex, now part of Hounslow

Hi·a·le·ah \,hī-ə-'lē-ə\ city SE Fla. N of Miami *pop* 188,004

Hibernia — see IRELAND — **Hi·ber·ni·an** \hī-'bər-nē-ən\ *adj or n*

Hick·o·ry \'hi-kə-rē\ city W *cen* N.C. *pop* 28,301

Hi·dal·go \hi-'dal-(,)gō, ē-'thäl-(,)gō\ state *cen* Mexico ✱ Pachuca *area* 8103 *sq mi* (20,987 *sq km*), *pop* 1,888,366

Hierosolyma — see JERUSALEM

Hier·ro \'yer-(,)ō\ *or* **Fer·ro** \'fer-(,)ō\ island Spain, westernmost of the Canary Islands *area* 107 *sq mi* (278 *sq km*)

Hi·ga·shi·ōsa·ka \hē-,gä-shē-'ō-sä-kä\ city Japan in S Honshu; suburb of Osaka *pop* 518,251

High Atlas — see ATLAS

High·land \'hī-land\ **1** city SE Calif. E of San Bernardino *pop* 34,439 **2** town NW Ind. S of Hammond *pop* 23,696 **3** region N Scotland, established 1975 ✳ Inverness *area* 9806 *sq mi* (25,398 *sq km*), *pop* 206,900

Highland Park **1** city NE Ill. N of Chicago *pop* 30,575 **2** city SE Mich. within city of Detroit *pop* 20,121

High·lands \'hī-landz\ the chiefly mountainous N part of Scotland N of a line connecting Firth of Clyde & Firth of Tay

Highlands of Navesink — see NAVESINK (Highlands of)

Highlands of the Hudson hilly region SE N.Y. on both sides of Hudson River; includes Storm King (W of the Hudson) 1355 *ft* (413 *m*)

High Plains the Great Plains esp. from Nebr. southward

High Point \'hī-,point\ city N *cen* N.C. SW of Greensboro *pop* 69,496

High Sierra the Sierra Nevada (in Calif.)

High Wyc·ombe \'wi-kəm\ borough SE *cen* England in Buckinghamshire WNW of London *pop* 60,516

Hii·u·maa \'hē-ə-,mä\ island Estonia in Baltic Sea N of Sarema Is. *area* 373 *sq mi* (966 *sq km*)

Hijāz, Al — see HEJAZ

Hil·des·heim \'hil-dəs-,hīm\ city N *cen* Germany SSE of Hannover *pop* 105,674

Hil·ling·don \'hi-liŋ-dən\ borough of W Greater London, England *pop* 225,800

Hills·boro \'hilz-,bər-ō\ city NW Oreg. W of Portland *pop* 37,520

Hi·lo \'hē-(,)lō\ city & port Hawaii in E Hawaii (island) *pop* 37,808

Hilton Head Island \'hil-t°n-'hed\ island comprising a town off S.C. coast *pop* 23,694

Hil·ver·sum \'hil-vər-səm\ city *cen* Netherlands in N. Holland SE of Amsterdam *pop* 84,674

Hi·ma·chal Pra·desh \hi-'mä-chəl-prə-'desh, -'däsh\ state NW India NW of Uttar Pradesh ✳ Simla *area* 21,490 *sq mi* (55,659 *sq km*), *pop* 5,170,877

Hi·ma·la·ya, the \,hi-mə-'lā-ə; hə-'mäl-yə, -'mä-lē-ə\ *or* **the Hi·ma·la·yas** \-əz\ mountains S Asia on border bet. India & Tibet & in Kashmir, Nepal, & Bhutan — see EVEREST (Mount) — **Hi·ma·la·yan** \,hi-mə-'lā-ən; hə-'mäl-yən, -'mä-lē-ən\ *adj or n*

Hi·me·ji \hē-'mā-jē\ city Japan in W Honshu *pop* 454,360

Hindenburg — see ZABRZE

Hin·du Kush \hin-(,)dü-'kush, -'kəsh\ *or anc* **Cau·ca·sus In·di·cus** \'kó-kə-səs-'in-di-kəs\ mountain range *cen* Asia SW of the Pamirs on border of Kashmir & in Afghanistan — see TIRICH MIR

Hin·du·stan \,hin-(,)dü-'stan, -də-, -'stän\ **1** region N India N of the Deccan including the plain drained by the Indus, the Ganges, & the Brahmaputra **2** the subcontinent of India **3** the Republic of India — **Hin·du·stani** *also* **Hin·do·stani** \,hin-dù-'sta-nē, -stä-nē\ *adj*

Hines·ville \'hīnz-,vil, -vəl\ town SE Ga. *pop* 21,603

Hing·ham \'hiŋ-əm\ town E Mass. SE of Boston *pop* 19,821

Hip·po \'hi-(,)pō\ *or* **Hippo Re·gi·us** \'rē-jəs, -jē-əs\ ancient city N Africa S of modern Bône, Algeria; chief town of Numidia

Hi·ra·ka·ta \,hē-rä-'kä-tä\ city Japan on Honshu *pop* 390,790

Hi·ro·shi·ma \,hir-ə-'shē-mə, hə-'rō-shə-mə\ city & port Japan in SW Honshu on Inland Sea *pop* 1,096,919

His·pa·nia \hi-'spā-nē-ə, -'spā-nyə, -'spa-\ IBERIAN PENINSULA

His·pan·io·la \,his-pə-'nyō-lə\ *or Sp* **Es·pa·ño·la** \,es-,pä-'nyō-lä\ *or formerly* **Hai·ti** \'hā-tē\ *or* **San·to Do·min·go** \,san-tə-də-'min-(,)gō\ *or* **San Domingo** \,san-də-\ island West Indies in the Greater Antilles; divided bet. Haiti (on W) & Dominican Republic (on E) *area* 29,371 *sq mi* (76,071 *sq km*)

His·sar·lik \,hi-sər-'lik\ site of ancient Troy NW Turkey in Asia 4 *mi* (6.4 *km*) SE of mouth of the Dardanelles

Hi·was·see \hī-'wä-sē\ river 150 *mi* (241 *km*) E U.S. flowing from NE Ga. WNW through W N.C. into Tennessee River in Tenn.

Ho·bart 1 \'hō-bərt\ city NW Ind. *pop* 21,822 2 \-,bärt\ city & port Australia ✳ of Tasmania *pop* 47,106

Hobbs \'häbz\ city SE corner of N.Mex. *pop* 29,115

Ho·bo·ken \'hō-,bō-kən\ city NE N.J. N of Jersey City *pop* 33,397

Ho Chi Minh City \'hō-,chē-'min\ *or formerly* **Sai·gon** \sī-'gän, 'sī-,\ city & port S Vietnam; formerly (as Saigon) ✳ of S. Vietnam *pop* 2,899,753

Hodeida — see AL HUDAYDAH

Hof \'hōf, 'hóf\ city Germany in Bavaria on the Saale near former E. Germany–W. Germany border *pop* 52,859

Hofei — see HEFEI

Hoff·man Estates \'häf-mən, 'hóf-\ village NE Ill. *pop* 46,561

Hofuf — see AL HUFUF

Hoggar — see AHAGGAR

Ho·hen·zol·lern \'hō-ən-,zä-lərn, -,tsó-lərn\ region SW Germany, formerly a province of Prussia — see WÜRTTEMBERG

Ho·he Tau·ern \,hō-ə-'taú(-ə)rn\ range of the E Alps W Austria bet. Carinthia & Tirol — see GROSSGLOCKNER

Hoh·hot \'hō-'hōt\ *or* **Hu·he·hot** \'hü-(')hä-'hōt\ *or* **Hu–ho–hao·t'e** \'hü-'hō-'haú-'tə\ city N China ✳ of Inner Mongolia *pop* 652,534

Ho·ho·kam Pi·ma National Monument \hō-'hō-kəm-'pē-mə\ reservation SE of Phoenix, Ariz.; not open to the public

Hok·kai·do \hä-'kī-(,)dō\ *or formerly* **Ye·zo** \'ye-(,)zō\ island N Japan N of Honshu *area with adjacent small islands* 30,313 *sq mi* (78,511 *sq km*), *pop* 5,643,715

Hol·guín \(h)ól-'gēn\ city E Cuba in plateau region *pop* 228,052

Hol·land \'hä-lənd\ 1 city W Mich. on Lake Michigan *pop* 30,745 2 medieval county of Holy Roman Empire bordering on North Sea, now forming N. & S. Holland provinces of the Netherlands 3 — see NETHERLANDS — **Hol·land·er** \-lən-dər\ *n*

Holland, Parts of district & former administrative county E England in SE Lincolnshire ✳ Boston *area* 418 *sq mi* (1083 *sq km*)

Hollandia — see JAYAPURA

Hol·lis·ter \'hä-lə-stər\ city W Calif. E of Monterey Bay *pop* 19,212

Hol·ly·wood \'hä-lē-,wúd\ 1 section of Los Angeles, Calif. NW of the downtown district 2 city SE Fla. N of Miami *pop* 121,697

Hol·stein \'hōl-ˌstīn, -ˌstēn; 'hól-ˌshtīn\ region N Germany S of Jutland Peninsula adjoining Schleswig; once a duchy of Denmark, became a part of Prussia 1866 — see SCHLESWIG-HOLSTEIN

Hol·ston \'hōl-stən\ river 140 *mi* (225 *km*) E Tenn. flowing SW to unite with French Broad River forming the Tennessee River

Holy Cross, Mount of the mountain 14,005 *ft* (4269 *m*) NW *cen* Colo. in Sawatch Range

Holy·head \'hä-lē-ˌhed\ **1** island NW Wales in St. George's Channel off W coast of Anglesey **2** urban area & port NW Wales in Gwynedd on Holy Is.

Ho·ly Island \'hō-lē\ or **Lin·dis·farne** \'lin-dəs-ˌfärn\ island N England off NE coast of Northumberland; connected to mainland at low tide *pop* 190

Holy Land a name for Palestine first used in Zech. 2:12

Holy Loch inlet of Firth of Clyde W Scotland on NW shore of the firth opposite mouth of the Clyde

Hol·yoke \'hōl-ˌyōk\ city SW Mass. N of Springfield *pop* 43,704

Holy Roman Empire realm of *cen* Europe in medieval & modern periods; of varying extent, but with Germany as chief component

Homel or **Homyel'** — see GOMEL

Home·stead \'hōm-ˌsted\ city SE Fla. SW of Miami *pop* 26,866

Homestead National Monument site SE Nebr. (W of Beatrice) of first homestead entered under General Homestead Act of 1862

Home·wood \'hōm-ˌwùd\ **1** city *cen* Ala. *pop* 22,922 **2** village NE Ill. S of Chicago *pop* 19,278

Homs \'hòmz, 'hüms\ or *anc* **Em·e·sa** \'e-mə-sə\ city W Syria on the Orontes *pop* 354,508

Honan — see HENAN

Hon·du·ras \hän-'dùr-əs, -'dyùr-; òn-'dü-räs\ country Central America bordering on the Caribbean & the Pacific; a republic ✻ Tegucigalpa *area* 43,277 *sq mi* (112,087 *sq km*), *pop* 4,604,800 — **Hon·du·ran** \-ən\ *adj or n* — **Hon·du·ra·ne·an** or **Hon·du·ra·ni·an** \ˌhän-dü-'rā-nē-ən, -dyü-\ *adj or n*

Honduras, Gulf of inlet of the Caribbean bet. S Belize, E Guatemala, & N Honduras

Hon·fleur \ōⁿ-'flœr\ town & port N France on Seine estuary *pop* 8346

Hong — see RED

Hong Kong \'häŋ-ˌkäŋ, -'käŋ; 'hóŋ-ˌkóŋ, -'kóŋ\ **1** special administrative region China on SE coast E of mouth of Zhu River including Hong Kong Is., Kowloon Peninsula & New Territories, & nearby islands; formerly a Brit. crown colony ✻ Victoria *area* 398 *sq mi* (1031 *sq km*), *pop* 4,986,560 **2** — see VICTORIA — **Hong Kong·er** \-ər\ *n*

Hong·shui or **Hung·shui** \'hùŋ-'shwē\ river S China flowing from E Yunnan E to E Guangxi Zhuangzu

Hong·ze or **Hung·tse** \'hùŋ-'dzə\ lake 65 *mi* (105 *km*) long E China in W Jiangsu; traversed by the Huang

Ho·ni·a·ra \ˌhō-nē-'är-ə\ town W Pacific ✻ of Solomon Islands on Guadalcanal Is. *pop* 35,288

Ho·no·lu·lu \ˌhä-nᵊl-'ü-(ˌ)lü, ˌhō-nᵊl-\ city & port ✻ of Hawaii on Oahu *pop* 365,272 — **Ho·no·lu·lan** \-'ü-lən\ *n*

Hon·shu \'hän-(,)shü, 'hon-\ *or* **Hon·do** \-(,)dō\ island Japan, chief island of the group *area* 86,246 *sq mi* (223,377 *sq km*), *pop* 100,254,208

Hood, Mount \'hud\ mountain 11,235 *ft* (3424 *m*) NW Oreg. in Cascade Range; highest point in state

Hood Canal inlet of Puget Sound 80 *mi* (129 *km*) long W Wash. along E shore of Olympic Peninsula

Hoofd·dorp \'hōft-,dorp\ commune W Netherlands *pop* 100,659

Hoogly — see HUGLI

Hook of Holland \'huk\ headland SW Netherlands in S. Holland on coast SW of The Hague

Hoorn Islands — see FUTUNA ISLANDS

Hoo·sac Mountains \'hü-sak\ mountain range NW Mass. & SW Vt., a southern extension of Green Mountains

Hoo·ver \'hü-vər\ city *cen* Ala. *pop* 39,788

Hoover Dam *or formerly* **Boul·der Dam** \'bōl-dər\ dam 726 *ft* (221 *m*) high in Colorado River bet. Nev. & Ariz. — see MEAD (Lake)

Ho·pat·cong, Lake \hə-'pat-,kän, -,kän\ lake 8 *mi* (13 *km*) long N N.J.

Hopeh *or* **Hopei** — see HEBEI

Hope·well \'hōp-,wel, -wəl\ city SE Va. *pop* 23,101

Hop·kins·ville \'häp-kənz-,vil\ city SW Ky. *pop* 29,809

Ho·reb, Mount \'hōr-,eb, 'hor-\ *or* **Mount Si·nai** \'sī-,nī *also* -nē-,ī\ mountain where according to the Bible the Law was given to Moses; thought to be in the Gebel Musa on Sinai Peninsula

Horlivka — see GORLOVKA

Hor·moz \'hor-,məz\ *or* **Hor·muz** *same or* hor-'müz\ island SE Iran in Strait of Hormuz

Hor·muz *or* **Or·muz** \'(h)or-,məz, (h)or-'müz\ ancient town S Iran on **Strait of Hormuz** (strait connecting Persian Gulf & Gulf of Oman)

Horn \'horn\ *or* **North Cape** cape NW Iceland

Horn, Cape headland S Chile on **Horn Island** in Tierra del Fuego; southernmost point of S. America, at 55°59′S

Horn·church \'horn-,chərch\ former urban district SE England in Essex, now part of Havering

Horn of Africa the easternmost projection of Africa; variously used of Somalia, SE or all of Ethiopia & sometimes Djibouti; its E tip is Cape Guardafui

Hor·sens \'hor-s°nz, -s°n(t)s\ city & port Denmark *pop* 54,940

Hos·pi·ta·let \(,)häs-,pi-t°l-'et, ,ōs-pē-tä-'let\ city NE Spain in Barcelona province, SW suburb of Barcelona *pop* 269,241

Ho·tan \'hō-'tän\ *or* **Ho·t'ien** \'hō-'tyen\ *or* **Kho·tan** \'kō-'tän\ town & oasis W China in SW Xinjiang Uygur on S edge of the Taklimakan

Hot Springs city W *cen* Ark. adjoining **Hot Springs National Park** (reservation containing hot mineral springs) *pop* 32,462

Hou·ma \'hō-mə, 'hü-\ city SE La. *pop* 30,495

Houns·low \'haunz-(,)lō\ borough of SW Greater London, England *pop* 193,400

Hou·sa·ton·ic \,hü-sə-'tä-nik, ,hü-zə-\ river 148 *mi* (238 *km*) W Mass. & W Conn. flowing from Berkshire Hills S into Long Island Sound

Hous·ton \'hyü-stən, 'yü-\ city & port SE Tex. connected with Galveston Bay by ship canal *pop* 1,630,553 — **Hous·to·nian** \hyü-'stō-nē-ən, yü-, -nyən\ *n* — **Hous·ton·ite** \'hyü-stə-ˌnīt, 'yü-\ *n*

Hove \'hōv\ town S England in E. Sussex *pop* 82,500

Ho·ven·weep National Monument \'hō-vən-ˌwēp\ site SE Utah & SW Colo. of prehistoric pueblos & cliff dwellings

How·rah *or* **Hao·ra** \'hau̇-rə\ city E India in W. Bengal on the Hugli opposite Calcutta *pop* 950,435

Hra·dec Krá·lo·ve \'(h)rä-ˌdets-'krä-lò-ˌvä\ *or G* **Kö·nig·grätz** \ˌkœ-nik-'grets\ city N *cen* Czech Republic *pop* 99,889

Hrodna *or* **Hrodno** — see GRODNO

Hsi — see XI

Hsia–men — see XIAMEN

Hsiang — see XIANG

Hsiang–t'an — see XIANGTAN

Hsin–chu \'shin-'chü\ city & port China in NW Taiwan on coast SW of Taipei *pop* 332,524

Hsin–hsiang — see XINXIANG

Hsi–ning — see XINING

Hsinkao — see YÜ SHAN

Hsüan–hua — see XUANHUA

Hsü–chou — see XUZHOU

Huai \hü-'ī, 'hwī\ river *over* 600 *mi* (966 *km*) E China flowing from S Henan E into Hongze Lake

Huai·nan \hü-'ī-ˌnän, 'hwī-\ city E China in N *cen* Anhui SW of Bengbu *pop* 703,934

Hual·la·ga \wä-'yä-gä, kwä-\ river 700 *mi* (1126 *km*) N *cen* Peru flowing N into the Marañón

Huam·bo \'wäm-(ˌ)bō, 'hwäm-\ *or formerly* **No·va Lis·boa** \'nò-və-ˌlēzh-'bō-ə\ city Angola in W *cen* highlands *pop* 49,823

Huang *or* **Hwang** \'hwäŋ\ *or* **Yellow** river *ab* 3000 *mi* (4828 *km*) N China flowing from Kunlun Mountains in Qinghai E into Bo Hai

Huang·pu *or* **Whang·poo** \'hwäŋ-'pü\ river 70 *mi* (113 *km*) E China flowing E & N past Shanghai into the Chang

Huas·ca·rán \ˌwäs-kä-'rän\ mountain 22,205 *ft* (6768 *m*) W Peru; highest in the country

Hu·bei *or* **Hu·peh** *or* **Hu·pei** \'hü-'bā, -'pā\ province E *cen* China ✳ Wuhan *area* 72,394 *sq mi* (188,224 *sq km*), *pop* 53,969,210

Hu·ber Heights \'hyü-bər, 'yü-\ city W Ohio *pop* 38,696

Hu·bli–Dhar·war \ˌhüb-lē-ˌdär-'wär\ city SW India in W Karnataka *pop* 648,298

Hudaydah, Al — see AL HUDAYDAH

Hud·ders·field \'hə-dərz-ˌfēld\ borough N England in W. Yorkshire NE of Manchester *pop* 123,888

Hud·son \'həd-sən\ river 306 *mi* (492 *km*) E N.Y. flowing from Adirondack Mountains S into New York Bay — **Hud·so·ni·an** \ˌhəd-'sō-nē-ən\ *adj*

Hudson Bay inlet of the Atlantic in N Canada; an inland sea 850 *mi* (1368 *km*) long

Hudson Strait strait 450 *mi* (724 *km*) long NE Canada bet. S Baffin Is. & N Que. connecting Hudson Bay with the Atlantic

Hue *or F* **Hué** \'hwä, 'wä, hü-'ā, hyü-'ā\ city & port *cen* Vietnam in Annam; formerly ✳ of Annam *pop* 211,718

Huel·va \'wel-vä, 'hwel-\ **1** province SW Spain in Andalusia on Gulf of Cádiz *area* 3894 *sq mi* (10,085 *sq km*), *pop* 443,476 **2** city, its ✻ *pop* 127,822

Hues·ca \'wes-kä, 'hwes-\ **1** province NE Spain in Aragon *area* 6051 *sq mi* (15,672 *sq km*), *pop* 207,810 **2** commune, its ✻ *pop* 44,165

Hufuf, Al — see AL HUFUF

Hu·gli *or* **Hoo·ghly** \'hü-glē\ river 120 *mi* (193 *km*) E India flowing S into Bay of Bengal; most westerly channel of the Ganges in its delta

Huhehot — see HOHHOT

Hui·la \'wē-(,)lä, 'hwē-\ volcano 18,865 *ft* (5750 *m*) SW *cen* Colombia

Hull \'həl\ **1** town Canada in SW Que. on Ottawa River opposite Ottawa, Ont. *pop* 60,707 **2** *or in full* **Kings·ton upon Hull** \'kiŋ(k)-stən\ city & borough & port N England in Humberside *pop* 242,200

Hu·ma·cao \,ü-mə-'kaú\ town E Puerto Rico *pop* 21,306

Hum·ber \'həm-bər\ estuary 40 *mi* (64 *km*) E England formed by Ouse & Trent rivers & flowing E & SE into North Sea

Hum·ber·side \'həm-bər-,sīd\ county E England; area formerly in Yorkshire; ✻ Kingston upon Hull *area* 1405 *sq mi* (3639 *sq km*), *pop* 835,200

Hum·boldt \'həm-,bōlt\ river 290 *mi* (467 *km*) N Nev. flowing W & SW into Rye Patch reservoir & formerly into Humboldt Lake

Humboldt Bay bay NW Calif. on which Eureka is situated

Humboldt Glacier glacier NW Greenland

Humboldt Lake lake W Nev. formerly receiving Humboldt River; has no outlet, but has an intermittent S extension **Humboldt Sink**

Hum·phreys Peak \'həmp-frēz\ mountain peak 12,633 *ft* (3851 *m*) N *cen* Ariz. — see SAN FRANCISCO PEAKS

Hu·nan \'hü-'nän\ province SE *cen* China ✻ Changsha *area* 81,274 *sq mi* (211,312 *sq km*), *pop* 60,659,754

Hun·ga·ry \'həŋ-gə-rē\ *or* **Hung Ma·gyar·or·szag** \,mȯ-,jȯr-'ȯr-,säg\ country *cen* Europe; formerly a kingdom, since 1946 a republic ✻ Budapest *area* 35,919 *sq mi* (93,030 *sq km*), *pop* 10,296,000 — **Hun·gar·i·an** \,hən-'ger-ē-ən, -'gar-\ *adj or n*

Hungshui — see HONGSHUI

Hungtse — see HONGZE

Hun·ter \'hən-tər\ river 287 *mi* (462 *km*) SE Australia in E New South Wales flowing E into the Pacific

Hun·ting·don \'hən-tiŋ-dən\ **1** *or* **Hun·ting·don·shire** \-,shir, -shər\ *or* **Huntingdon and Pe·ter·bor·ough** \'pē-tər-,bər-ō\ *or* **Hunts** \'hənts\ former county E *cen* England ✻ Huntingdon; since 1974 part of Cambridgeshire **2** town E *cen* England in Cambridgeshire *pop* 2859

Hun·ting·ton \'hən-tiŋ-tən\ city W W.Va. on Ohio River *pop* 54,844

Huntington Beach city SW Calif. SE of Los Angeles *pop* 181,519

Huntington Park city SW Calif. S of Los Angeles *pop* 56,065

Hunts·ville \'hənts-,vil, -vəl\ **1** city N Ala. *pop* 159,789 **2** city E Tex. N of Houston *pop* 27,925

Hu·on Gulf \'hyü-,än\ inlet of Solomon Sea on SE coast of North-East New Guinea S of Huon Peninsula

Hu·ron, Lake \'hyür-,än, 'yur-\ lake E *cen* N. America bet. the U.S. & Canada; one of the Great Lakes *area* 23,010 *sq mi* (59,826 *sq km*)

Hurst \'hərst\ city NE Tex. NE of Fort Worth *pop* 33,574

Hutch·in·son \'hə-chən-sən\ city *cen* Kans. *pop* 39,308

Huy \'wē, 'hwē\ commune E Belgium SW of Liège *pop* 18,197

Huy·ton with Ro·by \'hī-t°n-with-'rō-bē, -with-\ town NW England in Lancashire E of Liverpool *pop* 57,671

Hwaining — see ANQING

Hy·bla \'hī-blə\ ancient town in Sicily on S slope of Mt. Etna

Hydaspes — see JHELUM

Hy·der·a·bad \'hī-d(ə-)rə-,bad, -,bäd\ **1** former state S *cen* India in the Deccan ✳ Hyderabad **2** *or* **Hai·dar·a·bad** city S *cen* India ✳ of Andhra Pradesh *pop* 3,145,939 **3** city S Pakistan in Sind on the Indus *pop* 795,000

Hy·dra \'hī-drə\ *or* NGk **Ídhra** \'ēth-rä\ island Greece in S Aegean Sea off E coast of Peloponnese *area* 20 *sq mi* (52 *sq km*), *pop* 2794 — **Hy·dri·ot** \'hī-drē-ət, -drē-,ät\ *or* **Hy·dri·ote** \-,ōt, -ət\ *n*

Hydraotes — see RAVI

Hy·ères \ē-'er, 'yer\ commune SE France on Côte d'Azur E of Toulon *pop* 50,122

Hyères Islands *or* F **Îles d'Hyères** \,ēl-dē-'er, ēl-'dyer\ islands in the Mediterranean off SE coast of France

Hy·met·tus \hī-'me-təs\ mountain ridge *ab* 3370 *ft* (1027 *m*) *cen* Greece E & SE of Athens — **Hy·met·ti·an** \-'me-tē-ən\ *adj or n*

Hyr·ca·nia \(,)hər-'kā-nē-ə\ province of ancient Persia on SE coast of Caspian NE of Media & NW of Parthia — **Hyr·ca·ni·an** \-nē-ən\ *adj*

I

Ia·si \'yäsh, 'yä-shē\ *or* **Jas·sy** \'yä-sē\ city NE Romania *pop* 330,195

Iba·dan \i-'bä-d°n, -'ba-\ city SW Nigeria NNE of Lagos *pop* 1,263,000

Ibe·ria \ī-'bir-ē-ə\ **1** ancient Spain **2** IBERIAN PENINSULA **3** ancient region S of the Caucasus W of Colchis in modern Republic of Georgia — **Ibe·ri·an** \ī-'bir-ē-ən\ *adj or n*

Iberian Peninsula peninsula SW Europe bet. the Mediterranean & the Atlantic occupied by Spain & Portugal

Ibi·cuí \,ē-bi-'kwē\ river S Brazil in Rio Grande do Sul flowing W into Uruguay River

Ibi·za \ē-'vē-thä, -'bē-, -sə, -zə\ island Spain in the Balearics SW of Majorca *area ab* 220 *sq mi* (570 *sq km*)

Içá — see PUTUMAYO

Icaria — see IKARIA — **Icar·i·an** \ī-'ker-ē-ən, i-, -'kar-\ *adj or n*

Ice·land \'īs-lənd, 'īs-,land\ *or* Dan **Is·land** \'ēs-,län\ *or* Icelandic **Ís·land** \'ēs-,länt\ island bet. the Arctic & the Atlantic SE of Greenland; a republic formerly (1380–1918) belonging to Denmark, later

(1918–44) an independent kingdom in personal union with Denmark ✴ Reykjavik *area* 39,702 *sq mi* (102,828 *sq km*), *pop* 255,855 — **Ice·land·er** \'īs-,lan-dər, 'īs-lən-\ *n* — **Ice·lan·dic** \ī-'slan-dik\ *adj or n*

I–ch'ang — see YICHANG

Ichi·ka·wa \ē-'chē-,kä-wə\ city Japan in SE Honshu E of Tokyo *pop* 436,597

Iconium — see KONYA

Ida — see KAZ DAGI

Ida·ho \'ī-də-,hō\ state NW U.S. ✴ Boise *area* 83,557 *sq mi* (217,248 *sq km*), *pop* 1,006,749 — **Ida·ho·an** \ī-də-'hō-ən\ *adj or n*

Idaho Falls city SE Idaho on Snake River *pop* 43,929

Id·fu \'id-(,)fü\ city S Egypt on the Nile *pop* 34,858

Idhi \'ē-thē\ *or* **Ida** \'ī-də\ mountain 8058 *ft* (2456 *m*) Greece in *cen* Crete; highest on island

Idumaea *or* **Idumea** — see EDOM — **Id·u·mae·an** *or* **Id·u·me·an** \,id-yü-'mē-ən\ *adj or n*

Ie·per \'yā-pər\ *or F* **Ypres** \'ēprᵊ\ commune NW Belgium in W. Flanders *pop* 35,235

Ife \'ē-(,)fā\ city SW Nigeria NE of Ibadan *pop* 209,100

If·ni \'if-nē\ former territory SW Morocco; administered by Spain 1934–69 ✴ Sidi Ifni

Igua·cú *or* **Igua·zú** \,ē-gwə-'sü\ river S Brazil in Paraná state flowing W into Alto Paraná River; contains **Iguazú Falls** (waterfall over 2 *mi* or 3.2 *km* wide composed of numerous cataracts averaging 200 *ft or* 61 *m* in height)

IJs·sel \'ī-səl, 'ā-\ river 70 *mi* (113 *km*) E Netherlands flowing out of the Rhine N into IJsselmeer

IJs·sel·meer \,ī-səl-'mer, 'ā-\ *or* **Lake Ijs·sel** \'ī-səl, 'ā-\ freshwater lake N Netherlands separated from North Sea by a dike & bordered by reclaimed lands; part of former Zuider Zee (inlet of North Sea)

Ika·ria \ē-kä-'rē-ä\ *or* **Ni·ka·ria** \nē-\ *or anc* **Icar·ia** \ī-'kar-ē-ə, i-\ island Greece in Southern Sporades WSW of Samos *area* 99 *sq mi* (257 *sq km*)

Île–de–France \,ēl-də-'frä⁼s\ region & former province N *cen* France bounded on N by Picardy, on E by Champagne, on S by Orléanais, & on W by Normandy ✴ Paris

Ile des Pins \ēl-dā-'pa⁼\ *or* **Isle of Pines** \'pīnz\ island SW Pacific in New Caledonia territory SE of New Caledonia Is. *area* 58 *sq mi* (151 *sq km*)

Île du Diable — see DEVIL'S ISLAND

Îles de la Société — see SOCIETY ISLANDS

Îles du Vent — see WINDWARD ISLANDS

Îles sous le Vent — see LEEWARD ISLANDS

Il·ford \'il-fərd\ former municipal borough SE England in Essex, now part of Redbridge

Il·fra·combe \'il-fra-,küm\ town SW England in Devon on Bristol Channel *pop* 10,133

Ili \'ē-'lē\ river 800 *mi* (1287 *km*) *cen* Asia flowing from W Xinjiang Uygur, China, W & NW into Lake Balkhash in Kazakhstan

Ilía — see ELIS

Il·i·am·na \,i-lē-'am-nə\ volcano 10,016 *ft* (3053 *m*) NE of Iliamna Lake

Iliamna Lake lake 80 *mi* (129 *km*) long SW Alaska NE of Bristol Bay

Ilion *or* **Ilium** — see TROY — **Il·i·an** \'il-ē-ən\ *adj or n*

Il·lam·pu \ē-'yäm-(,)pü\ **1** *or* **So·ra·ta** \sə-'rä-tə\ massif in the Andes W Bolivia E of Lake Titicaca — see ANCOHUMA **2** peak 20,867 *ft* (6360 *m*) in the Illampu massif

Il·li·ma·ni \,ē-yē-'mä-nē\ mountain 21,201 *ft* (6462 *m*) Bolivia E of La Paz

Il·li·nois \,il-ə-'noi *also* -'noiz\ **1** river 273 *mi* (439 *km*) Ill. flowing SW into Mississippi River **2** state *cen* U.S. ✱ Springfield *area* 56,400 *sq mi* (146,640 *sq km*), *pop* 11,430,602 — **Il·li·nois·an** \,il-lə-'noi-ən *also* -'noi-z°n\ *adj or n*

Il·lyr·ia \i-'lir-ē-ə\ ancient region S Europe in Balkan Peninsula bordering on the Adriatic — **Il·lyr·i·an** \-ən\ *adj or n* — **Il·lyr·ic** \-'lir-ik\ *adj*

Il·lyr·i·cum \i-'lir-i-kəm\ province of Roman Empire in Illyria

Il·men \'il-mən\ lake W Russia in Europe S of Lake Ladoga

Ilo·ilo \,ē-lō-'ē-(,)lō\ city Philippines on Panay Is. *pop* 311,000

Im·pe·ria \im-'pir-ē-ə, -'per-\ commune & port NW Italy in Liguria SW of Genoa *pop* 40,171

Im·pe·ri·al Beach \im-'pir-ē-əl\ city SW Calif. S of San Diego *pop* 26,512

Imperial Valley valley U.S. & Mexico in SE Calif. & NE Baja California in Colorado Desert; most of area below sea level

Imp·hal \'imp-,həl\ city NE India ✱ of Manipur *pop* 196,268

Imroz — see GÖKÇEADA

Ina·gua \i-'nä-gwə\ two islands in SE Bahamas: **Great Inagua** (50 *mi* or 80 *km* long) & **Little Inagua** (8 *mi* or 13 *km* long)

In·chon \'in-,chän\ *or formerly* **Che·mul·po** \jə-'mùl-(,)pō\ city & port NW S. Korea W of Seoul *pop* 1,386,911

In·de·pen·dence \,in-də-'pen-dən(t)s\ city W Mo. E of Kansas City *pop* 112,301

In·dia \'in-dē-ə\ **1** peninsula region (often called a subcontinent) S Asia S of the Himalayas bet. Bay of Bengal & Arabian Sea occupied by India, Pakistan, & Bangladesh & formerly often considered as also including Burma (but not Ceylon) **2** those parts of India until 1947 under Brit. rule or protection together with Baluchistan & the Andaman & Nicobar islands; prior to 1937, Burma **3** country comprising major portion of peninsula; a republic within the Commonwealth of Nations; until 1947 a part of the Brit. Empire ✱ New Delhi *area* 1,195,063 *sq mi* (3,095,472 *sq km*), *pop* 896,567,000 — **In·di·an** \-ən\ *adj or n*

In·di·ana \,in-dē-'a-nə\ state E *cen* U.S. ✱ Indianapolis *area* 36,291 *sq mi* (94,357 *sq km*), *pop* 5,544,159 — **In·di·an·an** \-'a-nən\ *adj or n* — **In·di·an·i·an** \-'a-nē-ən\ *adj or n*

Indiana Harbor harbor district in E. Chicago, Ind., on Lake Michigan

In·di·a·nap·o·lis \,in-dē-ə-'na-pə-lis\ city *cen* Ind., its ✱ *pop* 731,327

Indian Ocean ocean E of Africa, S of Asia, W of Australia & Tasmania, & N of Antarctica *area ab* 28,350,500 *sq mi* (73,427,795 *sq km*)

Indian River lagoon 165 *mi* (266 *km*) long E Fla. bet. mainland & coastal islands

Indian States or **Native States** former semi-independent states of the Indian Empire ruled by native princes subject to varying degrees of Brit. authority — see BRITISH INDIA

Indian Territory former territory S U.S. in present state of Okla.

In·dies \'in-(,)dēz\ **1** EAST INDIES **2** WEST INDIES

In·di·gir·ka \,in-də-'gir-kə\ river over 1000 mi (1609 km) E cen Russia in Asia in NE Sakha Republic flowing N into E. Siberian Sea

In·dio \'in-dē-,ō\ city SE Calif. SE of San Bernardino pop 36,793

In·do·chi·na \,in-(,)dō-'chī-nə\ **1** peninsula SE Asia; includes Myanmar, Cambodia, Laos, Malay Peninsula, Thailand, & Vietnam **2** or **French Indochina** former country SE Asia comprising Annam, Cochin China, & Tonkin (all now a part of Vietnam), Cambodia, & Laos ✻ Hanoi — **In·do·Chi·nese** \-,chī-'nēz, -'nēs\ adj or n

In·do·ne·sia \,in-də-'nē-zhə, -shə\ **1** country SE Asia in Malay Archipelago comprising Sumatra, Java, S & E Borneo, Sulawesi, Timor, W New Guinea, the Moluccas, & many adjacent smaller islands; formerly (as **Netherlands East Indies**) an overseas territory of the Netherlands ✻ Jakarta area 779,675 sq mi (2,019,358 sq km), pop 188,216,000 **2** MALAY ARCHIPELAGO — **In·do·ne·sian** \,in-də-'nē-zhən, -shən\ adj or n

In·dore \in-'dōr, -'dȯr\ **1** former state cen India in Narmada valley ✻ Indore; area now in Madhya Pradesh **2** city NW cen India in W Madhya Pradesh pop 1,091,674

In·dus \'in-dəs\ river 1800 mi (2897 km) S Asia flowing from Tibet NW & SSW through Pakistan into Arabian Sea

In·gle·wood \'iŋ-gəl-,wu̇d\ city SW Calif. SW of Los Angeles pop 109,602

In·gol·stadt \'iŋ-gəl-,shtät, -,stät\ city S Germany in cen Bavaria pop 107,375

In·gu·she·tia \,in-gü-'shē-shə\ or **In·gu·she·ti·ya** \-'she-tē-yə\ or **Ingush Republic** \in-'güsh, iŋ-\ autonomous republic S Russia in Europe N of Caucasus Mts. ✻ Nazran area 1242 sq mi (3217 sq km), pop 1,234,000

Ink·ster \'iŋk-stər\ village SE Mich. W of Detroit pop 30,772

In·land Empire \'in-,land, -lənd\ region NW U.S. bet. Cascade Range & Rocky Mountains in E Wash., N Idaho, NW Mont., & NE Oreg.

Inland Sea inlet of the Pacific 240 mi (386 km) long SW Japan bet. Honshu on E & N, Kyushu on W, & Shikoku on S

Inn \'in\ river 320 mi (515 km) flowing from SE Switzerland NE through Austria into the Danube in SE Germany — see ENGADINE

Inner Hebrides — see HEBRIDES

Inner Mon·go·lia \-,män-'gōl-yə, -,män-, -'gō-lē-ə\ or **Nei Mong·gol** \'nā-'män-,gȯl, -'män-\ region N China in SE Mongolia & W Manchuria ✻ Hohhot area 454,633 sq mi (1,182,046 sq km), pop 21,456,798

In·nis·fil \'i-nəs-,fil, -fəl\ town Canada in SE Ont. pop 21,667

Inniskilling — see ENNISKILLEN

Inns·bruck \'inz-,bru̇k, 'in(t)s-\ city W Austria pop 118,112

Inside Passage protected shipping route from Puget Sound, Wash., to Skagway, Alaska, following channels bet. mainland & coastal islands

In·ter·la·ken \'in-tər-ˌlä-kən\ commune W *cen* Switzerland in Bern canton on the Aare bet. Lake of Thun & Lake of Brienz *pop* 5500

International Zone — see MOROCCO

In·ver·car·gill \in-vər-'kär-gill\ borough New Zealand on S coast of South Is. *pop* 56,059 — see BLUFF

In·ver Grove Heights \'in-vər\ city SE Minn. *pop* 22,477

In·ver·ness \ˌin-vər-'nes\ **1** *or* **In·ver·ness–shire** \-'nesh-ˌshir, -shər\ former county NW Scotland **2** burgh NW Scotland ✳ of Highland region *pop* 63,090

Io·an·ni·na \yō-'ä-nē-(ˌ)nä\ city NW Greece in N Epirus *pop* 56,496

Io·na \ī-'ō-nə\ island Scotland in S Inner Hebrides off SW tip of Mull Is. *area* 6 *sq mi* (16 *sq km*), *pop* 120

Io·nia \ī-'ō-nē-ə\ ancient region W Asia Minor bordering on the Aegean W of Lydia & Caria — **Io·ni·an** \-nē-ən\ *adj or n*

Io·ni·an Islands \ī-'ō-nē-ən\ islands W Greece in Ionian Sea *pop* 191,003

Ionian Sea arm of the Mediterranean Sea bet. SE Italy & W Greece

Io·wa \'ī-ə-wə\ **1** river 291 *mi* (468 *km*) Iowa flowing SE into Mississippi River **2** state *cen* U.S. ✳ Des Moines *area* 56,275 *sq mi* (145,752 *sq km*), *pop* 2,776,755 — **Io·wan** \-wən\ *adj or n*

Iowa City city E Iowa *pop* 59,738

I–pin — see YIBIN

Ipoh \'ē-(ˌ)pō\ city Malaysia (federation) in Perak *pop* 125,766

Ips·wich \'ip-(ˌ)swich\ **1** city E Australia in SE Queensland *pop* 73,299 **2** borough SE England ✳ of Suffolk *pop* 115,500

Iqa·lu·it \ē-'ka·lü-ət\ town Canada, on Baffin Is., Northwest Territories *pop* 3552

Iqui·que \ē-'kē-kā\ city & port N Chile on the Pacific *pop* 148,511

Iqui·tos \ē-'kē-(ˌ)tōs\ city NE Peru on the Amazon *pop* 269,500

Irák·li·on \i-'ra-klē-ən, ē-'rä-klē-ˌön\ *or* **Can·dia** \'kan-dē-ə\ city & port Greece ✳ of Crete *pop* 117,167

Iran \i-'rän, -'ran; ī-'ran\ *or esp formerly* **Per·sia** \'pər-zhə, *esp Brit* -shə\ country SW Asia bordering on N on Caspian Sea & in S on Persian Gulf & Gulf of Oman; an Islamic republic since 1979, formerly an empire ✳ Tehran *area* 635,932 *sq mi* (1,647,064 *sq km*), *pop* 59,570,000 — **Irani** \-'rä-nē, -ra\ *adj or n* — **Ira·ni·an** \i-'rä-nē-ən, -'ra-, -rä-, ī-\ *adj or n*

Iraq \i-'räk, -'rak\ country SW Asia in Mesopotamia; a republic since 1958, formerly a kingdom ✳ Baghdad *area* 168,927 *sq mi* (437,521 *sq km*), *pop* 18,838,000 — **Iraqi** \-'rä-kē, -'ra-\ *adj or n*

Irbīl — see ARBIL

Ire·land \'īr-lənd\ **1** *or L* **Hi·ber·nia** \hī-'bər-nē-ə\ island W Europe in the Atlantic, one of the British Isles *area* 32,052 *sq mi* (83,015 *sq km*); divided bet. Ireland (republic) & Northern Ireland **2** *or* **Eir·e** \'er-ə\ country occupying major portion of the island; a republic since 1949; a division of the United Kingdom of Great Britain and Ireland 1801–1921 & (as **Irish Free State**) a dominion of the Commonwealth of Nations 1922–37 ✳ Dublin *area* 26,602 *sq mi* (69,165 *sq km*), *pop* 3,523,401 **3** — see NORTHERN IRELAND — **Irish** \'ī-rish\ *adj or n* — **Irish·man** \-mən\ *n* — **Irish·wom·an** \-ˌwů-mən\ *n*

Iri·an Ja·ya \ir-ē-ˌän-'jī-ä\ *or* **West Irian** *or formerly* **Dutch New Guin·ea** \'gi-nē\ *or* **Netherlands New Guinea** territory of

Indonesia comprising the W half of New Guinea & adjacent islands; belonged to the Netherlands until 1963 ✳ Jayapura *area* 162,927 *sq mi* (421,981 *sq km*), *pop* 1,648,708

Irish Sea arm of the Atlantic bet. Great Britain & Ireland

Ir·kutsk \ir-'kütsk, ,ər-\ city S Russia in Asia on the Angara near Lake Baikal *pop* 639,000

Iron Gate \'ī(-ə)rn\ gorge 2 *mi* (3.2 *km*) long of the Danube where it cuts around Transylvanian Alps on border bet. Romania & Yugoslavia

Ir·ra·wad·dy \,ir-ə-'wä-dē\ river 1300 *mi* (2092 *km*) Myanmar flowing S into Bay of Bengal through several mouths

Ir·tysh \ir-'tish, ,ər-\ river *over* 2600 *mi* (4180 *km*) cen Asia flowing from Altai mountains in China, NW & N through Kazakhstan & into the Ob in W Russia in Asia

Irún \ē-'rün\ commune N Spain in Guipúzcoa *pop* 52,828

Ir·vine \'ər-,vīn\ city SW Calif. SE of Santa Ana *pop* 110,330

Ir·ving \'ər-vin\ city NE Tex. W of Dallas *pop* 155,037

Is·a·be·la Island \,i-zə-'be-lə, ,ē-sä-'vä-lä\ island Ecuador; largest of the Galápagos *area* 1650 *sq mi* (4290 *sq km*), *pop* 336

Isar \'ē-,zär\ river 163 *mi* (262 *km*) W Europe flowing from Tirol, Austria, through Bavaria, Germany, into the Danube

Isau·ria \ī-'sȯr-ē-ə\ ancient district in E Pisidia S Asia Minor on N slope of W Taurus Mountains — **Isau·ri·an** \-ē-ən\ *adj or n*

Is·chia \'is-kē-ə\ island Italy in Tyrrhenian Sea WSW of Naples *area* 18 *sq mi* (47 *sq km*)

Ise Bay \'ē-,sā\ inlet of the Pacific S Japan on S coast of Honshu

Iseo, Lake \ē-'zā-(,)ō\ lake 14 *mi* (22 *km*) long N Italy in Lombardy

Isère \ē-'zer\ river 150 *mi* (241 *km*) SE France flowing from Graian Alps WSW into the Rhône

Iser·lohn \,ē-zər-'lōn, 'ē-zər-,\ city W Germany *pop* 96,976

Isfahan — see ESFAHĀN

Ishim \i-'shim\ river 1330 *mi* (2140 *km*) flowing from N Kazakhstan N into the Irtysh in W Russia in Asia

Isis \'ī-səs\ the Thames River, England, at & upstream from Oxford

Is·ken·de·run \(,)is-,ken-də-'rün\ *or formerly* **Al·ex·an·dret·ta** \,a-lig-(,)zan-'dre-tə, ,e-\ city & port S Turkey on **Gulf of Iskenderun** (inlet of the Mediterranean) *pop* 154,807

Is·lam·a·bad \is-'lä-mə-,bäd, iz-, -'la-mə-,bad\ city ✳ of Pakistan in NE Pakistan NE of Rawalpindi *pop* 250,000

Island *or* **Ísland** — see ICELAND

Is·lay \'ī-(,)lā, -lə\ island Scotland in S Inner Hebrides *area* 234 *sq mi* (608 *sq km*), *pop* 3855

Isle au Haut \,ī-lə-'hō(t), ,ēl-ə-'hō\ island Maine at entrance to Penobscot Bay — see ACADIA NATIONAL PARK

Isle of Av·a·lon \'a-v-ə-,län\ district, orig. an island, SW England in Somerset including Glastonbury

Isle of Ely — see ELY (Isle of)

Isle of Man — see MAN (Isle of)

Isle of Pines — see YOUTH (Isle of)

Isle of Wight — see WIGHT (Isle of)

Isle Roy·ale \'īl-'rȯi(-ə)l\ island Mich. in NW Lake Superior in **Isle Royale National Park**

Is·ling·ton \'iz-lin-tən\ borough of N Greater London, England *pop* 155,200

Is·ma·i·lia \iz-mā-ə-'lē-ə, ,is-\ city NE Egypt on the Suez Canal *pop* 247,000

Isole Eolie — see LIPARI ISLANDS

Ison·zo \ē-'zòn(t)-(,)sō\ *or* **So·ča** \'sò-chä\ river *ab* 80 *mi* (129 *km*) W Slovenia & NE Italy flowing S into Gulf of Trieste

Ispahan — see ESFAHĀN

Is·par·ta \is-(,)pär-'tä\ city SW Turkey N of Antalya *pop* 112,117

Is·ra·el \'iz-rē-əl, -(,)rā- *also* 'is- *or* 'iz-rəl\ **1** ancient kingdom Palestine comprising the lands occupied by the Hebrew people; established *ab* 1025 B.C.; divided *ab* 933 B.C. into a S kingdom (Judah) & a N kingdom (Israel) **2** *or* **Northern Kingdom** *or* **Ephra·im** \'ē-frē-əm\ the N portion of the Hebrew kingdom after the division ✳ Samaria **3** country Palestine bordering on the Mediterranean; a republic established 1948 ✳ Jerusalem *area* 7993 *sq mi* (20,782 *sq km*), *pop* 4,037,620 — see PALESTINE — **Is·rae·li** \iz-'rā-lē *also* ,iz-rə-'ā-lē\ *adj or n* — **Is·ra·el·ite** \'iz-rē-ə-,līt, -rə-,līt\ *adj or n*

Is·sus \'i-səs\ ancient town S Asia Minor N of modern Iskenderun

Is·syk Kul *or* **Ys·yk–Köl** \i-sik-'kəl, -'kœl\ lake 115 *mi* (185 *km*) long in NE Kyrgyzstan *area* 2355 *sq mi* (6099 *sq km*)

Is·tan·bul \is-tən-'bül, -,tan-, -,tän-, -'bùl, 'is-tən-,\ *or with* m *for* n *or formerly* **Con·stan·ti·no·ple** \,kän-,stan-'t²n-'ō-pəl\ *or anc* **By·zan·ti·um** \bə-'zan-tē-əm, -'zan-sh(ē-)əm\ city NW Turkey on the Bosporus & Sea of Marmara; former ✳ of Turkey & of Ottoman Empire *pop* 6,620,241

Ister — see DANUBE

Is·tria \'is-trē-ə\ *or* **Is·tra** \-trə\ *or* **Is·tri·an Peninsula** \-trē-ən\ peninsula in Croatia & Slovenia projecting into the N Adriatic — **Istrian** *adj or n*

Itai·pu \ē-'tī-pü\ dam in Paraná River bet. Brazil & Paraguay

Italian East Africa former territory E Africa comprising Eritrea, Ethiopia, & Italian Somaliland

Italian Somaliland former Italian colony E Africa bordering on Indian Ocean ✳ Mogadishu; since 1960 part of Somalia

It·a·ly \'i-t²l-ē\ *or It* **Ita·lia** \ē-'täl-yä\ *or L* **Ita·lia** \ə-'tal-yə, i-\ **1** peninsula 760 *mi* (1223 *km*) long S Europe projecting into the Mediterranean bet. Adriatic & Tyrrhenian seas **2** country comprising the peninsula of Italy, Sicily, Sardinia, & numerous other islands; a republic since 1946, formerly a kingdom ✳ Rome *area* 116,313 *sq mi* (302,251 *sq km*), *pop* 57,235,000 — **Ital·ian** \ə-'tal-yən, i- *also* ī\ *adj or n* — **Ital·ian·ate** \-,nət, -,nät\ *adj*

Ita·na·gar \ē-tə-'nə-gər\ town NE India ✳ of Arunachal Pradesh

Itas·ca, Lake \ī-'tas-kə\ lake NW *cen* Minn.; generally considered as source of Mississippi River

Itén·ez — see GUAPORÉ

Ith·a·ca \'i-thi-kə\ **1** city S *cen* N.Y. on Cayuga Lake *pop* 29,541 **2** *or NGk* **Itha·ki** \ē-'thä-kē\ island W Greece in the Ionian Islands NE of Cephalonia *area* 37 *sq mi* (96 *sq km*) — **Ith·a·can** \'i-thi-kən\ *adj or n*

Itsu·ku·shi·ma \ēt-,sü-kə-'shē-mä\ island *ab* 5 *mi* (8 *km*) long Japan in Inland Sea SW of Hiroshima

It·u·raea *or* **It·u·rea** \i-tyù-'rē-ə\ ancient country NE Palestine S of Damascus — **It·u·rae·an** *or* **It·u·re·an** \-'rē-ən\ *adj or n*

Iva·no–Fran·kivs'k \i-'vä-nə-frän-'kifsk\ *or formerly* **Sta·ni·slav** \,stä-nə-'släf, -'släv\ city SW Ukraine *pop* 226,000

Iva·no·vo \ē-'vä-nə-və\ *or formerly* **Ivanovo Voz·ne·sensk** \,vəz-nə-'sen(t)sk\ city *cen* Russia in Europe WNW of Nizhniy Novgorod *pop* 480,000

Ivo·ry Coast \'ī-v(ə-)rē\ *or* **Côte d'Ivoire** \,kōt-dē-'vwär\ **1** region W Africa bordering on the Atlantic W of the Gold Coast **2** country W Africa including the Ivory Coast & its hinterland; a republic; formerly a territory of French West Africa * Abidjan *area* 124,503 *sq mi* (322,463 *sq km*), *pop* 13,459,000 — **Ivor·i·an** \(,)ī-'vōr-ē-ən, -'vōr-\ *adj or n* — **Ivory Coast·er** \'kō-stər\ *n*

Iwo \'ē-(,)wō\ city SW Nigeria NE of Ibadan *pop* 319,500

Iwo Ji·ma \ē-(,)wō-'jē-mə\ island Japan in W Pacific in the Volcano Islands *area* 8 *sq mi* (21 *sq km*)

Ix·elles \ēk-'sel\ *or* **Flem El·se·ne** \'el-sə-nə\ commune *cen* Belgium in Brabant; suburb of Brussels *pop* 72,610

Ix·ta·ci·huatl *or* **Iz·tac·ci·huatl** \,ēs-tä-sē-,wä-t°l\ extinct volcano 17,343 *ft* (5286 *m*) S Mexico N of Popocatepetl

Iza·bal, Lake \ē-zə-'bäl, -sä-'väl\ lake 25 *mi* (40 *km*) long E Guatemala

Izal·co \i-'zal-(,)kō, ē-'säl-\ volcano 7828 *ft* (2386 *m*) W El Salvador

Izhevsk \'ē-,zhefsk\ *or 1985–1987* **Usti·nov** \'üs-ti-,nóf, -,nóv\ city E Russia in Europe * of Udmurtia *pop* 651,000

Iz·ma·il *or Romanian* **Is·ma·il** \,iz-mä-'ēl, ,is-\ city SW Ukraine on the Danube delta *pop* 95,000

Iz·mir \iz-'mir\ *or formerly* **Smyr·na** \'smər-nə\ city & port W Turkey in Asia on an inlet of the Aegean *pop* 1,757,414

Iz·mit *or* **Is·mid** \iz-'mit\ *or anc* **As·ta·cus** \'as-tə-kəs\ *or* **Nic·o·me·dia** \,ni-kə-'mē-dē-ə\ city & port NW Turkey in Asia on **Gulf of Izmit** (E arm of Sea of Marmara) *pop* 256,882

Iz·nik \iz-'nik\ lake 14 *mi* (22 *km*) long NW Turkey in Asia

J

Jabal Katrinah — see KATHERINA (Gebel)

Ja·bal·pur \'jə-bəl-,pùr\ city *cen* India in *cen* Madhya Pradesh *pop* 739,961

Jack·son \'jak-sən\ **1** city S Mich. *pop* 37,446 **2** city * of Miss. on Pearl River *pop* 196,637 **3** city W Tenn. *pop* 48,949

Jackson Hole valley NW Wyo. E of Teton Range & partly in Grand Teton National Park; contains **Jackson Lake** (reservoir)

Jack·son·ville \'jak-sən-,vil\ **1** city *cen* Ark. NE of Little Rock *pop* 29,101 **2** city NE Fla. near mouth of St. Johns River *pop* 635,230 **3** city W *cen* Ill. *pop* 19,324 **4** city E N.C. *pop* 30,013

Jadotville — see LIKASI

Ja·én \hä-'än\ **1** province S Spain in N Andalusia *area* 5212 *sq mi* (13,499 *sq km*), *pop* 637,633 **2** commune, its * *pop* 101,938

Jaf·fa \'ja-fə, 'ya-, 'yä-\ *or* **Ya·fo** \'yä-'fō\ *or anc* **Jop·pa** \'jä-pə\ former city W Israel, since 1950 a S section of Tel Aviv

Jaff·na \'jäf-nə\ city N Sri Lanka on Jaffna Peninsula *pop* 129,000

Jaffna Peninsula peninsula N extremity of Sri Lanka extending into Palk Strait

Jain·tia Hills \'jīn-tē-ə\ hills E India in N *cen* Assam E of Khasi Hills

Jai·pur \'jī-,pu̇r\ **1** former state NW India; now part of Rajasthan **2** city, its ✳, now ✳ of Rajasthan *pop* 1,458,183

Ja·kar·ta *or* **Dja·kar·ta** \jə-'kär-tə\ *or formerly* **Ba·ta·via** \bə-'tā-vē-ə\ city & port ✳ of Indonesia in NW Java *pop* 6,503,449

Ja·lan·dhar \'jə-lən-dər\ city NW India in Punjab *pop* 509,510

Ja·la·pa \hə-'lä-pə\ city E Mexico ✳ of Veracruz *pop* 279,451

Ja·lis·co \hə-'lis-(,)kō\ state W *cen* Mexico ✳ Guadalajara *area* 30,941 *sq mi* (80,137 *sq km*), *pop* 5,302,689

Jal·u·it \'ja-lü-wət, 'jal-yü-wət\ island (atoll) W Pacific, in Ralik chain of the Marshalls

Ja·mai·ca \jə-'mā-kə\ island West Indies in the Greater Antilles; a dominion of the Commonwealth of Nations since 1962; formerly a Brit. colony ✳ Kingston *area* 4471 *sq mi* (11,580 *sq km*), *pop* 2,464,000 — **Ja·mai·can** \-kən\ *adj or n*

Jamaica Bay inlet of Atlantic Ocean SE N.Y. in SW Long Is.

Jam·bi \'jäm-bē\ city & port Indonesia in SE *cen* Sumatra *pop* 340,066

James \jāmz\ **1** *or officially* **Da·ko·ta** \də-'kō-tə\ river 710 *mi* (1143 *km*) N.Dak. & S.Dak. flowing S to Missouri River **2** river 340 *mi* (547 *km*) Va. flowing E into Chesapeake Bay at Hampton Roads

James Bay the S extension of Hudson Bay 280 *mi* (448 *km*) long & 150 *mi* (240 *km*) wide Canada bet. NE Ont. & W Que.

James·town \'jāmz-,taun\ **1** city SW N.Y. *pop* 34,681 **2** ruined village E Va. SW of Williamsburg on James River; first permanent English settlement in America (1607)

Jam·mu \jə-(,)mü\ city S of Srinagar, winter ✳ of Jammu & Kashmir *pop* 135,522

Jammu and Kash·mir \'kash-,mir, 'kazh-, kash-', kazh-\ *or* **Kashmir** state N India including Kashmir region & Jammu (to the S); claimed also by Pakistan; summer ✳ Srinagar, winter ✳ Jammu *area* 53,665 *sq mi* (138,992 *sq km*), *pop* 7,718,700

Jam·na·gar \jäm-'nə-gər\ city W India in W Gujarat on Gulf of Kachchh *pop* 350,544

Jam·shed·pur \'jäm-,shed-,pu̇r\ city E India in S Bihar SE of Ranchi *pop* 751,368

Ja·mu·na \'jə-mü-nə\ the lower Brahmaputra

Janes·ville \'jānz-,vil\ city S Wis. SE of Madison *pop* 52,133

Ja·nic·u·lum \jə-'ni-kyə-ləm\ hill in Rome, Italy, on right bank of the Tiber opposite the seven hills on which the ancient city was built — see AVENTINE

Jan Ma·yen Island \yän-'mī-ən\ island in Arctic Ocean E of Greenland & NNE of Iceland belonging to Norway *area* 147 *sq mi* (382 *sq km*)

Ja·pan \jə-'pan, ja-\ *or Jp* **Nip·pon** \ni-'pän, nē-'pōⁿ\ country E Asia comprising Honshu, Hokkaido, Kyushu, Shikoku, & other islands in the W Pacific; a constitutional monarchy ✳ Tokyo *area* 143,619 *sq mi* (371,973 *sq km*), *pop* 123,611,541 — **Jap·a·nese** \,ja-pə-'nēz, -'nēs\ *adj or n*

Japan, Sea of arm of the N Pacific W of Japan

Ja·pu·rá \zhä-pü-'rä\ river 1750 *mi* (2816 *km*) S Colombia & NW Brazil flowing SE into the Amazon

Ja·ra·bu·lus \ja-'rä-bü-ˌlús\ *or* **Je·ra·blus** \je-'rä-ˌblús\ town N Syria on the Euphrates near Turkish border

Jar·vis \'jär-vis\ island *cen* Pacific in the Line Islands; claimed by the U.S.

Jas·per National Park \'jas-pər\ reservation W Canada in W Alta. on E slopes of the Rockies NW of Banff National Park

Jassy — see IASI

Ja·strze·bie–Zdroj \yäs-'jä-bēz-'droi\ city S Poland *pop* 102,661

Ja·va \'jä-və, 'ja-və\ *or Indonesian* **Dja·wa** \'jä-və\ island Indonesia SE of Sumatra; chief city Jakarta *area* 51,007 *sq mi* (132,618 *sq km*), *pop* 107,581,306 — **Ja·va·nese** \ja-və-'nēz, jä-, -'nēs\ *adj or n*

Java Head cape Indonesia at W end of Java on Sunda Strait

Ja·va·rí \ˌzhä-vä-'rē\ *or Sp* **Ya·va·rí** \ˌyä-vä-'rē\ *or formerly* **Ya·ca·ra·na** \ˌyä-kä-'rä-nä\ river *ab* 600 *mi* (965 *km*) Peru & Brazil flowing NE on the boundary & into the Amazon

Java Sea arm of the Pacific bounded on S by Java, on W by Sumatra, on N by Borneo, & on E by Sulawesi

Jaxartes — see SYR DARYA

Jaya, Puncak — see PUNCAK JAYA

Ja·ya·pu·ra \ˌjä-yä-'pü-rä\ *or formerly* **Hol·lan·dia** \hȯ-'län-dē-ə\ *or* **Ko·ta·ba·ru** \ˌkō-tä-'bä-rü\ *or* **Su·kar·na·pu·ra** \sü-'kär-nä-ˌpü-rä\ city & port Indonesia ✳ in Irian Jaya

Ja·ya·pu·ra \ˌjä-yä-'pü-rä\ *or formerly* **Hol·lan·dia** \hȯ-'län-dē-ə\ *or* **Ko·ta·ba·ru** \ˌkō-tä-'bä-rü\ *or* **Su·kar·na·pu·ra** \sü-'kär-nä-ˌpü-rä\ city & port Indonesia ✳ in Irian Jaya

Jazirah, Al — see GEZIRA

Jebel, Bahr el — see BAHR EL GHAZAL

Je·bel ed Druz \'je-bəl-ed-'drüz\ *or* **Jebel Druz** region S Syria E of Sea of Galilee on border of Jordan

Jebel Musa — see MUSA (Jebel)

Jebel Toubkal — see TOUBKAL (Jebel)

Je·bus \'jē-bəs\ a Biblical name for Jerusalem

Jed·burgh \'jed-b(ə-)rə\ royal burgh SE Scotland in Borders region

Jef·fer·son \'je-fər-sən\ river over 200 *mi* (321 *km*) SW Mont. — see THREE FORKS

Jefferson, Mount mountain 10,495 *ft* (3199 *m*) NW Oreg. in Cascades

Jefferson City city ✳ of Mo. on Missouri River *pop* 35,481

Jef·fer·son·town \'je-fər-sən-ˌtaún\ city N Ky. E of Louisville *pop* 23,221

Jef·fer·son·ville \'je-fər-sən-ˌvil\ city S Ind. *pop* 21,841

Jehol — see CHENGDE

Je·mappes \zhə-'map\ commune SW Belgium W of Mons

Je·na \'yā-nə\ city E *cen* Germany E of Erfurt *pop* 100,967

Je·qui·ti·nho·nha \zhe-ˌkē-tē-'nyō-nyə, -'nō-nyə\ river 500 *mi* (805 *km*) E Brazil flowing NE into the Atlantic

Jer·ba *or* **Djer·ba** \'jər-bə, 'jer-\ *or* **Jar·bah** \'jär-bäh\ island SE Tunisia in the Mediterranean at entrance to Gulf of Gabes *area* 197 *sq mi* (510 *sq km*)

Je·rez \hə-ˈräs, hä-ˈreth, -ˈres\ *or* **Je·rez de la Fron·te·ra** \ˌthā-lä-frōn-ˈtā-rä\ *or formerly* **Xe·res** \ˈsher-ēz\ city SW Spain NE of Cádiz *pop* 182,939

Jer·i·cho \ˈjer-i-ˌkō\ **1** *or* Ar **Eri·ha** \ä-ˈrē-hä\ town W Jordan 5 *mi* (8 *km*) NW of Dead Sea **2** ancient Palestinian city near site of modern Jericho

Jer·sey \ˈjər-zē\ **1** island English Channel in the Channel Islands ❋ St. Helier *area* 45 *sq mi* (117 *sq km*) **2** NEW JERSEY — **Jer·sey·an** \-ən\ *n* — **Jer·sey·ite** \-ˌīt\ *n*

Jersey City city & port NE N.J. *pop* 228,537

Je·ru·sa·lem \jə-ˈrü-s(ə-)ləm, -ˈrü-z(ə-)ləm\ *or anc* **Hi·ero·sol·y·ma** \ˌhī-(ə-)rō-ˈsä-lə-mə\ city Palestine NW of Dead Sea; divided 1948–67 bet. Jordan (old city) & Israel (new city) ❋ of Israel since 1950 & formerly ❋ of ancient kingdoms of Israel & Judah; old city under Israeli control since 1967 *pop* 544,200 — **Je·ru·sa·lem·ite** \-lə-ˌmīt\ *n*

Jer·vis Bay \ˈjär-vis\ inlet of the Pacific SE Australia on SE coast of New South Wales on which is situated district (*area* 28 *sq mi or* 73 *sq km*) that is part of Australian Capital Territory

Jesselton — see KOTA KINABALU

Jewel Cave National Monument limestone cave SW S.Dak.

Jewish Autonomous Oblast *or* **Ye·vrey·ska·ya** \yi-ˈvrā-skə-yə\ autonomous oblast E Russia in Asia, bordering on the Amur ❋ Birobidzhan *area* 13,900 *sq mi* (36,001 *sq km*)

Jez·re·el \ˈjez-rē-ˌel, -ˌrēl\ ancient town *cen* Palestine in Samaria NW of Mt. Gilboa in Valley of Jezreel; now in N Israel

Jezreel, Valley of the E end of the Plain of Esdraelon

Jhan·si \ˈjän(t)-sē\ city N India in S Uttar Pradesh *pop* 313,491

Jhe·lum \ˈjā-ləm\ *or anc* **Hy·das·pes** \hī-ˈdas-(ˌ)pēz\ river 450 *mi* (724 *km*) NW India (subcontinent) flowing from Kashmir S & SW into the Chenab

Jia·mu·si \jyä-ˈmü-ˈsē\ *or* **Chia·mu·ssu** \jyä-ˈmü-ˈsü\ *or* **Kia·mu·sze** \jyä-ˈmü-ˈsü\ city NE China in E Heilongjiang *pop* 493,409

Jiang·su *or* **Kiang·su** \ˈjyäŋ-ˈsü\ province E China bordering on Yellow Sea ❋ Nanjing *area* 40,927 *sq mi* (106,001 *sq km*), *pop* 67,056,519

Jiang·xi *or* **Kiang·si** \ˈjyäŋ-shē\ province SE China ❋ Nanchang *area* 63,629 *sq mi* (165,435 *sq km*), *pop* 37,710,281

Jiao·zhou *or* **Kiao·chow** \jyaú-ˈjō\ bay of Yellow Sea E China in E Shandong *area* 200 *sq mi* (520 *sq km*)

Jid·da *or* **Jid·dah** \ˈji-də\ *or* **Jed·da** *or* **Jed·dah** \ˈje-də\ city W Saudi Arabia in Hejaz on Red Sea; port for Mecca *pop* 561,104

Jih-k'a-tse — see XIGAZÊ

Ji·lin \ˈjē-ˈlin\ *or* **Ki·rin** \ˈkē-ˈrin\ **1** province NE China in E Manchuria ❋ Changchun *area* 72,201 *sq mi* (187,723 *sq km*), *pop* 24,658,721 **2** *or formerly* **Yung·ki** \ˈyùŋ-ˈjē\ city NE China in E *cen* Jilin *pop* 1,036,858

Ji·nan *or* **Chi·nan** *or* **Tsi·nan** \ˈjē-ˈnän\ city E China ❋ of Shandong *pop* 1,500,000

Jin·ja \ˈjin-jä\ city & port SE Uganda on Lake Victoria *pop* 60,979

Jinmen — see QUEMOY

Jin·zhou *or* **Chin·chow** *or* **Chin·chou** \ˈjin-ˈjō\ city NE China in SW Liaoning *pop* 400,000

Jizah, Al — see GIZA

João Pes·soa \,zhwaüⁿ-pe-'sō-ə\ *or formerly* **Pa·ra·í·ba** \,pár-à-'ē-bə\ city NE Brazil ✳ of Paraíba *pop* 497,214

Jodh·pur \'jäd-pər, -,púr\ **1** *or* **Mar·war** \'mär-,wär\ former state NW India bordering on Thar Desert & Rann of Kachchh; since 1949 part of Rajasthan state **2** city, its ✳ *pop* 666,279

Jod·rell Bank \'jä-drəl\ locality W England in NE Cheshire near Macclesfield

Jogjakarta — see YOGYAKARTA

Jo·han·nes·burg \jō-'hä-nəs-,bərg, -'ha-\ city NE Republic of South Africa in Gauteng *pop* 654,232

John Day \'jän-'dā\ river 281 *mi* (452 *km*) N Oreg. flowing W & N into Columbia River

John Day Fossil Beds National Monument reservation N *cen* Oreg.

John o' Groat's \,jän-ō-'grōts\ *or* **John o' Groat's House** locality N Scotland; popularly considered the northernmost point of mainland of Scotland & Great Britain — see DUNNET HEAD

John·son City \'jän(t)-sən\ city NE Tenn. S of Va. border *pop* 49,381

John·ston \'jän(t)-stən\ **1** island (atoll) *cen* Pacific SW of Honolulu, Hawaii; belongs to the U.S. **2** town N R.I. SW of Providence *pop* 26,542

Johns·town \'jänz-,taún\ city SW Pa. *pop* 28,134

Jo·hor \jə-'hōr, -'hór\ state Malaysia in Peninsular Malaysia at S end of Malay Peninsula ✳ Johor Baharu *area* 7360 *sq mi* (19,062 *sq km*), *pop* 2,074,297

Johor Ba·ha·ru \'bä-hə-,rü\ city S Malaysia (federation) ✳ of Johor on an inlet opposite Singapore Is. *pop* 135,936

Join·vi·le *or formerly* **Join·vil·le** \zhäⁿ'-vē-lé\ city S Brazil NNW of Florianópolis *pop* 346,095

Jo·li·et \,jō-lē-'et, *chiefly by outsiders* ,jä-\ city NE Ill. *pop* 76,836

Jo·lo \hō-'lō\ island S Philippines, chief island of Sulu Archipelago *area* 345 *sq mi* (897 *sq km*)

Jones·boro \'jōnz-,bər-ō\ city NE Ark. *pop* 46,535

Jön·kö·ping \'yen-,shœ-piŋ\ city S Sweden at S end of Vättern Lake *pop* 309,867

Jon·quière \,zhōⁿ-'kyer\ town Canada in S *cen* Que. *pop* 57,933

Jop·lin \'jä-plin\ city SW Mo. *pop* 40,961

Joppa — see JAFFA

Jor·dan \'jór-dᵊn\ **1** river *cen* Utah flowing from Utah Lake N into Great Salt Lake **2** river 200 *mi* (322 *km*) NE Palestine flowing from Anti-Lebanon Mountains S through Sea of Galilee into Dead Sea **3** *or formerly* **Trans·jor·dan** \(,)tran(t)s-, (,)tranz-\ country SW Asia in NW Arabia ✳ Amman *area* 34,575 *sq mi* (89,549 *sq km*), *pop* 3,636,000 — **Jor·da·ni·an** \jór-'dā-nē-ən\ *adj or n*

Josh·ua Tree National Monument \'jä-shə-wə-,trē\ reservation S Calif. N of Salton Sea containing unusual desert flora

Jo·tun·heim \'yō-t°n-,häm\ *or Norw* **Jo·tun·hei·men** \-,hä-mən\ mountains S *cen* Norway — see GLITTERTIND

Juana Dí·az \,wä-nə-'dē-,äs, ,hwä-nä-'thē-äs\ municipality S Puerto Rico *pop* 45,198

Juan de Fu·ca, Strait of \,wän-də-'fyü-kə, ,hwän-dā-'fü-kä\ strait 100 *mi* (161 *km*) long bet. Vancouver Is., B.C., & Olympic Peninsula, Wash.

Juan Fer·nán·dez \\,wän-fər-'nan-dəs, ,hwän-fer-'nän-dās\ group of three islands SE Pacific W of Chile; belongs to Chile *area* 70 *sq mi* (182 *sq km*)

Juan–les–Pins \,zhwän-lā-'paⁿ\ town SE France on Cap d'Antibes

Juárez — see CIUDAD JUÁREZ

Jub·ba *or* **Ju·ba** \'jü-bə\ river 1000 *mi* (1609 *km*) E Africa flowing from S Ethiopia S through Somalia into Indian Ocean

Ju·by, Cape \'jü-bē, 'yü-\ cape NW Africa on NW coast of Western Sahara

Jú·car \'hü-,kär\ river *over* 300 *mi* (483 *km*) E Spain flowing S & E into the Mediterranean S of Valencia

Ju·daea *or* **Ju·dea** \ju-'dē-ə, -'dā-\ ancient region Palestine constituting the S division (Judah) of the country under Persian, Greek, & Roman rule; bounded on N by Samaria, on E by Jordan River & Dead Sea, on SW by Sinai Peninsula, & on W by the Mediterranean — **Ju·dae·an** *or* **Ju·de·an** \-ən\ *adj or n*

Ju·dah \'jü-də\ ancient kingdom S Palestine ✳ Jerusalem — see ISRAEL

Jugoslavia — see YUGOSLAVIA — **Ju·go·slav** \,yü-gō-'släv, -'slav\ *or* **Ju·go·sla·vi·an** \-'slä-vē-ən\ *adj or n*

Juiz de Fo·ra \,zhwēzh-də-'fōr-ə, -'fȯr-\ city E Brazil in S Minas Gerais *pop* 385,756

Ju·juy \hü-'hwē\ city NW Argentina N of Tucumán *pop* 44,188

Julian Alps \'jül-yən\ section of E Alps W Slovenia N of Istrian Peninsula; highest peak Triglav 9395 *ft* (2864 *m*)

Julian Venetia — see VENEZIA GIULIA

Junction City city NE *cen* Kans. *pop* 20,604

Ju·neau \'jü-(,)nō, jü-'\ city & port ✳ of Alaska in SE coastal strip *pop* 26,751

Jung·frau \'yùn̄-,fraù\ mountain 13,642 *ft* (4158 *m*) SW *cen* Switzerland in Berner Alpen bet. Bern & Valais cantons

Jung·gar \'jùn̄-'gär\ *or* **Dzun·gar·ian Basin** \,jəŋ-'gar-ē-ən, jùŋ-, -'ger-\ *or* **Dzun·gar·ia** \-ē-ə\ region W China in N Xinjiang Uygur N of the Tian Shan

Ju·ni·ata \,jü-nē-'a-tə\ river 150 *mi* (241 *km*) S *cen* Pa. flowing E into the Susquehanna

Ju·nín \hü-'nēn\ **1** city E Argentina W of Buenos Aires *pop* 62,080 **2** town *cen* Peru at S end of **Lake Junín** (25 *mi or* 40 *km* long)

Ju·pi·ter \'jü-pə-tər\ town SE Fla. *pop* 24,986

Jupiter Island island SE Fla. in the Atlantic

Ju·ra \'jùr-ə\ **1** canton W Switzerland *area* 322 *sq mi* (834 *sq km*), *pop* 65,376 **2** mountains France & Switzerland extending *ab* 145 *mi* (233 *km*) along the boundary; highest Mount Neige (in France) 5652 *ft* (1723 *m*) **3** island 24 *mi* (39 *km*) long W Scotland in the Inner Hebrides S of Mull

Juramento — see SALADO

Ju·ruá \,zhùr-(ə-)'wä\ river NW *cen* S. America flowing from E *cen* Peru NE into the Solimões in NW Brazil

Ju·rue·na \,zhùr-'wä-nə\ river 600 *mi* (966 *km*) W *cen* Brazil flowing N to unite with the Teles Pires forming the Tapajoz

Jut·land \'jət-lənd\ *or Dan* **Jyl·land** \'yūˌlán\ **1** peninsula N Europe projecting into North Sea & comprising mainland of Denmark & N portion of Schleswig-Holstein, Germany **2** the mainland of Denmark

K

Kaapland — see CAPE OF GOOD HOPE

Ka·ba·le·ga Falls \ˌkä-bä-'lē-gä, -'lä-\ *or* **Ka·ba·re·ga Falls** \-'rä-\ *or* **Mur·chi·son Falls** \'mər-chə-sən\ waterfall 130 *ft* (40 *m*) W Uganda in the Victoria Nile

Kab·ar·di·no–Bal·kar·ia \ˌka-bər-'dē-nō-ˌból-'kar-ē-ə, -ˌbál-\ autonomous republic S Russia in Europe on N slopes of the Caucasus ✻ Nalchik *area* 4826 *sq mi* (12,499 *sq km*), *pop* 784,000 — **Kab·ar·din·ian** \ˌka-bər-'dē-nē-ən\ *adj or n*

Ka·bul \'kä-bəl, kə-'bül\ **1** river 435 *mi* (700 *km*) Afghanistan & N Pakistan flowing E into the Indus **2** city ✻ of Afghanistan on Kabul River *pop* 1,424,400 — **Ka·buli** \'kä-bə-(ˌ)lē, kə-'bü-lē\ *adj or n*

Ka·bwe \'kä-(ˌ)bwā\ *or formerly* **Bro·ken Hill** \'brō-kən\ city *cen* Zambia *pop* 166,519

Ka·by·lia \kə-'bī-lē-ə, -'bi-\ mountainous region N Algeria on coast E of Algiers; comprises two areas: **Great Kabylia** (to W) & **Little Kabylia** (to E)

Kachchh, Gulf of \'kəch\ *or* **Gulf of Kutch** \'kəch\ inlet of Arabian Sea W India N of Kathiawar

Kachchh, Rann of *or* **Rann of Kutch** salt marsh in S Pakistan & W India stretching in an arc from the mouths of the Indus to the head of Gulf of Kachchh

Ka·desh–bar·nea \ˌkā-(ˌ)desh-'bär-nē-ə, -ˌbär-'nē-ə\ ancient town S Palestine SW of Dead Sea; exact location uncertain

Ka·di·koy \kä-'di-kȯi\ *or anc* **Chal·ce·don** \'kal-sə-ˌdän, kal-'sēdᵊn\ former city Asia on the Bosporus; now a district of Istanbul

Kadiyevka — see STAKHANOV

Kaerh — see GAR

Kae·song \'kā-ˌsȯŋ\ city SW N. Korea SE of Pyongyang *pop* 331,000

Kaf·fe·klub·ben \'kä-fə-ˌklü-bən, -ˌklə-\ island in Arctic Ocean off N coast of Greenland; northernmost point of land in the world, at 83°40'N

Kaf·frar·ia \kə-'frar-ē-ə, ka-, -'frer-\ region Republic of South Africa in Eastern Cape province S of Lesotho & bordering on Indian Ocean

Kafiristan — see NURISTAN

Ka·fue \kä-'fü-ā\ river 600 *mi* (965 *km*) Zambia flowing into the Zambezi

Ka·ge·ra \kä-'gä-rä\ river 430 *mi* (692 *km*) Burundi, Rwanda, & NW Tanzania flowing N & E into Lake Victoria on Uganda border

Ka·go·shi·ma \kä-gō-'shē-mä, kä-'gō-shē-\ city & port S Japan in S Kyushu on **Kagoshima Bay** (inlet of the Pacific) *pop* 536,685

Ka·hoo·la·we \kä-hō-ō-'lä-(,)vä, -(,)wä\ island Hawaii SW of Maui *area* 45 *sq mi* (117 *sq km*)

Kai·bab Plateau \'kī-,bab\ plateau N Ariz. & SW Utah N of Grand Canyon

Kai·e·teur Falls \'kī-ə-,túr, ,kī-'chúr\ waterfall 741 *ft* (226 *m*) high & 350 *ft* (107 *m*) wide *cen* Guyana

Kai·feng \'kī-'fəŋ\ city E *cen* China in NE Henan *pop* 318,000

Kai·lua \kī-'lü-ä\ city Hawaii in NE Oahu *pop* 36,818

Kair·ouan \ker-'wän\ city NE Tunisia *pop* 54,546

Kai·sers·lau·tern \,kī-zərz-'laú-tərn\ city SW Germany W of Ludwigshafen *pop* 100,541

Ka·ki·na·da \,kä-kə-'nä-də\ city & port E India in NE Andhra Pradesh on Bay of Bengal *pop* 279,875

Kalaallit Nunaat — see GREENLAND

Ka Lae \kä-'lä-ä\ *or* **South Cape** headland Hawaii, southernmost point of Hawaii (island)

Kalaeloa Point — see BARBERS POINT

Kal·a·ha·ri Desert \,ka-lə-'här-ē, ,kä-\ desert region S Africa N of Orange River & S of Lake Ngami in Botswana & NW Republic of South Africa

Ka·la·ma·zoo \,ka-lə-mə-'zü\ city SW Mich. *pop* 80,277

Ka·lat *or* **Khe·lat** \kə-'lät\ region NW Pakistan including S & *cen* Baluchistan; a former princely state ✻ Kalat

Ka·le·mie \kä-'lä-mē\ *or formerly* **Al·bert·ville** \al-,ber-'vēl, 'al-bərt-,vil\ city & port E Democratic Republic of the Congo on Lake Tanganyika *pop* 96,212

Kalgan — see ZHANGJIAKOU

Kal·goor·lie–Boul·der \kal-'gúr-lē-'bōl-dər\ town Australia in S *cen* W. Australia *pop* 25,016

Ka·li·man·tan \,ka-lə-'man-,tan, ,kä-lē-'män-,tän\ **1** an Indonesian name for Borneo **2** the S & E part of Borneo belonging to Indonesia; formerly (as **Dutch Borneo**) part of Netherlands India

Kalinin — see TVER'

Ka·li·nin·grad \kə-'lē-nən-,grad, -nyən-, -,grät\ *or G* **Kö·nigs·berg** \'kä-nigz-,bərg, *Ger* 'kœ-niks-,berk\ city & port W Russia in Europe near the Frisches Haff; formerly ✻ of E. Prussia *pop* 411,000

Ka·lisz \'kä-lēsh\ commune *cen* Poland W of Lodz *pop* 106,087

Kal·mar \'käl-,mär, 'kal-\ city & port SE Sweden *pop* 56,863

Kal·myk·ia \(,)kal-'mi-kē-ə\ autonomous republic S Russia in Europe on NW shore of Caspian Sea W of the Volga ✻ Elista *area* 29,305 *sq mi* (75,900 *sq km*) *pop* 322,000

Ka·lu·ga \kə-'lü-gə\ city W *cen* Russia in Europe on Oka River WNW of Tula *pop* 347,000

Ka·ma \'kä-mə\ river E Russia in Europe flowing SW into the Volga S of Kazan

Ka·ma·ku·ra \,kä-'mä-kə-,rä, ,kä-mä-'kúr-ä\ city Japan in SE Honshu on Sagami Sea S of Yokohama *pop* 174,299

Kam·chat·ka \kam-'chat-kə, -'chät-\ peninsula 750 *mi* (1207 *km*) long E Russia in Asia bet. Sea of Okhotsk & Bering Sea

Ka·met \kə-'mät, kə-'mēt\ mountain 25,447 *ft* (7756 *m*) N India in Uttar Pradesh in the NW Himalayas

Kam·loops \'kam-,lüps\ city Canada in S B.C. *pop* 67,057

Kam·pa·la \käm-'pä-lä, kam-\ city ✳ of Uganda N of Lake Victoria *pop* 773,463

Kampuchea — see CAMBODIA — **Kam·pu·che·an** \,kam-pù-'chē-ən\ *adj*

Kan — see GAN

Ka·nan·ga \kä-'nän-gä\ *or formerly* **Lu·lua·bourg** \lü-lwä-'bùr\ city S *cen* Democratic Republic of the Congo *pop* 371,862

Kananur — see CANNANORE

Ka·na·ta \kə-'nä-tə\ city Canada in SE Ont. *pop* 37,344

Ka·na·wha \kə-'nó-(w)ə\ river 97 *mi* (156 *km*) W W.Va. flowing NW into Ohio River

Ka·na·za·wa \kä-'nä-zä-wä, ,kä-nä-'zä-wä\ city & port Japan in W *cen* Honshu near Sea of Japan *pop* 442,872

Kan·chen·jun·ga \,kən-chən-'jəŋ-gə, -'jùn-\ *or* **Kang·chen·jun·ga** \,kəŋ-\ mountain 28,169 *ft* (8586 *m*) Nepal & Sikkim in the Himalaya; 3d highest in world

Kan·chi·pu·ram \kän-'chē-pə-rəm\ city SE India in N Tamil Nadu SW of Madras *pop* 145,028

Kan·da·har *or* **Qan·da·har** \'kən-də-,här\ city SE Afghanistan *pop* 130,212

Kan·dy \'kan-dē\ city W *cen* Sri Lanka ENE of Colombo *pop* 104,000 — **Kan·dy·an** \-dē-ən\ *adj*

Kane Basin \'kān\ section of the passage bet. NW Greenland & Ellesmere Is. N of Baffin Bay

Ka·ne·o·he Bay \,kä-nē-'ō-ā, -'ō-(,)hā\ inlet Hawaii on E Oahu

Kan·ka·kee \,kaŋ-kə-'kē\ **1** river 135 *mi* (217 *km*) Ind. & Ill. flowing SW & W to unite with Des Plaines River forming Illinois River **2** city NE Ill. on Kankakee River *pop* 27,575

Kan·nap·o·lis \kə-'na-pə-lis\ town S *cen* N.C. *pop* 29,696

Ka·no \'kä-(,)nō\ city N *cen* Nigeria *pop* 594,800

Kan·pur \'kän-,pùr\ city N India in S Uttar Pradesh on the Ganges *pop* 1,879,420

Kan·sas \'kan-zəs\ **1** *or* **Kaw** \'kó\ river 169 *mi* (272 *km*) E Kans. flowing E into Missouri River — see SMOKY HILL **2** state *cen* U.S. ✳ Topeka *area* 82,277 *sq mi* (213,097 *sq km*), *pop* 2,477,574 — **Kan·san** \'kan-zən\ *adj or n*

Kansas City 1 city NE Kans. adjacent to Kansas City, Mo. *pop* 149,767 **2** city W Mo. on Missouri River *pop* 435,146

Kansu — see GANSU

Kan·ton Island \'kan-tᵊn\ island (atoll) *cen* Pacific in Phoenix Islands

Kan·to Plain \'kän-(,)tō\ region Japan in E *cen* Honshu; Tokyo is situated on it

Kao–hsiung \'kaù-'shyùŋ, 'gaù-\ city & port SW Taiwan *pop* 1,405,860

Ka·pi·da·gi \,kä-pi-'daù\ *or anc* **Cyz·i·cus** \'si-zi-kəs\ peninsula NW Turkey in Asia projecting into Sea of Marmara

Ka·ra·chay–Cher·kes·sia \kär-ə-'chī-chir-'ke-syə\ *or formerly* **Ka·ra·cha·ye·vo–Cher·kess** \kär-ə-'chī-ə-,vō-chir-'kes\ autonomous region SE Russia in Europe in N Caucasus *area* 5444 *sq mi* (14,100 *sq km*), *pop* 431,000 ✳ Cherkessk

Ka·ra·chi \kə-'rä-chē\ city & port S Pakistan ✳ of Sind *pop* 5,103,000

Karafuto — see SAKHALIN

Ka·ra·gan·da \ˌkär-ə-'gän-də\ *or* **Qa·ra·ghan·dy** \-dē\ city *cen* Kazakhstan *pop* 608,600

Ka·raj \kä-'räj\ city N Iran NW of Tehran *pop* 275,100

Ka·ra·kal·pak \ˌkar-ə-ˌkäl-'päk\ autonomous republic NW Uzbekistan SE of Aral Sea ✻ Nukus *area* 63,938 *sq mi* (165,599 *sq km*), *pop* 1,273,800

Kar·a·ko·ram Pass \ˌkär-ə-'kōr-əm, -'kȯr-\ mountain pass 18,290 *ft* (5575 *m*) NE Kashmir through Karakoram Range

Karakoram Range mountain system ✻ *cen* Asia in N Kashmir & NW Tibet on Xinjiang Uygur border; westernmost system of the Himalaya complex, connecting the Himalayas with the Pamirs — see K2

Kar·a·ko·rum \ˌkar-ə-'kōr-əm\ ruined city Mongolia on the upper Orkhon ✻ of Mongol Empire

Ka·ra–Kum \ˌkar-ə-'küm, ˌkär-\ desert Turkmenistan S of Aral Sea bet. the Caspian Sea & the Amu Darya *area* 115,830 *sq mi* (300,000 *sq km*)

Kara Sea arm of Arctic Ocean off coast of Russia E of Novaya Zemlya

Ka·ra Su \ˌkar-ə-'sü, ˌkär-\ the Euphrates above its junction with the Murat in E *cen* Turkey

Kar·ba·lā' \ˌkär-bə-'lä, 'kär-bə-lə\ city *cen* Iraq SSW of Baghdad *pop* 83,301

Ka·re·lia \kə-'rē-lē-ə, -'rēl-yə\ autonomous republic NW Russia in Europe; formerly (1940–56), as the **Ka·re·lo–Finn·ish Republic** \kə-'rē-(ˌ)lō-'fi-nish\ constituent republic of the U.S.S.R. ✻ Petrozavodsk *area* 66,564 *sq mi* (172,401 *sq km*), *pop* 800,000 — **Ka·re·lian** \kə-'rē-lē-ən\ *adj or n*

Karelian Isthmus isthmus Russia in Europe bet. Gulf of Finland & Lake Ladoga

Ka·ri·ba, Lake \kä-'rē-bä\ lake 175 *mi* (282 *km*) long SE Zambia & N Zimbabwe formed in the Zambezi by **Kariba Dam**

Ka·ri·kal \ˌkär-ə-'käl\ **1** territory of former French India S of Pondicherry; incorporated 1954 in India *area* 52 *sq mi* (135 *sq km*) **2** *or* **Ka·rai·kal** \ˌkä-ri-'käl\ city & port, its ✻, on Bay of Bengal *pop* 22,252

Kar·kheh *or* **Ker·kheh** \kər-'kä\ *or anc* **Cho·as·pes** \kō-'as-(ˌ)pēz\ river flowing from W Iran S & W into marshlands E of the Tigris in SE Iraq

Karl–Marx–Stadt — see CHEMNITZ

Karls·kro·na \kär(-ə)lz-'krü-nə\ city & port SE Sweden on Baltic Sea *area pop* 59,753

Karls·ru·he \'kärl(-ə)z-ˌrü-ə\ city SW Germany in Baden-Württemberg on the Rhine *pop* 278,579 — **Karls·ru·her** \-ˌrü-ər\ *n*

Karl·stad \'kär(-ə)l-ˌstä(d)\ city SW Sweden *pop* 77,290

Kar·nak \'kär-ˌnak\ town S Egypt on the Nile N of Luxor on N part of site of ancient Thebes

Kar·na·ta·ka \kər-'nä-tə-kə\ *or formerly* **My·sore** \mī-'sȯr, -'sȯr\ state SW India ✻ Bangalore *area* 74,037 *sq mi* (191,756 *sq km*), *pop* 44,977,201

Ka·roo *or* **Kar·roo** \kə-'rü\ plateau region W Republic of South Africa W of Drakensberg Mountains divided into **Little Karoo** *or* **Southern Karoo** (in *cen* Western Cape province); **Great Karoo** *or* **Central Karoo** (in Western Cape & Eastern Cape provinces);

and **Northern Karoo** *or* **Upper Karoo** (in Northern Cape, Free State, & North West provinces)

Kár·pa·thos \'kär-pä-,thós\ island Greece in the S Dodecanese *area* 118 *sq mi* (307 *sq km*), *pop* 8129

Kars \'kärz, 'kärs\ city NE Turkey *pop* 79,496

Karst \'kärst\ *or* **Kras** \'kräs\ *or It* **Car·so** \'kär-(,)sō\ limestone plateau NE of Istrian Peninsula in W Slovenia extending into E Italy

Ka·run \kä-'rün\ river over 500 *mi* (804 *km*) W Iran flowing into Shatt-al-Arab

Ka·sai \kə-'sī\ **1** river 1338 *mi* (2153 *km*) N Angola & W Democratic Republic of the Congo flowing N & W into Congo River **2** region S *cen* Democratic Republic of the Congo

Kashi \'ka-shē, 'kä-\ *or* **Kash·gar** \'kash-,gär, 'käsh-\ city W China in SW Xinjiang Uygur *pop* 174,570

Ka·shi·wa \'kä-shē-(,)wä\ city Japan on Honshu *pop* 305,060

Kash·mir \'kash-,mir, 'kazh-, kash-, kazh-\ **1** *or formerly* **Cashmere** mountainous region N India (subcontinent) W of Tibet & SW of Xinjiang Uygur; includes valley (**Vale of Kashmir**) watered by the Jhelum **2** — see JAMMU AND KASHMIR — **Kash·miri** \kash-'mir-ē, kazh-\ *n*

Kas·kas·kia \ka-'skas-kē-ə\ river 320 *mi* (515 *km*) SW Ill. flowing SW into Mississippi River

Kas·sa·la \'ka-sə-lə\ city NE Sudan *pop* 99,000

Kas·sel \'ka-sᵊl, 'kä-\ city *cen* Germany WNW of Erfurt *pop* 196,828

Kas·ser·ine Pass \'ka-sə-,rēn\ mountain pass *cen* Tunisia

Ka·stel·lór·i·zon \,käs-te-'lór-ē-,zón\ *or* **Ca·stel·lo·ri·zo** \,käs-tə-'lór-ə-,zō\ *or It* **Cas·tel·ros·so** \,käs-,tel-'rō-(,)sō\ island Greece in the E Dodecanese off SW coast of Turkey *area* 9 *sq mi* (23 *sq km*)

Ká·stron \'käs-,trón\ town Greece on Lemnos

Ka·tah·din, Mount \kə-'tä-dᵊn\ mountain 5268 *ft* (1606 *m*) N *cen* Maine; highest point in state

Katanga — see SHABA — **Ka·tan·gese** \kə-täŋ-'gēz, -taŋ-, -'gēs\ *adj*

Ka·te·ri·ni \,kä-te-'rē-nē\ town N Greece *pop* 46,304

Kath·er·i·na, Ge·bel \'je-bəl-,kä-thə-'rē-nə\ *or* **Ja·bal Kat·ri·nah** \'jä-bəl-kä-'trē-nə\ *or* **Mount Cath·er·ine** \'ka-th(ə-)rən\ mountain 8652 *ft* (2637 *m*) NE Egypt on Sinai Peninsula; highest in the Gebel Musa

Ka·thi·a·war \,kä-tē-ə-'wär\ peninsula W India in Gujarat bet. Gulf of Kachchh & Gulf of Khambhat

Kath·man·du *or* **Kat·man·du** \,kat-,man-'dü, ,kät-,män-\ city ✳ of Nepal *pop* 235,211

Kat·mai, Mount \'kat-,mī\ volcano 6715 *ft* (2047 *m*) S Alaska in Aleutian Range at NE end of Alaska Peninsula

Katmai National Park reservation S Alaska including Mt. Katmai & Valley of Ten Thousand Smokes

Ka·to·wi·ce \,kä-tō-'vēt-se\ city S Poland in Silesia *pop* 367,041

Kat·rine, Loch \'ka-trən\ lake 9 *mi* (14 *km*) long *cen* Scotland in Central region E of Loch Lomond

Ka·tsi·na \'kät-sē-nä\ city N Nigeria ✳ of old kingdom of Katsina *pop* 182,400

Kat·te·gat \'ka-ti-,gat\ arm of North Sea bet. Sweden & Jutland Peninsula of Denmark

Kau·ai \kä-'wä-ē\ island Hawaii WNW of Oahu *area* 555 *sq mi* (1437 *sq km*)

Kau·nas \'kaú-nəs, -‚näs\ *or Russ* **Kov·no** \'kóv-(‚)nō, -nə\ city *cen* Lithuania on the Neman; a former (1918–40) ✳ of Lithuania *pop* 433,600

Ka·vá·la *or* **Ka·vál·la** \kä-'vä-lä\ city & port NE Greece in Macedonia *pop* 58,576

Kāveri — see CAUVERY

Kāveri Falls — see CAUVERY FALLS

Kaw — see KANSAS

Ka·wa·goe \kä-'wä-gō-wä\ city Japan on SE *cen* Honshu *pop* 304,860

Ka·wa·gu·chi \‚kä-wä-'gü-chē, kä-'wä-gü-(‚)chē\ city Japan in E Honshu N of Tokyo *pop* 438,667

Ka·war·tha Lakes \kə-'wôr-thə\ group of lakes Canada in SE Ont. E of Lake Simcoe; traversed by Trent Canal system

Ka·wa·sa·ki \‚kä-wä-'sä-kē\ city Japan in E Honshu on Tokyo Bay, S suburb of Tokyo *pop* 1,173,606

Kay·se·ri \kī-zə-'rē\ *or anc* **Cae·sa·rea** \‚sē-zə-'rē-ə, ‚se-zə-, ‚se-sə-\ *or* **Maz·a·ca** \'ma-zə-kə\ *or* **Caesarea Mazaca** city *cen* Turkey in Asia at foot of Erciyas Dagi; chief city of ancient Cappadocia *pop* 421,362

Ka·zakh·stan \‚ka-(‚)zak-'stan; ‚käk-(‚)zäk-'stän *also* kə-\ independent country NW *cen* Asia extending from Caspian Sea to Altai mountain range; a constituent republic of the U.S.S.R. 1936–91; ✳ Aqmola *area* 1,048,300 *sq mi* (2,715,097 *sq km*), *pop* 17,186,000

Ka·zan 1 \kə-'zan\ river 455 *mi* (732 *km*) Canada flowing through a series of lakes into Baker Lake **2** \kə-'zan, -'zän, -'zä-nyə\ city E *cen* Russia in Europe ✳ of Tatarstan *pop* 1,098,000

Kazan Retto — see VOLCANO

Kaz·bek \käz-'bek\ mountain 16,558 *ft* (5047 *m*) bet. Georgia & Russia in Europe in *cen* Caucasus Mountains

Kaz Da·gi \‚käz-'di\ *or* **Ida** \'ī-də\ mountain 5797 *ft* (1767 *m*) NW Turkey in Asia SE of ancient Troy

Kazvin — see QAZVIN

Kea \'kā-ä\ *or anc* **Ce·os** \'sē-‚äs\ island Greece in NW Cyclades; chief town Kea *area* 67 *sq mi* (174 *sq km*)

Ke·a·la·ke·kua Bay \kä-‚ä-lä-kä-'kü-ä\ inlet of the Pacific Hawaii in W Hawaii (island) on Kona coast W of Mauna Loa

Kear·ney \'kär-nē\ city S *cen* Nebr. on Platte River *pop* 24,396

Kear·ny \'kär-nē\ town NE N.J. N of Newark *pop* 34,874

Kecs·ke·met \'kech-ke-‚māt\ city *cen* Hungary *pop* 108,000

Ked·ah \'ke-də\ state Malaysia in N Peninsular Malaysia bordering on Strait of Malacca ✳ Alor Star *area* 3660 *sq mi* (9516 *sq km*), *pop* 1,304,800

Keeling — see COCOS

Keelung — see CHI-LUNG

Keene \'kēn\ city SW N.H. *pop* 22,430

Kee·wa·tin \kē-'wā-tᵊn, -'wä-\ former district Canada in E Northwest Territories N of Man. & Ont. & including the islands in Hudson Bay

Kefalliniá — see CEPHALONIA

Kef·la·vík \'kye-blä-‚vēk, 'ke-flə-\ town SW Iceland WSW of Reykjavik *pop* 7520

Keigh·ley \'kēth-lē—*sic*\ borough N England in W. Yorkshire, NW of Leeds *pop* 57,451

Kei·zer \'kī-zər\ city NW Oreg. N of Salem *pop* 21,884

Kej·im·ku·jik National Park \,ke-jə-mə-'kü-jik, ,kej-mə-\ reservation Canada in SW N.S.

Ke·lan·tan \kə-'lan-,tan\ state Malaysia in N Peninsular Malaysia on S. China Sea ✳ Kota Baharu *area* 5780 *sq mi* (14,970 *sq km*), *pop* 1,181,680

Ke·low·na \kə-'lō-nə\ city Canada in S B.C. *pop* 75,950

Keltsy — see KIELCE

Ke·me·ro·vo \'kye-mə-rə-və; 'ke-mə-,rō-və, -rə-,vō\ city Russia in Asia in Kuznetsk Basin on Tom River *pop* 521,000

Ke·nai Peninsula \'kē-,nī\ peninsula S Alaska E of Cook Inlet; site of **Kenai Fjords National Park** (ice field)

Ken·dal \'ken-dᵊl\ borough NW England in Cumbria *pop* 23,411

Ken·il·worth \'ke-nᵊl-,wərth\ town *cen* England in Warwickshire *pop* 19,315

Ke·ni·tra \kə-'nē-tra\ *or formerly* **Port Lyau·tey** \,pòr-lyō-'tā\ city N Morocco NE of Rabat *pop* 139,206

Ken·ne·bec \'ke-ni-,bek, ,ke-ni-\ river 150 *mi* (240 *km*) S Maine flowing S from Moosehead Lake into the Atlantic

Kennedy, Cape — see CANAVERAL (Cape)

Ken·ne·dy, Mount \'ke-nə-dē\ mountain 13,905 *ft* (4238 *m*) NW Canada in Yukon Territory in St. Elias Range near Alaska border

Ken·ner \'ke-nər\ city SE La. W of New Orleans *pop* 72,033

Ken·ne·saw Mountain \'ke-nə-,sò\ mountain 1809 *ft* (551 *m*) NW Ga. NW of Atlanta

Ken·ne·wick \'ke-nə-,wik\ city SE Wash. *pop* 42,155

Ke·no·sha \kə-'nō-shə\ city SE Wis. S of Racine *pop* 80,352

Ken·sing·ton and Chel·sea \'ken-ziŋ-tən-ənd-'chel-sē, ,ken(t)-siŋ-\ royal borough of W Greater London, England *pop* 127,600; includes former boroughs of Kensington & Chelsea

Kent \'kent\ **1** city NE Ohio SE of Cleveland *pop* 28,835 **2** city W Wash. S of Seattle *pop* 37,960 **3** county SE England bordering on Strait of Dover; one of kingdoms in Anglo-Saxon heptarchy ✳ Maidstone *area* 1493 *sq mi* (3867 *sq km*), *pop* 1,485,100 — **Kent·ish** \'ken-tish\ *adj*

Kent Island island Md. in Chesapeake Bay 15 *mi* (25 *km*) long; largest island in the bay

Ken·tucky \kən-'tə-kē\ **1** river 259 *mi* (417 *km*) N *cen* Ky. flowing NW into Ohio river **2** state E *cen* U.S. ✳ Frankfort *area* 40,395 *sq mi* (105,027 *sq km*), *pop* 3,685,296 — **Ken·tuck·i·an** \-kē-ən\ *adj or n*

Kent·wood \'kent-,wùd\ city SW Mich. *pop* 37,826

Ke·nya \'ke-nyə, 'kē-\ **1** extinct volcano 17,058 *ft* (5199 *m*) *cen* Kenya near equator **2** republic E Africa S of Ethiopia bordering on Indian Ocean; member of the Commonwealth of Nations, formerly Brit. crown colony & protectorate ✳ Nairobi *area* 224,960 *sq mi* (584,896 *sq km*), *pop* 28,113,000 — **Ke·nyan** \-nyən\ *adj or n*

Ker·a·la \'ker-ə-lə\ state SW India bordering on Arabian Sea ✳ Trivandrum *area* 15,007 *sq mi* (38,868 *sq km*), *pop* 29,098,518

Kerasun — see GIRESUN

Kerch \'kerch\ **1** peninsula projecting E from the Crimea **2** city & port in the Crimea on Kerch Strait *pop* 178,000

Kerch Strait strait bet. Kerch & Taman peninsulas connecting Sea of Azov & Black Sea

Ker·gue·len \\'kər-gə-lən, ,ker-gə-'len\\ island in the Kerguelen Archipelago

Kerguelen Islands archipelago S Indian Ocean belonging to France *area* 2394 *sq mi* (6200 *sq km*)

Ke·rin·ci *or* **Ke·rin·tji** \\kə-'rin-chē\\ volcano 12,484 *ft* (3805 *m*) Indonesia in W *cen* Sumatra; highest on the island

Kerkheh — see KARKHEH

Kerk·ra·de \\'kerk-,rä-də\\ commune SE Netherlands *pop* 53,364

Kérkyra — see CORFU

Ker·mad·ec Islands \\(,)kər-'ma-dək\\ islands SW Pacific NE of New Zealand; belong to New Zealand *area* 13 *sq mi* (34 *sq km*), *pop* 9

Ker·man \\kər-'män, ker-\\ **1** *or anc* **Car·ma·nia** \\kär-'mā-nē-ə, -nyə\\ region SE Iran bordering on Gulf of Oman & Persian Gulf S of ancient Parthia **2** *or anc* **Car·ma·na** \\kär-'mā-nə, -'ma-, -'mä-\\ city SE *cen* Iran in NW Kerman region *pop* 257,284

Kermanshah — see BAKHTARAN

Kern \\'kərn\\ river 150 *mi* (241 *km*) S *cen* Calif. flowing SW into a reservoir

Ker·ry \\'ker-ē\\ county SW Ireland in Munster ✳ Tralee *area* 1815 *sq mi* (4719 *sq km*), *pop* 121,894

Ker·u·len \\'ker-ə-,len\\ river E Mongolia flowing S & E into the Argun in Manchuria

Kes·te·ven, Parts of \\ke-'stē-vən, 'kes-ti-vən\\ district & former administrative county E England in SW Lincolnshire ✳ Sleaford *area* 734 *sq mi* (1901 *sq km*)

Kes·wick \\'ke-zik\\ town NW England in Cumbria in Lake District

Ket·ter·ing \\'ke-tə-riŋ\\ city SW Ohio S of Dayton *pop* 60,569

Keu·ka Lake \\'kyü-kə, kā-'yü-\\ lake 18 *mi* (29 *km*) long W *cen* N.Y.; one of the Finger Lakes

Kew \\'kyü\\ **1** city SE Australia in S Victoria, NE suburb of Melbourne *pop* 27,291 **2** parish S England in Surrey, now in the Greater London borough of Richmond upon Thames

Ke·wee·naw Peninsula \\'kē-wə-,nȯ\\ peninsula NW Mich. projecting from Upper Peninsula into Lake Superior W of Keweenaw Bay

Key Lar·go \\'lär-(,)gō\\ island S Fla. in the Florida Keys

Key West \\'west\\ city SW Fla. on Key West (island) at W end of Florida Keys *pop* 24,832 — **Key West·er** \\'wes-tər\\ *n*

Kha·ba·rovsk \\kə-'bär-əfsk, kə-\\ **1** territory E Russia in Asia bordering on Sea of Okhotsk *area* 318,378 *sq mi* (824,599 *sq km*), *pop* 1,855,000 **2** city, its ✳, on the Amur *pop* 615,000

Kha·kas·sia \\kə-'käs-yə, kə-; kə-'ka-zhə\\ autonomous region S Russia in Asia in SW Krasnoyarsk Territory N of the Sayan Mountains ✳ Abakan *area ab* 24,000 *sq mi* (62,400 *sq km*), *pop* 581,000

Khalkidiki — see CHALCIDICE

Khal·kís \\käl-'kēs, käl-\\ *or* **Chal·cis** \\'kal-səs, -kəs\\ city *cen* Greece ✳ of Euboea on Evripos Strait *pop* 51,482

Kham·bhat \\'kam-bət\\ *or* **Cam·bay** \\kam-'bā\\ city W India in Gujarat W of Vadodara *pop* 76,724

Khambhat, Gulf of *or* **Gulf of Cambay** inlet of Arabian Sea in India N of Bombay

Khan·ka \'kaŋ-kə\ lake E Asia bet. Maritime Territory, Russia & Heilongjiang, China *area* 1700 *sq mi* (4420 *sq km*)

Khan–Ten·gri \,kän-'teŋ-grē\ mountain 22,949 *ft* (6995 *m*) on border bet. Kyrgyzstan & Xinjiang Uygur (China) in Tian Shan

Kha·rag·pur \'kär-əg-,púr, 'kór-\ or **Kha·rak·pur** \-ək-\ city E India in SW N. Bengal WSW of Calcutta *pop* 279,736

Khar·kiv \'kär-kəf, 'kär-\ or **Khar·kov** \kär-,kóf, kär-, -,kóv, -kəf\ city NE Ukraine, its ✳ 1921–34, on edge of Donets Basin *pop* 1,623,000

Khar·toum \kär-'tüm\ city ✳ of Sudan at junction of White Nile & Blue Nile rivers *pop* 1,950,000

Khartoum North or **North Khartoum** city *cen* Sudan *pop* 151,000

Kha·si Hills \'kä-sē\ hills E India in NW *cen* Assam

Kha·tan·ga \kə-'täŋ-gə, -'taŋ-\ river 800 *mi* (1287 *km*) N Russia in Asia, in NE Krasnoyarsk Territory flowing N into Laptev Sea

Khelat — see KALAT

Kher·son \ker-'són\ city & port S Ukraine on the Dnieper near its mouth *pop* 365,000

Khí·os \'kē-,ós, 'kē-\ — see CHIOS

Khir·bat Qum·ran or **Khir·bet Qum·ran** \kir-'bat-küm-'rän\ locality Palestine in NW Jordan on Wadi Qumran near NW shore of Dead Sea; site of an Essene community (*ab* 100 B.C.–A.D. 68) near a series of caves in which the Dead Sea Scrolls were found

Khi·va \'kē-və\ **1** or **Kho·rezm** \kə-'re-zəm\ oasis Uzbekistan on the lower Amu Darya **2** or **Khwa·razm** \kwə-'ra-zəm, kwä-\ former khanate *cen* Asia including Khiva oasis **3** town in the oasis, ✳ of the khanate *pop* 41,300

Khmer Republic — see CAMBODIA

Khor·a·san \,kór-ə-'san, ,kór-\ or **Khu·ra·san** \,kúr-ə-'sän, ,kúr-\ region NE Iran; chief city Mashhad

Khor·ra·ma·bad \kó-'ra-mə-,bäd, -,bad\ or **Khur·ra·ma·bad** \kü-'rä-\ city W Iran *pop* 208,592

Khor·ram·shahr \,kór-əm-'shä(-hə)r, ,kór-\ city & port W Iran in Khuzistan on Shatt al Arab NNW of Abadan

Khotan — see HOTAN

Khums, Al — see AL KHUMS

Khu·zi·stan \,kü-zi-'stän, -'stan\ region SW Iran bordering on Persian Gulf; chief city Khorramshahr

Khy·ber Pass \'kī-bər\ mountain pass 33 *mi* (53 *km*) long on border bet. Afghanistan & Pakistan in Safed Koh Range WNW of Peshawar

Kiamusze — see JIAMUSI

Kiangsi — see JIANGXI

Kiangsu — see JIANGSU

Kiaochow — see JIAOZHOU

Ki·bo \'kē-(,)bō\ mountain peak 19,340 *ft* (5895 *m*) NE Tanzania; highest peak of Kilimanjaro & highest point in Africa

Kid·der·min·ster \'ki-dər-,min(t)-stər\ borough W *cen* England in Hereford and Worcester SW of Birmingham *pop* 51,261

Kid·ron \'ki-drən, 'kē-\ valley *cen* Palestine bet. Jerusalem & Mount of Olives; source of stream (Kidron) flowing E to Dead Sea

Kiel \'kēl\ **1** city & port N Germany ✳ of Schleswig-Holstein on SE coast of Jutland Peninsula *pop* 247,107 **2** or **Nord–Ost·see**

\,nȯrt-ˌȯst-ˈzä\ ship canal 61 *mi* (98 *km*) N Germany across base of Jutland Peninsula connecting Baltic Sea & North Sea

Kiel·ce \kē-ˈelt-(ˌ)sä, 'kyelt-\ *or Russ* **Kelt·sy** \'kelt-sē\ city S Poland S of Warsaw *pop* 212,901

Ki·ev *or* **Ki·yev** \ˈkē-ˌef, -ˌev, -if\ city ✶ of Ukraine on the Dnieper *pop* 2,587,000 — **Ki·ev·an** \ˈkē-ˌe-fən, -vən\ *adj or n*

Ki·ga·li \kē-ˈgä-lē\ city *cen* Rwanda, its ✶ *pop* 232,733

Kikládhes — see CYCLADES

Ki·lau·ea \ˌkē-ˌlä-ˈwā-ä\ volcanic crater 2 *mi* (3.2 *km*) wide Hawaii on Hawaii (island) in Hawaii Volcanoes National Park on E slope of Mauna Loa

Kil·dare \kil-ˈdar, -ˈder\ county E Ireland in Leinster ✶ Naas *area* 654 *sq mi* (1700 *sq km*), *pop* 122,656

Kil·i·man·ja·ro \ˌki-lə-mən-ˈjär-(ˌ)ō, -ˈjar-\ mountain Tanzania on NE mainland near Kenya border — see KIBO

Kil·ken·ny \kil-ˈke-nē\ **1** county SE Ireland in Leinster *area* 796 *sq mi* (2070 *sq km*), *pop* 73,635 **2** town, its ✶ *pop* 8513

Kil·lar·ney, Lakes of \ki-ˈlär-nē\ three lakes SW Ireland in County Kerry

Kill Dev·il \ˈkil-ˌde-vəl\ hill E N.C. near village of **Kit·ty Hawk** \ˈki-tē-ˌhȯk\ on sand barrier opposite Albemarle Sound

Kil·leen \ki-ˈlēn\ city *cen* Tex. N of Austin *pop* 63,535

Kil·lie·cran·kie \ˌki-lē-ˈkraŋ-kē\ mountain pass *cen* Scotland in Tayside in the SE Grampians NW of Pitlochry

Kill Van Kull \kil-(ˌ)van-ˈkəl, -vən-\ channel bet. N.J. & Staten Is., N.Y., connecting Newark Bay & Upper New York Bay

Kil·mar·nock \kil-ˈmär-nək\ burgh SW Scotland in Strathclyde *pop* 52,080

Kim·ber·ley \ˈkim-bər-lē\ city Republic of South Africa in E Northern Cape WNW of Bloemfontein *pop* 105,258

Kimberley Plateau *or* **The Kimberley** plateau region N Western Australia N of 19°30'S lat.

Kin·a·ba·lu *or* **Kin·a·bu·lu** \ˌkē-nä-ˈbä-lü\ mountain 13,455 *ft* (4101 *m*) N *cen* N. Borneo; highest in Borneo Is.

Kin·car·dine \kin-ˈkär-dᵊn\ *or* **Kin·car·dine·shire** \-ˌshir, -shər\ *or* **The Mearns** \ˈmᵊrnz, ˈmernz\ former county E Scotland ✶ Stonehaven

Ki·nesh·ma \ˈkē-nish-mə\ city *cen* Russia in Europe NE of Moscow *pop* 104,000

King·man \ˈkiŋ-mən\ reef *cen* Pacific at N end of Line Islands

King's — see OFFALY

Kings Canyon National Park \ˈkiŋz\ reservation SE *cen* Calif. in the Sierra Nevada N of Sequoia National Park

King's Lynn \ˈkiŋz-ˈlin\ *or* **Lynn** *or* **Lynn Re·gis** \ˈrē-jəs\ borough E England in Norfolk near The Wash *pop* 33,340

Kings Mountain ridge N.C. & S.C. SW of Gastonia, N.C.

Kings Peak mountain 13,528 *ft* (4123 *m*) NE Utah in Uinta Mountains; highest point in state

Kings·port \ˈkiŋz-ˌpōrt, -ˌpȯrt\ city NE Tenn. on the Holston *pop* 36,365

Kings·ton \ˈkiŋ-stən\ **1** city SE N.Y. on the Hudson *pop* 23,095 **2** city Canada in SE Ont. on Lake Ontario near head of St. Lawrence River; ✶ of Canada 1841–44 *pop* 56,597 **3** *or in full* **Kingston**

upon (*or* **on**) **Thames** royal borough of SW Greater London, England ✱ of Surrey *pop* 130,600   **4** city & port ✱ of Jamaica on **Kingston Harbor** (inlet of the Caribbean) *pop* 103,771

Kingston upon Hull — see HULL

Kings·town \'kiŋz-ˌtaún\ **1** town & port ✱ of St. Vincent and the Grenadines on St. Vincent Is. at head of Kingstown Bay *pop* 15,670   **2** — see DUN LAOGHAIRE

Kings·ville \'kiŋz-ˌvil, -vəl\ city S Tex. *pop* 25,276

Kinneret, Yam — see GALILEE (Sea of)

Kin·ross \kin-'rós\ *or* **Kin·ross–shire** \-'rósh-ˌshir, -shər\ former county E *cen* Scotland ✱ Kinross

Kin·sha·sa \kin-'shä-sə\ *or formerly* **Lé·o·pold·ville** \'lē-ə-ˌpóld-ˌvil, 'lā-\ city ✱ of Democratic Republic of the Congo on Congo River at outlet of Pool Malebo *pop* 3,804,000

Kin·ston \'kin-stən\ city E N.C. *pop* 25,295

Kin·tyre \kin-'tīr\ peninsula 40 *mi* (64 *km*) long SW Scotland bet. the Atlantic & Firth of Clyde; terminates in **Mull of Kintyre** \'məl\ (cape in N. channel)

Kioga — see KYOGA

Kirghiz Republic *or* **Kirgiz Republic** *or* **Kirghizia** — see KYRGYZSTAN

Ki·ri·ba·ti \'kir-ə-ˌbas—*sic*\ island nation W Pacific SSE of the Marshalls comprising Ocean Island and the Gilbert, Line, & Phoenix groups ✱ Tarawa *area* 277 *sq mi* (717 *sq km*), *pop* 78,600

Ki·rik·ka·le \kə-'ri-kə-ˌlä\ city *cen* Turkey E of Ankara *pop* 185,431

Kirin — see JILIN

Ki·riti·ma·ti \kə-'ris-məs—*sic*\ *or* **Christ·mas** \'kris-məs\ island (atoll) in the Line Islands; largest atoll in the Pacific *area* 234 *sq mi* (608 *sq km*), *pop* 674

Kirjath–arba — see HEBRON

Kirk·cal·dy \(ˌ)kər-'kò-dē, -'kòl-, -'kä-\ royal burgh & port E Scotland in Fife on Firth of Forth N of Edinburgh *pop* 46,314

Kirk·cud·bright \(ˌ)kər-'kü-brē\ *or* **Kirk·cud·bright·shire** \-ˌshir, -shər\ former county S Scotland ✱ Kirkcudbright

Kirk·land \'kərk-lənd\ city W Wash. NE of Seattle *pop* 40,052

Kirk·pat·rick, Mount \ˌkərk-'pa-trik\ mountain 14,856 *ft* (4528 *m*) E Antarctica in Queen Alexandra Range S of Ross Sea

Kir·kuk \kir-'kük\ city NE Iraq SE of Mosul *pop* 175,303

Kirk·wall \'kərk-ˌwòl\ burgh & port N Scotland ✱ of Orkney, on Mainland Is. *pop* 5947

Kirk·wood \'kərk-ˌwúd\ city E Mo. W of St. Louis *pop* 27,291

Ki·rov \'kē-ˌróf, -ˌróv, -rəf\ *or* **Vyat·ka** \vē-'at-kə, -'ät-\ city E *cen* Russia in Europe *pop* 493,000

Kirovabad — see GANCA

Ki·ro·vo·grad \ki-'rō-və-ˌgrad, -ˌgrät\ *or* **Ki·ro·vo·hrad** \-ˌkrät\ *or formerly* **Zi·nov·ievsk** \zə-'nóv-ˌyefsk\ *or* **Eli·sa·vet·grad** \i-ˌli-zə-'vet-ˌgrad, -ˌgrät\ city S *cen* Ukraine *pop* 278,000

Ki·ru·na \'kē-rü-ˌnä\ city N Sweden in Lapland *pop* 26,217

Ki·san·ga·ni \ˌkē-sän-'gä-nē\ *or formerly* **Stan·ley·ville** \'stan-lē-ˌvil\ city NE Democratic Republic of the Congo on Congo River *pop* 373,397

Kish \'kish\ ancient city of Sumer & Akkad E of site of Babylon

Kishinev — see CHIŞINĂU

Kis·ka \'kis-kə\ island SW Alaska; largest & westernmost of Rat Islands of the Aleutians

Kis·maa·yo \kēs-'mä-yō\ *or* **Kis·ma·yu** \kis-'mī-(ˌ)ü\ city & port S Somalia *pop* 30,115

Kis·sim·mee \ki-'si-mē\ **1** river 140 *mi* (225 *km*) S *cen* Fla. flowing SSE from Tohopekaliga Lake through **Lake Kissimmee** (12 *mi or* 19 *km* long) into Lake Okeechobee **2** city Fla. on Tohopekaliga Lake *pop* 30,050

Kistna — see KRISHNA

Ki·su·mu \kē-'sü-(ˌ)mü\ city W Kenya on Lake Victoria *pop* 152,643

Ki·ta·kyu·shu \kē-ˌtä-'kyü-(ˌ)shü\ city & port Japan in N Kyushu formed 1963 by amalgamation of former cities of Kokura, Moji, Tobata, Wakamatsu, & Yawata *pop* 1,026,467

Kitch·e·ner \'kich-nər, 'ki-chə-\ city Canada in SE Ont. *pop* 168,282

Kithairón — see CITHAERON

Kí·thi·ra *or* **Ký·the·ra** *or* **Ký·thi·ra** \'kē-thē-(ˌ)rä\ island W Greece, southernmost of Ionian Islands ✻ **Kíthira** *area* 110 *sq mi* (286 *sq km*)

Kit·ta·tin·ny Mountain \ˌki-tə-'ti-nē\ ridge E U.S. in the Appalachians extending from SE N.Y. through NW N.J. into E Pa.

Kit·tery Point \'ki-tə-rē\ cape Maine at S tip

Kitty Hawk — see KILL DEVIL

Kitz·bü·hel \'kits-ˌbyü(-ə)l, -ˌbü̇(-ə)l\ resort town W Austria in the Tirol *pop* 8119

Ki·vu, Lake \'kē-(ˌ)vü\ lake 60 *mi* (96 *km*) long & 30 *mi* (48 *km*) wide E Democratic Republic of the Congo in Great Rift Valley N of Lake Tanganyika *area* 1042 *sq mi* (2699 *sq km*)

Ki·zil Ir·mak \kə-ˌzil-ir-'mäk\ *or anc* **Ha·lys** \'hā-ləs\ river 715 *mi* (1150 *km*) N *cen* Turkey flowing W & NE into Black Sea

Kjö·len Mountains \'chȫ-lən\ mountains on border bet. NE Norway & NW Sweden; highest Kebnekaise (in Sweden) 6965 *ft* (2123 *m*)

Kla·gen·furt \'klä-gən-ˌfu̇rt\ city S Austria ✻ of Carinthia WSW of Graz *pop* 89,415

Klai·pe·da \'klī-pə-də\ *or* **Me·mel** \'mä-məl\ city & port W Lithuania on the Baltic *pop* 208,300

Klam·ath \'kla-məth\ river 250 *mi* (402 *km*) S Oreg. & NW Calif. flowing from Upper Klamath Lake SW into the Pacific

Klamath Mountains mountains S Oreg. & NW Calif. in the Coast Ranges; highest Mt. Eddy (in Calif.) 9038 *ft* (2755 *m*)

Kle·ve \'klā-və\ city W Germany WSW of Münster *pop* 46,450

Klon·dike \'klän-ˌdīk\ **1** river 90 *mi* (145 *km*) Canada in *cen* Yukon Territory flowing W into the Yukon **2** the Klondike River valley

Klu·ane National Park \klü-'ó-nē, -'ä-\ reservation Canada in SW Yukon Territory

Kly·az·ma \klē-'az-mə\ river *ab* 390 *mi* (630 *km*) *cen* Russia in Europe flowing E to join the Oka W of Nizhniy Novgorod

Knos·sos *or* **Cnos·sus** *or* **Gnos·sus** \'nä-səs\ ruined city ✻ of ancient Crete near N coast SE of modern Iraklion

Knox·ville \'näks-ˌvil, -vəl\ city E Tenn. on Tennessee River *pop* 165,121

Knud Ras·mus·sen Land \'(k)nüd-'ras-mə-sən, -'räs-,mü-s°n\ region N & NW Greenland NE of Baffin Bay

Ko·ba·rid \'kō-bə-,rēd\ *or It* **Ca·po·ret·to** \,ka-pə-'re-(,)tō, ,kä-pō-\ village W Slovenia on the Isonzo NE of Udine, Italy

Ko·be \'kō-bē, -,bā\ city & port Japan in S Honshu on Osaka Bay *pop* 1,477,423

København — see COPENHAGEN

Ko·blenz *or* **Co·blenz** \'kō-,blents\ city W Germany SSE of Cologne at confluence of the Rhine & the Moselle *pop* 109,046

Ko·buk Valley National Park \kō-'bùk\ reservation W Alaska N of the arctic circle along **Kobuk River**

Ko·ca \kō-'jä\ river *ab* 75 *mi* (121 *km*) S Turkey flowing SW & S into the Mediterranean

Ko·ca·bas \,kō-jə-'bäsh\ *or anc* **Gra·ni·cus** \grə-'nī-kəs\ river NW Turkey in Asia flowing NE to Sea of Marmara

Ko·chi \'kō-chē\ city & port Japan in S Shikoku *pop* 317,090

Ko·di·ak \'kō-dē-,ak\ island S Alaska in Gulf of Alaska E of Alaska Peninsula

Ko·dok \'kō-,däk\ *or formerly* **Fa·sho·da** \fə-'shō-də\ town SE Sudan on White Nile River

Ko·ha·la Mountains \kō-'hä-lä\ mountains Hawaii in N Hawaii (island); highest *ab* 5500 *ft* (1676 *m*)

Ko·hi·ma \'kō-,hē-mä, 'kō-hē-\ town NE India ✳ of Nagaland *pop* 53,122

Koil — see ALIGARH

Ko·kand \kō-'kand\ *or* **Qŭ·qon** \kú-'kòn\ **1** region & former khanate E Uzbekistan **2** city in Kokand region SE of Tashkent *pop* 175,000

Ko·ko·mo \'kō-kə-,mō\ city N cen Ind. *pop* 44,962

Koko Nor — see QINGHAI

Kok·so·ak \'käk-sō-,ak\ river 85 *mi* (136 *km*) Canada N Que. formed by confluence of the Caniapiskau and the Larch and flowing into Ungave Bay

Ko·la Peninsula \'kō-lə\ peninsula 250 *mi* (402 *km*) long & 150 *mi* (241 *km*) wide NW Russia in Europe bet. Barents & White seas

Ko·lar Gold Fields \kō-'lär\ city S India in SE Karnataka *pop* 156,398

Kold·ing \'kò-leŋ\ city & port Denmark *pop* 57,128

Kol·ha·pur \'kō-lə-,pùr\ city W India in SW Maharashtra SSE of Bombay *pop* 406,370

Kolmar — see COLMAR

Köln — see COLOGNE

Ko·ly·ma *or* **Ko·li·ma** \kə-'lē-mə, ,kə-li-'mä\ river 1110 *mi* (1786 *km*) NE Russia in Asia flowing from Kolyma Mountains NE into E. Siberian Sea

Kolyma Mountains *or* **Kolima Mountains** mountain range Russia in Asia in NE Khabarovsk Territory parallel to coast of Penzhinskaya Bay

Ko·man·dor·ski Islands \,kä-mən-'dòr-skē\ *or* **Com·mand·er Islands** \kə-'man-dər\ islands E Russia in Asia in Bering Sea E of Kamchatka Peninsula *area* 850 *sq mi* (2210 *sq km*)

Ko·ma·ti \kō-'mä-tē\ river 500 *mi* (805 *km*) S Africa flowing from N Drakensberg Mountains in NE Republic of South Africa E & N into Delagoa Bay in S Mozambique

Ko·mi Republic \'kō-mē\ autonomous republic NE Russia in Europe W of N Ural Mountains ✱ Syktyvkar *area* 160,579 *sq mi* (415,900 *sq km*), *pop* 1,255,000

Kommunizma, Pik — see COMMUNISM PEAK

Ko·mo·do \kə-'mō-(,)dō\ island Indonesia in the Lesser Sundas E of Sumbawa Is. & W of Flores Is. *area* 185 *sq mi* (481 *sq km*)

Kom·so·molsk \käm-sə-'mólsk\ city E Russia in Asia in S Khabarovsk Territory on the Amur

Ko·na \'kō-nä\ coast region Hawaii in W Hawaii (island)

Königgrätz — see HRADEC KRALOVE

Königsberg — see KALININGRAD

Kö·niz \'kā-nəts, 'kə(r)-, 'kē-\ commune W cen Switzerland SW of Bern *pop* 36,101

Kon·kan \'kän-kən\ region W India in W Maharashtra bordering on Arabian Sea & extending from Bombay S to Goa

Konstanz — see CONSTANCE

Kon·ya \kó-'nyä\ *or anc* **Ico·ni·um** \ī-'kō-nē-əm\ city SW cen Turkey on edge of cen plateau *pop* 513,346

Ko·o·lau \,kō-ō-'lä-(,)ü\ mountains Hawaii in E Oahu

Koo·te·nai *or (in Canada)* **Koo·te·nay** \'kü-t³n-,ā, -t³n-ē\ river 407 *mi* (655 *km*) SW Canada & NW U.S. in B.C., Mont., & Idaho flowing through **Kootenay Lake** (65 *mi* or 104 *km* long, in B.C.) into Columbia River

Kootenay National Park reservation Canada in SE B.C. including section of the upper Kootenay River

Ko·per \'kō-,per\ *or* **Ko·par** \-,pär\ *or It* **Ca·po·dis·tria** \,ka-pə-'dis-trē-ə, ,kä-pō-'dēs-\ town & port SW Slovenia at N end of Istrian Peninsula SSW of Trieste *pop* 25,272

Ko·peysk \kə-'pyäsk\ city SW Russia in Asia SE of Chelyabinsk *pop* 78,300

Kor·do·fan \,kór-də-'fan\ region cen Sudan W & N of White Nile River; chief city El Obeid

Ko·rea \kə-'rē-ə, esp Southern (,)kō-\ **1** peninsula 600 *mi* (966 *km*) long & 135 *mi* (217 *km*) wide E Asia bet. Yellow Sea & Sea of Japan **2** *or Jp* **Cho·sen** \'chō-'sen\ country coextensive with the peninsula; once a kingdom & (1910–45) a Japanese dependency ✱ Seoul; divided 1948 at 38th parallel into republics of **North Korea** \(,)kō-\ (*or* Pyongyang *area* 46,609 *sq mi or* 120,717 *sq km, pop* 22,646,000) & **South Korea** ✱ Seoul *area* 38,022 *sq mi or* 98,477 *sq km, pop* 44,042,000) — **Ko·re·an** \kə-'rē-ən esp Southern (,) kō-\

Korea Bay arm of Yellow Sea bet. Liaodong Peninsula & N. Korea

Korea Strait strait 120 *mi* (193 *km*) wide bet. S S. Korea & SW Japan connecting Sea of Japan & Yellow Sea

Kórinthos — see CORINTH

Kort·rijk \'kórt-,rīk\ *or* **Cour·trai** \kür-'trā\ commune NW Belgium in W. Flanders on the Leie NNE of Lille *pop* 76,141

Kos *or* **Cos** \'käs, 'kós\ **1** island Greece in the Dodecanese *area* 111 *sq mi* (289 *sq km*) **2** chief town on the island

Kos·ci·us·ko, Mount \,kä-zē-'əs-(,)kō, ,kä-sē-\ mountain 7310 *ft* (2228 *m*) SE Australia in SE New South Wales; highest in Great Dividing Range & in Australia

Ko·shi·ga·ya \kō-'shē-gä-yä; ,kō-shi-'gī-ə\ city Japan on Honshu *pop* 285,280

Ko·si·ce \'kò-shēt-,sā\ city E Slovakia *pop* 234,840

Ko·so·vo \'kò-sò-,vō, 'kä-\ autonomous province S Yugoslavia *area* 4203 *sq mi* (10,886 *sq km*), *pop* 1,954,747

Kos·rae \'kòs-,rī\ islands E Carolines, part of Federated States of Micronesia

Ko·stro·ma \,käs-trə-'mä\ city *cen* Russia in Europe on the Volga *pop* 282,000

Ko·sza·lin \kò-'shä-,lēn\ city NW Poland *pop* 107,580

Kotabaru — see JAYAPURA

Ko·ta Ba·ha·ru \,kō-tə-bä-hä-,rü\ city Malaysia in N Peninsular Malaysia ✳ of Kelantan *pop* 281,161

Ko·ta Kin·a·ba·lu \'kō-tə,-ki-nə-bə-'lü\ *or formerly* **Jes·sel·ton** \'je-səl-tən\ city & port Malaysia ✳ of Sabah *pop* 112,758

Ko·tor \'kō-,tòr\ *or It* **Cat·ta·ro** \'kä-tä-,rō\ town & port SW Yugoslavia in Montenegro on an inlet of the Adriatic *pop* 22,496

Kottbus — see COTTBUS

Kot·te \'kō-(,)tā\ town W Sri Lanka, a suburb ESE of Colombo *pop* 109,000

Kot·ze·bue Sound \'kät-si-,byü\ arm of Chukchi Sea NW Alaska NE of Bering Strait

Kou·chi·bou·guac National Park \kü-,shē-bü-'gwäk\ reservation SE Canada in E N.B.

Kou·dou·gou \kü-'dü-(,)gü\ town *cen* Burkina Faso *pop* 106,000

Kovno — see KAUNAS

Kow·loon \'kaù-'lün\ **1** peninsula SE China in Hong Kong opposite Hong Kong Is. **2** city on Kowloon Peninsula

Koy·u·kuk \'kī-ə-,kək\ river *ab* 500 *mi* (800 *km*) N *cen* Alaska flowing from Brooks Range SW into Yukon River

Kozhikode — see CALICUT

Kra, Isthmus of \'krä\ isthmus S Thailand in N *cen* Malay Peninsula; 40 *mi* (64 *km*) wide at narrowest part

Krak·a·tau \,kra-kə-'taù\ *or* **Krak·a·toa** \-'tō-ə\ island & volcano Indonesia bet. Sumatra & Java

Kra·ków *or* **Cra·cow** \'krä-,kaù, 'kra-; 'krä-, -(,)kō, *Pol* 'krä-,küf\ city S Poland on the Vistula *pop* 748,356

Kras — see KARST

Kras·no·dar \,kräs-nə-'där\ **1** territory S Russia in Europe in N Caucasus region *area* 32,278 *sq mi* (83,600 *sq km*), *pop* 5,004,000 **2** *or formerly* **Eka·te·ri·no·dar** \i-,kä-tə-'rē-nə-,där\ city, its ✳, on the Kuban *pop* 635,000

Kras·no·yarsk Territory \,kräs-nə-'yärsk\ **1** territory W *cen* Russia in Asia extending along valley of the Yenisey from Arctic Ocean to Sayan Mountains *area* 927,258 *sq mi* (2,401,598 *sq km*), *pop* 3,122,000 **2** city, its ✳, on the upper Yenisey *pop* 925,000

Kre·feld \'krä-,felt\ *or formerly* **Krefeld–Uer·ding·en** \-'ùr-diŋ-ən, -'ùr-\ city W Germany on the Rhine WSW of Essen *pop* 245,772

Krim — see CRIMEA

Krish·na \'krish-nə\ *or formerly* **Kist·na** \'kist-nə\ river 800 *mi* (1287 *km*) S India flowing from Western Ghats E into Bay of Bengal

Kristiania — see OSLO

Kris·tian·sand \'kris-chən-,sand, 'kris-tē-ən-,sän\ city & port SW Norway on the Skagerrak SW of Oslo *pop* 64,888

Kris·tian·sund \'kris-chən-,sənd, 'kris-tē-ən-,sún\ city & port W Norway *pop* 17,121

Kriti — see CRETE

Kri·voy Rog \,kri-,vói-'rōg, -'rók\ *or* **Kryv·yy Rih** \kri-'vē-'rik\ city SE *cen* Ukraine NE of Odessa *pop* 724,000

Kron·shtadt \'krōn-,shtät\ city W Russia in Europe on island in E Gulf of Finland W of St. Petersburg *pop* 45,300

Kru·ger National Park \'krü-gər\ game reserve NE Republic of South Africa in E parts of Northern & Mpumalanga provinces on Mozambique border

Kru·gers·dorp \'krü-gərz-,dórp\ city NE Republic of South Africa in Gauteng W of Johannesburg *pop* 92,725

Krung Thep — see BANGKOK

K2 \,kā-'tü\ *or* **God·win Aus·ten** \,gä-dwən-'ós-tən, ,gó-, -'äs-\ mountain 28,250 *ft* (8611 *m*) N Kashmir in Karakoram Range; 2d highest in the world

Kua·la Lum·pur \,kwä-lə-'lùm-,púr, -'ləm-, ,lùm-'\ city ✳ of Malaysia in Peninsular Malaysia *pop* 1,145,075

Kuang–chou — see GUANGZHOU

Ku·ban \kü-'banʸ, -'bän\ river over 550 *mi* (885 *km*) S Russia in Europe flowing from the Caucasus N & W into Sea of Azov

Ku·ching \'kü-chiŋ\ city & port Malaysia ✳ of Sarawak *pop* 231,490

Ku·dus \'kü-,düs\ city Indonesia in *cen* Java NE of Semarang

Kuei — see GUI

Kuei–lin — see GUILIN

Kuei–yang — see GUIYANG

Kufra — see AL KUFRAH

Ku·iu Island \'kü-(,)yü\ island SE Alaska in *cen* Alexander Archipelago

Ku·la Gulf \'kü-lə\ body of water 17 *mi* (27 *km*) long in the Solomons bet. New Georgia & adjacent islands

Kuldja — see YINING

Kum \'kùm\ river 247 *mi* (398 *km*) *cen* S. Korea flowing into Yellow Sea

Ku·ma·mo·to \,kü-mä-'mō-(,)tō\ city Japan in W Kyushu *pop* 636,144

Ku·ma·si \kü-'mä-sē, -'ma-\ city S *cen* Ghana in Ashanti *pop* 385,192

Kumgang — see DIAMOND

Kumilla — see COMILLA

Kunene — see CUNENE

Kun·lun \'kün-'lün\ mountains W China extending from the Pamirs & Karakoram Range E along N edge of Tibetan plateau to SE Qinghai — see MUZTAG

Kun·ming \'kün-'miŋ\ *or formerly* **Yun·nan** \'yü-'nän\ *or* **Yun·nan-fu** \-'fü\ city S China ✳ of Yunnan *pop* 1,127,411

Kun·san \'gün-,sän\ city & port W S. Korea on Yellow Sea at mouth of the Kum *pop* 218,216

Kuo·pio \'kwó-pē-,ó\ city S *cen* Finland *pop* 81,391

Ku·pre·a·nof \,kü-prē-'a-,nóf\ island SE Alaska in E Alexander Archipelago

Ku·ra \kə-'rä, 'kùr-ə\ river 941 *mi* (1514 *km*) W Asia flowing from NE Turkey ESE through Georgia & Azerbaijan into Caspian Sea

Ku·ra·shi·ki \kü-'rä-shē-kē, ˌkür-ä-'shē-kē\ city Japan on Honshu *pop* 416,703

Kur·di·stan \ˌkür-də-'stan, ˌkər-, -'stän; 'kər-də-ˌ\ region SW Asia chiefly in E Turkey, NW Iran, & N Iraq

Ku·re Atoll \'kür-ē, 'kyür-; \kü-(ˌ)rä\ *or* **Ocean Island** island *cen* Pacific in Hawaii, westernmost of the Leewards

Kurg — see COORG

Kur·gan \kür-'gan, -'gän\ city SW Russia in Asia E of Chelyabinsk *pop* 365,000

Ku·ria Mu·ria Islands \ˌkür-ē-ə-'mür-ē-ə, ˌkyür-, -'myür-\ islands Oman in Arabian Sea off SW coast *area* 28 *sq mi* (73 *sq km*), *pop* 85

Ku·ril Islands *or* **Ku·rile Islands** \'kyür-ˌēl, 'kür-; kyü-'rēl, kü-\ islands Russia in the Pacific bet. S Kamchatka & NE Hokkaido, Japan; belonged 1875–1945 to Japan *area* 6023 *sq mi* (15,600 *sq km*)

Kurisches Haff — see COURLAND LAGOON

Kur·nool \kər-'nül\ city S India in W Andhra Pradesh SSW of Hyderabad *pop* 236,313

Kursk \'kürsk\ city SW Russia in Europe on the Seym *pop* 435,000

Kush — see CUSH

Kus·ko·kwim \'kəs-kə-ˌkwim\ river *ab* 600 *mi* (965 *km*) SW Alaska flowing SW into **Kuskokwim Bay** (inlet of Bering Sea)

Kut, Al — see AL KUT

Ku·tah·ya *or* **Ku·ta·iah** \kü-'tä-yə\ city W *cen* Turkey *pop* 130,944

Kutch \'kəch\ former principality & state W India N of Gulf of Kachchh ✱ Bhuj; now part of Gujarat

Kutch, Gulf of — see KACHCHH (Gulf of)

Kutch, Rann of — see KACHCHH (Rann of)

Ku·wait \kü-'wāt\ **1** country SW Asia in Arabia at head of Persian Gulf; a sheikhdom, before 1961 under Brit. protection *area* 6880 *sq mi* (17,819 *sq km*), *pop* 1,355,827 **2** city & port, its ✱ *pop* 181,774 — **Ku·waiti** \-'wā-tē\ *adj or n*

Kuybyshev — see SAMARA

Kuz·netsk \küz-'netsk\ city SE *cen* Russia in Europe *pop* 101,000

Kuznetsk Basin basin of the Tom W *cen* Russia in Asia extending from Novokuznetsk to Tomsk

Kwa·ja·lein \'kwä-jə-lən, -ˌlān\ island (atoll) 78 *mi* (126 *km*) long W Pacific in Ralik chain of the Marshalls

Kwan·do \'kwän-(ˌ)dō\ river *ab* 500 *mi* (804 *km*) S Africa flowing from *cen* Angola SE & E into the Zambezi just above Victoria Falls

Kwang·cho·wan \'gwän-'jō-'wän, 'kwän-\ former territory SE China in Kwangtung on Leizhou Peninsula; leased 1898–1946 to France ✱ Fort Bayard *area* 325 *sq mi* (845 *sq km*)

Kwang·ju \'gwäŋ-(ˌ)jü, 'kwäŋ-\ city SW S. Korea *pop* 905,896

Kwangsi Chuang — see GUANGXI ZHUANGZU

Kwangtung — see GUANGDONG

Kwan·tung \'gwän-'düŋ, 'kwän-'tùŋ\ former territory NE China in S Manchuria at tip of Liaodong Peninsula; leased to Russia 1898–1905, to Japan 1905–45, & to Russia again 1945–55; included cities of Port Arthur & Dairen

Kwanza — see CUANZA

Kwathlamba — see DRAKENSBERG

Kwa·Zu·lu \kwä-'zü-(,)lü\ former group of noncontiguous black enclaves in E Republic of South Africa; incorporated into KwaZulu· Natal 1994

KwaZulu–Natal province E Republic of South Africa bet. Drakensberg Mountains & Indian Ocean *area* 35,591 *sq mi* (92,180 *sq km*), *pop* 8,553,000

Kweichow — see GUIZHOU

Kweilin — see GUILIN

Kyo·ga *or* **Kio·ga** \kē-'ō-gə\ lake *cen* Uganda N of Lake Victoria traversed by the Victoria Nile

Kyo·to \'kyō-(,)tō\ city Japan in W *cen* Honshu NNE of Osaka; formerly (794–1869) ✽ of Japan *pop* 1,461,140

Kyr·gyz·stan \,kir-gi-'stän, -'stän; 'kir-gi-,\ independent country W *cen* Asia; a constituent republic (**Kir·giz Republic** *or* **Kir·ghiz Republic** \(,)kir-'gēz\) of the U.S.S.R. 1936–91; ✽ Bishkek *area* 76,641 *sq mi* (198,500 *sq km*), *pop* 4,526,000

Kythera *or* **Kýthira** — see KÍTHIRA

Kyu·shu \'kyü-(,)shü\ island S Japan S of W end of Honshu *area* over 16,200 *sq mi* (41,958 *sq km*), *pop* 13,296,054

Ky·zyl \ki-'zil\ town S Russia in Asia ✽ of Tuva Republic *pop* 88,000

L

Laayoune — see AAIÚN, EL

Labe — see ELBE

Lab·ra·dor \'la-brə-,dȯr\ **1** peninsula E Canada bet. Hudson Bay & the Atlantic; divided bet. Que. & Nfld. *area* 625,000 *sq mi* (1,618,750 *sq km*) **2** the section of the peninsula belonging to Nfld. 102,485 *sq mi* (265,436 *sq km*) — **Lab·ra·dor·ean** *or* **Lab·ra·dor·ian** \,la-brə-'dȯr-ē-ən, -'dȯr-\ *adj or n*

Labrador Sea arm of the Atlantic bet. Labrador & Greenland

La·bu·an \lä-'bü-än\ island Malaysia off W coast of Sabah *pop* 14,904

La Ca·na·da–Flint·ridge \lä-kə-'nyä-də-'flint-(,)rij\ city SW Calif. NW of Pasadena *pop* 19,378

Lac·ca·dive Islands \'la-kə-,dēv, -,dīv, -div\ *or* **Can·na·nore Islands** \'ka-nə-,nȯr\ islands India in Arabian Sea N of Maldive Islands

Lacedaemon — see SPARTA — **Lac·e·dae·mo·nian** \,la-sə-di-'mō-nē-ən, -nyən\ *adj or n*

La·cey \'lā-sē\ city W Wash. E of Olympia *pop* 19,279

La Chaux–de–Fonds \lä-,shō-də-'fōⁿ\ commune W Switzerland in Neuchâtel canton in Jura Mountains WNW of Bern *pop* 36,107

La·chine \lä-'shēn\ town Canada in S Que. above the **Lachine Rapids** on St. Lawrence River SW of Montreal *pop* 35,266

La·chish \'lā-kish\ ancient city S Palestine W of Hebron

Lach·lan \'lä-klən\ river 800 *mi* (1287 *km*) SE Australia in *cen* New South Wales flowing W into the Murrumbidgee

Lack·a·wan·na \\,la-kə-'wä-nə\ city W N.Y. *pop* 20,585

Lac Mai–Ndombe — see MAI-NDOMBE (Lac)

La·co·nia \lə-'kō-nē-ə, -nyə\ ancient country S Greece in SE Peloponnese bordering on the Aegean & the Mediterranean ✻ Sparta — **La·co·ni·an** \-nē-ən, -nyən\ *adj or n*

Laconia, Gulf of inlet of the Mediterranean on S coast of Greece in Peloponnese bet. Capes Matapan & Malea

La Co·ru·ña \,lä-kō-'rü-nyä\ **1** province NW Spain in Galicia bordering on the Atlantic *area* 3041 *sq mi* (7876 *sq km*), *pop* 1,096,966 **2** *or* **Co·run·na** \kə-'rə-nə\ commune & port, its ✻ *pop* 246,953

La Crosse \lə-'krós\ city W Wis. *pop* 51,003

La·dakh \lə-'däk\ district N India in E Kashmir on border of Tibet ✻ Leh *area* 45,762 *sq mi* (118,981 *sq km*) — **La·dakhi** \-'dä-kē\ *adj or n*

Lad·o·ga, Lake \'la-də-gə, 'lä-\ lake W Russia in Europe near St. Petersburg *area* 6835 *sq mi* (17,703 *sq km*); largest in Europe

Ladrone — see MARIANA

La·dy·smith \'lā-dē-,smith\ city E Republic of South Africa in W KwaZulu-Natal *pop* 28,920

Lae \'lä-,ā\ city Papua New Guinea on Huon Gulf *pop* 80,655

La·fay·ette \,la-fē-'et, ,lä-\ **1** city W Calif. E of Berkeley *pop* 23,501 **2** city W cen Ind. *pop* 43,764 **3** city S La. *pop* 94,440

La·gash \'lā-,gash\ ancient city of Sumer bet. the Euphrates & the Tigris at modern village of Telloh \te-'lō\ in S Iraq

Lagoa dos Patos — see PATOS (Lagoa dos)

La·gos \'lā-,gäs, -,gōs\ city & port, former ✻ of Nigeria on an offshore island in Bight of Benin & on mainland opposite the island *pop* 1,340,000

La Goulette — see HALQ AL-WADI

La Grange \lə-'grānj\ city W Ga. *pop* 25,597

La Granja — see SAN ILDEFONSO

La Guai·ra \lə-'gwī-rə\ city N Venezuela on the Caribbean; port for Caracas *pop* 20,344

La·gu·na Beach \lə-'gü-nə\ city SW Calif. SE of Long Beach *pop* 23,170

Laguna Madre — see MADRE (Laguna)

La·gu·na Ni·guel \lä-'gü-nə-nē-'gel\ city Calif. *pop* 44,400

La Habana — see HAVANA

La Ha·bra \lə-'hä-brə\ city SW Calif. SE of Los Angeles *pop* 51,266

La Hogue \lə-'hōg\ roadstead NW France in English Channel off E coast of Cotentin Peninsula

La·hore \lə-'hōr, -'hór\ city Pakistan in E Punjab province near the Ravi *pop* 2,922,000

Lah·ti \'lä-tē\ city S Finland NNE of Helsinki *pop* 93,132

La Jol·la \lə-'hói-ə\ a NW section of San Diego, Calif.

Lake Charles \'chär(-ə)lz\ city SW La. *pop* 70,580

Lake Clark National Park \'klärk\ reservation S cen Alaska WSW of Anchorage

Lake District area NW England in S Cumbria & NW Lancashire containing many lakes & peaks

Lake Hav·a·su City \'ha-və-,sü\ city Ariz. *pop* 24,363

Lake Jack·son \'jak-sən\ city SE Tex. *pop* 22,776

Lake·land \'lāk-lənd\ city cen Fla. E of Tampa pop 70,576

Lake Os·we·go \ä-'swē-(,)gō\ city NW Oreg. S of Portland pop 30,576

Lake·ville \'lāk-,vil\ village SE Minn. SE of Minneapolis pop 24,854

Lake·wood \'lāk-,wúd\ **1** city SW Calif. NE of Long Beach pop 73,557 **2** city N cen Colo. N of Denver pop 126,481 **3** city NE Ohio on Lake Erie W of Cleveland pop 59,718

Lake Worth \'wərth\ city SE Fla. on Lake Worth (lagoon) S of W. Palm Beach pop 28,564

Lak·shad·weep \lək-'shä-,dwēp\ or formerly **Lac·ca·dive, Min·i·coy, and Amin·di·vi Islands** \'la-kə-,dēv, -,dīv; 'mi-ni-,kói; -mən-'dē-vē\ union territory India comprising the Laccadive group ✻ Kavaratti area 11 sq mi (29 sq km), pop 51,707

La Lí·nea \lä-'lē-nä-ä\ commune SW Spain on Bay of Algeciras pop 57,918

La Man·cha \lä-'män-chä, lə-'man-chə\ region S cen Spain in S New Castile — **Man·che·gan** \man-'chē-gən, män-'chä-\ adj or n

La Mau·ri·cie National Park \lä-,mòr-ē-'sē\ reservation SE Canada in S Quebec

Lam·ba·ré·né \,läm-bä-rä-'nä\ city W Gabon pop 17,770

Lam·beth \'lam-bəth, -,beth\ borough of S Greater London, England pop 220,100

La Me·sa \lə-'mā-sə\ city SW Calif. NE of San Diego pop 52,931

La·mia \lä-'mē-ä\ city E cen Greece NW of Thermopylae pop 43,898

La Mi·ra·da \,lä-mə-'rä-də\ city SW Calif. SE of Los Angeles pop 40,452

Lam·mer·muir \'la-mər-,myúr\ or **Lam·mer·moor** \-,múr\ hills SE Scotland in Lothian & Borders regions

Lam·pe·du·sa \,lam-pə-'dü-sə, ,läm-pe-'dü-zə\ island Italy in the Pelagians

La·nai \lə-'nī, lä-\ island Hawaii W of Maui area 141 sq mi (367 sq km)

Lan·ark \'la-nərk\ **1** or **Lan·ark·shire** \-,shir, -shər\ former county S cen Scotland; chief city Glasgow **2** burgh cen Scotland in Strathclyde SE of Glasgow pop 9778

Lan·ca·shire \'laŋ-kə-,shir, -shər\ or **Lan·cas·ter** \'laŋ-kəs-tər\ county NW England bordering on Irish Sea ✻ Preston area 1217 sq mi (3152 sq km), pop 1,365,100

Lan·cas·ter \'laŋ-kəs-tər; 'lan-,kas-tər, 'laŋ-\ **1** city SW Calif. NE of Los Angeles pop 97,291 **2** city S cen Ohio SE of Columbus pop 34,507 **3** city SE Pa. pop 55,551 **4** city NE Tex. S of Dallas pop 22,117 **5** city NW England in Lancashire pop 125,600 — **Lan·cas·tri·an** \laŋ-'kas-trē-ən, lan-\ adj or n

Landes \'länd\ coastal region SW France on Bay of Biscay bet. Gironde Estuary & the Adour

Land's End \'landz-'end\ cape SW England at SW tip of Cornwall; extreme W point of England, at 5°41′W

Lang·dale Pikes \'laŋ-,dāl\ two mountain peaks NW England in Cumbria in Lake District

Lang·ley \'laŋ-lē\ city Canada in B.C. ESE of Vancouver pop 66,040

Lan·gue·doc \laŋ-gə-'däk, ˌläŋ-'dȯk\ region & former province S France extending from Auvergne to the Mediterranean

Lan·sing \'lan-siŋ\ **1** village NE Ill. SSE of Chicago *pop* 28,086 **2** city S Mich., its ✳ *pop* 127,321

Lan Tau \'län-'daů\ island Hong Kong, China W of Hong Kong Is. *area* 58 *sq mi* (151 *sq km*)

La·nús \lä-'nüs\ city E Argentina S of Buenos Aires *pop* 466,755

Lan·zhou *or* **Lan-chou** \'län-'jō\ city N *cen* China ✳ of Gansu *pop* 1,194,640

La·od·i·cea \(ˌ)lā-ˌä-də-'sē-ə, ˌlā-ə-\ **1** ancient city W *cen* Asia Minor in Phrygia **2** — see LATAKIA — **La·od·i·ce·an** \-'sē-ən\ *adj or n*

Laoighis \'lāsh, 'lēsh\ *or* **Leix** \'lāsh, 'lēsh\ *or formerly* **Queen's** county *res* in Ireland in Leinster ✳ Portlaoighise *area* 664 *sq mi* (1726 *sq km*), *pop* 52,314

Laon \läⁿ\ commune N France NE of Paris *pop* 28,670

Laos \'laůs, 'lä-(ˌ)ōs, 'lä-ˌäs\ country SE Asia; a republic, until 1975 a kingdom; formerly a state of French Indochina; ✳ Vientiane *area* 91,428 *sq mi* (236,799 *sq km*), *pop* 4,533,000 — **Lao·tian** \lä-'ō-shən, 'laů-shən\ *adj or n*

La Pal·ma \lä-'päl-mä\ island Spain in Canary Islands; chief town Santa Cruz de la Palma *area* 280 *sq mi* (728 *sq km*)

La Paz \lä-'päz, -'päs, -'paz\ **1** city, administrative ✳ of Bolivia E of Lake Titicaca at altitude of 12,001 *ft* (3658 *m*), *metropolitan area pop* 711,036 **2** town W Mexico ✳ of Baja California Sur on **La Paz Bay** (inlet of Gulf of California) *pop* 46,011

Lap·land \'lap-ˌland, -lənd\ region N Europe above the arctic circle in N Norway, N Sweden, N Finland, & Kola Peninsula of Russia — **Lap·land·er** \-ˌlan-dər, -lən-\ *n* — **Lapp** \'lap\ *n* — **Lap·pish** \'la-pish\ *adj or n*

La Pla·ta \lä-'plä-tä\ city E Argentina SE of Buenos Aires *pop* 542,567

La Plata Peak \lə-'plä-tə, -'plä-\ mountain 14,336 *ft* (4370 *m*) *cen* Colo. in Sawatch Mountains

La Porte \lə-'pȯrt, -'pȯrt\ **1** city N Ind. *pop* 21,507 **2** city SE Tex. on Galveston Bay *pop* 27,910

Lap·tev Sea \'lap-ˌtef, -ˌtev\ *or formerly* **Nor·den·skjöld Sea** \'nȯr-d°n-ˌsheld, -ˌshůld, -ˌsheld\ arm of Arctic Ocean Russia bet. Taymyr Peninsula & New Siberian Islands

La Pu·en·te \lä-'pwen-tä\ city SW Calif. ESE of Los Angeles *pop* 36,955

L'Aqui·la \'lä-kwē-lä\ commune *cen* Italy NE of Rome ✳ of Abruzzi *pop* 66,863

Lar·a·mie \'lar-ə-mē\ **1** river 216 *mi* (348 *km*) N Colo. & SE Wyo. flowing N & NE into N. Platte River **2** city SE Wyo. *pop* 26,687

Larch \'lärch\ river 270 *mi* (434 *km*) Canada in W Que. flowing NE to unite with the Caniapiskau forming Koksoak River

La·re·do \lə-'rä-(ˌ)dō\ city S Tex. on Rio Grande *pop* 122,899

Lar·go \'lär-(ˌ)gō\ town W Fla. S of Clearwater *pop* 65,674

La Rio·ja \lä-rē-'ō-hä\ province N Spain along the upper Ebro ✳ Lagroño *area* 1944 *sq mi* (5035 *sq km*), *pop* 263,434

La·ris·sa \lə-'ri-sə\ city N *cen* Greece in E Thessaly *pop* 113,426

Lar·i·stan \ˌlar-ə-'stan\ region S Iran bordering on Persian Gulf

Larne \'lärn\ district NE Northern Ireland, established 1974 *area* 131 *sq mi* (341 *sq km*), *pop* 29,181

La Ro·chelle \,lä-rō-'shel\ city & port W France *pop* 72,936

Lar·vik \'lär-vik\ town & port SE Norway *pop* 38,019

La·Salle \lə-'sal\ town Canada in S Que. on the St. Lawrence *pop* 73,804

Las·caux \là-'skō\ cave SW *cen* France near town of Montignac

Las Cru·ces \läs-'krü-säs\ city S N.Mex. *pop* 62,126

La Se·re·na \lä-sä-'rā-nä\ city N *cen* Chile *pop* 83,283

Las Pal·mas \läs-'päl-mäs\ **1** province Spain comprising the E Canary Islands *area* 1569 *sq mi* (4064 *sq km*), *pop* 767,969 **2** city & port, its ✱, in NE Grand Canary Is. *pop* 342,040

La Spe·zia \lä-'spet-sē-ä\ city & port NW Italy in Liguria *pop* 104,511

Las·sen Peak \'la-sᵊn\ volcano 10,457 *ft* (3187 *m*) N Calif. at S end of Cascade Range; central feature of **Lassen Volcanic National Park**

Las Ve·gas \läs-'vā-gəs\ city SE corner of Nev. *pop* 258,295

Lat·a·kia \,la-tə-'kē-ə\ **1** region NW Syria bordering on the Mediterranean **2** *or anc* **La·od·i·cea** \(,)lä-,ä-də-'sē-ə, ,lä-ə-\ city & port, its chief town, on the Mediterranean *pop* 284,000

La·ti·na \lä-'tē-nä\ commune *cen* Italy *pop* 105,543

Lat·in America — \'la-tᵊn\ **1** Spanish America & Brazil **2** all of the Americas S of the U.S. — **Latin–American** *adj* — **Latin American** *n*

Latin Quarter section of Paris, France, S of the Seine frequented by students & artists

Lat·via \'lat-vē-ə\ independent country N *cen* Europe bordering on the Baltic; an independent republic 1918–40, a constituent republic (**Lat·vi·an Republic** \'lat-vē-ən\) of the U.S.S.R. 1940–91; ✱ Riga *area* 24,595 *sq mi* (63,701 *sq km*), *pop* 2,596,000 — **Lat·vi·an** *adj or n*

Lau·der·dale Lakes \'lȯ-dər-,dāl\ city SE Fla. *pop* 27,341

Lau·der·hill \'lȯ-dər-,hil\ city SE Fla. *pop* 49,708

Laun·ces·ton \'lȯn(t)-səs-tən, 'län(t)-\ city & port Australia in N Tasmania *pop* 62,504

Lau·ra·sia \lȯ-'rā-zhə, -shə\ hypothetical land area believed to have once connected the landmasses of the northern hemisphere except for the Indian subcontinent

Lau·rel \'lȯr-əl, 'lär-\ town S *cen* Md. NNE of Washington, D.C. *pop* 19,438

Lau·ren·tian Mountains \lȯ-'ren(t)-shən\ range Canada in S Que. N of the St. Lawrence on S edge of Canadian Shield

Laurentian Plateau — see CANADIAN SHIELD

Lau·ri·um \'lȯr-ē-əm, 'lär-\ mountain SE Greece at SE tip of Attica

Lau·sanne \lō-'zän, -'zan\ commune W Switzerland ✱ of Vaud canton on Lake Geneva *pop* 124,897

Lausitz — see LUSATIA

La·va Beds National Monument \'lä-və-,bedz, 'la-\ reservation N Calif. SE of Lower Klamath Lake

La·val \lə-'val\ town Canada in S Que. NW of Montreal *pop* 314,398

La Vendée — see VENDÉE

La Verne \lə-'vərn\ city SW Calif. E of Los Angeles *pop* 30,897

Lawn·dale \'lȯn-ˌdāl, 'län-\ city SW Calif. SSW of Los Angeles *pop* 27,331

Law·rence \'lȯr-ən(t)s, 'lär-\ **1** town *cen* Ind. NE of Indianapolis *pop* 26,763 **2** city NE Kans. WSW of Kansas City *pop* 65,608 **3** city NE corner of Mass. *pop* 70,207

Law·ton \'lȯ-tᵊn\ city SW Okla. *pop* 80,561

La'youn — see AAIÚN, EL

Lay·san \'lī-ˌsän\ island Hawaii in the Leewards NW of Niihau

Lay·ton \'lā-tᵊn\ city N Utah N of Salt Lake City *pop* 41,784

La·zio \'lät-sē-ˌō\ *or* **La·tium** \'lā-sh(ē-)əm\ region *cen* Italy bordering on Tyrrhenian Sea & traversed by the Tiber ✳ Rome *pop* 5,170,672

League City \'lēg\ city SE Tex. *pop* 30,159

Leam·ing·ton \'le-miŋ-tən\ *or* **Royal Leamington Spa** borough S *cen* England in Warwickshire *pop* 44,989

Leav·en·worth \'le-vən-ˌwərth\ city NE Kans. on Missouri River NW of Kansas City *pop* 38,495

Lea·wood \'lē-ˌwu̇d\ city E Kans. S of Kansas City *pop* 19,693

Leb·a·non **1** \'le-bə-nən\ city SE *cen* Pa. E of Harrisburg *pop* 24,800 **2** \-nən, -ˌnän\ country SW Asia bordering on the Mediterranean; a republic since 1944, formerly (1920–44) a French mandate ✳ Beirut *area* 3949 *sq mi* (10,228 *sq km*), *pop* 2,909,000 — **Leb·a·nese** \ˌle-bə-'nēz, -'nēs\ *adj or n*

Lebanon Mountains *or anc* **Lib·a·nus** \'li-bə-nəs\ mountains Lebanon running parallel to coast W of Bekaa Valley

Le Bour·get \lə-ˌbu̇r-'zhā\ commune N France, NE suburb of Paris

Lec·ce \'lā-chā, 'le-\ commune SE Italy in Puglia *pop* 100,233

Lec·co \'lā-(ˌ)kō, 'le-\ commune N Italy in Lombardy on SE arm (**Lake Lecco**) of Lake Como *pop* 45,859

Lech \'lek, 'leḵ\ river Austria & Germany flowing from Vorarlberg N into the Danube

Le·do \'lē-(ˌ)dō, 'lā-\ town NE India in NE Assam

Leeds \'lēdz\ city N England in W. Yorkshire *pop* 674,400

Lee's Summit \'lēz\ city W Mo. SE of Kansas City *pop* 46,418

Leeu·war·den \'lā-ü-ˌvär-də(n)\ commune N Netherlands ✳ of Friesland *pop* 86,405

Lee·ward Islands \'lē-wərd, 'lü-ərd\ **1** island chain *cen* Pacific extending 1250 *mi* (2012 *km*) WNW from main islands of the Hawaiian group; includes Nihoa, Necker, Laysan, Midway, & Kure islands **2** *or F* **Iles sous le Vent** \ˌēl-sü-lə-'väⁿ\ islands S Pacific, W group of the Society Islands *pop* 22,232 **3** islands West Indies in the N Lesser Antilles extending from Virgin Islands (on N) to Dominica (on S) **4** former colony Brit. West Indies in the Leewards including Antigua, St. Kitts-Nevis, & Montserrat

Leg·horn \'leg-ˌhȯrn\ *or* **It Li·vor·no** \lē-'vȯr-(ˌ)nō\ commune & port *cen* Italy in Tuscany on Tyrrhenian Sea *pop* 171,346

Leg·ni·ca \leg-'nēt-sä\ city SW Poland *pop* 104,196

Leh \'lā\ town India in E Kashmir on the Indus ✳ of Ladakh

Le Ha·vre \lə-'hävr°, -'häv\ *or formerly* **Le Havre–de–Grâce** \-də-'gräs\ city & port N France on English Channel on N side of Seine estuary *pop* 197,219

Le·high \'lē-ˌhī\ river 100 *mi* (161 *km*) E Pa. flowing SW & SE into Delaware River

Leh·man Caves \\'lē-mən\ limestone caverns E Nev. on E slope of Wheeler Peak in Great Basin National Park

Leices·ter \\'les-tər\ city *cen* England ✳ of Leicestershire *pop* 270,600

Leices·ter·shire \\'les-tər-ˌshir, -shər\ *or* **Leicester** \\'les-tər\ county *cen* England ✳ Leicester *area* 1021 *sq mi* (2644 *sq km*), *pop* 860,500

Lei·den *or* **Ley·den** \\'līd-ᵊn, *D usu* 'lā-də, -yə\ city W Netherlands in S. Holland on a branch of the lower Rhine *pop* 112,976

Leie — see LYS

Lei·ne \\'lī-nə\ river 119 *mi* (192 *km*) *cen* Germany

Lein·ster \\'len(t)-stər\ province E Ireland *area* 7581 *sq mi* (19,635 *sq km*), *pop* 1,382,560

Leip·zig \\'līp-sig, -sik\ city E Germany in Saxony *pop* 503,191

Lei·ria \lā-'rē-ə\ town W *cen* Portugal SSW of Coimbra *pop* 101,325

Leith \\'lēth\ port section of Edinburgh, Scotland, on Firth of Forth

Lei·tha \\'lī-(ˌ)tä\ river 112 *mi* (180 *km*) E Austria & NW Hungary flowing SE into the Raba

Lei·trim \\'lē-trəm\ county NW Ireland in Connacht ✳ Carrick on Shannon *area* 589 *sq mi* (1531 *sq km*), *pop* 25,301

Leix — see LAOIGHIS

Lei·xões \lā-'shoĩ"sh\ town NW Portugal on the Atlantic; port for Porto

Lei·zhou *or* **Lei·chou** \\'lā-'jō\ *or* **Lui·chow** \\'lwē-'jō, -'chaú\ peninsula SE China in Guangdong bet. S. China Sea & Gulf of Tonkin

Lek \\'lek\ river 40 *mi* (64 *km*) Netherlands flowing W into the Atlantic; the N branch of the lower Rhine

Lely·stad \\'lā-lē-ˌstät\ commune *cen* Netherlands ✳ of Flevoland

Le Maine — see MAINE

Leman, Lake — see GENEVA (Lake)

Le Mans \lə-'mä"\ city NW France on the Sarthe *pop* 148,465

Lemberg — see LVIV

Lem·nos \\'lem-ˌnäs, -nəs\ *or NGk* **Lím·nos** \\'lēm-ˌnós\ island Greece in the Aegean ESE of Chalcidice Peninsula; chief town Kástron *area* 177 *sq mi* (458 *sq km*)

Lem·on Grove \\'le-mən\ city S Calif. E of San Diego *pop* 23,984

Le·na \\'lē-nə, 'lā-, 'lye-nə\ river *ab* 2700 *mi* (4345 *km*) E Russia in Asia flowing from mountains W of Lake Baikal NE & N into Laptev Sea through wide delta

Le·nexa \lə-'nek-sə\ city E Kans. SW of Kansas City *pop* 34,034

Leningrad — see SAINT PETERSBURG 2 — **Len·in·grad·er** \\'le-nən-ˌgra-dər, -ˌgrä-\ *n*

Le·nin Peak \\'le-nən, 'lyā-ˌnēn\ mountain 23,405 *ft* (7134 *m*) on border bet. Kyrgyzstan & Tajikistan; highest in Trans Alai Range

Lens \\'lä"s\ city N France SW of Lille *pop* 35,278

Leom·in·ster \\'le-mən-stər\ city *cen* Mass. N of Worcester *pop* 38,145

Le·ón \lā-'ōn\ **1** *or* **León de Los Al·da·mas** \dā-ˌlòs-äl-'dä-mäs, thä-\ city *cen* Mexico in Guanajuato *pop* 872,453 **2** city W Nicaragua *pop* 90,897 **3** region & ancient kingdom NW Spain W of Old Castile **4** province NW Spain in N León region *area* 5972 *sq mi* (15,462 *sq km*), *pop* 525,896 **5** city, its ✳ *pop* 144,021

Le·o·ne, Mon·te \,mōn-tā-lā-'ō-nā\ mountain 11,657 ft (3553 m) on border bet. Switzerland & Italy SW of Simplon Pass; highest in Lepontine Alps

Leopold II, Lake — see MAI-NDOMBE (Lac)

Léopoldville — see KINSHASA

Le·pon·tine Alps \li-'pän-,tīn, 'le-pən-\ range of cen Alps on border bet. Switzerland & Italy — see LEONE (Monte)

Lep·tis Mag·na \,lep-təs-'mag-nə\ ancient seaport N Africa near present-day Al Khums

Lé·ri·da \'ler-i-də, 'lā-rē-thä\ **1** province NE Spain in NW Catalonia area 4644 sq mi (12,028 sq km), pop 353,455 **2** commune, its ✽ pop 111,880

Ler·wick \'lər-(,)wik, 'ler-\ burgh & port N Scotland ✽ of Shetland on Mainland Is. pop 7223

Les·bos \'lez-,bäs, -bəs, -,vòs\ or **Myt·i·le·ne** \,mit-ºl-'ē-nē, ,mē-tē-'lē-\ island Greece in the Aegean off NW Turkey area 630 sq mi (1632 sq km) pop 103,700

Les Ey·zies \,lāz-ā-'zē\ commune SW cen France SE of Périgueux

Le·so·tho \lə-'sō-(,)tō, -'sü-(,)tü\ or formerly **Ba·su·to·land** \bə-'sü-tō-,land\ country S Africa surrounded by Republic of South Africa; a constitutional monarchy, in the Commonwealth of Nations ✽ Maseru area 11,716 sq mi (30,462 sq km), pop 1,903,000

Lesser Antilles islands in the W. Indies including Virgin, Leeward, & Windward Islands, Trinidad, Barbados, Tobago, & islands in the S Caribbean N of Venezuela

Lesser Armenia — see LITTLE ARMENIA

Lesser Slave Lake \'slāv\ lake Canada in cen Alta. draining through the **Lesser Slave River** to Athabasca River area 461 sq mi (1199 sq km)

Lesser Sunda Islands — see SUNDA ISLANDS

Leth·bridge \'leth-(,)brij\ city Canada in S Alta. pop 60,974

Le·ti·cia \lā-'tē-sē-ä\ town SE Colombia on the Amazon

Leuc·tra \'lük-trə\ ancient village Greece in Boeotia SW of Thebes

Leuven — see LOUVAIN

Le·val·lois—Per·ret \lə-,vàl-'wä-pə-'rā\ commune N France on the Seine, NW suburb of Paris pop 47,788

Le·vant \lə-'vant\ the countries bordering on the E Mediterranean — **Le·van·tine** \'le-vən-,tīn, -,tēn, lə-'van-\ adj or n — **Le·vant·er** \lə-'van-tər\ n

Levant States — see SYRIA

Le·ven, Loch \'lē-vən\ **1** inlet of Loch Linnhe W Scotland in Highland region **2** lake 4 mi (6.4 km) long E Scotland SSE of Perth

Le·ver·ku·sen \'lā-vər-,kü-zºn\ city W Germany on the Rhine SE of Düsseldorf pop 161,147

Lé·vis—Lau·zon \'lē-vəs-lō-'zōⁿ, lā-'vē-\ town Canada in S Que. pop 39,452

Lev·kás \lef-'käs\ island Greece in the Ionians at entrance to Ambracian Gulf area 111 sq mi (289 sq km)

Lew·es \'lü-əs\ **1** the upper Yukon River S of its junction with the Pelly **2** borough S England ✽ of E. Sussex on Ouse River S of London

Lew·is and Clark Caverns \'lü-əs-ənd-'klärk\ *or formerly* **Mor·ri·son Cave** \'mȯr-ə-sən, 'mär-\ cavern *cen* Mont. WNW of Bozeman

Lewis and Clark Lake lake 30 *mi* (48 *km*) long SE S.Dak. & NE Nebr. formed by Gavins Point Dam

Lew·i·sham \'lü-ə-shəm\ borough of SE Greater London, England *pop* 215,300

Lew·is·ton \'lü-əs-tən\ **1** city NW Idaho on Wash. border *pop* 28,082 **2** city SW Maine on the Androscoggin opposite Auburn *pop* 39,757

Le·wis·ville \'lü-əs-,vil, -vəl\ city N Tex. *pop* 46,521

Lewis with Har·ris \'lü-əs-with-'har-əs, -with-\ island NW Scotland in the Outer Hebrides divided administratively into **Lewis** (in the N; chief town & port Stornoway) & **Harris** (in the S); largest of the Hebrides, in Western Isles regional division *area* 770 *sq mi* (2002 *sq km*)

Lex·ing·ton \'lek-siŋ-tən\ **1** city N *cen* Kentucky ESE of Frankfort *pop* 225,366 **2** town NE Mass. NW of Boston *pop* 28,974

Leyden — *see* LEIDEN

Ley·te \'lā-tē\ island Philippines in the Visayans W of **Leyte Gulf** (inlet of the Pacific); chief town Tacloban *area* 2785 *sq mi* (7241 *sq km*)

Ley·ton \'lāt-ᵊn\ former municipal borough SE England in Essex, now part of Waltham Forest

Lha·sa \'läs-ə, 'la-\ city SW China ✽ of Tibet *pop* 106,885

Lho·tse \'lȯt-'sā, 'hlȯt-\ mountain 27,923 *ft* (8511 *m*) in Mt. Everest massif S of Mt. Everest; 4th highest in the world

Lian·yun·gang \'lyän-'yün-'gän\ *or* **Lien–yün–kang** \le-'ən-'yün-'gän\ *or formerly* **Tung–hai** \'dùŋ-'hī\ city E China in N Jiangsu *pop* 354,139

Liao \'lyaù\ river 700 *mi* (1126 *km*) NE China flowing into Gulf of Liaodong

Liao·dong *or* **Liao·tung** \'lyaù-'dùŋ\ peninsula NE China in S Liaoning bet. Korea Bay & **Gulf of Liaodong** (arm of Bo Hai)

Liao·ning \'lyaù-'niŋ\ *or formerly* **Feng·tien** \'fəŋ-'tyen\ province NE China in S Manchuria ✽ Shenyang *area* 58,301 *sq mi* (151,583 *sq km*), *pop* 39,459,697

Liao·si \'lyaù-'shē\ former province (1948–54) NE China in S Manchuria bordering on Gulf of Liaodong ✽ Chin-chou

Liao·yang \'lyaù-'yäŋ\ city NE China in *cen* Liaoning NE of Anshan *pop* 492,559

Liaoyuan — *see* SHUANGLIAO

Li·ard \'lē-ərd\ river 755 *mi* (1215 *km*) W Canada flowing from Stikine Mountains in Yukon Territory E & N into Mackenzie River

Libanus — *see* LEBANON MOUNTAINS

Li·be·rec \'li-be-,rets\ city N Czech Republic in N Bohemia *pop* 104,158

Li·be·ria \lī-'bir-ē-ə\ country W Africa, a republic ✽ Monrovia *area* 43,000 *sq mi* (111,800 *sq km*), *pop* 2,101,628 — **Li·be·ri·an** \-ən\ *adj or n*

Lib·er·ty \'li-bər-tē\ city NW Mo. NNE of Kansas City *pop* 20,459

Liberty Island *or formerly* **Bed·loe's Island** \'bed-,lōz\ island SE N.Y. in Upper New York Bay; comprises **Statue of Liberty National Monument**

Lib·er·ty·ville \'li-bər-tē-,vil, -vəl\ city NE Ill. *pop* 19,174

Li·bre·ville \'lē-brə-,vil, -,vēl\ city & port ✴ of Gabon at mouth of Gabon River *pop* 352,000

Lib·ya \'li-bē-ə\ **1** the part of Africa N of the Sahara bet. Egypt & Syrtis Major (Gulf of Sidra) — an ancient name **2** N Africa W of Egypt — an ancient name **3** country N Africa bordering on the Mediterranean; a colony of Italy 1912–43, an independent kingdom 1951–69, a republic since 1969 ✴ Tripoli *area* 679,358 *sq mi* (1,766,331 *sq km*), *pop* 4,573,000 — **Lib·y·an** \'li-bē-ən\ *adj or n*

Lib·y·an Desert \'li-bē-ən\ desert N Africa W of the Nile in Libya, Egypt, & Sudan

Lich·field \'lich-,fēld\ city W *cen* England in Staffordshire *pop* 90,700

Lick·ing \'li-kiŋ\ river 320 *mi* (515 *km*) NE Ky. flowing NW into Ohio river

Li·di·ce \'li-də-sē, 'lē-dyēt-,sā\ village W *cen* Czech Republic in W *cen* Bohemia

Li·do \'lē-(,)dō\ island Italy in the Adriatic separating Lagoon of Venice & Gulf of Venice

Liech·ten·stein \'lik-tən-,stīn, 'lik-tən-,shtīn\ country W Europe bet. Switzerland & Austria bordering on the Rhine; a principality ✴ Vaduz *area* 62 *sq mi* (161 *sq km*), *pop* 28,877 — **Liech·ten·stein·er** \-,stī-nər, -,shtī-\ *n*

Li·ège \lē-'ezh, -'āzh\ *or Flem* **Luik** \'līk, 'lœik\ **1** province E Belgium *area* 1497 *sq mi* (3877 *sq km*), *pop* 999,646 **2** city, its ✴ *pop* 195,800

Lie·pa·ja \lē-'e-pə-yə, 'lye-pä-yä\ *or G* **Li·bau** \'lē-,baû\ city & port W Latvia on the Baltic *pop* 114,900

Lif·fey \'li-fē\ river 50 *mi* (80 *km*) E Ireland flowing into Dublin Bay

Lif·ford \'li-fərd\ town NW Ireland (republic) in Ulster ✴ of county Donegal *pop* 1478

Li·gu·ria \lə-'gyûr-ē-ə\ region NW Italy bordering on Ligurian Sea ✴ Genoa *pop* 1,727,212 — **Li·gu·ri·an** \-ē-ən\ *adj or n*

Ligurian Sea arm of the Mediterranean N of Corsica

Li·ka·si \lē-'kä-sē\ *or formerly* **Ja·dot·ville** \zha-dō-'vēl, zha-'dō-,vil\ city SE Democratic Republic of the Congo in SE Shaba *pop* 279,839

Lille \'lēl\ *or formerly* **Lisle** \'lēl, 'līl\ city N France; medieval ✴ of Flanders *pop* 178,301

Li·long·we \li-'loŋ-(,)gwā\ city ✴ of Malawi *pop* 223,318

Li·ma 1 \'lī-mə\ city NW Ohio *pop* 45,549 **2** \'lē-mə\ city ✴ of Peru, on the Rímac *pop* 5,825,900

Lim·a·vady \,li-mə-'va-dē\ district N Northern Ireland, established 1974 *area* 226 *sq mi* (588 *sq km*), *pop* 29,201

Li·may \lē-'mī\ river 250 *mi* (402 *km*) W Argentina flowing out of Lake Nahuel Huapí & joining the Neuquén forming Negro River

Lim·burg \'lim-,bərg\ **1** region W Europe E of the Meuse including parts of present Limburg province, Netherlands, & Limburg province, Belgium **2** province NE Belgium ✴ Hasselt *area* 935 *sq mi* (2422 *sq km*), *pop* 750,435 **3** province SE Netherlands ✴ Maastricht *area* 853 *sq mi* (2209 *sq km*), *pop* 1,119,942

Lime·house \'līm-,haûs\ district E London, England, in Tower Hamlets on N bank of Thames River

Lim·er·ick \'li-mə-rik, 'lim-rik\ **1** county SW Ireland in Munster *area* 1037 *sq mi* (2696 *sq km*), *pop* 109,873 **2** city & county borough & port, its *, on the Shannon *pop* 52,040

Limnos — see LEMNOS

Li·moges \lē-'mōzh, li-\ city SW *cen* France *pop* 136,407

Li·món \lē-'mōn\ *or* **Puer·to Limón** \'pwer-tō\ city & port E Costa Rica on the Caribbean *pop* 50,939

Li·mou·sin \,lē-mü-'za°\ region & former province S *cen* France W of Auvergne * Limoges

Lim·po·po \lim-'pō-(,)pō\ *or* **Croc·o·dile** \'krä-kə-,dīl\ river 1000 *mi* (1609 *km*) S Africa flowing from Northern province, Republic of South Africa, into Indian Ocean in Mozambique

Li·na·res \lē-'när-ās\ commune S Spain N of Jaén *pop* 58,039

Lin·coln \'liŋ-kən\ **1** city SE Nebr., its *, *pop* 191,972 **2** city E England * of Lincolnshire *pop* 81,900

Lincoln Park city SE of Detroit *pop* 41,832

Lin·coln·shire \'liŋ-kən-,shir, -shər\ *or* **Lincoln** county E England * Lincoln *area* 2354 *sq mi* (6097 *sq km*), *pop* 573,900

Lin·den \'lin-dən\ city NE N.J. SSW of Elizabeth *pop* 36,701

Lin·den·hurst \'lin-dən-,hərst\ village SE N.Y. in *cen* Long Is. *pop* 26,879

Lin·des·nes \'lin-dəs-,nās\ cape Norway at S tip on North Sea

Lindisfarne — see HOLY

Lind·sey, Parts of \'lin-zē\ district & former administrative county E England in N Lincolnshire * Lincoln *area* 1520 *sq mi* (3952 *sq km*)

Line Islands \'līn\ islands Kiribati in *cen* Pacific S of Hawaii formerly divided bet. the U.S. (Kingman Reef & Palmyra) & Great Britain (Teraina, Tabuaeran, & Kiritimati) *pop* 4782

Lin·ga·yen Gulf \,liŋ-gä-'yen\ inlet of S. China Sea Philippines in NW Luzon

Linguetta, Cape — see GJUHEZES (Cape)

Lin·kö·ping \'lin-,shə(r)-piŋ, -,shē-\ city SE Sweden *pop* 126,377

Lin·lith·gow \lin-'lith-(,)gō\ **1** *or* **Lin·lith·gow·shire** \-,shir, -shər\ — see WEST LOTHIAN **2** burgh SE Scotland in Lothian region W of Edinburgh *pop* 9524

Linn·he, Loch \'li-nē\ inlet of the Atlantic on W coast of Scotland extending NE from head of Firth of Lorne

Linz \'lints, 'linz\ city N Austria on the Danube *pop* 203,044

Li·on, Gulf of \'lī-ən\ *or* F **Golfe du Lion** \,gólf-dūē-'lyō°\ arm of the Mediterranean on S coast of France

Li·pa·ri \'li-pə-rē\ *or anc* **Lip·a·ra** \'li-pə-rə\ island, chief of the Lipari Islands

Lipari Islands *or It* **Iso·le Eo·lie** \'ē-zó-,lā-ā-'ó-lē-,ā\ islands Italy in SE Tyrrhenian Sea off NE Sicily *area ab* 45 *sq mi* (117 *sq km*) — see STROMBOLI

Li·petsk \'lē-,petsk, -,pitsk\ city SW *cen* Russia in Europe N of Voronezh *pop* 464,000

Lip·pe \'li-pə\ **1** river *ab* 150 *mi* (241 *km*) W Germany flowing from Teutoburger Wald W into the Rhine **2** former principality & state W Germany bet. Teutoburger Wald & the Weser * Detmold

Li·ri \'lir-ē\ river 100 *mi* (161 *km*) *cen* Italy flowing into Gulf of Gaeta

Lis·bon \'liz-bən\ *or Pg* **Lis·boa** \lēzh-'vō-ə\ city & port ✱ of Portugal on Tagus estuary *pop* 677,790 — **Lis·bo·an** \liz-'bō-ən\ *n*

Lis·burn \'liz-(,)bərn\ district E Northern Ireland, established 1974 *area* 171 *sq mi* (445 *sq km*), *pop* 99,162

Lis·burne, Cape \'liz-(,)bərn\ cape NW Alaska projecting into Arctic Ocean near W end of Brooks Range

Li·sieux \lēz-'yə(r), -'yœ\ city NW France E of Caen *pop* 24,506

Lisle \'līl\ village NE Ill. *pop* 19,512

Li·ta·ni \li-'tä-nē\ river 90 *mi* (144 *km*) S Lebanon flowing into Mediterranean

Lith·u·a·nia \,li-thə-'wā-nē-ə, ,li-thyə-, -nyə\ *or Lith* **Lie·tu·va** \lye-'tü-vä\ country N *cen* Europe bordering on the Baltic; remnant of a medieval principality extending from Baltic Sea to Black Sea; a republic 1918–40, a constituent republic (**Lithuanian Republic**) of the U.S.S.R. 1940–91; ✱ Vilnius *area* 25,174 *sq mi* (65,201 *sq km*), *pop* 3,753,000 — **Lith·u·a·nian** \,li-thə-'wā-nē-ən\ *adj or n*

Little Abaco — see ABACO

Little Armenia *or* **Lesser Armenia** region S Turkey corresponding to ancient Cilicia

Little Bighorn river 80 *mi* (129 *km*) N Wyo. & S Mont. flowing N into Bighorn River

Little Bighorn Battlefield National Monument site SE Mont. on the Little Bighorn River of battle 1876

Little Colorado river *ab* 300 *mi* (483 *km*) NE Ariz. flowing NW into Colorado River

Little Diomede — see DIOMEDE ISLANDS

Little Inagua — see INAGUA

Little Kabylia — see KABYLIA

Little Karroo — see KARROO

Little Minch — see MINCH

Little Missouri river 560 *mi* (901 *km*) W U.S. flowing from NE Wyo. N into Missouri River in W N.Dak.

Little Namaqualand — see NAMAQUALAND

Lit·tle Rock \'li-t°l-,räk\ city ✱ of Ark. on Arkansas River *pop* 175,795

Little Saint Ber·nard \,sänt-bər-'närd\ mountain pass 7178 *ft* (2188 *m*) over Savoy Alps bet. France & Italy S of Mont Blanc

Lit·tle·ton \'li-t°l-tən\ town N *cen* Colo. S of Denver *pop* 33,685

Little Walachia — see OLTENIA

Liv·er·more \'li-vər-,mōr, -,mòr\ city W Calif. SE of Oakland *pop* 56,741

Liv·er·pool \'li-vər-,pül\ city & port NW England in Merseyside on Mersey estuary *pop* 448,300 — **Liv·er·pud·li·an** \,li-vər-'pəd-lē-ən\ *adj or n*

Liv·ing·stone \'li-viŋ-stən\ city S Zambia on the Zambezi *pop* 82,218

Livingstone Falls rapids in lower Congo River W equatorial Africa below Pool Malebo; a series of cascades dropping *nearly* 900 *ft* (273 *m*) in 220 *mi* (352 *km*)

Li·vo·nia \li-'vō-nē-ə, -nyə\ **1** region *cen* Europe bordering on the Baltic in Latvia & Estonia **2** city SE Mich. W of Detroit *pop* 100,850 — **Li·vo·ni·an** \-nē-ən, -nyən\ *adj or n*

Livorno — see LEGHORN

Liz·ard Head \'li-zərd\ *or* **Lizard Point** headland SW England in S Cornwall at S tip of **The Lizard** (peninsula projecting into English Channel); extreme S point of Great Britain, at 49°57′30″N, 5°12′W

Lju·blja·na \lē-,ü-blē-'ä-nə\ city *cen* Slovenia, its ✻ *pop* 323,291

Llan·ber·is \lan-'ber-əs, hlan-\ village NW Wales in Gwynedd near Snowdon at entrance to **Pass of Llanberis** (1169 *ft or* 354 *m*)

Llan·drin·dod Wells \lan-'drin-,dȯd, hlan-\ town E Wales ✻ of Powys

Llan·dud·no \lan-'did-(,)nō, hlan-, -'dəd-\ town NW Wales on coast of Gwynedd *pop* 18,991

Lla·nel·li *or* **Lla·nel·ly** \hla-'ne-hlē; la-'ne-lē, hla-\ borough & port S Wales in Dyfed *pop* 73,500

Llan·gef·ni \lan-'gev-nē, hlan-\ town NW Wales in Gwynedd on Anglesey Is. *pop* 4265

Lla·no Es·ta·ca·do \'la-(,)nō,es-tə-'kä-(,)dō, 'lä-, 'yä-\ *or* **Staked Plain** \'stāk(t)-\ plateau region SE N.Mex. & NW Tex.

Llu·llai·lla·co \yü-,yī-'yä-(,)kō\ volcano 22,057 *ft* (6723 *m*) N Chile in Andes on Argentina border SE of Antofagasta

Lo·an·ge \lō-'aŋ-gə\ *or Pg* **Lu·an·gue** \lü-'aŋ-gə\ river 425 *mi* (684 *km*) NE Angola & SW Republic of the Congo flowing N into Kasai River

Lo·bi·to \lō-'bē-(,)tō\ city & port W Angola *pop* 59,528

Lo·bos, Point \'lō-(,)bōs\ **1** promontory Calif. in San Francisco on S side of entrance to the Golden Gate **2** promontory Calif. on the Pacific SW of Monterey

Lo·car·no \lō-'kär-(,)nō\ commune *cen* Switzerland *pop* 14,430

Loch·gilp·head \läk-'gilp-,hed, läk-\ burgh W Scotland on Loch Fyne

Lock·port \'läk-,pȯrt, -,pȯrt\ city W N.Y. NE of Buffalo *pop* 24,426

Lo·cris \'lō-krəs, 'lä-\ region of ancient Greece N of Gulf of Corinth — **Lo·cri·an** \-krē-ən\ *adj or n*

Lod \'lȯd\ city *cen* Israel *pop* 45,500

Lo·di **1** \'lō-,dī\ city *cen* Calif. SSE of Sacramento *pop* 51,874 **2** \'lō-,dī\ borough NE N.J. SE of Paterson *pop* 22,355 **3** \'lō-(,)dē\ commune N Italy in Lombardy SE of Milan *pop* 42,770

Lodz \'lüj, 'lädz\ city *cen* Poland WSW of Warsaw *pop* 851,690

Lo·fo·ten \'lō-,fō-tᵊn\ island group Norway off NW coast SW of Vesterålen *area* 475 *sq mi* (1235 *sq km*)

Lo·gan \'lō-gən\ city N Utah *pop* 32,762

Logan, Mount mountain 19,524 *ft* (5951 *m*) Canada in SW Yukon Territory; highest in St. Elias & Coast ranges & in Canada & 2d highest in N. America

Lo·gro·ño \lō-'grō-(,)nyō\ commune ✻ of La Rioja province, Spain, on the Ebro *pop* 121,066

Loire \lə-'wär, 'lwär\ river 634 *mi* (1020 *km*) *cen* France flowing from the Massif Central NW & W into Bay of Biscay

Lol·land \'lä-lənd\ island Denmark in the Baltic S of Sjælland *area* 477 *sq mi* (1240 *sq km*), *pop* 73,564

Lo·ma·mi \lō-'mä-mē\ river *cen* Democratic Republic of the Congo flowing N into Congo River

Lo·mas \'lō-,mäs\ *or* **Lo·mas de Za·mo·ra** \dā-zä-'mȯr-ä, thä-sä-'mō-rä\ city E Argentina SW of Buenos Aires *pop* 572,769

Lom·bard \'läm-,bärd\ village NE Ill. W of Chicago *pop* 39,408

Lom·bar·dy \-,bär-dē, -bər- *also* 'ləm-\ *or It* **Lom·bar·dia** \,läm-bər-'dē-ə, ,löm-\ region N Italy chiefly N of the Po ✳ Milan *pop* 8,911,995 — **Lom·bard** *n* — **Lom·bar·di·an** \läm-'bär-dē-ən\ *adj* — **Lom·bar·dic** \-dik\ *adj*

Lom·blen \läm-'blen\ island Indonesia in the Lesser Sundas E of Flores *area* 468 *sq mi* (1217 *sq km*)

Lom·bok \'läm-,bäk\ island Indonesia in the Lesser Sundas E of Bali; chief town Mataram *area* 1825 *sq mi* (4745 *sq km*), *pop* 1,300,234

Lo·mé \lō-'mā\ city & port ✳ of Togo *pop* 229,400

Lo·mi·ta \lō-'mē-tə\ city SW Calif. S of Los Angeles *pop* 19,382

Lo·mond, Ben \ben-'lō-mənd\ mountain 3192 *ft* (973 *m*) S *cen* Scotland on E side of Loch Lomond

Lomond, Loch lake 24 *mi* (39 *km*) S *cen* Scotland in Strathclyde & Central regions; largest in Scotland

Lom·poc \'läm-,päk\ city SW Calif. W of Santa Barbara *pop* 37,649

Lon·don \'lən-dən\ **1** city Canada in SE Ont. on Thames River *pop* 303,165 **2** city & port SE England formerly constituting an administrative county ✳ of United Kingdom; comprises **City of London** *or* **The City** (approximately coextensive with *anc* **Lon·din·i·um** \län-'di-nē-əm, ,lən-\; *pop* 4000) & 32 other boroughs which together are referred to as the metropolitan county of **Greater London** (*area* 632 *sq mi* *or* 1637 *sq km*, *pop* 6,377,900) — **Lon·don·er** \-də-nər\ *n*

Lon·don·der·ry **1** \'lən-dən-,der-ē\ town SE N.H. NE of Nashua *pop* 19,781 **2** — see DERRY **3** \,lən-dən-'der-ē, 'lən-dən-\ traditional county N Northern Ireland

Long Beach **1** city & port SW Calif. SE of Los Angeles *pop* 429,433 **2** city SE N.Y. on island S of Long Is. *pop* 33,510

Long Branch city E *cen* N.J. on the Atlantic *pop* 28,658

Long·ford \'lȯŋ-fərd\ **1** county E *cen* Ireland in Leinster *area* 403 *sq mi* (1048 *sq km*), *pop* 30,296 **2** town, its ✳ *pop* 6393

Long Island island 118 *mi* (190 *km*) long SE N.Y. S of Conn. *area* 1723 *sq mi* (4462 *sq km*)

Long Island City section of New York City in NW Queens

Long Island Sound inlet of the Atlantic bet. Conn. & Long Is.

Long·mont \'lȯŋ-,mänt\ city N Colo. N of Denver *pop* 51,555

Longs Peak \'lȯŋz\ mountain 14,255 *ft* (4345 *m*) N *cen* Colo. in Front Range in Rocky Mountain National Park

Lon·gueuil \lȯŋ-'gāl\ town Canada in S Que. E of Montreal *pop* 129,874

Long·view \'lȯŋ-,vyü\ **1** city NE Tex. *pop* 70,311 **2** city SW Wash. on Columbia River *pop* 31,499

Long Xuy·en \lȯŋ-'swē-ən\ city S Vietnam in SW Cochin China on S side of Mekong delta *pop* 128,817

Look·out, Cape \'lùk-,aùt\ cape E N.C. on the Atlantic SW of Cape Hatteras

Lookout Mountain ridge 2126 *ft* (648 *m*) SE Tenn., NW Ga., & NE Ala. near Chattanooga, Tenn.

Lo·rain \lə-'rān, lō-\ city N Ohio on Lake Erie W of Cleveland *pop* 71,245

Lor·ca \'lȯr-kə\ commune SE Spain SW of Murcia *pop* 65,832

Lord Howe Island \lȯrd-'haù\ island Australia in Tasman Sea ENE of Sydney belonging to New South Wales *area* 5 *sq mi* (13 *sq km*)

Lo·re·to \lə-'rā-(ˌ)tō, -'re-\ commune *cen* Italy in Marche S of Ancona *pop* 10,797

Lo·ri·ent \lȯr-ē-'äⁿ\ commune & port NW France in Brittany on Bay of Biscay *pop* 61,630

Lorn, Firth of \'lȯrn\ *or* **Firth of Lorne** \'lȯrn\ strait W Scotland bet. E Mull Is. & mainland

Lor·raine \lə-'rān, lȯ-\ *or G* **Lo·thring·en** \'lō-triŋ-ən\ region & former duchy NE France around the upper Moselle & the Meuse; remnant (Upper Lorraine) of medieval kingdom of **Lo·tha·rin·gia** \ˌlō-thə-'rin-j(ē-)ə\ including also territory to N (Lower Lorraine) bet. the Rhine & the Schelde — see ALSACE-LORRAINE

Los Al·tos \lȯs-'al-(ˌ)tōs\ city W Calif. SSE of Palo Alto *pop* 26,303

Los An·ge·les \lȯs-'an-jə-ləs *also* -ˌlēz, *sometimes* -'aŋ-gə-(ˌ)lēz\ city & port SW Calif. on the Pacific *pop* 3,485,398 — **Los An·ge·le·no** \ˌan-jə-'lē-(ˌ)nō *also* -ˌaŋ-gə-\ *n*

Los An·ge·les \lȯs-'äŋ-hā-ˌläs\ city S *cen* Chile *pop* 142,136

Los Gat·os \lȯs-'ga-təs\ city W Calif. S of San José *pop* 27,357

Lot \'lät, 'lȯt\ river 300 *mi* (483 *km*) S France flowing W into the Garonne

Lo·thi·an \'lō-thē-ən\ region S Scotland bordering on Firth of Forth, established 1975 ✳ Edinburgh *area* 662 *sq mi* (1716 *sq km*), *pop* 753,900; formerly divided into three counties (the **Lothians**): East Lothian, Midlothian, & West Lothian

Louang·phra·bang \'lwäŋ-prä-'bäŋ\ *or* **Luang Pra·bang** \'lwäŋ-prä-\ city NW Laos on the Mekong NNW of Vientiane

Lough·bor·ough \'ləf-ˌbər-ə, -ˌbə-rə, -b(ə-)rə\ borough *cen* England in Leicestershire S of Nottingham *pop* 47,647

Lou·ise, Lake \lu̇-'ēz\ lake W Canada in SW Alta. in Banff National Park

Lou·i·si·ade Archipelago \lü̇-ē-zē-'äd, -'äd\ island group in Solomon Sea SE of New Guinea; belongs to Papua New Guinea *pop* 14,599

Lou·i·si·ana \lu̇-ē-zē-'a-nə, ˌlü-ə-zē-, ˌlü-zē-\ state S U.S. ✳ Baton Rouge *area* 48,523 *sq mi* (126,160 *sq km*), *pop* 4,219,973 — **Lou·i·si·an·an** \-'a-nən\ *adj or n* — **Lou·i·si·an·i·an** \-'a-nē-ən, -a-nyən\ *adj or n*

Louisiana Purchase region W *cen* U.S. bet. Mississippi River & the Rockies purchased 1803 from France *area* 885,000 *sq mi* (2,301,000 *sq km*)

Lou·is·ville \'lü̇-i-ˌvil, -vəl\ city N Ky. on Ohio River *pop* 269,063

Loup \'lüp\ river 290 *mi* (467 *km*) with longest headstream (the Middle Loup) E *cen* Nebr. flowing E into Platte River

Lourdes \'lu̇rd, 'lu̇rdz\ commune SW France on the Gave de Pau SSW of Tarbes *pop* 16,581

Lourenço Marques — see MAPUTO

Louth \'lau̇th\ county E Ireland in Leinster bordering on Irish Sea ✳ Dundalk *area* 317 *sq mi* (824 *sq km*), *pop* 90,707

Lou·vain \lü-'vaⁿ\ *or Flem* **Leu·ven** \'lə(r)-və(n), 'lœ̅-\ city *cen* Belgium in Brabant E of Brussels *pop* 85,200

Love·land \'ləv-lənd\ city N Colo. N of Denver *pop* 37,352

Loveland Pass mountain pass N *cen* Colo. in Front Range of Rocky Mountains

Low Countries region W Europe bordering on North Sea & comprising modern Belgium, Luxembourg, & the Netherlands

Low·ell \'lō-əl\ city NE Mass. NW of Boston *pop* 103,439

Lower Canada the province of Canada 1791–1841 corresponding to modern Que. — see UPPER CANADA

Lower 48 the continental states of the U.S. excluding Alaska

Lower Klamath Lake lake N Calif. on Oreg. border SSE of Upper Klamath Lake (in Oreg.)

Lower Peninsula S part of Mich., S of Straits of Mackinac

Lower Saxony *or G* **Nie·der·sach·sen** \ˌnē-dər-'zäk-sən\ state of Germany & formerly of W. Germany bordering on North Sea ✳ Hannover *area* 18,305 *sq mi* (47,410 *sq km*), *pop* 7,387,200 — see SAXONY

Lowes·toft \'lō-stəf(t), -ˌstöft\ borough & port E England in E. Suffolk on North Sea *pop* 55,231

Low·lands \'lō-ləndz, -ˌlandz\ the *cen* & E part of Scotland lying bet. the Highlands & the Southern Uplands

Loy·al·ty Islands \'lòi-(ə)l-tē\ islands SW Pacific E of New Caledonia; a dependency of New Caledonia *area ab* 755 *sq mi* (1955 *sq km*), *pop* 17,912

Lu·a·la·ba \ˌlü-ä-'lä-bä\ river 400 *mi* (640 *km*) SE Democratic Republic of the Congo flowing N to join the **Lu·a·pu·la** \-'pü-lä\ (outlet of Lake Bangweulu) forming Congo River

Lu·an·da \lü-'än-də\ city & port ✳ of Angola *pop* 1,544,400

Luangue — see LOANGE

Lub·bock \'lə-bək\ city NW Tex. *pop* 186,206

Lü·beck \'lü-ˌbek, 'lē-\ city & port N Germany NE of Hamburg *pop* 215,999

Lu·blin \'lü-blən, -ˌblēn\ city E Poland SE of Warsaw *pop* 349,672

Lu·bum·ba·shi \ˌlü-büm-'bä-shē\ *or formerly* **Elis·a·beth·ville** \i-'li-zə-bəth-ˌvil\ city SE Democratic Republic of the Congo in SE Shaba *pop* 739,082

Lucania — see BASILICATA

Lu·ca·nia, Mount \lü-'kā-nē-ə, -nyə\ mountain 17,147 *ft* (5226 *m*) Canada in SW Yukon Territory in St. Elias Range N of Mt. Logan

Luc·ca \'lü-kə\ commune *cen* Italy in Tuscany NW of Florence *pop* 86,188

Lu·cerne \lü-'sərn\ *or G* **Lu·zern** \lüt-'sern\ **1** canton *cen* Switzerland *area* 577 *sq mi* (1494 *sq km*), *pop* 316,210 **2** commune, its ✳, on Lake of Lucerne *pop* 59,932

Lucerne, Lake of *or Ger* **Vier·wald·stät·ter See** \fir-'vält-ˌshter-ər-ˌzā\ lake 24 *mi* (39 *km*) long *cen* Switzerland *area* 44 *sq mi* (114 *sq km*)

Luchow — see HEFEI

Luck·now \'lək-ˌnaú\ city N India ESE of Delhi ✳ of Uttar Pradesh *pop* 1,619,115

Lüda — see DALIAN

Lü·de·ritz \'lü-də-rits, 'lē-\ town & port SW Namibia *pop* 6000

Lu·dhi·a·na \ˌlü-dē-'ä-nə\ city NW India in Punjab SE of Amritsar *pop* 1,042,740

Lud·wigs·burg \'lüd-vigz-ˌburg, 'lüt-viks-ˌbúrk\ city SW Germany in Baden-Württemberg N of Stuttgart *pop* 83,913

Lud·wigs·ha·fen am Rhein \ˌlüd-vigz-'hä-fᵊn-äm-'rīn, ˌlüt-viks-\ city SW Germany on the Rhine opposite Mannheim *pop* 165,368

Luf·kin \'ləf-kən\ city E Tex. NNE of Houston *pop* 30,206

Lu·ga·no \lü-'gä-(,)nō\ commune S Switzerland in Ticino canton on Lake Lugano *pop* 26,530

Lugano, Lake lake on border bet. Switzerland & Italy E of Lake Maggiore *area* 19 *sq mi* (49 *sq km*)

Lu·gansk \lü-'gän(t)sk\ *or* **Lu·hansk** \-'hän(t)sk\ *or alternately since 1935* **Vo·ro·shi·lov·grad** \,vȯr-ə-'shē-ləf-,grad, ,vär-, -ləv-, -,gräd\ city E Ukraine in Donets Basin *pop* 504,000

Lu·go \'lü-(,)gō\ **1** province NW Spain in NE Galicia on Bay of Biscay *area* 3785 *sq mi* (9803 *sq km*), *pop* 384,365 **2** commune, its ✳ *pop* 82,658

Luichow — see LEIZHOU

Luik — see LIÈGE

Lu·lea \lü-lā-,ö\ city & port N Sweden near head of Gulf of Bothnia *pop* 68,924

Lu·le·bur·gaz \,lü-lə-bùr-'gäz, ,lüē-\ city *cen* Turkey in Europe

Luluabourg — see KANANGA

Lund \'lùnd, 'lónd\ city SW Sweden NE of Malmö *pop* 92,027

Lun·dy Island \'lən-dē\ island SW England at mouth of Bristol Channel off coast of Devon *area* 2 *sq mi* (5.2 *sq km*)

Lü·ne·burg \'lü-nə-,bùrg, 'lœ-nə-,bùrk\ city N Germany SE of Hamburg & NE of **Lüneburg Heath** *or G* **Lü·ne·bur·ger Hei·de** \-,bùr-gər-,hī-də\ (tract of moorland *ab* 55 *mi or* 88 *km* long) *pop* 62,944

Lü·nen \'lü-nən, 'lœ-\ city W Germany S of Münster *pop* 88,443

Lu·nen·burg \'lü-nən-,bərg\ town Canada in S N.S. *pop* 25,720

Lu·né·ville \'lü-nə-,vil, lüē-ne-'vēl\ city NE France on the Meurthe SE of Nancy *pop* 22,393

Lungki — see ZHANGZHOU

Luo·yang \lü-'wō-'yäŋ\ *or* **Lo·yang** \'lō-'yäŋ\ city E China in N Henan in the Huang basin *pop* 759,752

Lu·ray Caverns \'lü-,rā, lù-'\ caverns N Va. in Blue Ridge Mountains

Lu·ri·stan \'lùr-ə-,stan, -,stän\ region W Iran; chief town Burujird

Lu·sa·ka \lü-'sä-kä\ city ✳ of Zambia *pop* 982,362

Lu·sa·tia \lü-'sā-sh(ē-)ə\ *or G* **Lau·sitz** \'laù-(,)zits\ region E Germany NW of Silesia E of the Elbe

Lü·shun \'lü-'shùn, 'lüē-\ *or* **Port Ar·thur** \'är-thər\ city & port NE China in S Liaoning at tip of Liaodong Peninsula *pop* 200,000

Lu·si·ta·nia — see PORTUGAL — **Lu·si·ta·ni·an** \,lü-sə-'tā-nē-ən, -nyən\ *adj or n*

Lu–ta — see DALIAN

Lutetia — see PARIS

Lu·ton \'lü-tᵊn\ borough SE *cen* England in SE Bedfordshire *pop* 167,300

Lüt·zen \'lüt-sən, 'lœt-\ town E Germany in Saxony SW of Leipzig

Lux·em·bourg *or* **Lux·em·burg** \'lək-səm-,bərg, 'lùk-səm-,bùrk\ **1** province SE Belgium ✳ Arlon *area* 1706 *sq mi* (4418 *sq km*), *pop* 232,813 **2** country W Europe bet. Belgium, France, & Germany; a grand duchy *area* 999 *sq mi* (2597 *sq km*), *pop* 392,000 **3** city, its ✳ *pop* 75,377 — **Lux·em·bourg·er** *or* **Lux·em·burg·er** \-,bər-gər, -,bùr-\ *n* — **Lux·em·bourg·i·an** *or* **Lux·em·burg·i·an** \,lək-səm-'bər-gē-ən, ,lùk-səm-'bùr-\ *adj*

Lux·or \'lək-,sȯr, 'lùk-\ city S Egypt on the Nile on S part of site of ancient Thebes *pop* 142,000

Lu·zon \lü-'zän\ island N Philippines, chief island of the group *area* 41,765 *sq mi* (108,171 *sq km*), *pop* 23,900,796

Lviv \lə-'vē-ü, -'vēf\ *or* **Lvov** \lə-'vȯf, -'vȯv\ *or Pol* **Lwów** \lə-'vüf, -'vüv\ *or G* **Lem·berg** \'lem-,bərg, -,berk\ city W Ukraine *pop* 802,000

Lyallpur — see FAISALABAD

Ly·ca·bet·tus *or Gk* **Ly·ka·bet·tos** \,li-kə-'be-təs, ,lī-\ mountain 909 *ft* (277 *m*) in NE part of Athens, Greece

Ly·ca·o·nia \,li-kā-'ō-nē-ə, ,lī-, -nyə\ ancient region & Roman province SE *cen* Asia Minor N of Cilicia

Ly·cia \'li-sh(ē-)ə\ ancient region & Roman province SW Asia Minor on coast SE of Caria — **Ly·cian** \'li-sh(ē-)ən\ *adj or n*

Lyd·ia \'li-dē-ə\ ancient country W Asia Minor bordering on the Aegean ✳ Sardis — **Lyd·i·an** \'li-dē-ən\ *adj or n*

Lyn·brook \'lin-,bru̇k\ village SE N.Y. on Long Is. *pop* 19,208

Lynch·burg \'linch-,bərg\ city S *cen* Va. on James River *pop* 66,049

Lynn \'lin\ **1** city NE Mass. NE of Boston *pop* 81,245 **2** *or* **Lynn Regis** — see KING'S LYNN

Lynn Canal narrow inlet of the Pacific 80 *mi* (129 *km*) long SE Alaska extending N from Juneau

Lynn·wood \'lin-,wu̇d\ city W Wash. N of Seattle *pop* 28,695

Lyn·wood \'lin-,wu̇d\ city SW Calif. S of Los Angeles *pop* 61,945

Ly·on·nais *or* **Ly·o·nais** \,lē-ȯ-'nä\ former province SE *cen* France NE of Auvergne & W of the Saône & the Rhône ✳ Lyon

Lyon \lyōⁿ\ *or* **Ly·ons** \lē-ənz\ \'lī-ənz\ *or anc* **Lug·du·num** \lu̇g-'dü-nəm, ,ləg-\ city SE *cen* France at confluence of the Saône & the Rhône *pop* 422,444

Lys \'lēs\ *or in Belgium* **Leie** \'lā-ə, 'lī-ə\ river 120 *mi* (193 *km*) France & Belgium flowing NE into the Schelde

Lyt·tel·ton \'li-tᵊl-tən\ borough New Zealand on South Is.; port for Christchurch, on **Port Lyttelton** (inlet) *pop* 3190

M

Maarianhamina — see MARIEHAMN

Maas — see MEUSE

Maas·tricht *or* **Maes·tricht** \'mä-,strikt, -,strikt; mä-'\ commune SE Netherlands on the Meuse ✳ of Limburg *pop* 118,152

Ma·cao *or* **Ma·cau** \mə-'kau̇\ **1** peninsula SE China in Guangdong in Xi delta W of Hong Kong **2** Portuguese overseas territory comprising peninsula on SE Macao Is. & adjacent islands *area* 6 *sq mi* (16 *sq km*), *pop* 488,000 **3** city & port; cap. ✳ *pop* 161,252 — **Mac·a·nese** \,ma-kə-'nēz, -'nēs\ *n*

Ma·ca·pá \,mä-kə-'pä\ city & port N Brazil ✳ of Amapá *pop* 179,609

Macassar — see MAKASSAR — **Ma·cas·sar·ese** \mə-,ka-sə-'rēz, -'rēs\ *n*

Mac·cles·field \'ma-kəlz-ˌfēld\ borough W England in E Cheshire SSE of Manchester *pop* 147,000

Mac·don·nell Ranges \mak-'dä-nᵊl\ series of mountain ridges *cen* Australia in S Northern Territory; highest point Mt. Ziel 5023 *ft* (1531 *m*)

Mac·e·do·nia \ˌma-sə-'dō-nē-ə, -nyə\ **1** region S Europe in Balkan Peninsula in NE Greece, the former Yugoslav section of Macedonia, & SW Bulgaria including territory of ancient kingdom of Macedonia (*or* **Mac·e·don** \'ma-sə-dən, -ˌdän\ ✳ Pella) **2** country S *cen* Balkan Peninsula; a federated republic of Yugoslavia 1946–92 ✳ Skopje *area* 9928 *sq mi* (25,714 *sq km*), *pop* 2,063,000 — **Mac·e·do·nian** \ˌma-sə-'dō-nyən\ *adj or n*

Ma·ceió \ˌma-sā-'ō\ city NE Brazil ✳ of Alagoas *pop* 628,209

Mac·gil·li·cud·dy's Reeks \mə-ˌgi-lə-ˌkə-dēz-'rēks\ mountain range SW Ireland in County Kerry — see CARRANTUOHILL

Ma·ches·ney Park \mə-'chez-nē\ village N Ill. N of Rockford *pop* 19,033

Ma·chi·da \mä-'chē-dä, 'mä-chē-ˌdä\ city Japan on Honshu *pop* 355,843

Ma·chi·li·pat·nam \ˌmə-chə-lə-'pət-nəm\ *or* **Ban·dar** \'bən-dər\ city & port SE India in E Andhra Pradesh SW of Kakinada *pop* 159,007

Ma·chu Pic·chu \ˌmä-(ˌ)chü-'pē-(ˌ)chü, -'pēk-\ site SE Peru of ancient Inca city on a mountain NW of Cuzco

Macías Nguema Biyogo — see BIOKO

Mac·ken·zie \mə-'ken-zē\ **1** river 1120 *mi* (1802 *km*) NW Canada flowing from Great Slave Lake NW into Beaufort Sea; sometimes considered to include the Finlay, Peace, & Slave rivers (total length 2635 *mi* or 4216 *km*) **2** former district Canada in W Northwest Territories in basin of Mackenzie River

Mackenzie Mountains mountain range NW Canada in the Rockies in Yukon Territory & W Northwest Territories

Mack·i·nac \'ma-kə-ˌnó, -ˌnak\ *or formerly* **Mich·i·li·mack·i·nac** \ˌmi-shə-lē-\ island N Mich. in Straits of Mackinac

Mackinac, Straits of channel N Mich. connecting Lake Huron & Lake Michigan; 4 *mi* (6.4 *km*) wide at narrowest point

Ma·comb \mə-'kōm\ city W Ill. SW of Peoria *pop* 19,952

Ma·con \'mā-kən\ city *cen* Ga. on the Ocmulgee *pop* 106,612

Mâ·con \mä-'kōⁿ\ city E *cen* France *pop* 38,508

Mac·quar·ie \mə-'kwär-ē\ river 590 *mi* (949 *km*) SE Australia in E *cen* New South Wales flowing NNW to Darling River

Mac·tan \mäk-'tän\ island S *cen* Philippines off E coast of Cebu

Mad·a·gas·car \ˌma-də-'gas-kər, -ˌkär\ island W Indian Ocean off SE Africa; formerly a French territory; became (1958) a republic of the French Community as the **Mal·a·gasy Republic** \ˌma-lə-'ga-sē\ *or* F **Ré·pu·blique Mal·gache** \rä-pü-ˈblēk-mäl-'gäsh\ *or since 1975* **Democratic Republic of Madagascar** ✳ Antananarivo *area* 226,657 *sq mi* (589,308 *sq km*), *pop* 13,255,000 — **Mad·a·gas·can** \ˌma-də-'gas-kən\ *adj or n*

Ma·dei·ra \mə-'dir-ə, -'der-ə\ **1** river 2013 *mi* (3239 *km*) W Brazil formed at Bolivian border by confluence of the Mamoré & the Beni & flowing NE to the Amazon **2** islands in N Atlantic N of the Canaries belonging to Portugal ✳ Funchal *area* 308 *sq mi* (798 *sq*

km), pop 253,000 **3** island, chief of group *area* 285 *sq mi (741 sq km)* — **Ma·dei·ran** \-'dir-ən, -'der-\ *adj or n*

Ma·de·ra \mə-'der-ə\ city *S cen* Calif. NW of Fresno *pop* 29,281

Madhya Bha·rat \ˌmä-dyə-'bär-ət\ former state *cen* India; a union of 20 states including Gwalior, Indore, & Malwa formed 1948; became part of Madhya Pradesh 1956

Madhya Pra·desh \prə-'desh, -'dāsh\ state *cen* India ✶ Bhopal *area* 171,220 *sq mi* (443,460 *sq km), pop* 66,181,170 — see CENTRAL PROVINCES AND BERAR, MADHYA BHARAT

Ma·di·nat ash Sha'b \mə-ˌdē-ˌnə-tash-'shab\ city *S* Yemen; formerly a national ✶ of People's Democratic Republic of Yemen & (as **Al It·ti·had** \al-ˌi-tə-'had\) ✶ of Federation of South Arabia

Mad·i·son \'ma-də-sən\ **1** river 180 *mi* (290 *km)* SW Mont. — see THREE FORKS **2** city *S* Wis., its ✶ *pop* 191,262

Madison Heights city SE Mich. N of Detroit *pop* 32,196

Ma·dras \mə-'dras, -'dräs\ **1** — see TAMIL NADU **2** city & port *S* India ✶ of Tamil Nadu *pop* 3,841,396 — **Ma·drasi** \-'dra-sē, -'drä-\ *n*

Ma·dre, La·gu·na \lə-ˌgü-nə-'mä-drä\ inlet of Gulf of Mexico *S* Tex. bet. Padre Is. & mainland

Ma·dre de Dios \ˌmä-drā-(ˌ)dā-dē-'ōs\ river *ab* 700 *mi* (1126 *km)* rising in SE Peru & flowing E into the Beni in Brazil

Ma·drid \mə-'drid\ **1** province *cen* Spain in NW old New Castile *area* 3087 *sq mi* (7995 *sq km), pop* 4,947,555 **2** city, its ✶ & ✶ of Spain *pop* 2,909,792 — **Mad·ri·le·nian** \ˌma-drə-'lē-nē-ən, -dri-, -nyən\ *adj or n* — **Ma·dri·le·ño** \ˌmä-drə-'lā-(ˌ)nyō, -drē-\ *n*

Ma·du·ra or **D Ma·doe·ra** \mə-'dúr-ə\ island Indonesia off coast of NE Java *area* (with adjacent islands) 2113 *mi* (5494 *sq km), pop* 1,858,183 — **Mad·u·rese** \ˌma-də-'rēz, ˌma-jə-, -'rēs\ *adj or n*

Ma·du·rai \ˌmä-də-'rī\ city *S* India in *S* Tamil Nadu *pop* 940,989

Maeander — see MENDERES

Ma·fia \'mä-fē-ə, 'ma-\ island Tanzania in Indian Ocean *S* of Zanzibar *area* 170 *sq mi* (442 *sq km), pop* 16,748

Maf·i·keng \'ma-fə-kin\ town N Republic of South Africa in North West province *pop* 6515

Ma·ga·dan \ˌmä-gə-'dan, -'dän\ city & port E Russia in Asia on N shore of Sea of Okhotsk *pop* 152,000

Ma·ga·dha \'mə-gə-də, 'mä-\ ancient kingdom, India including Bihar S of the Ganges

Magallanes — see PUNTA ARENAS

Mag·da·la \'mag-də-lə\ ancient city N Palestine on W shore of Sea of Galilee N of Tiberias

Mag·da·le·na \ˌmag-də-'lā-nə, -'lē-\ river 956 *mi* (1538 *km)* Colombia flowing N into the Caribbean

Mag·da·len Islands \'mag-də-lən\ or *F* **Îles de la Ma·de·leine** \ˌēl-də-là-màd-'len, -mäd-\ islands Canada in Que. in Gulf of St. Lawrence bet. Newfoundland & P.E.I. *area* 102 *sq mi* (265 *sq km), pop* 13,991

Mag·de·burg \'mäg-də-ˌbúrk, 'mag-də-ˌbərg\ city *cen* Germany on the Elbe WSW of Berlin *pop* 275,238

Ma·gel·lan, Strait of \mə-'je-lən, *chiefly Brit* -'ge-\ strait 350 *mi* (563 *km)* long at S end of S. America bet. mainland & Tierra del Fuego (Archipelago)

Mageröy — see NORTH CAPE

Mag·gio·re, Lake \mä-'jōr-ā, -'jŏr\ lake 40 *mi* (64 *km*) long N Italy & S Switzerland traversed by Ticino River

Magh·er·a·felt \'mär-ə,felt, 'ma-kə-rə,felt\ district *cen* Northern Ireland, established 1974 *area* 221 *sq mi* (575 *sq km*), *pop* 35,874

Ma·ghreb *or* **Ma·ghrib** \'mä-grəb\ **1** NW Africa &, at time of the Moorish occupation, Spain; now considered as including Morocco, Algeria, Tunisia, & sometimes Libya **2** *or* **El Ma·ghreb al Aq·sa** \el-'mä-grəb-äl-'äk-sä\ MOROCCO — **Ma·ghre·bi** *or* **Ma·ghri·bi** \'mä-grə-bē\ *adj or n* — **Ma·ghreb·i·an** \mə-'gre-bē-ən\ *or* **Ma·ghrib·i·an** \-'gri-\ *adj or n*

Mag·na Grae·cia \,mag-nə-'grē-shə\ the ancient Greek colonies in S Italian Peninsula including Tarentum, Sybaris, Crotona, Heraclea, & Neapolis

Mag·ne·sia \mag-'nē-shə, -zhə\ — see MANISA

Mag·ni·to·gorsk \mag-'nē-tə,gŏrsk\ city W Russia in Asia on Ural River *pop* 441,000

Magyarország — see HUNGARY

Ma·ha·jan·ga \,mə-hə-'jəŋ-gə\ city & port NW Madagascar *pop* 121,967

Mahalla El Kubra, El — see EL MAHALLA EL KUBRA

Ma·ha·na·di \mə-'hä-nə,dē\ river *ab* 560 *mi* (900 *km*) E India flowing into Bay of Bengal in Orissa through several mouths

Ma·ha·rash·tra \,mä-hə-'räsh-trə\ **1** region W *cen* India S of the Narbada; the original home of the Marathas **2** state W India bordering on Arabian Sea formed 1960 from SE part of former Bombay state ✳ Bombay *area* 118,637 *sq mi* (307,270 *sq km*), *pop* 78,937,187

Ma·hé \mä-'hā\ **1** island in Indian Ocean, chief of the Seychelles group *pop* 61,183 **2** *or formerly* **May·ya·li** \'mī-'yä-lē\ town SW India in N Kerala; a settlement of French India until 1954 *pop* 10,437

Ma·hil·yow *or* **Mo·gi·lev** \mə-gil-'yŏf\ city E Belarus on the Dnieper *pop* 363,000

Ma·hón \mə-'hōn, mä-'ōn\ *or* **Port Ma·hon** \mə-'hōn\ city & port Spain on Minorca Is. *pop* 21,564

Ma·hone Bay \mə-'hōn\ inlet of the Atlantic E Canada in S N.S.

Maid·en·head \'mā-d²n-,hed\ borough S England in Berkshire on Thames River W of London *pop* 49,038

Maid·stone \'mād-stən, -,stōn\ borough SE England ✳ of Kent on the Medway ESE of London *pop* 133,200

Main \'mīn, 'män\ river 325 *mi* (523 *km*) S *cen* Germany rising in N Bavaria in the Fichtelgebirge & flowing W into the Rhine

Mai–Ndom·be, Lac \,lak-,mīn-'dōm-bā\ *or formerly* **Lake Leo·pold II** \'lē-ə-,pōld\ lake W Democratic Republic of the Congo

Maine \'män\ **1** state NE U.S. ✳ Augusta *area* 33,265 *sq mi* (86,156 *sq km*), *pop* 1,227,928 **2** *or* **Le Maine** \lə-'men\ region & former province NW France S of Normandy ✳ Le Mans **3** — see MAYENNE — **Main·er** \'mā-nər\ *n*

Main·land \'mān-,land, -lənd\ **1** HONSHU **2** island N Scotland, largest of the Orkneys **3** island N Scotland, largest of the Shetlands

Mainz \'mīnts\ *or F* **Ma·yence** \mȧ-'yäⁿs\ city SW *cen* Germany on the Rhine ✳ of Rhineland-Palatinate *pop* 182,867

Mait·land \'māt-lənd\ city SE Australia in E New South Wales *pop* 46,909

Ma·jor·ca \mä-'jòr-kə, mə-, -'yòr-\ *or Sp* **Ma·llor·ca** \mä-'yòr-kä\ island Spain, largest of the Balearic Islands; chief city Palma *area* 1405 *sq mi* (3653 *sq km*) — **Ma·jor·can** \-'jòr-kən, -'yòr-\ *adj or n*

Ma·ju·ro \mə-'jùr-(,)ō\ island (atoll) W Pacific in SE Marshall Islands; contains ✳ of the group

Ma·ka·lu \'mä-kə-,lü\ mountain 27,824 *ft* (8481 *m*) in the Himalaya in NE Nepal SE of Mt. Everest; 5th highest in world

Ma·kas·sar \mə-'kas-ər\ **1** *or* **Ma·cas·sar** strait Indonesia bet. E Borneo & W Sulawesi **2** — see UJUNG PANDANG — **Ma·kas·sa·rese** \,mə-,kä-sə-'rēz, -'rēs\ *n*

Ma·ke·yev·ka *or* **Ma·ki·yiv·ka** \mə-'kā-yəf-kə\ city E Ukraine in Donets Basin NE of Donetsk *pop* 424,000

Ma·kga·di·kga·di Pans \mä-,kä-dē-'kä-dē\ large salt basin NE Botswana

Ma·khach·ka·la \mə-,käch-kə-'lä\ *or formerly* **Pe·trovsk** \pə-'tròfsk\ city SE Russia in Europe on the Caspian ✳ of Dagestan *pop* 339,000

Mal·a·bar Coast \'ma-lə-,bär\ region SW India on Arabian Sea in Karnataka & Kerala states

Ma·la·bo \mä-'lä-(,)bō\ *or formerly* **San·ta Is·a·bel** \,san-tə-'i-zə-,bel\ city ✳ of Equatorial Guinea on Bioko Is. *pop* 37,237

Malacca — see MELAKA — **Ma·lac·can** \-kən\ *adj*

Ma·lac·ca, Strait of \mə-'la-kə, -'lä-\ channel 500 *mi* (805 *km*) long bet. S Malay Peninsula & island of Sumatra

Má·la·ga \'ma-lə-gə, 'mä-lä-gä\ **1** province S Spain in Andalusia *area* 2809 *sq mi* (7275 *sq km*), *pop* 1,160,843 **2** city & port, its ✳, NE of Gibraltar *pop* 512,136

Malagasy Republic — see MADAGASCAR

Ma·lai·ta \mə-'lā-tə\ island SW Pacific in the SE Solomons NE of Guadalcanal

Ma·lang \mə-'läŋ\ city Indonesia in E Java S of Surabaja *pop* 695,618

Mä·lar·en \'mä-,lär-ən\ lake SE Sweden extending from Baltic Sea 70 *mi* (113 *km*) inland

Ma·la·tya \,mä-lä-,tyä\ *or anc* **Mel·i·te·ne** \,me-lə-'tē-nē\ city E Turkey NE of Gaziantep *pop* 281,776

Ma·la·wi \mə-'lä-wē\ *or formerly* **Ny·asa·land** \nī-'a-sə-,land, nē-\ country SE Africa bordering on Lake Malawi; formerly a Brit. protectorate; independent member of the Commonwealth of Nations since 1964; a republic since 1966 ✳ Lilongwe *area* 45,747 *sq mi* (118,485 *sq km*), *pop* 10,581,000 — **Ma·la·wi·an** \-ən\ *adj or n*

Malawi, Lake *or* **Lake Ny·asa** \nī-'a-sə, nē-\ lake SE Africa in Great Rift Valley in Malawi, Mozambique, & Tanzania

Ma·laya \mə-'lā-ə, mä-\ **1** MALAY PENINSULA **2** BRITISH MALAYA **3** *or* **Federation of Malaya** former country SE Asia; a Brit. dominion 1957–63, since 1963 a territory (now called **Peninsular Malaysia**) of Malaysia ✳ Kuala Lumpur *area* 50,690 *sq mi* (131,794 *sq km*) — **Ma·lay** \mə-'lā,'mä-,lā\ *adj or n* — **Ma·lay·an** \mə-'lā-ən, mä-; 'mä-,lā-\

Ma·lay Archipelago \mə-'lā, 'mä-,(,)lā\ archipelago SE Asia including Sumatra, Java, Borneo, Sulawesi, Moluccas, & Timor; usu. considered as including also the Philippines & sometimes New Guinea

Malay Peninsula peninsula 700 *mi* (1126 *km*) long SE Asia divided bet. Thailand & Malaysia

Ma·lay·sia \mə-'lā-zh(ē-)ə, -sh(ē-)ə\ **1** MALAY ARCHIPELAGO **2** *or* **Federation of Malaysia** country SE Asia, a union of Malaya, Sabah (N. Borneo), Sarawak, & (until 1965) Singapore; a limited constitutional monarchy in the Commonwealth of Nations ✳ Kuala Lumpur *area* 128,727 *sq mi* (333,403 *sq km*), *pop* 19,077,000 — **Ma·lay·sian** \mə-'lā-zhən, -shən\ *adj or n*

Malay Sea sea SE Asia surrounding the Malay Archipelago

Mal·den \'mȯl-dən\ **1** city E Mass. N of Boston *pop* 53,884 **2** island *cen* Pacific, one of the Line Islands

Mal·dives \'mȯl-,dēvz, -,dīvz *also* 'mal-, -divz\ islands in Indian Ocean S of the Laccadives; a sultanate under Brit. protection until 1965; now an independent member of the Commonwealth of Nations ✳ Male *area* 115 *sq mi* (299 *sq km*), *pop* 143,046 — **Mal·div·i·an** \mȯl-'di-vē-ən, mal-\ *adj or n*

Ma·le \'mä-lē\ island (atoll), chief of the Maldives; contains the nation's ✳

Ma·lea, Cape \mä-'lē-ä\ cape S Greece at extremity of E peninsula of the Peloponnese

Ma·le·bo, Pool *or* **Malebo Pool** \mä-'lā-,bō\ *or* **Stanley Pool** expansion of Congo River *ab* 20 *mi* (32 *km*) long 300 *mi* (483 *km*) above its mouth bet. Republic of the Congo & Democratic Republic of the Congo

Mal·e·ku·la *or* **Mal·a·ku·la** \,ma-lə-'kü-lə\ island SW Pacific in Vanuatu *area* 781 *sq mi* (2023 *sq km*), *pop* 19,289

Malgache, République — see MADAGASCAR

Mal·heur Lake \mal-'hu̇r\ lake SE Oreg. in Harney Basin

Ma·li \'mä-lē, 'ma-\ **1** federation 1959–60 of Senegal & Sudanese Republic **2** *or formerly* **Sudanese Republic** country W Africa in W Sahara & Sudan regions; a republic: before 1958 constituted **French Sudan** (a territory of France); ✳ Bamako *area* 478,652 *sq mi* (1,239,709 *sq km*), *pop* 8,646,000 — **Ma·li·an** \-lē-ən\ *adj or n*

Malines — see MECHLIN

Mal·in Head \'ma-lən\ cape Ireland (republic) in county Donegal; northernmost tip of Ireland

Mal·mé·dy \,mal-mə-'dē\ commune E Belgium SE of Liège; formerly in Germany, transferred (with Eupen) to Belgium 1919 *pop* 10,291

Malmö \'mal-,mœ, -(,)mō\ city & port SW Sweden on Öresund opposite Copenhagen, Denmark *pop* 232,908

Mal·ta \'mȯl-tə\ *or anc* **Mel·i·ta** \'me-lə-tə, mə-'lē-tə\ **1** *or* **Maltese Islands** \mȯl-'tēz, -'tēs\ group of islands in the Mediterranean S of Sicily; a dominion of the Commonwealth of Nations since 1964 ✳ Valletta *area* 122 *sq mi* (317 *sq km*), *pop* 362,000 **2** island, chief of the group *area* 95 *sq mi* (247 *sq km*) — **Maltese** *adj or n*

Maluku — see MOLUCCAS

Mal·vern Hills \'mȯ(l)-vərn\ hills W England in Hereford and Worcester

Malvinas, Islas — see FALKLAND ISLANDS

Mam·be·ra·mo \,mam-bə-'rä-(,)mō\ river 500 *mi* (805 *km*) W. New Guinea flowing NW into the Pacific

Mam·moth Cave \'ma-məth\ limestone caverns SW *cen* Kentucky in **Mammoth Cave National Park**

Mamoré   **194**

Ma·mo·ré \ˌmä-mō-ˈrā\ river 1200 *mi* (1931 *km*) Bolivia flowing N to unite with the Beni on Brazilian border forming Madeira River

Man, Isle of \ˈman\ *or anc* **Mo·na·pia** \mə-ˈnä-pē-ə\ *or* **Mo·na** \ˈmō-nə\ island British Isles in Irish Sea; a possession of the Brit. Crown; has own legislature & laws ✳ Douglas *area* 221 *sq mi* (575 *sq km*), *pop* 60,496 — **Manx·man** \ˈmaŋks-mən\ *n* — **Manx** \ˈmaŋks\ *adj or n*

Ma·na·do *or* **Me·na·do** \mə-ˈnä-(ˌ)dō\ city & port Indonesia on NE Sulawesi Is. on Celebes Sea *pop* 318,796

Ma·na·gua \mä-ˈnä-gwä\ city ✳ of Nicaragua on Lake Managua *pop* 552,900

Managua, Lake lake 38 *mi* (61 *km*) long W Nicaragua draining S to Lake Nicaragua

Ma·na·ma \mə-ˈna-mə\ city ✳ of Bahrain *pop* 136,999

Ma·nas·sas \mə-ˈna-səs\ city NE Va. *pop* 27,957

Ma·naus \mə-ˈnaús\ city W Brazil ✳ of Amazonas on Negro River 12 *mi* (19 *km*) from its junction with the Amazon *pop* 1,010,558

Mancha, La — see LA MANCHA

Manche, La — see ENGLISH CHANNEL

Man·ches·ter \ˈman-ˌches-tər, -chəs-tər\ **1** town *cen* Conn. E of Hartford *pop* 51,618 **2** city S N.H. on the Merrimack *pop* 99,567 **3** city NW England ENE of Liverpool *pop* 406,900 — see GREATER MANCHESTER — **Man·cu·ni·an** \man-ˈkyü-nē-ən, -nyən\ *adj or n*

Man·chu·kuo \ˈman-ˈchü-ˈkwō, man-ˈchü-\ former country (1931–45) E Asia in Manchuria & E Inner Mongolia ✳ Changchun

Man·chu·ria \man-ˈchùr-ē-ə\ region NE China S of the Amur including Heilongjiang, Jilin, & Liaoning provinces & part of Inner Mongolia — **Man·chu·ri·an** \-ē-ən\ *adj or n* — **Man·chu** \ˈman-ˌchü, man-ˈ\ *adj or n*

Man·da·lay \ˌman-də-ˈlā\ city *cen* Myanmar *pop* 453,000

Man·ga·ia \mäŋ-ˈgī-ə\ island S Pacific in SE Cook Islands; completely encircled by reef *area* 20 *sq mi* (52 *sq km*)

Man·ga·lore \ˈmaŋ-gə-ˌlōr, -ˌlór\ city S India in Karnataka on Malabar Coast W of Bangalore *pop* 272,819

Man·ga·re·va \ˌmäŋ-gä-ˈrā-vä, ˌmäŋ-ä-\ island S Pacific, chief of the Gambier Islands *area* 7 *sq mi* (18 *sq km*)

Man·hat·tan \man-ˈha-tᵊn, mən-\ **1** city NE *cen* Kans. on Kansas River *pop* 37,712 **2** island 13 *mi* (21 *km*) long SE N.Y. on New York Bay **3** borough of New York City comprising Manhattan Is., several small adjacent islands, & a small area (Marble Hill) on mainland *pop* 1,487,536 — **Man·hat·tan·ite** \-ˌīt\ *n*

Manhattan Beach city SW Calif. SW of Los Angeles *pop* 32,063

Ma·ni·hi·ki \ˌmä-nē-ˈhē-kē\ island, chief of the Northern Cook Islands; an atoll *pop* 408

Manihiki Islands — see NORTHERN COOK ISLANDS

Ma·ni·la \mə-ˈni-lə\ city & port ✳ of the Philippines on W coast of Luzon on Manila Bay (inlet of S. China Sea) *pop* 1,587,000

Man·i·pur \ˌma-ni-ˈpùr, mə-\ **1** river 210 *mi* (338 *km*) NE India & W Myanmar flowing into the Chindwin **2** state NE India bet. Assam & Myanmar ✳ Imphal *area* 8628 *sq mi* (22,433 *sq km*)

Ma·ni·sa *or* **Ma·nis·sa** \mä-nē-ˈsä\ *or anc* **Mag·ne·sia** \mag-ˈnē-shə, -zhə\ city W Turkey NE of Izmir *pop* 158,928

Man·i·to·ba \ma-nə-'tō-bə\ province S *cen* Canada ✳ Winnipeg *area* 211,468 *sq mi* (547,703 *sq km*), *pop* 1,091,942 — **Man·i·to·ban** \-bən\ *adj or n*

Manitoba, Lake lake over 120 *mi* (193 *km*) long Canada in S Man. *area* 1817 *sq mi* (4724 *sq km*)

Man·i·tou·lin Island \ma-nə-'tü-lən\ island 80 *mi* (129 *km*) long Canada in Ont. in Lake Huron *area* 1068 *sq mi* (2777 *sq km*)

Man·i·to·woc \ma-nə-tə-,wäk\ city E Wis. *pop* 32,520

Ma·ni·za·les \ma-nə-'za-ləs, ,mä-nē-'sä-läs\ city W *cen* Colombia in Cauca valley *pop* 327,100

Man·ka·to \man-'kā-(,)tō\ city S Minn. *pop* 31,477

Man·nar, Gulf of \mə-'när\ inlet of Indian Ocean bet. Sri Lanka & S tip of India S of Palk Strait

Mann·heim \'man-,hīm, 'män-\ city SW Germany at confluence of the Rhine & the Neckar *pop* 314,685

Mans·field \'manz-,fēld, 'man(t)s-\ **1** town *cen* Conn. *pop* 21,103 **2** city N *cen* Ohio *pop* 50,627 **3** town N *cen* England in Nottinghamshire N of Nottingham *pop* 98,800

Mansfield, Mount mountain 4393 *ft* (1339 *m*) N Vt.; highest in Green Mountains & in state

Mansûra, El *or* **Mansurah, Al** — see EL MANSÛRA

Man·te·ca \man-'tē-kə\ city *cen* Calif. S of Stockton *pop* 40,773

Man·tua \'man-chə-wə, 'manch-wə, 'män-tü-ä\ *or* **Man·to·va** \'män-tō-vä\ commune N Italy in Lombardy WSW of Venice *pop* 52,948 — **Man·tu·an** \'man-chə-wən, 'manch-wən, 'man-tə-wən\ *adj or n*

Ma·nua Islands \mä-'nü-ä\ islands SW Pacific in American Samoa E of Tutuila *area* 22 *sq mi* (57 *sq km*)

Ma·nus \'mä-nəs\ island SW Pacific in Admiralty Islands; largest of group *area* 600 *sq mi* (1560 *sq km*)

Man·za·la, Lake \man-'zä-lə\ *or anc* **Ta·nis** \'tā-nəs\ lagoon N Egypt in Nile delta W of N entrance of Suez Canal

Man·za·nil·lo \,man-zə-'ni-lō, ,män-sä-'nē-yō\ **1** city & port E Cuba on the Caribbean *pop* 107,650 **2** city & port SW Mexico in Colima *pop* 92,168

Mao·ke Mountains \'maù-kä\ *or formerly* **Snow Mountains** \'snō\ mountains W. Irian, Indonesia — see PUNCAK JAYA

Ma·ple Grove \'mā-pəl\ city SE *cen* Minn. *pop* 38,736

Maple Heights city NE Ohio SE of Cleveland *pop* 27,089

Maple Ridge municipality Canada in SW B.C. E of Vancouver *pop* 48,422

Ma·ple·wood \'mā-pəl-,wùd\ village SE Minn. *pop* 30,954

Ma·pu·to \mä-'pü-(,)tō\ *or formerly* **Lou·ren·ço Mar·ques** \lō-'rä^n-sü-'mär-kish\ city & port ✳ of Mozambique on Delagoa Bay *pop* 755,300

Ma·quo·ke·ta \mə-'kō-kə-tə\ river 150 *mi* (241 *km*) E Iowa flowing SE into Mississippi River

Mar·a·cai·bo \,mar-ə-'kī-(,)bō, ,mär-ä-\ city NW Venezuela on channel bet. Lake Maracaibo & Gulf of Venezuela *pop* 1,207,513

Maracaibo, Lake the S extension of Gulf of Venezuela in NW Venezuela *area* over 5000 *sq mi* (12,950 *sq km*)

Maracanda — see SAMARQAND

Ma·ra·cay \,mär-ä-'kī\ city N Venezuela WSW of Caracas *pop* 354,428

Marais des Cygnes \,mer-də-'zēn, -'sēn\ river 150 *mi* (241 *km*) E Kans. & W Mo. flowing into the Osage

Ma·ra·nhão \,mär-ə-'nyaủ⁵\ state NE Brazil bordering on the Atlantic ✷ São Luis *area* 127,242 *sq mi* (329,557 *sq km*), *pop* 4,922,339

Ma·ra·ñón \,mär-ə-'nyōn\ river N Peru flowing from the Andes NNW & E to join the Ucayali forming the Amazon

Mar·a·thon \'mar-ə-,thän\ **1** plain E Greece in Attica NE of Athens on the Aegean **2** ancient town on the plain

Mar·ble Canyon \'mar-bəl\ canyon of Colorado River N Ariz. just above the Grand Canyon, sometimes considered its upper portion

Mar·ble·head \'mär-bəl-,hed, ,mär-bəl-'\ town E Mass. *pop* 19,971

Mar·burg \'mär-,bůrk, -,bȯrg\ city W *cen* Germany in Hesse N of Frankfurt am Main *pop* 75,331

Marche \'märsh\ **1** region & former province *cen* France NW of Auvergne **2** region *cen* Italy on the Adriatic NW of Abruzzi ✷ Ancona *pop* 1,430,726

Mar·cus Island \'mär-kəs\ island W Pacific E of the Bonin Islands, belonging to Japan; occupied 1945–68 by U.S. *area* 1 *sq mi* (2.6 *sq km*)

Mar·cy, Mount \'mär-sē\ mountain 5344 *ft* (1629 *m*) NE N.Y.; highest in Adirondack Mountains & in state

Mar del Pla·ta \,mär-del-'plä-tä\ city & port E Argentina SSE of Buenos Aires *pop* 407,024

Mare Island \'mar, 'mer\ island W Calif. in San Pablo Bay

Ma·rem·ma \mä-'re-mä\ low-lying district W Italy on Tyrrhenian coast in SW Tuscany; formerly swampland

Ma·ren·go \mä-'reŋ-(,)gō\ village NW Italy in SE Piedmont

Mar·e·o·tis \,mar-ē-'ō-təs\ or Ar **Mar·yūt** \mar-'yüt\ lake N Egypt in Nile delta; Alexandria is situated bet. it & the Mediterranean

Ma·reth \'mär-əth, 'mar-\ town SE Tunisia SSE of Gabes

Mar·ga·ri·ta \,mär-gä-'rē-tä\ island N Venezuela in the Caribbean, chief of the **Nue·va Es·par·ta** \nwä-vä-e-'spär-tä\ group; chief town & port Porlamar *area* 414 *sq mi* (1072 *sq km*)

Mar·gate \'mär-,gāt\ **1** city SE Fla. *pop* 42,985 **2** \-,gāt, -gət\ borough SE England in Kent on coast of Isle of Thanet *pop* 53,280

Mar·iana Islands \,mar-ē-'ä-nə, ,mer-\ or formerly **La·drone Islands** \lə-'drōn\ islands W Pacific S of Bonin Islands; comprise commonwealth of Northern Mariana Islands & Guam

Ma·ri·a·nao \,mär-ē-ä-'naủ\ city W Cuba, W suburb of Havana *pop* 133,671

Ma·ri·án·ské Láz·ně \'mär-ē-,än(t)-ske-'läz-ne\ or G **Ma·ri·en·bad** \mə-'rē-ən-,bad, -,bät; 'mar-ē-ən-, 'mer-\ town W Czech Republic in NW Bohemia NE of Plzeň *pop* 15,378

Ma·ri·as \mə-'rī-əs, -əz\ river 210 *mi* (338 *km*) NW Mont. flowing SE to Missouri River

Marias Pass mountain pass 5215 *ft* (1590 *m*) NW Mont. in Lewis Range at SE corner of Glacier National Park

Ma·ri·bor \'mär-ē-,bȯr\ city NE Slovenia *pop* 153,053

Ma·rie Byrd Land \mə-,rē-'bərd\ region W Antarctica E of Ross Ice Shelf & Ross Sea

Ma·rie Ga·lante \má-,rē-gä-'länt\ island E W. Indies in the Leewards; a dependency of Guadeloupe *area* 60 *sq mi* (156 *sq km*), *pop* 13,463

Ma·rie·hamn \mə-'rē-ə-ˌhäm-ən\ *or* **Maa·rian·ha·mi·na** \'mär-
yän-ˌhä-mə-ˌnä\ seaport SW Finland ✳ of Ahvenanmaa *pop* 10,067

Mar·i·et·ta \ˌmar-ē-'e-tə, ˌmer-\ city NW Ga. NE of Atlanta *pop*
44,129

Ma·ri·na \mə-'rē-nə\ city W Calif. on Monterey Bay *pop* 26,436

Ma·rin·du·que \ˌmar-ən-'dü-(ˌ)kā, ˌmär-ēn-\ island Philippines in
Sibuyan Sea S of Luzon; chief town Boac *area* 355 *sq mi* (923 *sq
km*), *pop* 173,715

Mar·i·on \'mer-ē-ən, 'mar-\ **1** city N *cen* Ind. *pop* 32,618 **2** city E
Iowa NE of Cedar Rapids *pop* 20,403 **3** city *cen* Ohio *pop* 34,075

Ma·ri El *or* **Ma·riy El** \'mä-rē-'el\ autonomous republic E *cen*
Russia in Europe ✳ Yoshkar-Ola *area* 8958 *sq mi* (23,201 *sq km*),
pop 762,000

Mar·i·time Alps \'mar-ə-ˌtīm\ section of the W Alps SE France &
NW Italy extending to the Mediterranean; highest point Punta Ar-
gentera 10,817 *ft* (3297 *m*)

Maritime Provinces *or* **Maritimes** the Canadian provinces of
N.B., N.S., P.E.I. & sometimes thought to include Nfld. — see AT-
LANTIC PROVINCES

Maritime Territory *or Russ* **Pri·mor·skiy Kray** *or* **Pri·mor·ski
Krai** \prē-'mȯr-skē-'krī\ territory E Russia in Asia bordering on Sea
of Japan ✳ Vladivostok *area* 64,054 *sq mi* (165,900 *sq km*), *pop*
2,309,000

Ma·ri·tsa \mə-'rēt-sə\ *or Gk* **Év·ros** \'ev-ˌrȯs\ *or Turk* **Me·riç** \me-
'rēch\ river *ab* 300 *mi* (480 *km*) S Europe flowing from W Rhodope
Mountains in S Bulgaria E & S through Thrace into the Aegean

Ma·ri·u·pol' \ˌmar-ē-'ü-ˌpȯl, -pəl\ *or 1949–1989* **Zhda·nov** \zhə-
'dä-nəf\ city E Ukraine *pop* 417,000

Mark·ham \'mär-kəm\ **1** town Canada in SE Ont. NE of Toronto
pop 153,811 **2** river 200 *mi* (322 *km*) Papua New Guinea flowing
S & SE into Solomon Sea

Markham, Mount mountain 14,275 *ft* (4351 *m*) Antarctica W of
Ross Ice Shelf

Marl \'märl\ city W Germany in the Ruhr *pop* 91,864

Marl·bor·ough \'märl-ˌbər-ō, 'mȯl-\ city E Mass. E of Worcester
pop 31,813

Mar·ma·ra, Sea of \'mär-mə-rə\ *or anc* **Pro·pon·tis** \prə-'pän-təs\
sea NW Turkey connected with Black Sea by the Bosporus & with
Aegean Sea by the Dardanelles *area* 4429 *sq mi* (11,471 *sq km*)

Mar·mo·la·da \ˌmär-mō-'lä-dä\ mountain 10,965 *ft* (3342 *m*) NE Italy; highest in the Dolomites

Marne \'märn\ river 325 *mi* (523 *km*) NE France flowing W into the
Seine

Ma·ro·ni \mä-'rō-nē\ *or D* **Ma·ro·wij·ne** \ˌmär-ō-ˌvī-nə\ river 450
mi (720 *km*) on border bet. Suriname & French Guiana flowing N
into the Atlantic

Maros — see MURES

Mar·que·sas Islands \mär-'kā-zəz, -zəs, -səz, -səs\ *or F* **Îles Mar·
quises** \ēl-mär-'kēz\ islands S Pacific N of Tuamotu Archipelago in
French Polynesia ✳ Taiohae (on Nuku Hiva) *area* 480 *sq mi* (1248
sq km), *pop* 7358 — **Mar·que·san** \mär-'kā-zⁿn, -sⁿn\ *adj or n*

Mar·quette \mär-'ket\ city NW Mich. in Upper Peninsula on Lake
Superior *pop* 21,977

Mar·ra·kech or **Mar·ra·kesh** \,mar-ə-'kesh, 'mar-ə-,, mə-'rä-kish\ or formerly **Mo·roc·co** \mə-'rä-(,)kō\ city cen Morocco in foothills of the Grand Atlas pop 439,728

Mar·sa·la \mär-'sä-lä\ city & port Italy on W coast of Sicily S of Trapani pop 77,218

Marsa Matruh — see MATRUH

Mar·seille \mär-'sā\ or **Mar·seilles** \mär-'sā, -'sālz\ or anc **Mas·sil·ia** \mə-'si-lē-ə\ city & port SE France on Gulf of Lion pop 807,726 — **Mar·seil·lais** \,mär-sə-'yā, -'yäz; -sə-'lā, -'läz\ n

Mar·shall \'mär-shəl\ city NE Tex. pop 23,682

Marshall Islands islands W Pacific ✳ Majuro; part of former Trust Territory of the Pacific Islands; internally self-governing since 1980 — **Mar·shall·ese** \,mär-shə-'lēz, -'lēs\ adj or n

Mar·shall·town \'mär-shəl-,taün\ city cen Iowa pop 25,178

Marsh·field \'märsh-,fēld\ **1** town E Mass. N of Plymouth pop 21,531 **2** city N cen Wis. pop 19,291

Mar·ston Moor \'mär-stən\ locality N England in N. Yorkshire W of York

Mar·ta·ban, Gulf of \,mär-tə-'ban, -'bän\ arm of Andaman Sea S Myanmar

Mar·tha's Vine·yard \'mär-thəz-'vin-yərd\ island 20 mi (32 km) long SE Mass. in the Atlantic off SW coast of Cape Cod WNW of Nantucket — **Vine·yard·er** \'vin-yər-dər\ n

Mar·ti·nez \mär-'tē-nəs\ city W Calif. NE of Oakland pop 31,808

Mar·ti·nique \,mär-tᵊn-'ēk\ island W. Indies in the Windwards; department of France ✳ Fort-de-France area 425 sq mi (1101 sq km), pop 377,000 — **Mar·ti·ni·can** \-'ē-kən\ adj — **Mar·ti·ni·quais** \-,tē-ni-'kā\ adj

Marwar — see JODHPUR

Maryborough — see PORTLAOIGHISE

Mary·land \'mer-ə-lənd, locally also 'mər-lən(d)\ state E U.S. ✳ Annapolis area 10,460 sq mi (27,091 sq km), pop 4,781,468 — **Mary·land·er** \-lən-dər, -,lan-\ n

Maryland Heights city E Mo. W of St. Louis pop 25,407

Mary·ville \'mer-ē-,vil, 'mar-ē-, 'mä-rē-, -vəl\ city E Tenn. pop 19,208

Ma·sa·da \mə-'sä-də\ fortress town of ancient Palestine, site in SE Israel W of Dead Sea

Ma·san \'mä-,sän\ or formerly **Ma·sam·po** \'mä-,säm-,pō\ city & port SE S. Korea on an inlet of Korea Strait E of Pusan pop 448,746

Mas·ba·te \mäz-'bä-tē, mäs-\ island cen Philippines in the Visayans NE of Panay area 1571 sq mi (4085 sq km)

Mas·ca·rene Islands \,mas-kə-'rēn\ islands W Indian Ocean E of Madagascar including Mauritius, Réunion, and Rodrigues

Mas·couche \ma-'sküsh\ town Canada in S Que. N of Montreal pop 25,828

Mas·e·ru \'ma-sə-,rü, -zə-\ city ✳ of Lesotho pop 71,500

Mash·had \mə-'shad\ city NE Iran pop 1,463,508

Ma·son City \'mä-sᵊn\ city N Iowa pop 29,040

Mason–Dix·on Line \-'dik-sən\ the boundary line from the SW corner of Del. N to Pa. & W to approximately the SW corner of Pa. & often considered the boundary bet. the N & S states

Mas·qat \'məs-ˌkät\ *or* **Mus·cat** \-ˌkät, -ˌkat, -kət\ town & port ✻ of Oman on Gulf of Oman pop 100,000

Mas·sa·chu·setts \ˌma-sə-'chü-səts, -zəts\ state NE U.S. ✻ Boston *area* 8284 *sq mi* (21,456 *sq km*), *pop* 6,016,425

Massachusetts Bay inlet of the Atlantic E Mass.

Mas·sa·nut·ten Mountain \ˌma-sə-'nə-t°n\ ridge N Va. in Blue Ridge Mountains

Mas·sa·wa \mə-'sä-wə, -'sau̇-ə-\ *or* **Mits·'i·wa** \mit-'sē-wə\ city & port Eritrea on an inlet of Red Sea pop 16,579

Mas·sif Cen·tral \ma'-ˌsēf-(ˌ)sen-'träl, -(ˌ)sä°-\ plateau *cen* France rising sharply just W of the Rhône-Saône valley & sloping N to the Paris basin & W to the basin of Aquitaine

Mas·sil·lon \'ma-sə-lən, -ˌlän\ city NE Ohio *pop* 31,007

Mas·sive, Mount \'ma-siv\ mountain 14,421 *ft* (4396 *m*), *cen* Colo. in Sawatch Range W of Mt. Elbert

Ma·su·ria \mə-'zur-ē-ə, -'sur-\ *or* G **Ma·su·ren** \mä-'zur-ən\ region NE Poland SE of Gulf of Gdansk; formerly in E. Prussia, Germany — **Ma·su·ri·an** \-'zur-ē-ən, -'sur-\ *adj*

Mat·a·be·le·land \ˌma-tə-'bē-lē-ˌland, ˌmä-tä-'bä-lā-\ region SW Zimbabwe bet. the Limpopo & the Zambezi; chief town Bulawayo

Ma·ta·di \mä-tä-dē\ town & port W Democratic Republic of the Congo 172,926

Mat·a·gor·da Bay \ˌma-tə-'gör-də\ inlet of Gulf of Mexico 30 *mi* (48 *km*) long SE Tex.

Ma·ta·mo·ros \ˌmä-tä-'mör-ōs\ city NE Mexico in Tamaulipas on Rio Grande opposite Brownsville, Tex. *pop* 303,392

Mat·a·nus·ka \ˌma-tə-'nüs-kə\ river 90 *mi* (145 *km*) S Alaska flowing SW to head of Cook Inlet

Ma·tan·zas \mə-'tan-zəs, mä-'tän-säs\ city & port W Cuba on Straits of Florida E of Havana *pop* 113,724

Matapan — see TAÍNARON

Ma·thu·ra \'mə-tə-rə\ *or* **Mut·tra** \'mə-trə\ city N India in W Uttar Pradesh NW of Agra *pop* 226,850

Mat·lock \'mat-ˌläk\ town N England ✻ of Derbyshire *pop* 20,610

Ma·to Gros·so *or formerly* **Mat·to Gros·so** \ˌma-tə-'grō-(ˌ)sō, -(ˌ)sü\ 1 state SW Brazil ✻ Cuiabá *area* 352,400 *sq mi* (912,716 *sq km*), *pop* 2,020,581 2 plateau region in E *cen* Mato Grosso state

Ma·to Gros·so do Sul \dō-'sül, -dü-\ state SW Brazil ✻ Campo Grande *area* 140,219 *sq mi* (350,548 *sq km*), *pop* 1,778,494

Mato Tepee — SEE DEVILS TOWER

Ma·truh \mə-'trü\ *or* **Mar·sa Matruh** \'mar-sə\ town NW Egypt ✻ Matruh

Mats·qui \'mat-skwē\ municipality Canada in SW B.C. SE of Vancouver *pop* 68,064

Mat·su \'mät-sü, 'mat-, -(ˌ)sü\ island off SE China in Formosa Strait; administered by Taiwan *pop* 11,002

Mat·su·do \mät-'sü-(ˌ)dō\ city Japan on Honshu, a suburb of Tokyo *pop* 456,211

Mat·su·shi·ma \ˌmät-sü-'shē-mə, mät-'sü-shē-mə\ group of over 200 islets Japan off N Honshu NE of Sendai

Mat·su·ya·ma \ˌmät-sə-'yä-mä\ city & port Japan in W Shikoku *pop* 443,317

Mat·tag·a·mi \mə-'ta-gə-mē\ river 275 *mi* (442 *km*) Canada in E Ont.

Mat·ta·po·ni \ˌma-tə-pə-'nī\ river 125 *mi* (201 *km*) E Va.

Mat·ter·horn \'ma-tər-ˌhȯrn, 'mä-\ *or* F **Mont Cer·vin** \ˌmōⁿ-ser-'vaⁿ\ mountain 14,691 *ft* (4478 *m*) in Pennine Alps on border bet. Switzerland & Italy

Ma·tu·rín \ˌmä-tü-'rēn\ city NE Venezuela *pop* 207,382

Maui \'maúʻ-ē\ island Hawaii NW of Hawaii (island) *area* 728 *sq mi* (1893 *sq km*)

Mau·mee \ˌmò-'mē\ river 175 *mi* (282 *km*) NE Ind. & NW Ohio flowing NE into Lake Erie at Toledo

Mau·na Kea \ˌmaú-nä-'kā-ä, ˌmò-\ extinct volcano 13,796 *ft* (4205 *m*) Hawaii in N *cen* Hawaii (island)

Mauna Loa \'lō-ä\ volcano 13,680 *ft* (4170 *m*) Hawaii in S *cen* Hawaii (island) in Hawaii Volcanoes National Park — see KILAUEA

Maures, Monts des \ˌmōⁿ-dā-'mȯr, -'mȯr\ mountains SE France along the Riviera SW of Fréjus

Mau·re·ta·nia *or* **Mau·ri·ta·nia** \ˌmȯr-ə-'tā-nē-ə, ˌmär-, -nyə\ ancient country N Africa W of Numidia in modern Morocco & W Algeria — **Mau·re·ta·ni·an** *or* **Mau·ri·ta·ni·an** \-nē-ən, -nyən\ *adj or n*

Mauritania *or* F **Mau·ri·ta·nie** \mȯ-rē-tà-'nē\ country NW Africa bordering on the Atlantic N of Senegal River; a republic within the French Community, formerly a territory ✻ Nouakchott *area* 397,955 *sq mi* (1,030,807 *sq km*), *pop* 2,171,000 — **Mau·ri·ta·ni·an** \-'tā-nē-ən, ˌmär-, -nyən\ *adj or n*

Mau·ri·ti·us \mȯ-'ri-sh(ē-)əs\ island in Indian Ocean in *cen* Mascarenes; constitutes with Rodrigues & other dependencies a dominion of the Commonwealth of Nations ✻ Port Louis *area* 720 *sq mi* (1872 *sq km*), *pop* 1,103,000 — **Mau·ri·tian** \-'ri-shən\ *adj or n*

May, Cape \'mā\ cape S N.J. at entrance to Delaware Bay

May·a·gua·na \ˌmä-ə-'gwä-nə\ island in SE Bahamas NNE of Great Inagua Is. *area* 110 *sq mi* (285 *sq km*)

Ma·ya·güez \ˌmī-ä-'gwez, -'gwes\ city & port W Puerto Rico *pop* 100,371

Ma·ya·pán \ˌmī-ä-'pän\ ruined city ✻ of the Mayas SE Mexico in Yucatán SSE of Mérida

Mayence — see MAINZ

Ma·yenne \mä-'yen\ river 125 *mi* (201 *km*) NW France uniting with the Sarthe to form the **Maine** \'mān, 'men\ (8 *mi or* 13 *km* long, flowing into the Loire)

May·fair \'mā-ˌfar, -ˌfer\ district of W London, England, in Westminster borough

May·field Heights \'mā-ˌfēld\ city NE Ohio E of Cleveland *pop* 19,847

May·kop \mī-'kȯp\ city S Russia in Europe ✻ of Adygea *pop* 163,000

May·nooth \mä-'nüth\ town E Ireland in County Kildare *pop* 4768

Mayo 1 \'mī-(ˌ)ō\ river 250 *mi* (402 *km*) NW Mexico in Sonora flowing SW into Gulf of California **2** \'mā-(ˌ)ō\ county NW Ireland in Connacht ✻ Castlebar *area* 2084 *sq mi* (5418 *sq km*), *pop* 110,713

Ma·yon \mä-'yȯn\ volcano 8077 *ft* (2462 *m*) Philippines in SE Luzon

Ma·yotte \mä-'yät, -'yȯt\ island of the Comoro group; a French dependency *area* 144 *sq mi* (374 *sq km*) *pop* 90,000 — see COMORO ISLANDS

May·wood \'mā-ˌwùd\ **1** city SW Calif. W of Whittier *pop* 27,850 **2** village NE Ill. W of Chicago *pop* 27,139

Mayyali — see MAHÉ

Mazaca — see KAYSERI

Ma·za·tlán \ˌmä-zət-'län, -sät-\ city & port W Mexico in Sinaloa on the Pacific *pop* 314,249

Mba·ba·ne \ˌəm-bə-'bä-nā\ town ✻ of Swaziland *pop* 23,109

Mban·da·ka \ˌəm-bän-'dä-kä\ *or formerly* **Co·quil·hat·ville** \kō-kē-'at-ˌvil\ city W Democratic Republic of the Congo on Congo River *pop* 165,623

Mbi·ni \əm-'bē-nē\ *or formerly* **Río Mu·ni** \ˌrē-ō-'mü-nē\ mainland portion of Equatorial Guinea bordering on Gulf of Guinea ✻ Bata *area* 10,040 *sq mi* (26,104 *sq km*)

Mbomou — see BOMU

Mbu·ji-Ma·yi \əm-ˌbü-jē-'mī-ˌyē\ *or formerly* **Ba·kwan·ga** \bä-'kwän-gä\ city S Democratic Republic of the Congo *pop* 613,027

Mc·Al·len \mə-'ka-lən\ city S Tex. WNW of Brownsville *pop* 84,021

Mc·Kees·port \mə-'kēz-ˌpōrt, -ˌpórt\ city SW Pa. S of Pittsburgh *pop* 26,016

Mc·Kin·ley, Mount \mə-'kin-lē\ *or* **De·na·li** \də-'nä-lē\ mountain 20,320 *ft* (6194 *m*) *cen* Alaska in Alaska Range; highest in U.S. & N. America; in **Denali National Park**

Mc·Kin·ney \mə-'ki-nē\ city NE Tex. N of Dallas *pop* 21,283

M'Clure Strait \mə-'klùr\ channel N Canada bet. Banks Is. & Melville Is. opening on the W into Arctic Ocean

Mc·Mur·do Sound \mək-'mər-dō\ inlet of W Ross Sea Antarctica bet. Ross Is. & coast of Victoria Land

Mead, Lake \'mēd\ reservoir NW Ariz. & SE Nev. formed by Hoover Dam in Colorado River

Mearns, The — see KINCARDINE

Meath \'mēth, *by outsiders also* 'mēth\ county E Ireland in NE Leinster ✻ Trim *area* 903 *sq mi* (2348 *sq km*), *pop* 105,370

Meaux \'mō\ commune N France ENE of Paris *pop* 49,409

Mec·ca \'me-kə\ city Saudi Arabia ✻ of Hejaz *pop* 366,801 — **Mec·can** \-kən\ *adj or n*

Mech·lin \'me-klən\ *or Flem* **Me·che·len** \'mā-kə-lə(n)\ *or F* **Ma·lines** \mà-'lēn\ commune N Belgium *pop* 75,700

Meck·len·burg \'me-klən-ˌbərg, -ˌbùrk\ region NE Germany SE of Jutland Peninsula & E of the Elbe; in 18th & 19th centuries divided into duchies of **Mecklenburg–Schwerin** \-shvä-'rēn\ & **Meck·lenburg–Stre·litz** \-'shtrā-ləts,-'strā-\ which became grand duchies 1815 & states of Weimar Republic 1919

Me·dan \mā-'dän\ city Indonesia in NE Sumatra *pop* 1,730,752

Me·del·lín \ˌme-dᵊl-'ēn, ˌmā-thā-'yēn\ city NW Colombia NW of Bogotá *pop* 1,581,400

Med·ford \'med-fərd\ **1** city E Mass. N of Boston *pop* 57,407 **2** city SW Oreg. *pop* 46,951

Me·dia \'mē-dē-ə\ ancient country & province of Persian Empire SW Asia in NW modern Iran — **Mede** \'mēd\ *n* — **Me·di·an** \'mē-dē-ən\ *adj or n*

Media Atropatene — see AZERBAIJAN

Med·i·cine Bow \'me-də-sən-ˌbō\ river 120 *mi* (193 *km*) S Wyo. flowing into N. Platte River

Medicine Bow Mountains mountains N Colo. & S Wyo. in the Rockies; highest **Medicine Bow Peak** (in Wyo.) 12,013 *ft* (3662 *m*)

Medicine Hat city Canada in SE Alta. *pop* 43,625

Me·di·na 1 \mə-ˈdī-nə\ city N Ohio WNW of Akron *pop* 19,231 **2** \mə-ˈdē-nə\ city W Saudi Arabia *pop* 198,186

Mediolanum — see MILAN

Med·i·ter·ra·nean Sea \ˌme-də-tə-ˈrā-nē-ən, -nyən\ sea 2300 *mi* (3700 *km*) long bet. Europe & Africa connecting with the Atlantic through Strait of Gibraltar & with Red Sea through Suez Canal — **Mediterranean** *adj*

Mé·doc \mā-ˈdäk, -ˈdȯk\ district SW France N of Bordeaux

Med·way \ˈmed-ˌwā\ river 70 *mi* (113 *km*) SE England in Kent flowing NE into Thames River

Mee·rut \ˈmā-rət, ˈmir-ət\ city N India in NW Uttar Pradesh NE of Delhi *pop* 753,778

Meg·a·ra \ˈme-gə-rə\ city & port Greece on Saronic Gulf W of Athens *pop* 17,294; chief town of ancient **Meg·a·ris** \ˈme-gə-rəs\ (district bet. Saronic Gulf & Gulf of Corinth) — **Me·gar·i·an** \mə-ˈgar-ē-ən, me-, -ˈger-\ *adj or n*

Me·gha·la·ya \ˌmā-gə-ˈlā-ə\ state NE India ✳ Shillong *area* 8665 *sq mi* (22,442 *sq km*), *pop* 1,774,778

Megh·na \ˈmeg-nə\ the lower course of the Surma, India

Me·gid·do \mi-ˈgi-(ˌ)dō\ ancient city N Palestine N of Samaria

Meis·sen \ˈmī-sᵊn\ city E Germany NW of Dresden *pop* 33,997

Méjico — see MEXICO

Mek·nes \mek-ˈnes\ city N Morocco WSW of Fez; former ✳ of Morocco *pop* 248,369

Me·kong \ˈmā-ˈkȯŋ, -ˈkäŋ; ˈmā-\ river 2600 *mi* (4184 *km*) SE Asia flowing from Qinghai (China) S & SE into S. China Sea in S Vietnam

Mel·aka *or* **Ma·lac·ca** \mə-ˈla-kə, -ˈlä-\ **1** state Malaysia on W coast of Peninsular Malaysia *area* 640 *sq mi* (1648 *sq km*), *pop* 504,502 **2** city, its ✳ *pop* 250,635

Mel·a·ne·sia \ˌme-lə-ˈnē-zhə, -shə\ the islands in the Pacific NE of Australia & S of Micronesia including Bismarck Archipelago, the Solomons, Vanuatu, New Caledonia, & the Fijis — **Mel·a·ne·sian** \-zhən, -shən\ *adj or n*

Mel·bourne \ˈmel-bərn\ **1** city E Fla. SSW of Cape Canaveral *pop* 59,646 **2** city & port SE Australia ✳ of Victoria on Port Phillip Bay *metropolitan area pop* 2,761,995 — **Mel·bour·ni·an** *or* **Mel·bur·ni·an** \mel-ˈbər-nē-ən\ *n*

Me·lil·la \mə-ˈlē-yə\ city & port NE Morocco on coast NE of Fez; a Spanish presidio *pop* 56,497

Melita — see MALTA

Melitene — see MALATYA

Me·li·to·pol \ˌme-lə-ˈtȯ-pəl\ city S Ukraine near Sea of Azov *pop* 177,000

Melos — see MÍLOS

Mel·rose \ˈmel-ˌrōz\ city E Mass. N of Boston *pop* 28,150

Melrose Park village NE Ill. W of Chicago *pop* 20,859

Mel·ville, Lake \ˈmel-ˌvil\ lake Canada in Nfld. in Labrador; the inner basin of Hamilton Inlet *area* 1133 *sq mi* (2946 *sq km*)

Melville Island island Canada in N Northwest Territories in Parry Islands *area* over 16,250 *sq mi* (42,088 *sq km*)

Melville Peninsula peninsula Canada in E Northwest Territories bet. Foxe Basin & an arm of Gulf of Boothia

Memel — see KLAIPEDA

Mem·phis \'mem(p)-fəs\ **1** city SW Tenn. on Mississippi River *pop* 610,337 **2** ancient city N Egypt on the Nile S of modern Cairo; once ✻ of Egypt — **Mem·phi·an** \-fē-ən\ *adj or n* — **Mem·phite** \'mem-ˌfīt\ *adj or n*

Mem·phre·ma·gog, Lake \ˌmem(p)-fri-'mā-ˌgäg\ lake 30 *mi* (48 *km*) long on border bet. Canada & the U.S. in Que. & Vt.

Menado — see MANADO

Men·ai Strait \'me-ˌnī\ strait 14 *mi* (22 *km*) long N Wales bet. Anglesey Is. & mainland

Me Nam — see CHAO PHRAYA

Men·den·hall \'men-dən-ˌhȯl\ glacier SE Alaska N of Juneau

Men·de·res \ˌmen-də-'res\ **1** *or anc* **Mae·an·der** \mē-'an-dər\ river 240 *mi* (386 *km*) W Turkey in Asia flowing SW & W into the Aegean **2** *or anc* **Sca·man·der** \skə-'man-dər\ river 60 *mi* (96 *km*) NW Turkey in Asia flowing from Mt. Ida W & NW across the plain of ancient Troy into the Dardanelles

Men·dip \'men-ˌdip, -dəp\ hills SW England in NE Somerset; highest Blackdown 1068 *ft* (326 *m*)

Men·do·ci·no, Cape \ˌmen-də-'sē-(ˌ)nō\ headland NW Calif. SSW of Eureka; extreme W point of Calif., at 124°8′W

Men·do·ta, Lake \men-'dō-tə\ lake 6 *mi* (9.6 *km*) long S Wis. NW of Madison

Men·do·za \men-'dō-zə, -sä\ city W Argentina SE of Aconcagua *pop* 121,696

Men·lo Park \'men-(ˌ)lō\ city W Calif. SE of San Francisco *pop* 28,040

Me·nom·i·nee \mə-'nä-mə-nē\ river 125 *mi* (201 *km*) NE Wis. flowing SE on Mich.-Wis. border into Green Bay

Menominee Range iron-rich mountain range NE Wis. & NW Mich. in Upper Peninsula

Me·nom·o·nee Falls \mə-'nä-mə-nē\ village SE Wis. *pop* 26,840

Menorca — see MINORCA

Men·ton \mäⁿ-'tōⁿ\ *or It* **Men·to·ne** \men-'tō-nā\ city SE France on the Mediterranean ENE of Nice *pop* 29,474

Men·tor \'men-tər\ city NE Ohio NE of Cleveland *pop* 47,358

Men·zel Bour·gui·ba \men-'zel-búr-'gē-bə\ *or formerly* **Fer·ry·ville** \'fer-ē-ˌvil\ city N Tunisia on Lake Bizerte *pop* 42,111

Me·ra·no \mā-'rä-(ˌ)nō\ commune N Italy in Trentino-Alto Adige NW of Bolzano *pop* 32,600

Mer·ced \mər-'sed\ **1** river 150 *mi* (241 *km*) cen Calif. flowing W through Yosemite Valley into the San Joaquin **2** city cen Calif. in San Joaquin valley *pop* 56,216

Mer·cer Island \'mər-sər\ city W Wash. E of Seattle *pop* 20,816

Mer·cia \'mər-sh(ē-)ə\ ancient Anglian kingdom cen England; one of kingdoms in the Anglo-Saxon heptarchy — **Mer·cian** \'mər-sh(ē-)ən\ *adj or n*

Mer·gent·heim \'mer-gənt-ˌhīm\ *or* **Bad Mergentheim** \ˌbät-\ town S Germany in Baden-Württemberg NNE of Stuttgart

Meriç — see MARITSA

Mé·ri·da \'mer-ə-də, 'mä-rē-thä\ **1** city SE Mexico ✳ of Yucatán *pop* 557,340 **2** city W Venezuela S of Lake Maracaibo *pop* 167,992

Mer·i·den \'mer-ə-dᵊn\ city S *cen* Conn. S of Hartford *pop* 59,479

Mer·id·i·an \mə-'ri-dē-ən\ city E *cen* Miss. *pop* 41,036

Merín — see MIRIM (Lake)

Mer·i·on·eth \,mer-ē-'ä-nəth\ *or* **Mer·i·on·eth·shire** \-,shir, -shər\ former county NW Wales ✳ Dolgellau

Mer·oë \'mer-ō-(,)ē\ ancient city, site in N *cen* Sudan on the Nile — **Mero·ite** \'mer-ō-,īt\ *n* — **Mero·it·ic** \,mer-ō-'i-tik\ *adj*

Meroë, Isle of ancient region E Sudan bet. the Nile & Blue Nile rivers & the Atbara

Mer·rill·ville \'mer-əl-,vil, -vəl\ town NW Ind. *pop* 27,257

Mer·ri·mack \'mer-ə-,mak\ **1** river 110 *mi* (177 *km*) S N.H. & NE Mass. flowing S & NE into the Atlantic **2** town S N.H. *pop* 22,156

Mer·ritt Island \'mer-ət\ island 40 *mi* (64 *km*) long E Fla. W of Canaveral Peninsula bet. Indian & Banana rivers

Mer·sey \'mər-zē\ river 70 *mi* (113 *km*) NW England flowing NW & W into Irish Sea through a large estuary

Mer·sey·side \'mər-zē-,sīd\ metropolitan county NW England ✳ Liverpool *area* 261 *sq mi* (676 *sq km*), *pop* 1,376,800

Mer·sin \mer-'sēn\ city & port S Turkey on the Mediterranean WSW of Adana *pop* 422,357

Mer·thyr Tyd·fil \'mər-thər-'tid-,vil\ borough SE Wales in Mid Glamorgan *pop* 59,300

Mer·ton \'mər-tᵊn\ borough of SW Greater London, England *pop* 161,800

Me·ru, Mount \'mā-(,)rü\ mountain 14,979 *ft* (4566 *m*) NE Tanzania

Me·sa \'mā-sə\ city SW *cen* Ariz. E of Phoenix *pop* 288,091

Me·sa·bi Range \mə-'sä-bē\ range of hills NE Minn. NW of Duluth containing large deposits of iron

Me·sa Verde National Park \'mā-sə-'vərd, -'vər-dē\ reservation SW Colo. containing prehistoric cliff dwellings

Me·se·ta \me-'sā-tə\ the central plateau of Spain

Me·so·amer·i·ca \,me-zō-ə-'mer-i-kə, ,mē-, -sō-\ the parts of S N. America that were occupied by advanced peoples during pre-Columbian times — **Me·so·amer·i·can** \-kən\ *adj*

Mes·o·po·ta·mia \,me-s(ə-)pə-'tā-mē-ə, -myə\ **1** region SW Asia bet. the Tigris & the Euphrates extending from the mountains of E Asia Minor to the Persian Gulf **2** the entire Tigris-Euphrates valley — **Mes·o·po·ta·mian** \-mē-ən, -myən\ *adj* or *n*

Mes·quite \mə-'skēt, me-\ city N Tex. E of Dallas *pop* 101,484

Mes·se·ne *or* NGk **Mes·sí·ni** \me-'sē-nē\ town S Greece in SW Peloponnese, ancient ✳ of Messenia

Mes·se·nia \mə-'sē-nē-ə, -nyə\ region S Greece in SW Peloponnese bordering on Ionian Sea

Messenia, Gulf of inlet of the Mediterranean S Greece on S coast of Peloponnese

Mes·si·na \me-'sē-nä\ *or anc* **Mes·sa·na** \mə-'sä-nə\ *or* **Zan·cle** \'zaŋ-(,)klē\ city & port Italy in NE Sicily *pop* 272,461

Messina, Strait of channel bet. S Italy & NE Sicily

Mes·ta \me-'stä\ *or Gk* **Nés·tos** \'nes-,tòs\ river 150 *mi* (240 *km*) SW Bulgaria & NE Greece flowing from W end of Rhodope Mountains SE into the Aegean

Me·ta \'mā-tä\ river over 620 *mi* (998 *km*) NE Colombia flowing into the Orinoco on Venezuela-Colombia boundary

Met·air·ie \'me-tə-rē\ population center SE La. *pop* 149,428

Me·tau·ro \mə-'taùr-(,)ō\ *or anc* **Me·tau·rus** \-'tòr-əs\ river 70 *mi* (113 *km*) E *cen* Italy flowing E into the Adriatic

Me·thu·en \mə-'thü-ən, -'thyü-\ town NE Mass. *pop* 39,990

Metz \'mets, *F* 'mes\ city NE France on the Moselle *pop* 123,920

Meurthe \'mərt, 'mœrt\ river *ab* 100 *mi* (161 *km*) NE France flowing NW from Vosges Mountains to the Moselle

Meuse \'myüz, 'mə(r)z, 'mœz\ *or D* **Maas** \'mäs\ river *ab* 580 *mi* (933 *km*) W Europe flowing from NE France through S Belgium into North Sea in the Netherlands

Mewar — see UDAIPUR

Mex·i·cali \,mek-si-'ka-lē, -sē-'kä-\ city NW Mexico ✳ of Baja California state on Mexico-Calif. border *pop* 602,390

Mex·i·co \'mek-si-,kō\ *or Sp* **Mé·ji·co** \'me-hē-(,)kō\ *or MexSp* **Mé·xi·co** \'me-hē-(,)kō\ **1** country S N. America S of the U.S.; a republic ✳ Mexico *area* 759,530 *sq mi* (1,972,544 *sq km*), *pop* 89,995,000 **2** state S *cen* Mexico *area* 8286 *sq mi* (21,461 *sq km*), *pop* 9,815,795 **3** *or* **Mexico City** city ✳ of Mexico (republic) in Federal District (area surrounded on three sides by state of Mexico) — see TENOCHTITLÁN — **Mex·i·can** \'mek-si-kən\ *adj or n*

Mexico, Gulf of inlet of the Atlantic on SE coast of N. America

Mé·zenc, Mount \mā-'zeŋk\ volcanic mountain 5755 *ft* (1754 *m*) S France; highest in the Cévennes

Mez·zo·gior·no \,met-sō-'jòr-(,)nō, ,med-zō-\ the Italian Peninsula S of *ab* the latitude of Rome

Mi·ami \mī-'a-mē\ city & port SE Fla. on Biscayne Bay *pop* 358,548 — **Mi·ami·an** \-mē-ən\ *n*

Miami Beach city SE Fla. *pop* 92,639

Mich·i·gan \'mi-shi-gən\ state N U.S. in Great Lakes region including an upper (NW) & a lower (SE) peninsula ✳ Lansing *area* 58,527 *sq mi* (151,585 *sq km*), *pop* 9,295,297 — **Mich·i·gan·der** \,mi-shi-'gan-dər\ *n* — **Mich·i·gan·ite** \'mi-shi-gə-,nīt\ *n*

Michigan, Lake lake N *cen* U.S.; one of the Great Lakes *area* 22,400 *sq mi* (58,240 *sq km*)

Michigan City city N Ind. on Lake Michigan *pop* 33,822

Michilimackinac — see MACKINAC

Mi·cho·a·cán \,mē-chō-ä-'kän\ state SW Mexico bordering on the Pacific ✳ Morelia *area* 23,114 *sq mi* (59,865 *sq km*), *pop* 3,548,199

Mi·cro·ne·sia \,mī-krə-'nē-zhə, -shə\ the islands of the W Pacific E of the Philippines & N of Melanesia including the Caroline, Kiribati, Mariana, & Marshall groups — **Mi·cro·ne·sian** \-zhən, -shən\ *adj or n*

Micronesia, Federated States of islands W Pacific in the Carolines comprising Kosrae, Pohnpei, Chuuk, & Yap; part of former Trust Territory of the Pacific Islands; internally self-governing since 1986

Mid·del·burg \'mi-dᵊl-,bərg\ city SW Netherlands on Walcheren Is. ✳ of Zeeland *pop* 39,828

Middle Congo former French territory W *cen* Africa — see CONGO, FRENCH EQUATORIAL AFRICA

Middle East the countries of SW Asia & N Africa — usu. considered as including the countries extending from Libya on the W to Afghanistan on the E — **Middle Eastern** or **Mid·east·ern** \,mid-'ē-stərn\ *adj* — **Middle Easterner** *n*

Mid·dles·brough \'mi-d°lz-brə\ town N England ✳ of Cleveland on Tees River *pop* 141,100

Mid·dle·sex \'mi-d°l-,seks\ former county SE England, now absorbed in Greater London

Mid·dle·town \'mi-d°l-,taún\ **1** city *cen* Conn. S of Hartford *pop* 42,762 **2** city SE N.Y. *pop* 24,160 **3** city SW Ohio SW of Dayton *pop* 46,022 **4** town S R.I. N of Newport *pop* 19,460

Mid Gla·mor·gan \'mid-glə-'mór-gən\ county SE Wales *area* 393 *sq mi* (1022 *sq km*), *pop* 526,500

Mi·di \mē-'dē\ the south of France

Mid·i·an \'mi-dē-ən\ ancient region NW Arabia E of Gulf of Aqaba

Mid·land \'mid-lənd\ **1** city *cen* Mich. NW of Saginaw *pop* 38,053 **2** city W Tex. NE of Odessa *pop* 89,443

Mid·lands \'mid-ləndz\ the central counties of England usu. considered as comprising Bedfordshire, Buckinghamshire, Cambridgeshire, Derbyshire, Leicestershire, Lincolnshire, Northamptonshire, Nottinghamshire, Oxfordshire, Staffordshire, Warwickshire, W. Midlands, & part of Hereford and Worcester

Mid·lo·thi·an \mid-'lō-thē-ən\ or earlier **Ed·in·burgh** \'e-d°n-,bər-ə, -,bə-rə, -b(ə-)rə\ or **Ed·in·burgh·shire** \-,shir, -shər\ former county SE Scotland ✳ Edinburgh — see LOTHIAN

Mid·way \'mid-,wā\ islands (atoll) *cen* Pacific 1300 *mi* (2092 *km*) WNW of Honolulu, Hawaii, belonging to the U.S., in Hawaiian group but not incorporated in state of Hawaii *area* 2 *sq mi* (5.2 *sq km*)

Mid·west \,mid-'west\ or **Middle West** region N *cen* U.S. including area around Great Lakes & in upper Mississippi valley from Ohio & sometimes Ky. on the E to N.Dak., S.Dak., Nebr., & Kans. on the W — **Mid·west·ern** \,mid-'wes-tərn\ or **Middle Western** *adj* — **Mid·west·ern·er** \,mid-'wes-tə(r)-nər\ or **Middle Westerner** *n*

Midwest City city *cen* Okla. E of Oklahoma City *pop* 52,267

Mie·res \mē-'er-əs, 'myä-rās\ commune NW Spain in Asturias province *pop* 53,379

Mikonos — see MYKONOS

Mi·lan \mə-'lan, mē-'län\ or *It* **Mi·la·no** \mē-'lä-(,)nō\ or *anc* **Me·dio·la·num** \,me-dē-ō-'lä-nəm\ commune N Italy ✳ of Lombardy *pop* 1,449,403 — **Mil·a·nese** \,mi-lə-'nēz, -'nēs\ *adj* or *n*

Mi·laz·zo \mē-'lät-(,)sō\ or *anc* **My·lae** \'mī-(,)lē\ city & port Italy in NE Sicily W of Messina *pop* 31,559

Mi·le·tus \mī-'lē-təs, mə-\ ancient city on W coast of Asia Minor in Caria near mouth of Maeander River

Mil·ford \'mil-fərd\ **1** city S Conn. on Long Island Sound *pop* 49,938 **2** town E Mass. SE of Worcester *pop* 25,355

Milford Haven town & port SW Wales in Dyfed on Milford Haven (inlet of St. George's Channel) *pop* 13,934

Milk \'milk\ river 625 *mi* (1006 *km*) Canada & U.S. in Alta. & Mont. flowing SE into Missouri River

Mill·brae \'mil-ˌbrā\ city W Calif. on San Francisco Bay S of San Francisco *pop* 20,412

Mille Lacs \mi(l)-'lak(s)\ lake 20 *mi* (32 *km*) long E *cen* Minn.

Mill·ville \'mil-ˌvil\ city S N.J. *pop* 25,992

Mí·los or **Me·los** \'mē-ˌläs\ island Greece in SW Cyclades *area* 57 *sq mi* (148 *sq km*)

Mil·pi·tas \mil-'pē-təs\ city W Calif. N of San José *pop* 50,686

Mil·ton \'mil-t^n\ **1** town E Mass. S of Boston *pop* 25,725 **2** town Canada in SE Ont. SW of Toronto *pop* 32,075

Mil·wau·kee \mil-'wȯ-kē\ city & port SE Wis. on Lake Michigan *pop* 628,088 — **Mil·wau·kee·an** \-kē-ən\ *n*

Min \'min\ **1** river 350 *mi* (563 *km*) *cen* China in Szechwan flowing SE into the Chang **2** river 250 *mi* (402 *km*) SE China in Fujian flowing SE into E. China Sea

Mi·nas Basin \'mī-nəs\ landlocked bay E Canada in *cen* N.S.; the NE extension of Bay of Fundy; connected with it by **Minas Channel**

Mi·nas de Rí·o·tin·to \'mē-näs-thā-ˌrē-ō-'tēn-tō\ commune SW Spain in Huelva province NE of Huelva *pop* 5480

Mi·nas Ge·rais \ˌmē-nəs-zhə-'rīs\ state E Brazil ✻ Belo Horizonte *area* 226,707 *sq mi* (587,171 *sq km*), *pop* 15,746,200

Minch \'minch\ channel NW Scotland comprising **North Minch** & **Little Minch** bet. Outer Hebrides & NW coast of Scotland

Min·cio \'mēn-(ˌ)chō, 'min-chē-ˌō\ or *anc* **Min·cius** \'min(t)-sh(ē-)əs, -sē-əs\ river 115 *mi* (185 *km*) N Italy issuing from Lake Garda & emptying into the Po

Min·da·nao \ˌmin-də-'nä-ˌō, -'naú\ island S Philippines *area* (including adjacent islands) 38,254 *sq mi* (99,078 *sq km*), *pop* 13,966,000

Mindanao Sea sea S Philippines N of Mindanao

Min·do·ro \min-'dȯr-(ˌ)ō, -'dór-\ island *cen* Philippines SW of Luzon *area* 3759 *sq mi* (9773 *sq km*), *pop* 473,940

Minhow — see FUZHOU

Min·i·coy \'mi-ni-ˌkói\ island India, southernmost of the Laccadives *pop* 368,383 — **Min·ne·ap·o·lis** \ˌmi-nē-'a-pə-lis\ city SE Minn. on Mississippi River *pop* 84,068 *sq mi* (218,577 *sq km*), *pop* 4,375,099 — **Min·ne·ap·o·li·tan** \-nē-ə-'päl-ə-t^n\ *n*

Min·ne·so·ta \ˌmi-nə-'sō-tə\ **1** river 332 *mi* (534 *km*) S Minn. flowing from Big Stone Lake to Mississippi River **2** state N U.S. ✻ St. Paul *area* 84,068 *sq mi* (218,577 *sq km*), *pop* 4,375,099 — **Min·ne·so·tan** \-'sō-t^n\ *adj or n*

Min·ne·ton·ka \ˌmi-nə-'täŋ-kə\ city SE Minn. E of **Lake Minnetonka** (12 *mi* or 19 *km* long) *pop* 48,370

Minni — see ARMENIA

Mi·nor·ca \mə-'nȯr-kə\ or *Sp* **Me·nor·ca** \mā-'nȯr-kä\ island Spain in the Balearic Islands ENE of Majorca; chief city Mahón — **Mi·nor·can** \mə-'nȯr-kən\ *adj or n*

Mi·not \'mī-ˌnät, -nət\ city NW *cen* N.Dak. *pop* 34,544

Minsk \'min(t)sk\ city ✻ of Belarus *pop* 1,589,000

Minya, Al or **Minya, El** — see EL MINYA

Minya Konka — see GONGGA SHAN

Mi·que·lon \'mi-kə-ˌlän, ˌmē-kə-'lō^n\ island off S coast of Newfoundland, Canada, belonging to France — see SAINT PIERRE

Mir·a·mar \'mir-ə-ˌmär\ city SE Fla. *pop* 40,663

Mi·rim, Lake \mə-'rim\ *or Sp* **Me·rín** \mā-'rēn\ lake 108 *mi* (174 *km*) long on boundary bet. Brazil & Uruguay near Atlantic coast

Mir·za·pur \'mir-zə-ˌpu̇r\ city N India in SE Uttar Pradesh on the Ganges SW of Varanasi *pop* 169,368

Mi·se·num \mī-'sē-nəm\ ancient port & naval station S Italy at NW corner of Bay of Naples

Mish·a·wa·ka \ˌmi-shə-'wȯ-kə, -'wä-\ city N Ind. *pop* 42,608

Mis·kolc \'mish-ˌkōlts\ city NE Hungary NE of Budapest *pop* 207,300

Misr — see EGYPT

Mis·sion \'mi-shən\ **1** city S Tex. *pop* 28,653 **2** municipality Canada in SW B.C. *pop* 26,202

Mis·sion·ary Ridge \'mi-shə-ˌner-ē\ mountain SE Tenn. & NW Ga. SE of Chattanooga

Mission Vie·jo \vē-'ā-(ˌ)hō\ city SW Calif. SE of Santa Ana *pop* 72,820

Mis·sis·sau·ga \ˌmi-sə-'sȯ-gə\ city Canada in S Ont. SW of Toronto *pop* 463,388

Mis·sis·sip·pi \ˌmi-sə-'si-pē\ **1** river 2340 *mi* (3765 *km*) *cen* U.S. flowing from N *cen* Minn. to Gulf of Mexico — see ITASCA (Lake) **2** river 105 *mi* (169 *km*) Canada in SE Ont. flowing NE & N into Ottawa River **3** state S U.S. ✳ Jackson *area* 47,689 *sq mi* (123,514 *sq km*), *pop* 2,573,216 — **Mis·sis·sip·pian** \-pē-ən\ *adj or n*

Mississippi Sound inlet of Gulf of Mexico E of Lake Pontchartrain

Mis·sou·la \mə-'zü-lə\ city W Mont. *pop* 42,918

Mis·sou·ri \mə-'zu̇r-ē, *by some residents* mə-'zu̇r-ə\ **1** river 2466 *mi* (3968 *km*) W U.S. flowing from SW Mont. into Mississippi River in E Mo. — see THREE FORKS **2** state *cen* U.S. ✳ Jefferson City *area* 69,697 *sq mi* (180,515 *sq km*), *pop* 5,117,073 — **Mis·sou·ri·an** \-'zu̇r-ē-ən\ *adj or n*

Missouri City city SE Tex. *pop* 36,176

Mis·tas·si·ni \ˌmis-tə-'sē-nē\ **1** lake Canada in S *cen* Que. draining W to James Bay *area* 840 *sq mi* (2184 *sq km*) **2** river 185 *mi* (298 *km*) Canada in S Que. flowing S into Lake Saint-Jean

Mis·ti, El \el-'mēs-tē, -'mis-\ dormant volcano 19,101 *ft* (5822 *m*) S Peru

Mitch·am \'mi-chəm\ former municipal borough S England in Surrey, now part of Merton

Mitch·ell, Mount \'mi-chəl\ mountain 6684 *ft* (2037 *m*) W N.C. in Black Mountains of the Blue Ridge Mountains; highest point in U.S. E of Mississippi River

Mits'iwa — see MASSAWA

Mix·co \'mēs-(ˌ)kō\ city S *cen* Guatemala, a suburb of Guatemala City

Mi·ya·za·ki \mē-ˌyä-'zä-kē, mē-'yä-zä-(ˌ)kē\ city & port Japan in Kyushu on SE coast *pop* 287,367

Mi·zo·ram \mi-'zȯr-əm\ state NE India *area* 8142 *sq mi* (21,169 *sq km*), *pop* 689,756

Mma·ba·tho \mä-'bä-(ˌ)tō\ town N Republic of South Africa near Botswana border; formerly ✳ of Bophuthatswana

Mo·ab \'mō-,ab\ region Jordan E of Dead Sea; in biblical times a kingdom bet. Edom & the country of the Amorites — **Mo·ab·ite** \'mō-ə-,bīt\ adj or n — **Mo·ab·it·ish** \-,bī-tish\ adj

Mo·bile \mō-'bēl, 'mō-,bēl\ **1** river 38 mi (61 km) long SW Ala. formed by Alabama & Tombigbee rivers & flowing S into **Mobile Bay** (inlet of Gulf of Mexico) **2** city & port SW Ala. pop 196,278

Moçambique — see MOZAMBIQUE

Moçâmedes — see NAMIBE

Mo·cha \'mō-kə\ or Ar **Al Mu·khā** \,ȧl-mü-'kä\ town & port SW Yemen on the Red Sea

Mod·der \'mä-dər\ river 180 mi (290 km) Republic of South Africa in Free State; a tributary of the Vaal

Mo·de·na \'mō-dᵊn-ə, 'mȯ-dä-nä\ or anc **Mu·ti·na** \'myü-t²n-ə\ commune N Italy in Emilia SW of Venice pop 176,857 — **Mod·e·nese** \,mō-dᵊn-'ēz, -mō-, -'ēs\ n

Mo·des·to \mə-'des-(,)tō\ city cen Calif. on the Tuolumne pop 164,730

Moe·sia \'mē-sh(ē-)ə\ ancient country & Roman province SE Europe in modern Serbia & Bulgaria S of the Danube from the Drina to Black Sea

Mog·a·di·shu \,mä-gə-'di-(,)shü, ,mō-, -'dē-\ or **Mog·a·di·scio** \-(,)shō\ city & port ✳ of Somalia on Indian Ocean pop 349,245

Mogador — see ESSAOUIRA

Mogilev — see MAHILYOW

Mo·gol·lon Mountains \,mə-gə-'yōn, ,mō-\ mountains SW N.Mex.; highest Whitewater Baldy 10,895 ft (3320 m)

Mo·hacs \'mō-,hach, -,häch\ town S Hungary pop 20,700

Mo·hawk \'mō-,hȯk\ river 148 mi (238 km) E cen N.Y. flowing E into Hudson River

Mo·hen·jo Da·ro \mō-'hen-(,)jō-'där-(,)ō\ prehistoric city Pakistan in Indus valley NE of modern Karachi

Mo·ja·ve Desert or **Mo·ha·ve Desert** \mə-'hä-vē, mō-'\ desert S Calif. SE of S end of the Sierra Nevada

Mo·ji \'mō-(,)jē\ former city Japan in N Kyushu on Shimonoseki Strait — see KITAKYUSHU

Mok·po \'mäk-(,)pō\ city & port SW S. Korea on Yellow Sea SW of Kwangju pop 236,085

Mold \'mōld\ town NE Wales in Clwyd

Mol·da·via \mäl-'dā-vē-ə, -vyə\ **1** region Europe in NE Romania & Moldova bet. the Carpathians & Transylvanian Alps on the W & the Dniester on the E **2** — see MOLDOVA — **Mol·da·vian** \-vē-ən, -vyən\ adj or n

Mol·do·va \mäl-'dō-və, mȯl-\ independent country in E Moldavia region; formerly (as **Mcldavian Republic** or **Moldavia**) a constituent republic of the U.S.S.R.; ✳ Chişinău area 13,012 sq mi (33,701 sq km), pop 4,362,000

Mo·len·beek \'mō-lən-,bāk\ or **Molenbeek–Saint–Jean** \-saⁿ-'zhäⁿ\ commune cen Belgium in Brabant W of Brussels pop 68,759

Mo·line \mō-'lēn\ city NW Ill. on Mississippi River pop 43,202

Mo·li·se \mō-'lē-zā\ region cen Italy bet. the Apennines & the Adriatic S of Abruzzi ✳ Campobasso pop 335,348 — see ABRUZZI

Mo·lo·kai \,mä-lə-'kī, ,mō-lō-'kä-ē\ island cen Hawaii area 259 sq mi (673 sq km)

Mo·lo·po \mō-'lō-(,)pō\ river 600 *mi* (966 *km*) S Africa flowing W along border bet. Botswana & Republic of South Africa & thence S into Orange River; now usu. dry

Molotov — see PERM

Mo·luc·cas \mə-'luc-kəz\ *or Indonesian* **Ma·lu·ku** \mə-'lü-(,)kü\ islands Indonesia in Malay Archipelago bet. Sulawesi & New Guinea *area* 32,307 *sq mi* (83,675 *sq km*), *pop* 1,857,790 — see HALMAHERA — **Mo·luc·ca** \mə-'lə-kə\ *or* **Mo·luc·can** \-kən\ *adj*

Mom·ba·sa \mäm-'bä-sə\ **1** island Kenya on coast N of Pemba **2** city & port on Mombasa Is. & adjacent mainland *pop* 341,148

Mona 1 — see ANGLESEY **2** *or* **Monapia** — see MAN (Isle of)

Mo·na·co \'mä-nə-,kō *also* mə-'nä-(,)kō\ **1** country S Europe on the Mediterranean coast of France; a principality *area* 368 *acres* (147 *hectares*), *pop* 30,500 **2** commune, its ✻ — **Mo·na·can** \'mä-nə-kən, mə-'nä-kən\ *adj or n* — **Mon·e·gasque** \,mä-ni-'gask\ *adj or n*

Mo·nad·nock, Mount \mə-'nad-,näk\ mountain 3165 *ft* (965 *m*) SW N.H.

Mon·a·ghan \'mä-nə-hən, -,han\ **1** county NE Ireland (republic) in Ulster *area* 498 *sq mi* (1290 *sq km*), *pop* 51,293 **2** town, its ✻ *pop* 5754

Mo·na Passage \'mō-nə\ strait West Indies bet. Hispaniola & Puerto Rico connecting the Caribbean & the Atlantic

Monastir — see BITOLA

Mön·chen·glad·bach \,mən-kən-'glät-,bäk, ,mœn-kən-'glät-,bäk\ *or formerly* **Mün·chen-Glad·bach** \,m(y)ün-kən-, ,mœn-kən-\ city W Germany W of Düsseldorf *pop* 262,581

Monc·ton \'məŋk-tən\ city Canada in E N.B. *pop* 57,010

Mon·go·lia \män-'gōl-yə, mäŋ-, -'gō-lē-ə\ **1** region E Asia E of Altai Mountains; includes Gobi Desert **2** *or* **Outer Mongolia** country E Asia comprising major portion of Mongolia region; a republic ✻ Ulaanbaatar *area* 604,247 *sq mi* (1,565,000 *sq km*), *pop* 2,182,000 **3** INNER MONGOLIA — **Mon·gol** \'män-gəl; 'mäŋ-,gōl, 'mäŋ-\ *adj or n* — **Mon·go·lian** \män-'gōl-yən, mäŋ-, -gō-lē-ən\ *adj or n*

Mon·he·gan \män-'hē-gən\ island Maine E of Portland

Mon·mouth \'män-məth, 'mən-\ *or* **Mon·mouth·shire** \-,shir, -shər\ former county SE Wales, often regarded as part of England ✻ Newport

Mo·noc·a·cy \mə-'nä-kə-sē\ river 60 *mi* (96 *km*) S Pa. & N Md. flowing S into the Potomac

Mo·no Lake \'mō-(,)nō\ saline lake 14 *mi* (22 *km*) long E Calif.

Mo·non·ga·he·la \mə-,nän-gə-'hē-lə, -,näŋ-gə-, -'hā-lə\ river 128 *mi* (206 *km*) N W.Va. & SW Pa. flowing N to unite with Allegheny River at Pittsburgh forming Ohio River

Mon·roe \(,)mən-'rō\ **1** city N La. *pop* 54,909 **2** city SE Mich. SSW of Detroit on Lake Erie *pop* 22,902

Mon·roe·ville \(,)mən-'rō-,vil\ borough SW Pa. E of Pittsburgh *pop* 29,169

Mon·ro·via \(,)mən-'rō-vē-ə\ **1** city SW Calif. E of Pasadena *pop* 35,761 **2** city & port ✻ of Liberia, on the Atlantic *pop* 243,243

Mons \'mōⁿs\ *or Flem* **Ber·gen** \'ber-kə(n)\ commune SW Belgium ✻ of Hainaut *pop* 92,300

Mon·ta·na \män-'ta-nə\ state NW U.S. ✳ Helena *area* 147,046 *sq mi* (380,849 *sq km*), *pop* 799,065 — **Mon·tan·an** \-nən\ *adj or n*

Mont·au·ban \män-tō-'bän, mōⁿ-tō-'bäⁿ\ city SW France on the Tarn N of Toulouse *pop* 53,278

Mon·tauk Point \'män-,tȯk\ headland SE N.Y. at E tip of Long Is.

Mont Blanc \mōⁿ-'bläⁿ\ mountain peak 15,771 *ft* (4807 *m*) on border of France, Italy, and Switzerland in Savoy Alps; highest of the Alps

Mont Blanc Tunnel tunnel 7½ *mi* (12 *km*) long France & Italy under Mont Blanc

Mont·clair \mänt-'klar, -'kler\ city SW Calif. E of Los Angeles *pop* 28,434

Mon·te Al·bán \män-tē-äl-'bän, ,mōn-tä-äl-'vän\ ruined city of the Zapotecs S Mexico in Oaxaca state SW of Oaxaca

Mon·te·bel·lo \män-tə-'be-(,)lō\ city SW Calif. *pop* 59,564

Mon·te Car·lo \män-tē-'kär-(,)lō, ,mȯn-tä-\ commune Monaco *pop* 14,702

Mon·te·go Bay \män-'tē-(,)gō\ city & port NW Jamaica on Montego Bay (inlet of the Caribbean) *pop* 83,446

Mon·te·ne·gro \män-ə-'nē-(,)grō, -'nā-, -'ne-\ federated republic S Yugoslavia on the Adriatic; formerly a kingdom ✳ Podgorica *area* 5333 *sq mi* (13,812 *sq km*), *pop* 616,327 — **Mon·te·ne·grin** \-grən\ *adj or n*

Mon·te·rey \män-tə-'rā\ city W Calif. on peninsula at S end of **Monterey Bay** (inlet of the Pacific) *pop* 31,954

Monterey Park city SW Calif. E of Los Angeles *pop* 60,738

Mon·ter·rey \män-tə-'rā\ city NE Mexico ✳ of Nuevo León *pop* 1,064,197

Mon·te·vi·deo \män-tə-və-'dā-(,)ō, -'vi-dē-,ō; ,mȯn-tä-vē-'thä-ō\ city & port ✳ of Uruguay on N shore of Río de la Plata *pop* 1,260,753

Mon·te·zu·ma Castle National Monument \män-tə-'zü-mə\ reservation *cen* Ariz. containing prehistoric cliff dwellings

Mont·gom·ery \(,)mən(t)-'gə-mə-rē, män(t)-, -'gä-; -'gəm-rē, -'gäm-\ **1** city ✳ of Ala. on Alabama River *pop* 187,106 **2** ✳ **Mont·gom·ery·shire** \-,shir, -shər\ former county E Wales ✳ Welshpool

Mont·mar·tre \mōⁿ-'märtr\ section of Paris, France, on a hill in N *cen* part of the city

Mont·mo·ren·cy \mänt-mə-'ren(t)-sē, mōⁿ-mȯ-räⁿ-'sē\ commune N France, N suburb of Paris *pop* 20,927

Mont·mo·ren·cy Falls \mänt-mə-'ren(t)-sē\ waterfall *over* 270 *ft* (82 *m*) Canada in S Que. NE of Quebec (city) in **Montmorency River** (60 *mi or* 96 *km* flowing S into St. Lawrence River)

Mont·par·nasse \mōⁿ-(,)pär-'näs, -'nas\ section of Paris, France, in S *cen* part of the city — **Mont·par·nas·sian** \-'na-shən, -'na-sē-ən\ *adj*

Mont·pe·lier \mänt-'pēl-yər, -'pil-\ city ✳ of Vt. *pop* 8247

Mont·pel·lier \mōⁿ-pel-'yā\ city S France WNW of Marseille *pop* 210,866

Mon·tre·al \,män-trē-'ȯl, ,mən-\ *or* **Mont·ré·al** \mōⁿ-rā-'äl\ city & port Canada in S Que. on **Montreal Island** (32 *mi or* 51 *km* long, in St. Lawrence River) *pop* 1,017,666 — **Mon·tre·al·er** \,män-trē-'ȯ-lər, ,mən-\ *n*

Montreal North or **Montréal–Nord** \-'nȯr\ town Canada in S Que. on Montreal Is. *pop* 85,516

Mon·treuil \mōⁿ-'trœi\ or **Montreuil–sous–Bois** \-,sü-'bwä\ commune N France, E suburb of Paris *pop* 95,038

Mont–Roy·al \mōⁿ-rwä-'yäl\ or **Mount Roy·al** \maúnt-'rȯi(-ə)l\ height 769 *ft* (234 *m*) in Montreal, Que.

Mont–Saint–Mi·chel \,mōⁿ-saⁿ-mē-'shel\ small island NW France in Gulf of St-Malo

Mont·ser·rat \,män(t)-sə-'rat\ island Brit. West Indies in the Leewards SW of Antigua ✳ Plymouth *area* 40 *sq mi* (104 *sq km*), *pop* 12,100

Mon·u·ment Valley \'män-yə-mənt\ region NE Ariz. & SE Utah containing red sandstone buttes, mesas, & arches

Mon·za \'mōnt-sä, 'män-zə\ commune N Italy in Lombardy SE of Milan *pop* 121,151

Moore \'mȯr, 'mȯr\ city *cen* Okla. S of Oklahoma City *pop* 40,318

Mo·orea \,mō-ō-'rä-ä\ island S Pacific in Society Islands NW of Tahiti *area* over 50 *sq mi* (130 *sq km*)

Moor·head \'mȯr-,hed, 'mȯr-, 'mūr-\ city W Minn. on Red River opposite Fargo, N.Dak. *pop* 32,295

Moor·park \'mȯr-,pärk, 'mȯr-\ city SW Calif. W of Los Angeles *pop* 25,494

Moose \'müs\ river 50 *mi* (80 *km*) Canada in NE Ont. flowing NE into James Bay; estuary of Abitibi, Mattagami, & other rivers

Moose·head Lake \'müs-,hed\ lake 35 *mi* (56 *km*) long NW *cen* Maine

Moose Jaw city Canada in S Sask. W of Regina *pop* 33,593

Mo·rad·a·bad \mə-'rä-də-,bäd, -'ra-də-,bad\ city N India in NW Uttar Pradesh ENE of Delhi *pop* 429,214

Mo·ra·tu·wa \mə-'ra-tə-wə, 'mȯr-ə-,tü-wə\ city W Sri Lanka on Indian Ocean S of Colombo *pop* 170,000

Mo·ra·va \'mȯr-ä-vä\ **1** river *ab* 220 *mi* (354 *km*), *cen* Europe flowing S from E Czech Republic & forming part of the borders bet. the Czech Republic & Slovakia and Austria & Slovakia before entering the Danube **2** river 134 *mi* (216 *km*) Serbia flowing N into the Danube

Mo·ra·via \mə-'rä-vē-ə\ or **Mo·ra·va** \'mȯr-ä-vä\ region E Czech Republic S of Silesia traversed by Morava River; once an independent kingdom, later under shifting jurisdictions; chief city Brno

Mo·ra·vi·an Gate \mə-'rä-vē-ən\ mountain pass *cen* Europe bet. Sudety & Carpathian mountains — **Mo·ra·vi·an** \mə-'rä-vē-ən\ *adj or n*

Moravska Ostrava — see OSTRAVA

Mor·ay \'mər-ē\ or **Mor·ay·shire** \-,shir, -shər\ or **El·gin** \'el-gən\ or **El·gin·shire** \-,shir, -shər\ former county NE Scotland bordering on North Sea ✳ Elgin

Moray Firth inlet of North Sea N Scotland

Mord·vin·ia \mȯrd-'vi-nē-ə\ or **Mor·do·via** \(,)mȯr-'dō-vē-ə\ or **Mor·do·vi·an Republic** \-vē-ən\ autonomous republic *cen* Russia in Europe S & W of the middle Volga ✳ Saransk *area* 10,116 *sq mi* (26,200 *sq km*), *pop* 964,000 — **Mordvinian** *n*

Mo·reau \'mȯr-(,)ō, 'mȯr-\ river 290 *mi* (467 *km*) NW S.Dak. flowing E into Missouri River

More·cambe and Hey·sham \'mȯr-kəm-ənd-'hē-shəm, 'mȯr-\ borough NW England in N Lancashire on **Morecambe Bay** (inlet of Irish Sea) *pop* 41,187

Mo·re·lia \mə-'rāl-yə, mō-'rāl-yä\ city SW Mexico ✳ of Michoacán *pop* 489,756

Mo·re·los \mə-'rā-ləs, mō-'rā-lōs\ state S *cen* Mexico ✳ Cuernavaca *area* 1908 *sq mi* (4942 *sq km*), *pop* 1,195,059

Mo·re·no Valley \mə-'rē-(,)nō\ city S Calif. E of Riverside *pop* 118,779

More·ton Bay \'mȯr-tᵊn, 'mȯr-\ inlet of the Pacific Australia in SE Queensland at mouth of Brisbane River

Mor·gan Hill \'mȯr-gən\ city W Calif. SE of San Jose *pop* 23,928

Mor·gan·town \'mȯr-gən-,taún\ city N W.Va. *pop* 25,879

Mo·ri·ah \mə-'rī-ə\ hill *cen* Palestine in E part of Jerusalem

Mo·roc·co \mə-'rä-(,)kō\ **1** country NW Africa bordering on the Atlantic & the Mediterranean; a kingdom ✳ Rabat, summer ✳ Tangier *area* 172,413 *sq mi* (446,550 *sq km*), *pop* 20,419,555; formerly (1911–56) divided into **French Morocco** (protectorate ✳ Rabat), **Spanish Morocco** (protectorate ✳ Tetuán), **Southern Morocco** (Spanish protectorate, chief town Cabo Yubi), & the **International Zone** of Tangier **2** — see MARRAKECH — **Mo·roc·can** \-kən\ *adj or n*

Mo·ro Gulf \'mȯr-(,)ō, 'mȯr-\ arm of Celebes Sea S Philippines off SW coast of Mindanao

Mo·ro·ni \mȯ-'rō-nē\ city ✳ of Comoros *pop* 23,432

Mor·ris Jes·up, Cape \'mȯr-əs-'jes-əp, 'mär-\ headland N Greenland in Peary Land on Arctic Ocean; is world's northernmost dry land

Morrison, Mount — see YÜ SHAN

Morrison Cave — see LEWIS AND CLARK CAVERN

Mor·ris·town \'mȯr-əs-,taún, 'mär-\ city E Tenn. ENE of Knoxville *pop* 21,385

Mor·ton Grove \'mȯr-tᵊn\ village NE Ill. W of Evanston *pop* 22,408

Mos·cow \'mäs-(,)kō, -,kaú\ *or Russ* **Mos·kva** \másk-'vá\ **1** river 315 *mi* (507 *km*) W *cen* Russia in Europe flowing E into Oka River **2** city ✳ of Russia & formerly of U.S.S.R. & of Soviet Russia on Moscow River *pop* 8,769,000 — see MUSCOVY

Mo·selle \mō-'zel\ *or G* **Mo·sel** \'mō-zəl\ river *ab* 340 *mi* (545 *km*) E France & W Germany flowing from Vosges Mountains into the Rhine at Koblenz

Mos·qui·to Coast \mə-'skē-(,)tōt\ *or* **Mos·qui·tia** \mə-'skē-tē-ə\ region Central America bordering on the Caribbean in E Honduras & E Nicaragua

Mos·sel Bay \'mȯ-səl\ city & port S Republic of South Africa in S Western Cape on Mossel Bay (inlet of Indian Ocean) *pop* 17,574

Moss Point \'mȯs\ city SE Miss. E of Gulfport *pop* 17,837

Mos·tag·a·nem \mə-'sta-gə-,nem\ city & port NW Algeria *pop* 114,534

Mo·sul \mō-'sül, 'mō-səl\ city N Iraq on the Tigris *pop* 264,146

Moul·mein \mül-'mān, mōl-, -'mīn\ city S Myanmar on Gulf of Martaban at mouth of the Salween *pop* 171,977

Mound City Group National Monument \'maúnd\ reservation S Ohio N of Chillicothe containing prehistoric mounds

Moun·tain Brook \'maún-t⁸n\ city N *cen* Ala. E of Birmingham *pop* 19,810

Mountain View city W Calif. NW of San Jose *pop* 67,460

Mount De·sert Island \də-'zərt, 'de-zərt\ island S Maine in the Atlantic E of Penobscot Bay *area* 100 *sq mi* (260 *sq km*)

Mount·lake Terrace \'maúnt-,lāk\ city W Wash. N of Seattle *pop* 19,320

Mount Pearl \'pərl\ town Canada in Nfld. *pop* 23,689

Mount Pleasant \'ple-z⁸nt\   **1** city *cen* Mich. NW of Saginaw *pop* 23,285   **2** town SE S.C. on the coast *pop* 30,108

Mount Pros·pect \'prä-,spekt\ village NE Ill. *pop* 53,170

Mount Rainier National Park — see RAINIER (Mount)

Mount Rev·el·stoke National Park \'re-vəl-,stōk\ reservation Canada in SE B.C. on a plateau including Mt. Revelstoke W of Selkirk Mountains

Mount Royal — see MONT-ROYAL

Mount Saint Helens National Volcanic Monument — see SAINT HELENS (Mount)

Mount Ver·non \'vər-nən\ city SE N.Y. *pop* 67,153

Mourne Mountains mountains SE Northern Ireland

Moyle \'móil\ district N Northern Ireland, established 1974 *area* 191 *sq mi* (497 *sq km*), *pop* 14,617

Mo·zam·bique \,mō-zəm-'bēk\ *or Pg* **Mo·çam·bi·que** \,mü-säm-'bē-kə\   **1** channel 950 *mi* (1529 *km*) long SE Africa bet. Madagascar & Mozambique   **2** *or formerly* **Portuguese East Africa** country SE Africa bordering on Mozambique Channel; a republic, until 1975 a dependency of Portugal ✲ Maputo *area* 297,846 *sq mi* (771,421 *sq km*), *pop* 15,243,000 — **Mo·zam·bi·can** \,mō-zəm-'bē-kən\ *adj or n*

Mpu·ma·lan·ga \əm-,pü-mä-'län-gä\ *or formerly* **Eastern Transvaal** province NE Republic of South Africa *area* 30,259 *sq mi* (78,370 *sq km*), *pop* 2,911,000

Mtwa·ra \əm-'twär-ä\ city & port Tanzania in SE mainland

Mu·dan·jiang *or* **Mu–tan–chiang** *or* **Mu·tan·kiang** \'mü-'dän-'jyän\ city NE China in S Heilongjiang on the **Mudan River** (310 *mi or* 496 *km* flowing NE into Songhua River) *pop* 571,705

Mu·gu, Point \mə-'gü\ cape SW Calif. W of Los Angeles

Muir Woods National Monument \'myúr\ reservation N Calif. NW of San Francisco containing a redwood grove

Mui·zen·berg \'mī-z⁸n-,bərg\ town Republic of South Africa on False Bay, SSE suburb of Cape Town

Mukalla — see AL MUKALLA

Mukden — see SHENYANG

Mukhā, Al — see MOCHA

Mül·heim \'mül-,hīm, 'myül-, 'mœl-\ *or* **Mülheim an der Ruhr** \än-də(r)-'rúr\ city W Germany on Ruhr River *pop* 177,042

Mul·house \mə-'lüz\ commune NE France in Alsace *pop* 109,905

Mull \'məl\ island W Scotland in the Inner Hebrides *area* 351 *sq mi* (913 *sq km*), *pop* 1499

Mul·lin·gar \,mə-lən-'gär\ town N *cen* Ireland ✲ of Westmeath *pop* 8077

Mul·tan \mül-'tän\ city NE Pakistan SW of Lahore *pop* 742,000

Mult·no·mah Falls \,məlt-'nō-mə\ waterfall 620 *ft* (189 *m*) NW Oreg. E of Portland in a tributary of Columbia River

215 Muskogee

Mumbai — see BOMBAY 2

München–Gladbach — see MÖNCHENGLADBACH

Mun·cie \'mən(t)-sē\ city E cen Ind. *pop* 71,035

Mun·de·lein \'mən-də-,līn\ village NE Ill. NW of Chicago *pop* 21,215

Mu·nich \'myü-nik\ *or G* **Mün·chen** \'mu̇en-ken\ city S Germany ✻ of Bavaria on the Isar *pop* 1,229,052

Mun·ster \'mən(t)-stər\ 1 town NW Ind. *pop* 19,949 2 province S Ireland *area* 9316 *sq mi* (24,168 *sq km*), *pop* 789,869

Mün·ster \'mən(t)-stər, 'mu̇n(t)-, 'mu̇en-\ city W Germany; formerly ✻ of Westphalia *pop* 264,181

Mun·te·nia \,mən-'tē-nē-ə, mün-'te-nē-ə\ *or* **Greater Walachia** region SE Romania in E part of Walachia

Mur \'mu̇r\ *or* **Mu·ra** \'mu̇r-ə\ river 279 *mi* (449 *km*) Austria, NE Slovenia, & N tip of Croatia flowing into the Drava

Mu·rat \mü-'rät\ *or anc* **Ar·sa·ni·as** \är-'sä-nē-əs\ river 380 *mi* (612 *km*) E Turkey flowing WSW into the Euphrates

Mur·chi·son \'mər-chə-sən\ river 440 *mi* (708 *km*) Australia in W Western Australia flowing W into Indian Ocean

Murchison Falls — see KABALEGA FALLS

Mur·cia \'mər-sh(ē-)ə\ 1 region & ancient kingdom SE Spain bordering on the Mediterranean 2 province SE Spain bordering on the Mediterranean *area* 4369 *sq mi* (11,316 *sq km*), *pop* 1,045,601 3 commune, its ✻ & ✻ of ancient kingdom of Murcia *pop* 318,838

Mu·res \'mü-,resh\ *or Hung* **Ma·ros** \'mȯr-,ōsh\ river 450 *mi* (725 *km*), *cen* Romania & E Hungary flowing W into the Tisza

Mur·frees·boro \'mər-f(r)ēz-,bər-ō\ city *cen* Tenn. *pop* 44,922

Mur·mansk \mu̇r-'man(t)sk, -'män(t)sk\ city & port NW Russia in Europe on an inlet of Barents Sea *pop* 468,000

Mur·ray \'mər-ē, 'mə-rē\ 1 city N Utah *pop* 31,282 2 river 1609 *mi* (2589 *km*) SE Australia flowing from near Mt. Kosciusko in E Victoria W into Indian Ocean in SE S. Australia

Mur·rum·bidg·ee \,mər-əm-'bi-jē, ,mə-rəm-\ river *almost* 1000 *mi* (1609 *km*) SE Australia in New South Wales flowing W into Murray River

Murviedro — see SAGUNTO

Mu·sa, Ge·bel \'je-bəl-'mü-sə\ mountain group NE Egypt in S Sinai Peninsula — see HOREB (Mount), KATHERINA (Gebel)

Mu·sa, Je·bel \'je-bəl-'mü-sə\ *or anc* **Ab·i·la** *or* **Ab·y·la** \'a-bə-lə\ mountain 2775 *ft* (846 *m*) N Morocco opposite Rock of Gibraltar — see PILLARS OF HERCULES

Muscat — see MASQAT

Muscat and Oman — see OMAN

Mus·ca·tine \,məs-kə-'tēn\ city E Iowa *pop* 22,881

Mus·co·vy \'məs-kə-vē\ 1 the principality of Moscow (founded 1295) which in 15th century came to dominate Russia 2 RUSSIA — a former name

Mus·ke·gon \mə-'skē-gən\ 1 river 200 *mi* (322 *km*) W *cen* Mich. flowing SW into Lake Michigan 2 city & port SW Mich. *pop* 40,283

Mus·kin·gum \mə-'skin-əm, -gəm\ river 120 *mi* (193 *km*) E Ohio flowing SSE into Ohio River

Mus·ko·gee \(,)mə-'skō-gē\ city E Okla. *pop* 37,708

Mus·ko·ka, Lake \mə-ˈskō-kə\ lake Canada in SE Ont. E of Georgian Bay & N of Lake Simcoe *area* 54 *sq mi* (140 *sq km*)
Mus·sel·shell \ˈmə-səl-ˌshel\ river 300 *mi* (483 *km*) *cen* Mont. flowing E & N into Missouri River
Mutina — see MODENA
Mu·tsu Bay \ˈmüt-(ˌ)sü\ inlet N Japan on NE Honshu on Tsugaru Strait
Muttra — see MATHURA
Muz·tag \müs-ˈtäg, məz-\ *or* **Ulugh Muz·tagh** \ˌü-lə-müs-ˈtäg, -məz-\ mountain 25,340 *ft* (7724 *m*) W China in S Xinjiang Uygur; highest in Kunlun Mountains
Mwe·ru \ˈmwā-rü\ lake 76 *mi* (122 *km*) long on border bet. Democratic Republic of the Congo & Zambia SW of Lake Tanganyika
Myan·mar \ˈmyän-ˌmär\ *or formerly* **Bur·ma** \ˈbər-mə\ country SE Asia on Bay of Bengal; a federal republic ✻ Yangon *area* 261,789 *sq mi* (680,651 *sq km*), *pop* 45,573,000
Myc·a·le \ˈmi-kə-(ˌ)lē\ promontory W Turkey opposite Samos Is.
My·ce·nae \mī-ˈsē-(ˌ)nē\ ancient city S Greece in NE Peloponnese — **My·ce·nae·an** \ˌmī-sə-ˈnē-ən\ *adj or n*
My·ko·la·yiv \ˌmē-kə-ˈlá-yif\ *or* **Ni·ko·la·yev** \nē-\ city & port S Ukraine
Myk·o·nos \ˈmi-kə-ˌnōs\ *or NGk* **Mí·ko·nos** \ˈmē-kō-ˌnōs\ island Greece in the Aegean in NE Cyclades *area* 35 *sq mi* (91 *sq km*)
Mylae — see MILAZZO
My·men·singh \ˌmī-mən-ˈsin\ city N Bangladesh *pop* 198,662
My·ra \ˈmī-rə\ ancient city S Asia Minor on coast of Lycia
Myr·tle Beach \ˈmər-tᵊl\ city E S.C. on the Atlantic *pop* 24,848
My·sia \ˈmi-sh(ē-)ə\ ancient country NW Asia Minor bordering on the Propontis — **My·sian** \-sh(ē-)ən\ *adj or n*
My·sore \mī-ˈsōr, -ˈsȯr\ **1** — see KARNATAKA **2** city S India in S Karnataka *pop* 606,755
Mys·tic \ˈmis-tik\ river E Mass. flowing SE into Boston harbor
Mytilene — see LESBOS

N

Naas \ˈnäs\ town E Ireland in Leinster ✻ of Kildare *pop* 11,140
Nab·a·taea *or* **Nab·a·tea** \ˌna-bə-ˈtē-ə\ ancient Arab kingdom SE of Palestine — **Nab·a·tae·an** *or* **Nab·a·te·an** \-ˈtē-ən\ *adj or n*
Na·be·rezh·nye Chel·ny \ˌnä-bə-ˈrezh-nə-ˈchel-nē, nə-bir-ˈyezh-ni-yə-chil-ˈnē\ city E Russia in Europe in Tatarstan *pop* 514,000
Nab·lus \ˈna-bləs, ˈnä-\ *or* **Nā·bu·lus** \ˈnä-bü-lùs\ *or anc* **Shechem** \ˈshe-kəm, -ˌkem\ *or* **Ne·ap·o·lis** \nē-ˈa-pə-lis\ city *cen* Palestine in Samaria; now in W Jordan *pop* 106,944
Nac·og·do·ches \ˌna-kə-ˈdō-chəz, -chəs\ city E Tex. *pop* 30,872
Nafud *or* **Nafūd, An** — see AN NAFŪD
Na·ga Hills \ˈnä-gä\ hills E India & N Myanmar SE of the Brahmaputra; highest Saramati 12,553 *ft* (3826 *m*)

Na·ga·land \'nä-gə-,land\ state E India N of Manipur in Naga Hills ✴ Kohima *area* 6366 *sq mi* (16,488 *sq km*), *pop* 1,209,546

Na·ga·no \nä-'gä-(,)nō\ city Japan on Honshu *pop* 350,673

Na·ga·sa·ki \,nä-gä-'sä-kē, ,na-gə-'sa-kē\ city & port Japan in W Kyushu on E. China Sea *pop* 442,373

Na·gor·no–Ka·ra·bakh \nä-,gȯr-(,)nō-'kär-ə-,bäk\ autonomous oblast SW Azerbaijan ✴ Stepanakert *area* 1700 *sq mi* (4420 *sq km*), *pop* 193,300

Na·goya \nə-'gȯi-ə, 'nä-gȯ-(,)yä\ city Japan in S *cen* Honshu *pop* 2,154,664

Nag·pur \'näg-,pu̇r\ city E *cen* India in NE Maharashtra *pop* 1,624,752

Na·ha \'nä-(,)hä\ city & port Ryukyu Islands in SW Okinawa Is. ✴ of Okinawa *pop* 304,896

Na·han·ni National Park \nä-'hä-nē\ reservation W Canada in SW Northwest Territories

Na·huel Hua·pí \,nä-'wel-wä-'pē\ lake SW Argentina in the Andes in **Nahuel Huapí National Park**

Nairn \'narn, 'nern\ **1** *or* **Nairn·shire** \-,shir, -shər\ former county NE Scotland **2** burgh, its ✴, on Moray Firth *pop* 10,420

Nai·ro·bi \nī-'rō-bē\ city S *cen* Kenya, its ✴ *pop* 1,504,000

Najd — see NEJD — **Najdi** \'naj-dē, 'nazh-\ *adj or n*

Nal·chik \'näl-chik\ town S Russia in Europe ✴ of Kabardino-Balkaria *pop* 242,000

Na·ma·qua·land \nä-'mä-kwä-,land\ *or* **Na·ma·land** \'nä-mə-\ region SW Africa; divided by Orange River into **Great Namaqualand** (in Namibia) & **Little Namaqualand** (in Northern Cape province, Republic of South Africa, chief town Springbok)

Na·mi·be \nä-'mē-bä\ *or formerly* **Mo·çâ·me·des** \mə-'sä-mə-dish\ town & port SW Angola

Na·mib·ia \nə-'mi-bē-ə\ *or formerly* **South–West Africa** *or* **1884–1919 German Southwest Africa** country SW Africa on the Atlantic; until 1990 a territory administered by South Africa which captured it from Germany in World War I ✴ Windhoek *area* 318,321 *sq mi* (824,451 *sq km*), *pop* 1,511,600 — **Na·mib·ian** \-bē-ən, -byən\ *adj or n*

Nam·pa \'nam-pə\ city SW Idaho W of Boise *pop* 28,365

Nam·po \'nam-(,)pō, 'näm-\ *or formerly* **Chin·nam·po** \'chē(n)-,näm-(,)pō\ city & port SW N. Korea SW of Pyongyang *pop* 130,000

Na·mur \nə-'mu̇r, -'myu̇r\ **1** province S Belgium *area* 1413 *sq mi* (3674 *sq km*), *pop* 423,317 **2** commune, its ✴ *pop* 104,200

Nan \'nän\ river 390 *mi* (628 *km*) N Thailand flowing S to join the Ping forming the Chao Phraya

Na·nai·mo \nə-'nī-(,)mō\ city Canada in B.C. on SE Vancouver Is. *pop* 60,129

Nan·chang \'nän-'chäŋ\ city SE China ✴ of Jiangxi on the Gan SW of Poyang Lake *pop* 1,086,124

Nan·cy \'nan(t)-sē, näⁿ-'sē\ city NE France on the Meurthe *pop* 102,410

Nan·da De·vi \,nən-də-'dā-vē\ mountain 25,645 *ft* (7816 *m*) N India in the Himalayas in Uttar Pradesh

Nan·di *or* **Na·di** \'nän-(,)dē\ village Fiji on W Viti Levu Is.

Nan·ga Par·bat \\nəŋ-gə-'pər-bət\ mountain 26,660 *ft* (8126 *m*) NW Kashmir in the W Himalayas

Nan·jing \'nän-'jiŋ\ *or* **Nan·king** \'nan-'kiŋ, 'nän-\ city E China on the Chang ✻ of Jiangsu & (1928–37 & 1946–49) ✻ of China *pop* 2,090,204

Nan Ling \'nän-'liŋ\ mountain system SE China roughly separating Guangdong & Guangxi Zhuangzu from Hunan & Guizhou

Nan·ning \'nän-'niŋ\ *or formerly* **Yung·ning** \'yuŋ-'niŋ\ city S China ✻ of Guangxi Zhuangzu *pop* 721,877

Nan·terre \näⁿ-'ter\ commune N France W of Paris *pop* 86,627

Nantes \'nan(t)s, 'näⁿt\ city NW France on the Loire *pop* 252,029

Nan·ti·coke \'nan-ti-ˌkōk\ city Canada in SE Ont. *pop* 22,727

Nan·tong \'nän-'tuŋ\ *or* **Nan·tung** \-'tuŋ\ city & port E China in SE Jiangsu on Chang estuary NW of Shanghai *pop* 343,341

Nan·tuck·et \nan-'tə-kət\ island Mass. S of Cape Cod on **Nan-tucket Sound** (inlet of the Atlantic) *pop* 6012 — **Nan·tuck·et·er** \-kə-tər\ *n*

Napa \'na-pə\ city W Calif. N of Vallejo *pop* 61,842

Na·per·ville \'nā-pər-ˌvil\ city NE Ill. W of Chicago *pop* 85,351

Na·pi·er \'nā-pē-ər\ borough & port New Zealand in E North Is. on Hawke Bay *pop* 51,645

Na·ples \'nā-pəlz\ **1** city SW Fla. *pop* 19,505 **2** *or* It **Na·po·li** \'nä-pō-lē\ *or anc* **Ne·ap·o·lis** \nē-'a-pə-ləs\ city & port S Italy on **Bay of Naples** (inlet of Tyrrhenian Sea) ✻ of Campania *pop* 1,054,601 — **Ne·a·pol·i·tan** \ˌnē-ə-'pä-lə-tⁿn\ *adj or n*

Na·po \'nä-(ˌ)pō\ river 550 *mi* (885 *km*) NW S. America rising near Mt. Cotopaxi in *cen* Ecuador & flowing E & SE into the Amazon

Na·ra \'när-ä\ city Japan in W *cen* Honshu E of Osaka; an early ✻ of Japan *pop* 349,356

Nar·bonne \när-'bän, -'bən\ city S France *pop* 47,086

Na·rew \'när-ˌef, -ˌev\ *or Russ* **Na·rev** \'när-if\ river NE Poland flowing W & SW into Bug River

Nar·ma·da \nər-'mə-də\ river 800 *mi* (1287 *km*) *cen* India flowing W bet. Vindhya Mountains & Satpura Range into Gulf of Khambhat

Nar·ra·gan·sett Bay \ˌnar-ə-'gan(t)-sət\ inlet of the Atlantic SE R.I.

Nar·vik \'när-vik\ town & port N Norway *pop* 18,736

Nash·ua \'na-shə-wə *also* -ˌwä\ city S N.H. *pop* 79,662

Nash·ville \'nash-ˌvil, -vəl\ city N *cen* Tenn., its ✻ *pop* 488,374

Nas·sau 1 \'na-ˌsȯ\ city & port ✻ of Bahamas on New Providence Is. *pop* 172,196 **2** \'na-ˌsȯ, *G* 'nä-ˌsaů\ region Germany N & E of the Rhine; chief city Wiesbaden **3** — see SUDIRMAN

Nasser, Lake — see ASWAN

Na·tal \nə-'tal, -'täl\ **1** city & port NE Brazil ✻ of Rio Grande do Norte *pop* 606,541 **2** former province E Republic of South Africa bet. Drakensberg Mountains & Indian Ocean *area* 35,320 *sq mi* (91,479 *sq km*)

Natch·ez \'na-chəz\ city SW Miss. on Mississippi River *pop* 19,460

Natchez Trace pioneer road bet. Natchez, Miss., & Nashville, Tenn., used in the early 19th century

Na·tick \'nā-tik\ town E Mass. W of Boston *pop* 30,510

National City city SW Calif. S of San Diego *pop* 54,249

Native States — see INDIAN STATES

Natural Bridges National Monument reservation SE Utah

Nau·cra·tis \\'no-krə-təs\\ ancient Greek city N Egypt in Nile delta

Nau·ga·tuck \\'no-gə-,tək\\ borough SW cen Conn. pop 30,625

Nau·plia \\'no-plē-ə\\ or **Nau·pli·on** \\-plē-ən\\ or NGk **Náv·pli·on** \\'näf-plē-,ón\\ town & port S Greece in E Peloponnese near head of Gulf of Argolis pop 11,453

Na·u·ru \\nä-'ü-(,)rü\\ or formerly **Pleas·ant Island** \\'ple-zᵊnt\\ island (atoll) W Pacific 26 mi (42 km) S of the equator; formerly a joint Brit., New Zealand, & Australian trust territory; since 1968 an independent republic area 8 sq mi (21 sq km), pop 10,000 — **Na·u·ru·an** \\-'ü-rə-wən\\ adj or n

Na·va·jo National Monument \\'na-və-,hō-, 'nä\\ reservation N Ariz. SW of Monument Valley near Utah boundary containing cliff dwellings

Na·varre \\nə-'vär\\ or Sp **Na·var·ra** \\nä-'vär-ä\\ 1 region & former kingdom N Spain & SW France in W Pyrenees 2 province N Spain ✳ Pamplona area 4024 sq mi (10,422 sq km), pop 519,277

Navigators Islands — see SAMOA

Náv·pak·tos \\'näf-,pak-tós\\ town & port Greece on N shore of strait connecting Gulf of Corinth & Gulf of Patras

Nax·ci·van \\nək-chi-'vän\\ or **Na·khi·che·van** \\,na-ki-chə-'vän\\ 1 exclave of Azerbaijan separated from the rest of the country by Armenia area 2124 sq mi (5501 sq km), pop 305,700 2 city, its ✳, on the Araks pop 61,700

Nax·os \\'nak-səs, -,säs\\ 1 or NGk **Ná·xos** \\'näk-,sós\\ island Greece, largest of the Cyclades area 165 sq mi (427 sq km) 2 oldest Greek colony in Sicily; ruins SW of Taormina

Na·ya·rit \\,nä-yä-'rēt\\ state W Mexico bordering on the Pacific ✳ Tepic area 10,664 sq mi (27,620 sq km), pop 824,543

Naz·a·reth \\'na-zə-rəth\\ city N Israel in Galilee SE of Haifa pop 49,800 — **Naz·a·rene** \\,na-zə-'rēn\\ n

Naze, The \\'näz\\ headland SE England on E coast of Essex

Na·zil·li \\,nä-zē-'lē\\ city SW Turkey SE of Izmir

Naz·ran \\'näz-rən\\ town S Russia in Europe ✳ of Ingushetia

N'Dja·me·na \\ən-jä-'mä-nä, -'mē-\\ or formerly **Fort–La·my** \\,fòr-lə-'mē\\ city on the Chari ✳ of Chad pop 687,800

Neagh, Lough \\'nä\\ lake cen Northern Ireland area 153 sq mi (398 sq km); largest in British Isles

Neapolis 1 — see NABLUS 2 — see NAPLES

Near Islands \\'nir\\ islands SW Alaska at W end of the Aleutians — see ATTU

Near East 1 the Ottoman Empire at its greatest extent — a former usage 2 the countries of SW Asia & NE Africa — **Near Eastern** adj

Nebo, Mount — see PISGAH (Mount)

Ne·bras·ka \\nə-'bras-kə\\ state cen U.S. ✳ Lincoln area 77,355 sq mi (200,349 sq km), pop 1,578,385 — **Ne·bras·kan** \\-kən\\ adj or n

Ne·chako \\ni-'cha-(,)kō\\ river 287 mi (462 km) Canada in cen B.C. flowing N & E into the Fraser

Ne·ches \\'nä-chəz\\ river E Tex. flowing S & SE into Sabine Lake

Neck·ar \\'ne-kər, -,kär\\ river 228 mi (367 km) SW Germany rising in the Black Forest & flowing N & W into the Rhine

Neck·er \\'ne-kər\\ island Hawaii in Leewards NW of Niihau Is.

Need·ham \\'nē-dəm\\ town E Mass. WSW of Boston pop 27,557

Nee·nah \'nē-nə\ city E Wis. on Lake Winnebago *pop* 23,219

Ne·ge·ri Sem·bi·lan \'ne-grē-sən-'bē-lən\ state Malaysia in Peninsular Malaysia on Strait of Malacca ✱ Seremban *area* 2590 *sq mi* (6708 *sq km*), *pop* 691,200

Neg·ev \'ne-,gev\ *or* **Ha·Neg·ev** \,hä-\ *or* **Neg·eb** \-,geb\ region S Israel, a triangular wedge of desert touching Gulf of Aqaba in S

Ne·gro \'nā-(,)grō, 'ne-\ **1** river 400 *mi* (640 *km*) S *cen* Argentina flowing E into the Atlantic **2** river 1400 *mi* (2253 *km*) E Colombia & N Brazil flowing into the Amazon **3** river 434 *mi* (698 *km*) *cen* Uruguay flowing SW into Uruguay River

Ne·gros \'nā-(,)grōs, 'ne-\ island S *cen* Philippines in the Visayans SE of Panay Is. *area* 4905 *sq mi* (12,753 *sq km*)

Neige, Mount — see JURA 2

Nei·jiang *or* **Nei–chiang** \'nā-'jyän\ city *cen* China in S *cen* Szechwan SE of Chengdu *pop* 256,012

Nei Monggol — see INNER MONGOLIA

Neis·se \'nī-sə\ **1** *or* **Lau·sitz·er Neisse** \'laù-zit-sər-\ river 159 *mi* (256 *km*) N Europe flowing from N Czech Republic N into the Oder **2** — see NYSA

Nejd \'nejd, 'nezhd\ *or* **Najd** \'najd, 'nazhd\ region *cen* & E Saudi Arabia; *area* 447,000 *sq mi* (1,162,200 *sq km*), *pop* 1,200,000 — **Nejdi** \'nej-dē, 'nezh-\ *adj or n*

Nel·son \'nel-sən\ **1** river 400 *mi* (644 *km*) Canada in Man. flowing from N end of Lake Winnipeg to Hudson Bay **2** city & port New Zealand on N coast of South Is. *pop* 37,943

Ne·man \'ne-mən\ *or* **Ne·mu·nas** \'ne-mü-,näs\ river 582 *mi* (936 *km*) *cen* Europe flowing from *cen* Belarus N & W through Lithuania & along border with exclave of Russia into Courland Lagoon

Ne·mea \'nē-mē-ə\ valley & town Greece in NE Peloponnese W of Corinth — **Ne·me·an** \'nē-mē-ən, ni-'mē-\ *adj*

Ne·o·sho \nē-'ō-(,)shō, -shə\ *or in Okla* **Grand** river 460 *mi* (740 *km*) SE Kans. & NE Okla. flowing SE & S into Arkansas River; now largely submerged in dam-created lakes and reservoirs in its lower course

Ne·pal \nə-'pòl, nā-, -'päl *also* nə-'pal\ country Asia on NE border of India in the Himalaya; a kingdom ✱ Kathmandu *area* 54,362 *sq mi* (140,798 *sq km*), *pop* 20,220,000 — **Nep·a·lese** \,ne-pə-'lēz, -'lēs\ *adj or n* — **Ne·pali** \nə-'pò-lē, -'pä-, -'pa-\ *adj or n*

Ne·pe·an \'nē-pē-ən\ city Canada in SE Ont. SW of Ottawa *pop* 107,627

Ness, Loch \'nes\ lake 23 *mi* (37 *km*) long NW Scotland in Highland region

Néstos — see MESTA

Neth·er·lands \'ne-thər-ləndz\ **1** LOW COUNTRIES — an historical usage **2** *or* **Hol·land** \'hä-lənd\ *or D* **Ne·der·land** \'nā-dər-,länt\ country NW Europe on North Sea; a kingdom, official ✱ Amsterdam, de facto ✱ The Hague *area* 16,033 *sq mi* (41,525 *sq km*), *pop* 15,009,000 — **Neth·er·land** \'ne-thər-lənd\ *adj* — **Neth·er·land·er** \-,lan-dər, -lən-\ *n* — **Neth·er·land·ic** \-,lan-dik\ *adj* — **Neth·er·land·ish** \-,lan-dish, -lən-\ *adj*

Netherlands Antilles Dutch overseas territory, W. Indies comprising Bonaire, Curaçao, Saba, St. Eustatius, & S part of St. Martin ✱ Willemstad (on Curaçao) *area* over 370 *sq mi* (958 *sq km*), *pop* 190,566

Netherlands East Indies — see INDONESIA

Netherlands Guiana — see SURINAME

Netherlands New Guinea — see IRIAN JAYA

Netherlands Timor — see TIMOR

Néthou, Pic de — see ANETO (Pico de)

Net·tu·no \ne-'tü-(,)nō\ commune Italy on Tyrrhenian Sea SSE of Rome adjoining Anzio *pop* 34,653

Neu·châ·tel \,nü-shä-'tel, ,nyü-, ,nə(r)-, ,nᴈ-\ *or G* **Neu·en·burg** \'nói-ən-,bərg, -,búrk\ **1** canton W Switzerland in Jura Mountains *area* 308 *sq mi* (798 *sq km*), *pop* 159,543 **2** commune, its ✳, on **Lake of Neuchâtel** (*area* 84 *sq mi or* 218 *sq km*), *pop* 32,757

Neuil·ly–sur–Seine \,nə(r)-yē-,sür-'sän, ,nᴈ-'yē-sᴈr-'sen\ commune N France NW of Paris near the Bois de Boulogne *pop* 65,941

Neu·mün·ster \nói-'mün-stər\ city N Germany SSW of Kiel *pop* 81,175

Neu·quén \nyü-'kän, nā-ú-\ river 320 *mi* (515 *km*) W Argentina flowing from the Andes E to join the Limay forming Negro River

Neuse \nüs, 'nyüs\ river E *cen* N.C. flowing SE into Pamlico Sound

Neuss \'nóis\ city W Germany W of Düsseldorf *pop* 147,663

Neus·tria \'nü-strē-ə, 'nyü-\ **1** the western part of the dominions of the Franks after the conquest by Clovis in 511, comprising the NW part of modern France bet. the Meuse, the Loire, & the Atlantic **2** a name for Normandy used after 912 — **Neus·tri·an** \-ən\ *adj or n*

Ne·va \'nē-və, 'nā-, nye-'vä\ river 40 *mi* (64 *km*) W Russia in Europe flowing from Lake Ladoga to Gulf of Finland at St. Petersburg

Ne·va·da \nə-'va-də, -'vä-\ state W U.S. ✳ Carson City *area* 110,561 *sq mi* (286,353 *sq km*), *pop* 1,201,833 — **Ne·va·dan** \-'va-dᵉn, -'vä-\ *or* **Ne·va·di·an** \-'va-dē-ən, -'vä-\ *adj or n*

Ne·vers \nə-'ver\ city *cen* France SE of Orléans *pop* 43,889

Ne·ves \'nā-vəs\ city SE Brazil on Guanabara Bay *pop* 151,067

Ne·vis \'nē-vəs\ island Brit. West Indies, part of St. Kitts-Nevis, in the Leewards; chief town Charlestown *area* 50 *sq mi* (130 *sq km*) — **Ne·vis·ian** \nə-'vi-zh(ē-)ən\ *adj*

New Albany city S Ind. on Ohio River *pop* 36,322

New Amsterdam town founded 1625 on Manhattan Is. by the Dutch; renamed New York 1664 by the British

New·ark \'nü-ərk, 'nyü-; *esp 2 & 4* 'nü-,ärk, 'nyü-\ **1** city W Calif. SE of San Francisco *pop* 37,861 **2** city NE Del. W of Wilmington *pop* 25,098 **3** city & port NE N.J. on **Newark Bay** (W extension of Upper New York Bay) *pop* 275,221 **4** city *cen* Ohio *pop* 44,389

New Bedford city & port SE Mass. on W side of Buzzards Bay *pop* 99,922

New Ber·lin \'bər-lən\ city SE Wis. W of Milwaukee *pop* 33,592

New Braun·fels \'braún-fəlz\ city SE *cen* Tex. *pop* 27,334

New Brighton village SE Minn. N of St. Paul *pop* 22,207

New Britain **1** city *cen* Conn. *pop* 75,491 **2** island Bismarck Archipelago; largest of group *area* 14,160 *sq mi* (36,674 *sq km*), *pop* 263,500

New Brunswick **1** city N *cen* N.J. *pop* 41,711 **2** province SE Canada bordering on Gulf of Saint Lawrence & Bay of Fundy ✳ Fredericton *area* 27,633 *sq mi* (71,569 *sq km*), *pop* 723,900

New·burgh \'nü-,bərg, 'nyü-\ city SE N.Y. on Hudson River S of Poughkeepsie *pop* 26,454

New Caledonia island SW Pacific SW of Vanuatu; with nearby islands, constitutes an overseas department of France ✻ Nouméa *area* 7367 *sq mi* (19,081 *sq km*), *pop* 183,100

New Castile — see CASTILE

New·cas·tle \'nü-,ka-səl, 'nyü-, *3 is locally* nü-'\ **1** city & port SE Australia in E New South Wales at mouth of Hunter River *metropolitan area pop* 262,331 **2** town Canada in SE Ont. ENE of Toronto *pop* 49,479 **3** *or in full* **Newcastle upon Tyne** \'tīn\ city & port N England ✻ of Tyne and Wear *pop* 263,000 **4** *or in full* **Newcastle under Lyme** \'līm\ borough W *cen* England in Staffordshire *pop* 117,400

New Cas·tle \'nü-,ka-səl, 'nyü-\ city W Pa. ESE of Youngstown, Ohio *pop* 28,334

New Delhi city ✻ of India in Delhi Territory S of city of (old) Delhi *pop* 294,149

New England 1 the NE U.S. comprising the states of Maine, N.H., Vt., Mass., R.I., & Conn. **2** region SE Australia in NE New South Wales; in area of **New England Range** (part of Great Dividing Range) — **New En·gland·er** \'iŋ-glən-dər *also* 'iŋ-lən-\ *n* — **New En·glandy** \-dē\ *adj*

New Forest forested area S England in Hampshire bet. the Avon & Southampton Water; once a royal hunting ground

New·found·land \'nü-fən(d)-lənd, 'nyü-, -,land; ,nü-fən(d)-'land, ,nyü-\ **1** island Canada in the Atlantic E of Gulf of St. Lawrence *area* 43,359 *sq mi* (112,300 *sq km*) **2** province E Canada comprising Newfoundland (island) & part of Labrador ✻ St. John's *area* 143,488 *sq mi* (371,634 *sq km*), *pop* 568,474 — **New·found·land·er** \-lən-dər, -,lan-; -'lan-dər\ *n*

New France the possessions of France in N. America before 1763

New Georgia 1 island group W Pacific in *cen* Solomon Islands **2** island 50 *mi* (80 *km*) long, chief island of the group

New Gra·na·da \grə-'nä-də\ Spanish viceroyalty in NW S. America 1717–1819 comprising area included in modern Panama, Colombia, Venezuela, & Ecuador

New Guinea 1 island in Malay Archipelago N of E Australia divided bet. Irian Jaya on W & Papua New Guinea on E *area* over 315,000 *sq mi* (815,850 *sq km*) **2** the NE portion of the island of New Guinea with the Bismarck Archipelago, Bougainville, Buka, & adjacent small islands; part of Papua New Guinea — see NORTHEAST NEW GUINEA — **New Guin·ean** \'gi-nē-ən\ *adj or n*

New·ham \'nü-əm, 'nyü-\ borough of E Greater London, England *pop* 200,200

New Hamp·shire \'hamp-shər, -,shir\ state NE U.S. ✻ Concord *area* 9279 *sq mi* (24,033 *sq km*), *pop* 1,109,252 — **New Hamp·shire·man** \-mən\ *n* — **New Hamp·shir·ite** \-,īt\ *n*

New Ha·ven \'hā-vən\ city & port S Conn. *pop* 130,474 — **New Ha·ven·er** \'hā-və-nər\ *n*

New Hebrides — see VANUATU

New Hope \'nü-,hōp, 'nyü-\ village E Minn. N of Minneapolis *pop* 21,853

New Iberia city S La. SE of Lafayette *pop* 31,828

New·ing·ton \'nü-iŋ-tən, 'nyü-\ town *cen* Conn. SW of Hartford *pop* 29,208

New Ireland island W Pacific in Bismarck Archipelago N of New Britain ✳ Kavieng *area* 3340 *sq mi* (8684 *sq km*), *pop* (with adjacent islands) 48,774

New Jersey state E U.S. ✳ Trenton *area* 7787 *sq mi* (20,168 *sq km*), *pop* 7,730,188 — **New Jer·sey·an** \-ən\ *n* — **New Jer·sey·ite** \-ītٖ\ *n*

New London city & port SE Conn. on Long Island Sound at mouth of Thames River *pop* 28,540

New·mar·ket \'nü-ˌmär-kət, 'nyü-\ **1** town Canada in SE Ont. N of Toronto *pop* 45,474 **2** town E England in Suffolk *pop* 16,235

New Mex·i·co \'mek-si-ˌkō\ state SW U.S. ✳ Santa Fe *area* 121,593 *sq mi* (314,926 *sq km*), *pop* 1,515,069 — **New Mex·i·can** \-si-kən\ *adj or n*

New Milford city W Conn. *pop* 23,629

New Neth·er·land \'ne-thər-lənd\ Dutch colony in N. America 1613–64 occupying lands bordering on Hudson River & later also on lower Delaware River ✳ New Amsterdam

New Or·leans \'òr-lē-ənz, 'òr-lənz, 'òrl-yənz, (ˌ)òr-'lēnz\ city & port SE La. bet. Lake Pontchartrain & Mississippi River *pop* 496,938 — **New Or·lea·nian** \(ˌ)òr-'lē-nyən, -nē-ən\ *n*

New·port \'nü-ˌpòrt, 'nyü-, -pərt\ **1** city & port SE R.I. on Narragansett Bay *pop* 28,227 **2** borough S England ✳ of Isle of Wight *pop* 23,570 **3** borough SE Wales in Gwent WNW of Bristol *pop* 129,900 — **New·port·er** \-ˌpòr-tər, -ˌpòr-\ *n*

Newport Beach city SW Calif. SE of Long Beach *pop* 66,643

New·port News \'nü-ˌpòrt-'nüz, 'nyü-ˌpòrt-'nyüz, -ˌpòrt-, -pərt-\ city & port SE Va. on James River & Hampton Roads *pop* 170,045

New Providence island in NW *cen* Bahamas E of Andros; site of Nassau 80 *sq mi* (207 *sq km*)

New Quebec region Canada in N Que. N of the Eastmain bet. Hudson Bay & Labrador — see UNGAVA

New Quebec Crater *or formerly* **Chubb Crater** \'chəb\ lake-filled meteoric crater Canada in Que., in N Ungava Peninsula

New Ro·chelle \rə-'shel\ city SE N.Y. on Long Island Sound E of Mount Vernon *pop* 67,265

New·ry and Mourne \'nü-rē, 'nyü- . . . 'mòrn\ district S Northern Ireland *area* 345 *sq mi* (894 *sq km*), *pop* 82,288

New Siberian Islands islands NE Russia in Asia in Arctic Ocean bet. Laptev & E. Siberian seas *area* 11,000 *sq mi* (28,600 *sq km*)

New South Wales state SE Australia bordering on the Pacific ✳ Sydney *area* 309,433 *sq mi* (801,431 *sq km*), *pop* 5,732,032

New Spain Spanish viceroyalty 1535–1821 including territory now in SW U.S., Mexico, Central America N of Panama, much of the West Indies, & the Philippines ✳ Mexico City

New Sweden Swedish colony in N. America 1638–55 bordering on W bank of Delaware River from modern Trenton, N.J., to its mouth

New Territories Hong Kong exclusive of Hong Kong Is. & Kowloon Peninsula

New·ton \'nü-tᵊn, 'nyü-\ city E Mass. W of Boston *pop* 82,585

New·town \'nü-ˌtaún, 'nyü-\ town SW Conn. E of Danbury *pop* 20,779

New·town·ab·bey \ˌnü-tᵊn-'a-bē, ˌnyü-\ district E Northern Ireland, established 1974 *area* 58 *sq mi* (150 *sq km*), *pop* 73,832

New·town Saint Bos·wells \'nü-,taún-sənt-'bäz-wəlz, 'nyü-, -sänt-\ village S Scotland W of Kelso ✱ of Borders region

New West·min·ster \wes(t)-'min(t)-stər\ city Canada in SW B.C. on the Fraser ESE of Vancouver *pop* 43,585

New Windsor — see WINDSOR

New York 1 state NE U.S. ✱ Albany *area* 49,576 *sq mi* (121,898 *sq km*), *pop* 17,990,456 **2** *or* **New York City** city & port SE N.Y. at mouth of Hudson River; includes boroughs of Bronx, Brooklyn, Manhattan, Queens, & Staten Is. *pop* 7,322,564 **3** the borough of Manhattan in New York City — **New York·er** \'yòr-kər\ *n*

New York Bay inlet of the Atlantic SE N.Y. & NE N.J. at mouth of Hudson River forming harbor of metropolitan New York & consisting of **Upper New York Bay** & **Lower New York Bay** connected by the **Narrows** (strait separating Staten Is. & Long Is.)

New York State Barge Canal — see ERIE

New Zea·land \'zē-lənd\ country SW Pacific ESE of Australia comprising chiefly North Is. & South Is.; a dominion of the Commonwealth of Nations ✱ Wellington *area* 103,736 *sq mi* (269,714 *sq km*), *pop* 3,175,737 — **New Zea·land·er** \-lən-dər\ *n*

Ngaliema, Mount — see STANLEY (Mount)

Nga·mi, Lake \əŋ-'gä-mē\ marshy depression NW Botswana N of Kalahari Desert; formerly a large lake

Ngau·ru·hoe \əŋ-,gaú-rə-'hō-ē\ volcano 7515 *ft* (2291 *m*) New Zealand in *cen* North Is. in Tongariro National Park

Ni·ag·a·ra Falls \(,)nī-'a-g(ə-)rə\ **1** waterfalls on border bet. N.Y. & Ont. in the **Niagara River** (36 *mi* or 58 *km* flowing from Lake Erie N into Lake Ontario); divided by Goat Is. into Horseshoe, or Canadian, Falls (158 *ft* or 48 *m* high) & American Falls (167 *ft* or 51 *m* high) **2** city W N.Y. at the falls *pop* 61,840 **3** city Canada in SE Ont. *pop* 75,399

Nia·mey \nē-'ä-(,)mā, nyä-'mā\ city ✱ of Niger *pop* 392,165

Ni·as \'nē-,äs\ island Indonesia in Indian Ocean off W coast of Sumatra *area* 1569 *sq mi* (4079 *sq km*), *pop* 314,829 — **Ni·as·san** \'nē-ə-sən\ *n*

Ni·caea \nī-'sē-ə\ *or* **Nice** \'nīs\ ancient city of Byzantine Empire, site at modern village of Iznik in NW Turkey in Asia at E end of Iznik Lake — **Ni·cae·an** \nī-'sē-ən\ *adj* — **Ni·cene** \'nī-,sēn, nī-'\ *adj*

Nic·a·ra·gua \,ni-kə-'rä-gwə, ,nē-kä-'rä-gwä\ **1** lake *ab* 100 *mi* (161 *km*) long S Nicaragua **2** country Central America bordering on the Pacific & the Caribbean; a republic ✱ Managua *area* 49,579 *sq mi* (128,410 *sq km*), *pop* 4,265,000 — **Nic·a·ra·guan** \-'rä-gwən\ *adj or n*

Nice \'nēs\ *or anc* **Ni·caea** \nī-'sē-ə\ city & port SE France on the Mediterranean *pop* 345,674

Nic·o·bar Islands \'ni-kə-,bär\ islands India in Indian Ocean S of Andaman Islands *area* 740 *sq mi* (1917 *sq km*), *pop* 14,563 — see ANDAMAN AND NICOBAR

Nicomedia — see IZMIT

Ni·cop·o·lis \nə-'kä-pə-lis, nī-\ ancient city NW Greece in Epirus

Nic·o·sia \,ni-kə-'sē-ə\ city *cen* Cyprus, its ✱ *pop* 168,800

Nidwald, Nidwalden — see UNTERWALDEN

Niedersachsen — see LOWER SAXONY

Nieuw·poort or **Nieu·port** \'nü-,pōrt, 'nyü-, -,pȯrt, F nyœ-'pȯr\ commune NW Belgium in W. Flanders on the Yser *pop* 9572

Ni·ger \'nī-jər, nē-'zher\ **1** river 2600 *mi* (4184 *km*) W Africa flowing from Fouta Djallon NE, SE & S into Gulf of Guinea **2** country W Africa; a republic, until 1958 a territory of French West Africa ***** Niamey *area* 459,073 *sq mi* (1,188,999 *sq km*), *pop* 8,516,000 — **Ni·ger·ois** \,nē-zhər-'wä, -zher-\ *n*

Ni·ge·ria \nī-'jir-ē-ə\ country W Africa bordering on Gulf of Guinea; a republic within the Commonwealth of Nations, formerly a colony & protectorate ***** Abuja *area* 356,669 *sq mi* (927,339 *sq km*), *pop* 88,514,501 — **Ni·ge·ri·an** \-ē-ən\ *adj* or *n*

Nii·ga·ta \nē-'gä-tä, 'nē-gä-,tä\ city & port Japan in N Honshu on Sea of Japan *pop* 486,087

Nii·hau \'nē-,haü\ island Hawaii WSW of Kauai *area* 72 *sq mi* (187 *sq km*)

Nij·me·gen \'nī-,mā-gən, 'nā-, -,kə(n)\ commune E Netherlands in Gelderland on the Waal S of Arnhem *pop* 146,344

Nikaria — see IKARIA

Nikolayev — see MYKOLAYIV

Ni·ko·pol \'nē-kə-,pȯl, 'nyē-, -pəl\ city E *cen* Ukraine on the Dnieper *pop* 159,000

Nile \'nīl\ river 4160 *mi* (6693 *km*) E Africa flowing from Lake Victoria in Uganda N into the Mediterranean in Egypt; in various sections called specifically: **Vic·to·ria Nile** \vik-'tōr-ē-ə, -'tȯr-\ or **Som·er·set Nile** \'sə-mər-sət, -,set\ bet. Lake Victoria & Lake Albert; **Al·bert Nile** \'al-bərt\ bet. Lake Albert & Lake No; & **White Nile** from Lake No to Khartoum — see BLUE NILE — **Ni·lot·ic** \nī-'lä-tik\ *adj*

Niles \'nīlz\ **1** village NE Ill. NW of Chicago *pop* 28,284 **2** city NE Ohio SE of Warren *pop* 21,128

Nil·gi·ri Hills \'nil-gə-rē\ hills S India in W Tamil Nadu; highest point Mt. Dodabetta 8640 *ft* (2633 *m*)

Nîmes \'nēm\ city S France NE of Montpellier *pop* 133,607

Nimrud — see CALAH

Nin·e·veh \'ni-nə-və\ or L **Ni·nus** \'nī-nəs\ ancient city ***** of Assyria; ruins in Iraq on the Tigris opposite Mosul

Ning·bo or **Ning·po** \'niŋ-'bō\ or *formerly* **Ning·hsien** \'niŋ-'shyen\ city E China in N Zhejiang ESE of Hangzhou *pop* 552,540

Ninghsia, Ningsia — see YINCHUAN

Ning·xia Hui·zu \'niŋ-'shyä-'hwē-'dzü\ or **Ning·sia Hui** \'niŋ-'shyä-'hwē\ region N China; formerly a province ***** Yinchuan *area* 30,039 *sq mi* (78,101 *sq km*), *pop* 4,655,451

Ni·o·brara \,nī-ə-'brar-ə, -'brer-\ river 431 *mi* (694 *km*) E Wyo. & N Nebr. flowing E into Missouri River

Niort \nē-'ȯr\ city W France ENE of La Rochelle *pop* 58,660

Nip·i·gon, Lake \'ni-pə-,gän\ lake Canada in W Ont. N of Lake Superior *area* 1870 *sq mi* (4862 *sq km*)

Nip·is·sing, Lake \'ni-pə-siŋ\ lake Canada in SE Ont. NE of Georgian Bay *area* over 320 *sq mi* (829 *sq km*)

Nippon — see JAPAN — **Nip·pon·ese** \,ni-pə-nēz, -'nēs\ *adj* or *n*

Nip·pur \ni-'pür\ ancient city of Sumer SSE of Babylon

Nis or **Nish** \'nish, 'nēsh\ city E Yugoslavia in E Serbia *pop* 247,898

Ni·shi·no·mi·ya \,ni-shē-'nō-mē-,yä\ city Japan in *cen* Honshu on Osaka Bay E of Kobe *pop* 426,919

Ni·te·rói *or formerly* **Nic·the·roy** \,nē-te-'rôi\ city SE Brazil on Guanabara Bay opposite Rio de Janeiro *pop* 416,123

Ni·tra \'nĭ-trə, 'nyē-trä\ city W Slovakia *pop* 89,888

Ni·u·a·fo·'ou \nē-'ü-ä-,fō-ō\ island SW *cen* Pacific in the N Tongas *pop* 763

Ni·ue \nē-'ü-(,)ā\ island S *cen* Pacific; a self-governing territory of New Zealand *area* 100 *sq mi* (260 *sq km*), *pop* 2244 — **Ni·ue·an** \nyü-'wä-ən, 'nyü-,wä-\ n

Ni·velles \nē-'vel\ commune *cen* Belgium *pop* 23,217

Ni·ver·nais \,nē-vər-'nā\ region & former province *cen* France E of the upper Loire ✳ Nevers

Nizh·niy Nov·go·rod *or* **Nizh·ni Novgorod** \'nizh-nē-'näv-gə-,räd, -'nôv-gə-rət\ *or* 1932–89 **Gor·ki** \'gôr-kē\ city *cen* Russia in Europe at confluence of Oka & Volga rivers *pop* 1,433,000

Nizhniy Ta·gil *or* **Nizhni Tagil** \tə-'gil\ city W Russia in Asia on E slope of the Urals *pop* 437,000

No, Lake \'nō\ lake S *cen* Sudan where Bahr el Jebel & Bahr el Ghazal join to form the White Nile *area* 40 *sq mi* (104 *sq km*)

No·gal·es \nō-'ga-ləs, -'gä-läs\ **1** city S Ariz. on Mexican border *pop* 19,489 **2** city NW Mexico in Sonora *pop* 107,119

Nome, Cape \'nōm\ cape W Alaska on S side of Seward Peninsula

Noordwes — see NORTH WEST

Noot·ka Sound \'nút-kə, 'nüt-\ inlet of the Pacific Canada in SW B.C. on W coast of Vancouver Is.

Nor·co \'nôr-(,)kō, 'nôr-\ city SE Calif. W of Palm Springs *pop* 23,302

Nordenskjöld Sea — see LAPTEV SEA

Nord·kyn, Cape \'nôr-kən, 'nôr-; 'nür-kēn\ cape NE Norway on Barents Sea; northernmost point of European mainland, at 71°8′N

Nord–Ostsee — see KIEL 2

Nor·folk \'nôr-fək, *US also* -,fôk, -,fôrk\ **1** city NE Nebr. *pop* 21,476 **2** city & port SE Va. on Elizabeth River S of Hampton Roads *pop* 261,229 **3** county E England bordering on North Sea ✳ Norwich *area* 2152 *sq mi* (5574 *sq km*), *pop* 736,400

Norfolk Broads — see BROADS

Norfolk Island island S Pacific bet. New Caledonia & New Zealand; administered by Australia *area* 13 *sq mi* (34 *sq km*), *pop* 1912

Norge — see NORWAY

Nor·i·cum \'nôr-i-kəm, 'när-\ ancient country & Roman province S *cen* Europe S of the Danube in modern Austria & S Germany

No·rilsk \nə-'rēlsk\ city N Russia in Asia, N of arctic circle near mouth of the Yenisey *pop* 165,000

Nor·mal \'nôr-məl\ town *cen* Ill. N of Bloomington *pop* 40,023

Nor·man \'nôr-mən\ city *cen* Okla. on Canadian River *pop* 80,071

Nor·man·dy \'nôr-mən-dē\ *or F* **Nor·man·die** \nôr-mäⁿ-'dē\ region & former province NW France NE of Brittany ✳ Rouen — **Norman** \'nôr-mən\ *adj or n*

Nor·ris·town \'nôr-əs-,taún, 'när-\ borough SE Pa. *pop* 30,749

Norr·kö·ping \'nôr-,shē-piŋ\ city & port SE Sweden SW of Stockholm at head of an inlet of the Baltic *pop* 120,798

North·al·ler·ton \nôr-'tha-lər-t²n\ town N England ✳ of N. Yorkshire

North America continent of the western hemisphere NW of S. America bounded by Atlantic, Arctic, & Pacific oceans *area* 9,361,791 *sq mi* (24,247,039 *sq km*) — **North American** *adj or n*

North·amp·ton \nȯr-'tham(p)-tən, nȯrth-'ham(p)-\ **1** city W *cen* Mass. on Connecticut River N of Holyoke *pop* 29,289 **2** borough *cen* England ✳ of Northamptonshire *pop* 145,421

North·amp·ton·shire \-,shir, -shər\ *or* **Northampton** county *cen* England ✳ Northampton *area* 947 *sq mi* (2453 *sq km*), *pop* 572,900

North Andover town NE Mass. E of Lawrence *pop* 22,792

North Atlantic — see ATLANTIC OCEAN

North At·tle·bor·ough *or* **North At·tle·boro** \'a-t°l-,bər-ō\ town SE Mass. *pop* 25,038

North Bay \'nȯrth-,bā\ city Canada in SE Ont. *pop* 55,405

North Borneo — see SABAH

North Brabant *or D* **Noord–Bra·bant** \,nȯrt-'brä-,bänt\ province S Netherlands ✳ 's Hertogenbosch *area* 1971 *sq mi* (5105 *sq km*), *pop* 2,243,546

North·brook \'nȯrth-,brúk\ village NE Ill. NW of Chicago *pop* 32,308

North Canadian river *ab* 800 *mi* (1287 *km*) S *cen* U.S. flowing ESE from NE N.Mex. into Canadian River in E Okla. — see BEAVER

North Cape 1 cape New Zealand at N tip of North Is. **2** cape NE Norway on **Ma·ger·öy** \,mä-gə-'rói\ island (*area* 111 *sq mi or* 289 *sq km*) at 71°10'20"N **3** — see HORN

North Car·o·li·na \,kar(-ə)-'lī-nə\ state E U.S. ✳ Raleigh *area* 52,669 *sq mi* (136,413 *sq km*), *pop* 6,628,637 — **North Car·o·lin·ian** \-'li-nē-ən, -'li-nyən\ *adj or n*

North Cas·cades National Park \kas-'kādz, 'kas-,\ reservation N *cen* Wash. on Canadian border

North Channel strait bet. NE Ireland & SW Scotland connecting Irish Sea & the Atlantic

North Charleston city SE S.C. *pop* 70,218

North Chicago city NE Ill. S of Waukegan *pop* 34,978

North Da·ko·ta \də-'kō-tə\ state NW *cen* U.S. ✳ Bismarck *area* 70,665 *sq mi* (183,729 *sq km*), *pop* 638,800 — **North Da·ko·tan** \-'kō-t°n\ *adj or n*

North Down district E Northern Ireland, established 1974 *area* 28 *sq mi* (73 *sq km*), *pop* 70,308

North Downs hills S England chiefly in Kent & Surrey

North East Frontier Agency — see ARUNACHAL PRADESH

North–East New Guinea the NE part of mainland Papua New Guinea

Northern *or* **Noord** \'nȯrd, 'nȯrt\ *or formerly* **Northern Transvaal** province NE Republic of South Africa *area* 47,598 *sq mi* (123,280 *sq km*), *pop* 5,013,000

Northern Cape province W Republic of South Africa *area* 139,691 *sq mi* (361,800 *sq km*), *pop* 749,000

Northern Cir·cars \(,)sər-'kärz\ historic name for the coast region of E India now in E Andhra Pradesh

Northern Cook Islands \'kúk\ *or* **Ma·ni·hi·ki Islands** \,mä-nē-'hē-kē\ islands S *cen* Pacific N of Cook Islands; belong to New Zealand

Northern Ireland country NE Ireland; a division of the United Kingdom of Great Britain and Northern Ireland ✳ Belfast *area* 5452 *sq mi* (14,121 *sq km*), *pop* 1,543,000 — see ULSTER

Northern Karroo — see KARROO

Northern Kingdom — see ISRAEL

Northern Mar·i·ana Islands \,mar-ē-'a-nə, ,mer-\ islands W Pacific; in Trust Territory of the Pacific Islands 1947–76 & a U.S. commonwealth since 1986; *area* 184 *sq mi* (478 *sq km*), *pop* 45,400

Northern Rhodesia — see ZAMBIA

Northern Sporades — see SPORADES

Northern Territory territory *cen* & N Australia bordering on Arafura Sea ✳ Darwin *area* 520,280 *sq mi* (1,347,525 *sq km*), *pop* 169,300

Northern Yukon National Park reservation NW Canada

North Frisian — see FRISIAN ISLANDS

North·glenn \'nȯrth-,glen\ city N *cen* Colo. NE of Denver *pop* 27,195

North Ha·ven \'nȯrth-,hā-vən\ town S Conn. *pop* 22,247

North Holland *or D* **Noord–Hol·land** \,nȯrt-'hȯ-,länt\ province NW Netherlands ✳ Haarlem *area* 1124 *sq mi* (2911 *sq km*), *pop* 2,440,165

North Island island N New Zealand *area* 44,297 *sq mi* (114,729 *sq km*), *pop* 2,553,413

North Khartoum — see KHARTOUM, NORTH

North Kings·town \'kiŋ-stən\ town S R.I. *pop* 23,786

North Korea — see KOREA — **North Korean** *adj or n*

North Las Vegas city SE Nev. *pop* 47,707

North Lau·der·dale \'lȯ-dər-,dāl\ city SE Fla. *pop* 26,506

North Little Rock city *cen* Ark. *pop* 61,741

North Miami city SE Fla. *pop* 49,998

North Miami Beach city SE Fla. *pop* 35,359

North Minch — see MINCH

North Olm·sted \'əm-,sted\ city NE Ohio *pop* 34,204

North Ossetia — see ALANIA

North Pacific — see PACIFIC OCEAN

North Platte 1 river 680 *mi* (1094 *km*) W U.S. flowing from N Colo. N & E through Wyo. into Nebr. to unite with the S. Platte forming Platte River **2** city SW *cen* Nebr. *pop* 22,605

North Providence town NE R.I. *pop* 32,090

North Rhine–Westphalia *or G* **Nord·rhein–West·fa·len** \'nȯrt-,rīn-,vest-'fä-lən\ state of Germany & formerly of W. Germany formed 1946 by union of former Westphalia province, Lippe state, & N Rhine Province ✳ Düsseldorf *area* 13,142 *sq mi* (34,038 *sq km*), *pop* 17,349,700

North Rich·land Hills \'rich-lənd\ town N Tex. *pop* 45,895

North Ridge·ville \'rij-,vil\ village N Ohio *pop* 21,564

North Riding — see YORK

North River estuary of Hudson River bet. SE N.Y. & NE N.J.

North Roy·al·ton \'rȯi(-ə)l-tən\ city N Ohio *pop* 23,197

North Saskatchewan — see SASKATCHEWAN

North Sea arm of the Atlantic 600 *mi* (966 *km*) long & 350 *mi* (563 *km*) wide E of Great Britain

North Slope region N Alaska bet. Brooks Range & Arctic Ocean

North Ton·a·wan·da \ˌtä-nə-ˈwän-də\ city W N.Y. N of Buffalo *pop* 34,989

North Truchas Peak — see TRUCHAS PEAK

North·um·ber·land \ˈnȯr-ᵗhəm-bər-lənd\ county N England ✳ Newcastle upon Tyne *area* 2013 *sq mi* (5214 *sq km*), *pop* 300,600

Northumberland Strait strait 180 *mi* (290 *km*) long Canada in Gulf of St. Lawrence bet. P.E.I. & the mainland

North·um·bria \nȯr-ˈthəm-brē-ə\ ancient country Great Britain bet. the Humber & Firth of Forth; one of kingdoms in Anglo-Saxon heptarchy — **North·um·bri·an** \-ən\ *adj or n*

North Vancouver city Canada in SW B.C. *pop* 38,436

North Vietnam — see VIETNAM

North West or **Noord·wes** \ˌnȯrd-ˈwes, ˌnȯrt-\ province N Republic of South Africa *area* 44,861 *sq mi* (116,190 *sq km*), *pop* 3,349,000

North–West Frontier Province province of Pakistan & formerly of Brit. India on Afghanistan border ✳ Peshawar *pop* 11,658,000

Northwest Passage a passage by sea bet. the Atlantic & the Pacific along the N coast of N. America

Northwest Territories territory N Canada comprising the Arctic islands, the mainland N 60° bet. Yukon Territory & Hudson Bay, & the islands in Hudson Bay; ✳ Yellowknife *area* 1,253,432 *sq mi* (3,246,389 *sq km*), *pop* 57,649

North York city Canada in SE Ont. N of Toronto *pop* 562,564

North Yorkshire county N England ✳ Northallerton *area* 3327 *sq mi* (8617 *sq km*), *pop* 698,700

Nor·ton Shores \ˈnȯr-tᵊn\ city W Mich. S of Muskegon *pop* 21,755

Norton Sound arm of Bering Sea W Alaska

Nor·walk \ˈnȯr-ˌwȯk\ **1** city SW Calif. SE of Los Angeles *pop* 94,279 **2** city SW Conn. on Long Island Sound *pop* 78,331

Nor·way \ˈnȯr-ˌwā\ or Norw **Nor·ge** \ˈnȯr-gə\ country N Europe in Scandinavia bordering on Atlantic & Arctic oceans; a kingdom ✳ Oslo *area* 154,790 *sq mi* (400,906 *sq km*), *pop* 4,308,000 — **Nor·we·gian** \nȯr-ˈwē-jən\ *adj or n*

Norwegian Sea arm of the N Atlantic W of Norway

Nor·wich 1 \ˈnȯr-(ˌ)wich; ˈnȯr-ich, ˈnär-\ city SE Conn. *pop* 37,391 **2** \ˈnär-ij, -ich\ city E England ✳ of Norfolk *pop* 120,700

Nor·wood \ˈnȯr-ˌwu̇d\ **1** town E Mass. SW of Boston *pop* 28,700 **2** city SW Ohio within city of Cincinnati *pop* 23,674

Not·ta·way \ˈnä-tə-ˌwā\ river 400 *mi* (644 *km*) Canada in SW Que. flowing NW into James Bay

Not·ting·ham \ˈnä-tiŋ-əm, *US also* -ˌham\ borough N cen England ✳ of Nottinghamshire *pop* 261,500

Not·ting·ham·shire \ˈnä-tiŋ-əm-ˌshir, -shər, *US also* -ˌham-\ or **Nottingham** or **Notts** \ˈnäts\ county N cen England ✳ Nottingham *area* 866 *sq mi* (2243 *sq km*), *pop* 980,600

Nouak·chott \nu̇-ˈäk-ˌshät\ city ✳ of Mauritania near coast in SW *pop* 393,325

Nou·méa \nü-ˈmā-ə\ city & port ✳ of New Caledonia *pop* 65,110

No·va Igua·çu \ˌnȯ-və-ē-gwə-ˈsü\ city SE Brazil in Rio de Janeiro state NW of Rio de Janeiro *pop* 1,286,337

Nova Lisboa — see HUAMBO

No·va·ra \nō-ˈvär-ä\ commune NW Italy in Piedmont *pop* 102,473

No·va Sco·tia \ˌnō-və-ˈskō-shə\ province SE Canada comprising a peninsula (375 *mi or* 600 *km* long) & Cape Breton Is. ✳ Halifax area 20,402 *sq mi* (52,840 *sq km*), *pop* 899,942 — see ACADIA —

No·va Sco·tian \-shən\ *adj or n*

No·va·to \nō-'vä-(,)tō\ city W Calif. N of San Francisco *pop* 47,585

No·va·ya Zem·lya \'nō-və-yə-,zem-lē-'ä\ two islands NE Russia in Europe in Arctic Ocean bet. Barents Sea & Kara Sea *area* 31,382 *sq mi* (81,279 *sq km*), *pop* 400

Nov·go·rod \'näv-gə-,räd, 'nóv-gə-rət\ **1** medieval principality E Europe extending from Lake Peipus & Lithuania to the Urals **2** city W Russia in Europe *pop* 235,000

No·vi \'nō-,vī\ village SE Mich. NW of Detroit *pop* 32,998

No·vi Sad \,nō-vē-'säd\ city N Yugoslavia on the Danube; chief city of Vojvodina *pop* 264,533

No·vo·kuz·netsk \,nō-(,)vō-kùz-'netsk, ,nó-və-kùz-'nyetsk\ *or formerly* **Sta·linsk** \'stä-lin(t)sk, 'sta-; 'stäl-yin(t)sk\ city S Russia in Asia at S end of Kuznetsk Basin *pop* 600,000

No·vo·si·birsk \,nō-,vō-sə-'birsk, ,nó-və-\ *or formerly* **No·vo·ni·ko·la·evsk** \-,ni·kə-'lī-əfsk\ city S Russia in Asia on the Ob *pop* 1,442,000

Nu·bia \'nü-bē-ə, 'nyü-\ region & ancient kingdom NE Africa along the Nile in S Egypt & N Sudan — **Nu·bi·an** \'nü-bē-ən, 'nyü-\ *adj or n*

Nu·bi·an Desert \'nü-bē-ən, 'nyü-\ desert NE Sudan E of the Nile

Nu·e·ces \nù-'ā-səs, nyù-\ river over 300 *mi* (483 *km*) S Tex. flowing S & SE into Nueces Bay at head of Corpus Christi Bay

Nueva Esparta — see MARGARITA

Nue·vo La·re·do \'nwä-(,)vō-lä-'rä-(,)dō, -thō\ city N Mexico in Tamaulipas on Rio Grande opposite Laredo, Tex. *pop* 217,912

Nuevo Le·ón \lä-'ōn\ state N Mexico in the Sierra Madre Oriental ✱ Monterrey *area* 24,925 *sq mi* (64,556 *sq km*), *pop* 3,098,736

Nu·ku·'a·lo·fa \,nü-kü-ä-'lō-fä\ town ✱ of Tonga on Tongatapu Is. *pop* 21,383

Nu·ku Hi·va \,nü-kü-'hē-vä\ island S Pacific in the Marquesas; largest in group *area ab* 60 *sq mi* (155 *sq km*), *pop* 2100; chief town Taiohae

Null·ar·bor Plain \'nə-lə-,bór\ treeless plain SW Australia in Western Australia & S. Australia bordering on Great Australian Bight

Num·foor \'nüm-,fōr, -,fór\ island Irian Jaya in W Schouten Islands *area* 28 *sq mi* (73 *sq km*)

Nu·mid·ia \nù-'mid-ē-ə, nyù-\ ancient country N Africa E of Mauretania in modern Algeria; chief city Hippo — **Nu·mid·i·an** \-dē-ən\ *adj or n*

Nun·ea·ton \,nə-'nē-t°n\ borough *cen* England in Warwickshire E of Birmingham *pop* 71,530

Nu·ni·vak \'nü-nə-,vak\ island 50 *mi* (80 *km*) long W Alaska in Bering Sea

Nu·rem·berg \'nùr-əm-,bərg, 'nyùr-\ *or G* **Nürn·berg** \'nʉrn-,berk\ city S Germany in N *cen* Bavaria *pop* 497,496

Nu·ri·stan \,nùr-i-'stan, -'stän\ *or formerly* **Kaf·iri·stan** \,ka-fə-ri-'stan, -'stän\ district E Afghanistan S of the Hindu Kush ✱ Puchal — **Nur·i·stani** \,nùr-ə-'stä-nē\ *n*

Nuuk \'nük\ *or* **Godt·håb** \'gót-,hóp\ town ✱ of Greenland on SW coast *pop* 12,181

Nyasa, Lake — see MALAWI (Lake)

Nyasaland — see MALAWI

Nyir·a·gon·go \nē-,ir-ə-'gón̄-(,)gō, -'gän̄-, ,nyir-\ volcano *ab* 11,400 *ft* (3475 *m*) E Democratic Republic of the Congo in Virunga Mountains NE of Lake Kivu

Nyí·regy·há·za \'nē-,rej-,hä-zó\ city NE Hungary *pop* 120,600

Nysa \'ni-sə\ *or* G **Neis·se** \'nī-sə\ river 120 *mi* (193 *km*) SW Poland flowing NE into the Oder

O

Oa·he Reservoir \ō-'ä-(,)hē\ reservoir *ab* 225 *mi* (362 *km*) long N S.Dak. & S N.Dak. formed in Missouri River by **Oahe Dam**

Oa·hu \ō-'ä-(,)hü\ island Hawaii, site of Honolulu *area* 589 *sq mi* (1531 *sq km*)

Oak Creek \'ōk\ city SE Wis. *pop* 19,513

Oak Forest village NE Ill. S of Chicago *pop* 26,203

Oak·ham \'ō-kəm\ town E *cen* England in E Leicestershire; ✳ of former county of Rutlandshire *pop* 7996

Oak·land \'ō-klənd\ city & port W Calif. on San Francisco Bay opposite San Francisco *pop* 372,242

Oakland Park city SE Fla. N of Fort Lauderdale *pop* 26,326

Oak Lawn village NE Ill. SW of Chicago *pop* 56,182

Oak Park 1 village NE Ill. W of Chicago *pop* 53,648 **2** city SE Mich. N of Detroit *pop* 30,462

Oak Ridge city E Tenn. W of Knoxville *pop* 27,310

Oak·ville \'ōk-,vil\ town Canada in SE Ont. SW of Toronto *pop* 114,670

Oa·xa·ca \wä-'hä-kä\ **1** state SE Mexico bordering on the Pacific *area* 36,820 *sq mi* (95,364 *sq km*), *pop* 3,019,560 **2** city, its ✳ *pop* 212,943 — **Oa·xa·can** \-kən\ *adj*

Ob \'äb, 'ób\ river over 2250 *mi* (3620 *km*) W Russia in Asia flowing NW & N into **Gulf of Ob** (inlet of Arctic Ocean 500 *mi or* 800 *km* long)

Ober·am·mer·gau \,ō-bər-'ä-mər-,gaú\ town S Germany in Bavaria SSW of Munich *pop* 4906

Ober·hau·sen \'ō-bər-,haú-z°n\ city W Germany in the Ruhr WNW of Essen *pop* 224,559

Oberland — see BERNER ALPEN

Oberpfalz — see PALATINATE

Obwald *or* **Obwalden** — see UNTERWALDEN

Ocala \ō-'ka-lə\ city N *cen* Fla. S of Gainesville *pop* 42,045

Oce·a·nia \,ō-shē-'a-nē-ə, -'ä-\ the lands of the *cen* & S Pacific including Micronesia, Melanesia, Polynesia (including New Zealand), often Australia, & sometimes the Malay Archipelago — **Oce·a·ni·an** \-nē-ən\ *adj or n*

Ocean Island 1 — see BANABA **2** — see KURE ATOLL

Ocean·side \'ō-shən-,sīd\ city SW Calif. NNW of San Diego *pop* 128,398

Oc·mul·gee \ōk-'məl-gē\ river 255 *mi* (410 *km*) *cen* Ga. flowing SE to join the **Oco·nee** \ō-'kō-nē\ (250 *mi or* 402 *km*) forming the Altamaha

Ocmulgee National Monument reservation *cen* Ga. at Macon containing American Indian mounds & other remains

Ocra·coke Island \'ō-krə-,kōk\ island off *cen* N.C. coast bet. Pamlico Sound & the Atlantic — see CROATAN

Oden·se \'ō-d°n-sə, 'ü-ən-zə\ city Denmark in N Fyn Is. *pop* 174,948

Oder \'ō-dər\ *or* **Odra** \'ò-drə\ river *ab* 565 *mi* (909 *km*) *cen* Europe rising in the mountains of Silesia, Czech Republic & flowing N to join Neisse River & thence N into the Baltic Sea

Odes·sa \ō-'de-sə\ **1** city W Tex. *pop* 89,699 **2** city & port S Ukraine on Black Sea *pop* 1,101,000

Oea — see TRIPOLI

Oe·ta \'ē-tə\ mountains *cen* Greece, E spur of Pindus Mountains; highest point 7060 *ft* (2152 *m*)

Of·fa·ly \'ò-fə-lē, 'ä-\ *or formerly* **King's** county *cen* Ireland in Leinster ✳ Tullamore *area* 771 *sq mi* (2005 *sq km*), *pop* 58,494

Of·fen·bach \'ò-fən-,bäk, -,bäk\ city SW *cen* Germany on Main River E of Frankfurt am Main *pop* 115,790

Oga·den \ō-'gä-,dän\ plateau region SE Ethiopia

Ogasawara Islands — see BONIN ISLANDS

Og·bo·mo·sho \,ōg-bō-'mō-(,)shō\ city W Nigeria *pop* 644,200

Og·den \'òg-dən, 'äg-\ city N Utah *pop* 63,909

Ogee·chee \ō-'gē-chē\ river 250 *mi* (402 *km*) E Ga. flowing SE into the Atlantic

Ohio \ō-'hī-(,)ō, ə-, -ə\ **1** river *ab* 975 *mi* (1569 *km*) E U.S. flowing from junction of Allegheny & Monongahela rivers in W Pa. into Mississippi River **2** state E *cen* U.S. ✳ Columbus *area* 41,222 *sq mi* (107,177 *sq km*), *pop* 10,847,115 — **Ohio·an** \-'hī-ō-ən\ *n*

Ohře — see EGER

Oise \'wäz\ river 188 *mi* (302 *km*) N France flowing SW into the Seine

Oi·ta \'òi-,tä, ō-'ē-tä\ city & port Japan in NE Kyushu *pop* 417,051

Ojos del Sa·la·do \'ō-(,)hōs-,del-sä-'lä-(,)dō, -,thel-, -,thō\ mountain 22,664 *ft* (6908 *m*) NW Argentina in the Andes W of Tucumán

Oka \ō-'kä\ **1** river 530 *mi* (853 *km*) S *cen* Russia in Asia flowing N from the Sayan Mountains into the Angara **2** river 919 *mi* (1479 *km*) *cen* Russia in Europe flowing into the Volga

Oka·nog·an *or in Canada* **Oka·na·gan** \,ō-kə-'nä-gən\ river 300 *mi* (483 *km*) U.S. & Canada flowing from **Okanagan Lake** (in SE B.C.) into Columbia River in NE Wash.

Oka·van·go \,ō-kə-'väŋ-(,)gō\ *or* **Cu·ban·go** \kü-'bäŋ-(,)gü\ river 1000 *mi* (1609 *km*) SW *cen* Africa rising in *cen* Angola & flowing S & E to empty into **Okavango Swamps** *or* **Okavango Del·ta** (great marsh area N of Lake Ngami in NW Botswana)

Oka·ya·ma \,ō-kä-'yä-mä\ city & port Japan in W Honshu on Inland Sea *pop* 601,094

Oka·za·ki \ō-kä-'zä-kē, ō-'kä-zä-kē\ city Japan in S *cen* Honshu SE of Nagoya *pop* 306,821

Okee·cho·bee, Lake \,ō-kə-'chō-bē\ lake 37 *mi* (60 *km*) long S *cen* Fla.

Oke·fe·no·kee \ˌō-kə-fə-ˈnō-kē, ˌō-kē- *also* ˈōk-fə-ˌnōk\ swamp over 600 *sq mi* (1554 *sq km*) SE Ga. & NE Fla.

Okhotsk, Sea of \ō-ˈkätsk, ə-ˈkȯtsk\ inlet of the Pacific E Russia in Asia W of Kamchatka Peninsula & Kuril Islands

Oki Archipelago \ˈō-(ˌ)kē\ archipelago Japan in Sea of Japan off SW Honshu

Oki·na·wa \ˌō-kə-ˈnä-wə, -ˈnau̇-ə\ **1** island group Japan in *cen* Ryukyu Islands ✻ Naha; occupied by the U.S. 1945–1972 **2** island in the group; largest in the Ryukyus *area* 454 *sq mi* (1176 *sq km*) — **Oki·na·wan** \-ˈnä-wən, -ˈnau̇-ən\ *adj or n*

Okla·ho·ma \ˌō-klə-ˈhō-mə\ state S *cen* U.S. ✻ Oklahoma City *area* 69,956 *sq mi* (181,186 *sq km*), *pop* 3,145,585 — **Okla·ho·man** \-mən\ *adj or n*

Oklahoma City city ✻ of Okla. on the N. Canadian *pop* 444,719

Öland \ˈŎ(r)-ˌländ, ˈœ-\ island Sweden in Baltic Sea off SE coast; chief town Borgholm *area* 519 *sq mi* (1349 *sq km*)

Ola·the \ō-ˈlā-thə\ city NE Kans. SW of Kansas City *pop* 63,352

Old Castile — see CASTILE

Ol·den·burg \ˈōl-dən-ˌbȯrg, -ˌbu̇rk\ **1** former state NW Germany bordering on North Sea **2** city NW Germany W of Bremen *pop* 145,161

Old·ham \ˈōl-dəm\ borough NW England in Greater Manchester *pop* 211,400

Old Point Com·fort \ˈkəm-fərt\ cape SE Va. on N shore of Hampton Roads

Old Sar·um \ˈsar-əm, ˈser-\ *or anc* **Sor·bi·o·du·num** \ˌsȯr-bē-ə-ˈdü-nəm, -ˈdyü-\ ancient city S England in Wiltshire N of Salisbury

Ol·du·vai Gorge \ˈōl-də-ˌvī\ canyon Tanzania in N mainland SE of Serengeti Plain; fossil beds

Olek·ma \ō-ˈlek-mə\ river 794 *mi* (1278 *km*) E Russia in Asia rising in Yablonovy Mountains & flowing N into the Lena

Ole·nek \ˌä-lə-ˈnyȯk\ river N Russia in Asia flowing NE into Laptev Sea W of the Lena

Ol·i·fants \ˈä-lə-fən(t)s\ river 350 *mi* (563 *km*) S Africa in Republic of South Africa & Mozambique flowing into the Limpopo

Ol·ives, Mount of \ˈä-livz, -ləvz\ *or* **Ol·i·vet** \ˈä-lə-ˌvet, ˌä-lə-ˈ\ mountain ridge 2680 *ft* (817 *m*) W Jordan running N & S on E side of Jerusalem

Olo·mouc \ˈȯ-lə-ˌmōts\ *or G* **Ol·mütz** \ˈȯl-ˌmüts, -ˌmyüts, -ˌmuets\ city E Czech Republic in *cen* Moravia *pop* 105,690

Olsz·tyn \ˈȯl-shtən\ *or G* **Al·len·stein** \ˈä-lən-ˌshtīn\ city N Poland NNW of Warsaw *pop* 161,238

Olt \ˈȯlt\ river 308 *mi* (496 *km*) S Romania flowing S through the Transylvanian Alps into the Danube

Ol·te·nia \äl-ˈtē-nē-ə\ *or* **Little Walachia** region S Romania W of the Olt; the W division of Walachia

Olym·pia \ə-ˈlim-pē-ə, ō-\ **1** city ✻ of Wash. on Puget Sound *pop* 33,840 **2** plain S Greece in NW Peloponnese along the Alpheus — **Olym·pi·an** \-pē-ən\ *adj or n* — **Olym·pic** \-pik\ *adj*

Olympic Mountains mountains NW Wash. in *cen* Olympic Peninsula — see OLYMPUS (Mount)

Olympic National Park reservation NW Wash. including part of Olympic Mountains & strip of land along coast to W

Olympic Peninsula peninsula NW Wash. W of Puget Sound

Olym·pus \ə-'lim-pəs, ō-\ massif NE Greece in Thessaly near coast of Gulf of Salonika; highest point 9570 ft (2917 m)

Olympus, Mount 1 mountain 7965 ft (2428 m) NW Wash.; highest in Olympic Mountains **2** — see ULU DAG

Olyn·thus \ō-'lin(t)-thəs\ ancient city NE Greece in Macedonia on Chalcidice Peninsula

Om \'ōm\ river 450 mi (724 km) SW Russia in Asia flowing into the Irtysh

Omagh \'ō-mə, -(,)mä\ **1** district W Northern Ireland, established 1974 area 436 sq mi (1134 sq km), pop 45,343 **2** town W Northern Ireland in cen Omagh district pop 17,280

Oma·ha \'ō-mə-,hȯ, -,hä\ city E Nebr. on Missouri River pop 335,795

Oman \ō-'män, -'man\ or formerly **Muscat and Oman** country SW Asia in SE Arabia bordering on Arabian Sea; a sultanate ✻ Muscat area 82,000 sq mi (213,200 sq km), pop 2,000,000 — **Omani** \ō-'mä-nē, -'ma-\ adj or n

Oman, Gulf of arm of Arabian Sea bet. Oman & SE Iran

Om·dur·man \,äm-dər-'man, -'män\ city cen Sudan on the Nile opposite Khartoum & Khartoum North pop 526,287

Omi·ya \'ō-mē-,yä, ō-'mē-ä\ city Japan on Honshu, a suburb of Tokyo pop 403,779

Omo·lon \,ä-mə-'lȯn\ river 715 mi (1150 km) E Russia in Asia flowing from the Kolyma Range N into Kolyma River

Omsk \'ȯm(p)sk, 'äm(p)sk\ city SW Russia in Asia at confluence of the Irtysh & the Om pop 1,169,000

Omu·ra \ō-'mü-,rä, ō-'mü-rä\ city & port Japan in NW Kyushu on **Omura Bay** (inlet of E. China Sea) NNE of Nagasaki

One·ga, Lake \ō-'ne-gə\ lake NW Russia in Europe in S Karelia area over 3700 sq mi (9583 sq km)

Onei·da Lake \ō-'nī-də\ lake ab 22 mi (35 km) long cen N.Y. NE of Syracuse

On·tar·io \än-'ter-ē-,ō, -'tar-\ **1** city SW Calif. NW of Riverside pop 133,179 **2** province E Canada bet. Great Lakes & Hudson Bay ✻ Toronto area 353,951 sq mi (916,733 sq km), pop 10,084,885 — **On·tar·i·an** \-ē-ən\ adj or n

Ontario, Lake lake U.S. & Canada in N.Y. & Ont.; easternmost of the Great Lakes area ab 7600 sq mi (19,684 sq km)

Oos Kaap — see EASTERN CAPE

Ope·li·ka \,ō-pə-'lī-kə\ city E Alabama pop 22,122

Opo·le \ō-'pȯ-le\ or G **Op·peln** \'ȯ-pəln\ city SW Poland on the Oder pop 127,653

Oporto — see PORTO

Oquirrh Mountains \'ō-kər\ mountain range N cen Utah S of Great Salt Lake; highest point ab 11,000 ft (3353 m)

Ora·dea \ō-'rä-dē-ə\ city NW Romania in Transylvania near Hungarian border pop 225,416

Oral \ō-'räl\ or **Uralsk** \ü-'ralsk, yü-'ralsk\ city W Kazakhstan on Ural River pop 98,640

Oran \ō-'rän\ city & port NW Algeria pop 628,558

Or·ange \'är-inj, 'ȧr-(-ə)nj, 'ȯr-inj, 'ȯr(-ə)nj\ **1** city SW Calif. N of Santa Ana pop 110,658 **2** city E Tex. E of Beaumont on the Sabine pop 19,381 **3** river 1300 mi (2092 km) S Africa flowing from the Drakensberg in Lesotho W into the Atlantic

Orange \ȯ-ˈränzh\ city SE France N of Avignon *pop* 28,136
Orange Free State *or* **Oranje Vrystaat** — see FREE STATE
Orasul Stalin — see BRASOV
Ordzhonikidze — see VLADIKAVKAZ
Ore·bro \œr-ə-ˈbrü\ city S *cen* Sweden *pop* 123,188
Or·e·gon \ˈȯr-i-gən, -ˌär-, *chiefly by outsiders* -ˌgän\ 1 the Columbia River — an old name used esp. prior to discovery of mouth & re-naming of river (1791) by Capt. Robert Gray 2 state NW U.S. ✸ Salem *area* 97,073 *sq mi* (251,419 *sq km*), *pop* 2,842,321 — **Or·e·go·nian** \ˌȯr-i-ˈgō-nē-ən, -ˌär-, -ˈnyən\ *adj or n*
Oregon Caves limestone caverns SW Oreg. SW of Medford in **Oregon Caves National Monument**
Oregon Country region W N. America bet. Pacific coast & the Rockies and bet. N Calif. & Alaska — so called *ab* 1818–46
Oregon Trail pioneer route to the Pacific Northwest *ab* 2000 *mi* (3219 *km*) long from vicinity of Independence, Mo., to Fort Van-couver, Wash.; used esp. 1842–60
Orel \ȯ-ˈrel, ȯr-ˈyȯl\ city Russia in Europe SSW of Moscow
Orem \ˈȯr-əm, ˈȯr-\ city N *cen* Utah N of Provo *pop* 67,561
Oren·burg \ˈȯr-ən-ˌbȯrg, ˈȯr-, -ˌbȯrg\ *or formerly* **Chka·lov** \chə-ˈkä-ləf\ city SE Russia in Europe on Ural River *pop* 557,000
Oren·se \ȯ-ˈren-(ˌ)sā\ 1 province NW Spain *area* 2810 *sq mi* (7278 *sq km*), *pop* 353,491 2 city, its ✸ *pop* 101,623
Øre·sund \ˈȯr-ə-ˌsən\ strait bet. Sjælland Is., Denmark, & S Sweden connecting Kattegat with Baltic Sea
Or·gan Pipe Cactus National Monument \ˈȯr-gən-ˌpīp\ reserva-tion S Ariz. on Mexican border
Or·hon \ˈȯr-ˌhȯn, -ˌhȯn\ *or* **Or·khon** \ˈȯr-ˌkȯn, -ˌkȯn\ river N Mon-golia flowing NE from N edge of the Gobi into the Selenga
Oril·lia \ȯ-ˈril-yə\ city Canada in SE Ont. on Lake Simcoe *pop* 25,925
Ori·no·co \ˌȯr-ē-ˈnō-(ˌ)kō, ˌȯr-\ river 1600 *mi* (2575 *km*) Venezuela flowing from Brazilian border to Colombia border & thence into the Atlantic through wide delta
Oris·sa \ȯ-ˈri-sə\ state E India bordering on Bay of Bengal ✸ Bhu-baneswar *area* 60,178 *sq mi* (155,861 *sq km*), *pop* 31,659,736
Ori·za·ba \ˌȯr-ə-ˈzä-bə, ˌȯr-, ˌȯr-ē-ˈsä-vä\ 1 — see CITLALTEPETL 2 city E Mexico in Veracruz state *pop* 113,516
Ork·ney Islands \ˈȯrk-nē\ islands N Scotland constituting a region ✸ Kirkwall (on Mainland Is.) *area* 376 *sq mi* (978 *sq km*), *pop* 19,570 — **Ork·ca·dian** \ȯr-ˈkā-dē-ən\ *adj or n* — **Ork·ney·an** \ˈȯrk-nē-ən, ȯrk-\ *adj or n*
Or·lan·do \ȯr-ˈlan-(ˌ)dō\ city E *cen* Fla. NE of Tampa *pop* 164,693
Or·land Park \ˈȯr-lənd\ village NE Ill. SW of Chicago *pop* 35,720
Or·lé·a·nais \ˌȯr-lā-ə-ˈnā\ region & former province N *cen* France ✸ Orléans
Or·lé·ans \ˌȯr-lā-ˈäⁿ\ commune N *cen* France on the Loire SSW of Paris *pop* 107,965
Or·ly \ȯr-ˈlē, ˈȯr-lē\ commune France, SSE suburb of Paris
Or·moc Bay \ȯr-ˈmäk\ inlet of Camotes Sea Philippines in NW Leyte Is.
Or·mond Beach \ˈȯr-mənd\ city E Fla. upcoast from Daytona Beach *pop* 29,721
Ormuz — see HORMUZ

Orne \'órn\ river 95 *mi* (153 *km*) NW France flowing N into Bay of the Seine

Oron·tes \ò-'rän-(,)tēz\ river 246 *mi* (396 *km*) Syria & Turkey rising in Lebanon in the Bekaa & flowing into the Mediterranean

Or·ping·ton \'òr-piŋ-tən\ former urban district SE England in Kent, now part of Bromley

Or·re·fors \,ór-ə-'fórz, -'fórsh\ town SE Sweden NW of Kalmar

Orsk \'órsk\ city SE Russia in Europe on Ural River S of Magnitogorsk *pop* 273,000

Or·te·gal, Cape \,ór-tē-'gäl\ cape NW Spain

Ort·les \'órt-,läs\ *or G* **Ort·ler** \-lor\ mountain range of E Alps N Italy bet. Venezia Tridentina & Lombardy; highest peak Ortles 12,792 *ft* (3899 *m*)

Orū·mī·yeh \,ùr-ü-'mē-yə\ *or formerly* **Re·zā·'ī·yeh** \,re-zä-'ē-yə\ **1** shallow saline lake NW Iran *area* 1815 *sq mi* (4701 *sq km*) **2** city NW Iran *pop* 300,746

Oru·ro \ò-'ri-rō\ city W Bolivia *pop* 183,194

Or·vie·to \,ór-'vyä-(,)tō, -'vye-\ *or anc* **Vel·su·na** \vel-'sü-nə\ *or* **Vol·sin·ii** \väl-'si-nē-,ī\ commune *cen* Italy WNW of Terni *pop* 21,302

Osage \ō-'sāj, 'ō-,\ river E Kans. & Mo. flowing E into Missouri River; now partly submerged in Lake of the Ozarks

Osa·ka \ō-'sä-kä, 'ō-sä-,kä\ city & port Japan in S Honshu on **Osaka Bay** (inlet of the Pacific) *pop* 2,623,831

Osh·a·wa \'ä-shə-wə, -,wä, -,wò\ city Canada in SE Ont. on Lake Ontario ENE of Toronto *pop* 129,344

Osh·kosh \'äsh-,käsh\ city E Wis. on Lake Winnebago *pop* 55,006

Osi·jek \'ō-sē-,yek\ city E Croatia in Slavonia *pop* 129,792

Os·lo \'äz-(,)lō, 'äs-\ *or formerly* **Chris·ti·a·nia** *or* **Kris·ti·a·nia** \,kris-chē-'a-nē-ə, ,krish-chē-, ,kris-tē-, -'ä-\ city ✳ of Norway at N end of **Oslo Fjord** (inlet of the Skagerrak) *pop* 458,364

Os·na·brück \'äz-nə-,brük, ,ós-nə-'brük\ city NW Germany in Lower Saxony *pop* 165,143

Osor·no \ō-'sór-(,)nō\ volcano 8727 *ft* (2644 *m*) S *cen* Chile in lake district

Os·sa, Mount \'ä-sə\ mountain 6490 *ft* (1967 *m*) NE Greece in E Thessaly

Os·se·tia \ä-'sē-sh(ē-)ə\ region SE Russia in Europe in *cen* Caucasus — see ALANIA, SOUTH OSSETIA — **Os·sete** \'ä,sēt\ *also* **Os·set** \'ä-sət, -,set\ *n* — **Os·se·tian** \ä-'sē-shən\ *adj or n* — **Os·set·ic** \ä-'se-tik\ *n*

Os·si·ning \'ä-s⁸n-iŋ\ village SE N.Y. *pop* 22,582

Ost·end \ä-'stend, 'ä-,\ *or Flem* **Oost·en·de** \ō-'sten-də\ *or F* **Ostende** \ò-'stäⁿd\ city & port NW Belgium *pop* 68,500

Österreich — see AUSTRIA

Os·tia \'äs-tē-ə\ town *cen* Italy at mouth of the Tiber E of site of ancient town of the same name which was the port for Rome

Ostrasia — see AUSTRASIA

Ostra·va \'ós-trə-və\ *or formerly* **Mo·rav·ska Ostrava** \'mór-əf-skə\ city *cen* E Czech Republic in Moravia *pop* 327,553

Osu·mi Islands \'ō-sü-(,)mē, ō-'sü-mē\ island group Japan in N Ryukyus

Os·we·go \ä-'swē-(,)gō\ city N N.Y. on Lake Ontario *pop* 19,195

Oś·wię·cim \ˌȯsh-ˈfyen-chēm\ *or* **Ausch·witz** \ˈaùsh-ˌvits\ commune S Poland W of Kraków; site of Nazi concentration camp during World War II *pop* 45,282

Ota·go Harbor \ō-ˈtä-gō\ inlet of the Pacific S New Zealand on E coast of South Is.; Dunedin is situated on it

Otran·to \ō-ˈtran-(ˌ)tō, ˈō-trän-ˌtō\ commune & port S Italy on coast at SE tip of Puglia *pop* 5152

Otranto, Strait of strait bet. SE Italy & W Albania connecting Adriatic Sea & Ionian Sea

Ot·ta·wa \ˈä-tə-wə, -ˌwä, -ˌwȯ\ **1** river 696 *mi* (1120 *km*) E Canada in SE Ont. & S Que. flowing E into St. Lawrence River **2** city ✳ of Canada in SE Ont. *pop* 313,987

Ot·to·man Empire \ˈä-tə-mən\ former Turkish sultanate (✳ Constantinople) in SE Europe, W Asia, & N Africa including at greatest extent Turkey, Syria, Mesopotamia, Palestine, Arabia, Egypt, Barbary States, Balkans, & parts of Russia & Hungary — **Ottoman** *adj or n*

Ot·tum·wa \ə-ˈtəm-wə, ō-ˈtəm-\ city SE Iowa *pop* 24,488

Oua·chi·ta \ˈwä-shə-ˌtȯ\ river 605 *mi* (974 *km*) SW Ark. & E La. flowing into Black River

Ouachita Mountains mountains W Ark. & SE Okla. S of Arkansas River

Oua·ga·dou·gou \ˌwä-gä-ˈdü-(ˌ)gü\ city *cen* Burkina Faso, its ✳ *pop* 366,000

Ouar·gla \ˈwȯr-glə, ˈwär-, -ˌglä\ town & oasis Algeria in the Sahara *pop* 81,721

Oubangui — see UBANGI

Oubangui–Chari — see UBANGI-SHARI

Ou·den·aar·de \ˌaù-dᵊn-ˈär-də, ˌō-\ *or F* **Au·de·narde** \ˌō-dᵊn-ˈärd\ commune Belgium in E Flanders on the Schelde *pop* 27,162

Oudh \ˈaùd\ region N India in E *cen* Uttar Pradesh ✳ Lucknow

Oudts·hoorn \ˈōts-ˌhȯrn\ city S Republic of South Africa in Western Cape province E of Cape Town *pop* 26,907

Oues·sant, Île d' \ˌēl-dwe-ˈsäⁿ\ *or* **Ush·ant** \ˈə-shənt\ island NW France off tip of Brittany *pop* 1814

Ouj·da *or* **Oudj·da** \ùzh-ˈdä\ *or* **Ar Ujda** \ˈùj-də\ city NE Morocco near Algerian border *pop* 260,082

Ou·lu \ˈaù-(ˌ)lü, ˈō-\ *or Sw* **Uleå·borg** \ˈü-lā-ō-ˌbȯr-ē\ city N *cen* Finland on Gulf of Bothnia *pop* 100,281

Ou·ro Prê·to \ˌō-(ˌ)rü-ˈprā-(ˌ)tü\ city E Brazil in Minas Gerais *pop* 62,483

Ouse \ˈüz\ **1** *or* **Great Ouse** river 160 *mi* (257 *km*) *cen* & E England flowing into The Wash **2** river 60 *mi* (96 *km*) NE England flowing SE to unite with Trent River forming the Humber

Outer Banks chain of sand islands & peninsulas along N.C. coast

Outer Hebrides — see HEBRIDES

Outer Mongolia — see MONGOLIA — **Outer Mongolian** *adj or n*

Out Islands islands of the Bahamas group excepting New Providence

Ou·tre·mont \ˈü-trə-ˌmänt, *F* ü-trə-ˈmōⁿ\ town Canada in S Que. on Montreal Is. *pop* 22,935

Oval·le \ō-ˈvī-ˌä, -ˈvä-ˌyä\ city N *cen* Chile

Over·ijs·sel \ˌō-və-ˈrī-səl\ province E Netherlands ✳ Zwolle *area* 1518 *sq mi* (3932 *sq km*), *pop* 1,039,083

Over·land Park \'ō-vər-lənd\ city NE Kans. S of Kansas City *pop* 111,790

Ovie·do \ō-vē-'ā-(,)dō, ,ō-'vyā-thō\ **1** — see ASTURIAS 2 **2** city NW Spain ✳ of Asturias province *pop* 194,919

Owas·co Lake \ō-'wäs-(,)kō\ lake 11 *mi* (18 *km*) long *cen* N.Y.; one of the Finger Lakes

Owa·ton·na \,ō-wə-'tä-nə\ city SE Minn. *pop* 19,386

Ow·en Falls \'ō-ən\ former waterfall E Africa in Uganda in the Nile N of Lake Victoria; now submerged in water behind **Owen Falls Dam**

Ow·ens \'ō-ənz\ river E Calif. formerly flowing into **Owens Lake** (now dry), now supplying water to city of Los Angeles by way of Los Angeles Aqueduct

Ow·ens·boro \'ō-ənz-,bər-ō\ city NW Ky. *pop* 53,549

Owen Sound city Canada in SE Ont. on Georgian Bay *pop* 21,674

Owen Stan·ley Range \'stan-lē\ mountain range E New Guinea; highest peak Mt. Victoria 13,363 *ft* (4073 *m*)

Owy·hee \ō-'wī-(,)(h)ē\ river 250 *mi* (402 *km*) SW Idaho & SE Oreg. flowing N into Snake River

Ox·ford \'äks-fərd\ *or ML* **Ox·o·nia** \äk-'sō-nē-ə\ city S *cen* England ✳ of Oxfordshire *pop* 109,000 — **Ox·ford·ian** \äks-'fōr-dē-ən, -'fōr-\ *adj or n*

Ox·ford·shire \'äks-fərd-,shir, -shər\ *or* **Oxford** county S *cen* England ✳ Oxford *area* 1044 *sq mi* (2704 *sq km*), *pop* 553,800

Ox·nard \'äks-,närd\ city S Calif. SE of Santa Barbara *pop* 142,216

Oxus — see AMU DAR'YA

Oxy·rhyn·chus \,äk-si-'riŋ-kəs\ *or Ar* **El Bah·na·sa** \el-'bä-nə-,sä\ archaeological site Egypt N of El Minyâ & S of El Faiyûm

Oyrot — see GORNO-ALTAY

Ozark Plateau \'ō-,zärk\ *or* **Ozark Mountains** eroded tableland region 1500–2500 *ft* (457–762 *m*) high *cen* U.S. N of Arkansas River in N Ark., S Mo., & NE Okla. with E extension in S Ill. — **Ozark·er** \'ō-,zär-kər\ *n* — **Ozark·ian** \ō-'zär-kē-ən\ *adj or n*

Ozarks, Lake of the \'ō-,zärks\ reservoir 125 *mi* (200 *km*) long *cen* Mo. formed in Osage River by Bagnell Dam

P

Pa·ca·rai·ma Mountains \,pä-kä-'rī-mä\ mountain range N S. America in SE Venezuela, N Brazil, & W Guyana — see RORAIMA

Pa·chu·ca \pä-'chü-kä\ city *cen* Mexico ✳ of Hidalgo *pop* 179,440

Pa·cif·i·ca \pə-'si-fi-kə\ city W Calif. S of San Francisco on the Pacific *pop* 37,670

Pa·cif·ic Islands, Trust Territory of the \pə-'si-fik\ former U.S. trust territory comprising the Northern Mariana Islands (until 1978), the Federated States of Micronesia (until 1991), the Marshall Islands (until 1991), and Palau (until 1994)

Pacific Ocean ocean extending from the arctic circle to the antarctic regions & from W N. America & W S. America to E Asia &

Australia *area* 69,375,000 *sq mi* (180,375,000 *sq km*); often divided into **North Pacific Ocean** & **South Pacific Ocean** — **Pacific** *adj*

Pacific Rim the countries bordering on or located in the Pacific Ocean — used esp. of the rapidly developing Asian countries on the Pacific

Pacific Rim National Park reservation SW Canada in Vancouver Island

Pac·to·lus \pak-'tō-ləs\ river Asia Minor in ancient Lydia flowing into the Hermus (modern Gediz) near Sardis

Pa·dang \'pä-,däŋ\ city & port Indonesia in W Sumatra *pop* 631,543

Pad·ding·ton \'pa-diŋ-tən\ former metropolitan borough NW London, England, now part of Westminster

Pa·dre Island \'pä-drē, -drā\ island 113 *mi* (182 *km*) long S Tex. bet. Laguna Madre & Gulf of Mexico

Pad·ua \'pa-jə-wə, 'pa-dyü-wə\ *or It* **Pa·do·va** \'pä-dō-,vä\ commune NE Italy W of Venice *pop* 215,025 — **Pad·u·an** \'pa-jə-wən, 'pa-dyù-\ *adj or n*

Pa·du·cah \pə-'dü-kə, -'dyü-\ city W Ky. on Ohio River *pop* 27,256

Padus — see PO

Paes·tum \'pes-təm, 'pēs-\ *or earlier* **Po·sei·do·nia** \,pä-,sī-'dō-nē-ə, ,pō-\ ancient city S Italy in W Lucania on Gulf of Salerno (ancient **Bay of Paestum**)

Pa·go Pa·go \,pä-(,)gō-'pä-(,)gō, ,päŋ-(,)ō-'päŋ-(,)ō\ town & port ✱ of American Samoa on Tutuila Is.

Pa·hang \pə-'haŋ\ state E Malaysia (federation) bordering on S. China Sea ✱ Kuala Lipis *area* 13,920 *sq mi* (36,053 *sq km*), *pop* 1,036,724

Paint·ed Desert \'pān-təd\ region NE Ariz. E of the Little Colorado

Pais·ley \'pāz-lē\ burgh SW Scotland in Strathclyde *pop* 84,789

Pa·kan·ba·ru \,pä-kən-'bär-ü\ *or* **Pe·kan·ba·ru** \,pā-\ city Indonesia in *cen* Sumatra *pop* 398,694

Pa·ki·stan \'pa-ki-,stan, ,pä-ki-'stän\ country S Asia orig. comprising an E division & a W division; a dominion 1947–56, an Islamic republic since 1956, & a member of the Commonwealth of Nations 1956–72; formed from parts of former Brit. India; ✱ Islamabad *area* 310,403 *sq mi* (807,048 *sq km*), *pop* 131,434,000 — see EAST PAKISTAN, WEST PAKISTAN — **Pa·ki·stani** \,pa-ki-'sta-nē, ,pä-ki-'stä-\ *adj or n*

Pa·lat·i·nate \pə-'la-tᵊn-ət\ *or G* **Pfalz** \'(p)fälts\ either of two districts SW Germany once ruled by counts palatine of the Holy Roman Empire: **Rhenish Palatinate** *or* **Rhine Palatinate** *or G* **Rheinpfalz** \'rīn-,(p)fälts\ (on the Rhine E of Saarland) & **Upper Palatinate** *or G* **Ober·pfalz** \'ō-bər-,(p)fälts\ (on the Danube around Regensburg) — see RHINELAND-PALATINATE

Pal·a·tine \'pa-lə-,tīn\ **1** hill in Rome, Italy, one of seven on which the ancient city was built — see AVENTINE **2** village NE Ill. NW of Chicago *pop* 39,253

Pa·lau \pä-'laů\ *or* **Be·lau** \bə-\ island group W Pacific comprising a trust territory in association with U.S.; usu. considered part of the Carolines — **Pa·lau·an** \-laü-ən\ *n*

Pa·la·wan \pə-'lä-wən, -,wän\ island 278 *mi* (445 *km*) long W Philippines W of the Visayans *area* 4550 *sq mi* (11,830 *sq km*), *pop* (with adjacent islands) 528,287

Pa·lem·bang \ˌpä-ləm-ˈbäŋ\ city & port Indonesia in SE Sumatra *pop* 1,141,036

Pa·len·cia \pä-ˈlen-syä, -thyä\ **1** province N Spain *area* 3100 *sq mi* (8029 *sq km*), *pop* 185,479 **2** city, its ✱, NNE of Valladolid *pop* 77,772

Pa·len·que \pä-ˈleŋ-(ˌ)kä\ ruined Mayan city S Mexico in N Chiapas SW of modern town of Palenque

Pa·ler·mo \pə-ˈlər-(ˌ)mō, pä-ˈler-\ *or anc* **Pan·or·mus** \pa-ˈnȯr-məs\ *or* **Pan·hor·mus** \pan-ˈhȯr-\ city & port Italy ✱ of Sicily *pop* 697,162 — **Pa·ler·mi·tan** \pə-ˈlər-mə-tᵊn, -ˈler-\ *adj or n*

Pal·es·tine \ˈpa-lə-ˌstīn\ *or L* **Pal·aes·ti·na** \ˌpa-lə-ˈstē-nə, -ˈstī-\ **1** ancient region SW Asia bordering on E coast of the Mediterranean & extending E of Jordan River **2** former country bordering on the Mediterranean on W & Dead Sea on E; a part of the Ottoman Empire 1516–1917, a Brit. mandate 1923–48; now divided bet. Israel & Jordan with Arab Palestinians in the West Bank having limited self-rule since 1993 — **Pal·es·tin·ian** \ˌpa-lə-ˈsti-nē-ən, -nyən\ *adj or n*

Pal·i·sades \ˌpa-lə-ˈsädz\ line of cliffs 15 *mi* (24 *km*) long SE N.Y. & NE N.J. on W bank of Hudson River

Palk Strait \ˈpȯ(l)k\ strait 40 *mi* (64 *km*) wide bet. N Sri Lanka & SE India connecting Gulf of Mannar & Bay of Bengal

Pal·ma \ˈpäl-mä\ *or* **Palma de Mal·lor·ca** \dä-mä-ˈyȯr-kä, thä-\ commune & port Spain ✱ of Baleares province on Majorca *pop* 296,754

Pal·mas, Cape \ˈpäl-məs\ cape Liberia on extreme SE coast

Palm Bay \ˈpäm, ˈpälm, ˈpȯm, ˈpȯlm\ city E Fla. *pop* 62,632

Palm Beach Gardens city SE Fla. *pop* 22,965

Palm·dale \ˈpäm-ˌdäl, ˈpälm-\ city SW Calif. NE of Los Angeles *pop* 68,842

Palm Desert city SW Calif ESE of Riverside *pop* 23,252

Palm·er Archipelago \ˈpä-mər, ˈpäl-\ *or formerly* **Antarctic Archipelago** islands W of N end of Antarctic Peninsula in Falkland Islands Dependencies

Palmer Peninsula — see ANTARCTIC PENINSULA

Palmer Land the S section of Antarctic Peninsula

Palm·er·ston \ˈpä-mər-stən, ˈpäl-mər-\ island (atoll) *cen* Pacific NW of Rarotonga Is.; belongs to New Zealand *area* 1 *sq mi* (2.6 *sq km*)

Palmerston North city New Zealand on S North Is. NE of Wellington *pop* 70,318

Palm Springs city SW Calif. E of Los Angeles *pop* 40,181

Pal·my·ra \pal-ˈmī-rə\ *or bib* **Tad·mor** \ˈtad-ˌmȯr\ *or* **Ta·mar** \ˈtä-ˌmär, -mər\ ancient city Syria on N edge of Syrian Desert NE of Damascus — **Pal·my·rene** \ˌpal-mə-ˈrēn, -mī-\ *adj or n*

Palmyra Atoll island *cen* Pacific in Line Islands *area* 1 *sq mi* (2.6 *sq km*)

Palo Al·to \pa-lō-ˈal-(ˌ)tō\ city W Calif. SE of San Francisco on San Francisco Bay *pop* 55,900

Pal·o·mar, Mount *or* **Palomar Mountain** \ˈpa-lə-ˌmär\ mountain 6138 *ft* (1871 *m*) S Calif. NNE of San Diego

Pa·los \ˈpä-ˌlōs\ *or* **Pa·los de la Fron·te·ra** \ˌthä-lä-frȯn-ˈtä-rä\ town & former port SW Spain SE of Huelva

Pa·louse \pə-'lüs\ **1** river *ab* 140 *mi* (225 *km*) NW Idaho & SE Wash. flowing W & S into Snake River **2** fertile hilly region E Wash. & NW Idaho N of Snake & Clearwater rivers

Pa·mirs \pə-'mirz\ *or* **Pa·mir** \-'mir\ mountain region *cen* Asia in Tajikistan & on borders of Xinjiang Uygur, Kashmir, & Afghanistan from which radiate Tian Shan to N, Kunlun & Karakoram to E, & Hindu Kush to W; has many peaks over 20,000 *ft* (6096 *m*)

Pam·li·co \'pam-li-ˌkō\ river E N.C., estuary of Tar River, flowing E into **Pamlico Sound** (inlet of the Atlantic bet. the mainland & offshore islands)

Pam·pa \'pam-pə\ city NW Tex. ENE of Amarillo *pop* 19,959

Pam·phyl·ia \pam-'fi-lē-ə\ ancient district & Roman province S Asia Minor on coast S of Pisidia — **Pam·phyl·i·an** \-lē-ən\ *adj or n*

Pam·plo·na \pam-'plō-nə, päm-'plō-nä\ *or formerly* **Pam·pe·lu·na** \ˌpam-pə-'lü-nə\ city N Spain ✳ of Navarre province & once ✳ of Navarre kingdom *pop* 179,251

Pan·a·ji \'pə-nə-jē\ town & port W India ✳ of Goa & formerly ✳ of Portuguese India *pop* 42,915

Pan·a·ma *or Sp* **Pa·na·má** \'pa-nə-ˌmä, -ˌmö, ˌpa-nə-'; ˌpä-nä-'mä\ **1** country S Central America; a republic; before 1903 part of Colombia *area* (including Canal Zone) 33,659 *sq mi* (87,177 *sq km*), *pop* 2,563,000 **2** *or* **Panama City** city & port, its ✳, on Gulf of Panama *pop* 411,549 **3** ship canal 51 *mi* (82 *km*) *cen* Panama connecting the Atlantic (Caribbean Sea) & the Pacific (Gulf of Panama) — **Pan·a·ma·ni·an** \ˌpa-nə-'mä-nē-ən\ *adj or n*

Panama, Gulf of inlet of the Pacific on S coast of Panama

Panama, Isthmus of *or formerly* **Isthmus of Dar·i·en** \ˌdar-ē-'en, ˌder-, ˌdär-\ isthmus Central America connecting N. America & S. America & forming Panama (republic)

Panama Canal Zone — see CANAL ZONE

Panama City 1 city & port NW Fla. on Gulf of Mexico *pop* 34,378 **2** — see PANAMA

Pan·a·mint Mountains \'pa-nə-ˌmint, -mənt\ mountains E Calif. W of Death Valley — see TELESCOPE PEAK

Pa·nay \pə-'nī\ island Philippines in the Visayas; chief town Iloilo *area* 4446 *sq mi* (11,560 *sq km*)

Pan·gaea \pan-'jē-ə\ hypothetical land area believed to have once connected the landmasses of the southern hemisphere with those of the northern hemisphere — see GONDWANALAND, LAURASIA

Pang·pu — see BENGBU

Pa·ni·pat \'pä-ni-ˌpət\ city NW India in SE Haryana state *pop* 191,010

Panjab — see PUNJAB

Panj·nad \ˌpənj-'näd\ river 50 *mi* (80 *km*) Pakistan, the combined stream of the Chenab & the Sutlej, flowing SW into the Indus

Pan·kow \'päŋ-(ˌ)kō\ NE suburb of Berlin, Germany; formerly seat of E. German government

Pan·mun·jom \ˌpän-ˌmún-'jəm\ village on N. Korea—S. Korea border SE of Kaesong

Pan·no·nia \pə-'nō-nē-ə\ Roman province SE Europe including territory W of the Danube now in Hungary & adjacent parts of Croatia & Vojvodina

Pantar — see ALOR

Pan·tel·le·ria \pan-,te-lə-'rē-ə\ island Italy in the Mediterranean bet. Sicily & Tunisia

Pá·nu·co \'pä-nü-,kō\ river *cen* Mexico flowing from Hidalgo state NE into Gulf of Mexico

Pao-chi — see BAOJI

Pão de Açú·car \paủⁿ-dē-ə-'sü-kər\ *or* **Sugarloaf Mountain** peak 1296 *ft* (395 *m*) SE Brazil in city of Rio de Janeiro on W side of entrance to Guanabara Bay

Paoking — see SHAOYANG

Pao-ting — see BAODING

Pao-t'ou — see BAOTOU

Papal States temporal domain of the popes in *cen* Italy 755–1870

Pa·pee·te \,pä-pē-'ā-tē; pə-'pā-tē, -'pē-\ commune & port Society Islands on Tahiti ✲ of French Polynesia *pop* 23,555

Paph·la·go·nia \,pa-flə-'gō-nē-ə, -nyə\ ancient country & Roman province N Asia Minor bordering on Black Sea — **Paph·la·go·nian** \-nē-ən, -nyən\ *adj or n*

Pa·phos \'pā-,fäs, 'pä-,fòs\ town SW Cyprus on coast 10 *mi* (16 *km*) WNW of site of ancient city of Paphos *pop* 27,800 — **Pa·phi·an** \'pā-fē-ən\ *adj or n*

Pa·pua \'pa-pyù-wə, 'pä-pü-wə\ the SE portion of the island of New Guinea; part of Papua New Guinea — **Pap·u·an** \'pa-pyə-wən, -pə-\ *adj or n*

Papua, Gulf of arm of Coral Sea SE New Guinea

Papua New Guinea country comprising territories of Papua & New Guinea; independent from 1975, formerly a U.N. trust territory administered by Australia ✲ Port Moresby *area* 178,260 *sq mi* (461,693 *sq km*), *pop* 3,918,000 — **Papua New Guinean** *adj or n*

Pa·rá \pə-'rä\ 1 river 200 *mi* (322 *km*) N Brazil, the E mouth of the Amazon 2 state N Brazil S of the Amazon ✲ Belém *area* 481,869 *sq mi* (1,248,041 *sq km*), *pop* 5,084,726 3 — see BELÉM

Par·a·dise \'par-ə-,dīs, -,dīz\ 1 town N Calif. N of Sacramento *pop* 25,408 2 population center Nev. *pop* 124,682

Par·a·guay \'par-ə-,gwī, -,gwä; ,pä-rä-'gwī\ 1 river 1584 *mi* (2549 *km*) *cen* S. America flowing from Mato Grosso plateau in Brazil S into Paraná River in Paraguay 2 country *cen* S. America traversed by Paraguay river; a republic ✲ Asunción *area* 157,043 *sq mi* (406,741 *sq km*), *pop* 4,643,000 — **Par·a·guay·an** \,par-ə-'gwī-ən, -'gwä-\ *adj or n*

Pa·ra·í·ba \,par-ə-'ē-bə\ 1 *or* **Paraíba do Nor·te** \dü-'nòr-tē\ river *ab* 180 *mi* (290 *km*) NE Brazil flowing E into the Atlantic 2 *or* **Paraíba do Sul** \dü-'sül\ river *ab* 600 *mi* (965 *km*) SE Brazil flowing NE into the Atlantic 3 state NE Brazil bordering on the Atlantic ✲ João Pessoa *area* 20,833 *sq mi* (53,957 *sq km*), *pop* 3,200,620

Par·a·mar·i·bo \,par-ə-'mar-ə-,bō, ,pär-ä-'mär-ē-,bō\ city & port ✲ of Suriname on Suriname River *pop* 200,000

Par·a·mount \'par-ə-,maủnt\ city SW Calif. N of Long Beach *pop* 47,669

Par·a·mus \pə-'ra-məs\ borough NE N.J. *pop* 25,067

Pa·ra·ná \,pär-ä-'nä\ 1 *or in upper course* **Al·to Paraná** \'al-(,)tō, 'äl-\ river *ab* 2500 *mi* (4022 *km*) *cen* S. America flowing from junction of Rio Grande & Paranaíba River in Brazil SSW into the Río de la Plata in Argentina **2** state S Brazil E of Paraná River ✳ Curitiba *area* 76,959 *sq mi* (199,324 *sq km*), *pop* 8,415,659 **3** city NE Argentina on Paraná River *pop* 277,338

Pa·ra·ná·i·ba *or formerly* **Pa·ra·na·hi·ba** \,pär-ə-nə-'ē-bə, ,pär-ä-nä-\ river S Brazil flowing SW to unite with the Rio Grande forming Paraná River

Par·du·bi·ce \'pär-dü,bit-se\ city *cen* Czech Republic in Bohemia on the Elbe E of Prague *pop* 94,857

Pa·ria Peninsula \'pär-ē-ä\ peninsula NE Venezuela

Paria, Gulf of inlet of the Atlantic bet. Trinidad & Venezuela

Pa·ri·cu·tín \pä,,rē-kü-'tēn\ volcano *ab* 9100 *ft* (2775 *m*) SW Mexico in NW Michoacán; first eruption 1943

Parida, La — see BOLÍVAR (Cerro)

Par·is \'par-əs, *Fr* pá-'rē\ **1** city NE Tex. *pop* 24,699 **2** *or anc* **Lu·te·tia** \lü-'tē-sh(ē-)ə\ city ✳ of France on the Seine *pop* 2,175,200 — **Pa·ri·sian** \pə-'ri-zhən, -'rē-\ *adj or n*

Par·kers·burg \'pär-kərz-,bərg\ city NW W.Va. *pop* 33,862

Park Forest village NE Ill. S of Chicago *pop* 24,656

Park Ridge city NE Ill. NW of Chicago *pop* 36,175

Par·ma \'pär-mə\ **1** city NE Ohio S of Cleveland *pop* 87,876 **2** commune N Italy in Emilia-Romagna *pop* 168,905

Parma Heights city NE Ohio S of Cleveland *pop* 21,448

Par·na·í·ba *or formerly* **Par·na·hy·ba** \,pär-nə-'ē-bə\ river NE Brazil flowing NE into the Atlantic

Par·nas·sus \pär-'nas-əs\ *or NGk* **Par·nas·sós** \,pär-nä-'sós\ mountain 8061 *ft* (2457 *m*), *cen* Greece N of Gulf of Corinth

Pá·ros \'pär-,ós\ island Greece in *cen* Cyclades W of Naxos *area* 75 *sq mi* (194 *sq km*) — **Par·i·an** \'par-ē-ən, 'per-\ *adj*

Par·ra·mat·ta \,par-ə-'ma-tə\ city SE Australia, W suburb of Sydney, on **Parramatta River** (estuary, W arm of Port Jackson) *pop* 132,798

Par·ris Island \'par-əs\ island S S.C. in Port Royal Sound

Par·ry Islands \'par-ē\ islands Canada in N Northwest Territories in Arctic Ocean N of Victoria Is.

Parsnip — see FINLAY

Par·thia \'pär-thē-ə\ ancient country SW Asia in NE modern Iran — **Par·thi·an** \-ən\ *adj or n*

Pas·a·de·na \,pa-sə-'dē-nə\ **1** city SW Calif. E of Glendale *pop* 131,591 **2** city SE Tex. E of Houston *pop* 119,363 — **Pas·a·de·nan** \-nən\ *n*

Pa·sar·ga·dae \pə-'sär-gə-,dē\ city of ancient Persia built by Cyrus the Great; ruins NE of site of later Persepolis

Pa·say \'pä-,sī\ municipality Philippines in Luzon on Manila Bay S of Manila *pop* 354,000

Pas·ca·gou·la \,pas-kə-'gü-lə\ city & port SE Miss. *pop* 25,899

Pas·co \'pas-(,)kō\ city SE Wash. *pop* 20,337

Pasco, Cerro de — see CERRO DE PASCO

Pascua, Isla de — see EASTER

Pas de Calais — see DOVER (Strait of)

Pa·sig \'pä-sig\ river 14 *mi* (23 *km*) Philippines in Luzon flowing from the Laguna de Bay through Manila into Manila Bay

Pas·sa·ic \pə-'sā-ik\ **1** river 80 *mi* (130 *km*) NE N.J. flowing into Newark Bay **2** city NE N.J. SSE of Paterson *pop* 58,041

Pas·sa·ma·quod·dy Bay \pa-sə-mə-'kwä-dē\ inlet of Bay of Fundy bet. E Maine & SW N.B. at mouth of St. Croix River

Pas·se·ro, Cape \'pä-sə-ˌrō, 'pa-\ headland Italy at SE tip of Sicily

Pas·sy \pa-'sē\ section of Paris, France, on right bank of the Seine near the Bois de Boulogne

Pas·ta·za \pä-'stä-zə, -sä\ river 400 *mi* (644 *km*) Ecuador & Peru flowing S into the Marañón

Pat·a·go·nia \ˌpa-tə-'gō-nyə, -nē-ə\ region S. America in S Argentina & S Chile bet. the Andes & the Atlantic S of *ab* 40°S lat.; sometimes considered as including Tierra del Fuego — **Pat·a·go·nian** \-nyən, -nē-ən\ *adj or n*

Pa·tan \'pä-ˌtən\ city E *cen* Nepal adjoining Kathmandu *pop* 96,109

Pa·tap·sco \pə-'tap-(ˌ)skō, -si-ˌkō\ river 80 *mi* (129 *km*) N *cen* Md. flowing SE into Chesapeake Bay

Pat·er·son \'pa-tər-sən\ city NE N.J. N of Newark *pop* 140,891

Pa·ti·a·la \ˌpə-tē-'ä-lə\ **1** former state NW India, now part of Punjab state **2** city, its ✻, capital of Simla *pop* 253,341

Pat·mos \'pat-məs, 'pät-ˌmós\ island Greece in the NW Dodecanese

Pat·na \'pət-nə\ city NE India on the Ganges, ✻ of Bihar

Pa·tos, La·goa dos \'lä-'gō-ə-dəs-'pa-təs, -düs-ˌpä-(ˌ)tüs\ lagoon 124 *mi* (200 *km*) long S Brazil in Rio Grande do Sul

Pa·tras \'pa-trəs, pə-'tras\ *or Gk* **Pa·trai** \'pä-tre\ *or anc* **Pa·trae** \'pä-(ˌ)trē\ city & port W Greece in N Peloponnese on Gulf of Patras *pop* 155,180

Patras, Gulf of *or Gk* **Pa·tra·i·kós Kól·pos** \ˌpä-trä-ē-'kòs-ˌkól-(ˌ)pòs\ inlet of Ionian Sea W Greece W of Gulf of Corinth

Patrimony of St. Peter — see ROME (Duchy of)

Pa·tux·ent \pə-'tək-sənt\ river 100 *mi* (161 *km*) *cen* Md. flowing S & SE into Chesapeake Bay

Pau \'pō\ **1** *or F* **Gave de Pau** \ˌgàv-də-'pō\ river 100 *mi* (161 *km*) SW France rising in the Pyrenees SW of Pau & flowing to the Adour — see GAVARNIE **2** commune SW France on Pau River *pop* 83,928

Pa·via \pä-'vē-ä\ commune N Italy S of Milan *pop* 76,418

Pav·lof \'pav-ˌlòf\ volcano 8261 *ft* (2518 *m*) SW Alaska on SW Alaska Peninsula in Aleutian Range

Paw·tuck·et \pə-'tə-kət, pò-\ city NE R.I. *pop* 72,644

Pay·san·dú \ˌpī-ˌsän-'dü\ city & port W Uruguay *pop* 62,412

Pea·body \'pē-bə-dē, -ˌbä-dē\ city NE Mass. N of Lynn *pop* 47,039

Peace \'pēs\ river 1195 *mi* (1923 *km*) W Canada flowing E & NE in N B.C. & N Alta. into Slave River — see FINLAY

Peach·tree City \'pēch-ˌtrē\ city NW *cen* Ga. SSW of Atlanta *pop* 19,027

Pearl \'pər(-ə)l\ **1** river *ab* 410 *mi* (660 *km*) S Miss. flowing S into Gulf of Mexico **2** city S *cen* Miss. *pop* 19,588 **3** — see ZHU

Pearl City city Hawaii in S Oahu *pop* 30,993

Pearl Harbor inlet Hawaii on S coast of Oahu W of Honolulu; site of U.S. Navy base

Pea·ry Land \'pir-ē\ region N Greenland on Arctic Ocean

Pe·chen·ga \'pe-chən-gə, pe-'chen-gä\ *or Finn* **Pet·sa·mo** \'pet-sä-ˌmò\ town & port NW Russia in Europe on inlet of Barents Sea in district that belonged to Finland 1920–44 *pop* 3500

Pe·cho·ra \pi-'chòr-ə, -'chór-\ river over 1100 *mi* (1770 *km*) NE Russia in Europe flowing N into Barents Sea

Pe·cos \'pā-kəs\ river E N.Mex. & W Tex. flowing SE into the Rio Grande

Pecos National Monument archaeological site N *cen* N.Mex. SE of Santa Fe containing Indian villages & a Spanish mission

Pecs \'pāch\ city S Hungary W of the Danube *pop* 179,000

Ped·er·nal·es \,pər-d°n-'a-ləs\ river *cen* Tex. flowing E into Colorado River

Pee·bles \'pē-bəlz\ **1** *or* **Pee·bles·shire** \'pē-bəl-,shir, -shər\ *or* **Tweed·dale** \'twēd-,dāl\ former county SE Scotland including upper course of the Tweed **2** burgh SE Scotland in Borders region

Pee Dee \'pē-,dē\ river 233 *mi* (375 *km*) N.C. & S.C. flowing SE into Winyah Bay — see YADKIN

Peeks·kill \'pēk-,skil\ city SE N.Y. N of Yonkers *pop* 19,536

Peel \'pēl\ river 425 *mi* (684 *km*) NW Canada rising in W Yukon Territory & flowing E & N into the Mackenzie

Pee·ne \'pā-nə\ river 70 *mi* (113 *km*) NE Germany flowing E through Pomerania & forming **Peene Estuary** which flows N–S

Pee·ne·mün·de \'pā-nə-'mün-də, -'myün-, -'mœn-\ village NE Germany on island at mouth of Peene Estuary

Pei·pus \'pī-pəs\ *or Estonian* **Peip·si** \'pāp-sē\ *or Russ* **Chud·skoe** \chüt-'skó-yə, -'skói-(y)ə\ lake Europe, bet. Estonia & Russia *area* 1390 *sq mi* (3600 *sq km*)

Pekanbaru — see PAKANBARU

Pe·kin \'pē-kən, -,kin\ city N *cen* Ill. SSW of Peoria *pop* 32,254

Peking — see BEIJING — **Pe·king·ese** *or* **Pe·kin·ese** \,pē-kə-'nēz, -'nēs; -kiŋ-'ēz, -'ēs\ n

Pe·la·gian Islands \pə-'lā-j(ē-)ən\ islands Italy in the Mediterranean S of Sicily bet. Malta & Tunisia

Pe·lée, Mount \pə-'lā\ volcano French West Indies in N Martinique; erupted 1902

Pelee, Point — see POINT PELEE NATIONAL PARK

Pe·lee Island \'pē-lē\ island SE Canada in W Lake Erie SW of Point Pelee, Ont. *area* 18 *sq mi* (47 *sq km*), *pop* 272

Pel·e·liu \,pe-lə-'lē-(,)ü, 'pe-lel-,yü\ island W Pacific at S end of Palau Islands

Pe·li·on \'pē-lē-ən\ *or NGk* **Pí·lion** \'pēl-,yón\ mountain 5089 *ft* (1551 *m*) NE Greece in E Thessaly SE of Mt. Ossa

Pel·la \'pe-lə\ ancient city NE Greece, ancient ☀ of Macedonia

Pel·ly \'pe-lē\ river 330 *mi* (531 *km*) NW Canada in Yukon Territory flowing W into Yukon River

Pel·o·pon·nese \'pe-lə-pə-,nēz, -,nēs, ,pe-lə-pə-'\ *or* **Pel·o·pon·ne·sus** \,pe-lə-pə-'nē-səs\ *or* **Pel·o·pon·ni·sos** \,pe-lə-'pó-nē-,sós\ peninsula forming S part of mainland of Greece — **Pel·o·pon·ne·sian** \,pə-lə-pə-'nē-zhən, -shən\ *adj or n*

Pe·lo·tas \pā-'lō-təs\ city S Brazil in SE Rio Grande do Sul at S end of Lagoa dos Patos *pop* 289,484

Pem·ba \'pem-bə\ island Tanzania in Indian Ocean N of island of Zanzibar *pop* 265,039

Pem·broke \'pem-,brúk, *US also* -,brók\ *or* **Pem·broke·shire** \-,shir, -shər\ former county SW Wales ☀ Haverfordwest

Pembroke Pines \'pem-,brók\ city SE Fla. *pop* 65,452

Pe·nang \pə-'naŋ\ **1** island SE Asia at N end of Strait of Malacca *area* 108 *sq mi* (281 *sq km*) **2** state Malaysia (federation) comprising Penang Island & mainland opposite: until 1948 one of the

Straits Settlements ✳ George Town *area* 400 *sq mi* (1036 *sq km*), *pop* 1,065,075 **3** — see GEORGE TOWN

Pen·ch'i — see BENXI

Pen·del·i·kón \pen-de-lē-'kón\ mountain 3638 *ft* (1109 *m*) E Greece in Attica NE of Athens

Pend Oreille \pän-də-'rā\ river 100 *mi* (161 *km*) N Idaho & NE Wash. flowing from **Pend Oreille Lake** (35 *mi* or 56 *km* long, in Idaho) W & N into Columbia River in B.C.

Penedos de São Pedro e São Paulo — see SAINT PETER AND SAINT PAUL ROCKS

Pe·ne·us \pə-'nē-əs\ or *NGk* **Pi·niós** \pē-'nyòs\ or *formerly* **Sa·lam·bria** \sə-'lam-brē-ə\ river 125 *mi* (201 *km*) N Greece in Thessaly flowing E into Gulf of Salonika

P'eng-hu \'pəŋ-'hü\ or **Pes·ca·do·res** \pes-kə-'dōr-ēz, -'dòr-, -əs\ islands E China in Formosa Strait, attached to Taiwan; chief town Makung (on P'eng-hu, chief island) *area* 49 *sq mi* (127 *sq km*)

Peng-pu — see BENGBU

Pen-hsi — see BENXI

Peninsular Malaysia — see MALAYA

Pen·nine Alps \'pe-,nīn\ section of Alps on border bet. Switzerland & Italy NE of Graian Alps — see ROSA (Monte)

Pennine Chain mountains N England extending from Scotland border to Derbyshire & Staffordshire; highest Cross Fell 2930 *ft* (893 *m*)

Penn·syl·va·nia \,pen(t)-səl-'vā-nyə, -nē-ə\ state NE U.S. ✳ Harrisburg *area* 45,333 *sq mi* (117,866 *sq km*), *pop* 11,881,643 — **Penn·syl·va·nian** \-nyən, -nē-ən\ *adj or n*

Pe·nob·scot \pə-'näb-,skät, -skət\ river 101 *mi* (162 *km*) cen Maine flowing S into **Penobscot Bay** (inlet of the Atlantic)

Pen·rhyn \pen-'rin, 'pen-,\ or **Ton·ga·re·va** \,täŋ-(g)ə-'rā-və\ island S Pacific in the Manihiki Islands

Pen·sa·co·la \,pen(t)-sə-'kō-lə\ city & port NW Fla. on **Pensacola Bay** (inlet of Gulf of Mexico) *pop* 58,165

Pen·tap·o·lis \pen-'ta-pə-lis\ any one of several groups of five ancient cities in Italy, Asia Minor, & Cyrenaica

Pen·te·cost \'pen-ti-,kóst, -'käst\ island SW Pacific in Vanuatu *pop* 11,336

Pen·tic·ton \pen-'tik-tən\ city Canada in S B.C. *pop* 27,258

Pent·land Firth \'pent-lənd\ channel bet. Orkneys & mainland of Scotland

Pentland Hills hills S Scotland in Borders, Lothian, & Strathclyde regions; highest peak Scald Law 1898 *ft* (578 *m*)

Pen·za \'pen-zə\ city S *cen* Russia in Europe W of Kuibyshev *pop* 552,000

Pen·zance \pen-'zan(t)s, pən-\ borough & port SW England in Cornwall on English Channel *pop* 19,521

Pen·zhin·ska·ya \,pen-'zhin(t)-skə-yə, 'pen-,zhin(t)-\ or **Pen·zhi·na** \'pen-zhə-nə\ bay, an arm of Sea of Okhotsk, E Russia in Asia bet. Kamchatka Peninsula & mainland

People's Democratic Republic of Yemen — see YEMEN

People's Republic of China China exclusive of Taiwan

Pe·o·ria \pē-'ōr-ē-ə, -'òr-\ **1** town SW *cen* Ariz. *pop* 50,618 **2** city N *cen* Ill. on Illinois River *pop* 113,504

Pep·in, Lake \'pi-pən, 'pe-\ expansion of upper Mississippi River 34 *mi* (55 *km*) long bet. SE Minn. & W Wis.

Pera — see BEYOGLU

Pe·raea or **Pe·rea** \pə-'rē-ə\ ancient region of Palestine E of Jordan River

Pe·rak \'per-ə, 'pir-ə, 'per-,ak\ state Malaysia in W Peninsular Malaysia on Strait of Malacca ✳ Kuala Kangsar *area* 8030 *sq mi* (20,798 *sq km*), *pop* 1,880,016

Per·di·do \pər-'dē-(,)dō\ river 60 *mi* (96 *km*) rising in SE Ala. & flowing S into Gulf of Mexico forming part of Ala.-Fla. boundary

Per·ga \'pər-gə\ ancient city S Asia Minor in Pamphylia

Per·ga·mum \'pər-gə-məm\ or **Per·ga·mus** \-məs\ or **Per·ga·mos** \-məs, -,mäs\ **1** ancient Greek kingdom covering most of Asia Minor; at its height 263–133 B.C. **2** or modern **Ber·ga·ma** \bər-'gä-mə\ city W Turkey NNE of Izmir ✳ of ancient Pergamum

Pé·ri·gord \per-ə-'gór\ old division of N Guienne in SW France ✳ Périgueux

Pé·ri·gueux \per-ə-'gə(r), pā-rē-'gœ\ commune SW France NE of Bordeaux *pop* 34,848

Pe·rim \pə-'rim, -'rēm\ island in Bab el Mandeb Strait at entrance to Red Sea; belongs to Yemen

Per·lis \'per-lis\ state Malaysia bordering on Thailand & Andaman sea ✳ Kangar *area* 310 *sq mi* (803 *sq km*), *pop* 184,070

Perm \'pərm, 'perm\ or formerly **Mo·lo·tov** \'mä-lə-,tóf, 'mó-, 'mō-, -,tóv\ city E Russia in Europe *pop* 1,099,000

Per·nam·bu·co \,pər-nəm-'bü-(,)kō, -'byü-; ,per-nəm-'bü-(,)kü\ **1** state NE Brazil ✳ Recife *area* 39,005 *sq mi* (101,023 *sq km*), *pop* 7,109,626 **2** — see RECIFE

Per·nik \'per-nik\ or formerly **Di·mi·tro·vo** \də-'mē-trə-,vō\ city W Bulgaria S of Sofia *pop* 99,643

Per·pi·gnan \per-pē-'nyäⁿ\ city S France SE of Toulouse near Mediterranean coast *pop* 108,049

Per·ris \'per-əs\ city SE Calif. *pop* 21,460

Per·sep·o·lis \pər-'se-pə-lis\ city of ancient Persia, site in SW Iran NE of Shiraz

Persia — see IRAN — **Per·sian** \'pər-zhən, *esp Brit* -shən\ *adj or n*

Persian Gulf arm of Arabian Sea bet. SW Iran & Arabia

Persian Gulf States Kuwait, Bahrain, Qatar, & United Arab Emirates

Per·sis \'pər-sis\ ancient region SW Iran

Perth \'pərth\ **1** city ✳ of Western Australia on Swan River *pop* 80,517 — see FREMANTLE **2** or **Perth·shire** \-,shir, -shər\ former county *cen* Scotland **3** burgh *cen* Scotland *pop* 41,998

Perth Am·boy \,pərth-'am-,bói\ city & port NE N.J. on Raritan Bay at mouth of Raritan River *pop* 41,967

Pe·ru \pə-'rü, pā-\ country W S. America; a republic ✳ Lima *area* 496,222 *sq mi* (1,285,215 *sq km*), *pop* 22,916,000 — **Pe·ru·vi·an** \-'rü-vē-ən\ *adj or n*

Pe·ru·gia \pə-'rü-j(ē-)ə, pā-\ commune *cen* Italy bet. Lake Trasimeno & the Tiber ✳ of Umbria *pop* 143,698

Pe·sa·ro \'pā-zä-,rō\ commune & port *cen* Italy on the Adriatic NW of Ancona *pop* 88,500

Pe·sca·ra \pe-'skär-ä\ commune & port *cen* Italy on the Adriatic *pop* 121,367

Pe·sha·war \pə-'shä-wər, -'shaú(-ə)r\ city N Pakistan ESE of Khyber Pass *pop* 555,000

Pe·tach Tik·va *or* **Pe·tah Tiq·wa** \'pe-tə(k̲)-'tik-(,)vä, ,pā-\ city W Israel *pop* 148,900

Pet·a·lu·ma \,pe-tᵊl-'ü-mə\ city W Calif. N of San Francisco *pop* 43,184

Pe·ta·re \pe-'tär-(,)ā\ city N Venezuela, a SE suburb of Caracas *pop* 531,866

Pe·ter·bor·ough \'pē-tər-,bər-ō\ **1** city Canada in SE Ont. *pop* 68,371 **2** borough E *cen* England *pop* 88,346

Peterborough, Soke of \'sōk\ former administrative county E *cen* England in Northamptonshire; later part of Huntingdonshire & since 1974 in Cambridgeshire

Pe·ters·burg \'pē-tərz-,bərg\ **1** city SE Va. *pop* 38,386 **2** SAINT PETERSBURG

Pet·it·co·di·ac \,pe-tē-'kō-dē-,ak\ river 60 *mi* (96 *km*) SE Canada in SE N.B. flowing to head of Bay of Fundy

Pe·tra \'pē-trə, 'pe-\ ancient city of NW Arabia on slope of Mt. Hor, site now in SW Jordan; ✳ of the Edomites & Nabataeans

Pet·ri·fied Forest National Park \,pe-trə-'fīd\ reservation E Ariz. in Painted Desert containing natural exhibit of petrified wood

Pe·tro·dvo·rets \,pi-tro-dvár-'yets\ *or formerly* **Pe·ter·hof** \'pē-tər-,hôf, -,häf\ town W Russia in Europe W of St. Petersburg

Petrograd — see SAINT PETERSBURG 2

Pet·ro·pav·lovsk \,pe-trə-'pav-,lófsk, ,pi-trə-'páv-ləfsk\ city N Kazakhstan *pop* 248,300

Petropavlovsk–Kam·chat·skiy \-kam-'chat-skē, -'chät-\ city & port E Russia in Asia on Kamchatka Peninsula *pop* 273,000

Pe·tró·po·lis \pə-'trô-pü-ləs\ city SE Brazil in Rio de Janeiro state *pop* 255,211

Petrovsk — see MAKHACHKALA

Pet·ro·za·vodsk \,pi-trə-zə-'vòtsk\ city NW Russia in Europe ✳ of Karelia on Lake Onega *pop* 280,000

Petsamo — see PECHENGA

Pfalz — see PALATINATE

Pforz·heim \'(p)fôrts-,hīm\ city SW Germany SE of Karlsruhe *pop* 115,547

Phar·os \'far-,äs, 'fer-\ peninsula N Egypt in city of Alexandria; formerly an island

Pharr \'fär\ city S Tex. E of McAllen *pop* 32,921

Phar·sa·lus \fär-'sā-ləs\ *or modern* **Phar·sa·la** \'fär-sə-lə\ *or NGk* **Fár·sa·la** \'fär-sä-lä\ town NE Greece in E Thessaly in ancient district of **Phar·sa·lia** \fär-'säl-yə, -'sā-lē-ə\

Phe·nix City \'fē-niks\ city E Ala. *pop* 25,312

Phe·rae \'fir-ē\ ancient town SE Thessaly

Phil·a·del·phia \,fi-lə-'del-fyə, -fē-ə\ **1** city & port SE Pa. on Delaware River *pop* 1,585,577 **2** — see ALASEHIR **3** — see AMMAN — **Phil·a·del·phian** \-fyən, -fē-ən\ *adj or n*

Phi·lae \'fī-(,)lē\ former island S Egypt in the Nile above Aswân; now submerged

Philippeville — see SKIKDA

Phi·lip·pi \'fi-lə-,pī, fə-'li-,pī\ ancient town NE Greece in N *cen* Macedonia — **Phi·lip·pi·an** \fə-'li-pē-ən\ *adj or n*

249 Piedras Negras

Phil·ip·pine Islands \,fi-lə-'pēn, 'fi-lə-,\ islands of the Malay Archipelago NE of Borneo — see PHILIPPINES

Phil·ip·pines \-'pēnz, -,pēnz\ or Sp **Re·pú·bli·ca de Fi·li·pi·nas** \re-'pü-blē-kä-thä-,fē-lē-'pē-(,)näs\ or Pilipino **Re·pu·bli·ka ng Pi·li·pi·nas** \-näŋ-,pē-lē-'pē-(,)näs\ country E Asia comprising the Philippine Islands; a republic; once a Spanish possession & (1898–1945) a U.S. possession ✻ Manila land area 115,651 sq mi (299,536 sq km), pop 64,954,000 — **Fil·i·pi·na** \,fi-lə-'pē-nə\ n — **Fil·i·pi·no** \-'pē-,nō\ n — **Philippine** adj

Philippine Sea sea comprising the waters of the W Pacific E of & adjacent to the Philippine Islands

Philippopolis — see PLOVDIV

Phi·lis·tia \fə-'lis-tē-ə\ ancient country SW Palestine on the coast; the land of the Philistines — **Phil·is·tine** \'fi-lə-,stēn; fə-'lis-tən, -,tēn; 'fi-lə-stən\ adj or n

Phnom Penh \(pə-)'näm-'pen, (pə-)'nóm-\ city ✻ of Cambodia, on the Mekong pop 800,000

Pho·caea \fō-'sē-ə\ ancient city of Asia Minor on Aegean Sea in N Ionia — **Pho·cae·an** \-ən\ adj or n

Pho·cis \'fō-səs\ region cen Greece N of Gulf of Corinth — **Pho·cian** \'fō-sē-ən, -shən\ adj or n

Phoe·ni·cia \fi-'ni-sh(ē-)ə, -'nē-\ ancient country SW Asia at E end of the Mediterranean in modern Syria & Lebanon — **Phoe·ni·cian** \fi-'nē-shən, ni-\ adj or n

Phoe·nix \'fē-niks\ city ✻ of Ariz. on Salt River pop 983,403

Phoenix Islands islands cen Pacific belonging to Kiribati

Phra Nakhon Si Ayutthaya — see AYUTTHAYA

Phry·gia \'fri-j(ē-)ə\ ancient country W cen Asia Minor divided ab 400 B.C. into **Greater Phrygia** (the inland region) & **Lesser Phrygia** (region along the Hellespont) — **Phry·gian** \'fri-jē-ən, -jən\ adj or n

Pia·cen·za \pyä-'chen-sä\ or anc **Pla·cen·tia** \plə-'sen(t)-sh(ē-)ə\ commune N Italy on the Po SE of Milan pop 102,252

Pi·auí or formerly **Pi·au·hy** \pyaü-'ē, pē-,aú-\ state NE Brazil bordering on the Atlantic S of Parnaíba River ✻ Teresina area 97,017 sq mi (251,274 sq km), pop 2,581,054

Pia·ve \'pyä-(,)vä, pē-'ä-\ river 137 mi (220 km) NE Italy flowing S & SE into the Adriatic

Pic·ar·dy \'pi-kər-dē\ or F **Pi·car·die** \pē-kàr-'dē\ region & former province N France bordering on English Channel N of Normandy ✻ Amiens — **Pi·card** \'pi-,kärd, -kərd; pi-'kärd\ adj or n

Pi·ce·num \pī-'sē-nəm\ district of ancient Italy on the Adriatic SE of Umbria

Pick·er·ing \'pi-k(ə-)riŋ\ town Canada in SE Ont. pop 68,631

Pi·co Ri·ve·ra \pē-(,)kō-rə-'vir-ə\ city SW Calif. pop 59,177

Pied·mont \'pēd-,mänt\ **1** upland region E U.S. lying E of the Appalachian Mountains bet. SE N.Y. & cen Ala. **2** or It **Pie·mon·te** \pyä-'mōn-(,)tä\ region NW Italy bordering on France & Switzerland W of Lombardy ✻ Turin pop 4,357,559 — **Pied·mon·tese** \,pēd-mən-'tēz, -(,)män-, -'tēs\ adj or n

Pie·dras Ne·gras \pē-'ä-drəs-'ne-grəs, 'pyä-thräs-'nä-gräs\ city N Mexico in Coahuila on the Rio Grande opposite Eagle Pass, Tex. pop 98,177

Pi·er·ia \pī-'ir-ē-ə, -'er-\ ancient region NE Greece in Macedonia N of Thessaly

Pierre \'pir\ city ✳ of S.Dak. on Missouri River *pop* 12,906

Pierre·fonds \pē-,er-'fōⁿ, ,pyer-\ town Canada in S Que. W of Montreal *pop* 48,735

Pie·ter·mar·itz·burg \,pē-tər-'mar-əts-,bərg\ city E Republic of South Africa in S *cen* KwaZulu-Natal *pop* 128,598

Pigs, Bay of \'pigz\ *or* **Ba·hía de Co·chi·nos** \bä-'ē-ä-ṯẖä-kō-'chē-nōs\ bay W Cuba on S coast

Pikes Peak \'pīks\ mountain 14,110 *ft* (4301 *m*) E *cen* Colo. at S end of Front Range

Pik Pobedy — see POBEDA PEAK

Pi·la·tus \pē-'lä-túš\ mountain 6983 *ft* (2128 *m*) *cen* Switzerland in Unterwalden SW of Lucerne

Pil·co·ma·yo \,pēl-kō-'mä-yō\ river 1000 *mi* (1609 *km*) S *cen* S. America rising in Bolivia & flowing SE on Argentina-Paraguay boundary into Paraguay River

Pílion — see PELION

Pillars of Her·cu·les \'hər-kyə-,lēz\ the two promontories at E end of Strait of Gibraltar: Rock of Gibraltar (in Europe) & Jebel Musa (in Africa)

Pí·los \'pē-,lós\ town & port SW Greece in SW Peloponnese

Pim·li·co \'pim-li-,kō\ district of W London, England, in SW Westminster

Pi·nar del Río \pē-'när-ᵗẖel-'rē-(,)ō\ city & port W Cuba *pop* 121,774

Pi·na·tu·bo, Mount \,pē-nä-'tü-(,)bō, ,pi-nə-\ volcano N Philippines on Luzon

Pin·dus Mountains \'pin-dəs\ mountains N Greece bet. Epirus & Thessaly

Pine Bluff \'pīn-'bləf, -,bləf\ city SE *cen* Ark. *pop* 57,140

Pi·nel·las Park \pī-'ne-ləs\ city W Fla. NW of St. Petersburg *pop* 43,426

Pinellas Peninsula — peninsula W Fla. W of Tampa Bay

Pines, Isle of **1** — see YOUTH (Isle of) **2** — see ILE DES PINS

Ping \'piŋ\ river 360 *mi* (579 *km*) W Thailand flowing SSE to join Nan River forming the Chao Phraya

Piniós — see PENEUS

Pinkiang — see HARBIN

Pin·na·cles National Monument \'pi-ni-kəlz\ reservation W *cen* Calif. in Coast Range SSE of Hollister

Pinsk \'pin(t)sk\ city SW Belarus *pop* 123,800

Pio·tr·ków Try·bu·nal·ski \'pyó-tər-,küf-,tri-bü-'näl-skē, pē-'ó-, -,küv-\ commune C Poland SSE of Lodz *pop* 80,529

Pipe Spring National Monument \'pīp\ reservation NW Ariz. on Kaibab Plateau containing old Mormon fort

Pipe·stone National Monument \'pīp-,stōn\ reservation SW Minn. containing quarry once used by Indians

Piq·ua \'pi-(,)kwä, -kwə\ city W Ohio N of Dayton *pop* 20,612

Pi·rae·us \pī-'rē-əs, pi-'rā-\ *or* **Pi·rai·evs** \,pē-re-'efs\ city E Greece on Saronic Gulf; port of Athens *pop* 169,622

Pirineos — see PYRENEES

Pir·ma·sens \'pir-mə-,zen(t)s\ city SW Germany near French border E of Saarbrücken *pop* 47,801

Pir·na \\'pir-nə\\ city E Germany SE of Dresden *pop* 48,001

Pi·sa \\'pē-zə, *It* -sä\\ commune W *cen* Italy in Tuscany on the Arno *pop* 98,006 — **Pi·san** \\'pē-z°n\\ *adj or n*

Pis·cat·a·qua \\pi-'ska-tə-,kwō\\ river 12 *mi* (19 *km*) Maine & N.H. formed by junction of Cocheco & Salmon Falls rivers & flowing SE on Maine-N.H. boundary into the Atlantic

Pis·gah, Mount \\'piz-gə\\ ridge Palestine in Jordan E of N end of Dead Sea; highest point over 2630 *ft* (802 *m*) was alternatively called **Mount Ne·bo** \\'nē-bō\\

Pi·sid·ia \\pə-'si-dē-ə, pī-\\ ancient country S Asia Minor N of Pamphylia — **Pi·sid·i·an** \\-dē-ən\\ *adj*

Pi·sto·ia \\pē-'stō-yä\\ commune *cen* Italy NW of Florence *pop* 87,275

Pit \\'pit\\ river N Calif. flowing SW into the Sacramento

Pit·cairn Island \\'pit-,karn, -,kern\\ island S Pacific SE of Tuamotu Archipelago; a Brit. colony, with several smaller islands *pop* 62

Pi·tes·ti \\pē-'tesht, -'tesh-tē\\ city S *cen* Romania *pop* 162,395

Pitts·burg \\'pits-,bərg\\ city W Calif. NE of Oakland on San Joaquin River *pop* 47,564

Pitts·burgh \\'pits-,bərg\\ city SW Pa. at confluence of the Allegheny & the Monongahela where they form the Ohio *pop* 369,879 — **Pitts·burgh·er** \\-,bər-gər\\ *n*

Pitts·field \\'pits-,fēld\\ city W Mass. *pop* 48,622

Piz Bernina — see BERNINA

Pla·cen·tia \\plə-'sen(t)-shə\\ city SW Calif. *pop* 41,259

Placentia Bay inlet of the Atlantic E Canada in SE Newfoundland

Plac·id, Lake \\'pla-səd\\ lake 5 *mi* (8 *km*) long NE N.Y. in the Adirondacks

Plain·field \\'plān-,fēld\\ city N N.J. *pop* 46,567

Plains of Abra·ham \\'ā-brə-,ham\\ plateau Canada in W part of city of Quebec

Plain·view \\'plān-,vyü\\ city NW Tex. N of Lubbock *pop* 21,700

Pla·no \\'plā-(,)nō\\ city NE Tex. N of Dallas *pop* 128,713

Plan·ta·tion \\plan-'tā-shən\\ city SE Fla. W of Fort Lauderdale *pop* 66,692

Plant City \\'plant\\ city W *cen* Fla. E of Tampa *pop* 22,754

Plas·sey \\'pla-sē\\ village NE India in W. Bengal N of Calcutta

Pla·ta, Río de la \\'rē-ō-,thä-lä-'plä-tä\\ *or* River Plate \\'plāt\\ estuary of Paraná & Uruguay rivers S. America bet. Uruguay & Argentina

Pla·taea \\plə-'tē-ə\\ *or* **Pla·tae·ae** \\-'tē-,ē\\ ancient city Greece in SE Boeotia S of Thebes — **Pla·tae·an** \\-'tē-ən\\ *adj or n*

Platte \\'plat\\ **1** river 310 *mi* (499 *km*) *cen* Nebr. formed by junction of the N. Platte & S. Platte & flowing E into the Missouri **2** river 300 *mi* (483 *km*) SW Iowa & NW Mo. flowing into the Missouri

Plattensee — see BALATON (Lake)

Platts·burgh \\'plats-,bərg\\ city NE N.Y. on Lake Champlain *pop* 21,255

Plau·en \\'plaü-ən\\ *or* **Plauen im Vogt·land** \\im-'fōkt-,länt\\ city E Germany on the Weisse Elster *pop* 70,856

Pleasant — see NAURU

Pleas·ant Hill \\'ple-z°nt\\ city W Calif. ENE of Oakland *pop* 31,585

Pleas·an·ton \\'ple-z°n-tən\\ city W Calif. SE of Oakland *pop* 50,553

Plen·ty, Bay of \'plen-tē\ inlet of the S. Pacific N New Zealand on NE coast of North Is.

Ple·ven \'ple-ven\ city NW Bulgaria *pop* 138,323

Plock \'plótsk\ commune NE *cen* Poland *pop* 121,996

Plo·iesti *or* **Plo·esti** \plò-'yesht, -'yesh-tē\ city SE *cen* Romania *pop* 247,502

Plov·div \'plòv-,dif, -,div\ *or Gk* **Phil·ip·pop·o·lis** \,fē-lē-'pò-pō-,lēs\ city S Bulgaria on the Maritsa N of the Rhodope Mountains *pop* 379,083

Plum \'pləm\ city SW Pa. *pop* 25,609

Plym·outh \'pli-məth\ **1** town SE Mass. *pop* 45,608 **2** village SE Minn. NW of Minneapolis *pop* 50,889 **3** city & port SW England in Devon *pop* 238,800

Plzeň \'pal-,zen\ city W Czech Republic in Bohemia WSW of Prague *pop* 173,129

Po \'pò\ *or anc* **Pa·dus** \'pā-dəs\ river 405 *mi* (652 *km*) N Italy flowing from slopes of Mt. Viso E into the Adriatic through several mouths

Po·be·da Peak \pō-'be-də, pə-, -'bye-\ *or Russ* **Pik Po·be·dy** \,pēk-pə-'bye-dē, -'be-dē\ mountain 24,406 *ft* (7439 *m*) E Kyrgyzstan; highest in Tian Shan

Po·ca·tel·lo \,pō-kə-'te-(,)lō, -lə\ city SE Idaho *pop* 46,080

Po·co·no Mountains \'pō-kə-,nō\ mountains E Pa. NW of Kittatinny Mountain; highest point *ab* 1600 *ft* (488 *m*)

Pod·go·ri·ca \'pód-,gòr-ēt-sä\ *or 1946–92* **Ti·to·grad** \'tē-(,)tō-,grad, -,gräd\ city S Yugoslavia ✳ of Montenegro *pop* 152,242

Po·do·lia \pə-'dō-lē-ə, -'dòl-yə\ *or Russ* **Po·dolsk** \pə-'dólsk\ region W Ukraine N of middle Dniester River

Po·dolsk \pə-'dólsk\ city W *cen* Russia in Europe S of Moscow *pop* 208,000

Po Hai — see BO HAI

Pohn·pei \'pōn-,pā\ *or* **Po·na·pe** \'pō-nə-,pā\ island E Carolines, part of Federated States of Micronesia

Pointe-à-Pi·tre \,pwan-tə-'pētrᵇ\ city & port French West Indies in Guadeloupe on Grande-Terre *pop* 26,083

Pointe-Claire \'póint-'klar, pwant-, -'kler\ town Canada in S Que. on St. Lawrence River SW of Montreal *pop* 27,647

Pointe-Noire \,pwant-'nwär\ city & port SW Republic of the Congo on the Atlantic; formerly ✳ of Middle Congo *pop* 576,206

Point Pe·lee National Park \póint-'pē-lē\ reservation Canada in SE Ont. on **Point Pelee** (cape projecting into Lake Erie)

Poi·tiers *or formerly* **Poic·tiers** \pwä-'tyā, 'pwä-tē-,ā\ city W *cen* France SW of Tours *pop* 82,507

Poi·tou \pwä-'tü\ region & former province W France SE of Brittany ✳ Poitiers

Po·land \'pō-lənd\ *or Pol* **Pol·ska** \'pól-skä\ country E *cen* Europe bordering on Baltic Sea; in medieval period a kingdom, at one time extending to the lower Dnieper; partitioned 1772, 1793, 1795 among Russia, Prussia, & Austria; again a kingdom 1815–30; lost autonomy 1830–1918; since 1918 a republic ✳ Warsaw *area* 120,756 *sq mi* (312,758 *sq km*), *pop* 38,038,400 — **Pole** \pōl\ *n* — **Pol·ish** \'pō-lish\ *adj or n*

Polesye — see PRIPET

Polish Corridor strip of land N Europe in Poland that bet. World War I & World War II separated E. Prussia from main part of Germany; area was before 1919 part of Germany

Pol·ta·va \pəl-'tä-və\ city *cen* Ukraine on Vorskla River WSW of Kharkiv *pop* 320,000

Poltoratsk — see ASHKHABAD

Poly·ne·sia \päl-ə-'nē-zhə, -shə\ the islands of the *cen* & S Pacific including Hawaii, the Line, Phoenix, Tonga, Cook, & Samoa islands, Tuvalu, Easter Is., French Polynesia, & often New Zealand — **Poly·ne·sian** \-zhən, -shən\ *adj or n*

Pom·er·a·nia \päm-ə-'rā-nē-ə, -nyə\ *or G* **Pom·mern** \'pö-mərn\ *or Pol* **Po·mo·rze** \pö-'mö-zhe\ **1** region N Europe on Baltic Sea; formerly in Germany, now mostly in Poland **2** former province of Prussia — **Pom·er·a·nian** \-nē-ən, -nyən\ *adj or n*

Pom·er·e·lia \päm-ə-'rē-lē-ə, -'rēl-yə\ *or G* **Pom·me·rel·len** \,pö-mə-'re-lən\ region E Europe on the Baltic W of the Vistula & E of Pomerania; orig. part of Pomerania

Po·mo·na \pə-'mō-nə\ city SW Calif. E of Los Angeles *pop* 131,723

Pom·pa·no Beach \'päm-pə-,nō, 'pəm-\ city SE Fla. on the Atlantic N of Fort Lauderdale *pop* 72,411

Pom·pe·ii \päm-'pā, -'pā-,ē\ ancient city S Italy SE of Naples destroyed A.D. 79 by eruption of Mt. Vesuvius — **Pom·pe·ian** *or* **Pom·pei·ian** \-'pā-ən\ *adj or n*

Pon·ca City \'päŋ-kə\ city N Okla. on Arkansas River *pop* 26,359

Pon·ce \'pön(t)-(,)sā\ city & port S Puerto Rico *pop* 187,749

Pon·di·cher·ry \,pän-də-'cher-ē, -'sher-\ *or F* **Pon·di·ché·ry** \pöⁿ-dē-shā-'rē\ **1** union territory SE India SSW of Madras surrounded by Tamil Nadu; a settlement of French India before 1954, *area* 183 *sq mi* (474 *sq km*), *pop* 807,785 **2** city & port, its ✳ *pop* 202,648

Pon·ta Del·ga·da \,pön-tə-del-'gä-də\ city & port Azores on São Miguel Is. *pop* 21,091

Pont·char·train, Lake \'pänt-shər-,trān, ,pänt-shər-\ lake SE La. E of the Mississippi & N of New Orleans *area ab* 630 *sq mi* (1632 *sq km*)

Pon·te·fract \'pän-ti-,frakt, *formerly also* 'pəm(p)-frət, 'päm(p)-\ borough N England in W. Yorkshire, SE of Leeds *pop* 31,971

Pon·te·ve·dra \,pön-tā-'vā-drä\ **1** province NW Spain in SW Galicia on the Atlantic *area* 1729 *sq mi* (4478 *sq km*), *pop* 896,847 **2** commune & port, its ✳, NW of Vigo *pop* 68,645

Pon·ti·ac \'pän-tē-,ak\ city SE Mich. NW of Detroit *pop* 71,166

Pon·ti·a·nak \,pän-tē-'ä-,näk\ city Indonesia on SW coast of Borneo *pop* 398,357

Pon·tine Islands \'pän-,tīn, -,tēn\ islands Italy in Tyrrhenian Sea W of Naples; chief islands **Pon·za** \'pönt-sä\ & **Pon·ti·ne** \'pän-,tīn, -,tēn; pön-'tē-nä\

Pontine Marshes district *cen* Italy in SW Lazio, separated from sea by low sand hills that prevent natural drainage; now reclaimed

Pon·tus \'pän-təs\ **1** ancient country NE Asia Minor; a kingdom 4th century B.C. to 66 B.C., later a Roman province **2** *or* **Pontus Euxi·nus** — see BLACK SEA

Pon·ty·pool \,pän-ti-'pül\ town SE Wales in Gwent *pop* 36,761

Pon·ty·pridd \,pän-tə-'prēth\ town SE Wales in Mid Glamorgan *pop* 32,992

Poole \'pül\ borough S England in Dorset on English Channel *pop* 130,900

Poona — see PUNE

Po·o·pó, Lake \pō-ō-'pō, (,)pō-'pō\ lake 60 *mi* (96 *km*) long W *cen* Bolivia S of Lake Titicaca at altitude of 12,000 *ft* (3658 *m*)

Pop·lar \'pä-plǝr\ former metropolitan borough E London, England, on N bank of the Thames, now part of Tower Hamlets

Po·po·ca·te·petl \pō-pǝ-'ka-tǝ-,pe-tᵊl, -,ka-tǝ-; ,pō-pō-kä-'tä-,pet-ᵊl\ volcano 17,887 *ft* (5452 *m*) SE *cen* Mexico in Puebla

Porcupine river 448 *mi* (721 *km*) in N Yukon Territory & NE Alaska flowing N & W into the Yukon

Po·ri \'pȯr-ē\ city & port SW Finland *pop* 76,456

Pork·ka·la Peninsula \'pȯr-kä-,lä\ peninsula S Finland W of Helsinki

Por·la·mar \,pȯr-lä-'mär\ city & port NE Venezuela on Margarita Is.

Port Ad·e·laide \'a-dᵊl-,ād\ city SE S. Australia on Gulf of St. Vincent at mouth of Torrens River; port for Adelaide *pop* 38,205

Por·tage \'pȯr-tij, 'pȯr-\ **1** city NW Ind. E of Gary *pop* 29,060 **2** city SW Mich. S of Kalamazoo *pop* 41,042

Port Ar·thur \'är-thǝr\ **1** city & port SE Tex. on Sabine Lake *pop* 58,724 **2** — see THUNDER BAY **3** — see LÜ-SHUN

Port–au–Prince \,pȯrt-ō-'prin(t)s, ,pȯrt-; ,pȯr-(t)ō-'praⁿs\ city & port ✱ of Haiti on SE shore of Gulf of Gonave *pop* 752,600

Port Blair \'blär, 'bler\ town & port India on S. Andaman Is. ✱ of Andaman and Nicobar union territory

Port Ches·ter \'pȯrt-,ches-tǝr, 'pȯrt-\ village SE N.Y. NE of New Rochelle on Long Island Sound *pop* 24,728

Port Co·quit·lam \kō-'kwit-lǝm\ city Canada in SW B.C. E of Vancouver *pop* 36,773

Port Eliz·a·beth \i-'li-zǝ-bǝth\ city & port S Republic of South Africa in S Eastern Cape province on Algoa Bay *pop* 468,797

Por·ter·ville \'pȯr-tǝr-,vil, 'pȯr-\ city S *cen* Calif. *pop* 29,563

Port Ev·er·glades \'e-vǝr-,glädz\ seaport SE Fla. on the Atlantic S of Fort Lauderdale

Port Hed·land \'hed-lǝnd\ port Western Australia

Port Hue·ne·me \wī-'nē-mē\ city S Calif. near Oxnard *pop* 20,319

Port Hu·ron \'hyȯr-ǝn, 'yȯr-, -ǝn\ city E Mich. on Lake Huron & St. Clair River *pop* 33,694

Port Jack·son \'jak-sǝn\ inlet of S Pacific SE Australia in New South Wales; the harbor of Sydney

Port·land \'pȯrt-lǝnd, 'pȯrt-\ **1** city & port SW Maine on Casco Bay *pop* 64,358 **2** city & port NW Oreg. at confluence of Columbia & Willamette rivers *pop* 437,319

Portland Canal inlet of the Pacific *ab* 80 *mi* (129 *km*) long Canada & U.S. bet. B.C. & SE tip of Alaska

Port·laoigh·i·se \,pȯrt-'lē-shǝ, ,pȯrt-, -'lā-ǝ-\ *or* **Port Laoi·se** \'lē-shǝ\ *or* **Mary·bor·ough** \'mar-ē-,bǝr-ō\ town *cen* Ireland ✱ of County Laoighis *pop* 3773

Port Lou·is \'lü-ǝs, 'lü-ē\ city & port ✱ of Mauritius *pop* 142,645

Port Lyautey — see KENITRA

Port Mahon — see MAHON

Port Mores·by \'mȯrz-bē, 'mȯrz-\ city & port SE New Guinea in Papua ✱ of Papua New Guinea *pop* 193,242

Por·to \'pōr-(ˌ)tü, 'pȯr-\ *or* **Opor·to** \ō-'pōr-(ˌ)tü, -'pȯr-\ city & port NW Portugal on the Douro *pop* 310,600 — see LEIXŌES

Pôr·to Ale·gre \'pōr-(ˌ)tü-ä-'lä-grē\ city & port S Brazil ✷ of Rio Grande do Sul state at N end of Lagoa dos Patos *pop* 1,300,000

Por·to·be·lo \ˌpōr-tō-'be-(ˌ)lō, ˌpȯr-\ town & port Panama on Caribbean coast; the great emporium of S. American trade in 17th & 18th centuries

Port of Spain city & port ✷ of Trinidad and Tobago, on NW Trinidad Is. *pop* 50,878

Por·to-No·vo \ˌpȯr-tō-'nō-(ˌ)vō, ˌpȯr-\ city & port ✷ of Benin *pop* 192,000

Port Or·ange \'är-inj, 'är-(ə)nj, 'ȯr-inj, 'ȯr(-ə)nj\ city E Fla. *pop* 35,317

Porto Rico — see PUERTO RICO

Port Phil·lip Bay \'fi-ləp\ inlet of Bass Strait SE Australia in Victoria; the harbor of Melbourne

Port Roy·al \'roi(-ə)l\ town Jamaica at entrance to Kingston Harbor; early ✷ of Jamaica, destroyed by earthquakes 1692 & 1907 & partly engulfed by the sea

Port Royal Sound inlet of the Atlantic S S.C.

Port Said \sä-'ēd, 'sīd\ city & port NE Egypt on the Mediterranean at N end of Suez Canal *pop* 262,760

Port Saint Lu·cie \ˌsänt-'lü-sē\ city E Fla. *pop* 55,866

Ports·mouth \'pōrts-məth, 'pȯrts-\ **1** city & port SE N.H. on the Atlantic *pop* 25,925 **2** city S Ohio at junction of Ohio & Scioto rivers *pop* 22,676 **3** city & port SE Va. on Elizabeth River opposite Norfolk *pop* 103,907 **4** city S England in Hampshire on **Port·sea** \'pōrt-sē, 'pȯrt-\ (island in English Channel) *pop* 174,700

Port Stanley — see STANLEY

Port Sudan city & port NE Sudan on Red Sea *pop* 100,700

Por·tu·gal \'pȯr-chi-gəl, 'pȯr-; ˌpür-tü-'gäl\ *or anc* **Lu·si·ta·nia** \ˌlü-sə-'tā-nē-ə, -nyə\ country SW Europe in W Iberian Peninsula bordering on the Atlantic; a kingdom before 1910; now a republic ✷ Lisbon *area* (not including Azores & Madeira) 35,383 *sq mi* (91,642 *sq km*), *pop* 10,429,000 — **Por·tu·guese** \'pōr-chə-ˌgēz, ˌpȯr-, -ˌgēs; ˌpōr-chə-', ˌpȯr-\ *adj or n*

Portuguese East Africa — see MOZAMBIQUE

Portuguese Guinea — see GUINEA-BISSAU

Portuguese India former Portuguese possessions on W coast of India peninsula, annexed 1962 by India; comprised territory of Goa & districts of Daman & Diu

Portuguese Timor — see TIMOR

Portuguese West Africa — see ANGOLA

Port-Vi·la \'vē-lə, ˌpȯrt-\ *or* **Vila** town & port ✷ of Vanuatu in SW Efate Is. *pop* 18,905

Porz am Rhein \ˌpȯrts-äm-'rīn\ city W Germany ESE suburb of Cologne *pop* 76,762

Poseidonia — see PAESTUM

Potch·ef·stroom \'pȯ-chəf-ˌstrōm\ city NE Republic of South Africa in E North West province SW of Johannesburg *pop* 51,800

Po·to·mac \pə-'tō-mək, -mik\ river 287 *mi* (462 *km*) E U.S. flowing from W.Va. into Chesapeake Bay & forming S boundary of Md.

Po·to·sí \ˌpō-tō-'sē\ city S Bolivia *pop* 112,291

Pots·dam \'päts-ˌdam\ city NE Germany SW of Berlin *pop* 139,025

Potts·town \'päts-,taún\ borough SE Pa. ESE of Reading *pop* 21,831

Pough·keep·sie \pə-'kip-sē, pō-\ city SE N.Y. *pop* 28,844

Po·way \'paú-(,)wā\ city S Calif., a suburb of San Diego *pop* 43,516

Pow·der \'paú-dər\ **1** river 150 *mi* (241 *km*) E Oreg. flowing into the Snake **2** river 375 *mi* (604 *km*) N Wyo. & SE Mont. flowing N into the Yellowstone

Powell, Lake — see GLEN CANYON DAM

Pow·ys \'pō-əs\ county E cen Wales ✳ Llandrindod Wells *area* 1960 *sq mi* (5096 *sq km*), *pop* 116,500

Po·yang \'pō-'yäŋ\ lake 90 *mi* (145 *km*) long E China in Jiangxi

Poz·nan \'pōz-,nan, or *G* **Po·sen** \'pō-zⁿn\ city W *cen* Poland on the Warta *pop* 588,715

Poz·zuo·li \pót-'swò-lē\ or anc **Pu·te·o·li** \pyù-'tē-ə-,lī, pù-\ commune & port S Italy in Campania W of Naples *pop* 76,121

Prague \'präg\ or *Czech* **Pra·ha** \'prä-(,)hä\ city ✳ of Czech Republic & formerly of Czechoslovakia in Bohemia on Vltava River *pop* 1,214,772

Praia \'prī-ə\ town ✳ of Cape Verde on São Tiago Is. *pop* 61,797

Prai·rie Provinces \'prer-ē\ the Canadian provinces of Man., Sask., & Alta.

Prairie Village city NE Kans. S of Kansas City *pop* 23,186

Pra·to \'prä-tō\ commune *cen* Italy in Tuscany *pop* 165,888

Pratt·ville \'prat-,vil, -vəl\ city *cen* Ala. NW of Montgomery *pop* 19,587

Pres·cott \'pres-kət, -,kät\ city *cen* Ariz. *pop* 26,455

Presque Isle \presk-'īl\ peninsula NW Pa. in Lake Erie forming **Presque Isle Bay** (harbor of Erie, Pa.)

Pressburg — see BRATISLAVA

Pres·ton \'pres-tən\ **1** former town, Ont., Canada — see CAMBRIDGE **2** borough NW England NNW of Liverpool ✳ of Lancashire *pop* 126,200

Prest·wich \'prest-(,)wich\ borough NW England in Greater Manchester NNW of Manchester *pop* 31,198

Prest·wick \'prest-(,)wik\ burgh SW Scotland in Strathclyde N of Ayr *pop* 13,532

Pre·to·ria \pri-'tōr-ē-ə, -'tòr-\ city, administrative ✳ of Republic of South Africa & formerly ✳ of Transvaal *pop* 303,684

Pretoria–Witwatersrand–Vereeniging — see GAUTENG

Prib·i·lof Islands \'pri-bə-,lòf\ islands Alaska in Bering Sea

Prich·ard \'pri-chərd\ city SW Ala. N of Mobile *pop* 34,311

Primorski Krai or **Primorskiy Kray** — see MARITIME TERRITORY

Prince Al·bert \'al-bərt\ city Canada in *cen* Sask. *pop* 34,181

Prince Albert National Park reservation Canada in *cen* Sask. in watershed area

Prince Ed·ward Island \'ed-wərd\ island SE Canada in Gulf of Saint Lawrence off E N.B. & N N.S.; a province ✳ Charlottetown *area* 2185 *sq mi* (5660 *sq km*), *pop* 129,765

Prince Edward Island National Park reservation Canada on N coast of P.E.I.

Prince George \'jórj\ city Canada in E *cen* B.C. *pop* 69,653

Prince of Wales, Cape \'wālz\ cape Alaska at W tip of Seward Peninsula; most westerly point of mainland of N. America, at 168°W

Prince of Wales Island 1 island SE Alaska, largest in Alexander Archipelago **2** island N Canada bet. Victoria Is. & Somerset Is. *area* 12,830 *sq mi* (33,358 *sq km*)

Prince Ru·pert's Land \'rü-pərts\ historical region N & W Canada comprising drainage basin of Hudson Bay granted 1670 by King Charles II to Hudson's Bay Company; purchased 1869 by the Dominion

Prince Wil·liam Sound \'wil-yəm\ inlet of Gulf of Alaska S Alaska E of Kenai Peninsula

Prín·ci·pe Island \'prin(t)-si-pē\ island W Africa in Gulf of Guinea N of São Tomé — see SÃO TOMÉ

Prip·et \'pri-,pet, -pət\ *or Russ* **Pri·pyat** \'pri-pyət\ river 500 *mi* (805 *km*) E *cen* Europe in NW Ukraine & S Belarus flowing E through the marshlands called **Po·les·ye** \pò-'les-ye\ *or* **Pripet Marshes** *or* **Pripyat Marshes** to the Dnieper

Pro·gre·so \prə-'gre-(,)sō\ city SE Mexico on Yucatán Peninsula; port for Mérida *pop* 37,806

Pro·ko·pyevsk \prə-'kó-pyəfsk\ city S Russia in Asia at S end of Kuznetsk Basin NW of Novokuznetsk *pop* 272,000

Propontis — see MARMARA (Sea of)

Pro·vence \prə-'vän(t)s, prō-'väⁿs\ region & former province SE France bordering on the Mediterranean ✳ Aix-en-Provence — **Pro·ven·çal** \,prō-,vän-'säl, ,prä-vən-\ *adj or n*

Prov·i·dence \'prä-və-dən(t)s, -,den(t)s\ city & port N R.I., its ✳ *pop* 160,728

Pro·vo \'prō-(,)vō\ city N *cen* Utah on Utah Lake *pop* 86,835

Prud·hoe Bay \'prü,(,)dō, 'prə-; 'prüd-(,)hō, 'prəd-\ inlet of Beaufort Sea N Alaska

Prus·sia \'prə-shə\ *or G* **Preus·sen** \'prói-sⁿn\ **1** historical region N Germany bordering on Baltic Sea **2** former kingdom & state of Germany ✳ Berlin — see EAST PRUSSIA, WEST PRUSSIA — **Prus·sian** \'prə-shən\ *adj or n*

Prut \'prüt\ river 565 *mi* (909 *km*) E Europe flowing from the Carpathians SSE into the Danube; forming the Romanian boundary (World War II to 1991) with the U.S.S.R. & (since 1991) with Moldova & Ukraine

Pskov \pə-'skóf, -'skóv\ city W Russia in Europe near **Lake Pskov** (S arm of Peipus Lake) *pop* 209,000

Ptol·e·ma·is \,tä-lə-'mā-əs\ **1** ancient town in upper Egypt on left bank of the Nile NW of Thebes **2** ancient town in Cyrenaica NW of Barka; site at modern village of Tolmeta **3** — see ACRE

Pu·chon \'pü-,chón\ city NW S. Korea *pop* 456,292

Pueb·la \'pwe-blä\ **1** state SE *cen* Mexico *area* 13,096 *sq mi* (33,919 *sq km*), *pop* 4,126,101 **2** *or* **Puebla de Za·ra·go·za** \dä-,zar-ə-'gó-zə, thä-,sär-ä-'gō-sä\ city, its ✳, SE of Mexico (City) *pop* 1,054,921

Pueb·lo \'pwe-,blo\ city SE *cen* Colo. on the Arkansas *pop* 98,640

Puer·to Bar·rios \'pwer-tō-'bär-ē-,ōs\ city & port E Guatemala on Gulf of Honduras *pop* 39,088

Puerto La Cruz \lä-'krüz, -'krüs\ city NE Venezuela NE of Barcelona *pop* 60,546

Puerto Limón — see LIMÓN

Puerto Montt \'mónt\ city & port S *cen* Chile *pop* 84,410

Puer·to Ri·co \pȯr-tə-'rē-(,)kō, ˌpwer-tō-\ *or formerly* **Por·to Rico** \pȯr-tə, ˌpōr-tō\ island W. Indies E of Hispaniola; a self-governing commonwealth in union with the U.S. ✷ San Juan *area* 3435 *sq mi* (8931 *sq km*), *pop* 3,612,000 — **Puerto Ri·can** \'rē-kən\ *adj or n*

Pu·get Sound \'pyü-jət\ arm of the Pacific extending 80 *mi* (129 *km*) S into W Wash. from E end of Strait of Juan de Fuca

Pu·glia \'pül-yä\ *or* **Apu·lia** \ä-'pül-yä\ *or* **Le Pu·glie** \lə-pül-'yä\ region SE Italy on the Adriatic & Gulf of Taranto ✷ Bari *pop* 4,069,359

Pu·ka·pu·ka \ˌpü-kä-'pü-kä\ *or* **Dan·ger Islands** \'dān-jər\ atoll *cen* Pacific N of Cook Islands; chief island Pukapuka; administered with Cook Islands by New Zealand

Pu·la \'pü-lä\ city & port W Croatia at tip of Istrian Peninsula *pop* 62,690

Pul·ko·vo \'pül-kə-və, -,vō\ village W Russia in Europe S of St. Petersburg

Pull·man \'pùl-mən\ city SE Wash. *pop* 23,478

Pu·log, Mount \'pü-,lȯg\ mountain 9606 *ft* (2928 *m*) Philippines in N Luzon at S end of Cordillera Central; highest in Luzon

Pu·na de Ata·ca·ma \'pü-nä-ˌthä-,ä-tä-'kä-mä\ high plateau region NW Argentina NW of San Miguel de Tucumán

Pun·cak Jaya \'pün-,chäk-'jä-yə\ *or formerly* **Mount Car·stensz** \'kär-stənz\ mountain 16,535 *ft* (5040 *m*) in Sudirman Range, Irian Jaya, Indonesia; highest in New Guinea

Pu·ne \'pü-nə\ *or* **Poo·na** \'pü-nə\ city W India in Maharashtra ESE of Bombay *pop* 1,566,651

Pun·jab *or* **Pan·jab** \ˌpən-'jäb, -'jab, 'pən-,\ **1** region NW Indian subcontinent in Pakistan & NW India occupying valleys of the Indus & its five tributaries; formerly a province of Brit. India ✷ Lahore **2** *or* **East Punjab** former state NW India in E Punjab divided 1966 into two states of Punjabi Suba & Haryana **3** *or formerly* **West Punjab** province NE Pakistan ✷ Lahore **4** *or* **Punjabi Su·ba** \pən-'jä-bē-'sü-bə, -'ja-\ state NW India formed from N part of former state of Punjab ✷ Chandigarh *area* 19,448 *sq mi* (50,370 *sq km*), *pop* 20,289,969 — **Pun·jabi** \pən-'jä-bē, -'ja-\ *adj or n*

Punt \'pùnt\ ancient Egyptian name for a part of Africa not certainly identified, probably Somaliland

Pun·ta Are·nas \ˌpün-tä-ä-'rā-näs\ *or formerly* **Ma·gal·la·nes** \ˌmä-gä-'yä-näs\ city & port S Chile on Strait of Magellan *pop* 95,332

Punta del Es·te \thel-'es-tä\ town S Uruguay E of Montevideo *pop* 5272

Pu·ra·cé \ˌpü-rä-'sä\ volcano 15,604 *ft* (4756 *m*) SW *cen* Colombia

Pur·beck, Isle of \'pər-,bek\ peninsula region S England in Dorset extending E into English Channel

Pur·ga·toire \'pər-gə-,twär, 'pi-kə-,twir\ river 190 *mi* (306 *km*) SE Colo. flowing into the Arkansas

Pu·ri \'pùr-ē\ city & port E India in SE Orissa on Bay of Bengal *pop* 124,835

Pu·rus \pə-'rüs\ river 2000 *mi* (3219 *km*) NW *cen* S. America rising in the Andes in SE Peru & flowing NE into the Amazon in Brazil

Pu·san \'pü-,sän\ city & port SE S. Korea on Korea Strait *pop* 3,825,000

Push·kin \'pùsh-kən\ *or formerly* **Tsar·skoye Se·lo** \'(t)sär-skə-yə-sə-'lò\ *or* **Det·skoe Selo** \'dyet-skə-yə\ city W Russia in Europe S of St. Petersburg *pop* 95,300

Puteoli — see POZZUOLI

Put–in–Bay \'pùt-,in-'bā\ inlet of Lake Erie in Ohio on S. Bass Is. N of Sandusky Bay; site of **Perry's Victory and International Peace Memorial National Monument**

Pu·tu·ma·yo \,pü-tü-'mī-(,)ò\ *or (in Brazil)* **Içá** \ē-'sä\ river 980 *mi* (1577 *km*) NW S. America flowing from SW Colombia into the Amazon in NW Brazil

Puy·al·lup \pyü-'a-ləp\ city W *cen* Wash. *pop* 23,875

Puy de Dôme — see DÔME (Puy de)

Puy de Sancy — see SANCY (Puy de)

Pya·ti·gorsk \pi-tē-'gòrsk\ city S Russia in Europe in N Caucasus SE of Stravropol *pop* 132,000

Pyd·na \'pid-nə\ ancient town Macedonia on W shore of Gulf of Salonika

Pyong·yang \'pyòn-'yan, 'pyəŋ-, -'yän\ city ✳ of N. Korea on the Taedong *pop* 2,355,000

Pyr·a·mid Lake \'pir-ə-,mid\ lake 30 *mi* (48 *km*) long NW Nev. NE of Reno

Pyr·e·nees \'pir-ə-,nēz\ *or F* **Py·ré·nées** \pē-rā-'nā\ *or Sp* **Pi·ri·ne·os** \,pē-rē-'nä-(,)òs\ mountains along French-Spanish border from Bay of Biscay to Gulf of Lion — see ANETO (Pico de) — **Pyr·e·ne·an** \,pir-ə-'nē-ən\ *adj or n*

Q

Qandahar — see KANDAHAR

Qaraghandy — see KARAGANDA

Qa·tar \'kä-tər, 'gä-, 'gə-; kə-'tär\ country E Arabia on peninsula projecting into Persian Gulf; an independent emirate ✳ Doha *area* 4400 *sq mi* (11,395 *sq km*), *pop* 539,000 — **Qa·tari** \kə-'tär-ē, gə-\ *adj or n*

Qat·ta·ra Depression \kə-'tär-ə\ region NW Egypt, a low area 40 *mi* (64 *km*) from coast; lowest point 440 *ft* (134 *m*) below sea level

Qaz·vin *or* **Kaz·vin** \kaz-'vēn\ city NW Iran S of Elburz Mountains & NW of Tehran *pop* 248,591

Qe·na \'ke-nə, 'kā-\ city S Egypt N of Luxor *pop* 137,000

Qe·qer·tar·su·aq \,ke-ker,tär-'sü-äk\ *or* **Dis·ko** \'dis-kō\ island W Greenland in Davis Strait

Qeshm \'ke-shəm\ island S Iran in Strait of Hormuz *pop* 15,000

Qing·dao \'chin-'daù\ *or* **Tsing·tao** \'chin-'daù, '(t)sin-'daù\ city & port E China in E Shandong on Jiaozhou Bay *pop* 1,459,195

Qing·hai 1 \'chin-'hī\ *or* **Ko·ko Nor** \,kō-(,)kō-'nòr\ *or* **Ch'ing Hai** \'chin-'hī\ low saline lake W *cen* China in NE Qinghai province at altitude of 10,515 *ft* (3205 *m*) **2** *or* **Tsing·hai** \'chin-'hī\ province W China ✳ Xining *area* 278,378 *sq mi* (723,783 *sq km*), *pop* 4,456,946

Qin·huang·dao *or* **Ch'in–huang–tao** *or* **Chin·wang·tao** \'chin-'hwäŋ-'dau̇, -'wäŋ-\ city & port NE China in NE Hebei *pop* 210,000

Qi·qi·har \'chē-'chē-'här\ *or* **Ch'i–ch'i–ha–erh** \'chē-'chē-'hä-'ər\ *or* **Tsi·tsi·har** \'(t)sēt-sē-,här, 'chē-chē-\ city NE China in W Heilongjiang *pop* 1,500,000

Qi·shon \'kē-,shön, kē-'\ river 45 *mi* (72 *km*) N Israel flowing NW through Plain of Esdraelon to the Mediterranean

Qom \'kùm\ city NW *cen* Iran *pop* 543,139

Quad Cities \'kwäd\ the cities of Davenport, Iowa, Moline, Ill., Rock Island, Ill., & Bettendorf, Iowa

Quan·zhou *or* **Ch'üan–chou** *or* **Chuan–chow** \'chwän-'jō\ city SE China in SE Fujian on Formosa Strait *pop* 110,000

Qu'Ap·pelle \kwa-'pel\ river 270 *mi* (434 *km*) Canada in S Sask. flowing E into the Assiniboine

Que·bec \kwi-'bek, ki-\ *or* **Qué·bec** \kā-'bek\ **1** province E Canada extending from Hudson Bay to Gaspé Peninsula *area* 524,251 *sq mi* (1,357,811 *sq km*), *pop* 6,895,963 **2** city & port, its ✳, on the St. Lawrence *pop* 167,517 — **Que·bec·er** *or* **Que·beck·er** \kwi-'be-kər, ki-\ *n* — **Que·be·cois** *or* **Qué·be·cois** \,kā-bə-'kwä, -,be-\ *adj or n*

Queen Char·lotte Islands \'shär-lət\ islands Canada in W B.C. in Pacific Ocean *area ab* 4000 *sq mi* (10,360 *sq km*)

Queen Charlotte Sound sound S of Queen Charlotte Islands

Queen Eliz·a·beth Islands \i-'li-zə-bəth\ islands N Canada N of water passage extending from M'Clure Strait to Lancaster Sound; include Parry, Sverdrup, Devon, & Ellesmere islands

Queen Maud Land \'mȯd\ section of Antarctica on the Atlantic

Queens \'kwēnz\ borough of New York City on Long Is. E of Brooklyn *pop* 1,951,598

Queen's — see LAOIGHIS

Queens·land \'kwēnz-,land, -lənd\ state NE Australia ✳ Brisbane *area* 667,000 *sq mi* (1,727,530 *sq km*), *pop* 3,116,200 — **Queensland·er** \-,lan-dər, -,lən-\ *n*

Queenstown — see COBH

Quelpart — see CHEJU

Que·moy \ki-'mȯi, kwi-; 'kwē-,\ *or* *Chin* **Jin·men** \'jin-'mən\ island SE China in Formosa Strait 15 *mi* (24 *km*) E of Amoy; garrisoned by Taiwan since 1950 ✳ *pop* 60,544

Que·ré·ta·ro \kā-'rā-tä-,rō\ **1** state *cen* Mexico *area* 4544 *sq mi* (11,769 *sq km*), *pop* 1,051,235 **2** city, its ✳ *pop* 454,049

Quet·ta \'kwe-tə\ city N Baluchistan Pakistan *pop* 285,000

Que·zal·te·nan·go \ke(t)-,säl-tā-'näŋ-(,)gō\ city SW Guatemala *pop* 72,745

Que·zon City \'kā-,sȯn\ city Philippines in Luzon NE of Manila; former (1948–76) official ✳ of the Philippines *pop* 1,632,000

Quil·mes \'kēl-,mās, -,mes\ city E Argentina SE of Buenos Aires *pop* 509,445

Quim·per \kaⁿ-'per\ commune NW France W of Rennes near Bay of Biscay *pop* 62,541

Qui·nault \kwi-'nȯlt\ river 65 *mi* (105 *km*) W Wash. flowing to the Pacific

Quin·cy **1** \'kwin(t)-sē\ city W Ill. on the Mississippi *pop* 39,681 **2** \'kwin-zē\ city E Mass. SE of Boston *pop* 84,985

Quin·ta·na Roo \kēn-'tä-nä-'rō\ state SE Mexico in E Yucatán ✻ Chetumal *area* 16,228 *sq mi* (42,030 *sq km*), *pop* 493,277

Quin·te, Bay of \'kwin-tē\ inlet of Lake Ontario in Canada in SE Ont.; connected with Georgian Bay by Trent Canal

Quir·i·nal \'kwir-ə-nᵊl\ hill in Rome, Italy, one of seven on which the ancient city was built — see AVENTINE

Qui·to \'kē-(ˌ)tō\ city ✻ of Ecuador *pop* 1,100,847

Qumran, Khirbat — see KHIRBAT QUMRAN

Quoddy Bay PASSAMAQUODDY BAY

Qŭqon — see KOKAND

R

Ra·ba \'rä-bə\ river 160 *mi* (257 *km*) SE Austria & W Hungary flowing E & NE into the Danube

Ra·bat \rə-'bät\ city ✻ of Morocco on Atlantic coast *pop* 518,616

Ra·baul \rə-'baúl\ city Bismarck Archipelago at E end of New Britain; formerly ✻ of Territory of New Guinea *pop* 17,022

Rabbah Ammon, Rabbath Ammon — see AMMAN

Race, Cape \'räs\ headland, SE point of Newfoundland, Canada

Ra·ci·bórz \rä-'chē-ˌbúsh\ *or G* **Ra·ti·bor** \'rä-tə-ˌbór\ city SW Poland in Silesia on the Oder *pop* 62,833

Ra·cine \rə-'sēn, rä-\ city SE Wis. S of Milwaukee *pop* 84,298

Rad·cliff \'rad-ˌklif\ city *cen* Ky. *pop* 19,772

Rad·nor \'rad-nər, -ˌnór\ *or* **Rad·nor·shire** \-ˌshir, -shər\ former county E Wales ✻ Llandrindod Wells

Ra·dom \'rä-ˌdóm\ commune Poland NE of Kielce *pop* 226,317

Raetia — see RHAETIA — **Rae·tian** \'rē-shən\ *adj or n*

Ragae *or* **Rages** — see RHAGAE

Ra·gu·sa \rə-'gü-zə\ commune Italy in SE Sicily *pop* 68,850

Rah·way \'rò-ˌwā\ city NE N.J. SW of Elizabeth *pop* 25,325

Rain·bow Bridge National Monument \'rän-ˌbō\ reservation S Utah near Ariz. boundary containing **Rainbow Bridge** (large natural bridge)

Rai·nier, Mount \rə-'nir, rä-\ *or formerly* **Mount Ta·co·ma** \tə-'kō-mə\ mountain 14,410 *ft* (4392 *m*) W *cen* Wash., highest in the Cascade Range & in Wash.; in **Mount Rainier National Park**

Rainy \'rä-nē\ river 80 *mi* (129 *km*) on Canada-U.S. boundary bet. Ont. & Minn. flowing from Rainy Lake into Lake of the Woods

Rainy Lake lake Canada & U.S. bet. Ont. & Minn. *area* 360 *sq mi* (932 *sq km*)

Rai·pur \'rī-ˌpúr\ city E India in SE Madhya Pradesh E of Nagpur *pop* 438,639

Rai·sin \'rā-zᵊn\ river *ab* 115 *mi* (185 *km*) SE Mich. flowing into Lake Erie

Ra·jah·mun·dry \ˌrä-jə-'mún-drē\ city E India in E Andhra Pradesh on Godavari River W of Kakinada *pop* 324,881

Ra·jas·than \'rä-jə-ˌstän\ state NW India bordering on Pakistan ✻ Jaipur *area* 132,149 *sq mi* (342,266 *sq km*), *pop* 44,005,990

Raj·kot \'räj-ˌkōt\ **1** former state W India in N *cen* Kathiawar Peninsula **2** city, its **✳**, now in Gujarat *pop* 612,458

Raj·pu·ta·na \ˌräj-pə-'tä-nə\ *or* **Rajasthan** region NW India bordering on Pakistan & including part of Thar Desert

Ra·leigh \'rȯ-lē, 'rä-lē\ city E *cen* N.C., its **✳** *pop* 207,951

Ra·lik \'rä-lik\ the W chain of the Marshall Islands

Ram·a·po Mountains \'ra-mə-ˌpō\ mountains of the Appalachians N N.J. & S N.Y.; highest point 1164 *ft* (355 *m*)

Ra·mat Gan \rə-ˌmät-'gän, ˌrä-mät-\ city W Israel E of Tel Aviv *pop* 122,700

Ram·bouil·let \rän̄-bü-'yā\ town N France SW of Paris *pop* 25,293

Ram·gan·ga \räm-'gən-gə\ river *ab* 350 *mi* (563 *km*) N India in Uttar Pradesh flowing S into the Ganges

Ram·pur \'räm-ˌpu̇r\ **1** former state N India NW of Bareilly, now in Uttar Pradesh **2** city, its **✳**, ENE of Delhi *pop* 242,752

Rams·gate \'ramz-ˌgāt, -gət\ borough SE England in Kent on North Sea N of Dover *pop* 39,642

Ran·ca·gua \rän-'kä-gwä, rän̄-\ city *cen* Chile *pop* 139,925

Ran·chi \'rän-chē\ city E India in Bihar NW of Calcutta *pop* 599,306

Ran·cho Cu·ca·mon·ga \'ran-(ˌ)chō-ˌkü-kə-'mən-gə, 'rän-, -'mäŋ-\ city SW Calif. NW of Riverside *pop* 101,409

Rancho Pal·os Ver·des \-pa-ləs-'vər-dēz\ city SW Calif. on coast S of Torrance *pop* 41,659

Rand \'rand, 'ränd\ WITWATERSRAND

Ran·ders \'rä-nərs\ city & port NE Denmark *pop* 61,137

Ran·dolph \'ran-ˌdälf\ town E Mass. S of Boston *pop* 30,093

Range·ley Lakes \'rānj-lē\ chain of lakes W Maine & N N.H.

Ran·goon \ran-'gün, raŋ-\ **1** *or* **Yan·gon** \ˌyän-'gōn\ river 25 *mi* (40 *km*) S Myanmar, the E outlet of the Irrawaddy **2** — see YANGON

Ran·noch, Loch \'ra-nək, -nək\ lake 9 *mi* (14 *km*) long *cen* Scotland

Rann of Kachchh — see KACHCHH (Rann of)

Ra·pa \'rä-pə\ island S Pacific in SE Tubuai group *area* 15 *sq mi* (39 *sq km*) *pop* 516

Ra·pal·lo \rə-'pä-(ˌ)lō\ commune NW Italy in Liguria ESE of Genoa on Gulf of Rapallo (inlet of Ligurian Sea) *pop* 29,790

Rapa Nui — see EASTER

Rap·i·dan \ˌra-pə-'dan\ river 70 *mi* (113 *km*) N Va. rising in Blue Ridge Mountains & flowing E into the Rappahannock

Rap·id City \'ra-pəd\ city W S.Dak. in Black Hills *pop* 54,523

Rap·pa·han·nock \ˌra-pə-'ha-nək\ river 212 *mi* (341 *km*) NE Va. flowing into Chesapeake Bay

Rap·ti \'räp-tē\ river 400 *mi* (644 *km*) Nepal & N India flowing SE into the Gogra

Rar·i·tan \'rar-ə-tᵊn\ river 75 *mi* (121 *km*) N *cen* N.J. flowing E into **Raritan Bay** (inlet of the Atlantic S of Staten Is., N.Y.)

Rar·o·ton·ga \ˌrar-ə-'täŋ-gə, -'täŋ-ə\ island S Pacific in SW part of Cook Islands; site of Avarua, **✳** of the group *pop* 9826

Ra's al Khay·mah *or* **Ras al–Khai·mah** \ˌräs-al-'kī-mə, -'kī-\ sheikhdom, member of the United Arab Emirates

Ras Da·shen \ˌräs-də-'shen\ mountain 15,158 *ft* (4260 *m*) N Ethiopia NE of Lake Tana; highest in Ethiopia

Ra's at Tīb — see BON (Cape)

Rashid — see ROSETTA

Rasht \rasht\ city NW Iran near the Caspian *pop* 2,900,897

Ra·tak \'rä-ˌtäk\ the E chain of the Marshall Islands

Rat Islands \'rat\ islands SW Alaska in W Aleutians — see AMCHITKA, KISKA

Ra·ton \ra-'tōn, rə-, -'tün; *usu* -'tōn *in* N Mex, -'tün *in* Colo\ pass 7834 *ft* (2388 *m*) SE Colo. just N of Colo.-N.Mex. border in **Raton Range** (E spur of Sangre de Cristo Mountains)

Ra·ven·na \rä-'ve-nä\ commune N Italy NE of Florence *pop* 135,435

Ra·vi \'rä-vē\ *or anc* **Hy·dra·o·tes** \ˌhī-drə-'ō-(ˌ)tēz\ river 450 *mi* (724 *km*) N India flowing SW to the Chenab & forming part of boundary bet. E. Punjab (India) & W. Punjab (Pakistan)

Ra·wal·pin·di \ˌrä-wəl-'pin-dē, raúl-', rôl-'\ city NE Pakistan NNW of Lahore *pop* 966,000

Ray·town \'rā-ˌtaún\ city W Mo. SE of Kansas City *pop* 30,601

Read·ing \'re-diŋ\ **1** town E Mass. N of Boston *pop* 22,539 **2** city SE Pa. on the Schuylkill *pop* 78,380 **3** borough S England ✳ of Berkshire *pop* 122,600

Re·bild \'rā-ˌbil\ village N Denmark in N Jutland S of Ålborg in **Rebild Hills** (site of Rebild National Park)

Re·ci·fe \ri-'sē-fē\ *or formerly* **Per·nam·bu·co** \ˌpər-nəm-'bü-(ˌ)kō, -'byü-; ˌper-nəm-'bü-(ˌ)kü\ city & port NE Brazil ✳ of Pernambuco state *municipal area pop* 1,300,000

Reck·ling·hau·sen \ˌre-kliŋ-'hau-zᵊn\ city W Germany SW of Münster *pop* 125,966

Red \'red\ **1** river 1018 *mi* (1638 *km*) flowing E on Okla.-Tex. boundary & into the Atchafalaya & Mississippi in La. **2** river N *cen* U.S. & S *cen* Canada flowing N on Minn.-N.Dak. ŏoundary & into Lake Winnipeg in Man. **3** — see ARCTIC RED **4** *or* **Hong** \'hóŋ\ *or (in China)* **Yuan** \yü-'än, -'an\ river 500 *mi* (805 *km*) SE Asia rising in *cen* Yunnan, China, & flowing SE across N Vietnam into Gulf of Tonkin

Red·bridge \'red-(ˌ)brij\ borough of NE Greater London, England *pop* 220,600

Red Deer **1** river 385 *mi* (620 *km*) Canada in S Alta. flowing E & SE into the S Saskatchewan **2** city Canada in S *cen* Alta. S of Edmonton *pop* 58,134

Red·ding \'re-diŋ\ city N Calif. *pop* 66,462

Red Lake lake 38 *mi* (61 *km*) long N Minn. divided into **Upper Red Lake** & **Lower Red Lake**; drained by **Red Lake River** (196 *mi or* 315 *km* flowing W into Red River)

Red·lands \'red-lən(d)z\ city S Calif. SE of San Bernardino *pop* 60,394

Red·mond \'red-mənd\ city W *cen* Wash. NE of Seattle *pop* 35,800

Re·don·do Beach \ri-'dän-dō\ city SW Calif. *pop* 60,167

Red Sea sea 1450 *mi* (2334 *km*) long bet. Arabia & NE Africa

Red Volta river 200 *mi* (322 *km*) S Burkina Faso & N Ghana flowing into Lake Volta

Red·wood City \'red-ˌwúd\ city W Calif. SE of San Francisco *pop* 66,072

Redwood National Park reservation NW Calif.; groves of redwoods

Reel·foot \'rēl-ˌfu̇t\ lake NW Tenn. near the Mississippi

Re·gens·burg \'rā-gənz-ˌbərg, -gəns-ˌbu̇rk\ city SE Germany in Bavaria on the Danube NNE of Munich *pop* 123,002

Reg·gane \re-'gän, -'gan\ oasis *cen* Algeria in Tanezrouft SSE of Béchar

Reg·gio \'re-(ˌ)jō, -jē-(ˌ)ō\ **1** *or* **Reggio di Ca·la·bria** \dē-kä-'lä-brē-ä\ *or* **Reggio Calabria** *or anc* **Rhe·gi·um** \'rē-jē-əm\ commune & port S Italy on Strait of Messina *pop* 169,709 **2** *or* **Reggio nel·l'Emi·lia** \ˌne-le-'mēl-yä\ *or* **Reggio Emilia** commune N Italy in Emilia-Romagna NW of Bologna *pop* 131,419

Re·gi·na \ri-'jī-nə\ city Canada ✱ of Sask. *pop* 179,178

Reims *or* **Rheims** \'rēmz, *F* 'raⁿs\ city NE France ENE of Paris *pop* 185,164

Rein·deer Lake \'rān-ˌdir\ lake Canada on Man.-Sask. border *area ab* 2500 *sq mi* (6475 *sq km*)

Re·ma·gen \'rā-ˌmä-gən\ town W Germany on W bank of the Rhine NW of Koblenz *pop* 15,460

Rem·scheid \'rem-ˌshīt\ city W Germany in N. Rhine-Westphalia ESE of Düsseldorf *pop* 123,618

Ren·do·va \ren-'dō-və\ island W Pacific in *cen* Solomon Islands off SW *cen* coast of New Georgia Is.

Ren·frew \'ren-ˌfrü\ *or* **Ren·frew·shire** \-ˌshir, -shər\ former county SW Scotland ✱ Paisley

Rennes \'ren\ city NW France N of Nantes *pop* 203,533

Re·no \'rē-(ˌ)nō\ city W Nev. NNE of Lake Tahoe *pop* 133,850

Ren·ton \'ren-tᵊn\ city W Wash. SE of Seattle *pop* 41,688

Re·pen·ti·gny \rə-ˌpäⁿ-tē-'nyē\ town Canada in S Que. N of Montreal *pop* 49,630

Re·pub·li·can \ri-'pə-bli-kən\ river 445 *mi* (716 *km*) Nebr. & Kans. rising in E Colo. & flowing E to unite with the Smoky Hill forming Kansas River

Re·thondes \rə-'tōⁿd\ village N France E of Compiègne

Ré·union \rē-'yü-nyən, ˌrā-ᵾ-'nyōⁿ\ island W Indian Ocean in the W Mascarenes ✱ St.-Denis; an overseas department of France *area* 970 *sq mi* (2522 *sq km*), *pop* 634,000

Reut·ling·en \'ro̩it-liŋ-ən\ city S Germany in Baden-Württemberg S of Stuttgart *pop* 105,835

Revel — see TALLINN

Re·vere \ri-'vir\ city E Mass. NE of Boston *pop* 42,786

Re·vil·la Gi·ge·do \rā-'vē-yä-hē-'hä-(ˌ)thō\ islands Mexico in the Pacific SW of S end of Baja California

Re·vil·la·gi·ge·do Island \ri-ˌvi-lə-gə-'gē-(ˌ)dō, -'ge-\ island SE Alaska in SE Alexander Archipelago E of Prince of Wales Is.

Reyes, Point \'rāz\ cape W Calif. at S extremity of peninsula extending into the Pacific NW of Golden Gate

Reyk·ja·vík \'rā-kyə-ˌvik, -ˌvēk\ city & port ✱ of Iceland *pop* 97,648

Reyn·olds·burg \'re-nᵊl(d)z-ˌbərg\ village *cen* Ohio *pop* 25,748

Rey·no·sa \rā-'nō-sə\ city NE Mexico in Tamaulipas on the Rio Grande *pop* 281,618

Rezaïyeh — see ORŪMĪYEH

Rhae·tia *or* **Rae·tia** \'rē-sh(ē-)ə\ ancient Roman province *cen* Europe S of the Danube including most of modern Tirol & Vorarlberg

regions of Austria & Graubünden canton of E Switzerland —
Rhae·tian \-shən\ *adj or n*

Rhaetian Alps section of Alps E Switzerland in E Graubünden —
see BERNINA

Rha·gae *or* **Ra·gae** \-(,)jē, -,jī\ *or bib* **Ra·ges** \'rā-jəz\ city of ancient Media; ruins at modern village of **Rai** \'rī\ S of Tehran, Iran

Rheinpfalz — see PALATINATE

Rhenish Palatinate — see PALATINATE

Rheydt \'rīt\ city W Germany S of Mönchengladbach *pop* 100,300

Rhine \'rīn\ *or G* **Rhein** \'rīn\ *or F* **Rhin** \'raⁿ\ *or D* **Rijn** \'rīn\ river 820 *mi* (1320 *km*) W Europe flowing from SE Switzerland to
North Sea in Netherlands; forms W boundary of Liechtenstein &
Austria & SW boundary of Germany — **Rhe·nish** \'re-nish, 'rē-\
adj

Rhine·land \'rīn-,land, -lənd\ *or G* **Rhein·land** \'rīn-,länt\ **1** the
part of Germany W of the Rhine **2** RHINE PROVINCE — **Rhine-
land·er** \'rīn-,lan-dər, -lən-\ *n*

Rhineland–Palatinate *or G* **Rheinland–Pfalz** \'(p)fälts\ state of
Germany & formerly of W. Germany chiefly W of the Rhine ✳
Mainz *area* 7654 *sq mi* (19,900 *sq km*), *pop* 3,642,482

Rhine Palatinate — see PALATINATE

Rhine Province former province of Prussia, Germany, bordering
on Belgium ✳ Koblenz

Rhode Is·land \rōd-'ī-lənd\ **1** *or officially* **Rhode Island and
Providence Plantations** state NE U.S. ✳ Providence *area* 1212
sq mi (3139 *sq km*), *pop* 1,003,464 **2** — see AQUIDNECK — **Rhode
Islander** *n*

Rhodes \'rōdz\ *or NGk* **Ró·dhos** \'rȯ-,thȯs\ **1** island Greece in the
SE Aegean, chief island of the Dodecanese *area* 540 *sq mi* (1399
sq km) *pop* 103,295 **2** city, its ✳ *pop* 43,619 — **Rho·di·an** \'rō-
dē-ən\ *adj or n*

Rho·de·sia \rō-'dē-zh(ē-)ə\ **1** region *cen* S Africa S of Democratic
Republic of the Congo comprising Zambia & Zimbabwe; contains
rich archaeological findings **2** — see ZIMBABWE 2 — **Rho·de·sian**
\-zh(ē-)ən\ *adj or n*

Rhodesia and Nyasaland, Federation of former country S Africa comprising S. Rhodesia, N. Rhodesia, & Nyasaland; a federal
state within the Commonwealth; dissolved 1963

Rhod·o·pe \'rä-də-(,)pē, rō-'dō-pē\ mountains S Bulgaria & NE
Greece; highest Musala 9596 *ft* (2925 *m*)

Rhon·dda \'rän-də, '(h)rän-thə\ borough SE Wales in Mid Glamorgan *pop* 76,300

Rhône \'rōn\ river 505 *mi* (813 *km*) Switzerland & France rising in
the Alps and flowing through Lake Geneva into Gulf of Lion inlet
of the Mediterranean

Rhyl \'ril\ town & port NE Wales in Clwyd at mouth of the Clwyd
pop 22,714

Ri·al·to \rē-'al-(,)tō\ **1** city SW Calif. W of San Bernardino *pop*
72,388 **2** island & district of Venice, Italy

Ri·au *or Du* **Ri·ouw** \'rē-,aů\ archipelago Indonesia S of Singapore;
chief island Bintan *area* 2279 *sq mi* (5925 *sq km*), *pop* 278,966

Ri·bei·rão Prê·to \rē-bə-'raůⁿ-'prā-(,)tů\ city SE Brazil in N *cen*
São Paulo state *pop* 430,805

Rich·ard·son \'ri-chərd-sən\ city NE Tex. N of Dallas *pop* 74,840

Rich·e·lieu \'ri-shə-,lü, rē-shəl-'yœ\ river 210 *mi* (338 *km*) Canada in S Que. flowing N from Lake Champlain to head of Lake St. Peter in the St. Lawrence

Rich·field \'rich-,fēld\ village SE Minn.; a S suburb of Minneapolis *pop* 35,710

Rich·land \'rich-lənd\ city SE Wash. at confluence of Yakima & Columbia rivers *pop* 32,315

Rich·mond \'rich-mənd\ **1** city W Calif. NNW of Oakland on San Francisco Bay *pop* 87,425 **2** city E Ind. *pop* 38,705 **3** city *cen* Ky. *pop* 21,155 **4** borough of New York City — see STATEN ISLAND **5** city W Va. on the James *pop* 203,056 **6** city Canada in SW B.C. S of Vancouver *pop* 126,624 **7** *or in full* **Richmond upon Thames** borough of SW Greater London, England *pop* 154,600 — **Rich·mond·er** \-mən-dər\ *n*

Richmond Hill town Canada in SE Ont. N of Toronto *pop* 80,142

Ri·deau Canal \ri-'dō\ canal system Canada 124 *mi* (200 *km*) long in SE Ont. connecting Lake Ontario & Ottawa River & including **Rideau Lake** (20 *mi or* 32 *km* long) & **Rideau River** (flowing into the Ottawa)

Ridge·crest \'rij-,krest\ city S Calif. NE of Bakersfield *pop* 27,725

Ridge·field \'rij-,fēld\ town SW Conn. NW of Norwalk *pop* 20,919

Ridge·wood \'rij-,wùd\ village NE N.J. NNE of Paterson *pop* 24,152

Rid·ing Mountain National Park \'rī-diŋ\ reservation Canada in SW Man.; has game preserve

Rift Valley GREAT RIFT VALLEY

Ri·ga \'rē-gə\ city & port ✻ of Latvia at S extremity of the Gulf of Riga *pop* 915,000

Riga, Gulf of inlet of Baltic Sea bordering on Estonia & Latvia

Ri·je·ka *or* **Ri·e·ka** \rē-'ye-kə\ *or It* **Fiu·me** \'fyü-(,)mā, fē-'ü-\ city & port W Croatia *pop* 167,964

Rijs·wijk \'rīs-,vīk\ commune SW Netherlands *pop* 47,456

Ri·mac \'rē-,mäk\ river 80 *mi* (129 *km*) W Peru flowing SW through Lima into the Pacific

Ri·mi·ni \'ri-mi-(,)nē, 'rē-\ *or anc* **Arim·i·num** \ə-'ri-mə-nəm\ commune & port N Italy on the Adriatic ESE of Ravenna *pop* 128,119

Ri·mou·ski \ri-'müs-kē\ town Canada in E Que. on Gaspé Peninsula *pop* 30,873

Ring of Fire belt of volcanoes & frequent seismic activity nearly encircling the Pacific

Rio \'rē-(,)ō\ RIO DE JANEIRO

Rio Bran·co \,rē-(,)ō-'bran-(,)kō, ,rē-(,)ü-'brän-(,)kü\ **1** — see BRANCO **2** city W Brazil, ✻ of Acre *municipal area pop* 196,923

Rio de Ja·nei·ro \,rē-(,)ō-dā-zhə-'ner-(,)ō, -dē-; 'rē-ü-dē-zhə-'nā-rü\ **1** state SE Brazil *area* 17,092 *sq mi* (44,268 *sq km*), *pop* 12,584,108 **2** city, its ✻ & port on Guanabara Bay; former ✻ of Brazil *pop* 6,100,000

Río de la Plata — see PLATA (Río de la)

Río de Oro \,rē-(,)ō-dē-'ōr-(,)ō, -'ór-\ territory NW Africa comprising the S zone of Western Sahara

Rio Grande 1 \,rē-(,)ō-'grand, -'gran-dē *also* ,rī-ō-'grand\ *or MexSp* **Río Bra·vo** \,rē-(,)ō-'brä-(,)vō\ river 1885 *mi* (3034 *km*) SW U.S. forming part of Mexico-U.S. boundary & flowing from San Juan Mountains in SW Colo. to Gulf of Mexico **2** *or* **Rio Gran-**

de do Sul \ˌrē-ü-ˈgrän-dē-dü-ˈsül\ city S Brazil in Rio Grande do Sul state W of entrance to Lagoa dos Patos *pop* 172,435 **3** \ˌrē-(ˌ)ō-ˈgrän-dā, -dē\ municipality NE Puerto Rico *pop* 45,648 **4** — see GRANDE (Rio)

Rio Grande de Cagayan — see CAGAYAN

Rio Gran·de do Nor·te \ˈrē-(ˌ)ü-ˈgrän-dē-dü-ˈnȯr-tē\ state NE Brazil ✳ Natal *area* 20,528 *sq mi* (53,168 *sq km*), *pop* 2,413,618

Rio Grande do Sul \-ˈsül\ state SE Brazil bordering on Uruguay ✳ Pôrto Alegre *area* 108,951 *sq mi* (282,183 *sq km*), *pop* 9,127,611

Rioja, the — see LA RIOJA

Río Muni — see MBINI

Río Pie·dras \ˈrē-(ˌ)ō-ˈpyä-drəs, -ˌthräs\ former city, since 1951 part of San Juan, Puerto Rico

Rio Ran·cho \ˈrē-(ˌ)ō-ˈran-(ˌ)chō, -ˈrän-\ city *cen* N.Mex., a N suburb of Albuquerque *pop* 32,505

Rip·on Falls \ˈri-pən, -ˌpän\ former waterfall in the Victoria Nile N of Lake Victoria; submerged by Owen Falls Dam

Riv·er·side \ˈri-vər-ˌsīd\ city S Calif. *pop* 226,505

Riv·i·era \ˌri-vē-ˈer-ə\ coast region SE France & NW Italy bordering on the Mediterranean — see CÔTE D'AZUR

Riviera Beach city SE Fla. N of W. Palm Beach *pop* 27,639

Ri·yadh \rē-ˈyäd\ city ✳ of the Nejd & of Saudi Arabia *pop* 666,840

Rju·kan \rē-ü-ˌkän\ town S Norway W of Oslo near **Rjukan Falls** (waterfall 780 *ft or* 238 *m*)

Ro·a·noke \ˈrō-(ə-)ˌnōk\ **1** river 380 *mi* (612 *km*) S Va. & NE N.C. flowing E & SE into Albemarle Sound **2** city W *cen* Va. *pop* 96,397

Roanoke Island island N.C. S of entrance to Albemarle Sound

Rob·erts, Point \ˈrä-bərts\ cape NW Wash., tip of a peninsula extending S into Strait of Georgia from B.C. & separated from U.S. mainland by Boundary Bay

Rob·son, Mount \ˈräb-sən\ mountain 12,972 *ft* (3954 *m*) W Canada in E B.C.; highest in Canadian Rockies

Ro·ca, Cape \ˈrō-kə\ *or Pg* **Ca·bo da Ro·ca** \ˈkä-bü-də-ˈrō-kə\ cape Portugal; westernmost point of continental Europe, at 9°30′W

Roch·dale \ˈräch-ˌdāl\ borough NW England in Greater Manchester NNE of Manchester *pop* 92,704

Roche·fort \rȯsh-ˈfȯr, ˈrōsh-fȯrt\ *or* **Rochefort–sur–Mer** \-ˌsu̇r-ˈmer\ city W France SSE of La Rochelle *pop* 26,949

Roch·es·ter \ˈrä-chəs-tər, -ˌches-tər\ **1** city SE Minn. *pop* 70,745 **2** city SE N.H. *pop* 26,630 **3** city W N.Y. on the Genesee *pop* 231,636 **4** city SE England in Kent *pop* 52,505

Rochester Hills city SE Mich. N of Detroit *pop* 61,766

Rock \ˈräk\ river 300 *mi* (483 *km*) S Wis. & N Ill. flowing S & SW into the Mississippi at Rock Island

Rock·all \ˈrä-ˌkȯl\ islet N Atlantic NW of Ireland, at 57°36′N 13°41′W

Rock·ford \ˈräk-fərd\ city N Ill. NW of Chicago *pop* 139,426

Rock·hamp·ton \räk-ˈham(p)-tən, rä-ˈkam(p)-\ city & port E Australia in E Queensland on Fitzroy River *pop* 61,631

Rock Hill city N S.C. SSW of Charlotte, N.C. *pop* 41,643

Rock Island city NW Ill. on the Mississippi *pop* 40,552

Rock·lin \ˈrä-klin, -klən\ city E Calif. NE of Sacramento *pop* 19,033

Rock Springs city SW Wyo. near Utah border *pop* 19,050

Rock·ville \'räk-,vil, -vəl\ city SW Md. *pop* 44,835

Rockville Centre village SE N.Y. in W *cen* Long Is. *pop* 24,727

Rocky Mount \'rä-kē\ city NE *cen* N.C. *pop* 48,997

Rocky Mountain National Park reservation N Colo.

Rocky Mountains *or* **Rock·ies** \'rä-kēz\ mountains W N. America extending from N Alaska SE to N.Mex. — see ELBERT (Mount), ROBSON (Mount)

Rocky River city NE Ohio on Lake Erie W of Cleveland *pop* 20,410

Ródhos — see RHODES

Ro·dri·gues \rō-'drē-gəs\ island Indian Ocean in the Mascarenes; a dependency of Mauritius; chief town Port Mathurin *area* 40 *sq mi* (104 *sq km*), *pop* 37,782

Rog·ers \'rä-jərz\ city NW Ark. *pop* 24,692

Rogers Pass mountain pass Canada in SE B.C. in Selkirk Mountains

Rogue \'rōg\ river *ab* 200 *mi* (320 *km*) SW Oreg. rising in Crater Lake National Park & flowing W & SW into the Pacific

Ro·hil·khand \'rō-,hil-,kənd\ *or* **Ba·reil·ly** \bə-'rā-lē\ region N India in Uttar Pradesh; chief city Bareilly

Rohn·ert Park \'rō-nərt\ city W Calif. S of Santa Rosa *pop* 36,326

Roll·ing Meadows \'rō-liṇ\ city NE Ill. NW of Chicago *pop* 22,591

Ro·ma·gna \rō-'mä-nyä\ district N Italy on the Adriatic comprising the E part of Emilia-Romagna region

Roman Campagna — see CAMPAGNA DI ROMA

Ro·ma·nia \rú-'mä-nē-ə, rō-, -nyə\ *or* **Ru·ma·nia** \rú-\ country SE Europe bordering on Black Sea ✻ Bucharest *area* 91,699 *sq mi* (237,500 *sq km*), *pop* 22,789,000 — **Ro·ma·nian** \rú-'mä-nē-ən, rō-, -nyən\ *n* — **Ru·ma·nian** *or* **Rou·ma·nian** \rú-'mä-nē-ən, -nyən\ *adj or n*

Rom·blon \räm-'blōn\ **1** islands Philippines in N Visayan Islands in Sibuyan Sea *area* 524 *sq mi* (1357 *sq km*) **2** island in the group

Rome \'rōm\ **1** city NW Ga. NW of Atlanta *pop* 30,326 **2** city E *cen* N.Y. NW of Utica *pop* 44,350 **3** *or It* **Ro·ma** \'rō-mä\ *or anc* **Ro·ma** \'rō-mə\ city ✻ of Italy on the Tiber *pop* 2,693,383 **4** the Roman Empire — **Ro·man** \'rō-mən\ *adj or n*

Rome, Duchy of division of Byzantine Empire 6th to 8th century *cen* Italy comprising most of modern Lazio; later a province of the Papal States called **Patrimony of Saint Pe·ter** \'pē-tər\

Rom·ford \'räm(p)-fərd, 'rəm(p)-\ former municipal borough SE England in Essex, now part of Havering

Rom·u·lus \'rä-myə-ləs\ city SE Mich. *pop* 22,897

Ron·ces·va·lles \,rón(t)-səs-'vī-əs, *or F* **Ron·ce·vaux** \rōⁿs-'vō, rōⁿ-sə-\ commune N Spain 5 *mi* (8 *km*) from French boundary in the Pyrenees near **Pass of Roncesvalles**

Ron·dô·nia \rōⁿ-'dō-nyə\ *or formerly* **Gua·po·ré** \,gwä-pó-'rā\ state W Brazil ✻ Porto Velho *area* 93,839 *sq mi* (243,043 *sq km*), *pop* 1,130,400

Rong·er·ik \'rän-ə-,rik, 'róņ-\ island W *cen* Pacific in the Marshalls in Ratak chain E of Bikini

Ron·ne Ice Shelf \'rō-nə, 'rə-nə\ area of shelf ice Antarctica in Weddell Sea

Roo·de·poort \'rō-də-ˌpōrt, 'rō-i-ˌpōrt, -ˌpȯrt\ city Republic of South Africa in Gauteng W of Johannesburg *metropolitan pop* 141,764

Roo·se·velt \'rō-zə-ˌvelt, -ˌvȯlt *also* 'rü-\ river *ab* 400 *mi* (644 *km*) W *cen* Brazil flowing from W Mato Grosso state N into the Aripuanã

Ro·rai·ma \rȯ-'rī-mä\ mountain 9094 *ft* (2772 *m*) N S. America in Pacaraima Mountains on boundary bet. Venezuela, Guyana, & Brazil; has flat top

Ror·schach \'rȯr-ˌshäk, 'rōr-, -ˌshäk\ commune NE Switzerland on S shore of Lake Constance *pop* 9878

Ro·sa, Mon·te \'mȯn-tā-'rō-zä\ mountain 15,203 *ft* (4634 *m*) on Swiss-Italian border; highest in Pennine Alps

Ro·sa·rio \rō-'zär-ē-ˌō, -'sär-\ city E *cen* Argentina on the Paraná *pop* 591,428

Ros·com·mon \räs-'kä-mən\ 1 county *cen* Ireland in Connacht *area* 951 *sq mi* (2473 *sq km*), *pop* 51,897 2 town, its ✳ *pop* 1363

Rose, Mount \'rōz\ mountain 10,778 *ft* (3285 *m*) W Nev. in Carson Range SW of Reno

Ro·seau \rō-'zō\ seaport ✳ of Dominica *pop* 15,853

Ro·selle \rō-'zel\ 1 city NE Ill. *pop* 20,819 2 borough NE N.J. W of Elizabeth *pop* 20,314

Rose·mead \'rōz-ˌmēd\ city SW Calif. E of Los Angeles *pop* 51,638

Ro·sen·berg \'rō-z°n-ˌbərg\ city SE Tex. *pop* 20,183

Ro·set·ta \rō-'ze-tə\ *or Ar* Ra·shīd \rä-'shēd\ *or anc* Bol·bi·ti·ne \ˌbäl-bə-'tī-nē\ 1 river 146 *mi* (235 *km*) N Egypt forming W branch of the Nile in its delta 2 city N Egypt on the Rosetta *pop* 36,711

Rose·ville \'rōz-ˌvil\ 1 city W Calif. NE of Sacramento *pop* 44,685 2 city SE Mich. NE of Detroit *pop* 51,412 3 village SE Minn. N of St. Paul *pop* 33,485

Ross and Crom·ar·ty \'ròs-ənd-'krä-mər-tē\ former county N Scotland ✳ Dingwall

Ross Dependency section of Antarctica lying bet. 160° E and 150° W long.; claimed by New Zealand

Ross Ice Shelf area of shelf ice Antarctica in S Ross Sea

Ross Sea arm of S Pacific extending into Antarctica E of Victoria Land

Ros·tock \'räs-ˌtäk, 'rȯs-ˌtȯk\ city & port NE Germany on Warnow River near the Baltic coast *pop* 234,475

Ros·tov \rə-'stȯf, -'stȯv\ *or* Rostov–on–Don \-ˌän-'dän, -ˌȯn-\ city S Russia in Europe on the Don *pop* 1,027,000

Ros·well \'räz-ˌwel, -wəl\ 1 city NW *cen* Ga. N of Atlanta *pop* 47,923 2 city SE N.Mex. *pop* 44,654

Ro·ta \'rō-tə\ 1 island W Pacific at S end of the Marianas *area* 35 *sq mi* (91 *sq km*) 2 town & port SW Spain on the Atlantic NW of Cádiz

Roth·er·ham \'rä-thə-rəm\ borough N England in S. Yorkshire NE of Sheffield *area pop* 247,100

Rothe·say \'räth-sē\ royal burgh SW Scotland on island of Bute in Strathclyde *pop* 5408

Ro·to·rua \ˌrō-tō-'rü-ə\ city New Zealand in N *cen* North Is. *pop* 53,700

Rot·ter·dam \'rä-tər-ˌdam, -ˌdäm\ city & port SW Netherlands on the Nieuwe Maas *pop* 589,707 — **Rot·ter·dam·mer** \-ˌda-mər, -ˌdä-\ *n*

Ro·tu·ma \rō-'tü-mə\ island SW Pacific N of Fiji Islands *area* 14 *sq mi* (36 *sq km*); belongs to Fiji

Rou·baix \rü-'bā\ city N France NE of Lille *pop* 98,179

Rou·en \rü-'äⁿ\ city & port N France on the Seine *pop* 105,470

Round Rock town *cen* Tex. N of Austin *pop* 30,923

Rous·sil·lon \rü-sē-'yōⁿ\ region & former province S France bordering on the Pyrenees & the Mediterranean ❋ Perpignan

Rou·yn–No·ran·da \rü-ən-nə-'ran-də, rü-'aⁿ-\ town Canada in SW Que. *pop* 26,448

Row·lett \raú-lət\ city NE Tex., a suburb of Dallas *pop* 23,260

Rox·burgh \'räks-,bərə or -,bə-rə, -b(ə-)rə\ or **Rox·burgh·shire** \-,shir, -shər\ former county SE Scotland ❋ Jedburgh

Roy \'rói\ city NE Utah SW of Ogden *pop* 24,603

Roy·al Gorge \'rói-(ə)l\ section of the canyon of Arkansas River S *cen* Colo.

Royal Leamington Spa — see LEAMINGTON

Royal Oak city SE Mich. N of Detroit *pop* 65,410

Royal Tun·bridge Wells \'tən-brij\ borough SE England in Kent *pop* 44,506

Ru·an·da–Urun·di \rü-'än-də-ü-'rün-dē\ or **Belgian East Africa** former country E *cen* Africa bordering on Lake Tanganyika & comprising two districts, **Ruanda** (❋ Kigali) & **Urundi** (❋ Usumbura), administered by Belgium under League of Nations mandate 1919–45 & under U.N. trusteeship 1946–62 ❋ Usumbura — see BURUNDI, RWANDA

Ru·a·pe·hu, Mount \,rü-ə-'pā-(,)hü\ volcano 9175 *ft* (2796 *m*) New Zealand, highest peak in North Is., in Tongariro National Park

Rub' al-Kha·li \,rüb-al-'kä-lē, Ar -äl-'kä-\ desert region S Arabia extending from Nejd S to Hadhramaut *area ab* 250,000 *sq mi* (647,500 *sq km*)

Ru·bi·con \'rü-bi-,kän\ river 15 *mi* (24 *km*) N *cen* Italy flowing E into the Adriatic

Ru·da Slas·ka \,rü-də-'shlōⁿ-skə\ commune S Poland *pop* 169,789

Rudolf, Lake — see TURKANA Lake

Ru·fisque \rü-'fēsk\ city & port W Senegal *pop* 137,150

Rug·by \'rəg-bē\ town *cen* England in Warwick on the Avon *pop* 83,400

Rü·gen \'rü-gən, 'rǖ-\ island NE Germany in Baltic Sea off coast of Pomerania *area* 358 *sq mi* (927 *sq km*); chief town Bergen

Ruhr \'rúr\ 1 river 146 *mi* (235 *km*) W Germany flowing NW & W to the Rhine 2 industrial district in valley of the Ruhr

Ruis·lip North·wood \'rīs-ləp-'nórth-,wúd\ former urban district S England in Middlesex, now part of Hillingdon

Ru·me·lia \rü-'mēl-yə, -'mē-lē-ə\ a division of the old Ottoman Empire including Albania, Macedonia, & Thrace

Run·ny·mede \'rə-nē-,mēd\ meadow S England in Surrey at Egham on S bank of the Thames

Ru·pert \'rü-pərt\ river 380 *mi* (612 *km*) Canada in W Que. flowing W into James Bay

Rupert's Land PRINCE RUPERT'S LAND

Ru·se \'rü-(,)sä\ or **Turk Rus·chuk** \rús-'chük\ city NE Bulgaria on the Danube S of Bucharest *pop* 192,365

Rush·more, Mount \'rəsh-,mór, -,mór\ mountain 5600 *ft* (1707 *m*) W S.Dak. in Black Hills on which are carved faces of presidents

Washington, Jefferson, Lincoln, Theodore Roosevelt; a national memorial

Rus·sell Cave National Monument \\'rə-səl\\ reservation NE Ala. including cavern where remains of early pre-Columbian humans have been found

Rus·sell·ville \\'rə-səl-ˌvil\\ city NW *cen* Ark. *pop* 21,260

Rus·sia \\'rə-shə\\ *or Russ* **Ros·si·ya** \\rä-'sē-yə\\ **1** former empire E Europe & N Asia coextensive (except for Finland & Kars region) with the U.S.S.R. ✳ St. Petersburg **2** the U.S.S.R. **3** *or officially* **Russian Federation** independent country in E Europe & N Asia bordering on Arctic & Pacific oceans & on Baltic & Black seas; a constituent republic (**Russian Republic** *or* **Soviet Russia**) of the U.S.S.R. 1922–91 ✳ Moscow *area* 6,592,812 *sq mi* (17,075,383 *sq km*), *pop* 148,000,000 — **Rus·sian** \\'rə-shən\\ *adj or n*

Russian Turkestan region formerly comprising the republics of Soviet Central Asia

Rus·ton \\'rəs-tən\\ city N La. *pop* 20,027

Ruthenia — see ZAKARPATS'KA — **Ru·thene** \\rü-'thēn\\ *n* — **Ru·the·nian** \\-'thē-nyən, -nē-ən\\ *adj or n*

Rut·land \\'rət-lənd\\ *or* **Rut·land·shire** \\-lənd-ˌshir, -shər\\ former county E *cen* England ✳ Oakham

Ru·vu·ma *or Pg* **Ro·vu·ma** \\rü-'vü-mə\\ river *ab* 450 *mi* (724 *km*) SE Africa rising in S Tanzania & flowing E into Indian Ocean

Ru·wen·zo·ri \\ˌrü-ən-'zōr-ē, -'zór-\\ mountain group E *cen* Africa bet. Lake Albert & Lake Edward, on boundary bet. Uganda & Democratic Republic of the Congo — see STANLEY (Mount)

Rwan·da \\rü-'än-dä\\ *or formerly* **Ru·an·da** country E *cen* Africa; a republic ✳ Kigali *area* 10,169 *sq mi* (26,338 *sq km*), *pop* 7,584,000 — see RUANDA-URUNDI — **Rwan·dan** \\-dən\\ *adj or n* — **Rwan·dese** \\rü-ˌän-'dēz, -'dēs\\ *adj or n*

Rya·zan \\rē-ə-'zan, -'zän\\ city W *cen* Russia in Europe on Oka River SE of Moscow *pop* 529,000

Ry·binsk \\'ri-bən(t)sk\\ *or 1946–57* **Shcher·ba·kov** \\ˌsh(ch)er-bə-'kóf, -'kóv\\ *or 1984–89* **An·dro·pov** \\an-'drō-ˌpóf, -ˌpóv\\ city W *cen* Russia in Europe *pop* 252,000

Ryb·nik \\'rib-nik\\ commune S Poland *pop* 142,588

Rye \\'rī\\ borough SE England in E. Sussex *pop* 4293

Ryu·kyu Islands \\rē-'yü-(ˌ)kyü, -(ˌ)kü\\ islands W Pacific extending bet. Kyushu, Japan, & Taiwan; belonged to Japan 1895–1945; occupied by U.S. 1945; returned to Japan in 1953 (N islands) and 1972 (S islands) *area ab* 850 *sq mi* (2202 *sq km*), *pop* 1,222,458 — see AMAMI, OKINAWA, OSUMI ISLANDS, SAKISHIMA ISLANDS, TOKARA ISLANDS — **Ryu·kyu·an** \\ˌkyü-ən, -ˌkü-\\ *adj or n*

Rze·szow \\'zhe-ˌshüf\\ commune SE Poland *pop* 150,754

S

Saa·le \'zä-lə, 'sä-\ river 265 *mi* (426 *km*) E *cen* Germany rising in NE Bavaria in the Fichtelgebirge & flowing N into the Elbe

Saan·ich \'sa-nich\ municipality Canada in B.C. on SE Vancouver Is. N of Victoria *pop* 95,577

Saar \'sär, 'zär\ **1** *or* F **Sarre** \'sär\ river *ab* 150 *mi* (241 *km*) Europe flowing from Vosges Mountains in France N to the Moselle in W Germany **2** *or* **Saar·land** \'sär-,land, 'zär-\ region W Europe in basin of Saar River bet. France & Germany; once part of Lorraine, became part of Germany in 19th century; administered by League of Nations 1919–35; became a state of Germany 1935; came under control of France after World War II; to W. Germany by a plebiscite Jan. 1, 1957, as a state (**Saarland**) ✳ Saarbrücken *area* 991 *sq mi* (2567 *sq km*), *pop* 1,073,000

Saar·brück·en \zär-'brú-kən, sär-, -'brœ-\ city SW Germany ✳ of Saarland *pop* 192,030

Saaremaa — see SAREMA

Sa·ba 1 \'sä-bə, 'sä-bə\ island SE W. Indies in Leeward Islands; part of Netherlands Antilles ✳ The Bottom *area* 5 *sq mi* (13 *sq km*), *pop* 1119 **2** — see SHEBA

Sa·ba·dell \,sa-bə-'del, ,sä-\ commune NE Spain NW of Barcelona *pop* 184,460

Sa·bah \'sä-bə\ *or formerly* **North Borneo** state Malaysia in NE Borneo, formerly a Brit. colony ✳ Kota Kinabalu *area* 29,507 *sq mi* (76,423 *sq km*), *pop* 1,736,902

Sa·bar·ma·ti \,sä-bər-'mə-tē\ river *ab* 250 *mi* (402 *km*) W India flowing S into head of Gulf of Khambhat

Sa·bi \'sä-bē\ *or in Mozambique* **Sa·ve** \'sä-və\ river 400 *mi* (644 *km*) SE Africa rising in *cen* Zimbabwe & flowing E across S Mozambique to Indian Ocean

Sa·bine \sə-'bēn\ river E Tex. & W La. flowing SE through **Sabine Lake** (15 *mi or* 24 *km* long) & **Sabine Pass** (channel) into Gulf of Mexico

Sa·ble, Cape \'sä-bəl\ **1** cape at SW tip of Fla., southernmost point of U.S. mainland, at *ab* 25°7'N **2** headland E Canada on an islet S of **Cape Sable Island** (7 *mi or* 11 *km* long, at S end of N.S.)

Sable Island island Canada 20 *mi* (32 *km*) long in the Atlantic SE of Cape Canso; belongs to N.S.

Sab·ra·tha \'sa-brə-thə\ *or anc* **Sab·ra·ta** \-tə\ town Libya on the coast WNW of Tripoli *pop* 30,836

Sachsen — see SAXONY

Sa·co \'sò-(,)kō\ river 104 *mi* (167 *km*) E N.H. & SW Maine flowing SE into the Atlantic

Sac·ra·men·to \,sa-krə-'men-(,)tō\ **1** river 382 *mi* (615 *km*) N Calif. flowing S into Suisun Bay **2** city ✳ of Calif. on Sacramento River NE of San Francisco *pop* 369,365

Sacramento Mountains mountains S N.Mex. — see GUADALUPE MOUNTAINS, SIERRA BLANCA PEAK

Sa·fed Koh \sə-,fed-'kō\ mountain range E Afghanistan on Pakistan border; a S extension of the Hindu Kush

Sa·fi \'sa-fē\ city & port W Morocco SW of Casablanca *pop* 129,113

Sa·ga·mi Sea \sä-'gä-mē\ inlet of the Pacific Japan in *cen* Honshu SW of Tokyo Bay

Sa·ga·mi·ha·ra \sä-,gä-mē-'här-ä\ city Japan on Honshu *pop* 531,562

Saghalien — see SAKHALIN

Sag·i·naw \'sa-gə-,nò\ city E *cen* Mich. NNW of Flint *pop* 69,512

Saginaw Bay inlet of Lake Huron in E Mich.

Sa·gres \'sä-grish\ village SW Portugal E of Cape Saint Vincent

Sa·gua·ro National Monument \sə-'gwär-ō, -'wär-\ reservation SE Ariz. E of Tucson

Sag·ue·nay \'sa-gə-,nā, ,sa-gə-'\ river 105 *mi* (169 *km*) Canada in S Que. flowing from Lake Saint Jean E into the St. Lawrence

Sa·guia el Ham·ra \'sa-gyə-el-'ham-rə\ territory NW Africa, the N zone of Western Sahara

Sa·gun·to \sä-'gün-(,)tō\ *or formerly* **Mur·vie·dro** \,múr-vē-'ä-(,)drō, mür-'vyä-thrō\ commune E Spain NNE of Valencia *pop* 55,457

Sa·ha·ra \sə-'har-ə, -'her-, -'här-\ desert region N Africa N of the Sudan region extending from the Atlantic coast to Red Sea or, as sometimes considered, to the Nile — **Sa·ha·ran** \-ən\ *adj*

Sa·ha·ran·pur \sə-'här-ən-,púr\ city N India in NW Uttar Pradesh NNE of Delhi *pop* 374,945

Sa·hel \'sa·hil, sə-'hil\ the semidesert S fringe of the Sahara that stretches from Mauritania to Chad — **Sa·hel·ian** \sə-'hil-yən\ *adj*

Saida — see SIDON

Saigon — see HO CHI MINH CITY — **Sai·gon·ese** \,sī-gə-'nēz, -'nēs\ *adj or n*

Sai·maa \'sī-,mä\ group of lakes SE Finland of which **Lake Sai·maa** is the largest

Saint Al·bans \sānt-'ól-bənz\ borough SE England in Hertfordshire *pop* 122,400

Saint Al·bert \'al-bərt\ city Canada in *cen* Alta. *pop* 42,146

Saint Bar·thé·le·my \,san-bár-tā-lə-'mē\ island French West Indies in department of Guadeloupe; chief town Gustavia *pop* 2351

Saint Bernard — see GREAT SAINT BERNARD, LITTLE SAINT BERNARD

Saint–Bru·no–de–Mon·tar·ville \sānt-'brü-,nō-də-'män-tər-,vil, sənt-; ,saⁿ-brü-'nō-də-,mōⁿ-tär-'vēl\ town Canada in S Que. E of Montreal *pop* 23,849

Saint Cath·a·rines \'ka-th(ə-)rənz\ city Canada in SE Ont. NW of Niagara Falls on Welland Canal *pop* 129,300

Saint Charles \'chär(-ə)lz\ **1** city NE Ill. *pop* 22,501 **2** city E Mo. on the Missouri *pop* 54,555

Saint Clair, Lake \'klar, 'kler\ lake SE Mich. & SE Ont. *area* 460 *sq mi* (1196 *sq km*), connected by **Saint Clair River** (40 *mi or* 64 *km*) with Lake Huron & draining through Detroit River into Lake Erie

Saint Clair Shores city SE Mich. NE of Detroit *pop* 68,107

Saint–Cloud \sānt-'klaúd, sənt-; saⁿ-'klü\ commune France, WSW suburb of Paris *pop* 28,673

Saint Cloud \'klaúd\ city *cen* Minn. on the Mississippi *pop* 48,812

Saint Croix \sānt-'krói, sənt-\ **1** river 129 *mi* (208 *km*) Canada & U.S. bet. N.B. & Maine **2** river 164 *mi* (264 *km*) NW Wis. & E Minn. flowing into the Mississippi **3** *or* **San·ta Cruz** \,san-tə-'krüz\ island W. Indies, largest of the Virgin Islands of the U.S.

area 80 *sq mi* (208 *sq km*) *pop* 50,139; chief town Christiansted —
Cru·zan \krü-'zan\ *adj or n*

Saint Croix Island International Historic Site reservation E
Maine on Canada border on island in St. Croix River

Saint–Cyr–l'Ecole \saⁿ'sir-lā-'kȯl\ commune N France W of Versailles *pop* 17,795

Saint–De·nis \,saⁿ(t)-də-'nē\ **1** commune N France NNE of Paris
pop 90,806 **2** commune ✳ of Réunion Is. *pop* 100,926

Sainte–Foy \sänt-'fȯi, sənt-; saⁿt-'fwä, saⁿ-tə-\ town Canada in SE
Que. SW of Quebec city *pop* 71,133

Saint Eli·as, Mount \i-'lī-əs\ mountain 18,008 *ft* (5489 *m*) on
Alaska-Canada boundary in St. Elias Range

Saint Elias Range mountain range of the Coast Ranges SW Yukon
Territory & E Alaska — see LOGAN (Mount)

Sainte–Thé·rèse \,sänt-tə-'rāz, ,saⁿt-tā-'rez\ town Canada in S Que.
pop 24,158

Saint–Étienne \saⁿ-tā-'tyen\ city SE *cen* France *pop* 201,569

Saint–Eus·tache \,saⁿ-tyü-'stash\ town Canada in S Que. *pop*
37,278

Saint Eu·sta·ti·us \,sänt-yü-'stā-sh(ē-)əs\ *or* **Sta·tia** \'stā-shə\ island W. Indies in Netherlands Antilles NW of St. Kitts *area* 7 *sq mi*
(18 *sq km*) *pop* 1715

Saint Fran·cis \sänt-'fran(t)-səs, sənt-\ **1** river 425 *mi* (684 *km*) SE
Mo. & E Ark. flowing S into the Mississippi **2** *or* **Saint Fran·çois** \saⁿ-'frä⁀-swä\ river 165 *mi* (266 *km*) Canada in S Que. flowing NW into the St. Lawrence

Saint Francis, Lake expansion of St. Lawrence River Canada
above Valleyfield, Que.

Saint Gall \sänt-'gȯl, sənt-; saⁿ-'gäl\ *or G* **Sankt Gal·len** \zäŋkt-'gäl-ən\ **1** canton NE Switzerland *area* 778 *sq mi* (2015 *sq km*),
pop 416,578 **2** commune, its ✳ *pop* 73,889

Saint George \'jȯrj\ city SW corner of Utah *pop* 28,502

Saint George's \'jȯr-jəz\ town ✳ of Grenada *pop* 29,400

Saint George's Channel strait British Isles bet. SW Wales & Ireland

Saint–Ger·main \,saⁿ-zhər-'maⁿ\ *or* **Saint–Ger·main–en–Laye**
\-,ma°-,ä°-'lā\ commune N France WNW of Paris *pop* 41,710

Saint–Gilles \saⁿ-'zhēl\ *or* **Flem Sint–Gil·lis** \sint-'gi-ləs, -'ki-\
commune *cen* Belgium near Brussels *pop* 42,684

Saint Gott·hard \sänt-'gä-tərd, sənt-, 'gät-hərd; ,saⁿ-gə-'tär\ **1**
mountains Switzerland in Lepontine Alps bet. Uri & Ticino cantons **2** mountain pass 6916 *ft* (2108 *m*) in St. Gotthard Range

Saint He·le·na \sänt-ᵊl-'ē-nə, ,sänt-hə-'lē-\ island S Atlantic; a Brit.
colony ✳ Jamestown *area* 47 *sq mi* (122 *sq km*) *pop* 5644

Saint Hel·ens \sänt-'he-lənz, sənt-\ borough NW England in Merseyside ENE of Liverpool *pop* 98,769

Saint Helens, Mount volcanic peak 8366 *ft* (2550 *m*) SW Wash. in
Cascades; in **Mount Saint Helens National Volcanic Monument**

Saint Hel·ier \'hel-yər\ town Channel Islands ✳ of Jersey *pop*
28,123

Saint–Hu·bert \sänt-'hyü-bərt, sənt-; ,saⁿ-yü-'ber\ town Canada in
S Que. E of Montreal *pop* 74,027

Saint–Hy·a·cinthe \sänt-'hī-ə-(‚)sin(t)th, sənt-; ‚sant-yə-'sant\ town Canada in S Que. E of Montreal *pop* 39,292

Saint–Jean, Lake *or* **Lac Saint–Jean** \läk-saⁿ-zhäⁿ\ lake Canada in S Que. draining through the Saguenay to the St. Lawrence *area* 414 *sq mi* (1072 *sq km*)

Saint–Jean–de–Luz \saⁿ-‚zhäⁿ-də-'lüz, -'lüēz\ town SW France on Bay of Biscay SW of Biarritz *pop* 13,181

Saint–Jean–sur–Ri·che·lieu \saⁿ-'zhäⁿ-sùr-'ri-shə-‚lü, -‚rē-shəl-'yœ\ town Canada in S Que. SE of Montreal *pop* 37,607

Saint–Jé·rôme \‚saⁿ-zhā-'rōm, ‚sänt-jə-'rōm\ town Canada in S Que. NW of Montreal *pop* 23,384

Saint John \sänt-'jän, sənt-\ **1** river 418 *mi* (673 *km*) NE U.S. & SE Canada flowing from N Maine into Bay of Fundy in N.B. **2** city & port Canada in S N.B. at mouth of the St. John *pop* 74,969

Saint John Island island W. Indies, one of the Virgin Islands of the U.S. *area* 20 *sq mi* (52 *sq km*), *pop* 3504

Saint Johns \sänt-'jänz, sənt-\ river 285 *mi* (459 *km*) NE Fla. flowing N & E into the Atlantic

Saint John's \sänt-'jänz, sənt-\ **1** city Brit. West Indies ✱ of Antigua and Barbuda on Antigua Is. **2** city & port Canada ✱ of Nfld. *pop* 95,770

Saint Jo·seph \'jō-zəf *also* -səf\ city NW Mo. *pop* 71,852

Saint Kitts \'kits\ *or* **Saint Chris·to·pher** \'kris-tə-fər\ island Brit. West Indies in the Leewards; chief town Basseterre *area* 68 *sq mi* (177 *sq km*); with Nevis, forms independent state of **Saint Kitts–Nevis** (✱ Basseterre *area* 104 *sq mi or* 269 *sq km, pop* 41,800) — **Kit·ti·tian** \kə-'ti-shən\ *n*

Saint–Lau·rent \‚saⁿ-lȯ-'räⁿ, ‚sant-lȯ-'rent\ town Canada in S Que. on Montreal Is. *pop* 72,402

Saint Law·rence \sänt-'lȯr-ən(t)s, sənt-, -'lär-\ river 760 *mi* (1223 *km*) E Canada in Ont. & Que. bordering on the U.S. in N.Y., flowing from Lake Ontario NE into the Atlantic, & forming at its mouth a wide bay (the **Gulf of Saint Lawrence**)

Saint Lawrence, Lake expansion of St. Lawrence River Canada & U.S. WSW of Cornwall, Ont.

Saint Lawrence Island island 95 *mi* (153 *km*) long W Alaska in N Bering Sea

Saint Lawrence Islands National Park reservation SE Canada in SE Ont.

Saint Lawrence Seaway waterway Canada & U.S. in & along the St. Lawrence River bet. Lake Ontario & Montreal

Saint–Lé·o·nard \‚saⁿ-‚lā-ə-'när; sänt-'le-nərd, sənt-\ town Canada in S Que. N of Montreal *pop* 73,120

Saint–Lô \sänt-'lō, sənt-; saⁿ-'lō\ commune NW France *pop* 22,819

Saint–Lou·is \‚saⁿ-lü-'ē\ **1** city & port Senegal on island at mouth of Senegal River; formerly ✱ of Senegal *pop* 125,717 **2** city & port Réunion

Saint Lou·is \sänt-'lü-əs, sənt-\ **1** river 160 *mi* (257 *km*) NE Minn. flowing to W tip of Lake Superior **2** city E Mo. on the Mississippi *pop* 396,685 — **Saint Lou·i·san** \'lü-ə-sən\ *n* — **Saint Lou·i·sian** \'lü-ə-zhən, -shən\ *n*

Saint Lou·is, Lake \sänt-'lü-ē, sənt-\ expansion of St. Lawrence River Canada above Lachine Rapids

Saint Lou·is Park \'lü-əs\ city SE Minn. *pop* 43,787

Saint Lu·cia \sänt-'lü-shə, sȯnt-\ island Brit. West Indies in the Windwards S of Martinique; an independent member of the Commonwealth of Nations since 1979 ✻ Castries *area* 238 *sq mi* (616 *sq km*), *pop* 148,183

Saint–Ma·lo \saⁿ-mə-'lō\ city & port NW France in Brittany on island in Gulf of Saint-Malo *pop* 49,274

Saint–Malo, Gulf of arm of English Channel NW France bet. Cotentin Peninsula & Brittany

Saint Mar·tin \sänt-'mär-tᵊn, sȯnt-\ *or D* **Sint Maar·ten** \sint-\ island W. Indies in the N Leewards; divided bet. France & Netherlands *area* 33 *sq mi* (86 *sq km*)

Saint Mar·ys \'mer-ēz, 'mar-ēz, 'mā-rēz\ **1** river 175 *mi* (282 *km*) on Fla.-Ga. border flowing from Okefenokee Swamp to the Atlantic **2** river *ab* 70 *mi* (115 *km*) bet. Canada & U.S. in Ont. & Upper Peninsula of Mich. flowing from Lake Superior into Lake Huron; descends 20 *ft* (6.1 *m*) in a mile at **Saint Marys Falls** — see SAULT SAINTE MARIE CANALS

Saint–Maur–des–Fos·sés \saⁿ-ˌmȯr-dā-fō-'sā\ commune N France SE of Paris on the Marne *pop* 77,492

Saint Mau·rice \'mȯr-əs, sȯnt-, -'mär-; ˌsaⁿ-mə-'rēs\ river 325 *mi* (523 *km*) Canada in S Que. flowing S into the St. Lawrence

Saint–Mi·hiel \saⁿ-mē-'yel\ town NE France on the Meuse *pop* 5435

Saint Mo·ritz \ˌsänt-mə-'rits, ˌsaⁿ-mə-\ *or G* **Sankt Mo·ritz** \zäŋkt-mə-'rits\ town E Switzerland in Graubünden canton SSE of Chur *pop* 5900

Saint–Na·zaire \ˌsaⁿ-nə-'zar, -'zer\ commune & port NW France at mouth of the Loire *pop* 66,087

Sain·tonge \saⁿ-'tōⁿzh\ region & former province of France on Bay of Biscay N of the Gironde ✻ Saintes

Saint–Ouen \saⁿ-'twaⁿ\ commune France, N suburb of Paris *pop* 42,611

Saint Pan·cras \sänt-'paŋ-krəs, sȯnt-\ former metropolitan borough NW London, England, now part of Camden

Saint Paul \'pȯl\ city E Minn., its ✻ *pop* 272,235 — **Saint Paul·ite** \'pȯ-ˌlīt\ *n*

Saint Pe·ter, Lake \sänt-'pē-tər, sȯnt-\ expansion of St. Lawrence River Canada bet. Sorel & Trois-Rivières, Que.

Saint Peter and Saint Paul Rocks *or Pg* **Pe·ne·dos de São Pe·dro e São Pau·lo** \pə-'nä-düs-dē-ˌsaủⁿ-'päd-rü-ē-ˌsaủⁿ-'paủ-lü\ rocky islets in the Atlantic 600 *mi* (966 *km*) NE of Natal, Brazil; belong to Brazil

Saint Peter Port town Channel Islands ✻ of Guernsey *pop* 16,648

Saint Pe·ters \'pē-tərz\ city E Mo. WNW of St. Louis *pop* 45,779

Saint Pe·ters·burg \'pē-tərz-ˌbərg\ **1** city W Fla. on Pinellas Peninsula SW of Tampa *pop* 238,629 **2** *or 1914–24* **Pet·ro·grad** \'pe-trə-ˌgrad, -ˌgrät\ *or 1924–91* **Le·nin·grad** \'le-nən-ˌgrad, -ˌgrät\ city W Russia in Europe, at E end of Gulf of Finland; ✻ of Russian Empire 1712–1917, *pop* 4,952,000

Saint Pierre and Mi·que·lon \saⁿ-'pyer-ən(d)-ˌmē-kə-'lōⁿ\ French islands in the Atlantic off S Newfoundland ✻ St. Pierre, *area* 93 *sq mi* (242 *sq km*), *pop* 6400

Saint–Quen·tin \sänt-'kwen-tᵊn, sȯnt-, *F* saⁿ-käⁿ-'taⁿ\ commune N France on the Somme NW of Laon *pop* 62,085

Saint Si·mons Island \sānt-'sī-mənz, sənt-\ island SE Ga. in the Atlantic

Saint Thom·as \'tä-məs\ **1** island W. Indies, one of the Virgin Islands of the U.S. *area* 32 *sq mi* (83 *sq km*) **2** — see CHARLOTTE AMALIE **3** city Canada in SE Ont. S of London *pop* 29,990

Saint-Tro·pez \,saⁿ-trō-'pā\ commune SE France on the Mediterranean SW of Cannes *pop* 4484

Saint Vin·cent \sānt-'vin(t)-sənt, sənt-\ island Brit. West Indies in *cen* Windwards; with N Grenadines became independent 1979 as **Saint Vincent and the Grenadines** ✳ Kingstown *area* 150 *sq mi* (390 *sq km*), *pop* 109,000 — **Vin·cen·tian** \vin-'sen(t)-shən\ *adj or n*

Saint Vincent, Cape *or Pg* **Ca·bo de São Vi·cen·te** \'kä-bü-dē-,saůⁿ-vē-'sā²-tē\ cape SW Portugal

Saint Vincent, Gulf inlet of Indian Ocean Australia in S. Australia E of Yorke Peninsula

Sai·pan \sī-'pan, -'pän, 'sī-,\ island W Pacific in S *cen* Marianas *area* 70 *sq mi* (182 *sq km*), *pop* 38,896 — **Sai·pa·nese** \,sī-pə-'nēz, -'nēs\ *adj or n*

Sa·is \'sā-is\ ancient city Egypt in Nile delta

Sa·ja·ma \sä-'hä-mä\ mountain 21,391 *ft* (6520 *m*) W Bolivia near Chilean boundary

Sa·kai \(,)sä-'kī\ city Japan in S Honshu on Osaka Bay *pop* 807,859

Sak·a·ka·wea, Lake \,sa-kə-kə-'wē-ə\ reservoir *ab* 200 *mi* (322 *km*) long W N.Dak. formed in the Missouri by the Garrison Dam

Sa·kar·ya \sə-'kär-yə\ river *ab* 500 *mi* (804 *km*) NW Turkey in Asia flowing into the Black Sea E of the Bosporus

Sa·kha \'sä-kə\ *or* **Ya·ku·tia** \yə-'kü-sh(ē-)ə\ autonomous republic E *cen* Russia in Asia ✳ Yakutsk *area* 1,198,146 *sq mi* (3,103,198 *sq km*), *pop* 1,093,000

Sa·kha·lin \'sa-kə-,lēn, -,lon; ,sä-kä-'lēn\ *or formerly* **Sa·gha·lien** \'sa-gə-,lēn, ,sa-gə-'\ *or Jp* **Ka·ra·fu·to** \kä-'rä-fə-,tō\ island SE Russia in Asia in Sea of Okhotsk N of Hokkaido; formerly (1905–45) divided bet. Russia & Japan *area more than* 28,500 *sq mi* (73,815 *sq km*)

Sa·ki·shi·ma Islands \,sä-kē-'shē-mä, sä-'kē-shē-mä\ island group Japan in S Ryukyus off E coast of N Taiwan; occupied 1945–72 by the U.S. *area* 343 *sq mi* (892 *sq km*)

Sakkara — see SAQQĀRA

Sa·kon·net River \sə-'kä-nət\ inlet of the Atlantic SE R.I., E of Aquidneck Is.

Sal·a·ber·ry–de–Val·ley·field \'sa-lə-,ber-ē-də-'va-lē-,fēld\ *or* **Valleyfield** town Canada in S Que. SW of Montreal *pop* 27,598

Sa·la·do \sə-'lä-(,)dō, sä-'lä-thō\ **1** *or in upper course* **Ju·ra·men·to** \,hü-rä-'men-(,)tō\ river 1120 *mi* (1802 *km*) N Argentina flowing from the Andes SE into the Paraná **2** *or in upper course* **Des·agua·de·ro** \,thä,sä-gwä-'ther-(,)ō\ river 850 *mi* (1368 *km*) W *cen* Argentina flowing S into the Colorado

Sal·a·man·ca \,sa-lə-'maŋ-kə, ,sä-lä-'mäŋ-kä\ **1** province W Spain *area* 4763 *sq mi* (12,336 *sq km*), *pop* 357,801 **2** commune, its ✳, WNW of Madrid *pop* 162,888

Sal·a·maua \sä-lä-'maů-ä\ town Papua New Guinea on Huon Gulf

Salambria — see PENEUS

Sal·a·mis \'sa-lə-məs\ **1** ancient city Cyprus on E coast **2** island Greece in Saronic Gulf off Attica

Sal·da·nha Bay \sal-'da-nyə\ inlet of the Atlantic on W coast of Western Cape province, Republic of South Africa

Sa·lé \sa-'lā\ *or formerly* **Sal·lee** \'sa-lē\ city & port NW Morocco, N suburb of Rabat *pop* 289,391

Sa·lem \'sā-ləm\ **1** city & port NE Mass. NE of Lynn *pop* 38,091 **2** town SE N.H. E of Nashua *pop* 25,746 **3** city ✳ of Oreg. on Willamette river *pop* 107,786 **4** town W *cen* Va. WNW of Roanoke *pop* 23,756 **5** city S India in N Tamil Nadu SW of Madras *pop* 366,712

Sa·ler·no \sə-'lər-(,)nō, sä-'ler-\ commune & port S Italy on **Gulf of Salerno** (inlet of Tyrrhenian Sea) ESE of Naples *pop* 152,159 — **Sa·ler·ni·tan** \-'lər-nə-tən, -'ler-\ *adj or n*

Sal·ford \'sȯl-fərd\ urban area NW England in Greater Manchester *pop* 98,024

Sa·li·na \sə-'lī-nə\ city *cen* Kans. on Smoky Hill River *pop* 42,303

Sa·li·nas \sə-'lē-nəs\ **1** river 150 *mi* (241 *km*) W Calif. flowing NW into Monterey Bay **2** city W Calif. near Monterey Bay *pop* 108,777

Salinas National Monument reservation *cen* N. Mex. containing archaeological ruins

Salis·bury \'sȯlz-,ber-ē, -b(ə-)rē, *US also* 'salz-\ **1** city SE Md. *pop* 20,592 **2** city W *cen* N.C. SSW of Winston-Salem *pop* 23,087 **3** — see HARARE **4** city & borough S England in Wiltshire on the Avon *pop* 35,355

Salisbury Plain plateau S England in Wiltshire NW of Salisbury

Salm·on \'sa-mən\ river 420 *mi* (676 *km*) *cen* Idaho flowing into Snake River

Salmon River Mountains mountains *cen* Idaho; many peaks over 9000 *ft* (2743 *m*)

Salonika — see THESSALONÍKI

Sa·lon·i·ka, Gulf of \sə-'lä-ni-kə\ *or Gk* **Ther·ma·i·kós Kól·pos** \ther-,mä-ē-'kós-'kól-,pós\ arm of Aegean Sea N Greece W of Chalcidice

Sal·op — see SHROPSHIRE — **Sa·lo·pi·an** \sə-'lō-pē-ən\ *adj or n*

Salt \'sȯlt\ **1** river 200 *mi* (322 *km*) Ariz. flowing W into the Gila **2** river 100 *mi* (161 *km*) N *cen* Ky. flowing into Ohio River **3** river 200 *mi* (322 *km*) NE Mo. flowing SE into Mississippi River

Sal·ta \'säl-tä\ city NW Argentina *pop* 373,857

Sal·til·lo \säl-'tē-(,)yō, sal-\ city NE Mexico ✳ of Coahuila *pop* 440,845

Salt Lake City city N Utah, its ✳ *pop* 159,936

Sal·to \'säl-(,)tō\ city & port NW Uruguay on Uruguay River *pop* 74,881

Sal·ton Sea \'sȯl-tᵊn\ saline lake *ab* 235 *ft* (72 *m*) below sea level SE Calif. at N end of Imperial Valley formed by diversion of water from Colorado River into depression called **Salton Sink**

Salt Sea — see DEAD SEA

Sa·lu·da \sə-'lü-də\ river 200 *mi* (322 *km*) W *cen* S.C. flowing SE to unite with Broad River forming the Congaree

Sal·va·dor \'sal-və-ˌdȯr, ˌsal-və-'\ **1** EL SALVADOR **2** *or formerly*
São Salvador \saúⁿ-\ *or* **Ba·hia** \bä-'ē-ə\ port NE Brazil * of Ba-
hia *pop* 2,000,000 — **Sal·va·dor·an** \ˌsal-və-'dȯr-ən, -'dōr-\ *adj or
n* — **Sal·va·dor·ean** *or* **Sal·va·dor·ian** \-ē-ən\ *adj or n*

Sal·ween \'sal-ˌwēn\ river *ab* 1500 mi (2415 km) SE Asia flowing
from Tibet S into Gulf of Martaban in Myanmar

Salz·burg \'sōlz-ˌbərg, 'sälz-, 'salz-, G 'zälts-ˌbùrk\ city W
Austria ESE of Munich, Germany *pop* 143,971

Salz·git·ter \'zälts-ˌgi-tər\ *or formerly* **Wa·ten·stedt–Salzgitter**
\'vä-t°n-ˌshtet-, -ˌstet-\ city N *cen* Germany SW of Brunswick *pop*
115,381

Salz·kam·mer·gut \'zälts-ˌkä-mər-ˌgüt\ district N Austria E of
Salzburg; chief town Bad Ischl

Samanala — SEE ADAM'S PEAK

Sa·mar \'sä-ˌmär\ island *cen* Philippines in the Visayans N of Leyte
area 5050 *sq mi* (13,130 *sq km*)

Sa·ma·ra \sə-'mär-ə\ *or* 1935–91 **Kuy·by·shev** \'kwē-bə-ˌshef, 'kü-
ē-bə-, -ˌshev\ city E Russia in Europe in valley of the Volga *pop*
1,239,000

Sa·mar·ia \sə-'mer-ē-ə, -'mar-\ **1** district of ancient Palestine W of
the Jordan bet. Galilee & Judaea **2** city, its * & * of the Northern
Kingdom (Israel); rebuilt by Herod the Great & renamed **Se·bas·te**
\sə-'bas-tē\; site in Jordan at modern village of Sebastye — **Sa·**
mar·i·tan \-ə-tən\ *adj or n*

Sam·a·rin·da \ˌsa-mə-'rin-də\ city Indonesia in E Borneo *pop*
407,339

Sa·mar·qand *or* **Sam·ar·kand** \'sa-mər-ˌkand\ *or anc* **Mar·a·**
can·da \ˌmar-ə-'kan-də\ city E Uzbekistan *pop* 370,500

Sam·ni·um \'sam-nē-əm\ ancient country S *cen* Italy — **Sam·nite**
\-ˌnīt\ *adj or n*

Sa·moa \sə-'mō-ə\ *or formerly* **Navigators Islands** islands SW *cen*
Pacific N of Tonga Islands; divided at long. 171° W into American,
or Eastern, Samoa & Western Samoa *area* 1209 *sq mi* (3143 *sq km*)
— **Sa·mo·an** \sə-'mō-ən\ *adj or n*

Sa·mos \'sā-ˌmäs, 'sä-ˌmȯs\ island Greece in the Aegean off coast of
Turkey N of the Dodecanese *area* 184 *sq mi* (477 *sq km*) *pop*
41,850 — **Sa·mi·an** \'sā-mē-ən\ *adj or n*

Sam·o·thrace \'sa-mə-ˌthrās\ *or NGk* **Sa·mo·thrá·ki** \ˌsä-mō-
'thrä-kē\ island Greece in the NE Aegean — **Sam·o·thra·cian** \ˌsa-
mə-'thrā-shən\ *adj or n*

Sam·sun \säm-'sün\ city & port N Turkey on Black Sea NW of Ankara *pop* 303,979

San·aa *or* **Sana** \sa-'nä, 'sa-ˌnä\ city S Arabia * of Yemen & formerly * of Yemen Arab Republic *pop* 125,093

Sa·nan·daj \ˌsä-nən-'däj\ city NW Iran *pop* 204,537

San An·dre·as Fault \ˌsan-an-'drā-əs\ zone of faults Calif. extending from N coast toward head of Gulf of California

San An·ge·lo \san-'an-jə-ˌlō\ city W *cen* Tex. *pop* 84,474

San An·to·nio \ˌsan-ən-'tō-nē-ˌō\ **1** river *ab* 200 mi (322 km) S
Tex. flowing SE into Gulf of Mexico **2** city S Tex. on San Antonio
River *pop* 935,933 — **San An·to·ni·an** \-nē-ən\ *n*

San Be·ni·to \ˌsan-bə-'nē-(ˌ)tō\ city S Tex. NW of Brownsville *pop*
20,125

San Ber·nar·di·no \,san-,bər-nə(r)-'dē-(,)nō\ city SW Calif. E of Los Angeles *pop* 164,164

San Bernardino Mountains mountains S Calif. S of Mojave Desert; highest **San Gor·go·nio Mountain** \,san-gór-'gō-nē-(,)ō\ 11,502 *ft* (3506 *m*)

San Bru·no \san-'brü-(,)nō\ city W Calif. S of San Francisco *pop* 38,961

San Buenaventura — see VENTURA

San Car·los \san-'kär-lōs\ city W Calif. SE of San Francisco *pop* 26,167

San Carlos de Bariloche — see BARILOCHE

San Cle·men·te \,san-klə-'men-tē\ city SW Calif. NW of San Diego *pop* 41,100

San Clemente Island island S Calif., southernmost of Channel Islands

San Cris·to·bal \,san-kri-'stō-bəl\ island W Pacific in SE Solomons

San Cris·tó·bal \,san-kri-'stō-bəl\ **1** *or* **Chatham Island** island Ecuador in the Galápagos *pop* 1404 **2** city W Venezuela SSW of Lake Maracaibo *pop* 220,697

Sanc·ti Spí·ri·tus \,säŋk-tē-'spē-rē-,tüs\ city W *cen* Cuba SE of Santa Clara *pop* 85,499

San·cy, Puy de \,pwē-də-,sän̄-'sē\ mountain 6188 *ft* (1886 *m*) S *cen* France; highest in the Monts Dore & Auvergne Mountains

San·da·kan \san-'dä-kən\ city & port Malaysia in Sabah on Sulu Sea; former ✳ of N. Borneo *pop* 118,417

Sand·hurst \'sand-,hərst\ village S England in E Berkshire SE of Reading *pop* 6445

San·dia Mountains \san-'dē-ə\ mountains N *cen* N.Mex. E of Albuquerque; highest **Sandia Crest** 10,678 *ft* (3255 *m*)

San Di·e·go \,san-dē-'ā-(,)gō\ city & port SW Calif. on **San Diego Bay** (inlet of the Pacific) *pop* 1,110,549 — **San Di·e·gan** \-gən\ *adj or n*

San Di·mas \san-'dē-məs\ city SW Calif. NW of Pomona *pop* 32,397

San Domingo **1** — see HISPANIOLA **2** — see DOMINICAN REPUBLIC **3** — see SANTO DOMINGO

San·dring·ham \'san-driŋ-əm\ village E England in NW Norfolk

San·dus·ky \sən-'dəs-kē, san-\ **1** river 150 *mi* (241 *km*) N Ohio flowing N into Lake Erie **2** city N Ohio at entrance to **Sandusky Bay** (inlet of Lake Erie) *pop* 29,764

Sand·wich \'san(d)-(,)wich\ town SE England in Kent on Stour River *pop* 4227

Sandwich Islands — see HAWAII

Sandy \'san-dē\ city N Utah S of Salt Lake City *pop* 75,058

Sandy Hook peninsula E N.J. extending N toward New York Bay

San Fer·nan·do \,san-fər-'nan-(,)dō\ **1** valley S Calif. NW of Los Angeles; partly within Los Angeles city limits **2** city SW Calif. in San Fernando Valley *pop* 22,580

San·ford \'san-fərd\ **1** city NE Fla. *pop* 32,387 **2** town SW Maine *pop* 20,463

Sanford, Mount mountain 16,237 *ft* (4949 *m*) S Alaska at W end of Wrangell Mountains

San Fran·cis·co \san-frən-'sis-(,)kō\ city & port W Calif. on **San Francisco Bay** & the Pacific *pop* 723,959 — **San Fran·cis·can** \-kən\ *adj or n*

San Francisco Peaks mountain N *cen* Ariz. N of Flagstaff; includes three peaks: Mt. Humphreys 12,633 *ft* (3851 *m*), highest point in the state; Mt. Agassiz 12,340 *ft* (3761 *m*); & Mt. Fremont 11,940 *ft* (3639 *m*)

San Ga·bri·el \san-'gā-brē-əl\ city SW Calif. S of Pasadena *pop* 37,120

San Gabriel Mountains mountains S Calif. SW of Mojave Desert & NE of Los Angeles; highest San Antonio Peak 10,080 *ft* (3072 *m*)

San·ga·mon \'saŋ-gə-mən\ river *ab* 250 *mi* (400 *km*) *cen* Ill. flowing SW & W into Illinois River

San·gay \säŋ-'gī\ volcano 17,159 *ft* (5230 *m*) SE *cen* Ecuador

San·gi·he Islands \säŋ-gē-'ā\ *or* **San·gi Islands** \'säŋ-gē\ islands Indonesia NE of Sulawesi *pop* 194,253; largest of the group **Sangihe** *or* **Sangi**

San Gi·mi·gna·no \,sän-,jē-mē-'nyä-(,)nō\ commune *cen* Italy NW of Siena

San·gre de Cris·to Mountains \,saŋ-grē-də-'kris-(,)tō\ mountains S Colo. & N N.Mex. in Rocky Mountains — see BLANCA PEAK

San·i·bel Island \'sa-nə-bəl, -,bel\ island SW Fla. SW of Fort Myers

San Il·de·fon·so \,san-,il-də-'fän(t)-(,)sō, ,sän-,ēl-dā-'fòn-sō\ *or* **La Gran·ja** \lä-'grän-(,)hä\ commune *cen* Spain SE of Segovia

San Isi·dro \,san-ə-'sē-(,)drō\ city E Argentina *pop* 299,022

San Ja·cin·to \,san-jə-'sin-tō\ river SE Tex. flowing S into Galveston Bay

San Joa·quin \,san-wä-'kēn, -wò-\ river 350 *mi* (563 *km*) *cen* Calif. flowing from the Sierra Nevada SW & then NW into Sacramento River

San Jo·se \,san-(h)ō-'zā\ city W Calif. SSE of San Francisco *pop* 782,248

San Jo·sé \,säŋ-hō-'sā, ,san-(h)ō-'zā\ city *cen* Costa Rica, its ✳ *pop* 289,456

San Juan \san-'wän, ,sän-'hwän\ **1** river 360 *mi* (579 *km*) SW Colo., NW N.Mex., & SE Utah flowing W into Colorado River **2** city & port NE Puerto Rico, its ✳ *pop* 437,745 **3** city W Argentina N of Mendoza *pop* 106,564 — **San Jua·ne·ro** \,san-wä-'ner-(,)ō, -'hwä-\ *n*

San Juan Cap·is·tra·no \,ka-pə-'strä-(,)nō\ city SW Calif. SE of Los Angeles *pop* 26,183

San Juan Hill hill E Cuba near Santiago de Cuba

San Juan Islands islands NW Wash. bet. Vancouver Is. & the mainland

San Juan Mountains mountains SW Colo. in the Rocky Mountains — see UNCOMPAHGRE PEAK

Sankt An·ton am Arl·berg \zäŋkt-'än-,tōn-,äm-'är(-ə)l-,bərg, -,berk\ village W Austria in Tirol W of Innsbruck

Sankt Gallen — see SAINT GALL

Sankt Moritz — see SAINT MORITZ

San Le·an·dro \,san-lē-'an-(,)drō\ city W Calif. SE of Oakland *pop* 68,223

San Lo·ren·zo \,sän-lō-'ren-(,)zō\ city S Paraguay E of Asunción

San Lu·cas, Cape \san-ˈlü-kəs\ headland NW Mexico, the S extremity of Baja California

San Lu·is \san-ˈlü-əs\ valley S Colo. & N N.Mex. along the upper Rio Grande bet. the San Juan & Sangre de Cristo mountains

San Lu·is Obis·po \san-ˌlü-əs-ə-ˈbis-(ˌ)pō\ city W Calif. NW of Santa Barbara *pop* 41,958

San Lu·is Po·to·sí \san-lü̇-ēs-pō-tə-ˈsē\ 1 state *cen* Mexico *area* 24,266 *sq mi* (62,849 *sq km*), *pop* 2,003,187 2 city, its ✳, NE of León *pop* 525,819

San Mar·cos \san-ˈmär-kəs, -kōs\ 1 city SW Calif. NNW of San Diego *pop* 38,974 2 city S Tex. NE of San Antonio *pop* 28,743

San Ma·ri·no \san-mə-ˈrē-(ˌ)nō\ 1 country S Europe on Italian Peninsula SSW of Rimini; a republic *area* 24 *sq mi* (62 *sq km*), *pop* 24,000 2 town, its ✳ — **Sam·ma·ri·nese** \ˌsa(m)-ˌmar-ə-ˈnēz, -ˈnēs\ *n* — **San Mar·i·nese** \ˌsan-ˌmar-\ *adj or n*

San Mar·tín \san-mär-ˈtēn\ *or* **Ge·ne·ral San Martín** \hä-nā-ˈräl\ city E Argentina, NW suburb of Buenos Aires *pop* 407,506

San Ma·teo \ˌsan-mə-ˈtā-(ˌ)ō\ city W Calif. SSE of San Francisco *pop* 85,486

San Mi·guel de Tu·cu·mán \ˌsän-mē-ˈgel-dā-ˌtü-kü-ˈmän\ *or* **Tucumán** city NW Argentina at foot of E ranges of the Andes *pop* 473,014

San Pab·lo \san-ˈpa-(ˌ)blō\ city W Calif. N of Oakland on **San Pablo Bay** (N extension of San Francisco Bay) *pop* 25,158

San Pe·dro Channel \san-ˈpē-(ˌ)drō, -ˈpā-\ channel SW Calif. bet. Santa Catalina Is. & the mainland

San Pe·dro Su·la \ˌsän-ˈpā-(ˌ)thrō-ˈsü-lä\ city NW Honduras *pop* 300,400

San Ra·fael \ˌsan-rə-ˈfel\ city W Calif. N of San Francisco on San Pablo Bay *pop* 48,404

San Ra·mon \ˌsan-rə-ˈmōn\ city W Calif. E of Oakland *pop* 35,303

San Re·mo \sän-ˈrā-(ˌ)mō, san-ˈrē-\ city & port NW Italy in Liguria near French border *pop* 55,786

San Sal·va·dor \san-ˈsal-və-ˌdȯr, ˌsän-ˈsäl-vä-ˌthȯr\ 1 island *cen* Bahamas *area* 60 *sq mi* (156 *sq km*) 2 city W *cen* El Salvador, its ✳ *pop* 349,333

San Stefano — see YESILKOY

San·ta Ana \ˌsan-tə-ˈa-nə, ˌsän-tä-ˈä-nä\ 1 city SW Calif. ESE of Long Beach *pop* 293,742 2 city NW El Salvador NW of San Salvador *pop* 168,047

Santa Bar·ba·ra \ˈbär-b(ə-)rə\ city S Calif. *pop* 85,571

Santa Barbara Channel channel SW Calif. bet. the N Channel Islands & mainland

Santa Barbara Islands — see CHANNEL ISLANDS

Santa Catalina — see CATALINA

San·ta Ca·ta·ri·na \ˌsan-tə-ˌka-tə-ˈrē-nə\ state S Brazil bordering on the Atlantic ✳ Florianópolis *area* 37,060 *sq mi* (95,985 *sq km*), *pop* 4,536,433

Santa Clara \ˈklar-ə, ˈkler-\ 1 city W Calif. NW of San Jose *pop* 93,613 2 city W *cen* Cuba *pop* 194,354

San·ta Cla·ri·ta \klə-ˈrē-tə\ city Calif. *pop* 110,642

Santa Cruz \ˈkrüz\ 1 island SW Calif. in NW Channel Islands 2 city W Calif. S of San Jose on Monterey Bay *pop* 49,040 3 — see

SAINT CROIX 4 river 250 *mi* (402 *km*) S Argentina flowing E into the Atlantic 5 city E Bolivia *pop* 694,616

San·ta Cruz de Te·ne·ri·fe \\sän-tä-'krüs-dā-,te-nə-'rē-(,)fā, -'rēf, -'rif\ 1 province Spain comprising W Canary Islands *area* 1239 *sq mi* (3209 *sq km*), *pop* 725,815 2 city & port, its ✻, on NE Tenerife Is. *pop* 189,317

Santa Cruz Islands islands SW Pacific in SE Solomons N of Vanuatu; until 1978 administratively attached to Brit. Solomon Islands *area* 362 *sq mi* (938 *sq km*)

San·ta Fe \\san-tə-'fā\ 1 city ✻ of N.Mex. *pop* 55,859 2 city *cen* Argentina on Salado River *pop* 442,214 — Santa Fe·an \\fā-ən\ *n*

Santa Fe Trail pioneer route to the Southwest used esp. 1821–80 from vicinity of Kansas City, Mo., to Santa Fe, N.Mex.

San·ta Is·a·bel \\san-tə-'i-zə,bel\ 1 island W Pacific in the E *cen* Solomons NE of Guadalcanal *area ab* 1500 *sq mi* (3900 *sq km*) 2 — see MALABO

Santa Ma·ria \\mə-'rē-ə\ city W Calif. NW of Santa Barbara *pop* 61,284

San·ta Ma·ría \\sän-tä-mə-'rē-ə\ volcano *ab* 12,400 *ft* (3780 *m*) W Guatemala

Santa Mar·ta \\'mär-tə\ city & port N Colombia on the Caribbean E of Barranquilla *pop* 286,500

San·ta Mon·i·ca \\san-tə-'mä-ni-kə\ city SW Calif. adjacent to Los Angeles on Santa Monica Bay (inlet of the Pacific) *pop* 86,905

San·tan·der \\sän-,tän-'der, ,san-,tan-\ 1 — see CANTABRIA 2 city & port N Spain on Bay of Biscay ✻ of Cantabria province *pop* 191,079

San·ta Pau·la \\san-tə-'pȯ-lə\ city SW Calif. NW of Los Angeles *pop* 25,062

San·ta·rém \\san-tə-'rem\ city N Brazil in W Pará at confluence of the Tapajoz & the Amazon *pop* 265,105

San·ta Ro·sa \\san-tə-'rō-zə\ city W Calif. N of San Francisco *pop* 113,313

Santa Rosa Island island SW Calif. in NW Channel Islands

San·tee \\(,)san-'tē, 'san-\ 1 river 143 *mi* (230 *km*) S.C. flowing SE into the Atlantic — see CONGAREE 2 city S Calif., a suburb of San Diego *pop* 52,902

San·ti·a·go \\san-tē-'ä-(,)gō, sän-\ 1 city *cen* Chile, its ✻ *metropolitan area pop* 3,902,356 2 *or* Santiago de los Ca·bal·le·ros \\thä-lòs-,kä-vä-'yer-(,)ōs\ city N *cen* Dominican Republic *pop* 382,244 3 *or* Santiago de Com·pos·te·la \\də-,käm-pə-'ste-lə, -,kòm-\ commune NW Spain *pop* 87,807 — San·ti·a·gan \\san-tē-'ä-gən, sän-\ *or n*

Santiago de Cu·ba \\də-'kyü-bə, thä-'kü-vä\ city & port SE Cuba *pop* 405,354

Santiago del Es·te·ro \\(,)del-ə-'ster-(,)ō, (,)thel-ä-'stä-rō\ city N Argentina SE of San Miguel de Tucumán *pop* 201,709

San·to Do·min·go \\san-tə-'miŋ-(,)gō\ 1 *or* Santo Domingo de Guz·mán \\sän-tō-thō-'meŋ-gō-thä-güs-'män\ *or formerly* Tru·jil·lo \\trü-'hē-(,)yō\ *or* Ciu·dad Trujillo \\syü-'thä(th), ,sē-ü-'dad\ city & port ✻ of Dominican Republic on Caribbean Sea *pop* 654,757 2 — see HISPANIOLA 3 — see DOMINICAN REPUBLIC

San·to Do·min·gan \\san-tə-də-'miŋ-gən\ *adj or n*

San·tos \'san-tüs\ city & port SE Brazil in SE São Paulo state SSE of São Paulo on an island in a tidal inlet *pop* 428,526

San·tur·ce \sän-'túr-(,)sä\ a NE section of San Juan, Puerto Rico

São Fran·cis·co \,saủn-frən-'sēs-(,)kü\ river 1800 *mi* (2897 *km*) E Brazil flowing from S *cen* Minas Gerais NE & E into the Atlantic

São Luís \,saủn-lủ-'ēs\ city & port NE Brazil ✳ of Maranhão state on Maranhão Is. *pop* 695,780

São Manuel — see TELES PIRES

São Mi·guel \,saủn-mē-'gel\ island Portugal in E Azores; chief town Ponta Delgada *area* 288 *sq mi* (746 *sq km*)

Saône \'sōn\ river 298 *mi* (479 *km*) E France flowing SSW into the Rhône

São Pau·lo \saủn-'paủ-(,)lü, -(,)lō\ **1** state SE Brazil *area* 95,852 *sq mi* (248,257 *sq km*), *pop* 31,192,818 **2** city, its ✳ *pop* 10,900,000

São Ro·que, Cape \saủn-'ró-kə\ headland NE Brazil N of Natal

São Salvador — see SALVADOR

São Tia·go \,saủn-tē-'ä-(,)gü, -(,)gō\ island Cape Verde Islands, largest of the group; chief town Praia *area* 383 *sq mi* (992 *sq km*)

São To·mé \,saủn-tə-'mā\ island W Africa in Gulf of Guinea; with Príncipe Is., forms the republic (until 1975 a Portuguese territory) of **São Tomé and Príncipe** (✳ São Tomé *area* 372 *sq mi or* 963 *sq km, pop* 128,000)

São Tomé and Príncipe (✳ São Tomé *area* 372 *sq mi or* 963 *sq km, pop* 128,000)

São Vicente, Cabo de — see SAINT VINCENT (Cape)

Sap·po·ro \'sä-pō-,rō; sä-'pōr-(,)ō\ city Japan on W Hokkaido *pop* 1,671,765

Saq·qâ·ra *or* **Saq·qā·rah** *or* **Sak·ka·ra** \sä-'kär-ə\ village N Egypt SW of ruins of Memphis

Sarabat — see GEDIZ

Sar·a·gos·sa \,sar-ə-'gä-sə\ *or Span* **Za·ra·go·za** \,thä-rä-'gō-thä, ,sä-rä-'gō-sä\ city, ✳ of Zaragoza province, Spain *pop* 594,394

Sa·ra·je·vo \,sar-ə-'yä-(,)vō, ,sär-ə-; 'sär-ə-ye-,vò\ city SE *cen* Bosnia and Herzegovina, its ✳

Sar·a·nac \'sar-ə-,nak\ river 100 *mi* (161 *km*) NE N.Y. flowing NE from **Saranac Lakes** (three lakes in the Adirondacks: Upper Saranac, Middle Saranac, & Lower Saranac) into Lake Champlain

Sa·ransk \sə-'rän(t)sk\ city *cen* Russia in Europe ✳ of Mordvinia *pop* 322,000

Sar·a·so·ta \,sar-ə-'sō-tə\ city W Fla. S of Tampa *pop* 50,961

Sar·a·to·ga \,sar-ə-'tō-gə\ city W Calif. SW of San Jose *pop* 28,061

Saratoga Lake lake 7 *mi* (11 *km*) long E N.Y. S of Lake George

Saratoga Springs city NE N.Y. *pop* 25,001

Sa·ra·tov \sə-'rä-təf\ city S *cen* Russia in Europe on a reservoir of the Volga *pop* 909,000

Sa·ra·wak \sə-'rä-(,)wä(k), -,wak\ state Malaysia in N Borneo, formerly a Brit. colony ✳ Kuching *area* 48,342 *sq mi* (125,206 *sq km*), *pop* 1,648,217

Sardica — see SOFIA

Sar·din·ia \sär-'di-nē-ə, -'di-nyə\ *or It* **Sar·de·gna** \sär-'dā-nyä\ island Italy S of Corsica; with surrounding smaller islands, constitutes a region of Italy ✳ Cagliari *area ab* 9300 *sq mi* (24,087 *sq km*), *pop* 1,645,192 — **Sar·din·ian** \sär-'di-nē-ən, -'din-yən\ *adj or n*

Sar·dis \'sär-dəs\ *or* **Sar·des** \'sär-(,)dēz\ ancient city W Asia Minor ✳ of ancient kingdom of Lydia; site E of Izmir — **Sar·di·an** \'sär-dē-ən\ *adj or n*

Sa·re·ma *or Estonian* **Saa·re·maa** \'sär-ə-,mä\ island Estonia at mouth of Gulf of Riga *area ab* 1050 *sq mi* (2720 *sq km*)

Sa·re·ra Bay \sə-'rer-ə\ *or formerly* **Geel·vink Bay** \gāl-(,)viŋk, 'kāl-\ inlet Indonesia in N W. Irian

Sar·gas·so Sea \sär-'ga-(,)sō\ tract of comparatively still water N Atlantic lying chiefly bet. 25° & 35°N & 40° & 70°W

Sark \'särk\ island in the English Channel, one of the Channel Islands; a dependency of Guernsey *area* 2 *sq mi* (5.2 *sq km*) — **Sark·ese** \'sär-'kēz, -'kēs\ *n*

Sar·ma·tia \sär-'mā-sh(ē-)ə\ ancient region E Europe in modern Poland & Russia bet. the Vistula & the Volga — **Sar·ma·tian** \-shən\ *adj or n*

Sar·nia–Clear·wa·ter \'sär-nē-ə-'klir-,wȯ-tər, -,wä\ city Canada in SE Ont. on St. Clair River opposite Port Huron, Mich. *pop* 74,376

Sa·ron·ic Gulf \sə-'rä-nik\ inlet of the Aegean SE Greece bet. Attica & the Peloponnese

Sa·ros Gulf \'sar-,äs, 'ser-\ inlet of the Aegean SW Turkey in Europe N of Gallipoli Peninsula

Sarre — see SAAR

Sarthe \'särt\ river 175 *mi* (282 *km*) NW France flowing S to unite with the Mayenne forming Maine River

Sarum OLD SARUM

Sa·se·bo \'sä-se-,bō\ city & port Japan in NW Kyushu on an inlet of E. China Sea *pop* 245,017

Sas·katch·e·wan \sas-'ka-chə-wən, sa-, -,wän\ **1** river 340 *mi* (547 *km*) S *cen* Canada formed by confluence in *cen* Sask. of two branches rising in the Rockies in Alta.; the **North Saskatchewan** (760 *mi or* 1216 *km*) & the **South Saskatchewan** (865 *mi or* 1384 *km*), & flowing E into Lake Winnipeg **2** province SW Canada ✳ Regina *area* 220,121 *sq mi* (570,113 *sq km*), *pop* 988,928 — **Sas·katch·e·wan·ian** \-,ska-chə-'wä-nē-ən\ *adj or n*

Sas·ka·toon \,sas-kə-'tün\ city Canada in *cen* Sask. on S. Saskatchewan River *pop* 186,058

Sas·sa·ri \'sä-sä-(,)rē\ commune Italy in NW Sardinia *pop* 116,989

Sa·til·la \sə-'ti-lə\ river 220 *mi* (354 *km*) SE Ga. flowing E into the Atlantic

Sat·pu·ra Range \'sät-pə-rə\ range of hills W *cen* India bet. the Narmada & the Tapi

Sa·tu–Ma·re \,sä-(,)tü-'mär-(,)ā\ city NW Romania in Transylvania on the Somes *pop* 136,881

Sau·di Arabia \'saủ-dē, 'sȯ-dē, sä-'ü-dē\ country SW Asia occupying most of Arabian Peninsula; a kingdom, comprising former kingdoms of Nejd & Hejaz & principality of Asir ✳ Riyadh *area* 865,000 *sq mi* (2,240,350 *sq km*), *pop* 17,419,000 — **Saudi** *adj or n* — **Saudi Arabian** *adj or n*

Sau·gus \'sȯ-gəs\ town NE Mass. W of Lynn *pop* 25,549

Sault Sainte Ma·rie \'sü-(,)sānt-mə-'rē\ city Canada in Ont., across the St. Marys River from Michigan *pop* 81,476

Sault Sainte Marie Canals *or* **Soo Canals** \'sü\ three ship canals, two in the U.S. & one in Canada, at rapids in St. Marys River connecting Lake Superior & Lake Huron

Sau·mur \sō-'múr, -'myúr, -'mūer\ commune NW France on the Loire SE of Angers *pop* 31,894

Sau·rash·tra \saú-'räsh-trə\ former state (1948–56) W India on Kathiawar Peninsula; in Bombay state 1956–60 & since 1960 in Gujarat

Sa·va \'sä-və\ river 584 *mi* (940 *km*) flowing from Italian border E through Slovenia, into Croatia, along Croatia-Bosnia and Herzegovina border, & into Yugoslavia where it flows into the Danube at Belgrade

Sa·vaii \sə-'vī-,ē\ island SW *cen* Pacific, largest in Samoa, in W. Samoa

Sa·van·nah \sə-'va-nə\ **1** river 314 *mi* (505 *km*) E Ga. flowing SE to the Atlantic & forming Ga.-S.C. boundary **2** city & port E Ga. at mouth of Savannah River *pop* 137,560

Save — see SABI

Sa·vo \'sä-(,)vō\ island W Pacific in SE Solomons N of W Guadalcanal

Sa·vo·na \sä-'vō-nä\ commune & port NW Italy SW of Genoa *pop* 67,137

Sa·voy \sə-'vói, *or F* **Sa·voie** \sà-'vwä\ *or It* **Sa·vo·ia** \sä-'vò-yä\ region SE France in Savoy Alps SW of Switzerland & bordering on Italy; duchy 1416–1720, part of kingdom of Sardinia 1720–1860; became part of France 1860 — **Sa·voy·ard** \sə-'vói-,ärd, ,sa-,vói-'ärd, ,sa-,vwä-'yär(d)\ *adj or n*

Savoy Alps section of W Alps SE France — see MONT BLANC

Sa·watch Range \sə-'wäch\ mountain range *cen* Colo. in Rocky Mountains — see ELBERT (Mount)

Saxe \'saks\ SAXONY — its French form, used in English chiefly in names of former duchies in Thuringia: **Saxe–Al·ten·burg** \-'äl-t°n-,bùrg\, **Saxe–Co·burg** \-'kō-,bərg\, **Saxe–Go·tha** \-'gō-tə, -thə\, **Saxe–Mei·ning·en** \-'mī-niŋ-ən\, & **Saxe–Wei·mar–Ei·se·nach** \-'vī-,mär-'ī-z°n-,äk, -,äk\

Sax·o·ny \'sak-s(ə-)nē\ *or G* **Sach·sen** \'zäk-sən\ **1** region & former duchy NW Germany S of Jutland Peninsula between the Elbe & the Rhine — see LOWER SAXONY **2** region & former state E Germany N of the Erzgebirge — see SAXE — **Sax·on** \'sak-sən\ *adj or n*

Sa·yan Mountains \sə-'yän\ mountains S Russia in Asia on border of Tuva N of Altai Mountains

Sayre·ville \'sar-,vil, 'ser-\ borough E *cen* N.J. *pop* 34,986

Sa·zan \'sä-,zän\ *or It* **Sa·se·no** \sä-'zä-(,)nō, sä-\ island Albania in N Strait of Otranto

Sca Fell \,skó-'fel\ mountain 3162 *ft* (964 *m*) NW England in Cumbrians SW of Keswick; second highest peak in England

Sca·fell Pike \,skó-'fel\ mountain 3210 *ft* (978 *m*) NW England in Cumbria NE of Sca Fell; highest in the Cumbrians & in England

Scamander — see MENDERES

Scan·di·na·via \,skan-də-'nä-vē-ə, -vyə\ **1** peninsula N Europe occupied by Norway & Sweden **2** Denmark, Norway, Sweden, & sometimes also Iceland, the Faeroe Islands, & Finland — **Scan·di·na·vian** \-vē-ən, -vyən\ *adj or n*

Scapa Flow \,ska-pə-'flō\ sea basin N Scotland in the Orkneys

Scar·bor·ough \'skär-ˌbər-ō\ **1** city Canada in SE Ont. near Toronto *pop* 524,598 **2** town & port NE England in N. Yorkshire *pop* 107,800

Schaer·beek or Flem **Schaar·beek** \'skär-ˌbāk, 'skär-\ commune *cen* Belgium, NE suburb of Brussels *pop* 102,702

Schaff·hau·sen \'shäf-ˌhau̇-z°n\ **1** canton N Switzerland bordering on SW Germany *area* 115 *sq mi* (298 *sq km*), *pop* 71,210 **2** commune, its ✳ *pop* 34,101

Schaum·burg \'shäm-ˌ(ˌ)bərg\ village NE Ill. NW of Chicago *pop* 68,586

Schaum·burg–Lip·pe \'shauṁ-ˌburk-'li-pə\ state of Germany 1918–33 in NW bet. Westphalia & Hannover

Schel·de \'skel-də\ or **Scheldt** \'skelt\ or F **Es·caut** \e-'skō\ river 270 *mi* (434 *km*) W Europe flowing from N France through Belgium into North Sea in Netherlands

Sche·nec·ta·dy \skə-'nek-tə-dē\ city E N.Y. *pop* 65,566

Scher·er·ville \'shir-ər-ˌvil\ town NW Ind. *pop* 19,926

Sche·ve·ning·en \'skā-və-ˌniŋ-ə(n), 'skā-\ town SW Netherlands on North Sea W of The Hague

Schie·dam \skē-'däm, skē-\ commune SW Netherlands *pop* 71,117

Schles·wig \'shles-(ˌ)wig, -(ˌ)vik\ **1** or Dan **Sles·vig** \'slis-vē\ region N Germany & S Denmark in S Jutland Peninsula **2** city N Germany *pop ab* 26,938

Schleswig–Hol·stein \-'hōl-ˌstīn, -ˌshtīn\ state of Germany & formerly of W. Germany consisting of Holstein & part of Schleswig ✳ Kiel *area* 6046 *sq mi* (15,659 *sq km*), *pop* 2,626,100

Scho·field Barracks \'skō-ˌfēld\ city Hawaii in *cen* Oahu *pop* 19,597

Schou·ten Islands \'skau̇-t°n\ islands Indonesia in N W. Irian at mouth of Sarera Bay *area* 1230 *sq mi* (3198 *sq km*)

Schuyl·kill \'skü-k°l, 'skül-ˌkil\ river 131 *mi* (211 *km*) SE Pa. flowing SE into Delaware River at Philadelphia

Schwaben — see SWABIA

Schwarzwald — see BLACK FOREST

Schwein·furt \'shvīn-ˌfúrt\ city S *cen* Germany on Main River *pop* 54,520

Schweiz, der — see SWITZERLAND

Schwe·rin \shvā-'rēn\ city N Germany E of Hamburg *pop* 125,959

Schwyz \'shvēts\ **1** canton E *cen* Switzerland *area* 351 *sq mi* (909 *sq km*), *pop* 108,576 **2** town, its ✳, E of Lucerne *pop* 12,596

Scil·ly, Isles of \'si-lē\ island group SW England off Land's End comprising 140 islands ✳ Hugh Town (on St. Mary's, largest island) *area* 6 *sq mi* (16 *sq km*), *pop* 2900 — see CORNWALL 2

Scil·lo·ni·an \si-'lō-nē-ən\ *adj* or n

Sci·o·to \sī-'ō-tə\ river 237 *mi* (381 *km*) Ohio flowing S into Ohio River

Scone \'skün\ locality E Scotland NE of Perth *pop* 3713

Sco·pus, Mount \'skō-pəs\ mountain Palestine in W Jordan in small area belonging to Israel

Scores·by Sound \'skōrz-bē, 'skórz-\ inlet of Norwegian Sea E Greenland N of 70°N

Sco·tia Sea \'skō-shə\ part of the S Atlantic SE of Falkland Islands, W of S. Sandwich Islands, & N of S. Orkney Islands

Scot·land \'skät-lənd\ *or L* **Cal·e·do·nia** \,ka-lə-'dō-nyə, -nē-ə\ ML **Sco·tia** \'skō-shə\ country N Great Britain; a division of United Kingdom of Great Britain and Northern Ireland ✳ Edinburgh *area* 29,797 *sq mi* (77,174 *sq km*), *pop* 5,102,400 — **Scot** \'skät\ *n* — **Scots** \'skäts\ *adj* — **Scots·man** \-mən\ *n* — **Scots·wom·an** \-,wu̇-mən\ — **Scot·tish** \'skä-tish\ *adj or n*

Scotts Bluff National Monument \'skäts\ reservation W Nebr. on N. Platte River including **Scotts Bluff** (high butte that was a landmark on the Oregon Trail)

Scotts·dale \'skäts-,dāl\ city SW *cen* Ariz. E of Phoenix *pop* 130,069

Scran·ton \'skran-tᵊn\ city NE Pa. *pop* 81,805

Scun·thorpe \'skən-,thórp\ borough E England in Humberside WSW of Hull *pop* 60,500

Scu·ta·ri, Lake \'skü-tä-rē\ lake NW Albania & S Yugoslavia in Montenegro *area* 143 *sq mi* (370 *sq km*)

Scyth·ia \'si-thē-ə, -thē-\ the country of the ancient Scythians comprising parts of Europe & Asia in regions N & NE of Black Sea & E of Aral Sea

Sea Islands islands SE U.S. in the Atlantic off coast of S.C., Ga., & Fla. bet. mouths of Santee & St. Johns rivers

Seal Beach \'sēl\ city SW Calif. SE of Los Angeles *pop* 25,098

Sea·side \'sē-,sīd\ city W Calif. on Monterey Bay *pop* 38,901

Se·at·tle \sē-'a-tᵊl\ city & port W Wash. bet. Puget Sound & Lake Washington *pop* 516,259 — **Se·at·tle·ite** \-'a-tᵊl-,īt\ *n*

Se·ba·go Lake \sə-'bā-(,)gō\ lake 13 *mi* (21 *km*) long SW Maine

Sebaste 1 *or* **Sebastia** — see SIVAS **2** — see SAMARIA

Se·cun·der·a·bad \si-'kən-də-rə-,bad, -,bäd\ city S *cen* India in Andhra Pradesh, NE suburb of Hyderabad *pop* 167,461

Se·da·lia \si-'dāl-yə\ city W *cen* Mo. *pop* 19,800

Se·dan \si-'dan, *F* sə-'däⁿ\ city NE France on the Meuse NE of Reims *pop* 22,407

Sedge·moor \'sej-,mu̇r, -,mōr, -,mór\ tract of moorland SW England in *cen* Somerset

Se·dom \sə-'dōm\ town Israel near S end of Dead Sea

Se·go·via \sā-'gō-vyə, sə-, -vē-ə\ **1** — see COCO **2** province N *cen* Spain in Old Castile *area* 2683 *sq mi* (6949 *sq km*), *pop* 147,188 **3** commune, its ✳, NW of Madrid *pop* 54,142

Seim — see SEYM

Seine \'sān, 'sen\ river 480 *mi* (772 *km*) N France flowing NW into **Bay of the Seine** (inlet of English Channel)

Se·lang·or \sə-'laŋ-,ór, -'laŋ-gór\ state *cen* Malaysia (federation) on Strait of Malacca *area* 3074 *sq mi* (7962 *sq km*), *pop* 2,289,236

Se·len·ga \,se-lən-'gä\ river N *cen* Asia rising in W Mongolia & flowing to Lake Baikal

Se·leu·cia \sə-'lü-sh(ē-)ə\ **1** *or* **Seleucia Tra·che·o·tis** \,trä-kē-'ō-təs\ ancient city SE Asia Minor in Cilicia SW of Tarsus **2** ancient city, chief city of the Seleucid Empire; ruins now in Iraq on the Tigris SSE of Baghdad **3** *or* **Seleucia Pi·er·ia** \pī-'ir-ē-ə, -'er-\ ancient city Asia Minor N of mouth of the Orontes; port for Antioch

Sel·kirk \'sel-,kərk\ **1** *or* **Sel·kirk·shire** \-,shir, -shər\ former county SE Scotland **2** burgh *cen* Borders region SE of Edinburgh *pop* 5417

Selkirk Mountains mountains SW Canada in SE B.C. W of the Rockies; highest Mt. Sir Sandford 11,555 *ft* (3522 *m*)

Sel·ma \'sel-mə\ city *cen* Ala. W of Montgomery *pop* 23,755

Se·ma·rang \sə-'mär-,äŋ\ city & port Indonesia in *cen* Java on N coast *pop* 1,250,971

Se·mey \'se-mā\ *or* **Sem·i·pa·la·tinsk** \,se-mi-pə-'lä-,tin(t)sk\ city NE Kazakhstan on the Irtysh *pop* 841,900

Sem·i·nole, Lake \'se-mə-,nōl\ reservoir SW Ga. & NW Fla. formed by confluence of Chattahoochee & Flint rivers & emptying by the Apalachicola

Sen·dai \(,)sen-'dī\ city Japan in NE Honshu *pop* 918,378

Sen·e·ca Lake \'se-ni-kə\ lake 35 *mi* (56 *km*) long W *cen* N.Y.; one of the Finger Lakes

Sen·e·gal \se-ni-'gȯl, -'gäl, 'se-ni-,\ **1** river 1015 *mi* (1633 *km*) W Africa flowing from Fouta Djallon NW & W into the Atlantic **2** country W Africa on the Atlantic; a republic of the French Community, formerly a territory of French West Africa ✱ Dakar *area* 76,124 *sq mi* (197,161 *sq km*), *pop* 7,899,000 — **Sen·e·ga·lese** \,se-ni-gə-'lēz, -'lēs\ *adj or n*

Sen·e·gam·bia \,se-nə-'gam-bē-ə\ **1** region W Africa around Senegal & Gambia rivers **2** confederation of Senegal & Gambia 1982–89 — **Sen·e·gam·bi·an** \-ən\ *adj or n*

Sen·lac \'sen-,lak\ hill SE England in Sussex NW of Hastings

Sen·lis \sä*n*-lēs\ commune N France NNE of Paris *pop* 15,226

Sen·nar *or* **Sen·naar** \sə-'när\ region E Sudan chiefly bet. White Nile & Blue Nile rivers; an ancient kingdom

Sens \'sä*n*s\ city NE *cen* France WSW of Troyes *pop* 27,755

Seoul \'sōl\ city NW S. Korea on Han River; formerly ✱ of Korea, since 1948 ✱ of S. Korea *pop* 9,639,110

Se·pik \'sā-pik\ river 600 *mi* (966 *km*) N Papua New Guinea

Sept–Îles \se-'tēl\ *or* **Sev·en Islands** \'se-vən\ town Canada in E Que. at the mouth of St. Lawrence River *pop* 24,848

Se·quoia National Park \si-'kwȯi-ə\ reservation SE *cen* Calif.; includes Mt. Whitney

Seram — see CERAM

Ser·bia \'sər-bē-ə\ *or formerly* **Ser·via** \-vē-ə\ federated republic *cen* Yugoslavia traversed by Morava River; once a kingdom ✱ Belgrade *area* 34,115 *sq mi* (88,358 *sq km*), *pop* 9,823,000 — **Serb** \'sərb\ *adj or n* — **Ser·bi·an** \'sər-bē-ən\ *adj or n*

Serbs, Croats, and Slovenes, Kingdom of the — see YUGOSLAVIA

Serdica — see SOFIA

Se·re·kun·da \,se-re-'kün-də\ city W Gambia *pop* 68,824

Serendib — see CEYLON

Ser·en·geti Plain \,ser-ən-'ge-tē\ area N Tanzania including **Serengeti National Park** (wild game reserve)

Ser·gi·pe \sər-'zhē-pə\ state NE Brazil ✱ Aracajú *area* 8441 *sq mi* (21,862 *sq km*), *pop* 1,492,400

Se·rin·ga·pa·tam \sə-,riŋ-gə-pə-'tam\ town S India N of city of Mysore

Se·ro·we \sə-'rō-ā\ city E Botswana *pop* 30,264

Ser·ra da Es·tre·la \'ser-ə-(,)dä-ish-'tre-lə\ mountain range Portugal; highest point Malhão da Estrela (highest in Portugal) 6532 *ft* (1991 *m*)

Serra do Mar \dü-ˈmär\ mountain range S Brazil along coast

Ser·rai \ˈser-(ˌ)e, -ˌä\ city N Greece *pop* 50,875

Ser·ra Pa·ri·ma \ˈser-ə-pə-ˈrē-mə\ mountain range N S. America on Venezuela-Brazil border SW of Pacaraima Mountains; source of the Orinoco

Ses·tos \ˈses-təs\ ruined town Turkey in Europe on the Dardanelles (Hellespont) at narrowest point

Ses·to San Gio·van·ni \ˈses-tō-ˌsän-jō-ˈvä-nē\ commune N Italy *pop* 89,517

Sète \ˈset\ *or formerly* **Cette** \ˈset\ commune & port S France SSW of Montpellier *pop* 41,916

Se·te Que·das \ˈse-tē-ˈkä-dəsh\ *or formerly* **Guaí·ra** \ˈgwī-(ˌ)rä\ former cataract in Alto Paraná River on Brazil-Paraguay boundary; now submerged in reservoir formed by Itaipu Dam

Sé·tif \sā-ˈtēf\ commune NE Algeria *pop* 144,200

Se·tú·bal \sə-ˈtü-bəl, -ˌbäl\ city & port SW Portugal *pop* 77,285

Se·van \sə-ˈvän\ lake N Armenia *area* 525 *sq mi* (1360 *km*)

Se·vas·to·pol \sə-ˈvas-tə-ˌpōl, -ˌpȯl, -pəl; ˌsev-ə-ˈstō-pəl, -ˈstō-\ *or formerly* **Se·bas·to·pol** \-ˈbas-; ˌseb-ə\ city & port SW Crimea *pop* 366,000

Sev·ern \ˈse-vərn\ **1** inlet (**Severn River**) of Chesapeake Bay, in Md., on which Annapolis is situated **2** river 610 *mi* (982 *km*) Canada in NW Ont. flowing NE into Hudson Bay **3** river 210 *mi* (338 *km*) Great Britain flowing from E *cen* Wales into Bristol Channel in England

Se·ver·na·ya Zem·lya \ˈse-vər-nə-yə-ˌzem-lē-ˈä, ˌsye-vir-nə-yə-zim-ˈlyä\ islands N Russia in Asia N of Taymyr Peninsula in Arctic Ocean bet. Kara & Laptev seas *area* 14,300 *sq mi* (37,180 *sq km*)

Se·vier \sə-ˈvir\ river 280 *mi* (451 *km*) SW *cen* Utah flowing into **Sevier Lake** (25 *mi* or 40 *km* long; saline)

Se·ville \sə-ˈvil\ *or Sp* **Se·vil·la** \sā-ˈvē-(ˌ)yä\ **1** province SW Spain *area* 5406 *sq mi* (14,002 *sq km*), *pop* 1,619,703 **2** city, its ✷, on the Guadalquivir *pop* 659,126

Sè·vres \ˈsevrᵊ\ commune N France SW of Paris *pop* 22,057

Sew·ard Peninsula \ˈsü-ərd\ peninsula 180 *mi* (290 *km*) long & 130 *mi* (209 *km*) wide W Alaska projecting into Bering Sea bet. Kotzebue & Norton sounds — see PRINCE OF WALES (Cape)

Sey·chelles \sā-ˈshel(z)\ island group W Indian Ocean NE of Madagascar; formerly a Brit. colony, a republic in the Commonwealth of Nations since 1976 ✷ Victoria (on Mahé Is.) *area* 107 *sq mi* (277 *sq km*), *pop* 68,598

Sey·han \sā-ˈhän\ **1** *or* **Sei·hun** \-ˈhün\ river Turkey flowing SSW into the Mediterranean **2** — see ADANA

Seym *or* **Seim** \ˈsām\ river 460 *mi* (740 *km*) N Ukraine & Russia in Europe flowing W into the Desna

Sfax \ˈsfaks\ city & port Tunisia on Gulf of Gabes *pop* 221,770

's Gravenhage — see HAGUE (The)

Shaan·xi \ˈshän-ˈshē\ *or* **Shen·si** \ˈshen-ˈsē, ˈshən-ˈshē\ province N *cen* China bordering on the Huang ✷ Xi'an *area* 75,598 *sq mi* (195,799 *sq km*), *pop* 32,882,403

Sha·ba \ˈshä-bə\ *or formerly* **Ka·tan·ga** \kə-ˈtäŋ-gə, -ˈtäŋ-\ region SE Democratic Republic of the Congo; chief city Lubumbashi

Shah·ja·han·pur \ˌshä-jə-ˈhän-ˌpu̇r\ city N India in *cen* Uttar Pradesh NNW of Kanpur *pop* 237,663

Shah·pur \'shä·'pür\ ancient city SW Iran W of Shiraz

Shak·er Heights \'shā-kər\ city NE Ohio E of Cleveland *pop* 30,831

Shakh·ty \'shäk-tē, 'shak-\ *or formerly* **Ale·ksan·drovsk Gru·shev·ski** \a-lik-'sàn-drəfsk-grü-'shef-skē\ city S Russia in Europe NE of Rostov *pop* 228,000

Shan \'shän, 'shan\ *or formerly* **Federated Shan States** state E Myanmar comprising a mountainous region (the **Shan Hills**) ✳ Taunggyi

Shan·dong \'shän-'dȯŋ\ **1** *or* **Shan–tung** \'shan-'təŋ, 'shän-'dùŋ\ peninsula E China projecting ENE bet. Yellow Sea & Bo Hai **2** province E China including Shandong Peninsula ✳ Jinan *area* 59,189 *sq mi* (153,300 *sq km*), *pop* 84,392,827

Shang·hai \shaŋ-'hī\ municipality & port E China on the Huangpu near the Chang estuary *pop* 7,469,509

Shang·qiu *or* **Shang–ch'iu** \'shäŋ-'chyü\ city E China in E Henan *pop* 164,880

Shan·non \'sha-nən\ river 230 *mi* (370 *km*) W Ireland flowing S & W into the Atlantic

Shan·tou \'shän-'tō\ *or* **Swa·tow** \'swä-'taù\ city & port SE China in E Guangdong on S. China Sea *pop* 578,630

Shan·xi \'shän-'shē\ *or* **Shan·si** \-'sē, -'shē\ province N China bordering on the Huang ✳ Taiyuan *area* 60,656 *sq mi* (157,099 *sq km*), *pop* 28,759,014

Shao·xing *or* **Shao–hsing** \shaù-'shiŋ\ city E China in N Zhejiang SE of Hangzhou *pop* 179,818

Shao·yang \'shaù-'yäŋ\ *or formerly* **Pao·king** \'baù-'chiŋ\ city SE China in cen Hunan W of Hengyang *pop* 247,227

Shari — see CHARI

Sharjah — see ASH SHARIQAH

Shark Bay \'shärk\ inlet of Indian Ocean 150 *mi* (241 *km*) long W Western Australia, at ab 25°S

Shar·on, Plain of \'shar-ən, 'sher-\ region Israel on coast bet. Mt. Carmel & Jaffa

Sha·shi \'shä-'shē\ *or* **Sha–shih** \-'shir, -'shē\ city E cen China in S Hubei on the Chang *pop* 281,352

Shas·ta, Mount \'shas-tə\ mountain 14,162 *ft* (4316 *m*) N Calif. in Cascade Range; an isolated volcanic cone

Shatt al Ar·ab \shät-al-'ar-əb\ river 120 *mi* (193 *km*) SE Iraq formed by the Tigris & the Euphrates & flowing SE into Persian Gulf

Shaw·an·gunk Mountains \'shäŋ-gəm, shə-'wän-(,)gəŋk\ mountain ridge SE N.Y.; part of Kittatinny Mountain

Shaw·nee \shò-'nē, 'shò-,; shä-'nē, 'shä-,\ **1** city NE Kans. S of Kansas City *pop* 37,993 **2** city cen Okla. *pop* 26,017

Shcherbakov — see RYBINSK

She·ba \'shē-bə\ *or* **Sa·ba** \'sä-bə\ ancient country S Arabia, probably Yemen

She·boy·gan \shi-'bȯi-gən\ city & port E Wis. *pop* 49,676

Shechem — see NABLUS

Shef·field \'she-,fēld\ city N England in S. Yorkshire *pop* 499,700

Shel·i·kof \'she-li-,kȯf\ strait S Alaska bet. Alaska Peninsula & islands of Kodiak & Afognak

Shel·ton \'shel-tᵊn\ city SW Conn. *pop* 35,418

Shenandoah

Shen·an·do·ah \,she-nən-'dō-ə, ,sha-nə-'dō-ə\ river 55 *mi* (88 *km*) N Va. flowing NE bet. Allegheny & Blue Ridge Mountains across NE tip of W.Va. & into the Potomac; forms **Shenandoah Valley**

Shenandoah National Park reservation N Va. in Blue Ridge Mountains

Shensi — see SHAANXI

Shen·yang \'shən-'yäŋ\ *or* **Muk·den** \'mùk-dən, 'mək-; 'mùk'den\ *or formerly* **Feng·tien** \'fəŋ-'tyen\ city NE China ✳ of Liaoning; chief city of Manchuria *pop* 3,603,712

Sher·brooke \'shər-,brùk\ town E Canada in S Que. *pop* 76,429

Sher·man \'shər-mən\ city NE Tex. N of Dallas *pop* 31,601

's Her·to·gen·bosch \ser-,tō-gən-'bòs, -,kən-\ city S Netherlands ✳ of N. Brabant *pop* 81,471

Sher·wood Forest \'shər-,wùd- *also* 'sher-\ ancient royal forest *cen* England chiefly in Nottinghamshire

Shet·land \'shet-lənd\ **1** islands N Scotland NE of the Orkneys **2** *or* **Zet·land** \'zet-\ region comprising the Shetlands ✳ Lerwick (on Mainland Is.) *area* 550 *sq mi* (1430 *sq km*), *pop* 22,270 — **Shet·land·er** \'shet-lən-dər\ *n*

Shey·enne \shī-'an, -'en\ river 325 *mi* (523 *km*) SE *cen* N.Dak. flowing into Red River

Shi·bīn al–Kawm *or* **Shi·bîn el Kôm** \shi-,bēn-el-'kōm\ city N Egypt *pop* 153,000

Shigatse — see XIGAZÊ

Shi·jia·zhuang *or* **Shih–chia–chuang** \'shir-'jyä-'jwäŋ, 'shē-\ city NE China ✳ of Hebei *pop* 1,068,439

Shi·kar·pur \shi-'kär-,pùr\ city S *cen* Pakistan in Sind *pop* 88,000

Shi·ko·ku \shē-'kō-(,)kü\ island S Japan E of Kyushu *area* 7245 *sq mi* (18,765 *sq km*) *pop* 4,195,106

Shil·ka \'shil-ka\ river 345 *mi* (555 *km*) SE Russia in Asia flowing NE to unite with the Argun forming the Amur

Shil·long \shi-'lòŋ\ city NE India ✳ of Meghalaya *pop* 222,273

Shi·loh \'shī-(,)lō\ **1** locality SW Tenn., site of Civil War battle **2** ancient village Palestine W of Jordan River on slope of Mt. Ephraim

Shi·mi·zu \shē-'mē-(,)zü, 'shē-mē-,zü\ city & port Japan in *cen* Honshu on Suruga Bay; port for Shizuoka *pop* 241,524

Shi·mo·da \shē-'mò-də, -,dä\ city & port Japan in S Honshu SW of Yokohama on Sagami Sea *pop* 30,081

Shi·mo·no·se·ki \shē-mō-nō-'se-kē\ *or formerly* **Ba·kan** \'bä-,kän\ city & port Japan in SW Honshu on Shimonoseki Strait *pop* 262,643

Shimonoseki Strait strait Japan bet. Honshu & Kyushu connecting Inland Sea & Korea Strait

Shi·nar \'shī-nər, -,när\ a country known to the early Hebrews as a plain in Babylonia; prob. Sumer

Ship Rock \'ship\ isolated mountain 7178 *ft* (2188 *m*) N.Mex. in NW corner

Shi·raz \shi-'räz, -'raz\ city SW *cen* Iran *pop* 848,289

Shi·re \'shē-(,)rā, 'shir-ē\ river 250 *mi* (400 *km*) S Malawi & *cen* Mozambique flowing from Lake Malawi S into the Zambezi

Shi·shal·din \shi-'shal-dən\ volcano 9372 *ft* (2856 *m*) SW Alaska on Unimak Is.; highest in Aleutian Range

Shi·zu·o·ka \,shē-zü-'wō-kä\ city Japan in *cen* Honshu near Suruga Bay SW of Shimizu *pop* 472,199

Shko·dër \'shkō-dər\ city NW Albania *pop* 81,800

Sho·la·pur \'shō-lə-,púr\ *or* **So·la·pur** \'sō-\ city W India in SE Maharashtra SE of Bombay *pop* 514,461

Shore·ditch \'shōr-,dich, 'shór-\ former metropolitan borough N *cen* London, England, now part of Hackney

Shore·view \'shōr-,vyü, 'shór-\ city E Minn. *pop* 24,587

Short·land \'short-lənd\ islands W Pacific in the Solomons off S end of Bougainville

Sho·sho·ne \shə-'shō-nē, shə-'shōn\ river 120 *mi* (193 *km*) NW Wyo. flowing NE into Bighorn River

Shoshone Falls waterfall 210 *ft* (64 *m*) S Idaho in Snake River

Shreve·port \'shrēv-,pōrt, -,pórt\ city NW La. on Red River *pop* 198,525

Shrews·bury 1 \'sh(r)üz-,ber-ē, -b(ə-)rē\ town E Mass. E of Worcester *pop* 24,146 **2** *Brit often* 'shrōz-\ borough W England ✻ of Shropshire *pop* 59,826

Shrop·shire \'shräp-shər, -,shir\ *or* **Sal·op** \'sa-ləp, -,läp\ county W England bordering on Wales ✻ Shrewsbury *area* 1396 *sq mi* (3616 *sq km*), *pop* 401,600

Shuang·liao \'shwäŋ-'lyaü\ *or formerly* **Liao·yuan** \'lyaü-'ywen\ city NE China in W Jilin S of Changchun on the Liao

Shu·ma·gin \'shü-mə-gən\ islands SW Alaska S of Alaska Peninsula; largest Unga

Shushan — see SUSA

Shym·kent \shim-'kent\ *or* **Chim·kent** \chim-\ city S Kazakhstan N of Tashkent *pop* 438,800

Si — see XI

Si·al·kot \sē-'äl-,kōt\ city NE Pakistan NNE of Lahore *pop* 308,000

Siam — see THAILAND — **Si·a·mese** \,sī-ə-'mēz, -'mēs\ *adj or n*

Siam, Gulf of — see THAILAND (Gulf of)

Sian — see XI'AN

Siangtan — see XIANGTAN

Si·be·ria \sī-'bir-ē-ə\ region N Asia in Russia extending from the Urals to the Pacific; roughly coextensive with Russia in Asia — **Si·be·ri·an** \-ən\ *adj or n*

Si·biu \sē-'byü\ city W *cen* Romania in Transylvania *pop* 184,036

Si·bu·yan Sea \,sē-bü-'yän\ body of water *cen* Philippines bounded by Mindoro, S Luzon, & the Visayan Islands

Sic·i·ly \'si-s(ə-)lē\ *or It* **Si·ci·lia** \sē-'chēl-yä\ *or anc* **Si·cil·ia** \sə-'sil-yə\ *or* **Tri·nac·ria** \trə-'na-krē-ə, trī-\ island S Italy in the Mediterranean; a region ✻ Palermo *area* 9925 *sq mi* (25,706 *sq km*), *pop* 5,172,785 — **Si·cil·ian** \sə-'sil-yən\ *adj or n*

Si·cy·on \'si-shē-,än, 'si-sē-\ *or Gk* **Sik·y·on** \'sē-kē-,ón\ ancient city S Greece in NE Peloponnese NW of Corinth

Si·di Bar·râ·ni \'sē-dē-bə-'rä-nē\ village NW Egypt on coast

Sidi Bel Ab·bès \,sē-dē-,bel-ə-'bes\ commune NW Algeria *pop* 152,778

Si·don \'sī-d³n\ *or Ar* **Sai·da** \'sī-də\ city & port SW Lebanon; a chief city of ancient Phoenicia — **Si·do·ni·an** \sī-'dō-nē-ən\ *adj or n*

Sid·ra, Gulf of \'si-dra\ *or* **Gulf of Sir·te** \'sir-tə\ *or anc* **Syr·tis Major** \'sər-təs\ inlet of the Mediterranean on coast of Libya

Sie·ben·ge·bir·ge \'zē-bən-gə-‚bir-gə\ hills W Germany on right bank of the Rhine SSE of Bonn — see DRACHENFELS

Si·ena *or* **Si·en·na** \sē-'e-nä\ commune *cen* Italy in Tuscany *pop* 58,278 — **Si·en·ese** *or* **Si·en·nese** \‚sē-ə-'nēz, -'nēs\ *adj or n*

Si·er·ra Blan·ca Peak \sē-‚er-ə-'blaŋ-kə, 'syer-ä-'bläŋ-kä\ mountain 12,003 *ft* (3658 *m*) S *cen* N.Mex. in Sierra Blanca Range of the Sacramento Mountains

Sierra de Gre·dos \dā-'grā-(‚)dōs, thā-\ mountain range W *cen* Spain, SW extension of Sierra de Guadarrama; highest peak Plaza de Almanzor *ab* 8500 *ft* (2591 *m*)

Sierra de Gua·dar·ra·ma \dā-‚gwä-dä-'rä-mä\ mountain range *cen* Spain; highest peak Pico de Peñalara 7970 *ft* (2429 *m*)

Si·er·ra Le·one \sē-‚er-ə-lē-'ōn, ‚sir-ə-, -lē-'ō-nē\ country W Africa on the Atlantic; a dominion of the Commonwealth of Nations ✳ Freetown *area* 27,699 *sq mi* (71,740 *sq km*), *pop* 4,491,000 — **Si·er·ra Le·on·ean** \-'ō-nē-ən\ *adj or n*

Si·er·ra Ma·dre del Sur \sē-‚er-ə-'mä-drā-del-'sùr, 'syer-ä-'mä-thrä-thel-'sùr\ mountain range S Mexico along Pacific coast in Guerrero & Oaxaca

Sierra Madre Oc·ci·den·tal \‚äk-sə-‚den-'täl, ‚ōk-sē-‚then-'täl\ mountain range NW Mexico parallel to the Pacific coast

Sierra Madre Ori·en·tal \‚ōr-ē-‚en-'täl, ‚ōr-\ mountain range E Mexico parallel to coast of Gulf of Mexico

Sierra Mo·re·na \mō-'rā-nä\ mountain range SW Spain bet. the Guadiana & the Guadalquivir; highest peak Estrella 4339 *ft* (1322 *m*)

Sierra Ne·va·da \nə-'va-də, -'vä-\ **1** mountain range E Calif. — see WHITNEY (Mount) **2** mountain range S Spain; highest peak Mulhacén *ab* 11,410 *ft* (3478 *m*) — **Si·er·ran** \sē-'er-ən\ *adj or n*

Sierra Nevada de Mérida — see CORDILLERA DE MÉRIDA

Sierra Nevada de San·ta Mar·ta \dā-‚san-tə-'mär-tə, thā-‚sän-tä-\ mountain range N Colombia on Caribbean coast

Sierra Vis·ta \'vis-tə\ city SE Ariz. *pop* 32,983

Si·kang \'shē-'käŋ\ former province S China ✳ Yaan

Si·kho·te–Alin \'sē-kə-‚tä-ə-'lēn\ mountain range SE Russia in Asia in Maritime Territory

Sik·kim \'si-kəm, -‚kim\ former country SE Asia on S slope of the Himalayas bet. Nepal & Bhutan; since 1975 a state of India ✳ Gangtok *area* 2744 *sq mi* (7107 *sq km*), *pop* 406,457 — **Sik·kim·ese** \‚si-kə-'mēz, -'mēs\ *adj or n*

Si·le·sia \sī-'lē-zh(ē-)ə, sə-, -sh(ē-)ə\ region E *cen* Europe in valley of the upper Oder bordering on Sudety Mountains; formerly chiefly in Germany, now chiefly in E Czech Republic & SW Poland — **Si·le·sian** \-zh(ē-)ən, -sh(ē-)ən\ *adj or n*

Sim·birsk \sim-'birsk\ *or 1924–91* **Ul·ya·novsk** \ül-'yä-nəfsk\ city SE *cen* Russia in Europe on the Volga *pop* 656,000

Sim·coe, Lake \'sim-(‚)kō\ lake E Canada in SE Ont. SE of Georgian Bay *area* 280 *sq mi* (728 *sq km*)

Sim·fe·ro·pol \‚sim(p)-fə-'rò-pəl, -'rō-\ city in the Crimea *pop* 353,000

Si·mi Valley \sē-'mē\ city SW Calif. W of Los Angeles *pop* 100,217

Sim·la \'sim-lə\ city N India N of Delhi ✳ of Himachal Pradesh & former summer ✳ of India *pop* 81,463

Si·mons·town \'sī-mənz-,taun\ town & port SW Republic of South Africa in Western Cape province on False Bay S of Cape Town

Sim·plon Pass \'sim-,plän\ mountain pass 6590 *ft* (2009 *m*) in Lepontine Alps bet. Switzerland & Italy in Valais & Piedmont

Simplon Tunnel tunnel *ab* 12 *mi* (19 *km*) long through Monte Leone near Simplon Pass

Sims·bury \'simz-,ber-ē, -b(ə-)rē\ town N Conn. *pop* 22,023

Si·nai \'sī-,nī *also* -nē-,ī\ peninsula extension of continent of Asia NE Egypt bet. Red Sea & the Mediterranean — **Si·na·it·ic** \,sī-nē-'i-tik\ *adj*

Sinai, Mount — see HOREB (Mount)

Si·na·loa \,sē-nä-'lō-ä\ state W Mexico bordering on Gulf of California ✶ Culiacán *area* 22,429 *sq mi* (58,091 *sq km*), *pop* 2,204,054

Sind *or* **Sindh** \'sind\ province S Pakistan in lower Indus valley ✶ Karachi

Sin·ga·pore \'siŋ-ə-,pōr, -,pȯr *also* 'siŋ-gə-\ **1** island Malay Archipelago in S. China Sea off S end of Malay Peninsula; formerly a Brit. crown colony, from 1963 to 1965 a state of Malaysia (federation), an independent republic in the Commonwealth of Nations since 1965, *area* 225 *sq mi* (585 *sq km*), *pop* 2,685,400 **2** city & port, its ✶, on Singapore Strait *pop* 206,500 — **Sin·ga·por·ean** \,siŋ-ə-'pōr-ē-ən, -'pȯr- *also* 'siŋ-ə-\ *adj or n*

Singapore Strait channel SE Asia bet. Singapore Is. & Riau Archipelago connecting Strait of Malacca & S. China Sea

Sining — see XINING

Sinkiang Uighur — see XINJIANG UYGUR

Si·nop \sə-'nȯp\ *or anc* **Si·no·pe** \-'nō-pē\ town & port N Turkey on peninsula in Black Sea NW of Ankara *pop* 25,631

Sinsiang — see XINXIANG

Sint–Gillis — see SAINT-GILLES

Sint Maarten — see SAINT MARTIN

Sin·tra *or* **Cin·tra** \'sēn-trə\ city W Portugal NW of Lisbon *pop* 262,447

Sin·ui·ju \sin-'wē-,jü\ city W N. Korea on the Yalu opposite Dandong, China *pop* 289,000

Sion 1 \sē-'ōⁿ\ *or G* **Sit·ten** \'zi-tⁿn, 'si-\ commune SW *cen* Switzerland ✶ of Valais *pop* 25,350 **2** — see ZION 2

Sioux City \'sü\ city NW Iowa on Missouri River *pop* 80,505

Sioux Falls city SE S.Dak. on the Big Sioux *pop* 100,814

Si·ping \'sə-'piŋ\ *or* **Ssu·p'ing** \'sə-'piŋ\ *or formerly* **Sze·ping·kai** \'sə-'piŋ-'gī\ city NE China in Jilin SW of Changchun *pop* 317,223

Sip·par \si-'pär\ ancient city of Babylonia on the Euphrates SSW of modern Baghdad; Sargon's capital

Siracusa — see SYRACUSE

Si·ret \si-'ret\ river 280 *mi* (450 *km*) E Romania flowing from the Carpathians SE into the Danube

Sí·ros \'sē-,rȯs\ **1** *or* **Syros** island Greece in the Cyclades S of Andros **2** — see ERMOÚPOLIS

Sis·ki·you Mountains \'sis-ki-,yü\ mountains N Calif. & SW Oreg., a range of Klamath Mountains; highest Mt. Ashland (in Oreg.) 7533 *ft* (2296 *m*)

Sit·tang \'si-,täŋ\ river 260 *mi* (418 *km*) E *cen* Myanmar flowing S into Gulf of Martaban

Sit·twe \'si-ˌtwä\ *or formerly* **Ak·yab** \a-'kyab\ city & port W Myanmar; chief town of Arakan coast *pop* 42,329

Si·vas \si-'väs\ *or anc* **Se·bas·te** \sə-'bas-tē\ *or* **Se·bas·tia** \sə-'bas-ch(ē-)ə, -tē-ə\ city E *cen* Turkey on the upper Kizil Irmak *pop* 221,512

Si·wa \'sē-wə\ *or anc* **Am·mo·ni·um** \ə-'mō-nē-əm\ oasis & town NW Egypt W of Qattara Depression *pop* 4999

Si·wa·lik Range \si-'wä-lik\ foothills of the Himalayas N India extending SE from N Punjab into Uttar Pradesh

Sjæl·land \'she-ˌlän\ island, largest of islands of Denmark; site of Copenhagen *area* 2709 *sq mi* (7043 *sq km*) *pop* 1,971,946

Skag·er·rak \'ska-gə-ˌrak\ arm of the North Sea bet. Norway & Denmark

Skag·it \'ska-jət\ river 163 *mi* (262 *km*) SW B.C. & NW Wash. flowing S & W into Puget Sound

Skan·e·at·e·les Lake \ˌska-nē-'at-ləs, ˌski-nē-\ lake 16 *mi* (26 *km*) long *cen* N.Y. SW of Syracuse; one of the Finger Lakes

Skaw, The \'skȯ\ *or* **Ska·gens Od·de** \'skä-gənz-ˌȯ-də\ cape Denmark at N extremity of Jutland

Skee·na \'skē-nə\ river 360 *mi* (579 *km*) Canada in W B.C. flowing S & W into Hecate Strait

Skid·daw \'ski-ˌdȯ\ mountain 3053 *ft* (930 *m*) NW England in NW *cen* Cumbria

Skik·da \'skik-(ˌ)dä\ *or formerly* **Phi·lippe·ville** \'fi-ləp-ˌvil, fi-ˌlēp-'vēl\ city & port NE Algeria N of Constantine *pop* 128,747

Skí·ros \'skē-ˌrȯs\ island Greece in the Northern Sporades E of Euboea

Sko·kie \'skō-kē\ village NE Ill. N of Chicago *pop* 59,432

Skop·je \'skȯ-pye, -pyə\ city ✳ of Macedonia on the Vardar *pop* 563,301

Skunk \'skəŋk\ river 264 *mi* (425 *km*) SE Iowa flowing SE into Mississippi River

Skye \'skī\ island Scotland, one of the Inner Hebrides *area* 670 *sq mi* (1742 *sq km*)

Slave \'slāv\ river 258 *mi* (415 *km*) Canada flowing from W end of Lake Athabasca N into Great Slave Lake

Slave Coast region W Africa bordering on Bight of Benin bet. Benin & Volta rivers

Slav·kov \'släf-ˌkȯf, 'släv-ˌkȯv\ *or* **Aus·ter·litz** \'ȯ-stər-ˌlits, 'au̇-\ town SE Czech Republic ESE of Brno

Sla·vo·nia \slə-'vō-nē-ə, -nyə\ region E Croatia bet. the Sava, the Drava, & the Danube — **Sla·vo·ni·an** \-nē-ən, -nyən\ *adj or n*

Slea·ford \'slē-fərd\ town E England in SW Lincolnshire SSE of Lincoln

Slesvig — see SCHLESWIG

Sli·dell \slī-'del\ town SE La. NE of New Orleans *pop* 24,124

Slide Mountain \'slīd\ mountain 4204 *ft* (1281 *m*) SE N.Y. W of Kingston; highest in the Catskills

Sli·go \'slī-(ˌ)gō\ **1** county N Ireland (republic) in N Connacht *area* 693 *sq mi* (1795 *sq km*), *pop* 54,756 **2** municipal borough & port, its ✳, on **Sligo Bay** (inlet of Atlantic Ocean) *pop* 17,297

Slough \'slau̇\ borough SE *cen* England in Berkshire *pop* 98,600

Slo·va·kia \slō-'vä-kē-ə, -'va-\ *or* **Slo·ven·sko** \'slȯ-ven-ˌskȯ\ country *cen* Europe; a constituent republic of Czechoslovakia 1918–92

✳ Bratislava *area* 18,923 *sq mi* (49,011 *sq km*), *pop* 5,329,000 —
Slo·vak \'slō-ˌväk, -vak\ *adj or n* — **Slo·va·ki·an** \slō-vä-kē-ən, -'va-\ *adj or n*

Slo·ve·nia \slō-'vē-nē-ə, -nyə\ country S Europe N & W of Croatia; a federated republic of Yugoslavia 1946–91 **✳** Ljubljana *area* 7819 *sq mi* (20,251 *sq km*), *pop* 1,997,000 — **Slo·vene** \'slō-ˌvēn\ *adj or n* — **Slo·ve·nian** \slō-'vē-nē-ən, -nyən\ *adj or n*

Smith·field \'smith-ˌfēld\ city N R.I. NW of Providence *pop* 19,163

Smoky Hill \'smō-kē\ river 540 *mi* (869 *km*) *cen* Kans. flowing E to unite with Republican River forming the Kansas River

Smo·lensk \smō-'len(t)sk\ city W Russia in Europe on the upper Dnieper WSW of Moscow *pop* 352,000

Smyr·na \'smər-nə\ **1** town NW Ga. NW of Atlanta *pop* 30,981 **2** — see IZMIR

Snake \'snāk\ river 1038 *mi* (1670 *km*) NW U.S. flowing from NW Wyo. across S Idaho & into Columbia River in Wash.

Snake Range mountain range E Nevada

Sno·qual·mie Falls \snō-'kwäl-mē\ waterfall 270 *ft* (80 *m*) W *cen* Wash. in Snoqualmie River 70 *mi* (118 *km*)

Snow — see MAOKE

Snow·don \'snō-dⁿn\ massif 3560 *ft* (1085 *m*) NW Wales in Gwynedd; highest point in Wales

Snow·do·nia \snō-'dō-nē-ə, -nyə\ mountain region NW Wales centering around Snowdon

Snowy \'snō-ē\ river 278 *mi* (447 *km*) SE Australia flowing from Snowy Mountains to the Pacific in SE Victoria

Snowy Mountains mountains SE Australia in SE New South Wales

So·bat \'sō-ˌbat\ river 460 *mi* (740 *km*) W Ethiopia & SE Sudan flowing W into White Nile River

Soča — see ISONZO

So·chi \'sō-chē\ city & port S Russia in Europe on NE coast of Black Sea *pop* 344,000

So·ci·e·ty Islands \sə-'sī-ə-tē\ *or F* Îles de la So·cié·té \ˌēl-də-lä-sō-syä-'tā\ islands S Pacific belonging to France **✳** Papeete (on Tahiti) *area* 621 *sq mi* (1608 *sq km*), *pop* 162,573

So·cor·ro \sə-'kór-(ˌ)ō\ town Tex., a S suburb of El Paso *pop* 22,995

So·co·tra \sə-'kō-trə\ island Indian Ocean E of Gulf of Aden in Yemen **✳** Tamrida (Hadibu) *area* 1400 *sq mi* (3640 *sq km*), *pop* 8000

Söd·er·täl·je \ˌsə(r)-dər-'tel-yə, ˌsœ-\ town SE Sweden, a suburb of Stockholm *pop* 81,460

Sod·om \'säd-əm\ city of ancient Palestine in plain of Jordan River

So·fia \'sō-fē-ə, 'sò-, sō-'\ *or Bulg* So·fi·ya \'sò-fē-ə\ *or anc* Ser·di·ca \'sər-di-kə\ *or* Sar·di·ca \'sär-\ city W Bulgaria, its **✳** *pop* 1,141,142

Sog·di·a·na \ˌsäg-dē-'a-nə, -'ä-nə, -'ä-nə\ province of ancient Persian Empire bet. the Jaxartes (Syr Darya) & Oxus (Amu Darya) **✳** Maracanda (Samarqand) — **Sog·di·an** \'säg-dē-ən\ *adj or n*

Sogne Fjord \'sóŋ-nə\ inlet of Norwegian Sea SW Norway; longest fjord in Norway

So·hâg \sō-'haj\ city *cen* Egypt on the Nile SE of Asyût *pop* 85,300

So·ho \'sō-ˌhō\ district of *cen* London, England, in Westminster

Sois·sons \swä-'sōⁿ\ commune N France NW of Paris *pop* 32,144

Solapur — see SHOLAPUR

So·lent, The \'sō-lənt\ channel S England bet. Isle of Wight & the mainland

So·li·hull \ˌsō-li-'həl\ borough *cen* England in W. Midlands SE of Birmingham *pop* 194,100

So·li·mões \ˌsü-lē-'mōⁱⁿsh\ the upper Amazon, Brazil, from Peruvian border to the mouth of Negro River

So·ling·en \'zō-liŋ-ən, 'sō-\ city W Germany in the Ruhr ESE of Düsseldorf *pop* 165,924

Sol·na \'sól-ˌnä\ city E Sweden, N suburb of Stockholm *pop* 51,427

Sol·o·mon Islands \'sä-lə-mən\ islands W Pacific E of New Guinea divided bet. Papua New Guinea & the independent country (formerly a Brit. protectorate) of the Solomon Islands (✹ Honiara) *area* 11,500 *sq mi* (29,785 *sq km*), *pop* 349,000

Solomon Sea arm of Coral Sea W of Solomon Islands

So·lo·thurn \'zō-lə-ˌtúrn, 'sō-\ *or F* **So·leure** \sō-'lər, -'lœr\ **1** canton NW Switzerland *area* 305 *sq mi* (790 *sq km*), *pop* 223,803 **2** commune, its ✹, on the Aare *pop* 15,531

Sol·way Firth \'säl-ˌwä\ inlet of Irish Sea in Great Britain on boundary bet. England & Scotland

So·ma·lia \sō-'mä-lē-ə, sə-, -'mäl-yə\ country E Africa bordering on Gulf of Aden & Indian Ocean; formed 1960 by union of Brit. Somaliland & Italian Somaliland ✹ Mogadishu *area* 246,154 *sq mi* (637,539 *sq km*), *pop* 8,050,000 — **So·ma·lian** \-'mä-lē-ən, -'mäl-yən\ *adj or n* — **So·ma·li** \sō-'mä-lē, sə-\ *n*

So·ma·li·land \sō-'mä-lē-ˌland, sə-\ region E Africa comprising Somalia, Djibouti, & the Ogaden region of E Ethiopia

Som·er·set \'sə-mər-ˌset, -sət\ *or* **Som·er·set·shire** \-ˌshir, -shər\ county SW England ✹ Taunton *area* 1383 *sq mi* (3582 *sq km*), *pop* 459,100

Somerset Island island N Canada in Northwest Territories N of Boothia Peninsula *area* 9370 *sq mi* (24,362 *sq km*)

Somerset Nile — see NILE

Som·er·ville \'sə-mər-ˌvil\ city E Mass. N of Cambridge *pop* 76,210

So·mes \sō-'mesh\ *or Hung* **Sza·mos** \'sô-ˌmōsh\ river NE Hungary & NW Romania flowing NW into the Tisza

Somme \'säm, 'sam\ river *ab* 150 *mi* (241 *km*) N France flowing NW into the English Channel

Song·hua \'sòn-'hwä\ *or* **Sun·ga·ri** \'sún-gə-rē\ river *over* 1000 *mi* (1609 *km*) NE China in E Manchuria flowing from N. Korea border NW & NE into the Amur; dammed in upper part to form Songhua Reservoir

Song·nam \'sòŋ-'näm\ city W S. Korea *pop* 447,692

So·no·ra \sə-'nór-ə, -'nór-\ **1** river 250 *mi* (400 *km*) NW Mexico flowing SW into upper Gulf of California **2** state NW Mexico bordering on U.S. & Gulf of California ✹ Hermosillo *area* 71,403 *sq mi* (184,934 *sq km*), *pop* 1,823,606 — **So·no·ran** \-ən\ *adj or n*

Sonoran Desert desert SW U.S. & NW Mexico in S Ariz., SE Calif., & N Sonora

Soo Canals — see SAULT SAINTE MARIE CANALS

Soochow — see SUZHOU

Sop·ron \'shō-ˌprōn\ city W Hungary *pop* 57,500

Sorata — see ILLAMPU

Sorbiodunum — see OLD SARUM

So·ria \\'sōr-ē-ə, 'sȯr-\ **1** province N *cen* Spain *area* 3972 *sq mi* (10,287 *sq km*), *pop* 94,537 **2** commune, its ✳, W of Saragossa *pop* 32,360

So·ro·ca·ba \\,sōr-ə-'ka-bə, ,sȯr-, -'kä-\ city SE Brazil in SE São Paulo state *metropolitan area pop* 377,270

Sor·ren·to \sȯ-'ren-(,)tō\ *or anc* **Sur·ren·tum** \sə-'ren-təm\ commune & port S Italy on S side of Bay of Naples

Sos·no·wiec \sä-'snō-,vyets\ city SW Poland NE of Katowice *pop* 259,269

Sou·fri·ère \,sü-frē-'er\ **1** volcano 4813 *ft* (1467 *m*) French West Indies in S Basse-Terre, Guadeloupe **2** volcano 4048 *ft* (1234 *m*) Brit. West Indies on St. Vincent Is.

Sou·ris \\'sủr-əs\ river 450 *mi* (724 *km*) Canada & U.S. flowing from SE Sask. SE into N N.Dak. & N into the Assiniboine in SW Man.

Sousse \\'süs\ *or anc* **Had·ru·me·tum** \,ha-drə-'mē-təm\ city & port NE Tunisia *pop* 69,530

South Africa, Republic of country S Africa S of the Limpopo, Molopo, & Orange rivers bordering on Atlantic & Indian oceans; a republic, until 1961 (as **Union of South Africa**) a Brit. dominion; administrative ✳ Pretoria, legislative ✳ Cape Town, judicial ✳ Bloemfontein *area* 471,445 *sq mi* (1,221,043 *sq km*), *pop* 30,193,000 — **South African** *adj or n*

Sou·thall \\'saủ-,thȯl\ former municipal borough S England in Middlesex, now part of Ealing

South America continent of the western hemisphere lying bet. the Atlantic & Pacific oceans SE of N. America & chiefly S of the equator *area* 6,880,706 *sq mi* (17,821,029 *sq km*) — **South American** *adj or n*

South·amp·ton \saủ-'tham(p)-tən, saủth-'ham(p)-\ city & port S England in Hampshire on **Southampton Water** (estuary of Test River) *pop* 194,400

Southampton Island island N Canada in Northwest Territories, bet. Hudson Bay & Foxe Channel *area* 15,700 *sq mi* (40,820 *sq km*)

South Arabia, Federation of former Brit. protectorate comprising crown colony of Aden & numerous semi-independent Arab sultanates & emirates; made part of People's Democratic Republic of Yemen 1967

South Atlantic — see ATLANTIC OCEAN

South Australia state S Australia ✳ Adelaide *area* 380,070 *sq mi* (988,182 *sq km*), *pop* 1,462,900

South Bend \\'bend\ city N Ind. NW of Fort Wayne *pop* 105,511

South Canadian — see CANADIAN

South Cape — see KA LAE

South Car·o·li·na \,kar-(-ə)-'lī-nə\ state SE U.S. ✳ Columbia *area* 31,113 *sq mi* (80,583 *sq km*), *pop* 3,486,703 — **South Car·o·lin·ian** \-'li-nē-ən, -'li-nyən\ *adj or n*

South China Sea part of W Pacific enclosed by SE China, Taiwan, Philippines, Indochina, Malaya, & Borneo

South Da·ko·ta \də-'kō-tə\ state NW *cen* U.S. ✳ Pierre *area* 77,116 *sq mi* (199,730 *sq km*), *pop* 696,004 — **South Da·ko·tan** \-'kō-tᵊn\ *adj or n*

South Downs hills S England chiefly in Sussex

South El Monte city SW Calif. SE of Los Angeles *pop* 20,850

South·end on Sea \ˌsaủ-ˌthend-ˌón-ˈsē, -ˌän-\ borough SE England in Essex at mouth of Thames estuary *pop* 153,700

Southern Alps mountain range New Zealand in W South Is. extending almost the length of the island — see COOK (Mount)

Southern Morocco — see MOROCCO

Southern Ocean the Antarctic Ocean

Southern Rhodesia — see ZIMBABWE

Southern Up·lands \ˈəp-lən(d)z, -ˌlan(d)z\ elevated moorland region S Scotland in Dumfries and Galloway, Borders, Lothian, & SE Strathclyde administrative regions

Southern Yemen — see YEMEN

South Euclid city NE Ohio E of Cleveland *pop* 23,866

South·field \ˈsaủth-ˌfēld\ city SE Mich. NW of Detroit *pop* 75,728

South·gate \ˈsaủth-ˌgāt\ city SE Mich. S of Detroit *pop* 30,771

South Gate \ˌgāt\ city SW Calif. SE of Los Angeles *pop* 86,284

South Georgia island S Atlantic E of Tierra del Fuego in Falkland Islands Dependencies *area* 1450 *sq mi* (3770 *sq km*)

South Glamorgan county SE Wales ✳ Cardiff *area* 161 *sq mi* (417 *sq km*), *pop* 383,300

South Holland **1** village NE Ill. S of Chicago *pop* 22,105 **2** *or D* **Zuid–Hol·land** \ˈzīt-ˈhό-ˌlänt\ province SW Netherlands ✳ Rotterdam *area* 1259 *sq mi* (3261 *sq km*), *pop* 3,295,522

South·ing·ton \ˈsə-thiŋ-tən\ town W *cen* Conn. *pop* 38,518

South Island island S New Zealand *area* 59,439 *sq mi* (153,947 *sq km*), *pop* 881,537

South Kings·town \ˈkiŋ-stən, ˈkiŋz-ˌtaủn\ town S R.I. *pop* 24,631

South Korea — see KOREA

South Lake Tahoe city E Calif. on Lake Tahoe *pop* 21,586

South Milwaukee city SE Wis. on Lake Michigan *pop* 20,958

South Mountain ridge S Pa. & W Md. at N end of Blue Ridge

South Na·han·ni \nə-ˈha-nē\ river 350 *mi* (563 *km*) Canada in SW Northwest Territories flowing SE into the Liard

South Orkney Islands islands S Atlantic SE of the Falklands in Falkland Islands Dependencies *area* 240 *sq mi* (622 *sq km*)

South Os·se·tia \ä-ˈsē-sha\ autonomous region N Georgia ✳ Tskhinvali *area ab* 1500 *sq mi* (3900 *sq km*), *pop* 99,000

South Pacific — see PACIFIC OCEAN

South Pasadena city SW Calif. *pop* 23,936

South Pass broad level valley SW *cen* Wyo. crossing Continental Divide

South Plainfield borough NE N.J. SW of Elizabeth *pop* 20,489

South Platte river 424 *mi* (682 *km*) Colo. & Nebr. flowing E to join N. Platte River forming the Platte River

South·port \ˈsaủth-ˌpȯrt, -ˌpȯrt\ borough NW England in Merseyside on coast N of Liverpool *pop* 89,745

South Portland city SW Maine *pop* 23,163

South Saint Paul city SE Minn. on Mississippi River *pop* 20,197

South Sandwich Islands islands S Atlantic SE of S. Georgia Is. in Falkland Islands Dependencies *area* 120 *sq mi* (312 *sq km*)

South San Francisco city W Calif. *pop* 54,312

South Saskatchewan — see SASKATCHEWAN

South Seas the areas of the Atlantic, Indian, & Pacific oceans in the southern hemisphere, esp. the S Pacific

South Shetland Islands British islands S Atlantic SE of Cape Horn off tip of Antarctic Peninsula

South Shields \'shēldz\ borough N England in Tyne and Wear at mouth of the Tyne E of Newcastle *pop* 87,203

South Tirol — see ALTO ADIGE

South Vietnam — see VIETNAM

South·wark \'sə-thərk, 'saŭth-wərk\ borough of S London, England *pop* 196,500

South–West Africa — see NAMIBIA

South Windsor town N Conn. NE of Hartford *pop* 22,090

South Yemen — see YEMEN — **South Ye·me·ni** \'ye-mə-nē\ *adj*

South Yorkshire metropolitan county N England ✳ Barnsley *area* 624 *sq mi* (1616 *sq km*), *pop* 1,248,500

So·vetsk \sə-'vyetsk\ *or G* **Til·sit** \'til-sət, -zit\ city W Russia in Europe on the Neman *pop* 42,300

So·vet·ska·ya Ga·van \sə-'vyet-skə-yə-'gä-vən, -'gä-və-nyə\ city & port SE Russia in Asia on Tatar Strait *pop* 35,400

So·vi·et Central Asia \'sō-vē-,et, 'sä-;-vē-ət\ the portion of *cen* Asia formerly belonging to the U.S.S.R. & comprising the Kyrgyzstan, Tajikistan, Turkmenistan, & Uzbekistan republics & sometimes Kazakhstan

Soviet Russia **1** — see RUSSIA **2** the U.S.S.R.

Soviet Union — see UNION OF SOVIET SOCIALIST REPUBLICS — **Soviet** *adj or n*

So·we·to \sō-'wä-tō, -'we-, -tü\ township NE Republic of South Africa in Gauteng adjoining SW Johannesburg; a black residential complex

Spa \'spä\ town E Belgium SE of Liège *pop* 10,140

Spain \'spān\ *or Sp* **Es·pa·ña** \ā-'spä-nyä\ country SW Europe in the Iberian Peninsula; a kingdom ✳ Madrid *area* 194,881 *sq mi* (504,742 *sq km*), *pop* 39,141,000 — **Span·iard** \'span-yərd\ *n* — **Span·ish** \'spa-nish\ *adj or n*

Span·dau \'shpän-,daŭ, 'spän-\ a W section of Berlin, Germany

Spanish America **1** the Spanish-speaking countries of the Americas **2** the parts of America settled & formerly governed by the Spanish — **Spanish American** *adj or n*

Spanish Guinea former Spanish colony W Africa bordering on Gulf of Guinea including Río Muni (Mbini), Fernando Póo (Bioko), & other islands — see EQUATORIAL GUINEA

Spanish Main \'mān\ **1** the mainland of Spanish America esp. along N coast of S. America **2** the Caribbean Sea & adjacent waters esp. at the time when region was infested with pirates

Spanish Morocco — see MOROCCO

Spanish Peaks two mountains (**East Spanish Peak** 12,683 *ft or* 3866 *m* & **West Spanish Peak** 13,623 *ft or* 4152 *m*) S Colo.

Spanish Sahara former Spanish possessions Río de Oro & Saguia el Hamra — see WESTERN SAHARA

Spanish Town town SE *cen* Jamaica W of Kingston; former ✳ of Jamaica

Sparks \'spärks\ city W Nev. E of Reno *pop* 53,367

Spar·ta \'spär-tə\ *or* **Lac·e·dae·mon** \,la-sə-'dē-mən\ ancient city S Greece in Peloponnese S of Laconia — **Spar·tan** \'spär-tᵉn\ *adj or n*

Spar·tan·burg \'spär-tᵉn-,bərg\ city NW S.C. *pop* 43,467

Spen·cer Gulf \'spen(t)-sər\ inlet of Indian Ocean SE S. Australia

Spey \'spā\ river 110 *mi* (177 *km*) NE Scotland flowing into Moray Firth

Spey·er \'shpī(-ə)r, 'spī(-ə)r\ *or* **Spires** \'spīrz\ city SW Germany on W bank of the Rhine SW of Heidelberg *pop* 47,456

Spezia, La — see LA SPEZIA

Spits·ber·gen \'spits-,bər-gən\ group of islands in Arctic Ocean N of Norway; belongs to Norway *area* 23,641 *sq mi* (61,230 *sq km*) — see SVALBARD

Split \'split\ city & port S Croatia on Dalmatian coast *pop* 200,459

Spo·kane \spō-'kan\ **1** river 120 *mi* (193 *km*) N Idaho & E Wash. flowing from Coeur d'Alene Lake W into Columbia River **2** city E Wash. at Spokane Falls in Spokane River *pop* 177,196

Spo·le·to \spō-'lā-(,)tō, -'lē-\ commune *cen* Italy SE of Perugia *pop* 37,057

Spor·a·des \'spȯr-ə-,dēz, 'spär-\ two island groups Greece in the Aegean: the **Northern Sporades** (chief island Skíros, N of Euboea & E of Thessaly) & the **Southern Sporades** (chiefly Samos, Ikaria, & the Dodecanese, off SW Turkey)

Sprat·ly Islands \'sprat-lē\ islands *cen* S. China Sea SE of Cam Ranh Bay, Vietnam; claimed by several countries

Spree \'shprā, 'sprā\ river 247 *mi* (397 *km*) E Germany flowing N into the Havel

Spree·wald \-,vält\ marshy district E Germany in Spree valley

Spring·dale \'sprin-,dāl\ city NW Ark. *pop* 29,941

Spring·field \'sprin-,fēld\ **1** city ✻ of Ill. on the Sangamon *pop* 105,227 **2** city SW Mass. on Connecticut River *pop* 156,983 **3** city SW Mo. *pop* 140,494 **4** city N *cen* Ohio NE of Dayton *pop* 70,487 **5** city W Oreg. on the Willamette E of Eugene *pop* 44,683

Springs \'sprinz\ city NE Republic of South Africa in Gauteng *pop* 142,812

Spring Valley village SE N.Y. N of New York City *pop* 21,802

Spuy·ten Duy·vil Creek \,spī-t³n-'dī-vəl\ channel New York City N of Manhattan Is. connecting Hudson & Harlem rivers

Sri Lan·ka \(,)srē-'läŋ-kə, (,)shrē-, -'laŋ-\ *or formerly* **Cey·lon** \si-'län, sā-\ country coextensive with island of Ceylon; an independent republic in the Commonwealth of Nations ✻ Colombo *area* 25,332 *sq mi* (65,863 *sq km*), *pop* 17,829,500 — **Sri Lan·kan** \-'läŋ-kən, -'laŋ-\ *adj or n*

Sri·na·gar \srē-'nə-gər\ city India, summer ✻ of Jammu and Kashmir, in W Kashmir on the Jhelum NNE of Lahore *pop* 423,253

Ssu–p'ing — see SIPING

Staf·fa \'sta-fə\ islet W Scotland in the Inner Hebrides W of Mull — see FINGAL'S CAVE

Staf·ford \'sta-fərd\ borough W *cen* England ✻ of Staffordshire *pop* 117,000

Staf·ford·shire \'sta-fərd-,shir, -shər\ *or* **Stafford** county W *cen* England ✻ Stafford *area* 1086 *sq mi* (2813 *sq km*), *pop* 1,020,300

Staked Plain — see LLANO ESTACADO

Sta·kha·nov \stə-'kä-nəf, -'kä-\ *or formerly* **Ka·di·yev·ka** \kə-'dē-yəf-kə\ city E Ukraine *pop* 113,000

Stalin 1 — see BRASOV **2** — see DONETSK **3** — see VARNA

Stalinabad — see DUSHANBE

Stalingrad — see VOLGOGRAD

Stalino — see DONETSK

Stalinsk — see NOVOKUZNETSK

Stam·ford \'stam-fərd\ city SW Conn. *pop* 108,056

Stanislav — see IVANO-FRANKIVS'K

Stan·ley \'stan-lē\ *or* **Port Stanley** town ✶ of the Falklands

Stanley, Mount *or in Democratic Republic of the Congo* **Mount Nga·lie·ma** \ən-gäl-'yā-mä\ mountain with two peaks (higher 16,763 *ft or* 5109 *m*) E *cen* Africa; highest of Ruwenzori

Stanley Falls — see BOYOMA FALLS

Stanley Pool — see MALEBO, POOL

Stanleyville — see KISANGANI

Stan·o·voy \ˌsta-nə-'vȯi\ mountain range SE Russia in Asia N of the Amur

Stan·ton \'stan-tᵊn\ city SW Calif. SE of Los Angeles *pop* 30,491

Sta·ra Za·go·ra \ˌstär-ə-zə-'gȯr-ə, -'gȯr-\ city *cen* Bulgaria *pop* 164,553

State College borough *cen* Pa. NE of Altoona *pop* 38,923

Stat·en Island \'sta-tᵊn\ **1** island N.Y. SW of mouth of Hudson River **2** *or formerly* **Rich·mond** \'rich-mənd\ borough of New York City including Staten Is. *pop* 378,977

Statia — see SAINT EUSTATIUS

Statue of Liberty National Monument — see LIBERTY ISLAND

Staun·ton \'stan-tᵊn\ city NW *cen* Va. *pop* 24,461

Sta·vang·er \stə-'väŋ-ər, -'vaŋ-\ city & port SW Norway *pop* 97,570

Stav·ro·pol \sta-'vrō-pəl, -'vrō-, 'stä-vrə-pəl\ **1** territory S Russia in Europe N of the Caucasus *area* 31,120 *sq mi* (80,600 *sq km*), *pop* 2,536,000 **2** city, its ✶ *pop* 332,000 **3** — see TOL'YATTI

Stȩ·bark \'stem-ˌbärk\ *or G* **Tan·nen·berg** \'ta-nən-ˌbȯrg, 'tä-nən-ˌberk\ village NE Poland SW of Olsztyn

Steens Mountain \'stēnz\ mountain mass SE Oreg.; highest point *ab* 9700 *ft* (2955 *m*)

Stel·len·bosch \'ste-lən-ˌbäs, -ˌbäsh, *Afrik* ˌste-ləm-'bȯs\ city SW Republic of South Africa in SW Western Cape province *pop* 29,955

Step·ney \'step-nē\ *former* metropolitan borough E London, England, on N bank of Thames River, now part of Tower Hamlets

Ster·ling Heights \'stər-liŋ\ city SE Mich. N of Detroit *pop* 117,810

Steu·ben·ville \'stü-bən-ˌvil, 'styü-\ city E Ohio *pop* 22,125

Ste·vens Point \'stē-vənz\ city *cen* Wis. *pop* 23,006

Stew·art \'stü-ərt, 'styü-\ river 331 *mi* (532 *km*) Canada in *cen* Yukon Territory flowing W into Yukon River

Stewart Island island New Zealand S of South Is. *area* 675 *sq mi* (1748 *sq km*)

Sti·kine \sti-'kēn\ river 335 *mi* (539 *km*) Canada & Alaska flowing from **Stikine Mountains** (in B.C. & Yukon Territory) into the Pacific

Still·wa·ter \'stil-ˌwȯ-tər, -ˌwä-\ city N *cen* Okla. *pop* 36,676

Stir·ling \'stər-liŋ\ **1** *or* **Stir·ling·shire** \-ˌshir, -shər\ *former* county *cen* Scotland **2** burgh *cen* Scotland ✶ of Central region *pop* 38,638

Stock·holm \'stäk-ˌhō(l)m\ city & port ✶ of Sweden on Mälaren Lake *pop* 684,576 — **Stock·holm·er** \-ˌhō(l)-mər\ *n*

Stock·port \'stäk-ˌpȯrt, -ˌpȯrt\ borough NW England in Greater Manchester S of Manchester *pop* 276,800

Stock·ton \'stäk-tən\ city *cen* Calif. on the San Joaquin *pop* 210,943

Stoke New·ing·ton \stōk-'nü-iŋ-tən, -'nyü-\ former metropolitan borough N London, England, now part of Hackney

Stoke on Trent \stōk-,än-'trent, -,ȯn-\ city W *cen* England in Staffordshire *pop* 244,800

Stone·ham \'stō-nəm, 'stōn-,ham\ town E Mass. *pop* 22,203

Stone·ha·ven \stōn-'hā-vən, stän-'hī\ burgh & port E Scotland in Grampian region *pop* 7885

Stone·henge \'stōn-,henj, (,)stōn-'\ assemblage of megaliths S England in Wiltshire on Salisbury Plain erected by prehistoric peoples

Stone Mountain \'stōn\ mountain 1686 *ft* (514 *m*) NW *cen* Ga. E of Atlanta

Stones \'stōnz\ river 60 *mi* (96 *km*) *cen* Tenn. flowing NW into Cumberland River

Ston·ey Creek \'stō-nē\ city Canada in SE Ont. *pop* 49,968

Stor·mont \'stȯr-mənt\ E suburb of Belfast, Northern Ireland; site of Parliament House

Stor·no·way \'stȯr-nə-,wā\ burgh NW Scotland in Lewis ✻ of Western Isles region *pop* 8660

Stough·ton \'stō-tᵊn\ town E Mass. NW of Brockton *pop* 26,777

Stour 1 \'stu̇r\ river 47 *mi* (76 *km*) SE England flowing E bet. Essex & Suffolk into the North Sea 2 \'stau̇r, 'stu̇r\ river 55 *mi* (88 *km*) S England in Dorset & Hampshire flowing SE into Avon River 3 *or* **Great Stour** \'stu̇r *also* 'stau̇r\ river 40 *mi* (64 *km*) SE England in Kent flowing NE into the North Sea 4 \'stau̇r, 'stu̇r\ river 20 *mi* (32 *km*) *cen* England in Oxfordshire & Warwickshire flowing NW into Avon River 5 *same as* 4\ river 20 *mi* (32 *km*) W *cen* England in Staffordshire & Hereford and Worcester flowing S into Severn River

Stour·bridge \'stau̇r-(,)brij, 'stȯr-\ borough W *cen* England in W. Midlands W of Birmingham *pop* 54,661

Stow \'stō\ city NE Ohio NE of Akron *pop* 27,702

Stra·bane \strə-'ban\ district W Northern Ireland, established 1974 *area* 336 *sq mi* (874 *sq km*), *pop* 35,668

Straits Settlements former country SE Asia bordering on Strait of Malacca & comprising Singapore Is., Penang, & Meleka; now divided bet. Singapore (republic) & Malaysia (federation) *area* 1242 *sq mi* (3229 *sq km*)

Stral·sund \'shträl-,zu̇nt, 'sträl-, -,su̇nt\ city & port NE Germany on the Baltic opposite Rügen Is. *pop* 71,618

Stras·bourg \'sträs-,bu̇rg, 'sträz-, -,bȯrg\ *or* G **Strass·burg** \'shträs-,bu̇rk\ city NE France *pop* 255,937

Strat·ford \'strat-fərd\ 1 town SW Conn. *pop* 49,389 2 city Canada in SE Ont. W of Kitchener *pop* 27,666

Stratford–upon–Avon \-'ā-vən, -'a-\ borough *cen* England in Warwickshire SSE of Birmingham *pop* 20,858

Strath·clyde \strath-'klīd\ 1 Celtic kingdom of 6th to 11th centuries S Scotland & NW England ✻ Dumbarton; its S part called **Cum·bria** \'kəm-brē-ə\ 2 region SW Scotland, established 1975; ✻ Glasgow *area* 5214 *sq mi* (13,503 *sq km*), *pop* 2,286,800

Strath·more \strath-'mōr, -'mȯr\ great valley of E *cen* Scotland S of the Grampians

Stream·wood \'strēm-,wu̇d\ village NE Ill. E of Elgin *pop* 30,987

Stre·sa \'strā-zə\ town NW Italy in Piedmont on Lake Maggiore

Stret·ford \'stret-fərd\ borough NW England in Greater Manchester SW of Manchester *pop* 47,600

Stri·món, Gulf of \strē-'món\ *or* **Stri·mon·i·kós Kól·pos** \strē-ˌmó-nē-'kós-'kól-pós\ *or* **Stry·mon·ic Gulf** \strī-'mä-nik\ inlet of the Aegean NE Greece NE of Chalcidice Peninsula

Strom·bo·li \'sträm-bō-(ˌ)lē\ *or anc* **Stron·gy·le** \strän-jə-ˌlē\ **1** island Italy in Lipari Islands **2** volcano 3038 *ft* (926 *m*) on the island

Strom·lo, Mount \'sträm-(ˌ)lō\ hill 2500 *ft* (758 *m*) SE Australia in Australian Capital Territory W of Canberra

Strongs·ville \'strónz-ˌvil\ city NE Ohio SW of Cleveland *pop* 35,308

Stry·mon \'strī-ˌmän\ *or Bulg* **Stru·ma** \'strü-mə\ river W Bulgaria & NE Greece flowing SE into Gulf of Strimón

Stutt·gart \'shtút-ˌgärt, 'stút-, 'stət-\ city SW Germany ✳ of Baden-Württemberg on the Neckar *pop* 591,946

Styr \'stir\ river 271 *mi* (436 *km*) NW Ukraine flowing N into the Pripet in the Pripet Marshes

Styr·ia \'stir-ē-ə\ *or Ger* **Stei·er·mark** \'shtī-(-ə)r-ˌmärk, 'stī-(-ə)r-\ region *cen* & SE Austria; chief city Graz — **Styr·i·an** \'stir-ē-ən\ *adj or n*

Sua·kin \'swä-kən\ town & port NE Sudan on Red Sea

Su·bic \'sü-bik\ town Philippines in W Luzon at head of **Subic Bay** (inlet of S. China Sea NW of Bataan Peninsula) *pop* 30,340

Su·bo·ti·ca \'sü-bō-ˌtēt-sä\ city N Yugoslavia in N Vojvodina near Hungarian border *pop* 150,666

Süchow 1 — see XUZHOU **2** — see YIBIN

Su·cre \'sü-(ˌ)krā\ city, constitutional ✳ of Bolivia, SE of La Paz *pop* 130,952

Su·dan \sü-'dan, -'dän\ **1** region N Africa bet. the Atlantic & the upper Nile S of the Sahara including basins of Lake Chad & Niger River & the upper Nile **2** country NE Africa S of Egypt; a republic, until 1956 a territory (**Anglo-Egyptian Sudan**) under joint Brit. & Egyptian rule ✳ Khartoum *area* 967,500 *sq mi* (2,515,500 *sq km*), *pop* 25,000,000 — **Su·da·nese** \ˌsü-dᵊn-'ēz, -'ēs\ *adj or n*

Sudanese Republic — see MALI

Sud·bury \'səd-ˌber-ē, -b(ə-)rē\ city Canada in SE Ont. N of Georgian Bay *pop* 92,884

Sudd \'səd\ swamp region S Sudan drained by White Nile River

Su·de·ten·land \sü-'dā-tᵊn-ˌland, -ˌlänt\ region N Czech Republic in Sudety Mountains

Su·de·ty *Czech* 'sù-de-tē, *Polish* sù-'de-tē\ *or* **Su·de·ten** \sü-'dā-tᵊn\ mountains *cen* Europe N of the Carpathians bet. Czech Republic & Poland — **Sudeten** *adj or n*

Su·dir·man Range \'sü-'dir-mən\ *or formerly* **Nas·sau Range** \'na-ˌsó\ mountain range *cen* W. Irian — see DJAJA (Mount)

Su·ez \sü-'ez, 'sü-ˌez, *chiefly Brit* 'sü-iz\ city & port NE Egypt at S end of Suez Canal on **Gulf of Suez** (arm of Red Sea) *pop* 376,000

Suez, Isthmus of isthmus NE Egypt bet. Mediterranean & Red seas connecting Africa & Asia

Suez Canal canal over 100 *mi* (161 *km*) long NE Egypt traversing Isthmus of Suez

Suf·folk \'sə-fək, *US also* -ˌfòk\ **1** city SE Va. W of Chesapeake *pop* 52,141 **2** county E England bordering on North Sea ✳ Ipswich *area* 1520 *mi* (3937 *km*), *pop* 629,900; formerly divided into administrative counties of **East Suffolk** (✻ Ipswich) & **West Suffolk** (✻ Bury St. Edmunds)

Suffolk Broads — see BROADS

Sugar Land city SE Tex. SW of Houston *pop* 24,529

Sugarloaf Mountain — see PÃO DE AÇÚCAR

Suisse — see SWITZERLAND

Sui·sun Bay \sə-ˈsün\ the E extension of San Pablo Bay *cen* Calif.

Suisun City city *cen* Calif. SW of Sacramento *pop* 22,686

Su·i·ta \süˈē-tä\ city Japan on Honshu *pop* 345,187

Sukarnapura — see JAYAPURA

Su·khu·mi \ˈsü-kə-mē, sü-ˈkü-mē\ city & port NW Georgia ✻ of Abkhaz Republic on Black Sea *pop* 120,000

Suk·kur \ˈsü-kər\ city Pakistan in N Sind on the Indus *pop* 193,000

Su·la·we·si \ˌsü-lä-ˈwä-sē\ *or* **Ce·le·bes** \ˈse-lə-ˌbēz, sə-ˈlē-bēz\ island Indonesia E of Borneo ✻ Ujung Pandang *area* 72,775 *sq mi* (188,487 *sq km*), *pop* 12,520,711

Sul·grave \ˈsəl-ˌgrāv\ village England in S Northamptonshire

Sul·phur \ˈsəl-fər\ city SW La. *pop* 20,125

Su·lu Archipelago \ˈsü-(ˌ)lü\ archipelago SW Philippines SW of Mindanao

Sulu Sea sea W Philippines N of Celebes Sea

Su·ma·tra \sü-ˈmä-trə\ island W Indonesia S of Malay Peninsula *area* 182,542 *sq mi* (472,784 *sq km*) — **Su·ma·tran** \-trən\ *adj or n*

Sum·ba \ˈsüm-bə\ island Indonesia in the Lesser Sundas *area* 4306 *sq mi* (11,196 *sq km*), *pop* 251,126

Sum·ba·wa \süm-ˈbä-wə\ island Indonesia in the Lesser Sundas *area* 5693 *sq mi* (14,802 *sq km*), *pop* 195,554

Su·mer \ˈsü-mər\ the S division of ancient Babylonia — see AKKAD, SHINAR

Sum·ga·it \süm-ˈgī-it\ *or* **Sum·qay·it** \-ˈkī-\ city & port Azerbaijan on the Caspian NW of Baku *pop* 236,200

Sum·mer·ville \ˈsə-mər-ˌvil\ town SE S.C. NW of Charleston *pop* 22,519

Sum·mit \ˈsə-mət\ city NE N.J. W of Newark *pop* 19,757

Sum·ter \ˈsəm-tər\ city E *cen* S.C. E of Columbia *pop* 41,943

Sun·belt \ˈsən-ˌbelt\ region S & SW U.S.

Sun·da Islands \ˈsün-də, ˈsən-\ islands Malay Archipelago comprising the **Greater Sunda Islands** (Sumatra, Java, Borneo, Sulawesi, & adjacent islands) & the **Lesser Sunda Islands** (extending E from Bali to Timor); with exception of N Borneo, belongs to Indonesia

Sunda Strait strait bet. Java & Sumatra

Sun·der·land \ˈsən-dər-lənd\ borough N England in Tyne and Wear on North Sea *pop* 286,800

Sunds·vall \ˈsan(t)s-ˌväl, ˈsündz-\ city & port E Sweden on Gulf of Bothnia *pop* 94,329

Sungari — see SONGHUA

Sun·ny·vale \ˈsə-nē-ˌvāl\ city W Calif. WNW of San Jose *pop* 117,229

Sun·rise \ˈsən-ˌrīz\ city SE Fla. *pop* 64,407

Sun·set Crater \ˈsən-ˌset\ volcanic crater N *cen* Ariz. in **Sunset Crater National Monument**

Suomi — see FINLAND

Su·pe·ri·or \su̇-'pir-ē-ər\ city & port NW Wis. on Lake Superior *pop* 27,134

Superior, Lake lake U.S. & Canada; largest, northernmost, & westernmost of the Great Lakes *area* 31,800 *sq mi* (82,362 *sq km*)

Su·per·sti·tion Mountains \,sü-pər-'sti-shən\ range *S cen* Ariz. E of Phoenix

Sur \'su̇r\ *or* **Tyre** \'tīr\ town S Lebanon on the coast; ancient ✱ of Phoenicia

Sur, Point \'sər\ promontory Calif. on the Pacific SSW of Monterey — see BIG SUR

Su·ra·ba·ya \,su̇r-ə-'bī-ə\ city & port Indonesia in NE Java on **Surabaya Strait** (bet. Java & W end of Madura) *pop* 2,483,871

Su·ra·kar·ta \,su̇r-ə-'kär-tə\ city Indonesia in *cen* Java *pop* 504,176

Su·rat \'su̇r-ət, sə-'rat\ city W India in SE Gujarat *pop* 1,505,872

Sur·bi·ton \'sər-bə-tᵊn\ former municipal borough S England in Surrey WSW of London, now part of Kingston upon Thames

Su·ri·ba·chi, Mount \,su̇r-ē-'bä-chē\ volcano 548 *ft* (167 *m*) in the Volcano Islands at S end of Iwo Jima

Su·ri·na·me \,su̇r-ə-'nä-mə\ **1** *or formerly* **Dutch Guiana** *or* **Netherlands Guiana** country N S. America bet. Guyana & French Guiana; a republic, until 1975 territory of the Netherlands ✱ Paramaribo *area* 63,251 *sq mi* (163,820 *sq km*), *pop* 403,000 **2** river N Suriname flowing N into the Atlantic — **Su·ri·nam·er** \'su̇r-ə-,nä-mər, ,su̇r-ə-'nä-\ *n* — **Su·ri·nam·ese** \,su̇r-ə-nə-'mēz, -'mēs\ *adj or n*

Sur·ma \'su̇r-mə\ river 560 *mi* (901 *km*) NE India (subcontinent) in Manipur & Bangladesh — see MEGHNA

Surrentum — see SORRENTO

Sur·rey \'sər-ē, 'sə-rē\ **1** county SE England S of London ✱ Kingston upon Thames *area* 662 *sq mi* (1714 *sq km*), *pop* 998,000 **2** municipality Canada in SW B.C. SE of Vancouver *pop* 245,173

Surts·ey \'sərt-,sā, 'su̇rt-\ island Iceland off S coast *area* 1 *sq mi* (2.6 *sq km*); formed 1963 by volcanic eruption

Su·ru·ga Bay \'su̇r-ə-gə, su̇-'rü-gä\ inlet of the Pacific Japan on coast of SE Honshu W of Sagami Sea

Su·sa \'sü-zə\ *or bib* **Shu·shan** \'shü-shən, -,shan\ ancient city ✱ of Elam; ruins in SW Iran

Susiana — see ELAM

Sus·que·han·na \,səs-kwə-'ha-nə\ river 444 *mi* (714 *km*) E U.S. flowing from *cen* N.Y. S through Pa. & into Chesapeake Bay in N Md.

Sus·sex \'sə-siks, *US also* -,seks\ former county SE England bordering on English Channel; one of kingdoms in Anglo-Saxon heptarchy — see EAST SUSSEX, WEST SUSSEX

Suth·er·land \'sə-thər-lənd\ *or* **Suth·er·land·shire** \-lən(d)-,shir, -shər\ former county N Scotland ✱ Dornoch

Sutherland Falls waterfall 1904 *ft* (580 *m*) New Zealand in SW South Is.

Sut·lej \'sət-,lej\ river *ab* 900 *mi* (1448 *km*) N India (subcontinent) flowing from Tibet W & SW through the Punjab to join the Chenab

Sut·ton \'sə-tᵊn\ borough of S Greater London, England *pop* 164,300

Sutton Cold·field \'kōl(d)-,fēld\ borough *cen* England in W. Midlands NE of Birmingham *pop* 86,494

Sutton–in–Ash·field \-'ash-ˌfēld\ town N *cen* England in Nottinghamshire N of Nottingham *pop* 41,270

Su·va \'sü-va\ city & port ✳ of Fiji, on Viti Levu Is. *pop* 63,628

Su·wał·ki \sü-'vaü-kē\ **1** district NE Poland **2** city in the district

Su·wan·nee \sə-'wä-nē, 'swä-\ river 250 *mi* (400 *km*) SE Ga. & N Fla. flowing SW into Gulf of Mexico

Su·won \'sü-ˌwän\ city NW S. Korea S of Seoul *pop* 430,752

Su·zhou \'sü-'jō\ *or* **Soo·chow** \-'jō, -'chaü\ *or formerly* **Wu·hsien** \'wü-'shyen\ city E China in SE Jiangsu W of Shanghai *pop* 706,459

Sval·bard \'sväl-ˌbär\ islands in the Arctic Ocean including Spitsbergen, Bear Is., & other small islands *area* 23,958 *sq mi* (62,052 *sq km*); under Norwegian administration

Sverdlovsk — see YEKATERINBURG

Sver·drup Islands \'sver-drəp\ islands N Canada W of Ellesmere Is. including Axel Heiberg, Ellef Ringnes, & Amund Ringnes islands

Swa·bia \'swä-bē-ə\ *or G* **Schwa·ben** \'shvä-bən\ region and medieval county SW Germany chiefly in area comprising modern Baden-Wurttemberg & W Bavaria — **Swa·bi·an** \'swä-bē-ən\ *adj or n*

Swan \'swän\ *or in its upper course* **Av·on** \'a-vən\ river *ab* 240 *mi* (386 *km*) SW Western Australia flowing W into Indian Ocean

Swan Islands two islands in the Caribbean NE of Honduras

Swan·sea \'swän-zē\ *also* -ˌsē\ city & port SE Wales ✳ of W. Glamorgan *pop* 182,100

Swat \'swät\ river 400 *mi* (644 *km*) Pakistan flowing into Kabul River

Swatow — see SHANTOU

Swa·zi·land \'swä-zē-ˌland\ country SE Africa bet. Republic of South Africa & Mozambique; a former Brit. protectorate, an independent kingdom since 1968 ✳ Mbabane *area* 6705 *sq mi* (17,433 *sq km*), *pop* 494,534

Swe·den \'swē-dᵊn\ *or Sw* **Sve·ri·ge** \'sve-rē-yə\ country N Europe on Scandinavian Peninsula W of Baltic Sea; a kingdom ✳ Stockholm *area* 173,665 *sq mi* (449,792 *sq km*), *pop* 8,727,000 — **Swede** \swēd\ *n* — **Swed·ish** \'swē-dish\ *adj or n*

Swin·don \'swin-dən\ borough S England in NE Wiltshire *pop* 91,136

Świ·no·ujś·cie \ˌshfē-nō-'ü-ēsh-che\ city & port NW Poland on N coast of Uznam (Usedom) Is. NNW of Szczecin *pop* 42,886

Swin·ton and Pen·dle·bury \'swin-tᵊn-ənd-'pen-dᵊl-ˌber-ē, -b(ə-)rē\ borough NW England in Greater Manchester NW of Manchester *pop* 39,621

Swit·zer·land \'swit-sər-lənd\ *or F* **Suisse** \'swȳēs\ *or G* **der Schweiz** \der-'shvīts\ *or It* **Sviz·ze·ra** \'zvēt-tsä-rä\ *or L* **Hel·ve·tia** \hel-'vē-sh(ē-)ə\ country W Europe in the Alps; a federal republic ✳ Bern *area* 15,940 *sq mi* (41,444 *sq km*), *pop* 6,996,000 — **Swiss** \'swis\ *adj or n*

Syb·a·ris \'si-bə-rəs\ ancient Greek city S Italy on Gulf of Tarentum; destroyed 510 B.C. — **Syb·a·rite** \'si-bə-ˌrīt\ *n*

Syd·ney \'sid-nē\ **1** city & port SE Australia on Port Jackson ✳ of New South Wales *metropolitan area pop* 3,097,956 **2** city Canada in NE N.S. on Cape Breton Is. *pop* 26,063 — **Syd·ney·ite** \-,īt\ *n* — **Syd·ney·sid·er** \-,sī-dər\ *n*

Syene — see ASWÂN

Syk·tyv·kar \,sik-tif-'kär\ town NE Russia in Europe ✳ of Komi Republic *pop* 226,000

Sylt \'zilt, 'silt\ island NW Germany, chief of the N. Frisian Islands *area* 36 *sq mi* (94 *sq km*)

Syr·a·cuse \'sir-ə-,kyüs, -,kyüz\ **1** city *cen* N.Y. near Oneida Lake *pop* 163,860 **2** *or It* **Si·ra·cu·sa** \,sē-rä-'kü-zä\ *or anc* **Syr·a·cu·sae** \,sir-ə-'kyü-(,)sē, -(,)zē\ city & port Italy in SE Sicily *pop* 124,606 — **Syr·a·cu·san** \,sir-ə-'kyü-s°n\ *adj or n*

Syr Dar·ya \sir-'där-yə\ *or anc* **Jax·ar·tes** \jak-'sär-(,)tēz\ river *ab* 1370 *mi* (2204 *km*) Kyrgyzstan & S Kazakhstan flowing from Tian Shan W & NW into Lake Aral

Syr·ia \'sir-ē-ə\ **1** ancient region SW Asia bordering on the Mediterranean & covering modern Syria, Lebanon, Israel, & Jordan **2** former French mandate (1920–44) comprising the **Le·vant States** \lə-'vant\ (Syria, Lebanon, Latakia, & Jebel ed Druz), administrative ✳ Beirut, legislative ✳ Damascus **3** country SW Asia bordering on the Mediterranean; a republic 1944–58 & since 1961; a province of United Arab Republic 1958–61 ✳ Damascus *area* 71,498 *sq mi* (185,180 *sq km*), *pop* 13,398,000 — **Syr·i·an** \'sir-ē-ən\ *adj or n*

Syrian Desert desert W Asia bet. Mediterranean coast & the Euphrates covering N Saudi Arabia, NE Jordan, SE Syria, & W Iraq

Syros — see SÍROS 1

Syrtis Major — see SIDRA (Gulf of)

Syrtis Minor — see GABÈS (Gulf of)

Szamos — see SOMES

Szcze·cin \'shche-,chēn\ city & port NW Poland *pop* 412,058

Sze·chwan \'sech-'wän, 'sesh-\ *or* **Si·chuan** \'sēch-'wän\ province SW China ✳ Chengdu *area* 219,691 *sq mi* (571,197 *sq km*), *pop* 107,218,173

Sze·ged \'se-,ged\ city S Hungary *pop* 184,000

Sze·kes·fe·her·var \'sā-,kesh-,fe-här-,vär\ city W *cen* Hungary *pop* 111,200

Szepingkai — see SIPING

Szol·nok \'sōl-,nōk\ city E *cen* Hungary *pop* 82,900

Szom·bat·hely \'sōm-,bòt-,hā\ city W Hungary *pop* 87,700

T

Ta·bas·co \tə-'bas-(,)kō\ state SE Mexico on the Caribbean SW of Yucatán Peninsula ✳ Villahermosa *area* 9522 *sq mi* (24,662 *sq km*), *pop* 1,501,744

Ta·blas \'tä-bläs\ island *cen* Philippines in Romblon group

Ta·ble Bay \'tä-bəl\ harbor of Cape Town, Republic of South Africa

Table Mountain mountain 3563 *ft* (1086 *m*) Republic of South Africa S of Cape Town

Ta·bor, Mount \'tā-bər, -,bȯr\ mountain 1929 *ft* (588 *m*) N Palestine E of Nazareth

Ta·bo·ra \tä-'bȯr-ä, -'bȯr-\ city W *cen* Tanzania *pop* 67,392

Ta·briz \tə-'brēz\ city NW Iran in Azerbaijan *pop* 971,482

Ta·bu·ae·ran \tə-,bü-ə-'er-ən\ *or formerly* **Fan·ning Island** \'fa-niŋ\ island *cen* Pacific in the Line Islands *area* 15 *sq mi* (39 *sq km*), *pop* 376

Tac·na \'täk-nä\ city S Peru near Chilean border *pop* 150,200; in region (**Tacna–Ari·ca** \-ä-'rē-kä\) occupied 1884–1930 by Chile & now divided bet. Chile & Peru

Ta·co·ma \tə-'kō-mə\ city & port W Wash. on Puget Sound S of Seattle *pop* 176,664

Tacoma, Mount — see RAINIER (Mount)

Ta·con·ic Range \tə-'kä-nik\ mountains along N part of Conn.-N.Y. boundary, entire Mass.-N.Y. boundary & in SW Vt.; highest Mt. Equinox (in Vt.) 3816 *ft* (1163 *m*)

Ta·djou·ra, Gulf of \tə-'jür-ə\ inlet of Gulf of Aden in E Djibouti

Tadmor — see PALMYRA

Tae·dong \'tā-,dȯŋ, tī-\ river *cen* N. Korea flowing SW into Korea Bay

Tae·gu \ta-'gü, tī-\ city SE S. Korea NNW of Pusan *pop* 2,248,000

Tae·jon \ta-'jȯn, tī-\ city *cen* S. Korea NW of Taegu *pop* 1,064,000

Ta·gan·rog \'ta-gən-,räg\ city S Russia in Europe on **Gulf of Taganrog** (NE arm of Sea of Azov) *pop* 293,000

Ta·gus \'tā-gəs\ *or Sp* **Ta·jo** \'tä-(,)hō\ *or Pg* **Te·jo** \'tā-(,)zhü\ river 626 *mi* (1007 *km*) Spain & Portugal flowing W into the Atlantic

Ta·hi·ti \tə-'hē-tē\ island S Pacific in Windward group of the Society Islands; chief town Papeete *area* 402 *sq mi* (1045 *sq km*), *pop* 131,309 — **Ta·hi·tian** \tə-'hē-shən\ *adj or n*

Ta·hoe, Lake \'tä-,hō\ lake 22 *mi* (35 *km*) long on Calif.-Nev. boundary

Tai·chung \'tī-'chuŋ\ city W Taiwan *pop* 779,370

Tai Hu \'tī-'hü\ lake *ab* 45 *mi* (72 *km*) long E China in Jiangsu

T'ai·nan \'tī-'nän\ city SW Taiwan *pop* 702,237

Taí·na·ron \'tä-nä-,rȯn\ *or* **Mat·a·pan** \,ma-tə-'pan\ cape S Greece at S tip of Peloponnese bet. Gulfs of Laconia & Messenia

Tai·o·hae \,tī-ō-'hē\ town Nuku Hiva Is. ✳ of the Marquesas

Tai·pei \'tī-'pā, -'bā\ city ✳ of (Nationalist) Republic of China, on Taiwan *pop* 2,651,419

Tai Shan \'tī-'shän\ mountain 5000 *ft* (1524 *m*) E China in W Shandong

Tai·wan \'tī-'wän\ *or* **For·mo·sa** \fȯr-'mō-sə, fər-, -zə\ island China off SE coast E of Fujian; belonged to Japan 1895–1945; since 1949

seat of (Nationalist) Republic of China (✴ Taipei) *area* 13,807 *sq
mi* (35,760 *sq km*) *pop* 20,926,000 — **Tai·wan·ese** \ˌtī-wə-ˈnēz,
-ˈnēs\ *adj or n*

Tai·yu·an \ˈtī-ˈywen, -ˈywän\ *or formerly* **Yang·ku** \ˈyän-ˈkü\ city N
China ✴ of Shanxi *pop* 1,533,884

Tai·zhou *or* **T'ai–chou** \ˈtī-ˈjō\ city E China in *cen* Jiangsu

Ta·jik·i·stan \tä-ji-ki-ˈstan, tə-, -ˌjē, -ˈstän; -ˈji-ki-ˌ, -ˌjē\ country W
cen Asia bordering on China & Afghanistan; a constituent republic
(**Ta·dzhik Republic** \tä-ˈjik, tə-, -ˈjēk\ *or* **Ta·dzhik·i·stan** *same
as* TAJIKISTAN\) of the U.S.S.R. 1929–91 ✴ Dushanbe *area* 55,251
sq mi (143,100 *sq km*), *pop* 5,705,000

Ta·ju·mul·co \ˌtä-hü-ˈmül-(ˌ)kō\ mountain 13,845 *ft* (4220 *m*) W
Guatemala; highest in Central America

Ta·ka·mat·su \ˌtä-kä-ˈmät-(ˌ)sü, tä-ˈkä-mät-ˌsü\ city & port Japan in
NE Shikoku on Inland Sea *pop* 329,695

Ta·kat·su·ki \tä-ˈkät-sü-(ˌ)kē\ city Japan in S Honshu *pop* 359,867

Tak·ka·kaw \ˈta-kə-ˌkȯ\ waterfall 1650 *ft* (503 *m*) Canada in SE
B.C. in Yoho National Park; highest in Canada

Ta·kli·ma·kan *or* **Ta·kla Ma·kan** \ˌtä-klə-mə-ˈkän\ desert W China in *cen* Xinjiang Uygur bet. Tian Shan & Kunlun mountains

Ta·la·ud Islands \ˈtä-ˌlä-ˌüd\ *or* **Ta·laur Islands** \ˌlä-ˌur\ islands
Indonesia NE of Sulawesi *area* 494 *sq mi* (1284 *sq km*), *pop*
194,253

Tal·ca \ˈtäl-kä\ city *cen* Chile S of Santiago *pop* 128,544

Tal·ca·hua·no \ˌtäl-kä-ˈwä-(ˌ)nō, -ˈhwä-\ city & port S *cen* Chile
NW of Concepción *pop* 202,368

Ta–lien — see DALIAN

Tal·la·has·see \ˌta-lə-ˈha-sē\ city ✴ of Fla. *pop* 124,773

Tal·la·hatch·ie \ˌta-lə-ˈha-chē\ river 230 *mi* (370 *km*) N Miss. flowing SW

Tal·la·poo·sa \ˌta-lə-ˈpü-sə\ river 268 *mi* (431 *km*) NW Ga. & E Ala.
flowing SW to join the Coosa forming Alabama River

Tal·linn \ˈta-lən, tä-\ *or formerly* **Re·vel** \ˈrā-vəl\ city & port ✴ of
Estonia *pop* 482,000

Ta·ma·le \tä-ˈmä-lā\ town N Ghana *pop* 135,952

Tam·al·pais, Mount \ˌta-məl-ˈpī-əs\ mountain 2572 *ft* (784 *m*) W
Calif. NW of San Francisco

Ta·man \tə-ˈmän\ peninsula S Russia in Europe in Ciscaucasia bet.
Sea of Azov & Black Sea

Tam·an·ras·set \ˌta-mən-ˈra-sət\ wadi & oasis SE Algeria

Ta·mar \ˈtä-mər\ **1** river 40 *mi* (64 *km*) Australia in N Tasmania
flowing N to Bass Strait **2** river 60 *mi* (96 *km*) SW England flowing SE from NW Devon into English Channel **3** — see PALMYRA

Tam·a·rac \ˈta-mə-ˌrak\ city SE Fla. *pop* 44,822

Tamatave — see TOAMASINA

Ta·mau·li·pas \ˌtä-ˌmau̇-ˈlē-päs, -ˈli-\ state NE Mexico bordering on
Gulf of Mexico ✴ Ciudad Victoria *area* 30,822 *sq mi* (79,829 *sq
km*), *pop* 2,249,581

Tam·bo·ra \täm-ˈbȯr-ə, -ˈbȯr-\ volcano 9350 *ft* (2850 *m*) Indonesia
on Sumbawa Is.

Tam·bov \täm-ˈbȯf, -ˈbȯv\ city S *cen* Russia in Europe SE of Moscow *pop* 311,000

Tam·il Na·du \ˌta-məl-ˈnä-(ˌ)dü, ˌtä-\ *or formerly* **Madras** state SE India bordering on Bay of Bengal ✻ Madras *area* 50,180 *sq mi* (129,966 *sq km*), *pop* 55,858,946

Tam·pa \ˈtam-pə\ city W Fla. on **Tampa Bay** (inlet of Gulf of Mexico) *pop* 280,015 — **Tam·pan** \-pən\ *adj or n*

Tam·pe·re \ˈtam-pe-ˌrä, ˈtäm-\ city SW Finland *pop* 171,561

Tam·pi·co \tam-ˈpē-(ˌ)kō, tä-\ city & port E Mexico in S Tamaulipas on the Pánuco 7 *mi* (11 *km*) from its mouth *pop* 271,636

Ta·na \ˈtä-nä\ river 440 *mi* (708 *km*) E Africa in Kenya flowing into Indian Ocean

Ta·na, Lake \ˈtä-nä\ lake NW Ethiopia; source of Blue Nile River *area* 1418 *sq mi* (3687 *sq km*)

Ta·na·gra \ˈta-nə-grə, tə-ˈna-grə\ village E *cen* Greece E of Thebes; an important town of ancient Boeotia

Tan·a·na \ˈta-nə-ˌnȯ\ river 550 *mi* (885 *km*) E & *cen* Alaska flowing NW into Yukon River

Tananarive, Tananarivo — see ANTANANARIVO

Tan·ez·rouft \ˌta-nəz-ˈrüft\ extremely arid region of W Sahara in SW Algeria & N Mali

Tan·ga \ˈtaŋ-gə\ city & port Tanzania on NE coast *pop* 187,634

Tan·gan·yi·ka \ˌtan-gə-ˈnyē-kə, ˌtaŋ-gə-, -ˈnē-\ former country E Africa bet. Lake Tanganyika & Indian Ocean; administered by Britain 1920–61; became an independent member of the Commonwealth of Nations 1961 ✻ Dar es Salaam; since 1964 united with Zanzibar as Tanzania — see GERMAN EAST AFRICA — **Tan·gan·yi·kan** \-kən\ *adj or n*

Tanganyika, Lake lake E Africa in Great Rift Valley bet. Democratic Republic of the Congo & Tanzania *area* 12,700 *sq mi* (33,020 *sq km*)

Tan·gier \tan-ˈjir\ **1** city & port N Morocco on Strait of Gibraltar; summer ✻ of Morocco *pop* 187,894 **2** the International Zone of Tangier — see MOROCCO — **Tan·ger·ine** \ˌtan-jə-ˈrēn\ *adj or n*

Tang·shan \ˈdäŋ-ˌshän, ˈtäŋ-\ city NE China in E Hebei *pop* 1,044,194

Ta·nim·bar Islands \tə-ˈnim-ˌbär, tä-\ islands Indonesia in SE Moluccas ENE of Timor *pop* 50,000

Ta·nis \ˈtä-nəs\ *or bib* **Zo·an** \ˈzō-ˌan\ ancient city N Egypt in E Nile delta near Lake Tanis

Tanis, Lake — see MANZALA (Lake)

Tan·jung·ka·rang \ˌtän-jün-ˈkä-räŋ\ *or* **Ban·dar Lam·pung** \ˈbən-dər-ˈläm-pùŋ\ city & port Indonesia in S Sumatra *pop* 636,706

Tan·jung·pri·ok \ˌtän-ˌjün-prē-ˈòk\ port of Jakarta, Indonesia

Tan·na \ˈtä-nə\ island SW Pacific in Vanuatu *pop* 19,825

Tannenberg — see STĘBARK

Tan·ta \ˈtän-tə\ city N Egypt in *cen* Nile delta *pop* 372,000

Tan–tung — see DANDONG

Tan·za·nia \ˌtan-zə-ˈnē-ə, ˌtän-\ republic E Africa formed 1964 by union of Tanganyika & Zanzibar ✻ Dar es Salaam *area* 364,900 *sq mi* (945,091 *sq km*), *pop* 26,542,000 — **Tan·za·ni·an** \-ˈnē-ən\ *adj or n*

Taor·mi·na \ˌtaùr-ˈmē-nä\ *or anc* **Tau·ro·me·ni·um** \ˌtȯr-ə-ˈmē-nē-əm\ commune Italy in NE Sicily

Ta·pa·jos *or* **Ta·pa·joz** \ˌta-pə-ˈzhòs, ˌtä-\ river N Brazil flowing NE into the Amazon — see JURUENA

Ta·pi \'tä-pē\ river 436 *mi* (702 *km*) W India S of Satpura Range flowing W into Gulf of Khambhat

Tap·pan Zee \,ta-pən-'zē\ expansion of Hudson River SE N.Y.

Taprobane — see CEYLON

Ta·qua·ri \,ta-kwə-'rē, ,tä-\ river 350 *mi* (565 *km*) S *cen* Brazil rising in S *cen* Mato Grosso & flowing WSW into Paraguay River

Tar \'tär\ river 215 *mi* (346 *km*) NE N.C. — see PAMLICO

Tara \'tar-ə\ village Ireland in County Meath NW of Dublin near **Hill of Tara** (seat of ancient Irish kings)

Tarabulus — see TRIPOLI

Taranaki — see EGMONT (Mount)

Ta·ran·to \'tär-ən-,tō, tə-'ran-(,)tō\ *or anc* **Ta·ren·tum** \tə-'ren-təm\ city & port SE Italy on **Gulf of Taranto** (inlet of Ionian Sea) *pop* 244,512

Ta·ra·wa \tə-'rä-wə, 'tar-ə-,wä\ island *cen* Pacific * of Kiribati *area* 8 *sq mi* (21 *sq km*), *pop* 28,802

Tarbes \'tärb\ city SW France ESE of Pau *pop* 50,228

Ta·ri·fa, Cape \tä-'rē-fə, tə-\ cape S Spain; southernmost point of continental Europe, at 36°01'N

Ta·rim \'dä-'rēm, 'tä-\ river 1250 *mi* (2012 *km*) W China in Xinjiang Uygur in the Taklimakan flowing E & SE into a marshy depression

Tar·lac \'tär-,läk\ city Philippines in *cen* Luzon *pop* 688,457

Tarn \'tärn\ river 233 *mi* (375 *km*) S France flowing W into the Garonne

Tar·nów \'tär-,nüf\ city S Poland E of Kraków *pop* 120,385

Tar·qui·nia \tär-'kwē-nyə, -'kwi-, -nē-ə\ *or formerly* **Cor·ne·to** \kòr-'nā-(,)tō\ *or anc* **Tar·quin·ii** \tär-'kwi-nē-,ī\ town *cen* Italy in N Lazio NW of Viterbo

Tar·ra·go·na \,tär-ə-'gō-nə, ,tär-ä-'gō-nä\ **1** province NE Spain on the Mediterranean *area* 2426 *sq mi* (6283 *sq km*), *pop* 542,004 **2** commune & port, its *, SW of Barcelona *pop* 110,003

Tar·ra·sa \tä-'rä-sä\ commune NE Spain NNW of Barcelona *pop* 154,360

Tar·shish \'tär-(,)shish\ ancient maritime country referred to in the Bible, by some located in S Spain & identified with Tartessus

Tar·sus \'tär-səs\ city S Turkey near the Cilician Gates * of ancient Cilicia *pop* 187,508

Tar·tes·sus *or* **Tar·tes·sos** \tär-'te-səs\ ancient kingdom on SW coast of Spain identified with Tarshish — see TARSHISH

Tar·tu \'tär-(,)tü\ *or G* **Dor·pat** \'dòr-,pät\ city E Estonia W of Lake Peipus *pop* 113,410

Tash·kent \tash-'kent, täsh-\ city E of the Syr Darya * of Uzbekistan *pop* 2,073,000

Tas·man, Mount \'taz-mən\ mountain 11,475 *ft* (3498 *m*) New Zealand in South Is. in Southern Alps NE of Mt. Cook

Tas·ma·nia \taz-'mā-nē-ə, -nyə\ *or formerly* **Van Die·men's Land** \van-'dē-mənz\ island SE Australia S of Victoria; a state * Hobart *area* 26,383 *sq mi* (68,332 *sq km*), *pop* 471,400 — **Tas·ma·ni·an** \taz-'mā-nē-ən, -nyən\ *adj or n*

Tasman Sea the part of the S Pacific bet. SE Australia & W New Zealand

Ta·ta·ban·ya \'tò-tò-,bä-(,)nyò\ city NW Hungary *pop* 75,300

Ta·tar·stan \ˌta-tər-ˈstan, ˌtä-tər-ˈstän\ autonomous republic E *cen* Russia in Europe ✳ Kazan *area* 26,255 *sq mi* (68,000 *sq km*), *pop* 3,696,000

Ta·tar Strait \ˈtä-ˌtär, tə-ˈtär\ strait bet. Sakhalin Is. & mainland of Asia

Ta·try \ˈtä-trē\ *or* **Ta·tra** \ˈtä-trə\ mountain group N Slovakia & S Poland in *cen* Carpathian Mountains — see GERLACHOVKA

Tatung — see DATONG

Tau·ghan·nock Falls \tə-ˈga-nək\ waterfall 215 *ft* (66 *m*) S *cen* N.Y. NW of Ithaca

Taung·gyi \ˈtau̇n-ˌjē\ town E Myanmar ✳ of Shan state *pop* 8652

Taun·ton \ˈtȯn-tᵊn, ˈtän-\ city SE Mass. *pop* 49,832

Tau·nus \ˈtau̇-nəs\ mountain range SW *cen* Germany E of the Rhine & N of lower Main River; highest peak Grosser Feldberg 2886 *ft* (880 *m*)

Tauric Chersonese — see CHERSONESE

Tau·rus \ˈtȯr-əs\ *or* **Turk To·ros** \tȯ-ˈrȯs\ mountains S Turkey parallel to Mediterranean coast

Tax·co \ˈtäs-(ˌ)kō\ *or* **Taxco de Alar·cón** \thä-ˌä-ˌlär-ˈkȯn\ city S Mexico in Guerrero SSW of Mexico City *pop* 86,811

Tay \ˈtā\ river 120 *mi* (193 *km*) E *cen* Scotland flowing into North Sea through **Loch Tay** and **Firth of Tay**

Tay·lor \ˈtā-lər\ city SE Mich. SW of Detroit *pop* 70,811

Tay·myr Peninsula \tī-ˈmir\ peninsula N Russia in Asia bet. the Yenisey & the Khatanga — see CHELYUSKIN (Cape)

Tay·side \ˈtā-ˌsīd\ region E *cen* Scotland, established 1975 ✳ Dundee *area* 2893 *sq mi* (7492 *sq km*), *pop* 395,200

Tbi·li·si \tə-ˈbē-lə-sē, tə-bə-ˈlē-sē\ city ✳ of Republic of Georgia on the Kura *pop* 1,260,000

Tchad — see CHAD

Teche, Bayou \ˈtesh\ stream 175 *mi* (282 *km*) S La. flowing SE into the Atchafalaya

Tees \ˈtēz\ river 70 *mi* (113 *km*) N England flowing E into North Sea

Tees·side \ˈtē(z)-ˌsīd\ former county borough (1968–74) N England; since 1974 part of Cleveland

Te·gu·ci·gal·pa \tə-ˌgü-sə-ˈgal-pə, tä-ˌgü-sē-ˈgäl-pä\ city ✳ of Honduras *district pop* 608,100

Te·hach·a·pi Mountains \ti-ˈha-chə-pē\ mountains SE Calif. N of Mojave Desert running E–W bet. S end of Sierra Nevada & the Coast Ranges; highest Double Mountain 7988 *ft* (2435 *m*); at E end is **Tehachapi Pass** 3793 *ft* (1156 *m*)

Teh·ran \ˌtā-(ə-)ˈran, te-ˈran, -ˈrän\ city ✳ of Iran at foot of S slope of Elburz Mountains *pop* 6,042,584

Teh·ri \ˈtā-rē\ *or* **Tehri Garh·wal** \ˌ(ˌ)gər-ˈwäl\ former state N India in NW Uttar Pradesh on Tibet border; chief town Tehri

Te·huan·te·pec, Isthmus of \tā-ˈwän-tä-ˌpek\ the narrowest section of Mexico, bet. **Gulf of Tehuantepec** (on Pacific side) & Bay of Campeche; 137 *mi* (220 *km*) wide at narrowest point

Tejo — see TAGUS

Tel Aviv \ˌtel-ə-ˈvēv\ city W Israel on the Mediterranean *pop* 353,200 — see JAFFA — **Tel Avi·van** \-ˈvē-vən\ *n*

Tel el Amar·na \ˈtel-el-ə-ˈmär-nə\ locality *cen* Egypt on E bank of the Nile NW of Asyût; site of ruins

Tel·e·mark \ˈte-lə-ˌmärk\ mountain region SW Norway

Tele·scope Peak \\'te-lə-ˌskōp\\ mountain 11,049 *ft* (3368 *m*) E Calif., highest in Panamint Mountains

Te·les Pi·res \\'tā-lēs-'pē-rēs\\ *or formerly* **São Ma·nuel** \\ˌsaůⁿ-mȧ-'nwel\\ river 600 *mi* (966 *km*) E Brazil flowing NW to join the Juruena forming the Tapajos

Te·ma \\'tā-mä\\ city & port Ghana E of Accra *pop* 100,052

Te·mec·u·la \\tə-'me-kyü-lə\\ city S Calif. bet. Riverside & San Diego *pop* 27,099

Temeš — see TIMIŞ

Tem·pe \\tem-'pē, *chiefly by outsiders* 'tem-pē\\ city S *cen* Ariz. SE of Phoenix *pop* 141,865

Tempe, Vale of \\'tem-pē\\ *or NGk* **Tém·bi** \\'tem-bē\\ valley in NE Thessaly bet. Mounts Olympus & Ossa

Tem·ple \\'tem-pəl\\ city NE *cen* Tex. SSW of Waco *pop* 46,109

Temple City city SW Calif. SE of Pasadena *pop* 31,100

Te·mu·co \\tā-'mü-(ˌ)kō\\ city S *cen* Chile *pop* 157,634

Tenedos — see BOZCAADA

Te·ne·rife \\ˌte-nə-'rē-(ˌ)fā, -'rēf, -'rif\\ *or formerly* **Ten·er·iffe** \\ˌte-nə-'rif, -'rēf\\ island Spain, largest of the Canary Islands; chief town Santa Cruz de Tenerife *area* 795 *sq mi* (2059 *sq km*)

Ten·nes·see \\ˌte-nə-'sē, 'te-nə-ˌ\\ **1** river 652 *mi* (1049 *km*) E U.S. in Tenn., Ala., & Ky. flowing into Ohio River **2** state SE *cen* U.S. ✱ Nashville *area* 42,144 *sq mi* (109,153 *sq km*), *pop* 4,877,185 — **Ten·nes·se·an** *or* **Ten·nes·see·an** \\ˌte-nə-'sē-ən\\ *adj or n*

Tennessee–Tom·big·bee Waterway \\-täm-'big-bē\\ waterway 234 *mi* (374 *km*) long from Tennessee River on Tenn.-Miss. border to Tombigbee River in W *cen* Ala.

Te·noch·ti·tlán \\tā-ˌnóch-tēt-'län\\ name for Mexico City when it was capital of the Aztec Empire

Ten·sas \\'ten-ˌsó\\ river 250 *mi* (402 *km*) NE La. uniting with Ouachita River to form Black River

Ten·saw \\'ten-ˌsó\\ river 40 *mi* (64 *km*) SW Ala. formed by Tombigbee & Alabama rivers & flowing S into Mobile Bay

Te·o·ti·hua·cán \\tā-ō-ō-ˌtē-wä-'kän\\ city S *cen* Mexico in Mexico state NE of Mexico City; once ✱ of the Toltecs *pop* 2238

Te·pic \\tā-'pēk\\ city W Mexico ✱ of Nayarit *pop* 238,101

Te·quen·da·ma Falls \\ˌtā-kän-'dä-mä\\ waterfall *cen* Colombia S of Bogotá

Te·rai·na \\te-'rī-nə\\ *or formerly* **Washington Island** island *cen* Pacific in the Line Islands *pop* 437

Ter·cei·ra \\tər-'ser-ə, -'sir-\\ island *cen* Azores *area* 153 *sq mi* (396 *sq km*)

Te·re·si·na \\ˌtār-ā-'zē-nə\\ city NE Brazil ✱ of Piauí *pop* 598,449

Termonde — see DENDERMONDE

Ter·na·te \\ter-'nä-(ˌ)tä\\ **1** island Indonesia in N Moluccas off W Halmahera *pop* 33,964 **2** city & port, chief city on Ternate *pop* 24,287

Ter·ni \\'ter-nē\\ commune *cen* Italy NNE of Rome *pop* 110,020

Ter·ra·ci·na \\ˌter-ä-'chē-nä\\ city & port *cen* Italy in Lazio SE of Pontine Marshes *pop* 39,393

Ter·ra No·va National Park \\ˌter-ə-'nō-və\\ reservation E Canada in E Newfoundland (island)

Terre·bonne \\'ter-ə-ˌbän, ter-'bòn\\ town Canada in Que. N of Montreal *pop* 39,678

Ter·re Haute \ter-ə-'hōt *also* -'hət\ city W Ind. on the Wabash *pop* 57,483

Te·ruel \ter-ü-'wel\ **1** province E Spain in S Aragon *area* 5715 *sq mi* (14,802 *sq km*), *pop* 143,680 **2** commune, its ✳, S of Saragossa *pop* 28,487

Teschen — see CIESZYN

Tessin — see TICINO

Te·thys \'tē-thəs\ hypothetical sea believed to have extended into E Pangaea & later to have separated Laurasia to the N & Gondwanaland to the S with the Mediterranean being a remnant of it — **Te·thy·an** \-thē-ən\ *adj*

Te·ton Range \'tē-,tän, 'tē-tᵊn\ mountain range NW Wyo. — see GRAND TETON

Té·touan \tā-'twän\ *or Sp* **Te·tuán** \te-'twän\ city & port N Morocco on the Mediterranean *pop* 139,105

Teu·to·burg Forest \'tü-tə-,bərg, 'tyü-\ *or G* **Teu·to·bur·ger Wald** \'tȯi-tə-,bür-gər-,vält\ range of forested hills W Germany in region bet. Ems & Weser rivers; highest point 1530 *ft* (466 *m*)

Tewkes·bury \'tüks-,ber-ē, 'tyüks-, -b(ə-)rē\ borough SW *cen* England in Gloucestershire on Avon & Severn rivers *pop* 9554

Tewks·bury \'tüks-,ber-ē, 'tyüks-, -tüks-, -b(ə-)rē\ town NE Mass. *pop* 27,266

Tex·ar·ka·na \,tek-sər-'ka-nə, -sär-\ **1** city SW Ark. *pop* 22,631 **2** city NE Tex. adjacent to Texarkana, Ark. *pop* 31,656

Tex·as \'tek-səs, -siz\ state S U.S. ✳ Austin *area* 266,807 *sq mi* (691,030 *sq km*), *pop* 16,986,510 — **Tex·an** \-sən\ *adj or n*

Texas City city & port SE Tex. on Galveston Bay *pop* 40,822

Tex·co·co \tes-'kō-(,)kō\ city *cen* Mexico in Mexico state E of Mexico City *pop* 18,044

Thai·land \'tī-,land, -lənd\ *or formerly* **Si·am** \sī-'am\ country SE Asia on Gulf of Thailand; a kingdom ✳ Bangkok *area* 198,455 *sq mi* (513,998 *sq km*), *pop* 57,829,000 — **Thai·land·er** \-,lan-dər, -lən-\ *n* — **Thai** \'tī\ *adj or n*

Thailand, Gulf of *or formerly* **Gulf of Siam** arm of S China Sea bet. Indochina & Malay Peninsula

Thames **1** \'temz, 'thämz, 'tämz\ river 15 *mi* (24 *km*) SE Conn., an estuary flowing S into Long Island Sound **2** \'temz\ river 135 *mi* (217 *km*) Canada in SE Ont. flowing S & SW into Lake St. Clair **3** \'temz\ river *over* 200 *mi* (322 *km*) S England flowing from the Cotswolds in Gloucestershire E into the North Sea — see ISIS

Than·et, Isle of \'tha-nət\ tract of land SE England in NE Kent cut off from mainland by arms of Stour River *area* 42 *sq mi* (109 *sq km*)

Thar Desert \'tär\ *or* **Great Indian Desert** desert S Asia in Pakistan & India bet. Aravalli Range & the Indus

Thá·sos \'thä-,sȯs\ island Greece in the N Aegean E of Chalcidice Peninsula *area* 146 *sq mi* (378 *sq km*)

The·ba·id \thi-'bā-əd, 'thē-bā-,id\ ancient district surrounding Thebes in Egypt or in Greece

Thebes \'thēbz\ **1** *or anc* **The·bae** \'thē-(,)bē\ *or* **Di·os·po·lis** \dī-'äs-pə-lis\ ancient city S Egypt on the Nile S of modern Qena — see KARNAK, LUXOR **2** ancient city E Greece in Boeotia NNW of Athens — **The·ban** \'thē-bən\ *adj or n*

The Colony city N Tex. *pop* 22,113

The Hague — see HAGUE (The)

The·o·dore Roosevelt National Park \\thē-ə-,dōr, -,dȯr, -dər\ reservation W N.Dak. comprising three areas in badland region on the Little Missouri

Thermaïkós Kólpos — see SALONIKA (Gulf of)

Ther·mop·y·lae \(,)thər-'mä-pə-(,)lē\ locality E Greece bet. Mt. Oeta & Gulf of Lamia; once a narrow pass along the coast, now a rocky plain 6 *mi* (9.6 *km*) from the sea

Thes·sa·lo·ní·ki \,the-sä-lō-'nē-kē\ *or formerly* **Sa·lo·ni·ka** \sə-'lä-ni-kə\ *or anc* **Thes·sa·lo·ni·ca** \,the-sə-'lä-ni-kə, -lə-'nē-kə\ city & port N Greece in Macedonia *pop* 402,443

Thes·sa·ly \'the-sə-lē\ *or Gk* **Thes·sa·lía** \,the-sä-'lē-ä\ region E Greece bet. Pindus Mountains & the Aegean — **Thes·sa·lian** \the-'sä-lē-ən, -'sāl-yən\ *adj or n*

Thim·phu \thim-'pü\ city W *cen* Bhutan, its ✻

Thí·ra \'thē-rä\ *or anc* **The·ra** \'thir-ə\ island Greece in S Cyclades 29 *sq mi* (75 *sq km*)

Tho·hoy·an·dou \tō-,hȯi-an-'dü\ town NE Republic of South Africa; formerly ✻ of Venda

Thomp·son \'täm(p)-sən\ river 304 *mi* (489 *km*) Canada in S B.C. flowing S (as the **North Thompson**) & thence W & SW into the Fraser; joined by a branch, the **South Thompson**

Thorn·ton \'thȯrn-tᵊn\ city NE *cen* Colo. N of Denver *pop* 55,031

Thou·sand Islands \'thau̇-zᵊnd\ island group Canada & U.S. in St. Lawrence River in Ont. & N.Y.

Thousand Oaks city SW Calif. W of Los Angeles *pop* 104,352

Thrace \'thrās\ region SE Europe in Balkan Peninsula N of the Aegean; as ancient country (**Thra·ce** \'thrā-(,)sē\ *or* **Thra·cia** \'thrāsh(ē-)ə\), extended to the Danube; modern remnant divided bet. Greece (**Western Thrace**) & Turkey (**Eastern Thrace**, constituting Turkey in Europe) — **Thra·cian** \'thrā-shən\ *adj or n*

Thracian Chersonese — see CHERSONESE

Three Forks \'thrē\ locality SW Mont. where Missouri River is formed by confluence of Gallatin, Jefferson, & Madison rivers *pop* 1203

Three Rivers TROIS-RIVIÈRES

Thu·le \'tü-lē\ settlement & district NW Greenland N of Cape York

Thun \'tün\ commune E *cen* Switzerland *pop* 37,950

Thun, Lake of \'tün\ *or* **Thun·er·see** \'tü-nər-,zā\ lake 10 *mi* (16 *km*) long *cen* Switzerland; an expansion of Aare River

Thunder Bay city & port Canada in SW Ont. on Lake Superior, formed 1970 by consolidation of Fort William & Port Arthur *pop* 113,946

Thur·gau \'tu̇r-,gau̇\ *or F* **Thur·go·vie** \tēr-gȯ-'vē\ canton NE Switzerland ✻ Frauenfeld *area* 389 *sq mi* (1008 *sq km*), *pop* 201,773

Thu·rin·gia \thu̇-'rin-j(ē-)ə, thyu̇-\ *or G* **Thü·rin·gen** \'tē-riŋ-ən\ region *cen* Germany including the **Thu·rin·gian Forest** \thu̇-'rin-j(ē-)ən, thyu̇-\ *or G* **Thü·ring·er Wald** \'tē-riŋ-ər-,vält\ (wooded mountain range bet. the upper Werra & the Czech border) — **Thu·rin·gian** \thu̇-'rin-j(ē-)ən, thyu̇r-\ *adj or n*

Thur·rock \'thər-ək, 'thə-rək\ former urban district SE England in Essex

Thurs·day Island \'thərz-dē, -(,)dā\ island NE Australia off N Queensland in Torres Strait

Thyatira — see AKHISAR

Ti·a·hua·na·co \,tē-ä-wä-'nä-(,)kō\ locality W Bolivia near SE end of Lake Titicaca; site of prehistoric ruins

Tian·jin \'tyän-'jin\ or **Tien·tsin** \'tyen-'tsin, 'tin-\ municipality & port NE China SE of Beijing pop 7,764,141

Tian Shan \'tyän-'shän, -'shan\ or **Tien Shan** \'tyen-\ mountain system cen Asia extending from the Pamirs NE into Xinjiang Uygur — see POBEDA PEAK

Ti·ber \'tī-bər\ or It **Te·ve·re** \'tā-vā-rā\ river 252 mi (405 km) cen Italy flowing through Rome into Tyrrhenian Sea

Ti·ber·i·as \tī-'bir-ē-əs\ city N Palestine in Galilee on W shore of Sea of Galilee; now in NE Israel pop 23,900

Tiberias, Lake or **Tiberias, Sea of** — see GALILEE (Sea of)

Ti·bes·ti Mountains \tə-'bes-tē\ mountains N cen Africa in the Sahara in NW Chad; highest Emi Koussi 11,204 ft (3415 m)

Ti·bet \tə-'bet\ or **Xi·zang** \'shēd-'zäŋ\ region SW China on high plateau (average altitude 16,000 ft or 4877 m) N of the Himalayas ✻ Lhasa area 471,660 sq mi (1,226,316 sq km), pop 2,196,010 — **Ti·bet·an** \tə-'be-t⁾n\ adj or n

Ti·bu·rón \,tē-bü-'rōn\ island 34 mi (55 km) long NW Mexico in Gulf of California off coast of Sonora

Ti·ci·no \tē-'chē-(,)nō\ **1** river 154 mi (248 km) Switzerland & Italy flowing from slopes of St. Gotthard Range SE & SW through Lake Maggiore into the Po **2** or F **Tes·sin** \te-saⁿ\ canton S Switzerland bordering on Italy ✻ Bellinzona area 1085 sq mi (2821 sq km), pop 286,537 — **Ti·ci·nese** \,ti-chə-'nēz, -'nēs\ adj or n

Tientsin — see TIANJIN

Tier·ra del Fue·go \tē-'er-ə-(,)del-fü-'ā-(,)gō, 'tyer-ə-(,)thel-'fwä-gō\ **1** archipelago off S S. America S of Strait of Magellan; in Argentina & Chile area over 28,400 sq mi (73,556 sq km) **2** chief island of the archipelago; divided bet. Chile and Argentina area 18,530 sq mi (48,178 sq km)

Tiflis — see TBILISI

Ti·gard \'tī-gərd\ city NW Oreg. SSW of Portland pop 29,344

Ti·gre 1 \'tē-(,)grā\ city E Argentina, NNW suburb of Buenos Aires, on islands in Paraná delta pop 256,005 **2** \ti-'grā, 'ti-(,)grā\ region N Ethiopia bordering on Eritrea — **Ti·gre·an** \ti-'grā-ən\ adj or n

Ti·gris \'tī-grəs\ river 1180 mi (1899 km) Iraq & SE Turkey flowing SSE & uniting with the Euphrates to form the Shatt al Arab

Ti·jua·na \tē-ə-'wä-nə, ,tē-'hwä-nä\ city NW Mexico on U.S. border in Baja California pop 742,686

Ti·kal \tē-'käl\ ancient Mayan city N Guatemala

Til·burg \'til-,bərg\ commune S Netherlands SE of Rotterdam pop 160,618

Til·bury \'til-b(ə-)rē, US also -,ber-ē\ town & port SE England in Essex on Thames River E of London

Til·la·mook Bay \'ti-lə-,mək, -,múk\ inlet of the Pacific NW Oreg.

Tilsit — see SOVETSK

Ti·ma·ga·mi, Lake \tə-'mä-gə-mē\ lake Canada in Ont. N of Lake Nipissing

Timbuktu — see TOMBOUCTOU

Tim·gad \'tim-,gad\ ancient Roman city NE Algeria

Ti·miş \'tē-mesh\ *or* **Te·meš** \'te-mesh\ river *ab* 200 *mi* (322 *km*) Romania & Yugoslavia flowing W & S into the Danube downstream from Belgrade

Ti·mi·soa·ra \ˌtē-mē-'shwär-ä\ city W Romania *pop* 333,365

Tim·mins \'ti-mənz\ city Canada in E Ont. N of Sudbury *pop* 47,461

Ti·mor \'tē-ˌmȯr, tē-'\ **1** island E Indonesia in Lesser Sunda Islands *area* 13,094 *sq mi* (34,044 *sq km*), *pop* 3,000,000; W part (formerly **Netherlands Timor**) belonged to the Dutch until 1946, E part (formerly **Portuguese Timor**) to Portugal until 1975 **2** sea bet. Timor Is. & Australia — **Ti·mor·ese** \ˌtē-mȯ-'rēz, -'rēs\ *adj or n*

Tim·pa·no·gos, Mount \ˌtim-pə-'nō-gəs\ mountain 12,008 *ft* (3660 *m*) N *cen* Utah N of Provo; highest in Wasatch Range

Timpanogos Cave National Monument series of limestone caverns N *cen* Utah on N slope of Mt. Timpanogos

Ti·ni·an \ˌti-nē-'an\ island W Pacific in the S Marianas

Tin·ley Park \'tin-lē\ city NE Ill. *pop* 37,121

Ti·nos \'tē-ˌnos\ island Greece in N Cyclades SE of Andros

Tin·tag·el Head \tin-'ta-jəl\ headland SW England in NW Cornwall

Tip·pe·ca·noe \ˌti-pē-kə-'nü\ river 200 *mi* (322 *km*) N Ind. flowing SW into the Wabash

Tip·per·ary \ˌti-pə-'rer-ē\ **1** county S Ireland in Munster ✳ Clonmel *area* 1643 *sq mi* (4272 *sq km*), *pop* 132,772 **2** town in SW County Tipperary *pop* 4783

Ti·ra·në *or* **Ti·ra·na** \ti-'rä-nə, tē-\ city *cen* Albania, its ✳ *pop* 243,000

Tîr·gu—Mu·res \ˌtir-(ˌ)gü-'mü-ˌresh\ city NE *cen* Romania ESE of Cluj-Napoca *pop* 164,781

Ti·rich Mir \tir-ich-'mir\ mountain *ab* 25,260 *ft* (7699 *m*) Pakistan on Afghan border; highest in the Hindu Kush

Ti·rol *or* **Ty·rol** \tə-'rōl; 'tī-ˌrōl, tī-'; 'tir-əl\ *or It* **Ti·ro·lo** \tē-'rō-lē-ən, tē-; ti-rō-'; ˌtī-rə-\ region Europe in E Alps chiefly in Austria; the section S of Brenner Pass has belonged since 1919 to Italy — **Ti·ro·le·an** \tə-'rō-lē-ən, tē-; ˌti-rō-'; ˌtī-rə-\ *adj or n* — **Ti·ro·lese** \ˌtir-ə-'lēz, ˌtī-rə-, -'lēs\ *adj or n*

Ti·ruch·chi·rap·pal·li \tir-ə-chə-'rä-pə-lē\ city S India in *cen* Tamil Nadu *pop* 711,862

Ti·ryns \'tir-ənz, 'tī-ˌrənz\ city of pre-Homeric Greece; ruins in E Peloponnese SE of Argos

Ti·sza \'ti-ˌsȯ\ river *ab* 600 *mi* (965 *km*) E Europe flowing from the Carpathians in W Ukraine W & SW into the Danube

Ti·ti·ca·ca, Lake \ˌti-ti-'kä-kä, ˌtē-tē-\ lake on Peru-Bolivia boundary at altitude of 12,500 *ft* (3810 *m*), *area* 3200 *sq mi* (8320 *sq km*)

Titograd — see PODGORICA

Ti·tus·ville \'tī-təs-ˌvil, -vəl\ city E Fla. E of Orlando *pop* 39,394

Ti·vo·li \'ti-və-lē, 'tē-vō-\ *or anc* **Ti·bur** \'tī-bər\ commune *cen* Italy in Lazio ENE of Rome *pop* 50,559

Tjilatjap — see CILACAP

Tlax·ca·la \tlä-'skä-lä\ **1** state *cen* Mexico *area* 1511 *sq mi* (3913 *sq km*), *pop* 761,277 **2** city, its ✳, E of Mexico City *pop* 50,631

Tlem·cen \tlem-'sen\ *or* **Ti·lim·sen** \tə-lim-'sen\ city NW Algeria *pop* 126,882

Toa Al·ta \ˌtō-ä-'äl-tä\ municipality NE *cen* Puerto Rico *pop* 44,101

To·a Ba·ja \'bä-(ˌ)hä\ municipality NE Puerto Rico W of San Juan *pop* 89,454

To·a·ma·si·na \ˌtō-ə-mə-'sē-nə\ *or formerly* **Ta·ma·tave** \ˌtə-mə-'täv, ˌtä-\ city & port E coast of Madagascar *pop* 145,431

To·ba·go \tə-'bā-(ˌ)gō\ island SE W. Indies, a territory of Trinidad and Tobago; chief town Scarborough *area* 116 *sq mi* (302 *sq km*), *pop* 50,282 — **To·ba·go·ni·an** \ˌtō-bə-'gō-nē-ən, -nyən\ *n*

To·bol \tə-'bȯl\ river N Kazakhstan & SW Russia in Asia flowing from SE foothills of the Urals NNE into the Irtysh

To·bruk \tō-'brük, 'tō-\ city & port NE Libya *pop* 34,200

To·can·tins \ˌtō-kən-'tēnz, ˌtü-kən-'tēⁿs\ river *ab* 1700 *mi* (2736 *km*) E *cen* & NE Brazil rising in S *cen* Goiás & flowing N into Pará River

To·go \'tō-(ˌ)gō\ republic W Africa on Bight of Benin ✻ Lomé *area* 21,853 *sq mi* (56,599 *sq km*), *pop* 3,810,000 — **To·go·lese** \ˌtō-gə-'lēz, -'lēs\ *adj or n*

To·go·land \'tō-(ˌ)gō-ˌland\ region W Africa on Gulf of Guinea bet. Benin & Ghana; until 1919 a German protectorate, then divided into two trust territories: **British Togoland** (in W; since 1957 part of Ghana) & **French Togo** (in E; since 1958 Togo) — **To·go·land·er** \'tō-(ˌ)gō-ˌlan-dər\ *n*

To·ho·pe·kal·i·ga Lake \tə-ˌhō-pi-'ka-li-gə\ lake *cen* Fla. S of Orlando

To·ka·ra Islands \tō-'kär-ä\ island group Japan in N Ryukyus

To·ke·lau Islands \ˌtō-kə-ˌlaü\ islands *cen* Pacific N of Samoa belonging to New Zealand *pop* 1690 — **To·ke·lau·an** \ˌtō-kə-'laü-ən\ *n*

To·ko·ro·za·wa \ˌtō-kō-'rō-zä-(ˌ)wä\ city Japan on Honshu, a suburb of Tokyo *pop* 303,047

To·ku·shi·ma \ˌtō-kü-'shē-mä\ city & port Japan on E coast of Shikoku Is. *pop* 264,503

To·kyo \'tō-kē-ˌō, -ˌkyō\ *or formerly* **Edo** \'e-(ˌ)dō\ *or* **Ye·do** \'ye-(ˌ)dō\ city ✻ of Japan in SE Honshu on **Tokyo Bay** (inlet of the Pacific) *pop* 11,854,987 — **To·kyo·ite** \'tō-kē-(ˌ)ō-ˌīt\ *n*

To·le·do \tə-'lē-dō, -'lē-də, *for 2 & 3 also* tō-'lā-thō\ **1** city & port NW Ohio on the Maumee River *pop* 332,943 **2** province *cen* Spain in W New Castile *area* 5934 *sq mi* (15,369 *sq km*), *pop* 489,543 **3** commune, its ✻ *pop* 59,563 — **To·le·dan** \-'lē-dᵊn\ *adj or n* — **To·le·do·an** \-'lē-dō-ən\ *adj or n*

To·li·ma \tō-'lē-mä\ dormant volcano W *cen* Colombia 17,110 *ft* (5215 *m*)

To·lu·ca \tō-'lü-kä\ *or* **Toluca de Ler·do** \thä-'ler-(ˌ)dō\ city *cen* Mexico ✻ of Mexico state *pop* 487,630

Toluca, Ne·va·do de \nä-'vä-thō-thä-\ extinct volcano 15,016 *ft* (4577 *m*) S *cen* Mexico in Mexico state

Tol'·yat·ti *or* **To·gliat·ti** \tȯl-'yä-tē\ *or formerly* **Stav·ro·pol** \stav-'rō-pəl, -'rȯ-; 'stä-vrə-ˌpȯl\ city SE *cen* Russia in Europe NW of Samara *pop* 666,000

Tom \'täm, 'tȯm\ river 450 *mi* (724 *km*) S Russia in Asia rising in NW Altay Mountains & flowing into the Ob

Tom·big·bee \täm-'big-bē\ river NE Miss. & W Ala. flowing S to Mobile & Tensaw rivers

Tom·bouc·tou \tōⁿ-bük-'tü\ *or* **Tim·buk·tu** \ˌtim-ˌbək-'tü, tim-'bək-(ˌ)tü\ town W Africa in Mali near Niger River *pop* 31,925

Tomsk \'täm(p)sk, 'tóm(p)sk\ city S *cen* Russia in Asia on Tom River near its junction with the Ob *pop* 505,000

Ton·ga \'täŋ-gə, 'täŋ-ə\ islands SW Pacific E of Fiji; a kingdom in the Commonwealth of Nations ✳ Nukualofa *area* 270 *sq mi* (702 *sq km*), *pop* 94,649 — **Ton·gan** \'täŋ-gən *also* -ən\ *adj or n*

Tongareva — see PENRHYN

Ton·ga·ri·ro \,täŋ-gə-'rir-(,)ō, ,täŋ-ə-\ volcano 6516 *ft* (1986 *m*) New Zealand in *cen* North Is. in **Tongariro National Park**

Tong·hua \'tùŋ-'hwä, 'tòŋ-'wä\ *or* **T'ung–hua** *or* **Tung·hwa** \'tùŋ-\ city NE China in S Jilin *pop* 158,000

Tongue \'təŋ\ river 246 *mi* (396 *km*) N Wyo. & S Mont. flowing N into Yellowstone River

Ton·kin \'tän-kən; 'tän-'kin, 'täŋ-\ *or* **Tong·king** \'tän-'kiŋ\ region N Indochina bordering on China, since 1946 forming N part of Vietnam; chief city Hanoi — **Ton·kin·ese** \,tän-kə-'nēz, ,tän-, -'nēs\ *or* **Tong·king·ese** \,täŋ-kiŋ-'ēz, -'ēs\ *adj or n*

Tonkin, Gulf of arm of S. China Sea E of N Vietnam

Ton·le Sap \,tän-,lä-'sap\ *or* F **Grand Lac** \grän-'läk\ lake 87 *mi* (140 *km*) long SW Indochina in W Cambodia

Ton·to National Monument \'tän-(,)tō\ reservation S *cen* Ariz. E of Phoenix containing cliff-dweller ruins

Too·woom·ba \tə-'wùm-bə\ city E Australia in SE Queensland *pop* 81,043

To·pe·ka \tə-'pē-kə\ city ✳ of Kans. on Kansas River *pop* 119,883

To·po·lo·bam·po \tō-,pō-lō-'bäm-(,)pō\ town & port NW Mexico in Sinaloa on Gulf of California

Tor·bay \(,)tòr-'bā\ former county borough SW England in Devon on **Tor Bay** (inlet of English Channel); included Brixham, Paignton, & Torquay

Tor·cel·lo \tòr-'che-(,)lō\ island Italy in Lagoon of Venice

Tor·de·sil·las \,tòr-dā-'sē-yäs, -'sēl-yäs\ village NW Spain SW of Valladolid

Torino — see TURIN

Tor·ne \'tòr-nə\ *or Finn* **Tor·nio** \'tòr-nē-,ō\ river 354 *mi* (570 *km*) NE Sweden flowing S forming part of Finnish-Swedish border, to head of Gulf of Bothnia

To·ron·to \tə-'rän-(,)tō, -'rän-tə\ city & port Canada ✳ of Ont. on Lake Ontario *pop* 635,395 — **To·ron·to·ni·an** \tə-,rän-'tō-nē-ən; ,tòr-ən-, ,tär-ən-\ *adj or n*

Toros — see TAURUS

Tor·rance \'tòr-ən(t)s, 'tär-\ city SW Calif. SSW of Los Angeles *pop* 133,107

Tor·re An·nun·zi·a·ta \'tòr-ā-ä-,nün(t)-sē-'ä-tä\ commune S Italy on Bay of Naples SE of Naples *pop* 56,471

Torre de Cerredo — see CERREDO

Tor·re del Gre·co \'tòr-ā-del-'grā-(,)kō, -'grä-\ commune S Italy on Bay of Naples *pop* 103,577

Tor·rens, Lake \'tòr-ənz, 'tär-\ salt lake Australia in E S. Australia N of Spencer Gulf 92 *ft* (28 *m*) above sea level

Tor·re·ón \,tòr-ā-'ōn\ city N Mexico in Coahuila *pop* 459,809

Tor·res Strait \'tòr-əs\ strait 80 *mi* (129 *km*) wide bet. island of New Guinea & N tip of Cape York Peninsula, Australia

Tor·res Ve·dras \,tòr-iz-'ve-drəsh\ town W Portugal N of Lisbon

Tor·ring·ton \'tòr-iŋ-tən, 'tär-\ city NW Conn. *pop* 33,687

Tórs·havn \'tórs-,haún\ town & port ✱ of the Faeroe Islands *pop* 16,091

Tor·to·la \tòr-'tō-lə\ island Brit. West Indies, chief of the Brit. Virgin Islands; site of Road Town *area* 21 *sq mi* (54 *sq km*), *pop* 9730

Tor·tu·ga \tòr-'tü-gə\ island Haiti off N coast; a resort of pirates in 17th century *pop* 13,723

To·ruń \'tòr-,ün, -,ü-nyə\ city N Poland on the Vistula *pop* 200,822

Toscana — see TUSCANY

Tot·ten·ham \'tä-t^n-əm\ former municipal borough SE England in Middlesex, now part of Haringey

Toub·kal, Je·bel \'je-bəl-tüb-'käl\ mountain 13,665 *ft* (4165 *m*) W *cen* Morocco; highest in Atlas Mountains

Toug·gourt \tə-'gürt\ town & oasis NE Algeria S of Biskra *pop* 70,645

Tou·lon \tü-'lō^n\ commune & port SE France on the Mediterranean *pop* 170,167

Tou·louse \tü-'lüz\ city SW France on the Garonne *pop* 365,933

Tou·raine \tü-'rān, -'ren\ region & former province NW *cen* France ✱ Tours

Tourane — see DA NANG

Tour·coing \túr-'kwa^n\ city N France NE of Lille *pop* 94,425

Tour·nai *or* **Tour·nay** \túr-'nā\ *or Flem* **Door·nik** \'dōr-nik, 'dòr-\ commune SW Belgium on the Schelde *pop* 67,732

Tours \'túr\ city NW *cen* France *pop* 133,403

Tow·er Hamlets \'taú(-ə)r\ borough of E Greater London, England *pop* 153,500

Towns·ville \'taúnz-,vil, -vəl\ city & port NE Australia in NE Queensland *pop* 101,398

To·ya·ma \tō-'yä-mä\ city Japan in *cen* Honshu near **Toyama Bay** (inlet of Sea of Japan) *pop* 321,259

To·yo·ha·shi \,tòi-ō-'hä-shē\ city Japan in S Honshu SE of Nagoya *pop* 337,988

To·yo·na·ka \,tòi-ō-'nä-kə\ city Japan on Honshu *pop* 409,843

To·yo·ta \tòi-'ō-tä\ city Japan on Honshu *pop* 332,336

Trab·zon \trab-'zän\ *or* **Treb·i·zond** \'tre-bə-,zänd\ *or anc* **Trap·e·zus** \'tra-pi-zəs\ city & port NE Turkey on Black Sea *pop* 143,941

Tra·cy \'trā-sē\ city *cen* Calif. SSW of Stockton *pop* 33,558

Tra·fal·gar, Cape \tra-'fal-gər, *Sp* ,trä-fäl-'gär\ cape SW Spain SE of Cádiz at W end of Strait of Gibraltar

Tra·lee \tra-'lē\ seaport SW Ireland ✱ of Kerry *pop* 17,109

Trans Alai \,tran(t)s-ə-'lī, ,tranz-\ mountain range Kyrgyzstan & Tajikistan in NW Pamirs — see LENIN PEAK

Trans·al·pine Gaul \tran(t)s-'al-,pīn, tranz-\ the part of Gaul included chiefly in modern France & Belgium

Transcaucasia — see CAUCASIA — **Trans·cau·ca·sian** \,tran(t)s-kò-'kā-zhən, -'ka-\ *adj or n*

Transjordan — see JORDAN — **Trans·jor·da·ni·an** \,tran(t)s-jòr-'dä-nē-ən, ,tranz-\ *adj or n*

Trans·kei \(,)tran(t)s-'kī\ former black enclave in the Republic of South Africa ✱ Umtata; granted independence 1976; abolished 1994 — **Trans·kei·an** \-ən\ *adj or n*

Trans·vaal \tran(t)s-'väl, tranz-\ former province NE Republic of South Africa bet. the Vaal & the Limpopo; in 19th century a Boer republic (**South African Republic**) ✳ Pretoria *area* 109,621 *sq mi* (283,918 *sq km*)

Tran·syl·va·nia *or Romanian* **Tran·sil·va·nia** \,tran(t)-səl-'vā-nyə, -nē-ə\ region W Romania bounded on the N, E, & S by the Carpathians & the Transylvanian Alps; part of Hungary 1867–1918 — **Tran·syl·va·nian** \-nyən, -nē-ən\ *adj or n*

Transylvanian Alps a S extension of the Carpathian Mountains in *cen* Romania

Tra·pa·ni \'trä-pä-nē\ commune & port Italy at NW tip of Sicily *pop* 69,273

Tra·si·me·no, Lake \,trä-zē-'mā-nō\ lake 10 *mi* (16 *km*) wide *cen* Italy W of Perugia

Trav·an·core \'tra-vən-,kōr, -,kȯr\ region & former state SW India on Malabar Coast extending N from Cape Comorin; included (1949–56) in former **Travancore and Co·chin** \'kō-chən\ state (✳ Trivandrum) — see KERALA

Trav·erse, Lake \'tra-vərs\ lake NE S.Dak. & W Minn.; drained by the Bois de Sioux (headstream of Red River)

Treb·bia \'tre-bē-ä\ *or anc* **Tre·bia** \'trē-bē-ə\ river 71 *mi* (114 *km*) NW Italy flowing N into the Po

Treb·i·zond \'tre-bə-,zänd\ **1** — see TRABZON **2** Greek empire 1204–1461, an offshoot of Byzantine Empire; at greatest extent included Georgia, Crimea, & S coast of Black Sea E of the Sakarya

Treng·ga·nu \tren̄-'gä-(,)nü\ state Malaysia in NE Peninsular Malaysia on S. China Sea ✳ Kuala Trengganu *area* 5000 *sq mi* (12,950 *sq km*)

Trent \'trent\ **1** river 150 *mi* (241 *km*) Canada in SE Ont. flowing from Kawartha Lakes through Rice Lake into Lake Ontario (Bay of Quinte) **2** river 170 *mi* (274 *km*) *cen* England flowing NNE & uniting with Ouse River to form the Humber

Trent Canal canal system Canada 224 *mi* (360 *km*) long in SE Ont. connecting Lake Huron (Georgian Bay) with Lake Ontario (Bay of Quinte)

Tren·ti·no–Al·to Adi·ge \tren-'tē-nō-,äl-tō-'ä-dē-,jä\ region N Italy ✳ Trento *area* 5526 *sq mi* (13,613 *sq km*), *pop* 886,679

Tren·to \'tren-(,)tō\ commune N Italy *pop* 101,430

Tren·ton \'tren-t³n\ **1** city SE Mich. on Detroit River *pop* 20,586 **2** city ✳ of N.J. on Delaware River *pop* 88,675

Tre·vi·so \trā-'vē-(,)zō\ commune NE Italy NW of Venice *pop* 83,222

Trier \'trir\ city W Germany on the Moselle near Luxembourg border *pop* 98,752

Tri·este \trē-'est, -'es-tē, -'es-tā\ *or Slovenian and Serbo-Croatian* **Trst** \'tərst\ city & port NE Italy ✳ of Friuli-Venezia Giulia, on **Gulf of Trieste** (inlet at head of the Adriatic NW of the Istrian Peninsula) *pop* 229,216; once belonged to Austria; part of Italy 1919–47; in 1947 made with surrounding territory the **Free Territory of Trieste** under administration of the United Nations; city with N part of Free Territory returned to Italy 1953, S part of territory having previously been absorbed into Yugoslavia — **Tri·es·tine** \trē-'es-tən, -,tēn\ *adj*

Tri·ka·la *or* **Trik·ka·la** \'tri-kə-lə, 'trē-kä-lä\ city *cen* Greece *pop* 48,810

Trim \'trim\ town E Ireland ✳ of County Meath *pop* 1781

Trinacria — see SICILY — **Tri·nac·ri·an** \trə-'na-krē-ən, trī-\ *adj*

Trin·co·ma·lee \‚triŋ-kō-mə-'lē, ‚trin-'kə-mə-lē\ city & port NE Sri Lanka on Bay of Bengal *pop* 50,000

Trin·i·dad \'tri-nə-‚dad\ island SE W. Indies off coast of NE Venezuela *pop* 1,184,106; with Tobago, a dominion (**Trinidad and Tobago**) of the Commonwealth of Nations since 1962; formerly a Brit. colony ✲ Port of Spain *area* 1980 *sq mi* (5128 *sq km*), *pop* 1,234,388 — **Trin·i·da·di·an** \‚tri-nə-'dā-dē-ən, -'da-\ *adj or n*

Trin·i·ty \'tri-nə-tē\ river E Tex. flowing SE into Galveston Bay

Trip·o·li \'tri-pə-lē\ **1** *or Ar* **Ta·rā·bu·lus** \tə-'rä-bə-ləs\ *or anc* **Trip·o·lis** \'tri-pə-ə-'lē, -'lē\ city & port NW Lebanon NNE of Beirut *pop* 127,611 **2** *or Ar* **Tarābulus** *or anc* **Oea** \'ē-ə\ city & port NW Libya, its ✲ *pop* 591,062 **3** Tripolitania when it was one of the Barbary States — **Tri·pol·i·tan** \tri-'pä-lə-tᵊn\ *adj or n*

Trip·o·li·ta·nia \tri-‚pä-lə-'tā-nyə, ‚tri-pə-lə-\ *or anc* **Trip·o·lis** \'tri-pə-ləs\ region & former province NW Libya bordering on the Mediterranean — **Tri·po·li·ta·nian** \tri-‚pä-lə-'tā-nyən, ‚tri-pə-lə-\ *adj or n*

Tri·pu·ra \'tri-pə-rə\ state E India bet. Bangladesh & Assam ✲ Agartala *area* 4035 *sq mi* (10,451 *sq km*), *pop* 2,757,205

Tris·tan da Cu·nha \‚tris-tən-də-'kü-nə, -nyə\ island S Atlantic, chief of the Tristan da Cunha Islands attached to Brit. colony of St. Helena *area* 38 *sq mi* (98 *sq km*), *pop* 296; volcanic eruptions 1961

Tri·van·drum \tri-'van-drəm\ city & port S India NW of Cape Comorin ✲ of Kerala *pop* 699,872

Tro·as \'trō-‚as\ **1** *or* **Tro·ad** \-‚ad\ territory surrounding the ancient city of Troy in NW Mysia, Asia Minor **2** ancient city of Mysia S of site of Troy — **Tro·ad·ic** \trō-'a-dik\ *adj*

Tro·bri·and \'trō-brē-‚änd, -‚and\ islands SW Pacific in Solomon Sea; attached to Papua New Guinea *area* 170 *sq mi* (442 *sq km*) — **Tro·bri·and·er** \‚trō-brē-'än-dər, -'an-\ *n*

Trois-Ri·vières \‚t(r)wä-ri-'vyer\ town Canada in S Que. NE of Montreal on N bank of St. Lawrence River *pop* 49,426

Trom·sö \'träm-‚sö, -‚sœ\ city & port N Norway *pop* 50,548

Trond·heim \'trän-‚hām\ city & port *cen* Norway on **Trondheim Fjord** (80 *mi* or 128 *km* long), *pop* 137,346

Tros·sachs \'trä-səks, -‚saks\ valley *cen* Scotland bet. Loch Katrine & Loch Achray

Trou·ville \trü-'vēl\ *or* **Trouville–sur–Mer** \-(‚)sūer-'mer\ town & port N France on English Channel S of Le Havre *pop* 5645

Trow·bridge \'trō-(‚)brij\ town S England ✲ of Wiltshire *pop* 22,984

Troy \'trȯi\ **1** city SE Mich. N of Detroit *pop* 72,884 **2** city E N.Y. on Hudson River NNE of Albany *pop* 54,269 **3** city W Ohio *pop* 19,478 **4** *or* **Il·i·um** \'i-lē-əm\ *or* **Il·i·on** \'i-lē-‚än, -lē-ən\ *or* **Tro·ja** \'trō-jə, -yə\ ancient city NW Asia Minor in Troas SW of the Dardanelles — **Tro·jan** \'trō-jən\ *adj or n*

Troyes \'t(r)wä\ city NE France SE of Paris *pop* 60,755

Tru·chas Peak \'trü-chəs\ *or* **North Truchas Peak** mountain 13,110 *ft* (3996 *m*) N N.Mex. in Sangre de Cristo Mountains NE of Santa Fe; highest of three peaks forming **Truchas Peaks**

Trucial Oman, Trucial States — see UNITED ARAB EMIRATES

Truck·ee \'trə-kē\ river 120 *mi* (193 *km*) E Calif. & W Nev. flowing from Lake Tahoe into Pyramid Lake

Tru·ji·llo \trü-'hē-(ˌ)yō\ **1** city NW Peru NW of Lima *pop* 193,528 **2** — see SANTO DOMINGO

Trujillo Al·to \'äl-(ˌ)tō\ municipality NE *cen* Puerto Rico *pop* 61,120

Truk Islands \'trək, 'trúk\ islands *cen* Carolines, part of Federated States of Micronesia

Trum·bull \'trəm-bəl\ town SW Conn. N of Bridgeport *pop* 32,016

Tru·ro \'trúr-(ˌ)ō\ city & borough SW England, a ✳ of Cornwall and Isles of Scilly *pop* 16,277

Tsang·po \'(t)säŋ-'pó\ the upper Brahmaputra in Tibet

Tsaritsyn — see VOLGOGRAD

Tsarskoye Selo — see PUSHKIN

Tsinan — see JINAN

Tsinghai — see QINGHAI

Tsingtao — see QINGDAO

Tsitsihar — see QIQIHAR

Tskhin·va·li \'(t)skin-və-lē\ town N Republic of Georgia NW of Tbilisi ✳ of S. Ossetia Autonomous Oblast *pop* 42,600

Tsu·ga·ru Strait \'(t)sü-gä-ˌrü\ strait Japan bet. Honshu & Hokkaido

Tsu·shi·ma \(t)sü-'shē-mä\ island Japan in Korea Strait separated from Kyushu and Honshu by **Tsushima Strait** (the SE part of Korea Strait) *area* 271 *sq mi* (705 *sq km*)

Tu·a·mo·tu Archipelago \ˌtü-ä-'mō-(ˌ)tü\ archipelago S Pacific E of Society Islands; belongs to France *area* 330 *sq mi* (858 *sq km*), *pop* 11,754

Tü·bing·en \'tü-biŋ-ən, 'tyü-, 'tǖ-\ city SW Germany on the Neckar S of Stuttgart *pop* 82,483

Tuc·son \'tü-ˌsän, *esp locally* tü-'sän\ city SE Ariz. *pop* 405,390 — **Tuc·son·an** \'tü-ˌsä-nən\ *n*

Tucumán — see SAN MIGUEL DE TUCUMÁN

Tu·ge·la \tü-'gā-lä\ river 312 *mi* (502 *km*) E Republic of South Africa in *cen* KwaZulu-Natal flowing E to Indian Ocean; near its source on Mont Aux Sources are the **Tugela Falls** (3110 *ft or* 948 *m*)

Tu·la \'tü-lä\ **1** *or* **Tula de Al·len·de** \ˌ)thä-ä-'yen-dä\ city *cen* Mexico in SW Hidalgo N of Mexico City; ancient ✳ of the Toltecs *pop* 71,622 **2** city SW *cen* Russia in Europe S of Moscow on a tributary of Oka River *pop* 541,000

Tu·la·gi \tü-'lä-gē\ island S Pacific in S *cen* Solomons

Tu·lare \tü-'lar(-ē), -'ler(-ē)\ city S *cen* Calif. SE of Fresno *pop* 33,249

Tulare Lake former lake S *cen* Calif. S of Hanford; drained for farmland

Tul·la·more \ˌtə-lə-'mōr, -'mòr\ town *cen* Ireland ✳ of county Offaly *pop* 8623

Tul·sa \'təl-sə\ city NE Okla. on Arkansas River *pop* 367,302 — **Tul·san** \-sən\ *n*

Tu·ma·ca·co·ri National Monument \ˌtü-mə-'kä-kə-rē\ historic site S Ariz. S of Tucson; contains remains of Franciscan mission

Tu·men \'tü-mən\ river 324 *mi* (521 *km*) E Asia on border bet. N. Korea, China, & Russia flowing NE & SE into Sea of Japan

Tu·muc–Hu·mac Mountains \tü-,mü-kü-'mäk\ *or Pg* **Ser·ra Tu·mu·cu·ma·que** \'se-rə-tü-,mü-kü-'mä-kä, -kē\ range of low mountains NE Brazil on Suriname–French Guiana boundary

Tunbridge Wells — see ROYAL TUNBRIDGE WELLS

T'ung–hua — see TONGHUA

Tun·gus·ka \tüṅ-'gü-skə, tən-\ any of three rivers in *cen* Russia in Asia, tributaries of the Yenisey: **Lower Tunguska, Stony Tunguska,** & **Upper Tunguska** (lower course of the Angara)

Tu·nis \'tü-nəs, 'tyü-\ **1** city ✻ of Tunisia near site of ancient Carthage *pop* 620,149 **2** TUNISIA — used esp. of the former Barbary State

Tu·ni·sia \tü-'nē-zh(ē-)ə, tyü-, -'ni\ country N Africa bordering on the Mediterranean; formerly one of the Barbary States; a French protectorate 1881–1956, a monarchy 1956–57, & a republic since 1957 ✻ Tunis *area* 63,378 *sq mi* (164,149 *sq km*), *pop* 8,530,000 — **Tu·ni·sian** \-zh(ē-)ən\ *adj or n*

Tu·ol·um·ne \tü-'ä-lə-mē\ river 155 *mi* (249 *km*) *cen* Calif. flowing W from Yosemite National Park into the San Joaquin

Tu·pe·lo \'tü-pə-,lō, 'tyü-\ city NE Miss. *pop* 30,685

Tu·pun·ga·to \,tü-püṅ-'gä-(,)tō\ mountain 22,310 *ft* (6800 *m*) in the Andes on Argentina–Chile boundary ENE of Santiago, Chile

Tu·rin \'tür-ən, 'tyür-; tü-'rin, tyü-\ *or It* **To·ri·no** \tō-'rē-(,)nō\ commune NW Italy on the Po ✻ of Piedmont *pop* 961,916 — **Tu·rin·ese** \,tür-ə-'nēz, ,tyür-, -'nēs\ *adj or n*

Tur·ka·na, Lake \tər-'ka-nə\ *or* **Lake Ru·dolf** \'rü-,dȯlf, -,dälf\ lake N Kenya in Great Rift Valley *area* 2473 *sq mi* (6405 *sq km*)

Tur·key \'tər-kē\ country W Asia & SE Europe bet. Mediterranean & Black seas; formerly center of an empire (✻ Constantinople), since 1923 a republic ✻ Ankara *area* 301,380 *sq mi* (780,574 *sq km*), *pop* 50,664,458 — see OTTOMAN EMPIRE — **Turk** \'tərk\ *n* — **Turk·ic** \'tər-kik\ *adj or n* — **Turk·ish** \-kish\ *adj*

Tur·ki·stan *or* **Tur·ke·stan** \,tər-kə-'stan, -'stän; 'tər-kə-,\ region *cen* Asia bet. Iran & Siberia; now divided bet. Turkmenistan, Uzbekistan, Tajikistan, Kyrgyzstan, Kazakhstan, China, & Afghanistan — see CHINESE TURKESTAN, RUSSIAN TURKESTAN

Turk·men·i·stan \(,)tərk-,me-nə-'stan, -'stän; (,)tərk-'me-nə-,\ country *cen* Asia bordering on Afghanistan, Iran, & the Caspian Sea; a constituent republic (**Turk·men Republic** \'tərk-mən\) of the U.S.S.R. 1925–91 ✻ Ashkhabad *area* 188,455 *sq mi* (488,098 *sq km*), *pop* 3,958,000 — **Turk·man** \'tərk-mən\ *n, pl* **Turk·men** \-mən\ — **Turkmen** *n, pl* **Turk·mens** \-mənz\ — **Turkmen** *adj* — **Turk·me·ni·an** \tərk-'mē-nē-ən\ *adj* — **Tur·ko·man** *or* **Tur·co·man** \'tər-kə-mən\ *adj or n*

Turks and Cai·cos \'tərks-ənd-'kā-kəs, -,kōs\ two groups of islands (Turks Islands & Caicos Islands) Brit. West Indies at SE end of Bahamas; a Brit. colony; seat of government on **Grand Turk** (7 *mi or* 11 *km* long) *area* 166 *sq mi* (432 *sq km*), *pop* 12,350

Tur·ku \'tür-(,)kü\ city & port SW Finland *pop* 159,469

Tur·lock \'tər-,läk\ city *cen* Calif. SE of Modesto *pop* 42,198

Turn·hout \'türn-,haüt, tür-'nüt\ commune N Belgium *pop* 38,100

Tur·tle Bay \'tər-t⁹l\ section of New York City in E *cen* Manhattan on East River; site of United Nations headquarters

Tus·ca·loo·sa \,təs-kə-'lü-sə\ city W *cen* Ala. on Black Warrior River SW of Birmingham *pop* 77,759

Tus·ca·ny \'təs-kə-nē\ *or It* **To·sca·na** \tō-'skä-nä\ region NW *cen* Italy bordering on Ligurian & Tyrrhenian seas ✻ Florence area 8876 *sq mi* (22,989 *sq km*), *pop* 3,560,582 — **Tus·can** \'təs-kən\ *adj or n*

Tus·cu·lum \'təs-kyə-ləm, -kə-\ ancient town Italy in Lazio SE of Rome

Tus·tin \'təs-tən\ city SW Calif. E of Santa Ana *pop* 50,689

Tu·tu·i·la \,tü-tü-'wē-lä\ island, chief of American Samoa group *area* 52 *sq mi* (135 *sq km*) — **Tu·tu·i·lan** \-lən\ *adj or n*

Tu·va Republic \'tü-və\ autonomous republic S Russia in Asia N of Mongolia ✻ Kyzyl *area* 65,380 *sq mi* (169,334 *sq km*), *pop* 306,000

Tu·va·lu \tü-'vä-(,)lü, -'vär-(,)ü\ *or formerly* **El·lice Islands** \'e-lis\ islands W Pacific N of Fiji; a Brit. territory 1976–78; became an independent member of the Commonwealth of Nations 1978 ✻ Funafuti *area* 9 *sq mi* (23 *sq km*), *pop* 9700 — see GILBERT AND EL-LICE

Tux·tla \'tüst-lə\ *or* **Tuxtla Gu·tiér·rez** \gü-'tyer-es\ city SE Mexi-co ✻ of Chiapas *pop* 295,615

Tu·zi·goot National Monument \'tü-zi-,güt\ reservation *cen* Ariz. SW of Flagstaff containing ruins of prehistoric pueblo

Tver' \'tver\ *or 1932–90* **Ka·li·nin** \kä-'lē-nin\ city W *cen* Russia in Europe on the Volga *pop* 456,000

Tweed \'twēd\ river 97 *mi* (156 *km*) SE Scotland & NE England flowing E into North Sea

Tweeddale — see PEEBLES

Twick·en·ham \'twi-k°n-əm, 'twit-nəm\ former municipal borough SE England in Middlesex, now part of Richmond upon Thames

Twin Cities \'twin\ the cities of Minneapolis & St. Paul, Minn.

Twin Falls city S Idaho SW of Twin Falls (waterfall in Snake River) *pop* 27,591

Two Sic·i·lies \'tü-'si-s(ə-)lēz\ former kingdom consisting of Sicily & S Italy

Ty·chy \'ti-kē, -ki\ town S Poland *pop* 189,874

Ty·ler \'tī-lər\ city E Tex. ESE of Dallas *pop* 75,450

Tyn·dall, Mount \'tin-d°l\ **1** mountain 14,018 *ft* (4273 *m*) S *cen* Calif. in Sierra Nevada NW of Mt. Whitney **2** mountain 8280 *ft* (2524 *m*) New Zealand in *cen* South Is. in Southern Alps

Tyne \'tīn\ river 30 *mi* (48 *km*) N England flowing E into North Sea

Tyne and Wear \'wir\ metropolitan county N England ✻ Newcastle upon Tyne *area* 216 *sq mi* (559 *sq km*), *pop* 1,087,000

Tyne·mouth \'tīn-,maúth, -məth\ borough N England in Tyne and Wear on North Sea at mouth of the Tyne *pop* 60,022

Tyre — see SUR — **Tyr·i·an** \'tir-ē-ən\ *adj or n*

Ty·ree, Mount \tī-'rē\ mountain 16,290 *ft* (4965 *m*) W Antarctica in Ellsworth Mountains NW of Vinson Massif

Tyrol — see TIROL — **Ty·ro·le·an** \tə-'rō-lē-ən, tī-; ,tir-ə-', ,tī-rə-'\ *adj or n* — **Ty·ro·lese** \,tir-ə-'lēz, ,tī-rə-, -'lēs\ *adj or n*

Ty·rone \ti-'rōn\ former county W *cen* Northern Ireland ✻ Omagh *area* 1218 *sq mi* (3167 *sq km*)

Tyr·rhe·ni·an Sea \tə-'rē-nē-ən\ the part of the Mediterranean W of Italy, N of Sicily, & E of Sardinia & Corsica

Tyu·men \tyü-'men\ city W Russia in Asia on the **Tu·ra** \tü-'rä\ (a tributary of the Tobol) *pop* 496,000

Tzu–kung — see ZIGONG

Tzu–po — see ZIBO

U

Uap — see YAP

Uau·pés \waù-'pes\ *or Sp* **Vau·pés** \vaù-\ river Colombia & Brazil flowing ESE into Negro River

Uban·gi \ü-'bän-gē, yü-'ban-\ *or F* **Ou·ban·gui** \ü-bän̄-'gē\ river 700 *mi* (1126 *km*) W *cen* Africa on NW border of Democratic Republic of the Congo flowing W & S into Congo River — see UELE

Ubangi–Sha·ri \-'shär-ē\ *or F* **Oubangui–Cha·ri** \-shá-'rē\ former French territory N *cen* Africa — see CENTRAL AFRICAN REPUBLIC

Uca·ya·li \ü-kä-'yä-lē\ river *ab* 1000 *mi* (1609 *km*) *cen* & N Peru flowing N to unite with the Marañón forming the Amazon

Uc·cle \'ükl²,'ēkl²\ *or Flem* **Uk·kel** \'ə-kəl, 'œ-\ commune *cen* Belgium *pop* 73,721

Udai·pur \ù-'dī-,púr\ **1** *or* **Me·war** \mā-'wär\ former state NW India, now part of Rajasthan state **2** city, its ✳, *pop* 307,682

Udi·ne \'ü-dē-,nä\ commune NE Italy NE of Venice in Friuli-Venezia Giulia region *pop* 99,157

Ud·mur·tia \ùd-'múr-shə, -shē-ə\ *or* **Ud·mur·ti·ya** \-tē-yə\ autonomous republic E Russia in Europe in W foothills of the Urals ✳ Izhevsk *area* 16,255 *sq mi* (42,101 *sq km*), *pop* 1,637,000

Ue·le \'we-lē\ river 700 *mi* (1126 *km*) *cen* Africa flowing W in N Democratic Republic of the Congo to unite with the Bomu forming Ubangi River

Ufa \ü-'fä\ **1** river E Russia in Europe in S Urals flowing NW & SW into the Belaya **2** city E Russia in Europe ✳ of Bashkortostan *pop* 1,097,000

Ugan·da \ü-'gän-də, yü-'gän-\ republic E Africa N of Lake Victoria; member of the Commonwealth of Nations ✳ Kampala *area* 91,134 *sq mi* (236,037 *sq km*), *pop* 17,741,000 — **Ugan·dan** \-dən\ *adj or n*

Uga·rit \ü-'gär-it, yü-\ ancient city, Syria on Mediterranean coast — **Uga·rit·ic** \,yü-gə-'ri-tik, ,ü-gə-\

Uin·ta Mountains \yü-'in-tə\ mountain range NE Utah — see KINGS PEAK

Ujda — see OUJDA

Uj·jain \'ü-,jīn\ city NW *cen* India in W Madhya Pradesh NNW of Indore *pop* 362,633

Ujung Pan·dang \ü-,jùŋ-(,)pän-'däŋ\ *or formerly* **Ma·kas·sar** \mə-'ka-sər\ city & port Indonesia in SW Sulawesi *pop* 944,685

Ukraine \yü-'krān, 'yü-,, *also* yü-'krīn\ *or* **the Ukraine** country E Europe on N coast of Black Sea; a constituent republic of the U.S.S.R. 1923–91 ✳ Kiev *area* 233,089 *sq mi* (603,701 *sq km*), *pop* 52,344,000 — **Ukrai·ni·an** \yü-'krā-nē-ən *also* -'krī-\

Ulaan·baa·tar *or* **Ulan Ba·tor** \ü-,län-'bä-,tôr\ *or formerly* **Ur·ga** \'ûr-gə\ city N *cen* Mongolia (republic), its ✻ *pop* 548,400

Ulan–Ude \ü-,län-ü-'dä\ *or formerly* **Verkh·ne·u·dinsk** \,verk-nə-'ü-,din(t)sk\ city E Russia in Asia ✻ of Buryatia on the Selenga *pop* 366,000

Uleåborg — see OULU

Ulls·wa·ter \'əlz-,wo-tər, -,wä-\ lake 7 *mi* (11 *km*) long NW England in Cumbria

Ulm \'ùlm\ city S Germany in E Baden-Württemberg *pop* 112,173

Ul·san \'ül-'sän\ city SE S. Korea *pop* 551,014

Ul·ster \'əl-stər\ **1** region N Ireland (island) comprising Northern Ireland & N Ireland (republic); ancient kingdom, later a province comprising nine counties, three of which in 1921 joined Irish Free State (now Ireland) while the rest remained with United Kingdom **2** province N Ireland (republic) comprising counties Cavan, Donegal, & Mon·aghan *area* 3093 *sq mi* (8042 *sq km*) *pop* 232,206 **3** Northern Ireland comprising districts Antrim, Armagh, Down, Fermanagh, Londonderry, & Tyrone ✻ Belfast — **Ul·ster·ite** \-stə-,rīt\ *n* — **Ul·ster·man** \-stər-mən\ *n*

Ulu Dag \ü-lə-'dä(g)\ *or anc* **Mount Olym·pus** \ə-'lim-pəs, ō-\ mountain 8343 *ft* (2543 *m*) NW Turkey in Asia SE of Bursa

Ulugh Muztagh — see MUZTAG

Ulyanovsk — see SIMBIRSK

Uma·til·la \,yü-mə-'til-ə\ river 80 *mi* (129 *km*) NE Oreg. flowing W & N into Columbia River

Um·bria \'əm-brē-ə\ region *cen* Italy in the Apennines ✻ Perugia *pop* 820,316 — **Um·bri·an** \-ən\ *adj or n*

Umeå \'ü-mā-(,)ȯ\ city & port N Sweden on Gulf of Bothnia *pop* 94,912

Umm al Qay·wayn *or* **Umm al–Qai·wain** \'ùm-ȧl-kī-'wīn\ sheikhdom, member of United Arab Emirates

Um·nak \'üm-,nak\ island SW Alaska in Fox Islands

Ump·qua \'əm(p)-,kwȯ\ river 200 *mi* (322 *km*) SW Oreg. flowing into the Pacific

Um·ta·ta \üm-'tä-tə\ city Republic of South Africa, formerly ✻ of Transkei

Un·alas·ka \,ə-nə-'las-kə\ island SW Alaska in Fox Islands

Unalaska Bay bay SW Alaska on N coast of Unalaska Is.

Un·com·pah·gre Peak \,ən-kəm-'pä-grē\ mountain 14,309 *ft* (4361 *m*) SW Colo.; highest in San Juan Mountains

Uncompahgre Plateau tableland W Colo. SW of the Gunnison

Un·ga·va \,ən-'ga-və\ region Canada N of the Eastmain & W of Labrador including Ungava Peninsula, divided 1927 bet. Que. & Nfld. — see NEW QUEBEC

Ungava Bay inlet of Hudson Strait Canada in N Que.

Ungava Peninsula peninsula Canada in N Que. bet. Hudson Bay & Ungava Bay

Uni·mak \'yü-nə-,mak\ island SW Alaska in Fox Islands

Union City \'yün-yən\ **1** city W Calif. S of Oakland *pop* 53,762 **2** city NE N.J. N of Jersey City *pop* 58,012

Union of South Africa — see SOUTH AFRICA (Republic of)

Union of Soviet Socialist Republics *or* **Soviet Union** country 1922–91 E Europe & N Asia bordering on the Arctic & Pacific

United Arab Emirates

oceans & Baltic & Black seas; a union of 15 constituent republics ✱ Moscow *area* 8,649,512 *sq mi* (22,402,236 *sq km*)

United Arab Emir·ates \'e-mə-rəts, -,rāts\ *or formerly* **Tru·cial States** \'trü-shəl\ *or* **Trucial Oman** \ō-'män, -'man\ country NE Arabia on Persian Gulf between Qatar & Oman; a republic composed of seven sheikdoms (Abu Dhabi, 'Ajman, Al Fujayrah, Ash Shariqah, Dubayy, Ra's al Khaymah, & Umm al Qaywayn formerly under Brit. protection ✱ Abu Dhabi *area* 30,000 *sq mi* (77,700 *sq km*), *pop* 1,986,000

United Arab Republic former name (1961–71) of republic of Egypt & previously (1958–61) of union of Egypt & Syria

United Kingdom 1 *or* **United Kingdom of Great Britain and Northern Ireland** country W Europe in British Isles comprising Great Britain & Northern Ireland *area* 94,251 *sq mi* (244,110 *sq km*), *pop* 58,421,700 **2** *or* **United Kingdom of Great Britain and Ireland** country 1801–1921 comprising Great Britain & Ireland

United Nations political organization established 1945; headquarters in New York City in E *cen* Manhattan overlooking East River — see TURTLE BAY

United Provinces *or* **United Provinces of Agra and Oudh** former province N India formed 1902 ✱ Allahabad; as Uttar Pradesh, became a state of India (republic) 1950

United States of America *or* **United States** \yù-'nī-təd-'stāts, *esp Southern* 'yü-\ country N. America bordering on Atlantic, Pacific, & Arctic oceans; a federal republic ✱ Washington *area* 3,619,969 *sq mi* (9,375,720 *sq km*), *pop* 249,632,692

Uni·ver·si·ty City \,yü-nə-'vər-sə-tē\ city E Mo. WNW of St. Louis *pop* 40,087

University Park city NE Tex. within city of Dallas *pop* 22,259

Un·ter·wal·den \'ün-tər-,väl-dən\ former canton *cen* Switzerland, now divided into two cantons (formerly half cantons): **Nid·wal·den** \'nēt-,väl-dən\ *or* F **Nid·wald** \nēd-'väld\ (✱ Stans *area* 106 *sq mi or* 276 *sq km, pop* 35,393) & **Ob·wal·den** \'ȯp-,väl-dən\ *or* F **Ob·wald** \ȯb-'väld\ (✱ Sarnen *area* 189 *sq mi or* 490 *sq km, pop* 30,837)

Up·land \'əp-lənd\ city SW Calif. W of San Bernardino *pop* 63,374

Upo·lu \ü-'pō-(,)lü\ island S Pacific in Western Samoa

Upper Adige — see ALTO ADIGE

Upper Arlington city *cen* Ohio W of Columbus *pop* 34,128

Upper Canada the Canadian province 1791–1841 corresponding to the S part of modern Ont. — see LOWER CANADA

Upper Karroo — see KARROO

Upper Klamath Lake lake 30 *mi* (48 *km*) long S Oreg. SSE of Crater Lake National Park drained by Klamath River — see LOWER KLAMATH LAKE

Upper Palatinate — see PALATINATE

Upper Peninsula the N part of Mich. bet. Lakes Superior & Michigan

Upper Volta — see BURKINA FASO — **Upper Vol·tan** \'väl-tⁿn, 'vōl-, 'vȯl-\ *adj or n*

Upp·sa·la \'əp-,sä-lə, 'üp-, -lä\ city E Sweden NNW of Stockholm *pop* 174,554

Ur \'ər, 'ùr\ city of ancient Sumer; site in S Iraq NW of Basra

Ural \'yùr-əl\ river over 1500 *mi* (2414 *km*) Russia & Kazakhstan rising at S end of Ural Mountains & flowing S into the Caspian

Ural Mountains mountain system Russia & Kazakhstan extending from Kara Sea to steppes N of Aral Sea; usu. considered the dividing line bet. Asia & Europe; highest Narodnaya 6214 *ft* (1894 *m*) — **Ura·li·an** \yù-'rā-lē-ən, -'ra\ *adj*

Uralsk — see ORAL

Ura·ri·coe·ra \ù-,rär-i-'kwer-ə\ river *ab* 300 *mi* (483 *km*) N Brazil, a headstream of the Branco

Ura·wa \ù-'rä-wä\ city Japan in Honshu N of Tokyo *pop* 434,976

Ur·bana \ər-'ba-nə\ city E *cen* Ill. *pop* 36,344

Ur·ban·dale \'ər-bən-,dāl\ city N Iowa *pop* 23,500

Ur·bi·no \ùr-'bē-(,)nō\ commune *cen* Italy *pop* 15,125

Ur·fa \'ùr-fä\ *or anc* **Edes·sa** \i-'de-sə\ city SE Turkey *pop* 276,528

Urga — see ULAANBAATAR

Uri \'ùr-ē\ canton *cen* Switzerland S of Lake of Lucerne ✱ Altdorf *area* 415 *sq mi* (1079 *sq km*), *pop* 34,042

Urmia, Lake — see REZĀĪYEH

Uru·bam·ba \,ùr-ü-'bäm-bä\ river 450 *mi* (724 *km*) *cen* Peru flowing NNW to unite with the Apurímac forming the Ucayali

Uru·guay \'ùr-ə-,gwī, 'yùr-; 'yùr-ə-,gwä; ,ü-rü-'gwī\ **1** river *ab* 1000 *mi* (1609 *km*) SE S. America rising in Brazil & flowing into the Río de la Plata **2** *or* **Re·pú·bli·ca Ori·en·tal del Uru·guay** \rä-'pü-blē-(,)kä-,ōr-ē-,en-'täl-thel-\ country SE S. America bet. the lower Uruguay & the Atlantic; a republic ✱ Montevideo *area* 68,039 *sq mi* (176,221 *sq km*), *pop* 3,149,000 — see BANDA ORIENTAL — **Uru·guay·an** \ùr-ə-'gwī-ən, ,yùr-; ,yùr-ə-'gwä-\ *adj or n*

Ürüm·qi \'ē-'rēm-'chē\ *or* **Urum·chi** \ù-'rùm-chē, ,ùr-əm-\ *or* **Wu–lu–mu–ch'i** \'wü-'lü-'mü-'chē\ city NW China ✱ of Xinjiang Uygur on N side of Tian Shan *pop* 1,046,898

Urundi — see BURUNDI

Ushant — see OUESSANT, ÎLE D'

Us·hua·ia \ü-'swī-ä\ town S Argentina on S coast of Tierra del Fuego Is., at 54°48'S; southernmost city in the world *pop* 10,998

Usk \'əsk\ river 60 *mi* (96 *km*) S Wales & W England flowing E & S into Severn estuary

Üs·kü·dar \,üs-kē-'där\ suburb of Istanbul, Turkey, on Asian side of the Bosporus

Us·pal·la·ta Pass \,üs-pä-'yä-tä, -'zhä-\ *or* **La Cum·bre** \lä-'küm-(,)brā\ mountain pass (12,572 *ft or* 3832 *m*) & tunnel S S. America in the Andes bet. Mendoza, Argentina & Santiago, Chile

Us·su·ri \ù-'sùr-ē\ river 365 *mi* (587 *km*) E Asia on border bet. Russia & China flowing N into the Amur

Usti nad La·bem \'üs-tē-'näd-lä-,bem\ city NW Czech Republic in N Bohemia on the Elbe *pop* 99,739

Ustinov — see IZHEVSK

Usumbura — see BUJUMBURA

Utah \'yü-,tó, -,tä\ state W U.S. ✱ Salt Lake City *area* 84,899 *sq mi* (219,888 *sq km*), *pop* 1,722,850 — **Utah·an** \-,tó(-ə)n, -,tä(-ə)n\ *adj or n* — **Utahn** \-,tó(-ə)n, -,tä(-ə)n\ *n*

Utah Lake lake 23 *mi* (37 *km*) long N *cen* Utah drained by Jordan River

Uti·ca \'yü-ti-kə\ **1** city E *cen* N.Y. on Mohawk River *pop* 68,637 **2** ancient city N Africa on Mediterranean coast NW of Carthage

Utrecht \'yü-ˌtrekt, 'ē-ˌtrekt\ **1** province *cen* Netherlands S of the IJsselmeer *area* 538 *sq mi* (1393 *sq km*), *pop* 1,047,035 **2** city, its ✳ *pop* 232,705

Utsu·no·mi·ya \ˌüt-sə-'nō-mē-ˌyä\ city Japan in *cen* Honshu N of Tokyo *pop* 426,809

Ut·tar Pra·desh \ˌu̇-tər-prə-'desh, -'dāsh\ state N India bordering on Tibet & Nepal ✳ Lucknow *area* 113,655 *sq mi* (294,366 *sq km*), *pop* 139,112,287 — see UNITED PROVINCES

Ux·bridge \'əks-(ˌ)brij\ former municipal borough SE England in Middlesex, now part of Hillingdon

Ux·mal \üsh-'mäl, 'üs-\ site of ancient Maya city SE Mexico in W Yucatán

Uz·bek·i·stan \(ˌ)u̇z-ˌbe·ki-'stan, ˌəz-, -'stän; -'be·ki-\ country W *cen* Asia E of the Amu Darya; a constituent republic (**Uz·bek Re·public** \'u̇z-ˌbek, 'əz-, u̇z-'\) of the U.S.S.R. 1924–91 ✳ Tashkent *area* 173,591 *sq mi* (449,601 *sq km*), *pop* 21,179,000

Uzh·go·rod \'üzh-gə-rət\ city SW Ukraine ✳ of Zakarpats'ka *pop* 123,000

V

Vaal \'väl\ river 720 *mi* (1158 *km*) Republic of South Africa rising in Mpumalanga & flowing W into Orange River in Northern Cape province

Vaa·sa *or Sw* **Va·sa** \'vä-sə\ city & port W Finland *pop* 53,364

Vaca·ville \'va-kə-ˌvil\ city W Calif. SW of Sacramento *pop* 71,479

Va·do·da·ra \və-'dō-də-ˌrä\ *or* **Ba·ro·da** \bə-'rō-də\ city W India in SE Gujarat SE of Ahmadabad *pop* 1,061,598

Va·duz \vä-'düts\ commune ✳ of Liechtenstein on the upper Rhine

Váh \'väk\ *or Hung* **Vág** \'väg\ river over 240 *mi* (386 *km*) W Slovakia rising in Tatry Mountains & flowing W & S into the Danube

Va·lais \va-'lä\ *or G* **Wal·lis** \'vä-lis\ canton SW *cen* Switzerland bordering on France & Italy ✳ Sion *area* 2020 *sq mi* (5232 *sq km*), *pop* 249,473

Val·dai Hills \väl-'dī\ hills W Russia in Europe SE of Lake Ilmen; highest point 1053 *ft* (321 *m*)

Val·di·via \väl-'dē-vē-ä\ city & port S *cen* Chile *pop* 100,046

Val d'Or \'val-ˌdȯr\ town Canada in SW Que. *pop* 23,842

Val·dos·ta \val-'däs-tə\ city S Ga. *pop* 39,806

Va·lence \va-'läⁿs\ commune SE France S of Lyon *pop* 65,026

Va·len·cia \va-'len(t)-sh(ē-)ə, -sē-ə\ **1** region & ancient kingdom E Spain bet. Andalusia & Catalonia **2** province E Spain *area* 4156 *sq mi* (10,764 *sq km*), *pop* 2,117,927 **3** commune & port on the Mediterranean, its ✳ *pop* 752,909 **4** city N Venezuela WSW of Caracas *pop* 903,706

Va·len·ci·ennes \və-ˌlen(t)-sē-'en(z)\ city N France *pop* 39,276

Va·len·tia \və-'len(t)-sh(ē-)ə\ island SW Ireland in County Kerry in the Atlantic S of entrance to Dingle Bay

Val·la·do·lid \,va-lə-də-'lid, ,vä-yä-thō-'lēth\ **1** province NW *cen* Spain *area* 3166 *sq mi* (8200 *sq km*), *pop* 494,207 **2** commune, its ✳, NNW of Madrid *pop* 320,293

Val·lau·ris \,vä-lô-'rēs\ village SE France NE of Cannes

Val·le·cas \vä-'yā-käs\ commune *cen* Spain, SE suburb of Madrid

Val·le d'Ao·sta \vä-lā-dä-'ós-tä\ *or* **Val d'Ao·sta** \,väl-dä-\ autonomous region NW Italy bordering on France & Switzerland NW of Piedmont ✳ Aosta *area* 1260 *sq mi* (3263 *sq km*), *pop* 115,270

Val·le·jo \və-'lā-(,)ō\ city W Calif. on San Pablo Bay *pop* 109,199

Val·let·ta \və-'le-tə\ city & port ✳ of Malta *pop* 9210

Valley East town Canada in S Ont. N of Sudbury *pop* 21,939

Valleyfield — see SALABERRY-DE-VALLEYFIELD

Valley of Ten Thousand Smokes volcanic region SW Alaska in Katmai National Monument

Valley Stream village SE N.Y. on Long Is. *pop* 33,946

Va·lois \'val-,wä, väl-'wä\ medieval county & duchy N France in NE Île-de-France ✳ Crépy-en-Valois

Valona — see VLORE

Val·pa·rai·so \,val-pə-'rä-(,)zō\ city NW Ind. SE of Gary *pop* 24,414 **2** \-'rī-(,)zō, -'rä-\ *or Sp* **Val·pa·ra·í·so** \,väl-pä-rä-'ē-sō\ city & port *cen* Chile WNW of Santiago *pop* 265,718

Van \'van\ salt lake E Turkey in Armenia *area* 1419 *sq mi* (3675 *sq km*)

Van·cou·ver \van-'kü-vər\ **1** city SW Wash. on Columbia River opposite Portland, Oreg. *pop* 46,380 **2** city & port Canada in SW B.C. on Burrard Inlet *pop* 471,844 — **Van·cou·ver·ite** \-və-,rīt\ *n*

Vancouver, Mount mountain 15,700 *ft* (4785 *m*) on Alaska-Yukon boundary in St. Elias Range

Vancouver Island island W Canada in B.C. off SW coast; chief city Victoria *area* 12,408 *sq mi* (32,261 *sq km*)

Van Die·men Gulf \van-'dē-mən\ inlet of Arafura Sea N Australia in N Northern Territory

Van Diemen's Land — see TASMANIA

Vä·nern \'ve-nərn\ lake SW Sweden *area* 2156 *sq mi* (5584 *sq km*)

Van·taa \'vän-(,)tä\ town S Finland N of Helsinki *pop* 159,462

Va·nua Le·vu \və-,nü-ə-'le-(,)vü, ,vän-wä-'lä-\ island S Pacific in the Fijis NE of Viti Levu *area* 2137 *sq mi* (5535 *sq km*)

Van·u·a·tu \,van-wä-'tü, ,vän- *also* -'wä-(,)tü\ *or formerly* **New Heb·ri·des** \'he-brə-,dēz\ islands SW Pacific NE of New Caledonia & W of Fiji; formerly under joint Brit. & French administration, a republic since 1980 ✳ Vila (on Efate) *area* 5700 *sq mi* (14,820 *sq km*), *pop* 142,419

Va·ra·na·si \və-'rä-nə-sē\ *or* **Ba·na·ras** *or* **Be·na·res** \bə-'när-əs\ city N India in SE Uttar Pradesh *pop* 932,399

Var·dar \'vär-,där\ river 241 *mi* (388 *km*) Macedonia (country) & N Greece flowing S into Gulf of Salonika

Va·re·se \vä-'rā-sā\ commune N Italy NW of Milan *pop* 85,461

Var·na \'vär-nə\ *or formerly* **Sta·lin** \'stä-lən, 'sta-, -,lēn\ city & port E Bulgaria on Black Sea *pop* 314,913

Väs·ter·ås \,ves-tə-'rōs\ city E Sweden on Mälaren Lake NW of Stockholm *pop* 120,889

Vaté — see EFATE

Vat·i·can City \'va-ti-kən\ *or It* **Cit·tà del Va·ti·ca·no** \chēt-'tä-del-,yä-tē-'kä-nō\ independent papal state within commune of Rome, Italy; created Feb. 11, 1929 *area* 109 *acres* (43 *hectares*), *pop* 771

Vät·tern \'ve-tərn\ lake S Sweden *area* 738 *sq mi* (1911 *sq km*)

Vaud \'vō\ *or G* **Waadt** \'vät\ canton W Switzerland N of Lake Geneva ✻ Lausanne *area* 1240 *sq mi* (3212 *sq km*), *pop* 576,319

Vaughan \'vȯn, 'vän\ city Canada in SE Ont. N of Toronto *pop* 111,359

Vaupés — see UAUPÉS

Ve·ga Ba·ja \'vā-gə-'bä-(,)hä\ municipality N Puerto Rico *pop* 55,997

Vegas LAS VEGAS

Ve·ii \'vē-,ī, 'vā-\ ancient city of Etruria in *cen* Italy NNW of Rome

Vej·le \'vī-lə\ city & port Denmark *pop* 50,879

Vel·bert \'fel-bərt\ city W Germany in N. Rhine-Westphalia in Ruhr valley NE of Düsseldorf *pop* 89,347

Vel·la La·vel·la \'ve-lə-lə-'ve-lə\ island SW Pacific in *cen* Solomons

Vel·lore \ve-'lȯr, ve-, -'lȯr\ city SE India in N Tamil Nadu WSW of Madras *pop* 172,467

Vel·sen \'vel-sən, -zən\ commune W Netherlands; outer port for Amsterdam *pop* 61,506

Velsuna — see ORVIETO

Vence \'vä°s\ commune SE France W of Nice *pop* 7332

Ven·da \'ven-də\ former black enclave in the Republic of South Africa ✻ Thohoyandou; granted independence 1979; abolished 1994

Ven·dée \vä°-'dā\ *or* **La Vendée** \lä-\ region W France bordering on Bay of Biscay S of Brittany

Ven·dôme \vä°-'dōm\ town N *cen* France WSW of Orléans

Ve·ne·tia \və-'nē-sh(ē-)ə\ *or It* **Ve·ne·zia** \ve-'net-sē-ä\ **1** area NE Italy, W Slovenia, & W Croatia including territory bet. the lower Po & the Alps **2** VENEZIA EUGANEA — **Ve·ne·tian** \-'nē-shən\ *adj*

Ve·ne·to \'ve-nä-,tō, 'vā-\ region NE Italy comprising most of Venezia Euganea ✻ Venice *area* 7096 *sq mi* (18,379 *sq km*), *pop* 4,385,023

Ve·ne·zia Eu·ga·nea \vä-'net-sē-ä-,ä-ü-'gä-nē-ä\ the S portion of Venetia

Venezia Giu·lia \-'jül-yä\ the E portion of Venetia including Julian Alps & Istria; now mainly in Slovenia & Croatia

Venezia Tri·den·ti·na \,trē-,den-'tē-nä\ the NW portion of Venetia N of Lake Garda; included in Trentino-Alto Adige region

Ven·e·zu·e·la \,ve-nə-'zwā-lə, -zə-'wā\ *or* ✻ Caracas *area* 352,143 *sq mi* (912,050 *sq km*), *pop* 20,609,000 — **Ven·e·zu·e·lan** \-lən\ *adj or n*

Venezuela, Gulf of inlet of the Caribbean NW Venezuela N of Lake Maracaibo

Ven·iam·i·nof Crater \ve-'nya-mə-,nȯf\ volcano 8225 *ft* (2507 *m*) SW Alaska on *cen* Alaska Peninsula in Aleutian Range

Ven·ice \'ve-nəs\ *or It* **Ve·ne·zia** \ve-'net-sē-ä\ *or L* **Ve·ne·tia** \və-'nē-sh(ē-)ə\ city & port NE Italy ✻ of Veneto, on islands in La·goon of Venice (inlet of Gulf of Venice) *pop* 308,717 — **Ve·ne·tian** \və-'nē-shən\ *adj or n*

Venice, Gulf of arm of the Adriatic bet. Po delta & Istria

Ven·lo *or* **Ven·loo** \\'ven-(,)lō\\ commune SE Netherlands on Maas River near German border *pop* 64,890

Ven·ta \\'ven-tə\\ river 217 *mi* (349 *km*) in Lithuania & Latvia flowing into the Baltic

Ven·ti·mi·glia \\,ven-tē-'mēl-yä\\ commune NW Italy on Ligurian Sea W of San Remo near Menton, France *pop* 25,221

Vents·pils \\'vent-,spils, -,spilz\\ *or G* **Win·dau** \\'vin-,daù\\ city & port Latvia at mouth of the Venta *pop* 50,400

Ven·tu·ra \\ven-'tùr-ə, -'tyùr-\\ *or officially* **San Buen·a·ven·tu·ra** \\,san-,bwe-nə-,ven-\\ city & port SW Calif. on Santa Barbara Channel ESE of Santa Barbara *pop* 92,575

Venue, Ben — see BEN VENUE

Ve·ra·cruz \\,ver-ə-'krüz, -'krüs\\ **1** state E Mexico ✻ Jalapa *area* 28,114 *sq mi* (72,815 *sq km*), *pop* 6,228,239 **2** *or* **Vera Cruz Lla·ve** \\'yä-(,)vā\\ city & port E Mexico in Veracruz state on Gulf of Mexico *pop* 327,522

Ver·cel·li \\ver-'che-lē, (,)vər-\\ commune NW Italy *pop* 48,597

Ver·di·gris \\'vər-də-grəs\\ river 351 *mi* (565 *km*) SE Kans. & NE Okla. flowing into Arkansas River

Ver·dun \\(,)vər-'dən, ver-\\ **1** town Canada in S Que. on Montreal Is. *pop* 61,307 **2** *or* **Verdun–sur–Meuse** \\-,sùr-\\ city NE France on the Meuse ESE of Reims *pop* 23,427

Ver·ee·ni·ging \\fə-'rā-nə-giŋ, -nə-kəŋ\\ city NE Republic of South Africa in Gauteng on the Vaal S of Johannesburg *pop* 94,500

Verkhneudinsk — see ULAN-UDE

Ver·mont \\vər-'mänt\\ state NE U.S. ✻ Montpelier *area* 9609 *sq mi* (24,983 *sq km*), *pop* 562,758 — **Ver·mont·er** \\-'män-tər\\ *n*

Ver·non \\'vər-nən\\ **1** town N *cen* Conn. NE of Hartford *pop* 29,841 **2** city Canada in S B.C. *pop* 23,514

Vernyi — see ALMA-ATA

Vé·roia \\'ver-yä\\ *or anc* **Be·rea** *or* **Be·roea** \\bə-'rē-ə\\ town NE Greece in Macedonia W of Thessaloníki

Ve·ro·na \\ve-'rō-nä\\ commune NE Italy on the Adige *pop* 252,689 — **Ver·o·nese** \\,ver-ə-'nēz, -'nēs\\ *adj or n*

Ver·sailles \\(,)vər-'sī, ver-\\ city N France, WSW suburb of Paris *pop* 91,029

Vert, Cap \\kap-'ver\\ *or* **Cape Vert** \\'vərt\\ promontory W Africa in Senegal; westernmost point in Africa at 17°30'W

Ver·viers \\ver-'vyā\\ commune E Belgium E of Liège *pop* 53,700

Ves·ta·via Hills \\ve-'stā-vē-ə\\ city *cen* Ala. S of Birmingham *pop* 19,749

Ves·ter·ål·en \\'ves-tə-,rò-lən\\ island group Norway off NW coast NE of Lofoten island group

Ve·su·vi·us \\və-'sü-vē-əs\\ *or It* **Ve·su·vio** \\vā-'sü-vyō, -'zü-\\ volcano 4190 *ft* (1277 *m*) Italy in Campania on Bay of Naples

Vet·lu·ga \\vet-'lü-gä\\ river 528 *mi* (850 *km*) *cen* Russia in Europe flowing S into the Volga

Ve·vey \\və-'vā\\ commune W Switzerland in Vaud on NE shore of Lake Geneva *pop* 16,139

Vi·cen·te Ló·pez \\vē-'sen-tē-'lō-,pez, -,pes\\ city E Argentina, N suburb of Buenos Aires, on Río de la Plata *pop* 289,142

Vi·cen·za \\vē-'chen-sä\\ commune NE Italy W of Venice *pop* 107,076

Vi·chu·ga \vi-'chü-gə\ city *cen* Russia in Europe NE of Moscow *pop* 49,700

Vi·chy \'vi-shē, 've-\ commune *cen* France on the Allier *pop* 28,048

Vicks·burg \'viks-,bərg\ city W Miss. *pop* 20,908

Vic·to·ria \vik-'tōr-ē-ə, -'tor-\ **1** city SE Tex. on Guadalupe River *pop* 55,076 **2** city Canada ✱ of B.C. on SE Vancouver Is. *pop* 71,228 **3** river 350 *mi* (563 *km*) Australia in NW Northern Territory flowing N & NW to Timor Sea **4** state SE Australia ✱ Melbourne *area* 87,884 *sq mi* (228,498 *sq km*), *pop* 4,244,221 **5** or **Hong Kong** \'hän-,kän, -'kän; 'hon-,kon, -'kon\ city & port ✱ of Hong Kong special administrative region, China on NW Hong Kong Is. *pop* 1,026,870 — **Vic·to·ri·an** \vik-'tōr-ē-ən, -'tor-\ *adj or n*

Victoria, Lake lake E Africa in Tanzania, Kenya, & Uganda *area* 26,828 *sq mi* (69,484 *sq km*)

Victoria Falls waterfall 355 *ft* (108 *m*) S Africa in the Zambezi on border bet. Zambia & Zimbabwe

Victoria Island island N Canada SE of Banks Is. *area* 81,930 *sq mi* (213,018 *sq km*)

Victoria Land region E Antarctica S of New Zealand on W shore of Ross Sea & Ross Ice Shelf

Victoria Nile — see NILE

Vic·tor·ville \'vik-tər-,vil\ city SE Calif. N of San Bernardino *pop* 40,674

Vied·ma \'vyäd-mä\ town S *cen* Argentina *pop* 24,338

Vi·en·na \vē-'e-nə, -'a-\ *or* G **Wien** \'vēn\ city ✱ of Austria on the Danube *pop* 1,539,848 — **Vi·en·nese** \,vē-ə-'nēz, -'nēs\ *adj or n*

Vi·enne \vē-'en\ **1** river 217 *mi* (349 *km*) S *cen* France flowing NW into the Loire **2** city SE France on the Rhône *pop* 30,386

Vien·tiane \(,)vyen-'tyän\ city ✱ of Laos, near Thailand border *pop* 132,253

Vie·ques \vē-'ā-kās\ island W. Indies off E Puerto Rico, belonging to Puerto Rico; chief town Isabel Segunda

Vierwaldstätter See — see LUCERNE (Lake of)

Viet·nam \vē-'et-'näm, vyet-, ,vē-ət-, vēt-, -'nam\ country SE Asia in Indochina; state, including Tonkin & N Annam, set up 1945–46; with S Annam & Cochin China, an associated state of French Union 1950–54; after civil war, divided 1954–75 at 17th parallel into republics of **North Vietnam** (✱ Hanoi) & **South Vietnam** (✱ Saigon); reunited 1975 (✱ Hanoi) *area* 127,207 *sq mi* (330,738 *sq km*), *pop* 70,454,000 — **Viet·nam·ese** \vē-,et-nə-'mēz, ,vyet-, ,vē-ət-, ,vēt-, -na-, -nä-, -'mēs\ *adj or n*

Vi·go \'vē-(,)gō\ city & port NW Spain on **Vigo Bay** (inlet of the Atlantic) *pop* 276,109

Viipuri — see VYBORG

Vi·ja·ya·na·gar \,vi-jə-yə-'nə-gər\ Hindu kingdom (1336–1565) S India S of the Krishna

Vi·ja·ya·wa·da \,vi-jə-yə-'wä-də\ *or formerly* **Bez·wa·da** \be-'zwä-də\ city SE India in E Andhra Pradesh on the Krishna, at head of its delta *pop* 701,827

Vila — see PORT-VILA

Villa Cisneros — see DAKHLA

Villa Gustavo A. Madero — see GUSTAVO A. MADERO, VILLA

Vil·la·her·mo·sa \,vē-yä-,er-'mō-sä\ city SE Mexico ✱ of Tabasco state *pop* 158,216

Vil·la Park \'vi-lə\ village NE Ill. W of Chicago pop 22,253

Ville·franche \ˌvēl-'frän⁴sh, ˌvē-lə-\ **1** or **Villefranche–sur–Mer** \-sür-'mer\ commune & port SE France E of Nice pop 8123 **2** or **Villefranche–sur–Saône** \-'sōn\ commune E cen France NNW of Lyon pop 29,889

Vil·leur·banne \ˌ)vē-,œr-'ban, -'bän\ commune E France, E suburb of Lyon pop 119,848

Vil·ni·us \'vil-nē-əs\ city ✷ of Lithuania pop 582,000

Vi·lyui or **Vi·lyuy** \vil-'yü-ē\ river over 1500 mi (2414 km) cen Russia in Asia flowing E into the Lena

Vim·i·nal \'vi-mə-nᵊl\ hill in Rome, Italy, one of seven upon which the ancient city was built — see AVENTINE

Vi·my Ridge \'vē-mē, vi-'mē\ ridge near Vimy commune N France N of Arras

Vi·ña del Mar \ˌvē-nyä-(ˌ)thel-'mär\ city & port cen Chile E of Valparaiso pop 249,977

Vin·cennes \(ˌ)vin-'senz; for 2, F van⁴-'sen\ **1** city SW Ind. pop 19,859 **2** commune N France, E suburb of Paris pop 42,651

Vin·dhya Mountains \'vin-dyə-ˌdē-ə\ mountain range N cen India N of & parallel to the Narmada River

Vindhya Pra·desh \prə-'desh, -'dāsh\ former state NE cen India ✷ Rewa; became (1956) part of Madhya Pradesh

Vine·land \'vīn-lənd\ city S N.J. pop 54,780

Vin·land \'vin-lənd\ a portion of the coast of N. America visited & so called by Norse voyagers ab A.D. 1000; variously located from E or NE Canada to N.J.

Vin·ny·tsya or **Vin·ni·tsa** \'vi-nət-syə\ city W cen Ukraine pop 381,000

Vinson Massif \'vin(t)-sən\ mountain 16,066 ft (4897 m) W Antarctica S of Ellsworth Land in Ellsworth Mountains; highest in Antarctica

Vir·gin \'vər-jən\ river 200 mi (322 km) SW Utah & SE Nev. flowing to Lake Mead

Vir·gin·ia \vər-'ji-nyə, -'ji-nē-ə\ state E U.S. ✷ Richmond area 40,767 sq mi (105,586 sq km), pop 6,187,358 — **Vir·gin·ian** \-nyən, -nē-ən\ adj or n

Virginia Beach city SE Va. on the Atlantic pop 393,069

Virginia Capes Cape Charles & Cape Henry in Va. forming entrance to Chesapeake Bay

Virgin Islands group of islands W. Indies E of Puerto Rico — see BRITISH VIRGIN ISLANDS, VIRGIN ISLANDS OF THE UNITED STATES

Virgin Islands National Park reservation W. Indies in Virgin Islands of the U.S. on St. John Is.

Virgin Islands of the United States the W islands of the Virgin Islands group including St. Croix, St. John, & St. Thomas; a territory ✷ Charlotte Amalie (on St. Thomas Is.) area 132 sq mi (343 sq km), pop 101,809 — see DANISH WEST INDIES

Vi·run·ga \vē-'rün-gä\ volcanic mountain range E cen Africa in E Democratic Republic of the Congo, SW Uganda & NW Rwanda N of Lake Kivu; highest peak Karisimbi 14,780 ft (4505 m)

Vi·sa·lia \vī-'sāl-yə\ city S cen Calif. SE of Fresno pop 75,636

Vi·sa·yan Islands \və-'sī-ən\ islands cen Philippines bet. Luzon & Mindanao — see BOHOL, CEBU, LEYTE, MASBATE, NEGROS, PANAY, ROMBLON, SAMAR

Vis·by \'viz-bē\ city & port Sweden on Gotland Is. in the Baltic *pop* 19,319

Vish·a·kha·pat·nam \vi-ˌshä-kə-'pət-nəm\ *or* **Vis·a·kha·pat·nam** \vi-ˌsä-\ city & port E India in NE Andhra Pradesh *pop* 752,037

Vi·so \'vē-(ˌ)zō\ mountain 12,602 *ft* (3841 *m*) NW Italy in Piedmont SW of Turin near French border; highest in Cottian Alps

Vis·ta \'vis-tə\ city SW Calif. N of San Diego *pop* 71,872

Vis·tu·la \'vis-chə-lə, 'vish-chə-\ *or Pol* **Wis·ła** \'vē-(ˌ)swä\ river over 660 *mi* (1062 *km*) Poland flowing N from the Carpathians into Gulf of Gdansk

Vi·tebsk \'vē-ˌtepsk, -ˌtebsk, və-\ *or* **Vit·syebsk** \'vēt-syipsk\ city NE Belarus on Dvina River *pop* 1,434,200

Vi·ter·bo \vē-'ter-(ˌ)bō\ commune *cen* Italy in Lazio *pop* 58,353

Vi·ti Le·vu \vē-tē-'le-(ˌ)vü\ island SW Pacific, largest of the Fiji group *area* 4010 *sq mi* (10,386 *sq km*)

Vi·tim \və-'tēm\ river 1133 *mi* (1823 *km*) S Russia in Asia flowing NE & N into the Lena

Vi·to·ria \vi-'tōr-ē-ə, -'tòr-\ city N Spain ✳ of Álava province SSE of Bilbao *pop* 204,961

Vi·tó·ria \vi-'tōr-ē-ə, -'tòr-\ city & port E Brazil ✳ of Espírito Santo state on Espírito Santo Is. *pop* 258,243

Vi·try-sur-Seine \vē-ˌtrē-sər-'sän, -'sen\ commune N France, SSE suburb of Paris *pop* 82,820

Viz·ca·ya \vēs-'kī-ä\ *or* **Bis·ca·ya** \bēs-\ *or* **Bis·cay** \'bis-ˌkā, -kē\ province N Spain on Bay of Biscay; in Basque Country ✳ Bilbao *area* 853 *sq mi* (2209 *sq km*), *pop* 1,155,106

Vlaanderen — see FLANDERS

Vlaar·ding·en \'vlär-diŋ-ə(n)\ commune & port SW Netherlands W of Rotterdam *pop* 73,893

Vlad·i·kav·kaz \ˌvla-də-ˌkäf-'käz, -ˌkaf-'kaz\ *or 1932–43 &* *1955–91* **Or·dzha·ni·kid·ze** \ˌòr-jä-nə-'kid-zə\ *or 1944–54* **Dzau·dzhi·kau** \(d)zaù-'jē-ˌkaù\ city S Russia in Europe *pop* 325,000

Vla·di·mir \'vla-də-ˌmir, vlə-'dē-ˌmir\ city *cen* Russia in Europe on the Klyazma E of Moscow *pop* 356,000

Vlad·i·vos·tok \ˌvla-də-və-'stäk, -'väs-ˌtäk\ city & port SE Russia in Asia ✳ of Maritime Territory *pop* 648,000

Vlis·sing·en \'vli-siŋ-ə(n)\ *or* **Flush·ing** \'flə-shiŋ\ city & port SW Netherlands on Walcheren Is. *pop* 43,913

Vlo·rë \'vlòr-ə, 'vlòr-\ *or* **Va·lo·na** \və-'lō-nə\ *or formerly* **Av·lo·na** \av-'lō-nə\ city & port S Albania *pop* 73,800

Vlta·va \'vəl-tə-və\ river 270 *mi* (434 *km*) W Czech Republic in Bohemia flowing N into the Elbe

Vogelkop — see DOBERAI

Voiotía — see BOEOTIA

Voj·vo·di·na \'vòi-vò-ˌdē-nä\ autonomous region N Yugoslavia N of the Danube; chief city Novi Sad *area* 8683 *sq mi* (22,576 *sq km*), *pop* 2,012,605

Vol·ca·no Islands \väl-'kā-(ˌ)nō, vòl-\ *or Jp* **Ka·zan Ret·to** \ˌkä-ˌzän-'re-(ˌ)tō\ islands W Pacific S of Bonin Islands; belong to Japan; under U.S. control 1945–68 *area* 11 *sq mi* (29 *sq km*) — see IWO JIMA

Vol·ga \'väl-gə, 'vòl-, 'vōl-\ river *ab* 2300 *mi* (3700 *km*) Russia in Europe rising in Valdai Hills & flowing into the Caspian

Vol·go·grad \'väl-gə-ˌgrad, 'vȯl-, 'vōl-, -ˌgrät\ *or formerly* **Sta·lin·grad** \'stä-lən-ˌgrad, 'sta-, -ˌgrät\ *or* **Tsa·ri·tsyn** \(t)sə-'rēt-sən\ city S Russia in Europe on the Volga *pop* 1,006,000

Vo·log·da \'vȯ-ləg-də\ city *cen* Russia in Europe NNE of Moscow *pop* 290,000

Vó·los \'vȯ-ˌlós\ city & port E Greece on **Gulf of Volos** (inlet of the Aegean)

Volsinii — see ORVIETO

Vol·ta \'väl-tə, 'vōl-, 'vȯl-\ river W Africa flowing from **Lake Volta** (reservoir *area* 3275 *sq mi or* 8515 *sq km*) receiving the **Black Volta** & **White Volta**) in N *cen* Ghana & flowing S into Bight of Benin — see RED VOLTA

Vol·ta Re·don·da \'väl-tə-ri-'dän-də, 'vōl-, 'vȯl-\ city E Brazil on Paraíba River NW of city of Rio de Janeiro *pop* 220,086

Vol·tur·no \väl-'tùr-(ˌ)nō, vōl-, vȯl-\ river 110 *mi* (177 *km*) S *cen* Italy flowing from the Apennines SE & SW into Gulf of Gaeta

Vor·arl·berg \'fȯr-ˌärl-ˌbərg, 'fȯr-, -ˌberk\ province W Austria W of Tirol bordering on Switzerland ✱ Bregenz *pop* 333,128

Vo·ro·nezh \və-'rȯ-nish\ city S *cen* Russia in Europe near Don River *pop* 902,000

Voroshilovgrad — see LUGANSK

Vosges \'vōzh\ mountains NE France on W side of Rhine valley; highest 4672 *ft* (1424 *m*)

Voy·a·geurs National Park \ˌvȯi-ə-'zhərz\ reservation N Minn. on Canadian border S of Rainy Lake

Vrangelya — see WRANGEL

Vrystaat — see FREE STATE

Vyat·ka \vē-'ät-kə\ **1** river *ab* 800 *mi* (1287 *km*) E *cen* Russia in Europe flowing into the Kama **2** — see KIROV

Vy·borg \'vē-ˌbȯrg\ *or Finn* **Vii·pu·ri** \'vē-pü-rē\ city & port W Russia in Europe on arm of Gulf of Finland; belonged to Finland 1917–40 *pop* 81,100

Vy·cheg·da \'vi-chig-də\ river 700 *mi* (1120 *km*) NE *cen* Russia in Europe flowing W to the Northern Dvina

W

Waadt — see VAUD

Waal \'väl\ river Netherlands, the S branch of the lower Rhine

Wa·bash \'wȯ-ˌbash\ river 475 *mi* (764 *km*) Ind. & Ill. flowing into Ohio River

Wa·co \'wā-(ˌ)kō\ city NE *cen* Tex. on the Brazos *pop* 103,590

Wad·den Zee \ˌvä-dᵊn-'zā\ inlet of North Sea N Netherlands bet. W. Frisian Islands & IJsselmeer

Wad·ding·ton, Mount \'wä-diŋ-tən\ mountain 13,104 *ft* (3994 *m*) W Canada in SW B.C. in Coast Mountains; highest in the province

Wadi al-'Arabah, Wadi 'Arabah, Wadi el-'Arabah — see 'ARABAH, WADI

Wad Me·da·ni \wäd-'me-dᵊn-ē\ city E *cen* Sudan on the Blue Nile *pop* 106,715

Wa·gram \'vä-ˌgräm\ village Austria NE of Vienna

Wai·a·le·a·le, Mount \wī-ˌä-lä-'ä-lä\ mountain 5200 *ft* (1585 *m*) Hawaii in *cen* Kauai

Wai·ka·to \wī-'kä-(ˌ)tō\ river 264 *mi* (425 *km*) New Zealand in NW North Is. flowing NW into Tasman Sea

Wai·ki·ki \ˌwī-ki-'kē\ resort section of Honolulu, Hawaii NW of Diamond Head on **Waikiki Beach**

Wai·mea Canyon \wī-'mā-ä\ gorge Hawaii on SW coast of Kauai

Wai·pa·hu \wī-'pä-(ˌ)hü\ city Hawaii in SW Oahu *pop* 31,435

Wai·ta·ki \wī-'tä-kē\ river 130 *mi* (209 *km*) New Zealand in SE *cen* South Is. flowing ESE into the Pacific

Wa·ka·ya·ma \ˌwä-kä-'yä-mä\ city & port Japan in SW Honshu on Inland Sea *pop* 396,554

Wake Island \'wāk\ island N Pacific N of Marshall Islands belonging to the U.S.

Wake·field \'wāk-ˌfēld\ **1** town E Mass. N of Boston *pop* 24,825 **2** city & borough N England ∗ of W. Yorkshire *pop* 60,540

Wa·la·chia *or* **Wal·la·chia** \wä-'lā-kē-ä\ region S Romania bet. the Transylvanian Alps & the Danube; includes Muntenia & Oltenia; chief city Bucharest — **Wa·la·chi·an** *or* **Wal·la·chi·an** \-ən\ *adj or n*

Wał·brzych \'vaüb-ˌzhik, -ˌzhik\ city SW Poland *pop* 141,139

Wal·deck \'väl-ˌdek\ former county, principality, & state of Germany bet. Westphalia & Hesse-Nassau ∗ Arolsen

Wal·den Pond \'wol-dən\ pond NE Mass. S of Concord

Wales \'wālz\ *or* **W Cym·ru** \'kəm-ˌrē\ *or ML* **Cam·bria** \'kam-brē-ə\ principality SW Great Britain; a division of the United Kingdom of Great Britain and Northern Ireland ∗ Cardiff *area* 8016 *sq mi* (20,761 *sq km*), *pop* 2,799,000 — **Welsh** *also* **Welch** \'welsh *also* 'welch\ *adj or n* — **Welsh·man** \-mən\ *n* — **Welsh·wom·an** \-ˌwù-mən\ *n*

Wal·la·sey \'wä-lə-sē\ borough NW England in Merseyside on coast W of Liverpool *pop* 90,057

Wal·la Wal·la \ˌwä-lə-'wä-lə, 'wä-lə-ˌ\ city SE Wash. *pop* 26,478

Wal·ling·ford \'wä-liŋ-fərd\ town S Conn. NNE of New Haven *pop* 40,822

Wallis — see VALAIS

Wal·lis Islands \'wä-ləs\ islands SW Pacific NE of Fiji Islands; with Futuna Islands, constitute a French overseas territory (**Wallis and Futuna Islands** *pop* 14,000)

Wal·lops Island \'wä-ləps\ island E Va. in the Atlantic SW of Chincoteague Bay

Wal·lowa Mountains \wä-'laü-ə\ mountains NE Oreg. E of Blue Mountains; highest Sacajawea Peak 9838 *ft* (2999 *m*)

Wal·nut \'wol-(ˌ)nət\ city SW Calif. E of Los Angeles *pop* 29,105

Walnut Canyon National Monument reservation N *cen* Ariz. ESE of Flagstaff containing cliff dwellings

Walnut Creek city W Calif. E of Berkeley *pop* 60,569

Wal·pole \'wol-ˌpōl, 'wäl-\ town E Mass. SW of Boston *pop* 20,212

Wal·sall \'wol-ˌsol, -səl\ borough W *cen* England in W. Midlands NNW of Birmingham *pop* 255,600

Wal·tham \'wȯl-,tham, *chiefly by outsiders* -thəm\ city E Mass. W of Boston *pop* 57,878

Wal·tham Forest \'wȯl-thəm\ borough of NE Greater London, England *pop* 203,400

Wal·tham·stow \'wȯl-thəm-,stō\ former municipal borough SE England in Essex, now part of Waltham Forest

Wal·vis Bay \'wȯl-vəs\ town & port W Namibia on Walvis Bay (inlet) W of Windhoek; formerly an exclave of Republic of South Africa forming a district *area* (of district) 434 *sq mi* (1124 *sq km*)

Wands·worth \'wän(d)z-(,)wərth\ borough of SW Greater London, England *pop* 237,500

Wang·a·nui \,wäŋ-gə-'nü-ē, ,wäŋ-ə-\ **1** river 180 *mi* (290 *km*) New Zealand in SW *cen* North Is., flowing into Tasman Sea **2** city & port New Zealand in North Is. on Tasman Sea *pop* 41,400

Wan·ne-Eick·el \'vä-nə-'ī-kəl\ city W Germany in the Ruhr N of Bochum *pop* 100,300

Wan·stead and Wood·ford \'wän-stəd-ᵊn-'wu̇d-fərd\ former municipal borough S England in Essex, now part of Redbridge

Wap·si·pin·i·con \,wäp-si-'pi-ni-kən\ river 225 *mi* (362 *km*) SE Minn. & E Iowa flowing SE into Mississippi River

Wa·ran·gal \wə-'rəŋ-gəl\ city S *cen* India in N Andhra Pradesh NE of Hyderabad *pop* 447,653

War·bur·ton Creek \'wȯr-(,)bər-tᵊn\ river 275 *mi* (442 *km*) Australia in NE S. Australia flowing SW into Lake Eyre

Ware·ham \'war-əm, 'wer-, -,ham\ city SE Mass. ENE of New Bedford *pop* 19,232

War·ley \'wȯr-lē\ town W cen England, a NW suburb of Birmingham *pop* 152,455

War·ner Rob·ins \'wȯr-nər-'rä-bənz\ city *cen* Ga. *pop* 43,726

War·ren \'wȯr-ən, 'wär-\ **1** city SE Mich. N of Detroit *pop* 144,864 **2** city NE Ohio NW of Youngstown *pop* 50,793

War·ring·ton \'wȯr-iŋ-tən, 'wär-\ borough NW England in Cheshire on the Mersey E of Liverpool *pop* 57,389

War·saw \'wȯr-,sȯ\ *or Pol* **War·sza·wa** \vär-'shä-vä\ city ✽ of Poland on the Vistula *pop* 1,655,063 — **Var·so·vi·an** \,vär-'sō-vē-ən\ *n*

War·ta \'vär-tə\ *or G* **War·the** \'vär-tə\ river 502 *mi* (808 *km*) Poland flowing NW & W into the Oder

War·wick \'wär-ik, *US also* 'wik-ik, 'wȯr-(,)wik\ **1** city *cen* R.I. S of Providence on Narragansett Bay *pop* 85,427 **2** town *cen* England ✽ of Warwickshire *pop* 21,936

War·wick·shire \'wär-ik-,shir, -shər, *US also* 'wȯr-ik-, 'wȯr-(,)wik-\ *or* **Warwick** county *cen* England ✽ Warwick *area* 792 *sq mi* (2051 *sq km*), *pop* 477,000

Wa·satch Range \'wȯ-,sach\ mountain range SE Idaho & N & *cen* Utah — see TIMPANOGOS (Mount)

Wash, The \'wȯsh, 'wäsh\ inlet of North Sea E England bet. Norfolk & Lincoln

Wash·ing·ton \'wȯ-shiŋ-tən, 'wä-, *chiefly Midland also* 'wȯr-shiŋ- *or* 'wär-\ **1** state NW U.S. ✽ Olympia *area* 68,192 *sq mi* (177,299 *sq km*), *pop* 4,866,692 **2** city ✽ of the U.S., coextensive with District of Columbia *pop* 609,909 **3** — see TERAINA — **Wash·ing·to·nian** \,wȯ-shiŋ-'tō-nē-ən, ,wä-, -nyən\ *adj or n*

Washington, Lake lake 20 *mi* (32 *km*) long W Wash. E of Seattle

Washington, Mount

Washington, Mount mountain 6288 *ft* (1916 *m*) N N.H.; highest in White Mountains

Wash·i·ta \'wä-shə-,tò, 'wò-\ river 500 *mi* (805 *km*) NW Tex. & SW Okla. flowing SE into Red River

Wa·tau·ga \wä-'tò-gə\ river 60 *mi* (96 *km*) NW N.C. & NE Tenn. flowing into S fork of the Holston **2** town N Tex. *pop* 20,009

Watenstedt–Salzgitter — SEE SALZGITTER

Wa·ter·bury \'wò-tə(r)-,ber-ē, 'wä-\ city W *cen* Conn. *pop* 108,961

Wa·ter·ee \'wò-tə-,rē, 'wä-\ river S.C., lower course of the Catawba — see CONGAREE

Wa·ter·ford \'wò-tər-fərd, 'wä-\ **1** county S Ireland in Munster *area* 710 *sq mi* (1846 *sq km*), *pop* 51,296 **2** city & port, its ✻ *pop* 40,345

Wa·ter·loo \,wò-tər-'lü, ,wä-; 'wò-tər-,lü, 'wä-\ **1** city NE *cen* Iowa *pop* 66,467 **2** town *cen* Belgium S of Brussels *pop* 27,860 **3** city Canada in SE Ont. W of Kitchener *pop* 71,181

Wa·ter·ton–Glacier International Peace Park \'wò-tər-t°n, 'wä-\ reservation comprising **Glacier National Park** (reservation NW Mont.) & **Waterton Lakes National Park** (reservation Canada in Rocky Mountains in S Alta.)

Wa·ter·town \'wò-tər-,taùn, 'wä-\ **1** town SW Conn. NW of Waterbury *pop* 20,456 **2** town E Mass. W of Boston *pop* 33,284 **3** city N *cen* N.Y. SE of Kingston, Ont. *pop* 29,429 **4** city SE Wis. *pop* 19,142

Wat·ford \'wät-fərd\ town SE England in Hertfordshire NW of London *pop* 72,100

Wat·son·ville \'wät-sən-,vil\ city W Calif. *pop* 31,099

Wat·ten·scheid \'vä-t°n-,shīt\ city W Germany E of Essen *pop* 80,527

Watts \'wäts\ section of Los Angeles, Calif. S of the downtown district

Wau·ke·gan \wò-'kē-gən\ city NE Ill. N of Chicago *pop* 69,392

Wau·ke·sha \'wò-kə-,shò\ city SE Wis. *pop* 56,958

Wau·sau \'wò-,sò, -sä\ city N *cen* Wis. *pop* 37,060

Wau·wa·to·sa \,wò-wə-'tō-sə\ city SE Wis. *pop* 49,366

Wayne \'wān\ village SE Mich. SW of Detroit *pop* 19,899

Wa·zir·i·stan \wə-,zir-i-'stan, -'stän\ region W Pakistan on border of Afghanistan NE of Baluchistan

Weald \'wēld\ region SE England in Kent, Surrey, & Sussex, bet. N. Downs & S. Downs; once heavily forested

Wear \'wir\ river 67 *mi* (108 *km*) N England flowing into North Sea at Sunderland

Web·ster Groves \'web-stər\ city E Mo. *pop* 22,987

Wed·dell Sea \wə-'del, 'we-d°l\ arm of the S Atlantic E of Antarctic Peninsula

Wei \'wā\ river *ab* 535 *mi* (860 *km*) N *cen* China flowing E to join the Huang

Wei·fang \'wā-'fäŋ\ city E China in E *cen* Shandong *pop* 428,522

Wei·hai \'wā-'hī\ city & port E China in NE Shandong on Yellow Sea *pop* 128,888

Wei·mar \'vī-,mär, 'wī-\ city E *cen* Germany E of Erfurt *pop* 64,000

Weimar Republic the German republic 1919–33

Weir·ton \'wir-t°n\ city N W.Va. on Ohio River *pop* 22,124

Wel·land \\'we-lənd\\ city Canada in SE Ont. SW of Niagara Falls *pop* 47,914

Welland Canal *or* **Welland Ship Canal** canal 27 *mi* (44 *km*) Canada in SE Ont. connecting Lake Erie & Lake Ontario

Welles·ley \\'welz-lē\\ town E Mass. WSW of Boston *pop* 26,615

Wel·ling·ton \\'we-liŋ-tən\\ city & port ✳ of New Zealand in SW North Is. on Port Nicholson (Wellington Harbor) on Cook Strait *pop* 149,400

Wells \\'welz\\ city & borough SW England in Somerset *pop* 8374

Welsh·pool \\'welsh-ˌpül\\ town E Wales in Powys *pop* 7317

Wel·wyn Garden City \\'we-lən\\ town SE England in Hertfordshire N of London *pop* 40,369

Wem·bley \\'wem-blē\\ former municipal borough SE England in Middlesex, now part of Brent

We·natch·ee \\wə-'na-chē\\ city *cen* Wash. *pop* 21,756

Wen·zhou *or* **Wen·chow** *or* **Wen–chou** \\'wən-'jō\\ city & port E China in S Zhejiang on E. China Sea *pop* 401,871

Wer·ra \\'ver-ə\\ river 180 *mi* (290 *km*), *cen* Germany flowing N

We·ser \\'vā-zər\\ river 273 *mi* (439 *km*) *cen* & NW Germany flowing into North Sea

Wes·la·co \\'wes-li-ˌkō\\ city S Tex. W of Harlingen *pop* 21,877

Wes·sex \\'we-siks\\ ancient Anglian kingdom S England ✳ Winchester; one of kingdoms in Anglo-Saxon heptarchy

West Al·lis \\'a-ləs\\ city SE Wis. *pop* 63,221

West Antarctica — see ANTARCTICA

West Bank area Palestine W of Jordan River; occupied by Israel since 1967 — **West Bank·er** \\'baŋ-kər\\ *n*

West Bend \\'bend\\ city SE Wis. NNW of Milwaukee *pop* 23,916

West Bengal state E India comprising the W third of former Bengal province ✳ Calcutta *area* 33,852 *sq mi* (87,677 *sq km*), *pop* 68,077,965

West Beskids — see BESKIDS

West Brom·wich \\'brä-mich\\ borough W *cen* England in W. Midlands NW of Birmingham *pop* 154,930

West Co·vi·na \\kō-'vē-nə\\ city SW Calif. *pop* 96,086

West Des Moines city S *cen* Iowa *pop* 31,702

Wes·ter·ly \\'wes-tər-lē\\ town SW R.I. *pop* 21,605

Western — see HEBRIDES

Western Australia state W Australia on Indian Ocean ✳ Perth *area* 975,920 *sq mi* (2,537,392 *sq km*), *pop* 1,676,400

Western Cape *or* **Wes–Kaap** \\'wes-ˌkäp, 'ves-\\ province SW Republic of South Africa *area* 49,950 *sq mi* (129,370 *sq km*), *pop* 3,635,000

Western Ghats \\'gäts, 'gòts, 'gäts\\ chain of mountains SW India extending SSE parallel to coast from mouth of the Tapi to Cape Comorin; highest 8842 *ft* (2695 *m*) — see EASTERN GHATS

Western Isles **1** the Outer Hebrides, constituting since 1975 a region of W Scotland ✳ Stornoway *area* 1120 *sq mi* (2912 *sq km*), *pop* 29,410 **2** — used unofficially of the entire Hebrides group

Western Reserve tract of land NE Ohio on S shore of Lake Erie; part of W lands of Conn., ceded 1800 *area ab* 5470 *sq mi* (14,222 *sq km*)

Western Sahara *or formerly* **Spanish Sahara** territory NW Africa *area* 102,703 *sq mi* (266,001 *sq km*) *pop* 213,000; formerly a Spanish possession, divided 1975 bet. Mauritania, which gave up its claim in Aug. 1979, & Morocco, which subsequently occupied the entire territory

Western Samoa group of islands of Samoa W of 171°W; until 1962 a territory administered by New Zealand; became an independent member of the Commonwealth of Nations 1962 ✳ Apia (on Upolu Is.) *area* 1100 *sq mi* (2850 *sq km*), *pop* 156,349

Western Thrace — see THRACE

Wes·ter·ville \'wes-tər-ˌvil, -vəl\ city *cen* Ohio *pop* 30,269

West·field \'west-ˌfēld\ **1** city SW Mass. WNW of Springfield *pop* 38,372 **2** town NE N.J. WSW of Elizabeth *pop* 28,870

West Flanders province NW Belgium bordering on North Sea ✳ Brugge *area* 1210 *sq mi* (3134 *sq km*), *pop* 1,106,829

West Frisian — see FRISIAN ISLANDS

West Germany — see GERMANY

West Glamorgan county SE Wales ✳ Swansea *area* 317 *sq mi* (820 *sq km*), *pop* 357,800

West Ham \'ham\ former county borough SE England in Essex, now part of Newham

West Hartford town *cen* Conn. *pop* 60,110

West Ha·ven \'west-ˌhā-vən\ city S Conn. *pop* 54,021

West Hollywood city SW Calif. *pop* 36,118

West Indies **1** the islands lying bet. SE N. America & N S. America bordering the Caribbean & comprising the Greater Antilles, Lesser Antilles, & Bahamas **2** or **West Indies Federation** former country including all of the Brit. West Indies except the Bahamas & the Brit. Virgin Islands; established 1958, dissolved 1961 — **West Indian** *adj or n*

West Irian — see IRIAN JAYA

West Jordan city N *cen* Utah *pop* 42,892

West Lafayette city W *cen* Ind. *pop* 25,907

West·lake \'west-ˌlāk\ city N Ohio W of Cleveland *pop* 27,018

West·land \'west-lənd\ city SE Mich. W of Detroit *pop* 84,724

West Lo·thi·an \'lō-thē-ən\ *or earlier* **Lin·lith·gow** \lin-'lith-(ˌ)gō\ *or* **Lin·lith·gow·shire** \-ˌshir, -shər\ former county SE Scotland bordering on Firth of Forth ✳ Linlithgow — see LOTHIAN

West Malaysia the peninsular part of Malaysia — see MALAYA 3

West·meath \(ˌ)west-'mēth, -'mēth\ county E *cen* Ireland in Leinster ✳ Mullingar *area* 681 *sq mi* (1771 *sq km*), *pop* 61,880

West Memphis city E Ark. on Mississippi River *pop* 28,259

West Midlands metropolitan county W *cen* England ✳ Birmingham *area* 360 *sq mi* (932 *sq km*), *pop* 2,499,300

West Miff·lin \'mi-fl∂n\ borough SW Pa. SE of Pittsburgh *pop* 23,644

West·min·ster \'wes(t)-ˌmin(t)-stər\ **1** city SW Calif. E of Long Beach *pop* 78,118 **2** city N *cen* Colo. NW of Denver *pop* 74,625 **3** *or* **City of Westminster** borough of W *cen* Greater London, England *pop* 181,500

West·mont \'west-ˌmänt\ city NE Ill. *pop* 21,228

West·mor·land \'west-mər-lənd, *US also* west-'mōr- *or* -'mȯr-\ former county NW England ✳ Kendal

West New York town NE N.J. on Hudson River *pop* 38,125

Wes·ton–su·per–Mare \'wes-tən-,sü-pər-'mar, -'mer\ borough SW England in Avon on Bristol Channel *pop* 57,980

West Pakistan the former W division of Pakistan, now coextensive with Pakistan

West Palm Beach city SE Fla. on Lake Worth inlet *pop* 67,643

West·pha·lia \west-'fāl-yə, -'fā-lē-ə\ *or G* **West·fa·len** \,vest-'fä-lən\ region W Germany bordering on Netherlands E of the Rhine; includes Ruhr valley; a province of Prussia 1816–1945 ✳ Münster — see NORTH RHINE-WESTPHALIA — **West·pha·lian** \west(t)-'fāl-yən, -'fä-lē-ən\ *adj or n*

West·port \'west-,pōrt, -,pȯrt\ town SW Conn. *pop* 24,410

West Prussia region N Europe bordering on the Baltic bet. Pomerania & E. Prussia; since 1945 in Poland

West Punjab — see PUNJAB

West Quod·dy Head \'kwä-dē\ cape NE Maine at entrance to Passamaquoddy Bay

Wes·tra·lia \we-'strāl-yə, -'strä-lē-ə\ WESTERN AUSTRALIA

West Riding — see YORK

West Sacramento city Calif. *pop* 28,898

West Saint Paul city SE Minn. S of St. Paul *pop* 19,248

West Springfield town SW Mass. on Connecticut River *pop* 27,537

West Suffolk — see SUFFOLK

West Sus·sex \'sə-siks, *US also* -,seks\ county S England ✳ Chichester *area* 806 *sq mi* (2088 *sq km*), *pop* 692,800

West Valley City city N Utah bordering Salt Lake City on the S *pop* 86,976

West Vancouver municipality Canada in SW B.C. N of Vancouver *pop* 38,783

West Virginia state E U.S. ✳ Charleston *area* 24,181 *sq mi* (62,871 *sq km*), *pop* 1,793,477 — **West Virginian** *adj or n*

West Warwick town *cen* R.I. *pop* 29,268

West Yorkshire metropolitan county NW England ✳ Wakefield *area* 816 *sq mi* (2113 *sq km*), *pop* 1,984,700

Weth·ers·field \'we-tharz-,fēld\ town *cen* Conn. *pop* 25,651

Wex·ford \'weks-fərd\ **1** county SE Ireland in Leinster *area* 908 *sq mi* (2352 *sq km*), *pop* 102,069 **2** town & port, its ✳ *pop* 9537

Wey·mouth \'wā-məth\ town E Mass. SE of Boston *pop* 54,063

Whales, Bay of \'hwālz, 'wālz\ inlet of Ross Sea Antarctica in Ross Ice Shelf

Whangpoo — see HUANGPU

Whea·ton \'hwēt-tᵊn, 'wē-\ city NE Ill. W of Chicago *pop* 51,464

Wheat Ridge \'hwēt, 'wēt\ city N *cen* Colo. W of Denver *pop* 29,419

Whee·ler Peak \'hwē-lər, 'wē-\ **1** mountain 13,065 *ft* (3980 *m*) E Nev. in Snake Range **2** mountain 13,160 *ft* (4010 *m*) N N.Mex. in Sangre de Cristo Mountains; highest in the state

Whee·ling \'hwē-liŋ, 'wē-\ **1** village NE Ill. NNE of Chicago *pop* 29,911 **2** city N W.Va. on Ohio River *pop* 34,882

Whid·bey Island \'hwid-bē, 'wid-\ island 40 *mi* (64 *km*) long NW Wash. at N end of Puget Sound E of Admiralty Inlet

Whit·by \'hwit-bē, 'wit-\ town Canada in S Ont. *pop* 61,281

White \'hwīt, 'wīt\ **1** river 690 *mi* (1110 *km*) N Ark. & SW Mo. flowing SE into Mississippi River **2** river NW Colo. & E Utah flowing W into Green River **3** river 50 *mi* (80 *km*) SW Ind. flowing W into the Wabash **4** river 325 *mi* (523 *km*) S S.Dak. flowing E into Missouri River **5** river NW Tex.

White Bear Lake city E Minn. NE of St. Paul *pop* 24,704

White·chap·el \'hwit-,cha-pəl, 'wit-\ district of E London, England, N of Thames River in Tower Hamlets

White·friars \'hwīt-,frī(-ə)rz, 'wīt-\ district of *cen* London, England, on Thames River

White·hall \-,hȯl\ city *cen* Ohio, E suburb of Columbus *pop* 20,572

White·horse \'hwīt-,hȯrs, 'wīt-\ city NW Canada ✳ of Yukon Territory on upper Yukon River *pop* 17,925

White Mountains **1** mountains E Calif. & SE Nev. **2** mountains N N.H. in the Appalachians — see WASHINGTON (Mount)

White Nile — see NILE

White Pass mountain pass 2890 *ft* (881 *m*) SE Alaska N of Skagway

White Plains city SE N.Y. NE of Yonkers *pop* 48,718

White Sands National Monument reservation S N.Mex. SW of Alamogordo comprising an area of gypsum sand dunes

White Sea *or Russ* **Be·lo·ye Mo·re** \'bye-lə-yə-'mȯr-yə, 'be-lə-\ inlet of Barents Sea NW Russia in Europe enclosed on the N by Kola Peninsula

White Volta — see VOLTA

Whit·ney, Mount \'hwit-nē, 'wit-\ mountain 14,495 *ft* (4418 *m*) SE *cen* Calif. in Sierra Nevada in Sequoia National Park; highest in the U.S. outside of Alaska

Whit·ti·er \'hwit-tē-ər, 'wi-\ city SW Calif. SE of Los Angeles *pop* 77,671

Wich·i·ta \'wi-chə-,tȯ\ **1** city S *cen* Kans. on Arkansas River *pop* 304,011 **2** river 250 *mi* (402 *km*) N Tex. flowing ENE into Red River

Wichita Falls city N Tex. on Wichita River *pop* 96,259

Wichita Mountains mountains SW Okla.; highest Mt. Scott 2464 *ft* (751 *m*)

Wick·low \'wi-(,)klō\ **1** county E Ireland in Leinster *area* 782 *sq mi* (2033 *sq km*), *pop* 97,265 **2** town & port, its ✳, SSE of Dublin *pop* 5847

Wicklow Mountains mountains Ireland along E coast; highest Lugnaquilla 3039 *ft* (926 *m*)

Wien — see VIENNA

Wies·ba·den \'vēs-,bä-dᵊn\ city SW *cen* Germany on the Rhine W of Frankfurt am Main ✳ of Hesse *pop* 264,022

Wig·an \'wi-gən\ borough NW England in Greater Manchester W of Manchester *metropolitan area pop* 301,900

Wight, Isle of \'wīt\ island S England in English Channel constituting **Isle of Wight** county (✳ Newport *area* 152 *sq mi or* 394 *sq km, pop* 126,600)

Wig·town \'wig-tən, -,taún\ *or* **Wig·town·shire** \-,shir, -shər\ former county SW Scotland = Wigtown

Wil·der·ness Road \'wil-dər-nəs\ trail from SW Va. to *cen* Ky. through Cumberland Gap blazed to site of Boonesborough by Daniel Boone 1775 & later extended to falls of the Ohio at Louisville

Wil·helms·ha·ven \,vil-,helmz-'hä-fən, 'vi-ləmz-,\ city & port NW Germany NW of Bremen *pop* 91,149

Wilkes–Barre \'wilks-,bar-ə, -,bar-ē, -,bar\ city NE Pa. on the Susquehanna SW of Scranton *pop* 47,523

Wilkes Land \'wilks\ coast region E Antarctica extending along Indian Ocean S of Australia

Wil·kins·burg \'wil-kənz-,bərg\ borough SW Pa. *pop* 21,080

Wil·lam·ette \wə-'la-mət\ river 300 *mi* (485 *km*) NW Oreg. flowing N into Columbia River

Wil·la·pa Bay \'wi-lə-,pȯ, -,pä\ inlet of the Pacific SW Wash.

Wil·lem·stad \'vi-ləm-,stät\ city ✳ of Netherlands Antilles on Curaçao Is. *pop* 43,547

Willes·den \'wilz-dən\ former municipal borough SE England in Middlesex, now part of Brent

Wil·liams·burg \'wil-yəmz-,bərg\ city SE Va. NNW of Newport News; ✳ of Virginia 1699–1780; site of large-scale restoration (Colonial Williamsburg) *pop* 11,530

Wil·liam·son, Mount \'wil-yəm-sən\ mountain 14,375 *ft* (4382 *m*) SE *cen* Calif. in Sierra Nevada NNW of Mt. Whitney

Wil·liams·port \'wil-yəmz-,pȯrt, -,pȯrt\ city N *cen* Pa. on W branch of the Susquehanna *pop* 31,933

Wil·lough·by \'wi-lə-bē\ city NE Ohio NE of Cleveland *pop* 20,510

Wil·mette \wil-'met\ village NE Ill. N of Chicago *pop* 26,690

Wil·ming·ton \'wil-miŋ-tən\ **1** city & port N Del. *pop* 71,529 **2** city & port SE N.C. *pop* 55,530

Wil·son \'wil-sən\ city E *cen* N.C. E of Raleigh *pop* 36,930

Wilson, Mount mountain 5710 *ft* (1740 *m*) SW Calif. NE of Pasadena

Wilt·shire \'wilt-,shir, -shər\ county S England ✳ Trowbridge *area* 1392 *sq mi* (3605 *sq km*), *pop* 553,300

Wim·ble·don \'wim-bəl-dən\ former municipal borough SE England in Surrey, now part of Merton

Win·ches·ter \'win-,ches-tər, -chəs-tər\ **1** town E Mass. NW of Boston *pop* 20,267 **2** city N Va. *pop* 21,947 **3** city & borough S England ✳ of Hampshire *pop* 30,642

Wind \'wind\ river W *cen* Wyo., the upper course of Bighorn River

Windau — see VENTSPILS

Wind Cave limestone cavern SW S. Dak. in Black Hills in **Wind Cave National Park**

Win·der·mere \'win-də(r)-,mir\ lake 10 *mi* (16 *km*) long NW England in Cumbria; largest in England

Wind·ham \'win-dəm\ town E *cen* Conn. *pop* 22,039

Wind·hoek \'vint-,hůk\ city ✳ of Namibia *pop* 144,558

Wind River Canyon gorge of Bighorn River W *cen* Wyo.

Wind River Range mountain range W *cen* Wyo. — see GANNETT PEAK

Wind·sor \'win-zər\ **1** town N *cen* Conn. N of Hartford *pop* 27,817 **2** city Canada in SE Ont. on Detroit River opposite Detroit, Mich. *pop* 191,435 **3** *or* **New Windsor** royal borough S England in Berkshire on Thames River W of London *pop* 30,065

Wind·ward Islands \'wind-wərd\ **1** islands W. Indies in the S Lesser Antilles extending S from Martinique but not including Barbados, Tobago, or Trinidad **2** former colony Brit. West Indies comprising territories of St. Lucia, St. Vincent, & Grenada in the Windward group & Dominica in the Leewards **3** *or F* **Îles du Vent** \ēl-dē-vä"\ islands S Pacific, E group of the Society Islands, including Tahiti *pop* 140,341

Windward Passage channel bet. Cuba & Hispaniola

Win·ne·ba·go, Lake \,wi-nə-'bā-(,)gō\ lake 30 *mi* (48 *km*) long E Wis.

Win·ni·peg \'wi-nə-,peg\ **1** river *ab* 500 *mi* (804 *km*) Canada in W Ont. & SE Man. flowing from Lake of the Woods to Lake Winnipeg **2** city Canada ✳ of Man. *pop* 616,790 — **Win·ni·peg·ger** \-pe-gər\ *n*

Winnipeg, Lake lake *ab* 260 *mi* (418 *km*) long Canada in S *cen* Man. drained by Nelson River

Win·ni·pe·go·sis, Lake \,wi-nə-pə-'gō-səs\ lake Canada in W Man. W of Lake Winnipeg *area* 2075 *sq mi* (5374 *sq km*)

Win·ni·pe·sau·kee, Lake \,wi-nə-pə-'sò-kē\ lake *cen* N.H. *area* 71 *sq mi* (185 *sq km*)

Wi·no·na \wə-'nō-nə\ city SE Minn. *pop* 25,399

Wi·noo·ski \wə-'nüs-kē\ river 100 *mi* (161 *km*) N *cen* Vt. flowing into Lake Champlain

Win·ston–Sa·lem \,win(t)-stən-'sā-ləm\ city N N.C. *pop* 143,485

Win·ter Haven \'win-tər-,hā-vən\ city *cen* Fla. E of Lakeland *pop* 24,725

Winter Park city E Fla. N of Orlando *pop* 22,242

Winter Springs city E *cen* Fla. N of Orlando *pop* 22,151

Win·ter·thur \'vin-tər-,túr\ commune N Switzerland in Zurich canton NE of Zurich *pop* 86,600

Win·yah Bay \'win-,yò\ inlet of the Atlantic E S.C.

Wis·con·sin \wi-'skän(t)-sən\ **1** river 430 *mi* (692 *km*) *cen* Wis. flowing S & W into Mississippi River **2** state N *cen* U.S. ✳ Madison *area* 56,154 *sq mi* (145,439 *sq km*), *pop* 4,891,769 — **Wis·con·sin·ite** \-sə-,nīt\ *n*

Wisconsin Dells — see DELLS OF THE WISCONSIN

Wisła — see VISTULA

Wis·mar \'vis-,mär, 'wiz-,mär\ city & port N Germany *pop* 54,471

Wis·sa·hick·on Creek \,wi-sə-'hi-kən\ stream SE Pa. flowing into the Schuylkill at Philadelphia

With·la·coo·chee \,with-lə-'kü-chē\ **1** river 110 *mi* (177 *km*) S Ga. & NW Fla. flowing SE into the Suwannee **2** river 120 *mi* (193 *km*) NW *cen* Fla. flowing NW into Gulf of Mexico

Wit·ten \'vi-t³n\ city W Germany SW of Dortmund *pop* 105,242

Wit·ten·berg \'wi-t³n-,bərg, 'vi-t³n-,berk\ city E *cen* Germany E of Dessau *pop* 48,718

Wit·wa·ters·rand \'wit-,wò-tərz-,rand, -,wä-, -,ränd, -,ränt\ ridge of auriferous rock 62 *mi* (100 *km*) long & 23 *mi* (37 *km*) wide NE Republic of South Africa in Gauteng and North West provinces

Wło·cła·wek \vwòt-'swä-,vek\ commune N *cen* Poland on the Vistula *pop* 120,823

Wo·burn \'wü-bərn, 'wō-\ city E Mass. NW of Boston *pop* 35,943

Wo·dzi·sław Ślą·ski \vò-'jē-swäf-'shlòn-skē\ town S Poland *pop* 111,329

Wolds, The \'wōldz\ chalk hills NE England in N. Yorkshire, Humberside, & N Lincolnshire

Wolfs·burg \'wúlfs-,bərg, 'vólfs-,búrk\ city N *cen* Germany *pop* 128,955

Wol·lon·gong \'wú-lən-,gän, -,gón\ city SE Australia in E New South Wales S of Sydney *pop* 211,417

Wol·ver·hamp·ton \,wúl-vər-'ham(p)-tən\ borough W *cen* England in W. Midlands NW of Birmingham *pop* 239,800

Won·san \'wən-,sän\ city & port N. Korea on E coast *pop* 274,000

Wood Buffalo National Park \'wúd\ reservation W Canada in N Alta. & S Northwest Territories

Wood·bury \'wúd-,ber-ē, -bə-rē\ city E Minn., a suburb of St. Paul *pop* 20,075

Wood Green former municipal borough SE England in Middlesex, now part of Haringey

Wood·land \'wúd-lənd\ city W Calif. NW of Sacramento *pop* 39,802

Wood·lark \'wúd-,lärk\ island W Pacific in Solomon Sea off SE end of New Guinea; attached to Papua New Guinea *area* 400 *sq mi* (1040 *sq km*)

Wood·ridge \'wúd-(,)rij\ city NE Ill. *pop* 26,256

Woods, Lake of the lake S Canada & N U.S. in Ont., Man., & Minn. SE of Lake Winnipeg *area* 1679 *sq mi* (4349 *sq km*)

Wood·stock \'wúd-,stäk\ city Canada in SE Ont. *pop* 30,075

Wool·wich \'wú-lij, -lich\ former metropolitan borough E London, England, now part of Greenwich

Woom·era \'wú-mə-rə\ town S. Australia W of Lake Torrens

Woon·sock·et \wün-'sä-kət, 'wün-,\ city N R.I. *pop* 43,877

Woos·ter \'wús-tər\ city N *cen* Ohio SW of Akron *pop* 22,191

Worces·ter \'wús-tər\ **1** city E *cen* Mass. W of Boston *pop* 169,759 **2** *or* **Worces·ter·shire** \-tə(r)-,shir, -shər\ former county W *cen* England — see HEREFORD AND WORCESTER **3** city, ✳ of Hereford and Worcester *pop* 81,000

Worms \'wərmz, 'vórm(p)s\ city SW Germany on the Rhine NNW of Mannheim *pop* 77,429

Worth, Lake \'wərth\ inlet (lagoon) of the Atlantic SE Fla.

Wor·thing \'wər-thin\ borough S England in W. Sussex on English Channel *pop* 94,100

Wound·ed Knee \,wün-dəd-'nē\ locality SW S. Dakota; site of 1890 massacre of American Indians by U.S. troops

Wran·gel \'raŋ-gəl\ *or Russ* **Vran·ge·lya** \'vrän-gəl-yə\ island in Arctic Ocean off NE coast of Russia in Asia

Wran·gell \'raŋ-gəl\ island SE Alaska NE of Prince of Wales Is.

Wrangell, Cape cape on Attu Is. in Aleutians

Wrangell, Mount active volcano 14,163 *ft* (4317 *m*) S Alaska in Wrangell Mountains NW of Mt. Blackburn

Wrangell Mountains mountain range S Alaska NW of St. Elias Range — see BLACKBURN (Mount)

Wrangell–Saint Eli·as National Park \-sänt-i-'lī-əs\ reservation S *cen* Alaska; largest park in the world covering 8,331,604 *acres* (3,374,300 *hectares*)

Wrath, Cape \'rath, *Sc* 'röth *or* 'räth\ extreme NW point of Scotland, at 58°35′N

Wrex·ham \'rek-səm\ borough NE Wales in Clwyd *pop* 40,272

Wro·cław \'vròt-,swäf, -,släv\ *or G* **Bres·lau** \'bres-,laủ, 'brez-\ city SW Poland, chief city of Silesia *pop* 642,334

Wu \'wü\ river 700 *mi* (1126 *km*) *cen* China rising in W Guizhou & flowing through Szechwan into the Chang

Wu·chang \'wü-'chäŋ\ former city E *cen* China — see WUHAN

Wu·han \'wü-'hän\ city E *cen* China ❋ of Hubei at junction of Han & Chang rivers; formed from the former separate cities of Hankow, Hanyang, & Wuchang *pop* 3,284,229

Wuhsien — see SUZHOU

Wu·hu \'wü-'hü\ city E China in E Anhui *pop* 425,740

Wu·lu·mu·ch'i — see ÜRÜMQI

Wu·pat·ki National Monument \wü-'pat-kē\ reservation N Ariz. NNE of Flagstaff containing prehistoric Indian dwellings

Wup·per·tal \'vủ-pər-,täl\ city W Germany in Ruhr valley ENE of Düsseldorf *pop* 385,463

Würt·tem·berg \'wər-təm-,bərg, 'wủr-; 'vẻr-təm-,berk\ region SW Germany bet. Baden & Bavaria; chief city Stuttgart; once a duchy, kingdom 1813–1918, state 1918–45; divided 1945–51, S part being joined to Hohenzollern forming **Württemberg–Hohenzollern** state & N part to N Baden forming **Württemberg–Baden** state; since 1951 part of Baden-Württemberg state

Würz·burg \'wẻrts-,bərg, 'wủrts-; 'vẻrts-,bủrk\ city S *cen* Germany on Main River in N Bavaria NW of Nuremberg *pop* 128,512

Wu·xi *or* **Wu—hsi** *or* **Wu·sih** \'wü-'shē\ city E China in S Jiangsu NW of Suzhou

Wu·zhou *or* **Wu–chou** *or* **Wu·chow** \'wü-'jō\ city S China in E Guangxi Zhuangzu at junction of the Gui & the Xi *pop* 210,452

Wy·an·dotte \'wī-ən-,dät *also* 'wīn-\ city SE Mich. *pop* 30,938

Wye \'wī\ river 130 *mi* (209 *km*) E Wales & W England flowing into Severn River

Wy·o·ming \wī-'ō-miŋ\ **1** state NW U.S. ❋ Cheyenne *area* 97,914 *sq mi* (254,576 *sq km*), *pop* 453,588 **2** valley NE Pa. along the Susquehanna **3** city SW Mich. *pop* 63,891 — **Wy·o·ming·ite** \-miŋ-,īt\ *n*

X

Xan·thus \'zan(t)-thəs\ city of ancient Lycia; its site near mouth of Koca River in SW Turkey

Xe·nia \'zē-nyə, -nē-ə\ city SW *cen* Ohio *pop* 24,664

Xeres — see JEREZ

Xi *or* **Hsi** *or* **Si** \'shē\ river 300 *mi* (483 *km*) SE China in Guangxi Zhuangzu & Guangdong flowing E into S. China Sea

Xia·men *or* **Hsia–men** \'shyä-'men\ *or* **Amoy** \ä-'mòi, a-, ə-\ city & port SE China in S Fujian on two islands *pop* 308,000

Xi'·an *or* **Si·an** \'shē-'än\ *or formerly* **Chang·an** \'chäŋ-'än\ city E *cen* China ❋ of Shaanxi on the Wei *pop* 1,959,044

Xiang *or* **Hsiang** \'shyäŋ\ river 350 *mi* (560 *km*) SE *cen* China flowing from N Guangxi Zhuangzu N into Hunan

Xiang·tan *or* **Hsiang–t'an** *or* **Siang·tan** \'shyäŋ-'tän, -'tan\ city SE China in E Hunan on the Xiang S of Changsha *pop* 441,968

Xi·ga·zê \'shē-'gä-'dzə\ *or* **Shi·ga·tse** \shi-'gä-'dzə\ *or* **Jih–k'a–tse** \'zhir-'kä-'dzə\ town W China in SE Tibet on the Tsangpo W of Lhasa

Xin·gu \shēŋ-'gü\ river 1230 *mi* (1979 *km*) *cen* & N Brazil rising on Mato Grosso plateau & flowing N into the Amazon near its mouth

Xi·ning *or* **Si·ning** *or* **Hsi–Ning** \'shē-'niŋ\ city NW China ✻ of Qinghai *pop* 551,776

Xin·jiang Uy·gur *or* **Sin·kiang Ui·ghur** \'shin-'jyäŋ-'wē-gər\ region W China bet. the Kunlun & Altay mountains; formerly a province ✻ Ürümqi *area* 635,829 *sq mi* (1,653,154 *sq km*), *pop* 15,155,778

Xin·xiang *or* **Hsin–hsiang** *or* **Sin·siang** \'shin-'shyäŋ\ city E China in N Henan N of Zhengzhou *pop* 473,762

Xizang — see TIBET

Xo·chi·mil·co \,sō-chē-'mēl(,)-kō, ,sō-shi-, -'mil-\ city S *cen* Mexico, SE suburb of Mexico City *pop* 271,020

Xuan·hua *or* **Hsüan–hua** \'shwän-'hwä, 'shwan-, -'wä\ city NE China in NW Hebei NW of Beijing *pop* 114,000

Xu·zhou \'shü-'jō\ *or* **Hsü–chou** *or* **Sü·chow** \'shü-'jō, 'sü-; 'sü-'chaú\ city E China in NW Jiangsu *pop* 805,695

Y

Ya·blo·no·vy Mountains *or* **Ya·blo·no·vyy Mountains** \,yä-blə-nə-'vē\ mountain range S Russia in Asia

Yacarana — see JAVARI

Yad·kin \'yad-kən\ river 202 *mi* (325 *km*) *cen* N.C., the upper course of the Pee Dee

Yafo — see JAFFA

Yak·i·ma \'ya-kə-,mó\ **1** river 200 *mi* (322 *km*) S Wash. flowing SE into Columbia River **2** city S *cen* Wash. *pop* 54,827

Yak·u·tat Bay \'ya-kə-,tat\ inlet of the Pacific SE Alaska

Yakutia — see SAKHA

Ya·kutsk \yə-'kütsk\ city E *cen* Russia in Asia *pop* 198,000

Ya·long *or* **Ya·lung** \'yä-'lúŋ\ river SW China in W Szechwan flowing S into the Chang

Yal·ta \'yól-tə\ city & port on S coast of Crimea *pop* 89,000

Ya·lu \'yä-(,)lü\ river *ab* 500 *mi* (804 *km*) SE Manchuria & NW N. Korea flowing N, W, & SW into Korea Bay

Ya·mal \yə-'mäl\ peninsula NW Russia in Asia at N end of Ural Mountains bet. Gulf of Ob & Kara Sea

Ya·mous·sou·kro \,yä-mə-'sü-krō\ town *cen* Ivory Coast

Yam·pa \'yam-pə\ river 250 *mi* (400 *km*) NW Colo. flowing W into Green River in Dinosaur National Monument

Ya·mu·na \'yə-mə-nə\ river 860 *mi* (1384 *km*) N India in Uttar Pradesh flowing from the Himalayas S & SE into the Ganges

Ya·na \'yä-nə\ river N Russia in Asia flowing N into Laptev Sea

Yan'an \'yä-'nän\ *or* **Yen·an** \'ye-'nän\ city NE *cen* China in *cen* Shaanxi *pop* 113,277

Yangku — see TAIYUAN

Yan·gon \'yän-'gōn\ **1** — see RANGOON 1 **2** *or formerly* **Rangoon** city & port ✳ of Myanmar on Rangoon River 21 *mi* (34 *km*) from its mouth *pop* 1,717,649

Yang·quan *or* **Yang–chüan** \'yäŋ-'chwän, -'chwen\ city N China in E Shanxi E of Taiyuan *pop* 362,268

Yangtze — see CHANG

Yang·zhou *or* **Yang–chou** \'yäŋ-'jō\ city E China in SW Jiangsu NE of Nanjing *pop* 312,892

Yan·tai \'yän-'tī\ *or* **Yen–t'ai** \'yən-\ *or* **Che·foo** \'jə-'fü\ city & port E China in NE Shandong on Shandong Peninsula on Bo Hai *pop* 452,127

Yao \'yaü\ city Japan on Honshu, a suburb of Osaka *pop* 277,724

Yaoun·dé *or* **Yaun·de** \yaün-'dā\ city S *cen* Cameroon, its ✳ *pop* 649,000

Yap \'yap, 'yäp\ *or* **Uap** \'wäp\ islands W Carolines, part of Federated States of Micronesia — **Yap·ese** \ya-'pēz, yä-, -'pēs\ *adj*

Ya·quí \yä-'kē\ river 420 *mi* (676 *km*) NW Mexico in Sonora flowing SW into Gulf of California

Yar·kand \yär-'känd\ *or* **Yar·kant** \-'känt\ river Kashmir & China flowing from Karakoram Range N & W to join the Hotan in Xinjiang Uygur forming the Tarim

Yar·mouth \'yär-məth\ **1** city SE Mass. E of Barnstable *pop* 21,174 **2** *or* **Great Yarmouth** borough & port E England in Norfolk on North Sea *pop* 50,152

Ya·ro·slavl \ˌyär-ə-'slä-vᵊl\ city *cen* Russia in Europe on the Volga NE of Moscow *pop* 637,000

Yau·co \'yaü-ˌkō\ municipality SW Puerto Rico *pop* 42,058

Yavarí — see JAVARI

Ya·wa·ta \yä-'wä-tä\ former city Japan in N Kyushu — see KITA-KYUSHU

Yazd \'yazd\ *or* **Yezd** \'yezd\ city *cen* Iran *pop* 230,483

Yaz·oo \ya-'zü, 'ya-(ˌ)zü\ river 189 *mi* (304 *km*) Miss. flowing SW into Mississippi River

Yedo — see TOKYO

Ye·gor'·yevsk \yə-'gȯr-yəfsk, -əfsk\ city W *cen* Russia in Europe SE of Moscow *pop* 74,200

Ye·ka·te·rin·burg \yi-'ka-tə-rən-ˌbərg, yi-ˌka-ti-rēm-'bùrk\ *or 1924–91* **Sverd·lovsk** \sverd-'lȯfsk\ city W Russia in Asia in *cen* Ural Mountains *pop* 1,371,000

Yelizavetpol — see GANCA

Yellow — see HUANG

Yel·low·knife \'ye-lō-ˌnīf\ city Canada ✳ of Northwest Territories on Great Slave Lake *pop* 15,179

Yellow Sea \'ye-(ˌ)lō\ inlet of E. China Sea bet. N China, N. Korea, & S. Korea

Yel·low·stone \'ye-lō-ˌstōn\ river 671 *mi* (1080 *km*) NW Wyo. & S & E Mont. flowing N through **Yellowstone Lake** (*area* 140 *sq mi* *or* 364 *sq km*) & **Grand Canyon of the Yellowstone** in Yellowstone National Park & NE into Missouri River in NW N.Dak. near Mont. border

Yellowstone Falls two waterfalls NW Wyo. in Yellowstone River at head of Grand Canyon of the Yellowstone; upper fall 109 *ft* (33 *m*), lower fall 308 *ft* (94 *m*)

Yellowstone National Park reservation NW Wyo., E Idaho, & S Mont. including plateau region notable for numerous geysers & hot springs

Ye·men \'ye-mən\ country S Arabia bordering on Red Sea & Gulf of Aden; a republic formed 1990 by merger of **Yemen Arab Republic** (✳ Sanaa) with **People's Democratic Republic of Yemen** or **Southern Yemen** (✳ Aden) ✳ Sanaa *area* 203,849 *sq mi* (527,969 *sq km*), *pop* 12,961,000 — **Ye·me·ni** \'ye-mə-nē\ *adj or n* — **Ye·men·ite** \-mə-ˌnīt\ *n or adj*

Yen·i·sey \ˌyi-ni-'sā\ river over 2500 *mi* (4022 *km*) Russia in Asia flowing N into Arctic Ocean

Yen-t'ai — see YANTAI

Ye·re·van \ˌyer-ə-'vän\ city ✳ of Armenia *pop* 1,199,000

Ye·şil Ir·mak \yə-ˌshēl-ir-'mäk\ river N Turkey in Asia flowing N into Black Sea

Ye·şil·koy \ye-(ˌ)shēl-'kói\ or formerly **San Ste·fa·no** \san-'ste-fə-ˌnó\ town Turkey in Europe on Sea of Marmara W of Istanbul

Yevreyskaya — see JEWISH AUTONOMOUS OBLAST

Yezo — see HOKKAIDO

Yi·bin \'yē-'bēn\ or **I–pin** \'ē-'bēn, -'pin\ or formerly **Su·chow** \'shü-'jō, 'sü-; 'sü-'chaú\ city *cen* China in S Szechwan *pop* 805,695

Yi·chang \'yē-'chäŋ\ or **I–ch'ang** \'ē-'chäŋ\ city *cen* China in W Hubei *pop* 371,601

Yin·chuan \'yin-'chwän, -'chwen\ or formerly **Ning·sia** or **Ning·hsia** \'niŋ-'shyä\ city N China ✳ of Ningxia Huizu on the Huang *pop* 356,652

Ying·kou \'yiŋ-'kó\ or **Ying·kow** \-'kaú, -'kó\ city & port NE China in *cen* Liaoning on Gulf of Liaodong *pop* 421,589

Yi·ning \'yē-'niŋ\ or **Gul·ja** \'gül-(ˌ)jä\ or **Kul·dja** \'kül-(ˌ)jä\ city W China in NW Xinjiang Uygur *pop* 177,193

Yog·ya·kar·ta \ˌyō-gyə-'kär-tə\ or **Jog·ja·kar·ta** \ˌjōg-yə-\ city Indonesia in S Java *pop* 412,392

Yo·ho National Park \'yō-(ˌ)hō\ reservation W Canada in SE B.C. on Alta. border

Yo·ko·ha·ma \ˌyō-kō-'hä-mä\ city & port Japan in SE Honshu on Tokyo Bay S of Tokyo *pop* 3,220,350

Yo·ko·su·ka \ˌyō-'kó-s(ə-)kä\ city & port Japan in Honshu W of entrance to Tokyo Bay *pop* 433,361

Yon·kers \'yäŋ-kərz\ city SE N.Y. N of New York City *pop* 188,082

Yonne \'yän, 'yón\ river 182 *mi* (293 *km*) NE *cen* France flowing NNW into the Seine

Yor·ba Lin·da \ˌyór-bə-'lin-də, ˌyór-\ city SW Calif. SE of Los Angeles *pop* 52,422

York \'yórk\ **1** city SE Pa. SE of Harrisburg *pop* 42,192 **2** city Canada in SE Ont. near Toronto *pop* 140,525 **3** or **York·shire** \-ˌshir, -shər\ former county N England bordering on North Sea comprising city of York & (former) administrative counties of **East Rid·ing** \'rī-diŋ\ (✳ Beverley), **North Riding** (✳ Northallerton),

& **West Riding** (✳ Wakefield) — see HUMBERSIDE, NORTH YORK-
SHIRE, SOUTH YORKSHIRE, WEST YORKSHIRE **4** *or anc* **Ebo·ra·cum** \i-
'bōr-ə-kəm, -'bär-\ N England in N. Yorkshire on Ouse River
pop 100,600

York, Cape — see CAPE YORK PENINSULA

Yorke Peninsula \'yȯrk\ peninsula Australia in SE S. Australia bet.
Spencer Gulf and Gulf St. Vincent

York River estuary 40 *mi* (64 *km*) E Va. flowing SE into Chesapeake Bay

Yo·sem·i·te Falls \yō-'se-mə-tē\ waterfall E *cen* Calif. descending
from rim of Yosemite Valley in two falls (upper fall 1430 *ft or* 436
m, lower fall 320 *ft or* 98 *m* connected by a cascade)

Yosemite Valley glaciated valley of Merced River E *cen* Calif. on
W slope of Sierra Nevada in **Yosemite National Park**

Yosh·kar–Ola \yəsh-'kär-ə-'lä\ town E Russia in Europe ✳ of Mari
El *pop* 249,000

Yo·su \'yō-(,)sü\ city & port S S. Korea on Korea Strait *pop*
171,933

Yough·io·ghe·ny \,yä-kə-'gā-nē, ,yȯ-hə-, -'ge-nē\ river 135 *mi* (217
km) NE W.Va., NW Md., & Pa. flowing N & W into the
Monongahela

Youngs·town \'yəŋz-,taůn\ city NE Ohio E of Akron *pop* 95,732

Youth, Isle of \'yüth\ *or formerly* **Isle of Pines** island W Cuba in
the Caribbean *area* 1180 *sq mi* (3068 *sq km*)

Ypres — see IEPER

Yp·si·lan·ti \ip-sə-'lan-tē\ city SE Mich. *pop* 24,846

Yser \ē-'zer\ river 48 *mi* (77 *km*) France & Belgium flowing into
North Sea

Yssyk–Köl — see ISSYK KUL

Yu·an \'ywen, 'ywän\ **1** river 500 *mi* (805 *km*) SE *cen* China flowing from Guizhou NE to NE Hunan **2** — see RED

Yu·ba City \'yü-bə\ city N Calif. N of Sacramento *pop* 27,437

Yu·cai·pa \yü-'kī-pə\ city S Calif. E of Riverside *pop* 32,824

Yu·ca·tán \,yü-kə-'tan, -kä-'tän\ **1** peninsula SE Mexico & N Central America including Belize & part of Guatemala **2** state SE
Mexico at N end of Yucatán Peninsula ✳ Mérida *area* 16,749 *sq mi*
(43,380 *sq km*), *pop* 1,362,940 — **Yu·ca·te·can** \-'te-kən\ *adj*

Yucatán Channel channel bet. Yucatán & W end of Cuba

Yuc·ca House National Monument \'yə-kə\ reservation SW
Colo.; contains prehistoric ruins

Yu·go·sla·via *also* **Ju·go·sla·via** \,yü-gō-'slä-vē-ə, ,yü-gə-\ country
S Europe on Balkan Peninsula comprising Serbia, Montenegro,
Vojvodina, & Kosovo; together with Slovenia, Croatia, Bosnia and
Herzegovina, & Macedonia established 1918 as a kingdom (**Kingdom of the Serbs, Croats, and Slovenes**), became a federal republic 1945; ✳ Belgrade *area* 39,449 *sq mi* (102,173 *sq km*), *pop*
10,561,000 — **Yu·go·slav** \,yü-gō-'släv, -'slav; 'yü-gō-,\ *or* **Yu·go-
sla·vi·an** \,yü-gō-'slä-vē-ən, -gə-\ *adj or n*

Yu·kon \'yü-,kän\ **1** city *cen* Okla. *pop* 20,935 **2** river 1979 *mi*
(3185 *km*) Yukon Territory & Alaska flowing NW & SW into Bering Sea — see LEWES **3** *or* **Yukon Territory** territory NW Canada
bet. Alaska & B.C. bordering on Arctic Ocean ✳ Whitehorse *area*
205,345 *sq mi* (531,843 *sq km*), *pop* 27,797

Yu·ma \'yü-mə\ city SW Ariz. on Colorado River *pop* 54,923

Yungki — see JILIN

Yungning — see NANNING

Yun·nan \'yü-'nän\ **1** province SW China bordering on Indochina & Myanmar ✻ Kunming *area* 168,417 *sq mi* (437,884 *sq km*), *pop* 36,972,610 **2** *or* **Yunnanfu** — see KUNMING — **Yun·nan·ese** \,yü-nə-'nēz, -'nēs\ *adj or n*

Yun·que, El \el-'yün-(,)kā\ mountain 3496 *ft* (1066 *m*) E Puerto Rico

Yü Shan \'yē-'shän, 'yü-\ *or* **Hsin·kao** \'shin-'kaủ\ *or* **Mount Mor·ri·son** \'mȯr-ə-sən, 'mär-\ mountain 13,113 *ft* (3997 *m*) cen Taiwan; highest on island

Yver·don \ē-ver-'dōⁿ\ commune W Switzerland N of Lausanne *pop* 20,802

Z

Zaan·dam \'zän-,däm\ commune W Netherlands *pop* 129,341

Zab·rze \'zäb-(,)zhā\ *or G* **Hin·den·burg** \'hin-dən-bərg, -,bủrk\ city SW Poland in Silesia *pop* 203,367

Za·ca·te·cas \,za-kə-'tā-kəs, ,sä-kä-'tā-käs\ **1** state N cen Mexico *area* 28,973 *sq mi* (75,040 *sq km*), *pop* 1,276,323 **2** city, its ✻ *pop* 100,051

Za·dar \'zä-,där\ *or It* **Za·ra** \'zä-rä\ city & port Croatia; held by Italy 1920–47 *pop* 80,355

Zag·a·zig \'za-gə-,zig\ *or* **Az–Za·qā·zīq** \,az-zə-,kä-'zēk\ city N Egypt NNE of Cairo *pop* 279,000

Za·greb \'zä-,greb\ city ✻ of Croatia *pop* 867,865

Zag·ros Mountains \'za-grəs, -,grōs\ mountains W & S Iran bordering on Turkey, Iraq, & Persian Gulf; highest over 14,000 *ft* (4267 *m*)

Za·he·dan \,zä-hi-'dän\ city E Iran *pop* 281,923

Zaire \'zyir\ **1** river in Africa — see CONGO 1 **2** — see CONGO 2 — **Zair·ean** *or* **Zair·ian** \zä-'ir-ē-ən\ *adj or n*

Za·kar·pat·s'ka \,zä-kər-'pät-skä\ *or formerly* **Car·pa·thi·an Ru·the·nia** \kär-'pā-thē-ən-rü-'thē-nyə, -nē-ə\ *or* **Ruthenia** region W Ukraine S of the Carpathian Mountains; part of Hungary before 1918 & 1939–45; a province of Czechoslovakia 1918–38 ✻ Uzhgorod *area* 4942 *sq mi* (12,800 *sq km*), *pop* 1,265,900

Zá·kin·thos \'zä-kēn-,thōs\ **1** island W Greece, one of the Ionian Islands, SSE of Cephalonia *area* 157 *sq mi* (407 *sq km*) *pop* 32,746 **2** its chief town *pop* 10,205

Za·ma \'zä-mə, 'zä-\ ancient town N Africa SW of Carthage

Zam·be·zi *or* **Zam·be·si** \zam-'bē-zē, zäm-'bā-zē\ river *ab* 1700 *mi* (2735 *km*) SE Africa flowing from NW Zambia into Mozambique Channel

Zam·bia \'zam-bē-ə\ *or formerly* **Northern Rhodesia** country S Africa; formerly a Brit. protectorate; independent republic within the Commonwealth of Nations since 1964 ✻ Lusaka *area* 290,585

sq mi (752,615 *sq km*), *pop* 9,132,000 — **Zam·bi·an** \'zam-bē-ən\ *adj or n*

Zam·bo·an·ga \,zam-bō-'än-gə\ city & port Philippines on SW coast of Mindanao *pop* 442,000

Za·mo·ra \zə-'mōr-ə, -'mòr-\ **1** province NW Spain in *cen* León *area* 4077 *sq mi* (10,559 *sq km*), *pop* 213,668 **2** city, its ✳ *pop* 64,631

Zancle — see MESSINA

Zanes·ville \'zānz-,vil\ city E *cen* Ohio *pop* 26,778

Zan·jan \zan-'jän\ city NW Iran *pop* 215,261

Zan·zi·bar \'zan-zə-,bär\ **1** island E Africa off NE Tanzania mainland *area* 600 *sq mi* (1554 *sq km*), *pop* 375,539; formerly a sultanate, with Pemba & adjacent islands forming a Brit. protectorate; became independent 1963; united 1964 with Tanganyika to form Tanzania **2** city & port ✳ of the island & formerly of protectorate *pop* 157,634 — **Zan·zi·bari** \,zan-zə-'bär-ē\ *n or adj*

Za·po·rizh·zhya *or Russ* **Za·po·rozh'·ye** \,zä-pə-'rō-zhə\ *or formerly* **Ale·ksan·drovsk** \,a-lik-'san-drəfsk\ city SE Ukraine *pop* 897,000

Za·ra·go·za \,zar-ə-'gō-zə\ *or* **Sar·a·gos·sa** \,sar-ə-'gä-sə\ **1** province NE Spain in W Aragon *area* 6639 *sq mi* (17,195 *sq km*), *pop* 837,327 **2** — see SARAGOSSA

Zee·brug·ge \'zā,brə-gə, -,brü-\ town NW Belgium; port for Brugge

Zee·land \'zē-lənd, 'zā-; 'zā-,länt\ province SW Netherlands ✳ Middelburg *area* 1043 *sq mi* (2701 *sq km*), *pop* 361,195

Zeist \'zīst\ commune *cen* Netherlands E of Utrecht *pop* 59,096

Zem·po·al·te·pec \,zem-pō-'äl-tä-,pek\ *or* **Zem·po·al·te·petl** \-,äl-'tä-,pe-t°l, -,äl-tə-\ mountain 11,138 *ft* (3395 *m*) SE Mexico in Oaxaca

Zer·matt \(t)ser-'mät\ village SW *cen* Switzerland in Valais in Pennine Alps NE of the Matterhorn

Zetland — see SHETLAND

Zhang·jia·kou \'jäŋ-'jyä-'kō\ *or* **Ch'ang-chia-k'ou** \'chäŋ-'jyä-'kō\ *or* **Kal·gan** \'kal-'gan\ city NE China in NW Hebei NW of Beijing *pop* 529,136

Zhang·zhou *or* **Chang-chou** \'jäŋ-'jō\ *or formerly* **Lung-ki** \'lüŋ-kē\ city SE China in S Fujian

Zhda·nov — see MARIUPOL

Zhe·jiang *or* **Che·kiang** \'jə-'jyäŋ\ province E China bordering on E. China Sea ✳ Hangzhou *area* 39,305 *sq mi* (102,193 *sq km*), *pop* 41,445,930

Zheng·zhou *or* **Cheng-chou** *or* **Cheng·chow** \'jəŋ-'jō\ city NE *cen* China ✳ of Henan on the Huang *pop* 1,159,679

Zhen·jiang *or* **Chen-chiang** \'jən-'jyäŋ\ city & port E China in NW *cen* Jiangsu *pop* 368,316

Zhi·to·mir *or* **Zhy·to·myr** \zhi-'tò-,mir\ city W Ukraine *pop* 298,000

Zhou·shan *or* **Chou–shan** \'jō-'shän\ archipelago E China in E. China Sea at entrance to Hangzhou Bay

Zhu \'jü\ *or* **Chu** \'jü, 'chü\ *or* **Pearl** river SE China SE of Guangzhou

Zhu·zhou *or* **Chu-chou** *or* **Chu·chow** \'jü-'jō\ city SE China in E Hunan *pop* 409,924

Zi·bo _or_ **Tzu–po** \'(d)zə-'bō\ city E China in _cen_ Shandong _pop_ 1,138,074

Zie·lo·na Go·ra \zhe-'lô-nä-'gûr-ä\ city W _cen_ Poland _pop_ 113,322

Zi·gong _or_ **Tzu–kung** \'(d)zə-'gúŋ\ city S _cen_ China in S _cen_ Szechwan _pop_ 393,184

Zi·li·na \'zhē-lē-,nä\ city N Slovakia _pop_ 83,853

Zim·ba·bwe \zim-'bä-bwē, -(,)bwä\ **1** archaeological site NE Zimbabwe (country) **2** _or formerly_ **Southern Rhodesia** _or 1970–79_ **Rhodesia** country S Africa S of the Zambezi; a self-governing Brit. colony which declared itself a republic 1970; adopted majority rule 1979 ✻ Harare _area_ 150,820 _sq mi_ (390,624 _sq km_), _pop_ 7,550,000 — **Zim·ba·bwe·an** \-ən\ _adj or n_

Zinovievsk — see KIROVOGRAD

Zi·on \'zī-ən\ **1** city NE Ill. N of Waukegan _pop_ 19,775 **2** _or_ **Mount Zion** _or_ **Sion** \'sī-ən, 'zī-\ _or_ **Mount Sion** hill E Jerusalem, Israel; orig. the stronghold of Jerusalem conquered by David; occupied in ancient times by the Jewish Temple

Zi·on National Park \'zī-ən\ reservation SW Utah centering around **Zion Canyon** of Virgin River

Zi·pan·gu \zə-'paŋ-(,)gü\ the name for Japan used by Marco Polo

Zi·pa·qui·rá \,sē-pä-kē-'rä\ town _cen_ Colombia N of Bogotá

Zla·to·ust \,zlä-tə-'üst\ city W Russia in Asia in the S Urals _pop_ 208,000

Zoan — see TANIS

Zom·ba \'zäm-bə, 'zōm-\ city SE Malawi S of Lake Malawi _pop_ 51,838

Zon·gul·dak \,zòŋ-gəl-'däk\ city & port NW Turkey _pop_ 116,725

Zug \'(t)sük, 'züg\ _or F_ **Zoug** \'züg\ **1** canton N Switzerland _area_ 92 _sq mi_ (238 _sq km_), _pop_ 84,742 **2** commune, its ✻, on Lake of Zug _pop_ 21,752

Zug, Lake of lake N _cen_ Switzerland in Zug & Schwyz cantons N of Lake of Lucerne _area_ 15 _sq mi_ (39 _sq km_)

Zug·spit·ze \'(t)sük-,shpit-sə, 'züg-, -,spit-\ mountain 9721 _ft_ (2963 _m_) S Germany; highest in Bavarian Alps & in Germany

Zui·der Zee \,zī-dər-'zā, -'zē\ former inlet of North Sea N Netherlands — see IJSSELMEER

Zuidholland — see SOUTH HOLLAND

Zu·lu·land \'zü-(,)lü-,land\ territory E Republic of South Africa in NE KwaZulu-Natal bordering on Indian Ocean N of the Tugela _area_ 10,362 _sq mi_ (26,838 _sq km_)

Zu·rich \'zúr-ik\ _or G_ **Zü·rich** \'tsü̇e-rik\ **1** canton N Switzerland _area_ 668 _sq mi_ (1730 _sq km_), _pop_ 1,152,769 **2** city, its ✻, at NW end of Lake of Zurich _pop_ 347,021 — **Zü·rich·er** \-i-kər, -ri-kər\ _n_

Zurich, Lake of lake 25 _mi_ (40 _km_) long N _cen_ Switzerland

Zut·phen \'zət-fən\ commune E Netherlands on the IJssel _pop_ 31,117

Zwick·au \'tsfi-,kaú, 'zwi-\ city E Germany S of Leipzig _pop_ 112,565

Zwol·le \'zvò-lə, 'zwò-\ city E Netherlands ✻ of Overijssel _pop_ 98,318